INTRODUCTION TO
JAVA™
PROGRAMMING

CORE VERSION
FIFTH EDITION

Y. Daniel Liang

School of Computing
Armstrong Atlantic State University

PEARSON
Prentice Hall

D1309708

Upper Saddle River, NJ 07458

...-Publication Data

...nprehensive Version of this book.

...d Editorial Director,
...i J. Horton
...in R. Apt
...litor: Toni Dianne Holm
...ssistant: Patrick Lindner
...ident and Director of Production
...Manufacturing, ESM: David W. Riccardi
...tive Managing Editor: Vince O'Brien
...aging Editor: Camille Trentacoste
...oduction Editor: John Keegan
...Director of Creative Services: Paul Belfanti
Art Director: Jonathan Boylan
Interior & Cover Designer: Dina Curro

Managing Editor, AV Management
    and Production: Patricia Burns
Art Editor: Xiaohong Zhu
Front Cover Photo: © Rick Strange/AGE Fotostock America, Inc.
Director, Image Resource Center: Melinda Reo
Manager, Rights and Permissions: Zina Arabia
Manager, Visual Research: Beth Brenzel
Manager, Cover Visual Research
    and Permissions: Karen Sanatar
Manufacturing Manager: Trudy Pisciotti
Manufacturing Buyer: Lisa McDowell
Executive Marketing Manager: Pamela Hersperger
Marketing Assistant: Barrie Reinhold

© 2005, 2003, 2001, 1999, 1998 Pearson Education, Inc.
Pearson Prentice Hall
Pearson Education, Inc.
Upper Saddle River, NJ 07458

The author and publisher of this book have used their best efforts in preparing this book. These efforts include the development, research, and testing of the theories and programs to determine their effectiveness. The author and publisher make no warranty of any kind, expressed or implied, with regard to these programs or the documentation contained in this book. The author and publisher shall not be liable in any event for incidental or consequential damages in connection with, or arising out of, the furnishing, performance, or use of these programs.

Printed in the United States of America

10   9   8   7   6   5   4   3   2

ISBN: 0-13-148953-4 (Custom Version)

ISBN: 0-13-154748-8 (Unbound Edition)

Pearson Education Ltd., London
Pearson Education Australia Pty. Ltd., Sydney
Pearson Education Singapore, Pte. Ltd.
Pearson Education North Asia Ltd., Hong Kong
Pearson Education Canada, Inc., Toronto
Pearson Educación de Mexico, S.A. de C.V.
Pearson Education—Japan, Tokyo
Pearson Education Malaysia, Pte. Ltd.
Pearson Education, Inc., Upper Saddle River, New Jersey

To Samantha, Michael, and Michelle

PREFACE

In the past seven years, five editions of *Introduction to Java Programming* have been published. Each new edition substantially improved the previous edition in clarity, content, presentation, examples, and exercises, thanks to comments and suggestions by instructors and students. The Fifth Edition is a gigantic leap forward. I invite you to take a close look and be the judge. I am constantly improving the book. Please continue to send me your comments and suggestions to help further improve it.

Custom Versions

The book is published in a comprehensive version of twenty-nine chapters and can also be printed in custom versions with substantial savings for students. The first sixteen chapters form the custom core. You can customize the book by adding new chapters to the custom core. The following diagram summarizes the materials in the comprehensive version.

Introduction to Java Programming, 5E, Comprehensive Version

Part I Fundamentals of Programming
  Chapter 1 Introduction to Computers, Programs, and Java
  Chapter 2 Primitive Data Types and Operations
  Chapter 3 Control Statements
  Chapter 4 Methods
  Chapter 5 Arrays

Part II Object-Oriented Programming
  Chapter 6 Objects and Classes
  Chapter 7 Strings
  Chapter 8 Inheritance and Polymorphism
  Chapter 9 Abstract Classes and Interfaces
  Chapter 10 Object-Oriented Modeling

Part III GUI Programming
  Chapter 11 Getting Started with GUI Programming
  Chapter 12 Event-Driven Programming
  Chapter 13 Creating User Interfaces
  Chapter 14 Applets, Images, and Audio

Part IV Exception Handling and IO
  Chapter 15 Exceptions and Assertions
  Chapter 16 Simple Input and Output

Custom Core

Part V Data Structures and Collections Framework
  Chapter 17 Object-Oriented Data Structures
  Chapter 18 Java Collections Framework

Part VI Threads and Internationalization
  Chapter 19 Multithreading
  Chapter 20 Internationalization

Part VII Advanced GUI Programming
  Chapter 21 JavaBeans, Bean Events, and MVC
  Chapter 22 Containers, Layout Managers, and Borders
  Chapter 23 Menus, Toolbars, Dialogs, and Internal Frames
  Chapter 24 Advanced Swing Components

Part VIII Web Programming
  Chapter 25 Java Database Programming
  Chapter 26 Servlets
  Chapter 27 JavaServer Pages

Part IX Distributed Computing
  Chapter 28 Networking
  Chapter 29 Remote Method Invocation

Appendixes

Please contact your Prentice Hall sales representative or your Pearson Custom Editor to order custom versions.

Teaching Strategies

There are three popular strategies in teaching Java. The first, known as *GUI-first*, is to mix Java applets and GUI programming with object-oriented programming concepts. The second, known as *object-first*, is to introduce object-oriented programming (OOP) from the start. The third strategy, known as *fundamentals-first*, is a step-by-step approach, first laying a sound foundation on programming concepts, control statements, methods, and arrays, then introducing object-oriented programming, and then moving on to graphical user interface (GUI), applets, and finally to exception handling, simple I/O, and other advanced subjects.

GUI-first

The GUI-first strategy, starting with GUI and applets, seems attractive, but requires substantial knowledge of object-oriented programming and a good understanding of the Java event-handling model; thus, students may never fully understand what they are doing.

object-first

The object-first strategy is based on the notion that objects should be introduced first because Java is an object-oriented programming language. This notion, however, overlooks the importance of the fundamental techniques required for writing programs in any programming language. Furthermore, this approach inevitably mixes static and instance variables and methods before students can fully understand classes and objects and use them to develop useful programs. Students are overwhelmed by having to master object-oriented programming and basic rules of programming simultaneously in the early stage of learning Java. This is a common source of frustration for first-year students learning object-oriented programming.

fundamentals-first

From my own experience, confirmed by the experiences of many colleagues, I have found that learning basic logic and fundamental programming techniques like loops is a struggle for most first-year students. *Students who cannot write code in procedural programming are not able to learn object-oriented programming.* A good introduction on primitive data types, control statements, methods, and arrays prepares students to learn object-oriented programming. Therefore, this text adopts the fundamentals-first strategy, proceeding at a steady pace through all the necessary and important basic concepts, then moving to object-oriented programming, and then to the use of the object-oriented approach to build interesting GUI applications and applets with exception handling, simple I/O, and advanced features. The fundamentals-first approach can reinforce object-oriented programming by first presenting the procedural solutions and demonstrating how they can be improved using the object-oriented approach. Students can learn when and how to apply OOP effectively.

problem solving

This book is not simply about how to program, for it teaches, as well, how to solve problems using programs. Applying the concept of abstraction in the design and implementation of software projects is the key to developing software. The overriding objective of the book, therefore, is to teach students to use many levels of abstraction in solving problems and to see problems in small and in large. *The examples and exercises throughout the book foster the concept of developing reusable components and using them to create practical projects.*

Learning Strategies

practice

A programming course is quite different from other courses. In a programming course, you learn from examples, from practice, and from mistakes. You need to devote a lot of time to writing programs, testing them, and fixing errors.

programmatic solution

For first-time programmers, learning Java is like learning any high-level programming language. The fundamental point in learning programming is to develop the critical skills of formulating programmatic solutions for real problems and translating them into programs using selection statements, loops, and methods.

object-oriented
programming

Once you acquire the basic skills of writing programs using loops, methods, and arrays, you can begin to learn object-oriented programming. You will learn how to develop object-oriented software using class encapsulation and class inheritance.

Java API

Once you understand the concept of object-oriented programming, learning Java becomes a matter of learning the Java API. The Java API establishes a framework for programmers to develop applications using Java. You have to use these classes and interfaces in the API and follow their conventions and rules to create applications. The best way to learn the Java API is to imitate examples and do exercises. The following diagram highlights the API covered in the book.

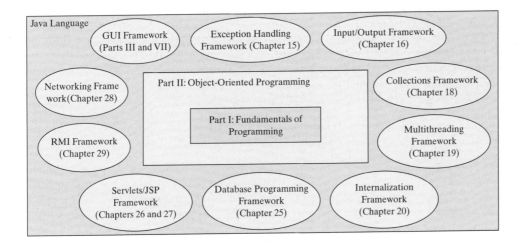

Pedagogical Features

The philosophy of the Liang Java Series is *teaching by example and learning by doing*. Basic features are explained by example so that you can learn by doing. The book uses the following elements to get the most from the material:

teaching by example
learning by doing

- ◆ **Objectives** list what students should have learned from the chapter. This will help them to determine whether they have met the objectives after completing the chapter.

- ◆ **Introduction** opens the discussion with a brief overview of what to expect from the chapter.

- ◆ **Examples**, carefully chosen and presented in an easy-to-follow style, teach programming concepts. Each example has a problem statement, solution steps, complete source code, sample run, and review.

- ◆ **Chapter Summary** reviews the important subjects that students should understand and remember. It helps them to reinforce the key concepts they have learned in the chapter.

- ◆ **Review Questions** are grouped by sections to help students track their progress and evaluate their learning.

- ◆ **Programming Exercises** are grouped by sections to provide students with opportunities to apply the skills on their own. The level of difficulty is rated easy (no asterisk), moderate (*), hard (**), or challenging (***). The trick of learning programming is practice, practice, and practice. To that end, the book provides a large number of exercises.

- ◆ **Interactive Self-Test** lets students test their knowledge interactively online. The Self-Test is accessible from the Companion Website. It provides more than nine hundred multiple-choice questions organized by sections in each chapter.

- ◆ **Notes**, **Tips**, and **Cautions** are inserted throughout the text to offer valuable advice and insight on important aspects of program development.

 NOTE
Provides additional information on the subject and reinforces important concepts.

 TIP
Teaches good programming style and practice.

🌱 **CAUTION**

Helps students steer away from the pitfalls of programming errors.

Flexible Chapter Orderings

The book provides flexible chapter orderings to enable GUI, IO, or Collections to be covered earlier. Many of the chapters after Chapter 14 can be covered immediately after Chapter 14. The following diagram shows the chapter dependencies.

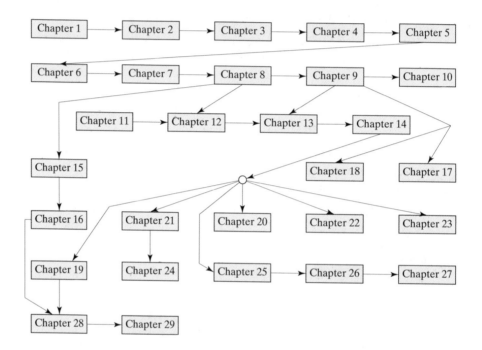

🌱 **NOTE**

Some of the optional examples and exercises in a later chapter may be dependent on earlier chapters. In such cases the examples and exercises can be omitted. For example, Chapter 25 has an example that uses JTable from Chapter 24. If you have not covered JTable, this type of examples and excercises can be skipped.

What's New in This Edition?

This edition improves upon *Introduction to Java Programming, Fourth Edition*. The major changes are as follows:

✦ The book is completely revised in every detail to improve clarity, content, presentation, examples, and exercises.

✦ The book provides many new illustrations and uses short examples to demonstrate concepts and techniques. Longer examples are presented in case studies with overall discussions and thorough line-by-line explanations.

✦ Part I, "Fundamentals of Programming," focuses on problem-solving and basic programming techniques with many new illustrations and practical examples. This part uses JOptionPane input dialog to receive input, but console input using the MyInput class and the JDK 1.5 Scanner class are also introduced to provide alternative ways for input.

✦ Part II, "Object-Oriented Programming," is expanded into five chapters to give a comprehensive introduction on OOP and how to use it to design programs. New organization improves the presentation of object-oriented programming and enables GUI programming to be covered earlier.

✦ Part III, "GUI Programming," is expanded into four chapters to introduce GUI programming, event-driven programming, creating user interfaces, and applets. Advanced GUI features are now covered in Part VII, "Advanced GUI Programming."

✦ Chapter 16, "Simple Input and Output," is completely overhauled. It first introduces the File class, then text I/O, binary I/O, object I/O, and random access files. Short examples are used to demonstrate concepts and techniques. Three cases studies on using various I/O classes are presented in this chapter.

✦ The comprehensive version covers the Java collections framework, threads, JavaBeans, advanced GUI components, JDBC, Servlets, JSP, networking, and RMI.

✦ Purely mathematical examples, such as computing deviations and matrix multiplications, have been replaced by practical examples, such as computing loan payments, taxes, and printing payroll statements.

✦ The number of exercises is almost doubled to cover a variety of problems with simple or complex solutions. The level of difficulty is rated easy (no asterisk), moderate (*), hard (**), or challenging (***).

✦ The book is updated to JDK 1.5.

How are the New Features in JDK 1.5 Treated?

There are already more features in Java than an introductory course can cover. This edition does not aim to cover all the new features in JDK 1.5. Nevertheless, some of the useful features of JDK 1.5 are appropriately introduced to beginners. Specifically,

✦ Formatted output (System.out.printf) is covered in Chapter 2.

✦ The enhanced for loop is covered in Chapters 5 and 18.

✦ The java.util.Scanner class is covered in Chapter 2 and Supplement T for console input, and in Chapter 7 to complement the StringTokenizer class.

✦ Boxing and unboxing of primitives is covered in Chapter 9.

✦ Static import is covered in Chapter 11.

✦ Generic types are covered in Chapter 18 and Supplement Q.

To facilitate the use of this book in courses based on JDK 1.4 and to enable instructors to choose JDK 1.5 topics freely, all the sections on JDK 1.5 are marked *JDK 1.5 Features* and can be skipped.

 NOTE

Sun MicroSystems recently renamed JDK 1.5 to JDK 5.0. Since most programmers are familiar with JDK 1.5, Sun uses JDK 5.0 and JDK 1.5 interchangeably. So does this book.

JDK 1.5 = JDK 5.0

Java Development Tools

You can use a text editor, such as the Windows Notepad or WordPad, to create Java programs, and compile and run the programs from the command window. You can also use a Java development tool, such as TextPad, JBuilder, NetBeans, or Eclipse. These tools support an integrated development environment (IDE) for rapidly developing Java programs. Editing, compiling, building, and executing programs are integrated in one graphical user interface. Using these tools effectively will greatly increase your programming productivity. TextPad is a primitive IDE tool. JBuilder, NetBeans, and Eclipse are more sophisticated. It may take a while to become familiar with a tool, but the time you invest will pay off in the long run. Tutorials on TextPad, JBuilder, NetBeans, and Eclipse are in the supplements on the Companion Website.

Companion Website

The Companion Website accessible from `www.prenhall.com/liang` contains the following resources:

+ Interactive Self-Test

+ Supplements

+ Answers to review questions

+ Solutions to even-numbered programming exercises

+ Source code for the examples in the book

+ Download links for JDK 1.5, JBuilder, NetBeans, Eclipse, TextPad, JCreator LE, JEdit, JGrasp, BlueJ, WinZip, MySQL, and Apache Tomcat.

Instructor Resource Website

The Instructor Resource Website accessible from `www.prenhall.com/liang` contains the following resources:

+ Microsoft PowerPoint slides with interactive buttons to view full-color, syntax-highlighted source code and to run programs without leaving the slides.

+ Sample exams. In general, each exam has four parts:

   1. Multiple-choice questions or short-answer questions (most of these are different from the ones in the Self-Test on the Companion Website)

   2. Correct programming errors

   3. Trace programs

   4. Write programs

+ Solutions to all the exercises. Students will have access to the solutions of even-numbered exercises from the Companion Website.

+ Quiz generator developed using Java.

Some readers have requested the materials in the Instructor Resource Website. Please understand that these are for instructors only. Such requests will not be answered.

Supplements

The text covers the core subjects. The supplements extend the text to introduce additional topics that might be of interest to readers. The following supplements are available from the Companion Website.

A. Installing and Configuring JDK 1.5
B. Compiling and Running Java from the Command Window
C. Compiling and Running Java from TextPad
D. Java Coding Style Guidelines
E. HTML Tutorial
F. Glossary
G. SQL statements for creating and initializing tables for Chapters 25, 26, 27, and 29
H. JBuilder Tutorial
I. NetBeans Tutorial
J. Eclipse Tutorial
K. Tutorial for MySQL
L. Tutorial for Oracle
M. Tutorial for Microsoft Access
N. Tutorial for Tomcat
O. Creating Shortcuts for Java Applications on Windows
P. Supplemental Case Study for Chapter 10: Design a `GenericMatrix` Class
Q. Creating Generic Types (JDK 1.5)
R. Enumerated Types (JDK 1.5)
S. Semaphores (JDK 1.5)
T. Obtaining Input from the Console Using the `Scanner` Class (JDK 1.5)

Acknowledgments

I would like to thank Ray Greenlaw, Chuck Shipley, and my colleagues at Armstrong Atlantic State University for enabling me to teach what I write and for supporting me in writing what I teach. Teaching is the source of inspiration for continuing to improve the book. I am grateful to the instructors and students who have offered comments, suggestions, bug reports, and praise. Their enthusiastic support has contributed to the success of my Java series.

This book was greatly improved thanks to outstanding reviews by James Chegwidden of Tarrant County College, Dan Lipsa of Armstrong Atlantic State University, Vladan Jovanovic of Georgia Southern University, Kenrick Mock of the University of Alaska—Anchorage, Ronald F. Taylor of Wright State University, and Lixin Tao of Pace University. Professors Mutsumi Nakamura and Lian Yu of Arizona State University are so kind to provide us with the errata and suggestions, which came just in time before the book is finished.

It is a great pleasure and privilege to work with the legendary computer science team at Prentice Hall. I would like to thank Alan Apt, Toni Holm, Patrick Lindner, Sarah Parker, Camille Trentacoste, John Keegan, Xiaohong Zhu, Pamela Hersperger, Barrie Reinhold, Toni Callum, Barbara Taylor-Laino, Meredith Maresca, and their colleagues for organizing, managing, and promoting this project, and to Robert Milch for copy editing.

During the production of this book, I was in Asia. I thank Pearson Education in Taiwan, Malaysia, and Singapore for their hospitality and valuable assistance.

As always, I am indebted to my wife, Samantha, for her love, support, and encouragement.

Y. Daniel Liang
liang@armstrong.edu
www.cs.armstrong.edu/liang/intro5e.html

BRIEF CONTENTS

CONTENTS

PART IV ✦ EXCEPTION HANDLING AND IO

Chapter 15   Exceptions and Assertions

Chapter 16   Simple Input and Output

The Following Chapters are Available as Custom Chapters

PART V ✦ DATA STRUCTURES AND COLLECTIONS FRAMEWORK

Chapter 17   Object-Oriented Data Structures

SUPPLEMENTS ARE POSTED ON THE COMPANION WEBSITE

PART I

FUNDAMENTALS OF PROGRAMMING

By now you have heard a lot about Java and are anxious to start writing Java programs. The first part of the book is a stepping stone that will prepare you to embark on the journey of learning Java. You will begin to know Java and will develop fundamental programming skills. Specifically, you will learn how to write simple Java programs with primitive data types, control statements, methods, and arrays.

Chapter 1
Introduction to Computers, Programs, and Java

Chapter 2
Primitive Data Types and Operations

Chapter 3
Control Statements

Chapter 4
Methods

Chapter 5
Arrays

Prerequisites for Part I

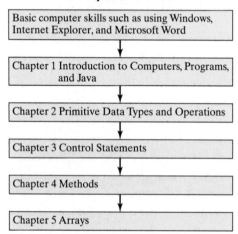

Basic computer skills such as using Windows, Internet Explorer, and Microsoft Word

↓

Chapter 1 Introduction to Computers, Programs, and Java

↓

Chapter 2 Primitive Data Types and Operations

↓

Chapter 3 Control Statements

↓

Chapter 4 Methods

↓

Chapter 5 Arrays

chapter

1

INTRODUCTION TO COMPUTERS, PROGRAMS, AND JAVA

Objectives

- ✦ To review computer basics, programs, and operating systems (§§1.2–1.4).

- ✦ To represent numbers in binary, decimal, and hexadecimal (§1.5 Optional).

- ✦ To understand the relationship between Java and the World Wide Web (§1.6).

- ✦ To know Java's advantages (§1.7).

- ✦ To distinguish the terms API, IDE, and JDK (§1.8).

- ✦ To write a simple Java program (§1.9).

- ✦ To create, compile, and run Java programs (§1.10).

- ✦ To know the basic syntax of a Java program (§1.11).

- ✦ To display output on the console and on the dialog box (§1.12).

1.1 Introduction

You use word-processors to write documents, Web browsers to explore the Internet, and e-mail programs to send e-mails over the Internet. Word-processors, browsers, and e-mail programs are all examples of software that runs on computers. Software is developed using programming languages. There are many programming languages. So why Java? The answer is that Java enables users to deploy applications on the Internet for servers, desktop computers, and small hand-held devices. The future of computing will be profoundly influenced by the Internet, and Java promises to remain a big part of that future. Java is *the* Internet programming language.

You are about to begin an exciting journey, learning a powerful programming language. Before the journey, it is helpful to review computer basics, programs, and operating systems, and to become familiar with number systems. You may skip the review in Sections 1.2, 1.3, and 1.4 if you are familiar with such terms as CPU, memory, disks, operating systems, and programming languages. You may also skip Section 1.5 and use it as reference when you have questions regarding binary and hexadecimal numbers.

1.2 What Is a Computer?

A computer is an electronic device that stores and processes data. A computer includes both *hardware* and *software*. In general, hardware is the physical aspect of the computer that can be seen, and software is the invisible instructions that control the hardware and make it work. Computer programming consists of writing instructions for computers to perform. You can learn a programming language without knowing computer hardware, but you will be better able to understand the effect of the instructions in the program if you do. This section gives a brief introduction to computer hardware components and their functionality.

hardware
software

A computer consists of the following major hardware components, as shown in Figure 1.1.

✦ Central Processing Unit (CPU)

✦ Memory (main memory)

✦ Storage Devices (disks, CDs, tapes)

✦ Input and Output Devices (monitors, keyboards, mouses, printers)

✦ Communication Devices (modems and network interface cards (NICs))

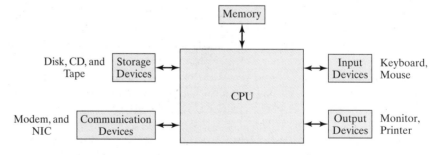

FIGURE 1.1 *A computer consists of a CPU, memory, hard disk, floppy disk, monitor, printer, and communication devices.*

1.2.1 Central Processing Unit

CPU

The *central processing unit* (CPU) is the brain of a computer. It retrieves instructions from memory and executes them. The CPU usually has two components: a *control unit* and an *arithmetic/logic unit*. The control unit controls and coordinates the actions of the other components. The arithmetic and logic unit performs numeric operations (addition, subtraction, multiplication, division) and logical operations (comparisons).

Today's CPU is built on a small silicon semiconductor chip with millions of transistors. The *speed* of the CPU is mainly determined by clock speed. Every computer has an internal clock. The clock emits electronic pulses at a constant rate, and these are used to control and synchronize the pace of operations. The faster the clock speed, the more instructions are executed in a given period of time. The clock speed is measured in *megahertz* (MHz), with 1 megahertz equaling 1 million pulses per second. The speed of the CPU has been improved continuously. If you buy a PC now, you can get an Intel Pentium 4 Processor at 3 *gigahertz* (1 gigahertz is 1000 megahertz).

megahertz

gigahertz

1.2.2   Memory

Computers use zeros and ones because digital devices have two stable states, referred to as *zero* and *one* by convention. Data of various kinds, such as numbers, characters, and strings, are encoded as a series of bits (*binary digits*: zeros and ones). *Memory* stores data and program instructions for the CPU to execute. A memory unit is an ordered sequence of *bytes*, each holding eight bits, as shown in Figure 1.2.

bit

byte

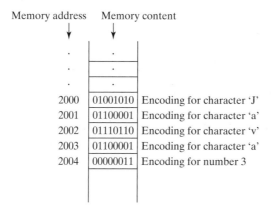

FIGURE 1.2   *Memory stores data and program instructions.*

The programmer need not be concerned about the encoding and decoding of data, which is performed automatically by the system based on the encoding scheme. The encoding scheme varies. For example, character 'J' is represented by 01001010 in one byte in the popular ASCII encoding. A small number such as 3 can be stored in a single byte. If a computer needs to store a large number that cannot fit into a single byte, it uses several adjacent bytes. No two data items can share or split the same byte. A byte is the minimum storage unit.

A program and its data must be brought to memory before they can be executed. A memory byte is never empty, but its initial content may be meaningless to your program. The current content of a memory byte is lost whenever new information is placed in it.

Every byte has a unique address. The address is used to locate the byte for storing and retrieving data. Since bytes can be accessed at any location, the memory is also referred to as *RAM* (random-access memory). Today's personal computers usually have at least 128 megabytes of RAM. A *megabyte* is about 1 million bytes. Like the CPU, memory is built on silicon semiconductor chips containing thousands of transistors embedded on their surface. Compared to the CPU chips, memory chips are less complicated, slower, and less expensive.

RAM

megabyte

1.2.3   Storage Devices

Memory is volatile, because information is lost when the power is off. Programs and data are permanently stored on storage devices and are moved to memory when the computer actually uses them. The reason for that is that memory is much faster than storage devices. There are three main types of storage devices:

◆ Disk drives (hard disks and floppy disks)

◆ CD drives (CD-R and CD-RW)

◆ Tape drives

drive

Drives are devices for operating a medium, such as disks, CDs, and tapes.

1.2.3.1 Disks

hard disk
floppy disk

There are two kinds of disks: *hard disks* and *floppy disks*. Personal computers usually have a 3.5-inch floppy disk drive and a hard drive. A floppy disk has a fixed capacity of about 1.44 MB. Hard disk capacities vary. The capacity of the hard disks of the latest PCs is in the range of 30 gigabytes to 120 gigabytes. Hard disks provide much faster performance and larger capacity than floppy disks. Both disk drives are often encased inside the computer. A floppy disk is removable. A hard disk is mounted inside the case of the computer. Removable hard disks are also available.

1.2.3.2 CDs

CD-R

CD-RW

CD stands for compact disc. There are two types of CD drives: CD-R and CD-RW. A *CD-R* is for read-only permanent storage, and the user cannot modify its contents once they are recorded. A *CD-RW* can be used like a floppy disk. A single CD can hold up to 650 MB. Most software is distributed through CD-Rs. Most new PCs are equipped with a CD-RW drive that can work with both CD-R and CD-W.

1.2.3.3 Tapes

Tapes are mainly used for backup of data and programs. Unlike disks and CDs, tapes store information sequentially. The computer must retrieve information in the order it was stored. Tapes are very slow. It would take one to two hours to back up a 1-gigabyte hard disk.

1.2.4 Input and Output Devices

The common input devices are *keyboards* and *mouses*. The output devices are *monitors* and *printers*. Input devices let the user talk to the computer. Output devices let the computer communicate to the user.

1.2.4.1 The Keyboard

A computer *keyboard* resembles a typewriter keyboard except that it has extra keys for certain special functions.

Function keys are located at the top of the keyboard with prefix F. Their use depends on the software.

Numeric keypad, located on the right-hand corner of the keyboard, is a separate set of number keys for quick input of numbers.

Arrow keys, located between the main keypad and the numeric keypad, are used to move the cursor up, down, left, and right.

Insert, delete, page up, page down keys, located above the arrow keys, are used in word processing for performing insert, delete, page up, and page down.

1.2.4.2 The Mouse

A mouse is a pointing device. It is used to move an electronic pointer called a cursor around the screen or to click on an object on the screen to trigger it to respond. In Java GUI programming, you can use the mouse to click on a button to trigger an event.

1.2.4.3 The Monitor

The monitor displays information (text and graphics). The resolution and dot pitch determine the quality of the display.

The *resolution* specifies the number of pixels per square inch. Pixels (short for "picture elements") are tiny dots that form an image on the screen. The resolution can be set manually. The higher the resolution, the sharper and clearer the image is.

resolution

The *dot pitch* is the amount of space between pixels. The smaller the dot pitch, the better the display.

dot pitch

1.2.5 Communication Devices

Computers can be networked through communication devices. The commonly used communication devices are the regular *modem*, *DSL*, cable modem, and *network interface card*. A regular modem uses a phone line and can transfer data at a speed up to 56,000 bps (bits per second). A DSL (digital subscriber line) also uses a phone line and can transfer data at a speed twenty times faster than a regular modem. A cable modem uses the TV cable line maintained by the cable company. A cable modem is as fast as a DSL. A network interface card (NIC) is a device that connects a computer to a *local area network* (LAN). The LAN is commonly used in business, universities, and government organizations. A typical NIC, called *10BaseT*, can transfer data at 10 mbps (million bits per second).

modem
DSL

NIC

LAN

mbps

1.3 Programs

Computer *programs*, known as *software*, are instructions to the computer. You tell a computer what to do through programs. Without programs, a computer is an empty machine. Computers do not understand human languages, so you need to use computer languages to communicate with them.

software

The language a computer speaks is the computer's native language or machine language. The *machine language* is a set of primitive instructions built into every computer. The instructions are in the form of binary code, so you have to enter binary codes for various instructions. Programming using a native machine language is a tedious process. Moreover, the programs are highly difficult to read and modify. For example, to add two numbers, you might have to write the instruction in binary like this:

machine language

```
1101101010011010
```

Assembly language is a low-level programming language in which a mnemonic is used to represent each of the machine language instructions. For example, to add two numbers, you might write an instruction in assembly code like this:

assembly language

```
ADDF3 R1, R2, R3
```

Assembly languages were developed to make programming easy. Since the computer cannot understand assembly language, however, a program called an *assembler* is used to convert assembly language programs into machine code, as shown in Figure 1.3.

assembler

Since assembly language is machine-dependent, an assembly program can only be executed on a particular machine. Assembly programs are written in terms of machine instructions with easy-to-remember mnemonic names. The high-level languages were developed in order to overcome the platform-specific problem and make programming easier.

The *high-level languages* are English-like and easy to learn and program. Here, for example, is a high-level language statement that computes the area of a circle with radius 5:

high-level language

```
area = 5 * 5 * 3.1415;
```

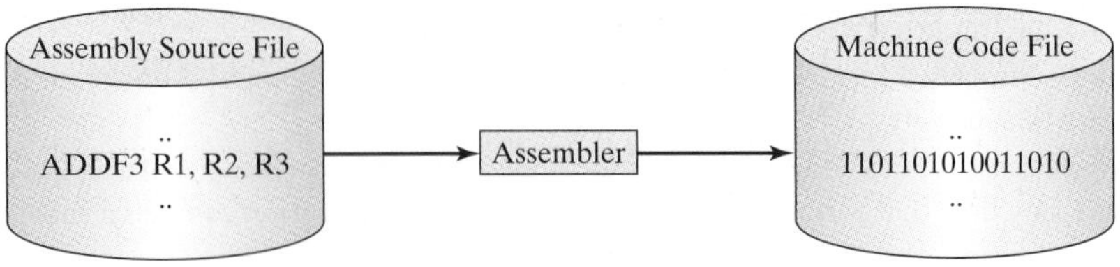

Assembly Source File

ADDF3 R1, R2, R3

→ Assembler →

Machine Code File

1101101010011010

FIGURE 1.3 *Assembler translates assembly language instructions to machine code.*

There are over one hundred high-level languages. The popular languages used today are:

✦ Java

✦ COBOL (COmmon Business Oriented Language)

✦ FORTRAN (FORmula TRANslation)

✦ BASIC (Beginner All-purpose Symbolic Instructional Code)

✦ Pascal (named for Blaise Pascal)

✦ Ada (named for Ada Lovelace)

✦ C (whose developer designed B first)

✦ Visual Basic (Basic-like visual language developed by Microsoft)

✦ Delphi (Pascal-like visual language developed by Borland)

✦ C++ (an object-oriented language, based on C)

Each of these languages was designed for a specific purpose. COBOL was designed for business applications and now is used primarily for business data processing. FORTRAN was designed for mathematical computations and is used mainly for numeric computations. BASIC, as its name suggests, was designed to be learned and used easily. Ada was developed for the Department of Defense and is mainly used in defense projects. C combines the power of an assembly language with the ease of use and portability of a high-level language. Visual BASIC and Delphi are used in developing graphical user interfaces and in rapid application development. C++ is popular for system software projects like writing compilers and operating systems. The Microsoft Windows operating system was coded using C++.

source program
compiler

A program written in a high-level language is called a *source program*. Since a computer cannot understand a source program, a program called a *compiler* is used to translate the source program into a machine-language program called an *object program*. The object program is often then linked with other supporting library code to form an executable file. The executable file can be executed on the machine, as shown in Figure 1.4. On Windows, executable files have extension .exe.

You can port a source program to any machine with appropriate compilers. The source program must be recompiled, however, because the object program can only run on a specific

FIGURE 1.4 *A source program is compiled into an object file, and the object file is linked with the system library to form an executable file.*

documents on the Internet, and bringing images, sound, and video alive on the Web. However, it cannot interact with the user except through simple forms. Web pages in HTML are essentially static and flat.

Java initially became attractive because Java programs can be run from a Web browser. Java
programs that run from a Web browser are called *applets*. Applets use a modern graphical user in-   applet
terface with buttons, text fields, text areas, radio buttons, and so on, to interact with users on the
Web and process their requests. Applets make the Web responsive, interactive, and fun to use.
Figure 1.8 shows an applet running from a Web browser. To run applets from a Web browser, you
need to use Netscape 7 or Internet Explorer 6, or higher.

 TIP

For a demonstration of Java applets, visit `java.sun.com/applets`. This site provides
a rich Java resource as well as links to other cool applet demo sites. `java.sun.com`
is the official Sun Java Web site.

Java can also be used to develop applications on the server side. These applications, called
Java servlets or *JavaServer Pages (JSP)*, can be run from a Web server to generate dynamic Web   servlet
pages. The Self-Test Web site for this book, as shown in Figure 1.9, was developed using Java   JSP
servlets. The Web pages for the questions and answers are dynamically generated by the servlets.

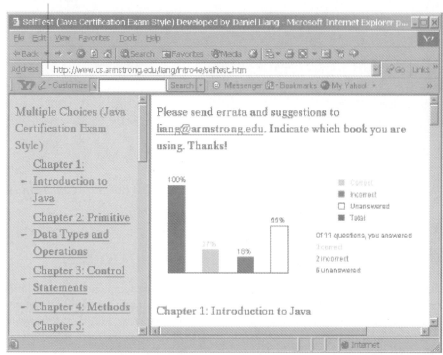

FIGURE 1.9 *Java was used to develop the self-test in the Companion Website for this book.*

Java is a versatile programming language. You can use it to develop applications on your desktop and on the server. You can also use it to develop applications for small hand-held devices, such
as personal digital assistants and cell phones. Figure 1.10 shows a Java program that displays the
calendar on a Palm PDA and on a cell phone.

FIGURE 1.10 *Java can be used to develop applications for hand-held and wireless devices, such as a Palm PDA (left) and a cell phone (right).*

1.7 Characteristics of Java (Optional)

Java has become enormously popular. Java's rapid rise and wide acceptance can be traced to its design and programming features, particularly its promise that you can write a program once and run it anywhere. As stated in the Java-language white paper by Sun, Java is *simple, object-oriented, distributed, interpreted, robust, secure, architecture-neutral, portable, high-performance, multithreaded*, and *dynamic*. Let's analyze these often-used buzzwords.

1.7.1 Java Is Simple

No language is simple, but Java is a bit easier than the popular object-oriented programming language C++, which was the dominant software-development language before Java. Java is partially modeled on C++, but greatly simplified and improved. For instance, pointers and multiple inheritance often make programming complicated. Java replaces the multiple inheritance in C++ with a simple language construct called an *interface*, and eliminates pointers.

Java uses automatic memory allocation and garbage collection, whereas C++ requires the programmer to allocate memory and collect garbage. Also, the number of language constructs is small for such a powerful language. The clean syntax makes Java programs easy to write and read. Some people refer to Java as "C++--" because it is like C++ but with more functionality and fewer negative aspects.

1.7.2   Java Is Object-Oriented

Java is inherently object-oriented. Although many object-oriented languages began strictly as procedural languages, Java was designed from the start to be object-oriented. Object-oriented programming (OOP) is a popular programming approach that is replacing traditional procedural programming techniques.

Software systems developed using procedural programming languages are based on the paradigm of procedures. Object-oriented programming models the real world in terms of objects. Everything in the world can be modeled as an object. A circle is an object, a person is an object, and a Windows icon is an object. Even a loan can be perceived as an object. A Java program is object-oriented because programming in Java is centered on creating objects, manipulating objects, and making objects work together.

Part I, "Fundamentals of Programming," introduces primitive data types and operations, control statements, methods, and arrays. These are the fundamentals for all programming languages. You will learn object-oriented programming in Part II, "Object-Oriented Programming."

One of the central issues in software development is how to reuse code. Object-oriented programming provides great flexibility, modularity, clarity, and reusability through encapsulation, inheritance, and polymorphism—all of which you will learn about in this book. For years, object-oriented technology was perceived as elitist, requiring a substantial investment in training and infrastructure. Java has helped object-oriented technology enter the mainstream of computing. Its simple, clean syntax makes programs easy to write and read. Java programs are quite *expressive* in terms of designing and developing applications.

1.7.3   Java Is Distributed

Distributed computing involves several computers working together on a network. Java is designed to make distributed computing easy. Since networking capability is inherently integrated into Java, writing network programs is like sending and receiving data to and from a file.

1.7.4   Java Is Interpreted

You need an interpreter to run Java programs. The programs are compiled into the Java Virtual Machine code called *bytecode*. The bytecode is machine-independent and can run on any machine that has a Java interpreter, which is part of the Java Virtual Machine (JVM).   bytecode

Most compilers, including C++ compilers, translate programs in a high-level language to machine code. The code can only run on the native machine. If you run the program on other machines, it has to be recompiled on the native machine. For instance, if you compile a C++ program in Windows, the executable code generated by the compiler can only run on the Windows platform. With Java, you compile the source code once, and the bytecode generated by a Java compiler can run on any platform with a Java interpreter. The Java interpreter translates the bytecode into the machine language of the target machine.

1.7.5   Java Is Robust

Robust means *reliable*. No programming language can ensure complete reliability. Java puts a lot of emphasis on early checking for possible errors, because Java compilers can detect many problems that would first show up at execution time in other languages. Java has eliminated certain types of error-prone programming constructs found in other languages. It does not support pointers, for example, thereby eliminating the possibility of overwriting memory and corrupting data.

Java has a runtime exception-handling feature to provide programming support for robustness. Java forces the programmer to write the code to deal with exceptions. Java can catch and respond to an exceptional situation so that the program can continue its normal execution and terminate gracefully when a runtime error occurs.

1.7.6 Java Is Secure

As an Internet programming language, Java is used in a networked and distributed environment. If you download a Java applet (a special kind of program) and run it on your computer, it will not damage your system because Java implements several security mechanisms to protect your system against harm caused by stray programs. The security is based on the premise that *nothing should be trusted*.

1.7.7 Java Is Architecture-Neutral

architecture-neutral
platform-independent

Java is interpreted. This feature enables Java to be *architecture-neutral*, or to use an alternative term, *platform-independent*. With a Java Virtual Machine (JVM), you can write one program that will run on any platform, as shown in Figure 1.5 on page 9.

Java's initial success stemmed from its Web-programming capability. You can run Java applets from a Web browser, but Java is for more than just writing Web applets. You can also run stand-alone Java applications directly from operating systems, using a Java interpreter. Today, software vendors usually develop multiple versions of the same product to run on different platforms (Windows, OS/2, Macintosh, and various UNIX, IBM AS/400, and IBM mainframes). Using Java, developers need to write only one version that can run on every platform.

1.7.8 Java Is Portable

Because Java is architecture-neutral, Java programs are portable. They can be run on any platform without being recompiled. Moreover, there are no platform-specific features in the Java language. In some languages, such as Ada, the largest integer varies on different platforms. But in Java, the range of the integer is the same on every platform, as is the behavior of arithmetic. The fixed range of the numbers makes the program portable.

The Java environment is portable to new hardware and operating systems. In fact, the Java compiler itself is written in Java.

1.7.9 Java's Performance

Java's performance is sometimes criticized. The execution of the bytecode is never as fast as it would be with a compiled language, such as C++. Because Java is interpreted, the bytecode is not directly executed by the system, but is run through the interpreter. However, its speed is more than adequate for most interactive applications, where the CPU is often idle, waiting for input or for data from other sources.

CPU speed has increased dramatically in the past few years, and this trend will continue. There are many ways to improve performance. Users of the earlier Sun Java Virtual Machine certainly noticed that Java was slow. However, the new JVM is significantly faster. The new JVM uses the technology known as *just-in-time compilation*. It compiles bytecode into native machine code, stores the native code, and reinvokes the native code when its bytecode is executed. Sun recently developed the Java HotSpot Performance Engine, which includes a compiler for optimizing the frequently used code. The HotSpot Performance Engine can be plugged into a JVM to dramatically boost its performance.

1.7.10 Java Is Multithreaded

Multithreading is a program's capability to perform several tasks simultaneously. For example, downloading a video file while playing the video would be considered multithreading. Multithread programming is smoothly integrated in Java, whereas in other languages you have to call procedures specific to the operating system to enable multithreading.

Multithreading is particularly useful in graphical user interface (GUI) and network programming. In GUI programming, there are many things going on at the same time. A user can listen to an audio recording while surfing a Web page. In network programming, a server can serve multiple clients at the same time. Multithreading is a necessity in multimedia and network programming.

1.7.11 Java Is Dynamic

Java was designed to adapt to an evolving environment. New class can be loaded on the fly without recompilation. There is no need for developers to create, and for users to install, major new software versions. New features can be incorporated transparently as needed.

1.8 The Java Language Specification, API, JDK, and IDE

Computer languages have strict rules of usage. If you do not follow the rules when writing a program, the computer will be unable to understand it. Sun Microsystems, the originator of Java, intends to retain control of this important new computer language—and for a very good reason: to prevent it from losing its unified standards. The Java language specification and Java API define the Java standard.

The Java language specification is a technical definition of the language that includes the syntax and semantics of the Java programming language. The complete reference of the Java language specification can be found at `java.sun.com/docs/books/jls`.

The *application program interface* (API) contains predefined classes and interfaces for developing Java programs. The Java language specification is stable, but the API is still expanding. At the Sun Java Web site (`java.sun.com`), you can view and download the latest version and updates to the Java API.

API

Java was introduced in 1995. Sun announced the Java 2 platform in December 1998. Java 2 is the overarching brand that applies to current Java technology. There are three editions of the Java API: *Java 2 Standard Edition (J2SE), Java 2 Enterprise Edition (J2EE),* and *Java 2 Micro Edition (J2ME)*. Java is a full-fledged and powerful language that can be used in many ways. J2SE can be used to develop client-side standalone applications or applets. J2EE can be used to develop server-side applications, such as Java servlets and JavaServer Pages. J2ME can be used to develop applications for mobile devices, such as cell phones. This book uses J2SE to introduce Java programming.

There are many versions of J2SE. The latest version is J2SE 5.0, which will be used in this book. Sun releases each version of J2SE with a *Java Development Toolkit* (JDK). For J2SE 5.0, the Java Development Toolkit is called JDK 5.0, formerly known as JDK 1.5. Since most Java programmers are familiar with the name JDK 1.5, this book uses the names JDK 5.0 and JDK 1.5 interchangeably.

J2SE 5.0

JDK 5.0
JDK 1.5

JDK consists of a set of separate programs for developing and testing Java programs, each of which is invoked from a command line. Besides JDK, there are more than a dozen Java development tools on the market today. The major development tools are:

✦ JBuilder by Borland (`www.borland.com`)

✦ NetBeans Open Source by Sun (`www.netbeans.org`)

> ✦ Sun ONE, a commercial version of NetBeans by Sun (java.sun.com)
>
> ✦ Eclipse Open Source by IBM (www.eclipse.org)

Java IDE

These tools provide an *integrated development environment* (IDE) for rapidly developing Java programs. Editing, compiling, building, debugging, and online help are integrated in one graphical user interface. Just enter source code in one window or open an existing file in a window, then click a button, menu item, or function key to compile the source code.

1.9 A Simple Java Program

A Java program can be written in many ways. This book introduces Java applications and applets. *Applications* are standalone programs. This includes any program written with a high-level language. Applications can be executed from any computer with a Java interpreter. *Applets* are special kinds of Java programs that can run directly from a Java-compatible Web browser. Applets are suitable for deploying Web projects. Applets will be introduced in Chapter 14, "Applets, Images, and Audio."

application
applet

Let us begin with a simple Java program that displays the message "Welcome to Java!"

EXAMPLE 1.1 A SIMPLE APPLICATION

Problem

Write a program that displays the message "Welcome to Java!" on the console.

Solution

Listing 1.1 gives the solution to the problem.

LISTING 1.1 Welcome.java (Displaying a Message)

```
Comments ──▶ // This application program prints Welcome to Java!
Class
heading ──▶ public class Welcome {    Class Name
Main method    public static void main(String[] args) {
signature
                System.out.println("Welcome to Java!");    String
        }
    }
```

Review

class name

Every Java program must have at least one class. Each class begins with a class declaration that defines data and methods for the class. In this example, the *class name* is Welcome.

main method

The class contains a method named main. The main method in this program contains the System.out.println statement. The main method is invoked by the interpreter.

console output

In this program, println("Welcome to Java!") is actually the statement that prints the message. So why use the other statements in the program? Because Java, like any other programming language, has its own syntax, and you need to write code that obeys the syntax rules. The Java compiler will report syntax errors if your program violates the syntax rules.

EXAMPLE 1.1 (CONTINUED)

 NOTE

You are probably wondering about such points as why the `main` method is declared this way and why `System.out.println(...)` is used to display a message to the console. Your questions cannot be fully answered yet. For the time being, you will just have to accept that this is how things are done. You will find the answers in the coming chapters.

1.10   Creating, Compiling, and Executing a Java Program

You have to create your program and compile it before it can be executed. This process is iterative, as shown in Figure 1.11. If your program has compilation errors, you have to fix them by modifying the program, then recompile it. If your program has runtime errors or does not produce the correct result, you have to modify the program, recompile it, and execute it again.

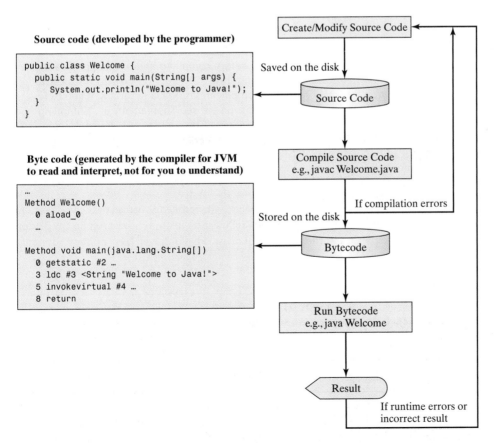

FIGURE 1.11   *The Java programming-development process consists of creating/modifying source code, compiling, and executing programs.*

editor

You can use any text *editor* to create and edit a Java source code file, or you can use an IDE like JBuilder and NetBeans. Figure 1.12 shows how to use the NotePad to create and edit the source code file.

![Welcome - Notepad window showing Java source code]

```
public class welcome {
  public static void main(String[] args) {
    System.out.println("welcome to Java!");
  }
}
```

FIGURE 1.12 *You can create the Java source file using Windows NotePad.*

.java source file

This file must end with the extension .java and should have the exact same name as the public class name. For example, the file for the source code in Example 1.1 should be named Welcome.java, since the public class name is `Welcome`.

compile

To *compile* the program is to translate the Java source code into Java bytecode using the software called a *compiler*. The following command compiles Welcome.java:

```
javac Welcome.java
```

 NOTE

You must first install and configure JDK before compiling and running programs. See Supplement A, "Installing and Configuring JDK 5.0," on how to install JDK and how to set up the environment to compile and run Java programs. If you have trouble compiling and running programs, please see Supplement B, "Compiling and Running Java from the Command Window." This supplement also contains information on how to use basic DOS commands and how to use Windows NotePad and WordPad to create and edit files. All the supplements are accessible from the Companion Website.

.class bytecode file

If there are no syntax errors, the *compiler* generates a bytecode file named `Welcome.class`. The bytecode is similar to machine instructions but is architecture-neutral and can run on any platform that has the Java interpreter and runtime environment. This is one of Java's primary advantages: *Java bytecode can run on a variety of hardware platforms and operating systems.*

 CAUTION

Java source programs are case-sensitive. It would be wrong, for example, to replace main in the program with Main. Program filenames are case-sensitive on UNIX but generally not on PCs; JDK treats filenames as case-sensitive on any platform. If you try to compile the program using javac welcome.java, you will get a file-not-found error.

run

To execute a Java program is to run the program's bytecode. You can execute the bytecode on any platform with a Java interpreter.

The following command *runs* the bytecode:

```
java Welcome
```

Figure 1.13 shows the javac command for compiling Welcome.java. The compiler generated the Welcome.class file. This file is executed using the java command.

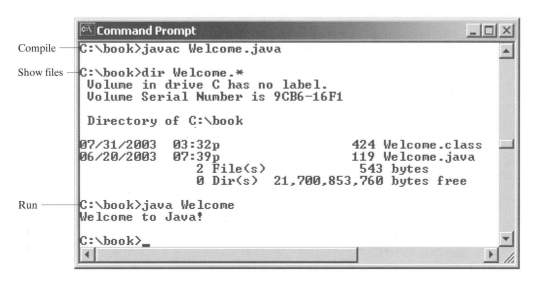

Compile
Show files
Run

```
C:\book>javac Welcome.java

C:\book>dir Welcome.*
 Volume in drive C has no label.
 Volume Serial Number is 9CB6-16F1

 Directory of C:\book

07/31/2003  03:32p                    424 Welcome.class
06/20/2003  07:39p                    119 Welcome.java
               2 File(s)              543 bytes
               0 Dir(s)  21,700,853,760 bytes free

C:\book>java Welcome
Welcome to Java!

C:\book>_
```

FIGURE 1.13 *The output of Example 1.1 displays the message Welcome to Java!*

 CAUTION

Do not use the extension .class in the command line when executing the program. The Java interpreter assumes that the first argument in the command is the filename and then fetches filename.class to execute. It would fetch filename.class.class if you used java filename.class in the command line.

 TIP

If you execute a class file that does not exist, a NoClassDefFoundError exception will occur. If you execute a class file that does not have a main method or you mistype the main method (e.g., by typing Main instead of main), a NoSuchMethodError will occur.

NoClassDefFoundError

NoSuchMethodError

1.11 Anatomy of the Java Program

The application program in Example 1.1 has the following components:

✦ Comments

✦ Reserved words

✦ Modifiers

✦ Statements

✦ Blocks

✦ Classes

✦ Methods

✦ The main method

To build a program, you need to understand these basic elements. They are explained in the sections that follow.

1.11.1 Comments

The first line in welcome.java on page 20 is a *comment* that documents what the program is and how the program is constructed. Comments help programmers and users to communicate and understand the program. Comments are not programming statements and are ignored by the compiler. In Java, comments are preceded by two slashes (`//`) on a line, called a *line comment*, or enclosed between `/*` and `*/` on one or several lines, called a *paragraph comment*. When the compiler sees `//`, it ignores all text after `//` on the same line. When it sees `/*`, it scans for the next `*/` and ignores any text between `/*` and `*/`.

line comment

paragraph comment

Here are examples of the two types of comments:

```
// This application program prints Welcome to Java!
/* This application program prints Welcome to Java! */
/* This application program
   prints Welcome to Java! */
```

javadoc comment

 NOTE

In addition to the two comment styles, `//` and `/*`, Java supports comments of a special type, referred to as *javadoc comments*. javadoc comments begin with `/**` and end with `*/`. They are used for documenting classes, data, and methods. They can be extracted into an HTML file using JDK's `javadoc` command. For more information, see `java.sun.com/j2se/javadoc`.

1.11.2 Reserved Words

reserved word

Reserved words, or *keywords*, are words that have a specific meaning to the compiler and cannot be used for other purposes in the program. For example, when the compiler sees the word `class`, it understands that the word after `class` is the name for the class. Other reserved words in Example 1.1 are `public`, `static`, and `void`. Their use will be introduced later in the book.

case-sensitive

 TIP

Because Java is *case-sensitive*, public is a reserved word, but Public is not. Nonetheless, for clarity and readability, it would be best to avoid using reserved words in other forms. (See Appendix A, "Java Keywords.")

1.11.3 Modifiers

modifier

Java uses certain reserved words called *modifiers* that specify the properties of the data, methods, and classes and how they can be used. Examples of modifiers are `public` and `static`. Other modifiers are `private`, `final`, `abstract`, and `protected`. A `public` datum, method, or class can be accessed by other classes. A `private` datum or method cannot be accessed by other classes.

1.11.4 Statements

statement

A *statement* represents an action or a sequence of actions. The statement `System.out`
`.println("Welcome to Java!")` in the program in Example 1.1 is a statement to display the greeting "Welcome to Java!" Every statement in Java ends with a *semicolon* (`;`).

semicolon

2. Compile the source file.

3. Run the bytecode.

4. Replace "Welcome to Java" with "My first program" in the program; save, compile, and run the program. You will see the message "My first program" displayed.

5. Replace `main` with `Main`, and recompile the source code. The compiler returns an error message because the Java program is case-sensitive.

6. Change it back, and compile the program again.

7. Instead of the command `javac Welcome.java`, use `javac welcome.java`. What happens?

8. Instead of the command `java Welcome`, use `java Welcome.class`. What happens? (The interpreter searches for `Welcome.class.class`.)

chapter

PRIMITIVE DATA TYPES AND OPERATIONS

Objectives

✦ To write Java programs to perform simple calculations (§2.2).

✦ To use identifiers to name variables, constants, methods, and classes (§2.3).

✦ To use variables to store data (§§2.4–2.5).

✦ To program with assignment statements and assignment expressions (§2.5).

✦ To use constants to store permanent data (§2.6).

✦ To declare Java primitive data types: `byte`, `short`, `int`, `long`, `float`, `double`, `char`, and `boolean` (§§2.7–2.10).

✦ To use Java operators to write expressions (§§2.7–2.10).

✦ To know the rules governing operand evaluation order, operator precedence, and operator associativity (§§2.11–2.12).

✦ To represent a string using the `String` type (§2.13).

✦ To obtain input using the `JOptionPane` input dialog boxes (§2.14).

✦ To obtain input from the console (§2.16 Optional).

✦ To format output using JDK 1.5 `printf` (§2.17 Optional).

✦ To become familiar with Java documentation, programming style, and naming conventions (§2.18).

✦ To distinguish syntax errors, runtime errors, and logic errors (§2.19).

✦ To debug logic errors (§2.20).

2.1 Introduction

In the preceding chapter, you learned how to create, compile, and run a Java program. In this chapter, you will be introduced to Java primitive data types and related subjects, such as variables, constants, data types, operators, and expressions. You will learn how to write programs using primitive data types, input and output, and simple calculations.

2.2 Writing Simple Programs

To begin, let's look at a simple program that computes the area of a circle. The program reads in the radius of the circle and displays its area. The program will use variables to store the radius and the area, and will use an expression to compute the area.

Writing this program involves designing algorithms and data structures, as well as translating algorithms into programming codes. An *algorithm* describes how a problem is solved in terms of the actions to be executed, and it specifies the order in which the actions should be executed. Algorithms can help the programmer plan a program before writing it in a programming language. The algorithm for this program can be described as follows:

algorithm

1. Read in the radius.

2. Compute the area using the following formula:

   area = radius $\times$ radius $\times$ π

3. Display the area.

Many of the problems you will meet when taking an introductory course in programming using this text can be described with simple, straightforward algorithms. As your education progresses, and you take courses on data structures or on algorithm design and analysis, you will encounter complex problems that require sophisticated solutions. You will need to design accurate, efficient algorithms with appropriate data structures in order to solve such problems.

Data structures involve data representation and manipulation. Java provides data types for representing integers, floating-point numbers (i.e., numbers with a decimal point), characters, and Boolean types. These types are known as *primitive data types.* Java also supports array and string types as objects. Some advanced data structures, such as stacks, sets, and lists, have built-in implementation in Java.

primitive data types

To novice programmers, coding is a daunting task. When you *code*, you translate an algorithm into a programming language understood by the computer. You already know that every Java program begins with a class declaration in which the keyword `class` is followed by the class name. Assume that you have chosen `ComputeArea` as the class name. The outline of the program would look like this:

```
public class ComputeArea {
  // Data and methods to be given later
}
```

As you know, every application must have a `main` method that controls the execution of the program. So the program is expanded as follows:

```
public class ComputeArea {
  public static void main(String[] args) {
    // Step 1: Read in radius

    // Step 2: Compute area

    // Step 3: Display the area
  }
}
```

The program needs to read the radius entered by the user from the keyboard. This raises two important issues:

✦ Reading the radius.

✦ Storing the radius in the program.

variable

descriptive names

Let's address the second issue first. In order to store the radius, the program needs to declare a symbol called a *variable* that will represent the radius. Variables are used to store data and computational results in the program.

Rather than using x and y, choose *descriptive names*: in this case, radius for radius, and area for area. Specify their data types to let the compiler know what radius and area are, indicating whether they are integer, float, or something else. Declare radius and area as double-precision floating-point numbers. The program can be expanded as follows:

```
public class ComputeArea {
  public static void main(String[] args) {
    double radius;
    double area;

    // Step 1: Read in radius

    // Step 2: Compute area

    // Step 3: Display the area
  }
}
```

The program declares radius and area as variables. The reserved word double indicates that radius and area are double-precision floating-point values stored in the computer.

The first step is to read in radius. Reading a number is not a simple matter. For the time being, let us assign a fixed number to radius in the program. In Section 2.14, "Getting Input from Input Dialogs," you will learn how to obtain a numeric value from an input dialog.

The second step is to compute area by assigning the expression radius * radius * 3.14159 to area.

In the final step, print area on the console by using the System.out.println method.

The complete program is shown in Listing 2.1. A sample run of the program is shown in Figure 2.1.

LISTING 2.1 ComputeArea.java (Computing Area for a Circle)

```
1   public class ComputeArea {
2     /** Main method */
3     public static void main(String[] args) {
4       double radius;
5       double area;
6
7       // Assign a radius
8       radius = 20;
9
10      // Compute area
11      area = radius * radius * 3.14159;
12
13      // Display results
14      System.out.println("The area for the circle of radius " +
15        radius + " is " + area);
16    }
17  }
```

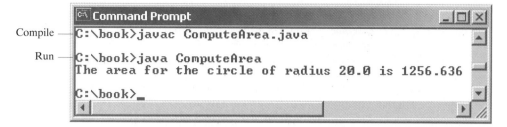

— C:\book>javac ComputeArea.java

— C:\book>java ComputeArea
The area for the circle of radius 20.0 is 1256.636

C:\book>_

FIGURE 2.1 *The program displays the area of the circle.*

The plus sign (+) is called a *string concatenation operator* if one of the operands is a string. The string concatenation operator connects two strings if two operands are strings. If one of the operands is a non-string (e.g., a number), the non-string value is converted into a string and concatenated with the other string. So the plus signs (+) in Lines 14–15 concatenate strings into a longer string, which is then displayed in the output. More on strings and string concatenation will be discussed in Section 2.13, "The String Type."

concatenating strings

concatenating strings with numbers

 CAUTION

A string constant should not cross lines in the source code. Thus the following statement would result in a compilation error:

```
System.out.println("Introduction to Java Programming,
  by Y. Daniel Liang");
```

To fix the error, break the string into substrings, and use the concatenation operator (+) to combine them:

```
System.out.println("Introduction to Java Programming, " +
  "by Y. Daniel Liang");
```

breaking a long string

2.3 Identifiers

Just as every entity in the real world has a name, so you need to choose names for the things you will refer to in your programs. Programming languages use special symbols called *identifiers* to name such programming entities as variables, constants, methods, classes, and packages. Here are the rules for naming identifiers:

identifier

◆ An identifier is a sequence of characters that consists of letters, digits, underscores (_), and dollar signs ($).

◆ An identifier must start with a letter, an underscore (_), or a dollar sign ($). It cannot start with a digit.

◆ An identifier cannot be a reserved word. (See Appendix A, "Java Keywords," for a list of reserved words.)

◆ An identifier cannot be true, false, or null.

◆ An identifier can be of any length.

For example, $2, ComputeArea, area, radius, and showMessageDialog are legal identifiers, whereas 2A and d+4 are illegal identifiers because they do not follow the rules. The Java compiler detects illegal identifiers and reports syntax errors.

case-sensitive

> ✿ **NOTE**
> Since Java is *case-sensitive*, X and x are different identifiers.

descriptive names

> ✿ **TIP**
> Identifiers are used for naming variables, constants, methods, classes, and packages. Descriptive identifiers make programs easy to read. Besides choosing *descriptive names* for identifiers, there are naming conventions for different kinds of identifiers. Naming conventions are summarized in Section 2.18, "Programming Style and Documentation."

2.4 Variables

Variables are used to store data in a program. In the program in Listing 2.1, radius and area are variables of double-precision, floating-point type. You can assign any numerical value to radius and area, and the values of radius and area can be reassigned. For example, you can write the code shown below to compute the area for different radii:

```
// Compute the first area
radius = 1.0;
area = radius * radius * 3.14159;
System.out.println("The area is " + area + " for radius " + radius);

// Compute the second area
radius = 2.0;
area = radius * radius * 3.14159;
System.out.println("The area is " + area + " for radius " + radius);
```

2.4.1 Declaring Variables

Variables are for representing data of a certain type. To use a variable, you declare it by telling the compiler the name of the variable as well as what type of data it represents. This is called a *variable declaration*. Declaring a variable tells the compiler to allocate appropriate memory space for the variable based on its data type. Here is the syntax for declaring a variable:

declaring variable

```
datatype variableName;
```

Here are some examples of variable declarations:

```
int x;              // Declare x to be an integer variable;
double radius;      // Declare radius to be a double variable;
double interestRate; // Declare interestRate to be a double variable;
char a;             // Declare a to be a character variable;
```

The examples use the data types int, double, and char. Later in this chapter you will be introduced to additional data types, such as byte, short, long, float, char, and boolean.
If variables are of the same type, they can be declared together, as follows:

```
datatype variable1, variable2, …, variablen;
```

The variables are separated by commas.

naming variables

> ✿ **NOTE**
> By convention, variable names are in lowercase. If a name consists of several words, concatenate all of them and capitalize the first letter of each word except the first. Examples of variables are radius and interestRate.

2.5   Assignment Statements and Assignment Expressions

After a variable is declared, you can assign a value to it by using an *assignment statement*. In Java, the equal sign (=) is used as the *assignment operator*. The syntax for assignment statements is as follows:

assignment statement
assignment operator

```
variable = expression;
```

An *expression* represents a computation involving values, variables, and operators that evaluates to a value. For example, consider the following code:

expression

```
int x = 1;                        // Assign 1 to variable x;
double radius = 1.0;              // Assign 1.0 to variable radius;
a = 'A';                          // Assign 'A' to variable a;
x = 5 * (3 / 2) + 3 * 2;          // Assign the value of the expression to x;
x = y + 1;                        // Assign the addition of y and 1 to x;
area = radius * radius * 3.14159; // Compute area
```

The variable can also be used in the expression. For example,

```
x = x + 1;
```

In this assignment statement, the result of x + 1 is assigned to x. If x is 1 before the statement is executed, then it becomes 2 after the statement is executed.

To assign a value to a variable, the variable name must be on the left of the assignment operator. Thus, 1 = x would be wrong.

In Java, an assignment statement can also be treated as an expression that evaluates to the value being assigned to the variable on the left-hand side of the assignment operator. For this reason, an assignment statement is also known as an *assignment expression*. For example, the following statement is correct:

assignment expression

```
System.out.println(x = 1);
```

which is equivalent to

```
x = 1;
System.out.println(x);
```

The following statement is also correct:

```
i = j = k = 1;
```

which is equivalent to

```
k = 1;
j = k;
i = j;
```

 NOTE

In an assignment statement, the data type of the variable on the left must be compatible with the data type of the value on the right. For example, int x = 1.0 would be illegal because the data type of x is int. You cannot assign a double value (1.0) to an int variable without using type casting. Type casting is introduced in Section 2.8, "Numeric Type Conversions."

2.5.1   Declaring and Initializing Variables in One Step

Variables often have initial values. You can declare a variable and initialize it in one step. Consider, for instance, the following code:

```
int x = 1;
```

This is equivalent to the next two statements:

```
int x;
x = 1;
```

You can also use a shorthand form to declare and initialize variables of the same type together. For example,

```
int i = 1, j = 2;
```

 TIP

A variable must be declared before it can be assigned a value. A variable declared in a method must be assigned a value before it can be used.

Whenever possible, declare a variable and assign its initial value in one step. This will make the program easy to read and avoid programming errors.

2.6 Constants

constant

The value of a variable may change during the execution of the program, but a *constant* represents permanent data that never changes. In our ComputeArea program, π is a constant. If you use it frequently, you don't want to keep typing 3.14159; instead, you can define a constant for π. Here is the syntax for declaring a constant:

```
final datatype CONSTANTNAME = VALUE;
```

The word final is a Java keyword which means that the constant cannot be changed. For example, in the ComputeArea program, you could define π as a constant and rewrite the program as follows:

```
// ComputeArea.java: Compute the area of a circle
public class ComputeArea {
  /** Main method */
  public static void main(String[] args) {
    final double PI + 3.14159; // Declare a constant

    // Assign a radius
    double radius = 20;

    // Compute area
    double area = radius * radius * PI;

    // Display results
    System.out.println("The area for the circle of radius " +
      radius + " is " + area);
  }
}
```

---

naming constants

 CAUTION

A constant must be declared and initialized before it can be used. You cannot change a constant's value once it is declared. By convention, constants are named in uppercase: PI, not pi or Pi.

---

benefits of constants

NOTE

There are three benefits of using constants: (1) you don't have to repeatedly type the same value; (2) the value can be changed in a single location, if necessary; (3) the program is easy to read.

2.7   Numeric Data Types and Operations

Every data type has a range of values. The compiler allocates memory space to store each variable or constant according to its data type. Java provides several primitive data types for numeric values, characters, and Boolean values. In this section, numeric data types are introduced.

Java has six numeric types: four for integers and two for floating-point numbers. Table 2.1 lists the six numeric data types, their ranges, and their storage sizes.

TABLE 2.1   **Numeric Data Types**

Name	Range	Storage Size
byte	-2^7 (-128) to $2^7 - 1$ (127)	8-bit signed
short	-2^{15} (-32768) to $2^{15} - 1$ (32767)	16-bit signed
int	-2^{31} (-2147483648) to $2^{31} - 1$ (2147483647)	32-bit signed
long	-2^{63} to $2^{63} - 1$ (i.e., -9223372036854775808 to 9223372036854775807)	64-bit signed
float	$-3.4E38$ to $3.4E38$ (6 to 7 significant digits of accuracy)	32-bit IEEE 754
double	$-1.7E308$ to $1.7E308$ (14 to 15 significant digits of accuracy)	64-bit IEEE 754

> **NOTE**
> IEEE 754 is a standard approved by the Institute of Electrical and Electronics Engineers for representing floating-point numbers on computers. The standard has been widely adopted. Java has adopted the 32-bit IEEE 754 for the `float` type and the 64-bit IEEE 754 for the `double` type. The IEEE 754 standard also defines special values and operations in Appendix F, "Special Floating-Point Values."

2.7.1   Numeric Operators

The operators for numeric data types include the standard arithmetic operators: addition (+), subtraction (−), multiplication (*), division (/), and remainder (%). For examples, see the following code:

operators +, −, *, /, %

```
int i1 = 34 + 1;        // i1 becomes 35
double d1 = 34.0 - 0.1; // d1 becomes 33.9
long i2 = 300 * 30;     // i2 becomes 9000
double d2 = 1.0 / 2.0;  // d2 becomes 0.5
int i3 = 1 / 2;         // i3 becomes 0; Note that the result is
                        // the integer part of the division
byte i4 = 20 % 3;       // i4 becomes 2; Note that the result is
                        // the remainder after the division
```

The result of integer division is an integer. The fractional part is truncated. For example, $5/2 = 2$, not 2.5, and $-5/2 = -2$, not -2.5.

The % operator yields the remainder after division. Therefore, 7 % 3 yields 1, and 20 % 13 yields 7. This operator is often used for integers but also can be used with floating-point values.

$\sqrt[3]{\dfrac{\dfrac{2}{7}}{\dfrac{6}{1}}}$

Remainder is very useful in programming. For example, an even number % 2 is always 0 and an odd number % 2 is always 1. So you can use this property to determine whether a number is even or odd. Suppose you know that January 1, 2005 is a Saturday, you can find that the day for February 1, 2005 is Tuesday using the following expression:

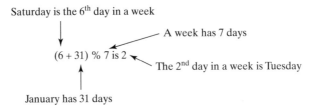

Saturday is the 6th day in a week

A week has 7 days

(6 + 31) % 7 is 2

The 2nd day in a week is Tuesday

January has 31 days

unary operator
binary operator

The + and − operators can be both unary and binary. A *unary operator* has only one operand; a *binary operator* has two operands. For example, the − operator in −5 can be considered a unary operator to negate number 5, whereas the − operator in 4 − 5 is a binary operator for subtracting 5 from 4.

---

approximation

> **NOTE**
>
> Calculations involving floating-point numbers are approximated because these numbers are not stored with complete accuracy. For example,
>
> ```
> System.out.println(1 - 0.1 - 0.1 - 0.1 - 0.1 - 0.1);
> ```
>
> displays 0.5000000000000001, not 0.5, and
>
> ```
> System.out.println(1.0 - 0.9);
> ```
>
> displays 0.09999999999999998, not 0.1. Integers are stored precisely. Therefore, calculations with integers yield a precise integer result.

2.7.2 Numeric Literals

literal

A *literal* is a constant value that appears directly in a program. For example, 34, 1,000,000, and 5.0 are literals in the following statements:

```
int i = 34;
long k = 1000000;
double d = 5.0;
```

2.7.2.1 Integer Literals

An integer literal can be assigned to an integer variable as long as it can fit into the variable. A compilation error would occur if the literal were too large for the variable to hold. The statement byte b = 1000, for example, would cause a compilation error, because 1000 cannot be stored in a variable of the byte type.

suffix L or l

An integer literal is assumed to be of the int type, whose value is between -2^{31} (-2147483648) and $2^{31} - 1$ (2147483647). To denote an integer literal of the long type, append the letter L or l to it (e.g., 2147483648L). L is preferred because l (lowercase L) can easily be confused with 1 (the digit one). Since 2147483648 exceeds the range for the int value, it must be denoted as 2147483648L.

---

octal and hex literals

> **NOTE**
>
> By default, an integer literal is a decimal number. To denote an octal integer literal, use a leading 0 (zero), and to denote a hexadecimal integer literal, use a

leading *0x* or *0X* (zero x). For example, the following code displays the decimal value 65535 for hexadecimal number FFFF:

```
System.out.println(0xFFFF);
```

Hexadecimal numbers, binary numbers, and octal numbers were introduced in Section 1.5, "Number systems."

2.7.2.2   Floating-Point Literals

Floating-point literals are written with a decimal point. By default, a floating-point literal is treated as a double type value. For example, 5.0 is considered a double value, not a float value. You can make a number a float by appending the letter f or F, and you can make a number a double by appending the letter d or D. For example, you can use 100.2f or 100.2F for a float number, and 100.2d or 100.2D for a double number.

suffix f or F

suffix d or D

 NOTE

The double type values are more accurate than the float type values. For example,

double vs. float

```
System.out.println("1.0 / 3.0 is " + 1.0 / 3.0);
```

displays 1.0 / 3.0 is 0.3333333333333333.

```
System.out.println("1.0F / 3.0F is " + 1.0F / 3.0F);
```

displays 1.0F / 3.0F is 0.33333334.

2.7.2.3   Scientific Notations

Floating-point literals can also be specified in scientific notation; for example, 1.23456e + 2, the same as 1.23456e2, is equivalent to $1.23456 \times 10^2 = 123.456$, and 1.23456e − 2 is equivalent to $1.23456 \times 10^{-2} = 0.0123456$. E (or e) represents an exponent and can be either in lowercase or uppercase.

2.7.3   Arithmetic Expressions

Writing numeric expressions in Java involves a straightforward translation of an arithmetic expression using Java operators. For example, the arithmetic expression

$$\frac{3 + 4x}{5} - \frac{10(y - 5)(a + b + c)}{x} + 9\left(\frac{4}{x} + \frac{9 + x}{y}\right)$$

can be translated into a Java expression as:

```
(3 + 4 * x) / 5 - 10 * (y - 5) * (a + b + c) / x +
9 * (4 / x + (9 + x) / y)
```

The numeric operators in a Java expression are applied the same way as in an arithmetic expression. Operators contained within pairs of parentheses are evaluated first. Parentheses can be nested, in which case the expression in the inner parentheses is evaluated first. Multiplication, division, and remainder operators are applied next. If an expression contains several multiplication, division, and remainder operators, they are applied from left to right. Addition and subtraction operators are applied last. If an expression contains several addition and subtraction operators, they are applied from left to right.

integer vs. decimal division

> **CAUTION**
>
> Be careful when applying division. Division of two integers yields an integer in Java. For example, the formula for converting a Fahrenheit degree is
>
> $$celsius = \left(\tfrac{5}{9}\right)(fahrenheit - 32)$$
>
> Because 5 / 9 yields 0 in Java, the preceding formula should be translated into a Java statement shown below:
>
> ```
> celsius = (5.0 / 9) * (fahrenheit - 32)
> ```

2.7.4 Shortcut Operators

Very often the current value of a variable is used, modified, and then reassigned back to the same variable. For example, consider the following code:

```
i = i + 8;
```

This statement is equivalent to

```
i += 8;
```

shortcut operator

The += is called a *shortcut operator*. Other shortcut operators are shown in Table 2.2.

TABLE 2.2 **Shortcut Operators**

Operator	Name	Example	Equivalent
+=	Addition assignment	i += 8	i = i + 8
-=	Subtraction assignment	f -= 8.0	f = f - 8.0
*=	Multiplication assignment	i *= 8	i = i * 8
/=	Division assignment	i /= 8	i = i / 8
%=	Remainder assignment	i %= 8	i = i % 8

++ and −−

There are two more shortcut operators for incrementing and decrementing a variable by 1. This is handy because that's often how much the value needs to be changed. These two operators are ++ and --. They can be used in prefix or suffix notation, as shown in Table 2.3.

TABLE 2.3 **Increment and Decrement Operators**

Operator	Name	Description
++var	preincrement	The expression (++var) increments var by 1 and evaluates to the *new* value in var *after* the increment.
var++	postincrement	The expression (var++) evaluates to the *original* value in var and increments var by 1.
--var	predecrement	The expression (--var) decrements var by 1 and evaluates to the *new* value in var *after* the decrement.
var--	postdecrement	The expression (var--) evaluates to the *original* value in var and decrements var by 1.

preincrement, predecrement

If the operator is *before* (prefixed to) the variable, the variable is incremented or decremented by 1, then the *new* value of the variable is returned. If the operator is *after* (suffixed to) the variable, the original *old* value of the variable is returned, then the variable is incremented or decremented by 1. Therefore, the prefixes ++x and --x are referred to, respectively, as the *preincrement operator* and the *predecrement operator*; and the suffixes x++ and x-- are referred to, respectively, as the *postincrement operator* and the *postdecrement operator*. The prefix form of ++ (or −−) and the suffix form of ++ (or −−) are the same if they are used in isolation, but they have different effects when used in an expression. The following code illustrates this:

postincrement, postdecrement

```
int i = 10;                 Same effect as      int newNum = 10 * i;
int newNum = 10 * i++;                          i = i + 1;
```

In this case, i is incremented by 1, then the *old* value of i is returned and used in the multiplication. So newNum becomes 100. If i++ is replaced by ++i as follows,

```
int i = 10;                 Same effect as      i = i + 1;
int newNum = 10 * (++i);                        int newNum = 10 * i;
```

i is incremented by 1, and the new value of i is returned and used in the multiplication. Thus newNum becomes 110.

Here is another example:

```
double x = 1.0;
double y = 5.0;
double z = x-- + (++y);
```

After all three lines are executed, y becomes 6.0, z becomes 7.0, and x becomes 0.0.

The increment operator ++ and the decrement operator −− can be applied to all integer and floating-point types. These operators are often used in loop statements. A *loop statement* is a structure that controls how many times an operation or a sequence of operations is performed in succession. This structure, and the subject of loop statements, is introduced in Chapter 3, "Control Statements."

 TIP

Using increment and decrement operators makes expressions short, but it also makes them complex and difficult to read. Avoid using these operators in expressions that modify multiple variables or the same variable multiple times, such as this one: int k = ++i + i.

 NOTE

Like the assignment operator (=), the operators (+=, −=, *=, /=, %=, ++, and −−) can be used to form an assignment statement as well as an expression. Prior to Java 2, all expressions could be used as statements. Since Java 2, only the following types of expressions can be statements:

```
variable op= expression; // Where op is +, -, *, /, or %
++variable;
variable++;
--variable;
variable--;
```

The code shown below has a compilation error in Java 2:

```
public static void main(String[] args) {
  3 + 4; // Correct prior to Java 2, but wrong in Java 2
}
```

> ※ **CAUTION**
> There are no spaces in the shortcut operators. For example, + = should be +=.

2.8 Numeric Type Conversions

Sometimes it is necessary to mix numeric values of different types in a computation. Consider the following statements:

```
byte i = 100;
long k = i * 3 + 4;
double d = i * 3.1 + k / 2;
```

Are these statements correct? Java allows binary operations on values of different types. When performing a binary operation involving two operands of different types, Java automatically converts the operand based on the following rules:

converting operands

1. If one of the operands is `double`, the other is converted into `double`.

2. Otherwise, if one of the operands is `float`, the other is converted into `float`.

3. Otherwise, if one of the operands is `long`, the other is converted into `long`.

4. Otherwise, both operands are converted into `int`.

For example, the result of 1/2 is 0, and the result of 1.0/2 is 0.5.

You can always assign a value to a numeric variable whose type supports a larger range of values; thus, for instance, you can assign a `long` value to a `float` variable. You cannot, however, assign a value to a variable of a type with smaller range unless you use *type casting*. Casting is an operation that converts a value of one data type into a value of another data type. Casting a variable of a type with a small range to a variable of a type with a larger range is known as *widening a type*. Casting a variable of a type with a large range to a variable of a type with a smaller range is known as *narrowing a type*. Widening a type can be performed automatically without explicit casting. Narrowing a type must be performed explicitly.

type casting

widening a type

narrowing a type

The syntax for casting gives the target type in parentheses, followed by the variable's name or the value to be cast. The code that follows is an example.

```
float f = (float)10.1;
int i = (int)f;
```

In the first line, the `double` value 10.1 is cast into `float`. In the second line, i has a value of 10; the fractional part in f is truncated.

> ※ **CAUTION**
> Casting is necessary if you are assigning a value to a variable of a smaller type range, such as assigning a `double` value to an `int` variable. A compilation error will occur if casting is not used in situations of this kind. Be careful when using casting. Lost information might lead to inaccurate results, as will be shown in Example 2.3, "Monetary Units," in Section 2.15, "Case Studies."

possible loss of precision

> ※ **NOTE**
> Casting does not change the variable being cast. For example, d is not changed after casting in the following code:
> ```
> double d = 4.5;
> int i = (int)d; // d is not changed
> ```

NOTE

To assign a variable of the int type to a variable of the short or byte type, explicit casting must be used. For example, the following statements have a syntax error:

```
int i = 1;
byte b = i; // Error because explicit casting is required
```

However, so long as the integer literal is within the permissible range of the target variable, explicit casting is not needed to assign an integer literal to a variable of the short or byte type. Please refer to Section 2.7.2.1, "Integer Literals."

2.9   Character Data Type and Operations

The character data type, char, is used to represent a single character. A character literal is enclosed in single quotation marks. Consider the following code:

char type

```
char letter = 'A';
char numChar = '4';
```

The first statement assigns character A to the char variable letter. The second statement assigns the digit character 4 to the char variable numChar.

 CAUTION

A string literal must be enclosed in quotation marks. A character literal is a single character enclosed in single quotation marks. So "A" is a string, and 'A' is a character.

char literal

2.9.1   Unicode and ASCII code

Computers use binary numbers internally. A character is stored as a sequence of 0s and 1s in a computer. To convert a character to its binary representation is called *encoding*. There are different ways to encode a character. How characters are encoded is defined by an encoding scheme.

character encoding

Java uses *Unicode*, a 16-bit encoding scheme established by the Unicode Consortium to support the interchange, processing, and display of written texts in the world's diverse languages. (See the Unicode Web site at www.unicode.org for more information.) Unicode takes two bytes, preceded by \u, expressed in four hexadecimal digits that run from '\u0000' to '\uFFFF'. For example, the word "coffee" is translated into Chinese using two characters. The Unicodes of these two characters are "\u5496\u5561". The following statement displays three Greek letters, as shown in Figure 2.2.

Unicode

```
JOptionPane.showMessageDialog(null, "\u03b1 \u03b2 \u03b3",
    "Display Greek Letters", JOptionPane.INFORMATION_MESSAGE);
```

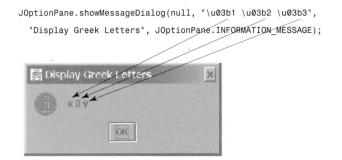

FIGURE 2.2 *You can use Unicode to represent international characters.*

ASCII

Unicode can represent 65,536 characters, since FFFF in hexadecimal is 65535. Most computers use ASCII (American Standard Code for Information Interchange), a 7-bit encoding scheme for representing all uppercase and lowercase letters, digits, punctuation marks, and control characters. Unicode includes ASCII code, with '\u0000' to '\u007F' corresponding to the 128 ASCII characters. (See Appendix B, "The ASCII Character Set," for a list of ASCII characters and their decimal and hexadecimal codes.) You can use ASCII characters like 'X', '1', and '$' in a Java program as well as Unicodes. Thus, for example, the following statements are equivalent:

```
char letter = 'A';
char letter = '\u0041'; // Character A's Unicode is 0041
```

Both statements assign character A to char variable letter.

char increment and
decrement

 NOTE

The increment and decrement operators can also be used on char variables to get the next or preceding Unicode character. For example, the following statements display character b:

```
char ch = 'a';
System.out.println(++ch);
```

2.9.2   Escape Sequences for Special Characters

Java allows you to use escape sequences to represent special characters, as shown in Table 2.4. An escape sequence begins with the backslash character (\) followed by a character that has a special meaning to the compiler.

TABLE 2.4   **Java Escape Sequences**

Description	Character Escape Sequence	Unicode
Backspace	\b	\u0008
Tab	\t	\u0009
Linefeed	\n	\u000A
Formfeed	\f	\u000C
Carriage Return	\r	\u000D
Backslash	\\	\u005C
Single Quote	\'	\u0027
Double Quote	\"	\u0022

Suppose you want to print the quoted message shown below:

```
He said "Java is fun"
```

Here is how to write the statement:

```
System.out.println("He said \"Java is fun\"");
```

2.9.3   Casting between char and Numeric Types

A char can be cast into any numeric type, and vice versa. When an integer is cast into a char, only its lower sixteen bits of data are used; the other part is ignored. When a floating-point value is cast into a char, the floating-point value is first cast into an int, which is then cast into a char. When a char is cast into a numeric type, the character's Unicode is cast into the specified numeric type.

Implicit casting can be used if the result of a casting fits into the target variable. Otherwise, explicit casting must be used. For example, since the Unicode of '0' is 48, which is within the range of a byte, these implicit castings are fine:

```
byte b = '0';
int i = '0';
```

But the next casting is incorrect, because the Unicode \uFFF4 cannot fit into a byte:

```
byte b = '\uFFF4';
```

To force a casting, use explicit casting, as follows:

```
byte b = (byte)'\uFFF4';
```

Any positive integer between 0 and FFFF in hexadecimal can be cast into a character implicitly. Any number not in this range must be cast into a char explicitly.

 NOTE

All numeric operators can be applied to the char operands. The char operand is cast into a number if the other operand is a number or a character. If the other operand is a string, the character is concatenated with the string. For example, the following statements:

numeric operators on characters

```
int i = '1' + '2'; // (int)'1' is 49 and (int)'2' is 50
System.out.println("i is " + i);

int j = 1 + 'a'; // (int)'a' is 97
System.out.println("j is " + 98);
System.out.println(j + " is the Unicode for character " + (char)j);

System.out.println("Chapter " + '2');
```

display

```
i is 99
j is 98
98 is the Unicode for character b
Chapter 2
```

 NOTE

It is worthwhile to note that the Unicodes for lowercase letters are consecutive integers starting from the Unicode for 'a', then for 'b', 'c', ..., and 'z'. The same is true for the uppercase letters. Furthermore, the Unicode for 'a' is greater than the Unicode for 'A'. So 'a' – 'A' is the same as 'b' – 'B'. For a lowercase letter *ch*, its corresponding uppercase letter is (char)('A' + (ch - 'a')).

2.10 **boolean** Data Type and Operations

Often in a program you need to compare two values, such as whether i is greater than j. Java provides six *comparison operators* (also known as *relational operators*) in Table 2.5 that can be used to compare two values. The result of the comparison is a Boolean value: true or false. For example, the following statement displays true:

comparison operators

```
System.out.println(1 < 2);
```

TABLE 2.5   Comparison Operators

Operator	Name	Example	Answer
<	less than	1 < 2	true
<=	less than or equal to	1 <= 2	true
>	greater than	1 > 2	false
>=	greater than or equal to	1 >= 2	false
==	equal to	1 == 2	false
!=	not equal to	1 != 2	true

compare characters

> **NOTE**
> You can also *compare characters*. Comparing characters is the same as comparing the Unicodes of the characters. For example, 'a' is larger than 'A' because the Unicode of 'a' is larger than the Unicode of 'A'.

(== vs. =)

> **CAUTION**
> The equality comparison operator is two equal signs (==), not a single equal sign (=). The latter symbol is for assignment.

Boolean variable

A variable that holds a Boolean value is known as a *Boolean variable*. The boolean data type is used to declare Boolean variables. The domain of the boolean type consists of two literal values: true and false. For example, the following statement assigns true to the variable lightsOn:

```
boolean lightsOn = true;
```

Boolean operators

Boolean operators, also known as *logical operators*, operate on Boolean values to create a new Boolean value. Table 2.6 contains a list of *Boolean operators*. Table 2.7 defines the not (!) operator. The not (!) operator negates true to false and false to true. Table 2.8 defines the and (&&)

TABLE 2.6   Boolean Operators

Operator	Name	Description
!	not	logical negation
&&	and	logical conjunction
||	or	logical disjunction
^	exclusive or	logical exclusion

TABLE 2.7   Truth Table for Operator !

p	!p	Example
true	false	!(1 > 2) is true, because (1 > 2) is false.
false	true	!(1 > 0) is false, because (1 > 0) is true.

TABLE 2.8   Truth Table for Operator &&

p1	p2	p1 && p2	Example
false	false	false	(2 > 3) && (5 > 5) is false, because either (2 > 3) or (5 > 5) is false.
false	true	false	
true	false	false	(3 > 2) && (5 > 5) is false, because (5 > 5) is false.
true	true	true	(3 > 2) && (5 >= 5) is true, because (3 > 2) and (5 >= 5) are both true.

TABLE 2.9   Truth Table for Operator ¦¦

p1	p2	p1 ¦¦ p2	Example
false	false	false	(2 > 3) ¦¦ (5 > 5) is false, because (2 > 3) and (5 > 5) are both false.
false	true	true	
true	false	true	(3 > 2) ¦¦ (5 > 5) is true, because (3 > 2) is true.
true	true	true	

TABLE 2.10   Truth Table for Operator ^

p1	p2	p1 ^ p2	Example
false	false	false	
false	true	true	(2 > 3) ^ (5 > 1) is true, because (2 > 3) is false and (5 > 1) is true.
true	false	true	
true	true	false	(3 > 2) ^ (5 > 1) is false, because both (3 > 2) and (5 > 1) are true.

operator. The and (&&) of two Boolean operands is true if and only if both operands are true. Table 2.9 defines the or (¦¦) operator. The or (¦¦) of two Boolean operands is true if at least one of the operands is true. Table 2.10 defines the exclusive or (^) operator. The exclusive or (^) of two Boolean operands is true if and only if the two operands have different Boolean values.

The following statements check whether a number is divisible by 2 and 3, whether a number is divisible by 2 or 3 and whether a number is divisible by 2 or 3 but not both:

```java
System.out.println("Is " + number + " divisible by 2 and 3? " +
  ((number % 2 == 0) && (number % 3 == 0)));

System.out.println("Is " + number + " divisible by 2 or 3? " +
  ((number % 2 == 0) || (number % 3 == 0)));

System.out.println("Is " + number +
  " divisible by 2 or 3, but not both? " +
  ((number % 2 == 0) ^ (number % 3 == 0)));
```

2.10.1   Unconditional vs. Conditional Boolean Operators

If one of the operands of an && operator is false, the expression is false; if one of the operands of an ¦¦ operands is true, the expression is true. Java uses these properties to improve the performance of these operators.

When evaluating p1 && p2, Java first evaluates p1 and then evaluates p2 if p1 is true; if p1 is false, it does not evaluate p2. When evaluating p1 ¦¦ p2, Java first evaluates p1 and then evaluates p2 if p1 is false; if p1 is true, it does not evaluate p2. Therefore, && is referred to as the *conditional* or *short-circuit AND* operator, and ¦¦ is referred to as the *conditional* or *short-circuit OR* operator.

Java also provides the & and ¦ operators. The & operator works exactly the same as the && operator, and the ¦ operator works exactly the same as the ¦¦ operator with one exception: the & and ¦ operators always evaluate both operands. Therefore, & is referred to as the *unconditional AND* operator, and ¦ is referred to as the *unconditional OR* operator. In some rare situations, you can

conditional operator
short-circuit operator

unconditional operator

use the & and ¦ operators to guarantee that the right-hand operand is evaluated regardless of whether the left-hand operand is `true` or `false`. For example, the expression (width < 2) & (height-- < 2) guarantees that (height-- < 2) is evaluated. Thus, the variable `height` will be decremented regardless of whether `width` is less than 2 or not.

 TIP

Avoid using the & and ¦ operators. The benefits of the & and ¦ operators are marginal. Using them will make the program difficult to read and could cause errors. For example, the expression (x != 0) & (100 / x) results in a runtime error if x is 0. However, (x != 0) && (100 / x) is fine. If x is 0, (x != 0) is false. Since && is a short-circuit operator, Java does not evaluate (100 / x) and returns the result as false for the entire expression (x != 0) && (100 / x).

---

bitwise operations

 NOTE

The & and ¦ operators can also apply to *bitwise operations*. See Appendix G, "Bit Operations," for details.

 NOTE

As shown in the preceding section, a `char` value can be cast into an `int` value, and vice versa. A Boolean value, however, cannot be cast into a value of other types, nor can a value of other types be cast into a Boolean value.

Boolean literals

 NOTE

`true` and `false` are literals, just like a number such as 10, so they are not keywords, but you cannot use them as identifiers, just as you cannot use 10 as an identifier.

2.11 Operator Precedence and Associativity

Operator precedence and associativity determine the order in which operators are evaluated. Suppose that you have this expression:

```
3 + 4 * 4 > 5 * (4 + 3) - 1
```

What is its value? How does the compiler know the execution order of the operators? The expression in the parentheses is evaluated first. (Parentheses can be nested, in which case the expression in the inner parentheses is executed first.) When evaluating an expression without parentheses, the operators are applied according to the precedence rule and the associativity rule. The *precedence* rule defines precedence for operators, as shown in Table 2.11, which contains the operators you have learned in this chapter. Operators are listed in decreasing order of precedence from top to bottom. Operators with the same precedence appear in the same group. (See Appendix C, "Operator Precedence Chart," for a complete list of Java operators and their precedence.)

associativity

If operators with the same precedence are next to each other, their *associativity* determines the order of evaluation. All binary operators except assignment operators are *left-associative*. For example, since + and − are of the same precedence and are left-associative, the expression

$$a - b + c - d \quad \underline{\text{equivalent}} \quad ((a - b) + c) - d$$

Assignment operators are *right-associative*. Therefore, the expression

$$a = b \mathrel{+}= c = 5 \quad \underline{\text{equivalent}} \quad a = (b \mathrel{+}= (c = 5))$$

precedence

TABLE 2.11   Operator Precedence Chart

Precedence	Operator
Highest Order	var++ and var-- (Postincrement and postdecrement)
	+, – (Unary plus and minus), ++var and --var (prefix)
	(type) (Casting)
	! (Not)
	*, /, % (Multiplication, division, and remainder)
	+, – (Binary addition and subtraction)
	<, <=, >, >= (Comparison)
	==, != (Equality)
	& (Unconditional AND)
	^ (Exclusive OR)
	¦ (Unconditional OR)
	&& (Conditional AND)
	¦¦ (Conditional OR)
Lowest Order	=, +=, –=, *=, /=, %= (Assignment operator)

Suppose a, b, and c are 1 before the assignment; after the whole expression is evaluated, a becomes 6, b becomes 6, and c becomes 5.

Applying the operator precedence and associativity rule, the expression 3 + 4 * 4 > 5 * (4 + 3) – 1 is evaluated as follows:

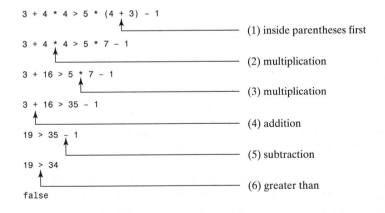

```
3 + 4 * 4 > 5 * (4 + 3) – 1
                    └──────────────── (1) inside parentheses first
3 + 4 * 4 > 5 * 7 – 1
    └──────────────────────────── (2) multiplication
3 + 16 > 5 * 7 – 1
        └──────────────────────── (3) multiplication
3 + 16 > 35 – 1
  └────────────────────────────── (4) addition
19 > 35 – 1
      └──────────────────────────── (5) subtraction
19 > 34
 └────────────────────────────────── (6) greater than
false
```

> **Tip**
> You can use parentheses to force an evaluation order as well as to make a program easy to read. Use of redundant parentheses does not slow down the execution of the expression.

2.12 Operand Evaluation Order

The precedence and associativity rules specify the order of the operators but not the order in which the operands of a binary operator are evaluated. Operands are evaluated strictly from left to right in Java. *The left-hand operand of a binary operator is evaluated before any part of the right-hand*

from left to right

operand is evaluated. This rule takes precedence over any other rules that govern expressions. Consider this expression:

```
a + b * (c + 10 * d) / e
```

a, b, c, d, and e are evaluated in this order. *If no operands have side effects that change the value of a variable, the order of operand evaluation is irrelevant.* Interesting cases arise when operands do have a side effect. For example, x becomes 1 in the following code because a is evaluated to 0 before ++a is evaluated to 1:

```
int a = 0;
int x = a + (++a);
```

But x becomes 2 in the following code because ++a is evaluated to 1, then a is evaluated to 1:

```
int a = 0;
int x = ++a + a;
```

The order for evaluating operands takes precedence over the operator precedence rule. In the former case, (++a) has higher precedence than addition (+), but since a is a left-hand operand of the addition (+), it is evaluated before any part of its right-hand operand (e.g., ++a in this case).

In summary, the rule of evaluating an expression is:

evaluation rule

✦ Rule 1: Evaluate whatever subexpressions you can possibly evaluate from left to right.

✦ Rule 2: The operators are applied according to their precedence, as shown in Table 2.11.

✦ Rule 3: The associativity rule applies for two operators next to each other with the same precedence.

Applying the rule, the expression 3 + 4 * 4 > 5 * (4 + 3) - 1 is evaluated as follows:

```
3 + 4 * 4 > 5 * (4 + 3) - 1
```
     (1) 4 * 4 is the first subexpression that can be evaluated from the left.

```
3 + 16 > 5 * (4 + 3) - 1
```
     (2) 3 + 16 is evaluated now.

```
19 > 5 * (4 + 3) - 1
```
     (3) 4 + 3 is now the leftmost subexpression that should be evaluated.

```
19 > 5 * 7 - 1
```
     (4) 5 * 7 is evaluated now.

```
19 > 35 - 1
```
     (5) 35 - 1 is evaluated now.

```
19 > 34
```
     (6) 19 > 34 is evaluated now.

```
false
```

The result happens to be the same as applying Rule 2 and Rule 3 without applying Rule 1. In fact, Rule 1 is not necessary if no operands have side effects that change the value of a variable in an expression.

2.13 The `String` Type

The char type only represents one character. To represent a string of characters, use the data type called String. For example, the following code declares the message to be a string that has an initial value of "Welcome to Java":

```
String message = "Welcome to Java";
```

String is actually a predefined class in the Java library just like the System class and JOptionPane class. The String type is not a primitive type. It is known as a *reference type*. Any Java class can be used as a reference type for a variable. Reference data types will be thoroughly discussed in Chapter 6, "Classes and Objects." For the time being, you only need to know how to declare a String variable, how to assign a string to the variable, and how to concatenate strings.

As first shown in Listing 2.1, two strings can be concatenated. The plus sign (+) is the concatenation operator if one of the operands is a string. If one of the operands is a non-string (e.g., a number), the non-string value is converted into a string and concatenated with the other string. Here are some examples:

concatenating strings and numbers

```
// Three strings are concatenated
String message = "Welcome " + "to " + "Java";

// String Chapter is concatenated with number 2
String s = "Chapter" + 2; // s becomes Chapter2

// String Supplement is concatenated with character B
String s1 = "Supplement" + 'B'; // s becomes SupplementB
```

If none of the operands is a string, the plus sign (+) is the addition operator that adds two numbers.

The short hand += operator can also be used for string concatenation. For example, the following code appends the string " and Java is fun" with the string "Welcome to Java" in message:

```
message += " and Java is fun";
```

So the new message is "Welcome to Java and Java is fun".

The operator precedence order and associativity rule for the operators + and += apply to strings in the same way as to numbers. Suppose that i = 1 and j = 2, what is the output of the following statement?

```
System.out.println("i + j is " + i + j);
```

The output is "i + j is 12" because "i + j is " is concatenated with the value of i first. To force i + j to be executed first, enclose i + j in the parentheses, as follows:

```
System.out.println("i + j is " + (i + j));
```

2.14   Getting Input from Input Dialogs

In Listing 2.1, the radius is fixed in the source code. To use a different radius, you have to modify the source code and recompile it. Obviously, this is not convenient. You can use the showInputDialog method in the JOptionPane class to get input at runtime. When this method is executed, a dialog is displayed to enable you to enter an input, as shown in Figure 2.3.

showInputDialog

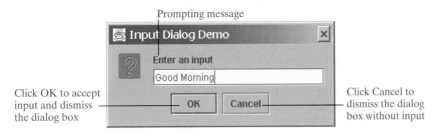

FIGURE 2.3   *The input dialog box enables the user to enter a string.*

After entering a string, click OK to accept the input and dismiss the dialog box. The input is returned from the method as a string. You can invoke the method with four arguments, as follows:

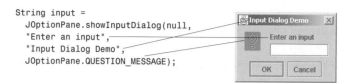

```
String input =
    JOptionPane.showInputDialog(null,
    "Enter an input",
    "Input Dialog Demo",
    JOptionPane.QUESTION_MESSAGE);
```

The first argument can always be null. The second argument is a string that prompts the user. The third argument is the title of the input box. The fourth argument can be JOptionPane.QUESTION_MESSAGE, which causes the icon () to be displayed in the input box.

---

showInputDialog method

 NOTE

There are several ways to use the showInputDialog method. For the time being, you only need to know two ways to invoke it.

One is to use a statement as shown in the example:

```
String string = JOptionPane.showInputDialog(null, x,
    y, JOptionPane.QUESTION_MESSAGE));
```

where x is a string for the prompting message, and y is a string for the title of the input dialog box.

The other is to use a statement like this one:

```
JOptionPane.showMessageDialog(x);
```

where x is a string for the prompting message.

2.14.1 Converting Strings to Numbers

The input returned from the input dialog box is a string. If you enter a numeric value such as 123, it returns "123". You have to convert a string into a number to obtain the input as a number.

Integer.parseInt method

To convert a string into an int value, use the parseInt method in the Integer class, as follows:

```
int intValue = Integer.parseInt(intString);
```

where intString is a numeric string such as "123".

Double.parseDouble method

To convert a string into a double value, use the parseDouble method in the Double class, as follows:

```
double doubleValue = Double.parseDouble(doubleString);
```

where doubleString is a numeric string such as "123.45".

The Integer and Double classes are both included in the java.lang package. These classes will be further discussed in Chapter 9, "Abstract Classes and Interfaces."

 NOTE

You can also convert a string into a value of the byte type, short type, long type, float type, char type, or boolean type. You will learn the conversion methods later in the book.

EXAMPLE 2.1   ENTERING INPUT FROM DIALOG BOXES

Problem

This example shows you how to enter input from dialog boxes. As shown in Figure 2.4, the program prompts the user to enter a year as an int value and checks whether it is a leap year; then it prompts the user to enter a double value and checks whether it is positive.

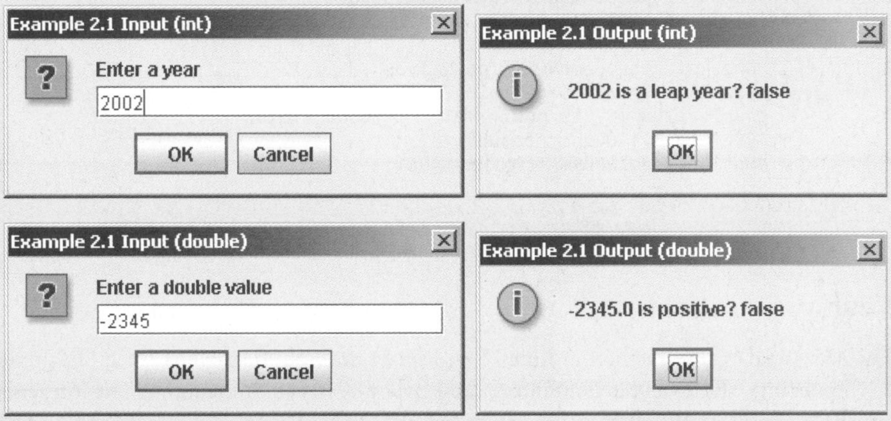

Example 2.1 Input (int)	Example 2.1 Output (int)
? Enter a year `2002` OK Cancel	**i** 2002 is a leap year? false OK

Example 2.1 Input (double)	Example 2.1 Output (double)
? Enter a double value `-2345` OK Cancel	**i** -2345.0 is positive? false OK

FIGURE 2.4   *The input dialog box enables the user to enter a string.*

Solution

A year is a *leap year* if it is divisible by 4 but not by 100 or if it is divisible by 400. So you can use the following Boolean expression to check whether a year is a leap year:

leap year

```
((year % 4 == 0) && (year % 100 != 0)) || (year % 400 == 0)
```

LISTING 2.2   InputDialogDemo.java (Entering Input from Dialogs)

```
1   import javax.swing.JOptionPane;
2
3   public class InputDialogDemo {
4     /** Main method */
5     public static void main(String args[]) {
6       // Prompt the user to enter a year
7       String yearString = JOptionPane.showInputDialog(null,
8         "Enter a year", "Example 2.1 Input (int)",
9         JOptionPane.QUESTION_MESSAGE);
10
11      // Convert the string into an int value
12      int year = Integer.parseInt(yearString);
13
14      // Check if the year is a leap year
15      boolean isLeapYear =
16        ((year % 4 == 0) && (year % 100 != 0)) || (year % 400 == 0);
17
```

show input dialog

convert to int

EXAMPLE 2.1 (CONTINUED)

show message dialog

show input dialog

converting to double

show message dialog

```
18        // Display the result in a message dialog box
19        JOptionPane.showMessageDialog(null,
20          year + " is a leap year? " + isLeapYear,
21          "Example 2.1 Output (int)", JOptionPane.INFORMATION_MESSAGE);
22
23        // Prompt the user to enter a double value
24        String doubleString = JOptionPane.showInputDialog(null,
25          "Enter a double value", "Example 2.1 Input (double)",
26          JOptionPane.QUESTION_MESSAGE);
27
28        // Convert the string into a double value
29        double doubleValue = Double.parseDouble(doubleString);
30
31        // Check if the number is positive
32        JOptionPane.showMessageDialog(null,
33          doubleValue + " is positive? " + (doubleValue > 0),
34          "Example 2.1 Output (double)",
35          JOptionPane.INFORMATION_MESSAGE);
36      }
37    }
```

Review

The showInputDialog method in Lines 7–9 displays an input dialog box titled "Example 2.1 Input (int)." Enter a year as an integer and click OK to accept the input. The integer is returned as a string that is assigned to the String variable yearString. The Integer.parseInt(yearString) (Line 12) is used to convert the string into an int value. If you entered an input other than an integer, a runtime error would occur. In Chapter 15, "Exceptions and Assertions," you will learn how to handle the exception so that the program can continue to run.

The showMessageDialog method in Lines 19–21 displays the output in a message dialog box titled "Example 2.1 Output (int)."

The showInputDialog method in Lines 24–26 displays an input dialog box titled "Example 2.1 Input (double)." Enter a floating-point value and click OK to accept the input. The floating-point value is returned as a string that is assigned to the String variable doubleString. The Double.parseDouble(doubleString) (Line 29) is used to convert the string into an int value. If you entered a non-numeric value, a runtime error would occur.

 NOTE
If you click *Cancel* in the input dialog box, no string is returned. A runtime error would occur.

2.15 Case Studies

In the preceding sections, you learned about variables, constants, primitive data types, operators, and expressions. You are now ready to use them to write interesting programs. This section presents three examples: computing loan payments, breaking a sum of money down into smaller units, and displaying the current time.

EXAMPLE 2.2 COMPUTING LOAN PAYMENTS

Problem

This example shows you how to write a program that computes loan payments. The loan can be a car loan, a student loan, or a home mortgage loan. The program lets the user enter the interest rate, number of years, and loan amount, and then computes the monthly payment and the total payment. It concludes by displaying the monthly and total payments.

Solution

The formula to compute the monthly payment is as follows:

$$\frac{loanAmount \times monthlyInterestRate}{1 - \dfrac{1}{(1 + monthlyInterestRate)^{numberOfYears \times 12}}}$$

You don't have to know how this formula is derived. Nonetheless, given the monthly interest rate, number of years, and loan amount, you can use it to compute the monthly payment.

Here are the steps in developing the program:

1. Prompt the user to enter the annual interest rate, number of years, and loan amount.

2. Obtain the monthly interest rate from the annual interest rate.

3. Compute the monthly payment using the preceding formula.

4. Compute the total payment, which is the monthly payment multiplied by 12 and multiplied by the number of years.

5. Display the monthly payment and total payment in a message dialog.
   The program follows, and the output is shown in Figure 2.5.

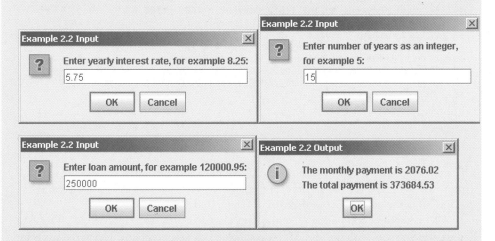

FIGURE 2.5 *The program accepts the annual interest rate, number of years, and loan amount, then displays the monthly payment and total payment.*

EXAMPLE 2.2 (CONTINUED)

LISTING 2.3   ComputeLoan.java (Computing Loan Payments)

```
1   import javax.swing.JOptionPane;
2
3   public class ComputeLoan {
4     /** Main method */
5     public static void main(String[] args) {
6       // Enter yearly interest rate
7       String annualInterestRateString = JOptionPane.showInputDialog(
8         null, "Enter yearly interest rate, for example 8.25:",
9         "Example 2.2 Input", JOptionPane.QUESTION_MESSAGE);
10
11      // Convert string to double
12      double annualInterestRate =
13        Double.parseDouble(annualInterestRateString);
14
15      // Obtain monthly interest rate
16      double monthlyInterestRate = annualInterestRate / 1200;
17
18      // Enter number of years
19      String numberOfYearsString = JOptionPane.showInputDialog(null,
20        "Enter number of years as an integer, \nfor example 5:",
21        "Example 2.2 Input", JOptionPane.QUESTION_MESSAGE);
22
23      // Convert string to int
24      int numberOfYears = Integer.parseInt(numberOfYearsString);
25
26      // Enter loan amount
27      String loanString = JOptionPane.showInputDialog(null,
28        "Enter loan amount, for example 120000.95:",
29        "Example 2.2 Input", JOptionPane.QUESTION_MESSAGE);
30
31      // Convert string to double
32      double loanAmount = Double.parseDouble(loanString);
33
34      // Calculate payment
35      double monthlyPayment = loanAmount * monthlyInterestRate / (1
36        - 1 / Math.pow(1 + monthlyInterestRate, numberOfYears * 12));
37      double totalPayment = monthlyPayment * numberOfYears * 12;
38
39      // Format to keep two digits after the decimal point
40      monthlyPayment = (int)(monthlyPayment * 100) / 100.0;
41      totalPayment = (int)(totalPayment * 100) / 100.0;
42
43      // Display results
44      String output = "The monthly payment is " + monthlyPayment +
45        "\nThe total payment is " + totalPayment;
46      JOptionPane.showMessageDialog(null, output,
47        "Example 2.2 Output", JOptionPane.INFORMATION_MESSAGE);
48    }
49  }
```

monthlyPayment — Line 35

totalPayment — Line 37

formatting numbers — Lines 40–41

preparing output — Lines 44–47

Review

Each new variable in a method must be declared once and only once. Choose the most appropriate data type for the variable. For example, numberOfYears is best declared as int (Line 24), although it could be declared as long, float, or double.

pow method

The method for computing b^p in the Math class is pow(b, p) (Lines 35–36). The Math class, which comes with the Java API, is available to all Java programs. The Math class is introduced in Chapter 4, "Methods."

EXAMPLE 2.2 (CONTINUED)

The statements in Lines 40–41 are for formatting the number to keep two digits after the decimal point. For example, if monthlyPayment is 2076.0252175, (int)(monthlyPayment * 100) is 207602. Therefore, (int)(monthlyPayment * 100) / 100.0 yields 2076.02.

formatting numbers

The strings are concatenated into output in Lines 44–45. The linefeed escape character '\n' is in the string to display the text after '\n' in the next line.

EXAMPLE 2.3 MONETARY UNITS

Problem

Write a program that classifies a given amount of money into smaller monetary units. The program lets the user enter an amount as a double value representing a total in dollars and cents, and outputs a report listing the monetary equivalent in dollars, quarters, dimes, nickels, and pennies.

Your program should report the maximum number of dollars, then the maximum number of quarters, and so on, in this order.

Solution

Here are the steps in developing the program:

1. Prompt the user to enter the amount as a decimal number such as 11.56.

2. Convert the amount (e.g., 11.56) into cents (1156).

3. Divide the cents by 100 to find the number of dollars. Obtain the remaining cents using the cents remainder 100.

4. Divide the remaining cents by 25 to find the number of quarters. Obtain the remaining cents using the remaining cents remainder 25.

5. Divide the remaining cents by 10 to find the number of dimes. Obtain the remaining cents using the remaining cents remainder 10.

6. Divide the remaining cents by 5 to find the number of nickels. Obtain the remaining cents using the remaining cents remainder 5.

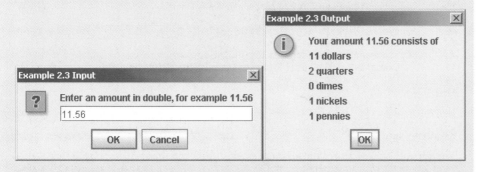

FIGURE 2.6   *The program receives an amount in decimals and breaks it into singles, quarters, dimes, nickels, and pennies.*

EXAMPLE 2.3 (CONTINUED)

7. The remaining cents are the pennies.

8. Display the result.

The program follows, and the output is shown in Figure 2.6.

LISTING 2.4   ComputeChange.java (Monetary Units)

```java
1 import javax.swing.JOptionPane;
2
3 public class ComputeChange {
4   /** Main method */
5   public static void main(String[] args) {
6     // Receive the amount entered from the keyboard
7     String amountString = JOptionPane.showInputDialog(null,
8       "Enter an amount in double, for example 11.56",
9       "Example 2.3 Input", JOptionPane.QUESTION_MESSAGE);
10
11    // Convert string to double
12    double amount = Double.parseDouble(amountString);
13
14    int remainingAmount = (int)(amount * 100);
15
16    // Find the number of one dollars
17    int numberOfOneDollars = remainingAmount / 100;
18    remainingAmount = remainingAmount % 100;
19
20    // Find the number of quarters in the remaining amount
21    int numberOfQuarters = remainingAmount / 25;
22    remainingAmount = remainingAmount % 25;
23
24    // Find the number of dimes in the remaining amount
25    int numberOfDimes = remainingAmount / 10;
26    remainingAmount = remainingAmount % 10;
27
28    // Find the number of nickels in the remaining amount
29    int numberOfNickels = remainingAmount / 5;
30    remainingAmount = remainingAmount % 5;
31
32    // Find the number of pennies in the remaining amount
33    int numberOfPennies = remainingAmount;
34
35    // Display results
36    String output = "Your amount " + amount + " consists of \n" +
37      numberOfOneDollars + " dollars\n" +
38      numberOfQuarters + " quarters\n" +
39      numberOfDimes + " dimes\n" +
40      numberOfNickels + " nickels\n" +
41      numberOfPennies + " pennies";
42    JOptionPane.showMessageDialog(null, output,
43      "Example 2.3 Output", JOptionPane.INFORMATION_MESSAGE);
44  }
45 }
```

Margin notes (aligned with code):
- dollars
- quarters
- dimes
- nickels
- pennies

Review

The variable amount stores the amount entered from the input dialog box (Lines 7–12). This variable is not changed because the amount has to be used at the end of the program to display the results. The program introduces the variable remainingAmount (Line 14) to store the changing remainingAmount.

EXAMPLE 2.3 (CONTINUED)

The variable `amount` is a `double` decimal representing dollars and cents. It is converted to an `int` variable `remainingAmount`, which represents all the cents. For instance, if `amount` is 11.56, then the initial `remainingAmount` is 1156. The division operator yields the integer part of the division. So 1156 / 100 is 11. The remainder operator obtains the remainder of the division. So 1156 % 100 is 56.

The program extracts the maximum number of singles from the total amount and obtains the remaining amount in the variable `remainingAmount` (Lines 17–18). It then extracts the maximum number of quarters from `remainingAmount` and obtains a new `remainingAmount` (Lines 21–22). Continuing the same process, the program finds the maximum number of dimes, nickels, and pennies in the remaining amount.

One serious problem with this example is the possible *loss of precision* when casting a `double` amount to an `int remainingAmount`. This could lead to an inaccurate result. If you try to enter the amount 10.03, 10.03 * 100 becomes 1002.9999999999999. You will find that the program displays 10 dollars and 2 pennies. There are two ways to fix the problem. One is to enter the amount as an `int` value representing cents (see Exercise 2.14); the other is to read the decimal number as a string and extract the dollars part and the cents part separately as `int` values. Processing strings will be introduced in Chapter 7, "Strings."

loss of precision

As shown in Figure 2.6, 0 dimes, 1 nickels, and 1 pennies are displayed in the result. It would be better not to display 0 dimes, and to display 1 nickel and 1 penny using the singular forms of the words. You will learn how to use selection statements to modify this program in the next chapter (see Exercise 3.1).

EXAMPLE 2.4 DISPLAYING THE CURRENT TIME

Problem

Write a program that displays the current time in GMT (Greenwich Meridian Time) in the format hour:minute:second, such as 1:45:19.

Solution

The `currentTimeMillis` method in the `System` class returns the current time in milliseconds since midnight, January 1, 1970 GMT (also known as the *Unix time* because 1970 was the year when the Unix operating system was formally introduced). You can use this method to obtain the current time, and then compute the current second, minute, and hour as follows.

`currentTimeMillis`
Unix time

1. Obtain the total milliseconds since midnight, Jan 1, 1970 in `totalSeconds` by invoking `System.currentTimeMillis()`.

2. Obtain the total seconds `totalSeconds` by dividing 1000 from `totalMilliseconds`.

3. Compute the current second in the minute in the hour from `totalSeconds % 60`.

4. Obtain the total minutes `totalMinutes` by dividing 60 from `totalSeconds`.

5. Compute the current minute in the hour from `totalMinutes % 60`.

EXAMPLE 2.4 (CONTINUED)

FIGURE 2.7 *The program displays the current time.*

6. Obtain the total hours `totalHours` by dividing 60 from `totalMinutes`.

7. Compute the current hour from `totalHours % 24`.

The program follows, and the output is shown in Figure 2.7.

LISTING 2.5 ShowCurrentTime.java (Displaying Current Time)

```
 1 import javax.swing.JOptionPane;
 2
 3 public class ShowCurrentTime {
 4   public static void main(String[] args) {
 5     // Obtain the total milliseconds since the midnight, Jan 1, 1970
 6     long totalMilliseconds = System.currentTimeMillis();
 7
 8     // Obtain the total seconds since the midnight, Jan 1, 1970
 9     long totalSeconds = totalMilliseconds / 1000;
10
11     // Compute the current second in the minute in the hour
12     int currentSecond = (int)(totalSeconds % 60);
13
14     // Obtain the total minutes
15     long totalMinutes = totalSeconds / 60;
16
17     // Compute the current minute in the hour
18     int currentMinute = (int)(totalMinutes % 60);
19
20     // Obtain the total hours
21     long totalHours = totalMinutes / 60;
22
23     // Compute the current hour
24     int currentHour = (int)(totalHours % 24);
25
26     // Display results
27     String output = "Current time is " + currentHour + ":"
28       + currentMinute + ":" + currentSecond + " GMT";
29
30     JOptionPane.showMessageDialog(null, output,
31       "Example 2.4 Output", JOptionPane.INFORMATION_MESSAGE);
32   }
33 }
```

totalSeconds

currentSecond

totalMinutes

currentMinute

totalHours

currentHour

preparing output

Review

When `System.currentTimeMillis()` (Line 6) is invoked, it returns the difference, measured in milliseconds, between the current time and midnight, January 1, 1970 GMT. This method returns the milliseconds as a `long` value.

This example finds the current time. To find the date (day, month, and year), see Exercise 4.18.

2.16   Getting Input from the Console (Optional)

The previous editions of this book used the `MyInput` class to let the user enter input from the command window. If you wish to use it, download MyInput.java from the Companion Website to the directory that contains your program. `MyInput` is like `JOptionPane`. `JOptionPane` is a class in the Java library, whereas I developed `MyInput`. You can use the methods in `JOptionPane` without knowing how the class is implemented. Likewise, you can use the methods in `MyInput` without having to be concerned about its implementation. The implementation of `MyInput` will be introduced in Chapter 7. You may also use the new JDK 1.5 `Scanner` class for console input. (See Supplement T, "Obtaining Input from the Console Using the `Scanner` Class."

MyInput

The `MyInput` class contains the methods `readByte()`, `readShort()`, `readInt()`, `readLong()`, `readFloat()`, `readDouble()`, `readChar()`, `readBoolean()`, and `readString()` to read numeric values, characters, `boolean` values, and strings from the console.

Listing 2.6 is an example that uses the methods in `MyInput`. A sample run of this program is shown in Figure 2.8.

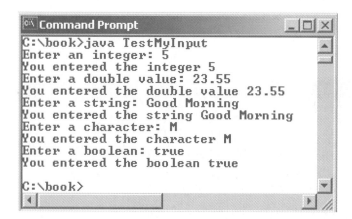

FIGURE 2.8   *You can enter input from a command window.*

LISTING 2.6   TestMyInput.java (Using Console Input)

```java
1 public class TestMyInput {
2   public static void main(String args[]) {
3     // Prompt the user to enter an integer
4     System.out.print("Enter an integer: ");
5     int intValue = MyInput.readInt();
6     System.out.println("You entered the integer " + intValue);
7
8     // Prompt the user to enter a double value
9     System.out.print("Enter a double value: ");
10    double doubleValue = MyInput.readDouble();
11    System.out.println("You entered the double value "
12      + doubleValue);
13
14    // Prompt the user to enter a string
15    System.out.print("Enter a string: ");
16    String string = MyInput.readString();
17    System.out.println("You entered the string " + string);
18
19    // Prompt the user to enter a character
20    System.out.print("Enter a character: ");
21    char charValue = MyInput.readChar();
22    System.out.println("You entered the character " + charValue);
23
```

```
24      // Prompt the user to enter a boolean
25      System.out.print("Enter a boolean: ");
26      boolean booleanValue = MyInput.readBoolean();
27      System.out.println("You entered the boolean " + booleanValue);
28    }
29 }
```

🌸 NOTE

The print method displays a string to the console. This method is identical to the println method except that println moves the cursor to the next line after displaying the string, but print does not advance the cursor to the next line when completed.

---

input from a file

🌸 TIP

One benefit of using the console input is that you can store the input values in a text file and pass the file from the command line using the following command:

```
java TestMyInput < input.txt
```

where input.txt is a text file that contains the data, as shown in Figure 2.9(a). The output of java TestMyInput < input.txt is shown in Figure 2.9(b).

(a)

```
C:\book>java TestMyInput < input.txt
Enter an integer: You entered the integer 5
Enter a double value: You entered the double value 23.55
Enter a string: You entered the string Good Morning
Enter a character: You entered the character M
Enter a boolean: You entered the boolean true

C:\book>
```

(b)

FIGURE 2.9 *(a) You can create a text file using NotePad. (b) The data in the text file are passed to the program.*

You can also save the output into a file using the following command:

output to a file

```
java TestMyInput < input.txt > out.txt
```

2.17 Formatting Output (JDK 1.5 Feature)

You already know how to display console output using the print or println methods. JDK 1.5 introduced a new printf method that enables you to format output. The syntax to invoke this method is

printf

```
System.out.printf(format, items)
```

specifier

where format is a string that may consist of substrings and format specifiers. A format *specifier* specifies how an item should be displayed. An item may be a numeric value, a character, a boolean value, or a string. Each specifier begins with a percent sign. Table 2.12 lists some frequently used specifiers:

Another common source of runtime errors is division by zero. This happens when the divisor is zero for integer divisions. For instance, the following program would cause a runtime error, as shown in Figure 2.12.

```
// ShowRuntimeErrors.java: Program contains runtime errors
public class ShowRuntimeErrors {
  public static void main(String[] args) {
    int i = 1 / 0;                                                    runtime error
  }
}
```

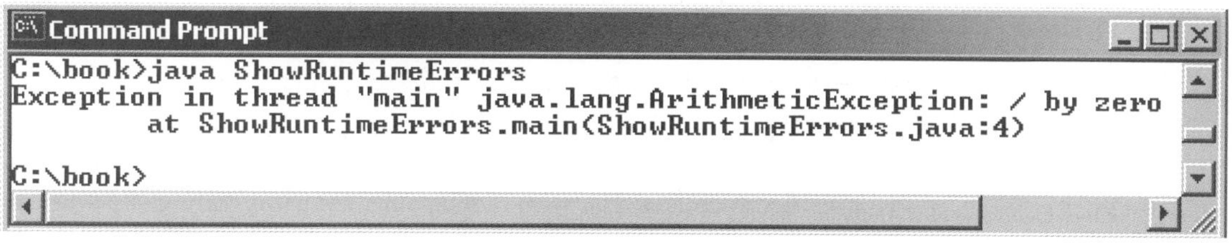

FIGURE 2.12 *The runtime error causes the program to terminate.*

2.19.3 Logic Errors

Logic errors occur when a program does not perform the way it was intended to. Errors of this kind occur for many different reasons. For example, suppose you wrote the following program to add number1 to number2:

```
// ShowLogicErrors.java: The program contains a logic error
public class ShowLogicErrors {
  public static void main(String[] args) {
    // Add number1 to number2
    int number1 = 3;
    int number2 = 3;
    number2 += number1 + number2;
    System.out.println(number2 is + number2);
  }
}
```

The program does not have syntax errors or runtime errors, but it does not print the correct result for number2. See if you can find the error.

2.20 Debugging

In general, syntax errors are easy to find and easy to correct, because the compiler gives indications as to where the errors came from and why they are there. Runtime errors are not difficult to find either, since the Java interpreter displays them on the console when the program aborts. Finding logic errors, on the other hand, can be very challenging.

Logic errors are called *bugs*. The process of finding and correcting errors is called *debugging*. A common approach to debugging is to use a combination of methods to narrow down to the part of the program where the bug is located. You can *hand-trace* the program (i.e., catch errors by reading the program), or you can insert print statements in order to show the values of the variables or the execution flow of the program. This approach might work for a short, simple program. But for a large, complex program, the most effective approach for debugging is to use a debugger utility.

bugs
debugging
hand-traces

JDK includes a command-line debugger (jdb), which is invoked with a class name. jdb is itself a Java program, running its own copy of the Java interpreter. All the Java IDE tools, such as JBuilder, NetBeans, and Eclipse, include integrated debuggers. The debugger utilities let you follow the execution of a program. They vary from one system to another, but they all support most of the following helpful features:

✦ **Executing a single statement at a time:** The debugger allows you to execute one statement at a time so that you can see the effect of each statement.

✦ **Tracing into or stepping over a method:** If a method is being executed, you can ask the debugger to enter the method and execute one statement at a time in the method, or you can ask it to step over the entire method. You should step over the entire method if you know that the method works. For example, always step over system-supplied methods, such as `System.out.println`.

✦ **Setting breakpoints:** You can also set a breakpoint at a specific statement. Your program pauses when it reaches a breakpoint and displays the line with the breakpoint. You can set as many breakpoints as you want. Breakpoints are particularly useful when you know where your programming error starts. You can set a breakpoint at that line and have the program execute until it reaches the breakpoint.

✦ **Displaying variables:** The debugger lets you select several variables and display their values. As you trace through a program, the content of a variable is continuously updated.

✦ **Displaying call stacks:** The debugger lets you trace all of the method calls and lists all pending methods. This feature is helpful when you need to see a large picture of the program-execution flow.

✦ **Modifying variables:** Some debuggers enable you to modify the value of a variable when debugging. This is convenient when you want to test a program with different samples but do not want to leave the debugger.

KEY TERMS

algorithm 33	increment operator (++) 43
assignment operator (=) 37	indentation 67
assignment statement 37	int type 39
backslash (\) 46	literal 40
Boolean value 47	logic error 69
boolean type 48	long type 39
byte type 39	narrowing (of types) 44
casting 44	operand evaluation order 51
char type 45	operator associativity 50
constant 38	operator precedence 50
debugging 69	primitive data type 33
decrement operator (--) 43	runtime error 68
double type 39	short type 39
encoding 45	short-circuit operator 49
final 38	syntax error 68
float type 39	Unicode 45
floating-point number 33	Unix time 61
expression 37	variable declaration 36
identifier 35	widening (of types) 44

Key Classes and Methods

◆ `java.lang.Math` is a class that contains static methods for mathematical operations.

◆ `Math.pow(a, b)` returns a raised to the power of b (a^b).

◆ `JOptionPane.showInputDialog(`...`)` displays an input dialog.

◆ `Integer.parseInt(string)` parses a string into an `int` value.

◆ `Integer.parseDouble(string)` parses a string into a `double` value.

◆ `System.currentTimeMills()` returns the current time in milliseconds since midnight, January 1, 1970 GMT (the Unix time).

CHAPTER SUMMARY

◆ Java provides four integer types (`byte`, `short`, `int`, `long`) that represent integers of four different sizes, and two floating-point types (`float`, `double`) that represent floating-point numbers of two different precisions. Character type (`char`) represents a single character, and `boolean` type represents a `true` or `false` value. These are called primitive data types. Java's primitive types are portable across all computer platforms. They have exactly the same values on all platforms. When they are declared, the variables of these types are created and assigned memory space.

◆ Java provides operators that perform numeric operations: + (addition) , - (subtraction) , * (multiplication) , / (division) , and % (remainder). Integer division (/) yields an integer result. The remainder operator (%) yields the remainder of the division.

◆ The increment operator (++) and the decrement operator (--) increment or decrement a variable by 1. If the operator is prefixed to the variable, the variable is first incremented or decremented by 1, then used in the expression. If the operator is a suffix to the variable, the variable is incremented or decremented by 1, but then the original old value is used in the expression.

◆ All the numeric operators can be applied to characters. When an operand is a character, the character's Unicode value is used in the operation.

◆ You can use casting to convert a value of one type into another type. Casting a variable of a type with a small range to a variable of a type with a larger range is known as *widening a type*. Casting a variable of a type with a large range to a variable of a type with a smaller range is known as *narrowing a type*. Widening a type can be performed automatically without explicit casting. Narrowing a type must be performed explicitly.

◆ The Boolean operators &&, &, ¦¦, ¦, !, and ^ operate with Boolean values and variables. The relational operators (<, <=, ==, !=, >, >=) work with numbers and characters, and yield a Boolean value.

◆ When evaluating `p1 && p2`, Java first evaluates `p1` and then evaluates `p2` if `p1` is `true`; if `p1` is `false`, it does not evaluate `p2`. When evaluating `p1 ¦¦ p2`, Java first evaluates `p1` and then evaluates `p2` if `p1` is `false`; if `p1` is `true`, it does not evaluate `p2`. Therefore, && is referred to as the *conditional* or *short-circuit AND* operator, and ¦¦ is referred to as the *conditional* or *short-circuit OR* operator.

✦ Java also provides the & and ¦ operators. The & operator works exactly the same as the && operator, and the ¦ operator works exactly the same as the ¦¦ operator with one exception: the & and ¦ operators always evaluate both operands. Therefore, & is referred to as the *unconditional AND* operator, and ¦ is referred to as the *unconditional OR* operator.

✦ The operands of a binary operator are evaluated from left to right. No part of the right-hand operand is evaluated until all the operands before the binary operator are evaluated.

✦ The operators in arithmetic expressions are evaluated in the order determined by the rules of parentheses, operator precedence, and associativity.

✦ Parentheses can be used to force the order of evaluation to occur in any sequence. Operators with higher precedence are evaluated earlier. The associativity of the operators determines the order of evaluation for operators of the same precedence.

✦ All binary operators except assignment operators are left-associative, and assignment operators are right-associative.

✦ You can receive input from an input dialog box using the method `JOptionPane.showInputDialog`. The input from an input dialog box is a string. To convert it to a double number, use the `Double.parseDouble` method; to convert it to an `int` value, use the `Integer.parseInt` method.

✦ You can use the `Math.pow(a, b)` method to compute a^b and use the `System.currentTimeMillis()` to return the current time in milliseconds since midnight, January 1, 1970 GMT (the Unix time).

✦ Programming errors can be categorized into three types: syntax errors, runtime errors, and logic errors. Errors that occur during compilation are called *syntax errors* or *compilation errors*. *Runtime errors* are errors that cause a program to terminate abnormally. *Logic errors* occur when a program does not perform the way it was intended to.

REVIEW QUESTIONS

Sections 2.2–2.6

2.1 Are the following identifiers valid?

```
applet, Applet, a++, --a, 4#R, $4, #44, apps
```

2.2 Which of the following are Java keywords?

```
class, public, int, x, y, radius
```

2.3 Declare an `int` variable `count` with initial value 100, and declare an `int` constant `SIZE` with value 20.

2.4 What are the benefits of using constants?

Section 2.7 Numeric Data Types and Operations

2.5 Assume that `int a = 1` and `double d = 1.0`, and that each expression is independent. What are the results of the following expressions?

```
a = 46 / 9;
a = 46 % 9 + 4 * 4 - 2;
a = 45 + 43 % 5 * (23 * 3 % 2);
```

```
a %= 3 / a + 3;
d = 4 + d * d + 4;
d += 1.5 * 3 + (++a);
d -= 1.5 * 3 + a++;
```

2.6   Find the largest and smallest byte, short, int, long, float, and double. Which of these data types requires the least amount of memory?

2.7   What is the result of 25 / 4? How would you rewrite the expression if you wished the result to be a floating-point number?

2.8   Are the following statements correct? If so, show the output.

```
System.out.println("the output for 25 / 4 is " + 25 / 4);
System.out.println("the output for 25 / 4.0 is " + 25 / 4.0);
```

2.9   How would you write the following arithmetic expression in Java?

$$\frac{4}{3(r + 34)} - 9(a + bc) + \frac{3 + d(2 + a)}{a + bd}$$

2.10   Which of these statements are true?

  a. Any expression can be used as a statement.
  b. The expression x++ can be used as a statement.
  c. The statement x = x + 5 is also an expression.
  d. The statement x = y = x = 0 is illegal.
  e. All the operators of the same precedence are evaluated from left to right.

2.11   Which of the following are correct literals for floating-point numbers?
        12.3, 12.3e + 2, 23.4e − 2, −334.4, 20, 39F, 40D

2.12   Identify and fix the errors in the following code:

```
1   public class Test {
2     public void main(string[] args) {
3       int i;
4       int k = 100.0;
5       int j = i + 1;
6
7       System.out.println("j is " + j + " and
8         k is " + k);
9     }
10  }
```

Section 2.8 Numeric Type Conversions

2.13   Can different types of numeric values be used together in a computation?

2.14   What does an explicit conversion from a double to an int do with the fractional part of the *double* value? Does casting change the variable being cast?

2.15   Show the following output.

```
float f = 12.5F;
int i = (int)f;
System.out.println("f is " + f);
System.out.println("i is " + i);
```

Section 2.9 Character Data Type and Operations

2.16   Use print statements to find out the ASCII code for '1', 'A', 'B', 'a', 'b'. Use print statements to find out the character for the decimal code 40, 59, 79, 85, 90. Use print statements to find out the character for the hexadecimal code 40, 5A, 71, 72, 7A.

2.17 Which of the following are correct literals for characters?
'1' , '\u345dE', '\u3fFa', '\b', \t

2.18 How do you display characters \ and "?

2.19 Evaluate the following:

```
int i = '1';
int j = '1' + '2';
int k = 'a';
char c = 90;
```

Section 2.10 `boolean` Data Type and Operations

2.20 List six comparison operators.

2.21 Assume that x is 1, show the result of the following Boolean expressions:

```
(true) && (3 > 4)
!(x > 0) && (x > 0)
(x > 0) || (x < 0)
(x != 0) || (x == 0)
(x >= 0) || (x < 0)
(x != 1) == !(x == 1)
```

2.22 Write a Boolean expression that evaluates to true if the number is between 1 and 100.

2.23 Write a Boolean expression that evaluates to true if the number is between 1 and 100 or the number is negative.

2.24 Assume that x and y are int type. Which of the following expressions are correct?

```
x > y > 0
x = y && y
x /= y
x or y
x and y
(x != 0) || (x = 0)
```

2.25 List the precedence order of the Boolean operators. Evaluate the following expressions:

```
true | true && false
true || true && false
true | true & false
```

Sections 2.11–2.12

2.26 Show and explain the output of the following code:

a.
```
int i = 0;
System.out.println(--i + i + i++);
System.out.println(i + ++i);
```

b.
```
int i = 0;
i = i + (i = 1);
System.out.println(i);
```

c.
```
int i = 0;
i = (i = 1) + i;
System.out.println(i);
```

2.27 Assume that int a = 1 and double d = 1.0, and that each expression is independent. What are the results of the following expressions?

```
a = (a = 3) + a;
a = a + (a = 3);
a += a + (a = 3);
```

```
a = 5 + 5 * 2 % a--;
a = 4 + 1 + 4 * 5 % (++a + 1);
d += 1.5 * 3 + (++d);
d -= 1.5 * 3 + d++;
```

Section 2.13

2.28 Show the output of the following statements.

```
System.out.println("1" + 1);
System.out.println('1' + 1);
System.out.println("1" + 1 + 1);
System.out.println("1" + (1 + 1));
System.out.println('1' + 1 + 1);
```

Sections 2.14–2.16

2.29 How do you convert a decimal string into a `double` value? How do you convert an integer string into an `int` value?

2.30 How do you obtain the current minute using the `System.currentTimeMillis()` method?

Section 2.18

2.31 What are the specifiers for outputting a boolean value, a character, a decimal integer, a floating-point number, and a string?

2.32 What is wrong in the following statements?

a. `System.out.printf("%5d %d", 1, 2, 3);`
b. `System.out.printf("%5d %f", 1);`
c. `System.out.printf("%5d %f", 1, 2);`

2.33 Show the output of the following statements:

a. `System.out.printf("amount is %f %e\n", 32.32, 32.32);`
b. `System.out.printf("amount is %5.4f %5.4e\n", 32.32, 32.32);`
c. `System.out.printf("%6b\n", (1 > 2));`
d. `System.out.printf("%6s\n", "Java");`

Sections 2.19–2.20

2.34 How do you denote a comment line and a comment paragraph?

2.35 What are the naming conventions for class names, method names, constants, and variables? Which of the following items can be a constant, a method, a variable, or a class according to the Java naming conventions?

`MAX_VALUE, Test, read, readInt`

2.36 Reformat the following program according to the programming style and documentation guidelines. Use the next-line brace style.

```
public class Test
{
  // Main method
  public static void main(String[] args) {
  /** Print a line */
  System.out.println("2 % 3 = "+2%3);
  }
}
```

2.37 Describe syntax errors, runtime errors, and logic errors.

Comprehensive

2.38 Evaluate the following expression:

```
1 + "Welcome " + 1 + 1
1 + "Welcome " + (1 + 1)
1 + "Welcome " + ('\u0001' + 1)
1 + "Welcome " + 'a' + 1
```

2.39 Can the following conversions involving casting be allowed? If so, find the converted result.

```
char c = 'A';
i = (int)c;

boolean b = true;
i = (int)b;

float f = 1000.34f;
int i = (int)f;

double d = 1000.34;
int i = (int)d;

int i = 97;
char c = (char)i;

int i = 1000;
boolean b = (boolean)i;
```

2.40 Suppose that x is 1. What is x after the evaluation of the following expression?

```
(x > 1) & (x++ > 1)
```

2.41 Suppose that x is 1. What is x after the evaluation of the following expression?

```
(x > 1) && (x++ > 1)
```

2.42 Show the output of the following program:

```
public class Test {
  public static void main(String[] args) {
    char x = 'a';
    char y = 'c';

    System.out.println(++y);
    System.out.println(y++);
    System.out.println(x > y);
    System.out.println(x - y);
  }
}
```

PROGRAMMING EXERCISES

 NOTE

Solutions to even-numbered exercises are on the Companion Website. Solutions to all exercises are on the Instructor Resource Web site. The level of difficulty is rated easy (no star), moderate (*), hard (**), or challenging (***).

Sections 2.2–2.8

2.1 (*Converting Fahrenheit to Celsius*) Write a program that reads a Fahrenheit degree in double from an input dialog box, then converts it to Celsius and displays the result in a message dialog box. The formula for the conversion is as follows:

celsius = (5 / 9) * (fahrenheit − 32)

HINT

In Java, 5 / 9 is 0, so you need to write 5.0 / 9 in the program to obtain the correct result.

2.2 (*Computing the volume of a cylinder*) Write a program that reads in the radius and length of a cylinder and computes volume using the following formulas:

area = radius * radius * π
volume = area * length

2.3 (*Converting feet into meters*) Write a program that reads a number in feet, converts it to meters, and displays the result. One foot is 0.305 meters.

2.4 (*Converting pounds into kilograms*) Write a program that converts pounds into kilograms. The program prompts the user to enter a number in pounds, converts it to kilograms, and displays the result. One pound is 0.454 kilograms.

2.5* (*Calculating tips*) Write a program that reads the subtotal and the gratuity rate, and computes the gratuity and total. For example, if the user enters 10 for subtotal and 15 percent for gratuity rate, the program displays $1.5 as gratuity and $11.5 as total.

2.6** (*Summing the digits in an integer*) Write a program that reads an integer between 0 and 1000 and adds all the digits in the integer. For example, if an integer is 932, the sum of all its digits is 14.

 HINT

Use the % operator to extract digits, and use the / operator to remove the extracted digit. For instance, 932 % 10 = 2 and 932 / 10 = 93.

Section 2.9 Character Data Type and Operations

2.7* (*Converting an uppercase letter to lowercase*) Write a program that converts an uppercase letter to a lowercase letter. The character is typed in the source code. In Chapter 7, "Strings," you will learn how to enter a character from an input dialog box.

 HINT

In the ASCII table (see Appendix B), uppercase letters appear before lowercase letters. The offset between any uppercase letter and its corresponding lowercase letter is the same. So you can find a lowercase letter from its corresponding uppercase letter, as follows:

```
int offset = (int)'a' - (int)'A';
char lowercase = (char)((int)uppercase + offset);
```

2.8* (*Finding the character of an ASCII code*) Write a program that receives an ASCII code (an integer between 0 and 128) and displays its character. For example, if the user enters 97, the program displays character a.

Section 2.10 `boolean` Data Type and Operations

2.9* (*Validating triangles*) Write a program that reads three edges for a triangle and determines whether the input is valid. The input is valid if the sum of any two edges is greater than the third edge. For example, if your input for three edges is 1, 2, 1, the output should be:

```
Can edges 1, 2, and 1 form a triangle? false
```

if your input for three edges is 2, 2, 1, the output should be:

```
Can edges 2, 2, and 1 form a triangle? true
```

2.10 (*Checking whether a number is even*) Write a program that reads an integer and checks whether it is even. For example, if your input is 25, the output should be:

```
Is 25 an even number? false
```

If your input is 2000, the output should be:

```
Is 2000 an even number? true
```

2.11* (*Using the &&, || and ^ operators*) Write a program that prompts the user to enter an integer and determines whether it is divisible by 5 and 6, whether it is divisible by 5 or 6, and whether it is divisible by 5 or 6, but not both. For example, if your input is 10, the output should be

```
Is 10 divisible by 5 and 6? false
Is 10 divisible by 5 or 6? true
Is 10 divisible by 5 or 6, but not both? true
```

Section 2.15 Case Studies

2.12* (*Calculating the future investment value*) Write a program that reads in investment amount, annual interest rate, and number of years, and displays the future investment value using the following formula:

```
futureInvestmentValue =
    investmentAmount x (1 + monthlyInterestRate)
```
^{numberOfYears*12}

For example, if you entered amount 1000, annual interest rate 3.25%, and number of years 1, the future investment value is 1032.98.

 HINT

Use the `Math.pow(a, b)` method to compute a raised to the power of b.

2.13* (*Payroll*) Write a program that reads the following information and prints a payroll statement, as shown in Figure 2.13.

Employee's full name (e.g., John Doe)

Number of hours worked in a week (e.g., 10)

Hourly pay rate (e.g., 6.75)

Federal tax withholding rate (e.g., 20%)

State tax withholding rate (e.g., 9%)

2.14* (*Monetary units*) Rewrite Example 2.3 to fix the possible loss of accuracy when converting a `double` value to an `int` value. Enter the input as an integer whose last two digits represent the cents. For example, the input 1156 represents 11 dollars and 56 cents.

Sections 2.16–2.17

2.15* (*Using the console input*) Rewrite Exercise 2.13 using the `MyInput` class.

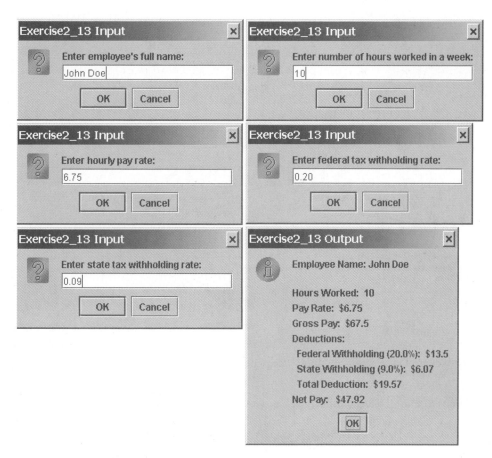

FIGURE 2.13 *The program prints a payroll statement.*

chapter

3

CONTROL STATEMENTS

Objectives

- ◆ To understand the flow of control in selection and loop statements (§§3.2–3.7).

- ◆ To use Boolean expressions to control selection statements and loop statements (§§3.2–3.7).

- ◆ To implement selection control using `if` and nested `if` statements (§§3.2.1-3.2.3).

- ◆ To implement selection control using `switch` statements (§3.2.4).

- ◆ To write expressions using the conditional operator (§3.2.5).

- ◆ To use `while`, `do-while`, and `for` loop statements to control the repetition of statements (§§3.4.1-3.4.3).

- ◆ To write nested loops (§3.4.4).

- ◆ To know the similarities and differences of three types of loops (§3.5).

- ◆ To implement program control with `break` and `continue` (§3.6).

3.1   Introduction

Program control specifies the order in which statements are executed in a program. The programs that you have written so far execute statements in sequence. Often, however, you are faced with situations in which you must provide alternative steps.

In Chapter 2, "Primitive Data Types and Operations," if you assigned a negative value for radius in Listing 2.1 ComputeArea.java, the program would print an invalid result. If the radius is negative, you don't want the program to compute the area. Like all high-level programming languages, Java provides selection statements that let you choose actions with two or more alternative courses. You can use selection statements in the following *pseudocode* (i.e., natural language mixed with Java code) to rewrite Listing 2.1:

pseudocode

```
if the radius is negative
  the program displays a message indicating a wrong input;
else
  the program computes the area and displays the result;
```

Like other high-level programming languages, Java provides iteration structures in order to control the repeated execution of statements. Suppose that you need to print the same message a hundred times. It would be tedious to have to write the same code a hundred times in order to print the message a hundred times. Java provides a powerful control structure called a *loop*, which controls how many times an operation or a sequence of operations is performed in succession. Using a loop statement, you simply tell the computer to print the message a hundred times without having to code the print statement a hundred times. Java has three types of loop statements: while loops, do-while loops, and for loops.

In this chapter, you will learn various selection and loop control statements.

3.2   Selection Statements

This section introduces selection statements. Java has several types of selection statements: simple if statements, if ... else statements, nested if statements, switch statements, and conditional expressions.

3.2.1   Simple if Statements

A simple if statement executes an action only if the condition is true. The syntax for a simple if statement is shown below:

```
if (booleanExpression) {
  statement(s);
}
```

if statement

The execution flow chart is shown in Figure 3.1(a).

If the booleanExpression evaluates as true, the statements in the block are executed. As an example, see the following code:

```
if (radius >= 0) {
  area = radius * radius * PI;
  System.out.println("The area for the circle of radius " +
    radius + " is " + area);
}
```

The flow chart of the preceding statement is shown in Figure 3.1(b). If the value of radius is greater than or equal to 0, then the area is computed and the result is displayed; otherwise, the two statements in the block will not be executed.

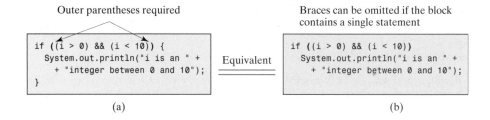

FIGURE 3.1 *An* `if` *statement executes statements if the* `booleanExpression` *evaluates as* `true`.

🌿 **NOTE**

The `booleanExpression` is enclosed in parentheses for all forms of the `if` statement. Thus, for example, the outer parentheses in the following `if` statements are required.

Outer parentheses required

Braces can be omitted if the block contains a single statement

```
if ((i > 0) && (i < 10)) {
  System.out.println("i is an " +
    + "integer between 0 and 10");
}
```
Equivalent
```
if ((i > 0) && (i < 10))
  System.out.println("i is an " +
    + "integer between 0 and 10");
```

(a)   (b)

The braces can be omitted if they enclose a single statement.

🌿 **CAUTION**

Forgetting the braces when they are needed for grouping multiple statements is a common programming error. If you modify the code by adding new statements in an `if` statement without braces, you will have to insert the braces if they are not already in place.

The following statement determines whether a number is even or odd:

```
// Prompt the user to enter an integer
String intString = JOptionPane.showInputDialog(
  "Enter an integer:");

// Convert string into int
int number = Integer.parseInt(intString);

if (number % 2 == 0)
  System.out.println(number + " is even.");

if (number % 2 != 0)
  System.out.println(number + " is odd.");
```

CAUTION

Adding a semicolon at the end of an `if` clause, as shown in (a) in the following code, is a common mistake.

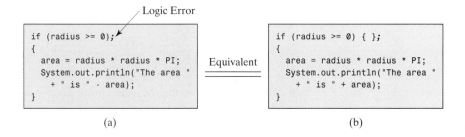

Logic Error

```
if (radius >= 0);
{
   area = radius * radius * PI;
   System.out.println("The area "
      + " is " + area);
}
```
(a)

Equivalent

```
if (radius >= 0) { };
{
   area = radius * radius * PI;
   System.out.println("The area "
      + " is " + area);
}
```
(b)

This mistake is hard to find, because it is not a compilation error or a runtime error; it is a logic error. The code in (a) is equivalent to (b).

This error often occurs when you use the next-line block style. Using the end-of-line block style will prevent this error.

3.2.2 if ... else Statements

A simple `if` statement takes an action if the specified condition is `true`. If the condition is `false`, nothing is done. But what if you want to take alternative actions when the condition is `false`? You can use an `if ... else` statement. The actions that an `if ... else` statement specifies differ based on whether the condition is `true` or `false`.

Here is the syntax for this type of statement:

```
if (booleanExpression) {
   statement(s)-for-the-true-case;
}
else {
   statement(s)-for-the-false-case;
}
```

The flow chart of the statement is shown in Figure 3.2.

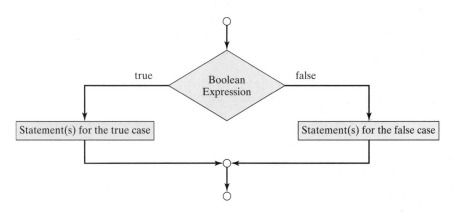

FIGURE 3.2 *An if ... else statement executes statements for the true case if the boolean expression evaluates as true; otherwise, statements for the false case are executed.*

If the booleanExpression evaluates as true, the statement(s) for the true case is executed; otherwise, the statement(s) for the false case is executed. For example, consider the following code:

```
if (radius >= 0) {
  area = radius * radius * PI;
  System.out.println("The area for the circle of radius " +
    radius + " is " + area);
}
else {
  System.out.println("Negative input");
}
```

If radius >= 0 is true, area is computed and displayed; if it is false, the message "Negative input" is printed.

As usual, the braces can be omitted if there is only one statement within them. The braces enclosing the System.out.println("Negative input") statement can therefore be omitted in the preceding example.

Using the if … else statement, you can rewrite the code for determining whether a number is even or odd in the preceding section, as follows:

```
if (number % 2 == 0)
  System.out.println(number + " is even.");
else
  System.out.println(number + " is odd.");
```

This is more efficient because whether number % 2 is 0 is tested only once.

3.2.3 Nested if Statements

The statement in an if or if … else statement can be any legal Java statement, including another if or if … else statement. The inner if statement is said to be *nested* inside the outer if statement. The inner if statement can contain another if statement; in fact, there is no limit to the depth of the nesting. For example, the following is a nested if statement:

```
if (i > k) {
  if (j > k)
    System.out.println("i and j are greater than k");
}
else
  System.out.println("i is less than or equal to k");
```

The if (j > k) statement is nested inside the if (i > k) statement.

The nested if statement can be used to implement multiple alternatives. The statement given in Figure 3.3(a), for instance, assigns a letter grade to the variable grade according to the score, with multiple alternatives.

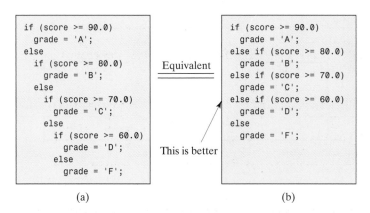

(a) Equivalent This is better (b)

FIGURE 3.3 *A preferred format for multiple alternative if statements is shown in (b).*

The execution of this `if` statement proceeds as follows. The first condition (`score >= 90.0`) is tested. If it is `true`, the grade becomes `'A'`. If it is `false`, the second condition (`score >= 80.0`) is tested. If the second condition is `true`, the grade becomes `'B'`. If that condition is `false`, the third condition and the rest of the conditions (if necessary) continue to be tested until a condition is met or all of the conditions prove to be `false`. If all of the conditions are `false`, the grade becomes `'F'`. Note that a condition is tested only when all of the conditions that come before it are `false`.

The `if` statement in Figure 3.3(a) is equivalent to the `if` statement in Figure 3.3(b). In fact, Figure 3.3(b) is the preferred writing style for multiple alternative `if` statements. This style avoids deep indentation and makes the program easy to read.

NOTE

The `else` clause matches the most recent unmatched `if` clause in the same block. For example, the following statement in (a) is equivalent to the statement in (b):

matching else with if

```
int i = 1;
int j = 2;
int k = 3;

if (i > j)
    if (i > k)
        System.out.println("A");
else
        System.out.println("B");
```
(a)

Equivalent

This is better with correct indentation

```
int i = 1;
int j = 2;
int k = 3;

if (i > j)
    if (i > k)
        System.out.println("A");
    else
        System.out.println("B");
```
(b)

The compiler ignores indentation. Nothing is printed from the statement in (a) and (b). To force the `else` clause to match the first `if` clause, you must add a pair of braces:

```
int i = 1; int j = 2; int k = 3;

if (i > j) {
  if (i > k)
    System.out.println("A");
}
else
  System.out.println("B");
```

This statement prints B.

TIP

Often new programmers write the code that assigns a test condition to a `boolean` variable like the code in (a):

assign boolean variable

```
if (number % 2 == 0)
    even = true;
else
    even = false;
```
(a)

Equivalent

This is better

```
boolean even
= number % 2 == 0;
```
(b)

The code can be simplified by assigning the test value directly to the variable, as shown in (b).

☙ CAUTION

To test whether a `boolean` variable is `true` or `false` in a test condition, it is redundant to use the equality comparison operator like the code in (a):

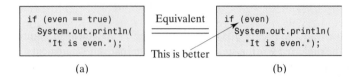

```
if (even == true)
    System.out.println(
        "It is even.");
```

Equivalent
═════════

```
if (even)
    System.out.println(
        "It is even.");
```

This is better

(a)   (b)

Instead, it is better to use the `boolean` variable directly, as shown in (b). Another good reason to use the `boolean` variable directly is to avoid errors that are difficult to detect. Using the `=` operator instead of the `==` operator to compare equality of two items in a test condition is a common error. It could lead to the following erroneous statement:

```
if (even = true)
    System.out.println("It is even.");
```

This statement does not have syntax errors. It assigns `true` to `even` so that `even` is always `true`.

EXAMPLE 3.1 COMPUTING TAXES

Problem

The United States federal personal income tax is calculated based on filing status and taxable income. There are four filing statuses: single filers, married filing jointly, married filing separately, and head of household. The tax rates for 2002 are shown in Table 3.1. If you are, say, single with a taxable income of $10,000, the first $6,000 is taxed at 10% and the other $4,000 is taxed at 15%. So your tax is $1,200.

TABLE 3.1 2002 U.S. Federal Personal Tax Rates

Tax rate	Single filers	Married filing jointly or qualifying widow/widower	Married filing separately	Head of household
10%	Up to $6,000	Up to $12,000	Up to $6,000	Up to $10,000
15%	$6,001–$27,950	$12,001–$46,700	$6,001–$23,350	$10,001–$37,450
27%	$27,951–$67,700	$46,701–$112,850	$23,351–$56,425	$37,451–$96,700
30%	$67,701–$141,250	$112,851–$171,950	$56,426–$85,975	$96,701–$156,600
35%	$141,251–$307,050	$171,951–$307,050	$85,976–$153,525	$156,601–$307,050
38.6%	$307,051 or more	$307,051 or more	$153,526 or more	$307–051 or more

Write a program that prompts the user to enter the filing status and taxable income and computes the tax for the year 2002. Enter 0 for single filers, 1 for married filing jointly, 2 for married filing separately, and 3 for head of household. A sample run of the program is shown in Figure 3.4.

EXAMPLE 3.1 (CONTINUED)

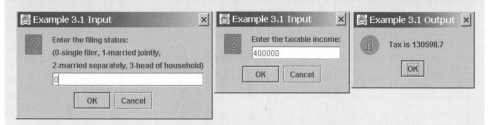

FIGURE 3.4 *The program computes the tax using* if *statements.*

Solution

Your program computes the tax for the taxable income based on the filing status. The filing status can be determined using if statements outlined as follows:

```
if (status == 0) {
  // Compute tax for single filers
}
else if (status == 1) {
  // Compute tax for married file jointly
}
else if (status == 2) {
  // Compute tax for married file separately
}
else if (status == 3) {
  // Compute tax for head of household
}
else {
  // Display wrong status
}
```

For each filing status, there are six tax rates. Each rate is applied to a certain amount of taxable income. For example, of a taxable income of \$400,000 for single filers, \$6,000 is taxed at 10%, $(27950 - 6000)$ at 15%, $(67700 - 27950)$ at 27%, $(141250 - 67700)$ at 35%, and $(400000 - 307050)$ at 38.6%.

Listing 3.1 gives the solution to compute taxes for single filers. The complete solution is left as an exercise.

LISTING 3.1 ComputeTaxWithSelectionStatement.java (Computing Tax)

```
1 import javax.swing.JOptionPane;
2
3 public class ComputeTaxWithSelectionStatement {
4   public static void main(String[] args) {
5     // Prompt the user to enter filing status
6     String statusString = JOptionPane.showInputDialog(null,
7       "Enter the filing status:\n" +
8       "(0-single filer, 1-married jointly,\n" +
9       "2-married separately, 3-head of household)",
10      "Example 3.1 Input", JOptionPane.QUESTION_MESSAGE);
11     int status = Integer.parseInt(statusString);
12
13     // Prompt the user to enter taxable income
14     String incomeString = JOptionPane.showInputDialog(null,
15       "Enter the taxable income:",
16       "Example 3.1 Input", JOptionPane.QUESTION_MESSAGE);
17     double income = Double.parseDouble(incomeString);
18
19     // Compute tax
20     double tax = 0;
21
```

import class

input dialog

convert string to int

input dialog

convert string to double

compute tax

message dialog

EXAMPLE 3.1 (CONTINUED)

```
22    if (status == 0) { // Compute tax for single filers
23      if (income <= 6000)
24        tax = income * 0.10;
25      else if (income <= 27950)
26        tax = 6000 * 0.10 + (income - 6000) * 0.15;
27      else if (income <= 67700)
28        tax = 6000 * 0.10 + (27950 - 6000) * 0.15 +
29          (income - 27950) * 0.27;
30      else if (income <= 141250)
31        tax = 6000 * 0.10 + (27950 - 6000) * 0.15 +
32          (67700 - 27950) * 0.27 + (income - 67700) * 0.30;
33      else if (income <= 307050)
34        tax = 6000 * 0.10 + (27950 - 6000) * 0.15 +
35          (67700 - 27950) * 0.27 + (141250 - 67700) * 0.30 +
36          (income - 141250) * 0.35;
37      else
38        tax = 6000 * 0.10 + (27950 - 6000) * 0.15 +
39          (67700 - 27950) * 0.27 + (141250 - 67700) * 0.30 +
40          (307050 - 141250) * 0.35 + (income - 307050) * 0.386;
41    }
42    else if (status == 1) { // Compute tax for married file jointly
44      // Left as exercise
44    }
45    else if (status == 2) { // Compute tax for married separately
46      // Left as exercise
47    }
48    else if (status == 3) { // Compute tax for head of household
49      // Left as exercise
50    }
51    else {
52      System.out.println("Error: invalid status");
53      System.exit(0);
54    }
55
56    // Display the result
57    JOptionPane.showMessageDialog(null, "Tax is " +
58      (int)(tax * 100) / 100.0,
59      "Example 3.1 Output", JOptionPane.INFORMATION_MESSAGE);
60  }
61 }
```

Review

The `import` statement (Line 1) makes the class `javax.swing.JOptionPane` available for use in this example.

The program receives the filing status and taxable income. The multiple alternative `if` statements (Lines 22, 42, 45, 48, 51) check the filing status and compute the tax based on the filing status.

Like the `showMessageDialog` method, `System.exit(0)` (Line 53) is also a static method. This method is defined in the `System` class. Invoking this method terminates the program. The argument 0 indicates that the program is terminated normally.

Note that an initial value of 0 is assigned to `tax` (Line 20). A syntax error would occur if it had no initial value because all of the other statements that assign values to `tax` are within the `if` statement. The compiler thinks that these statements may not be executed and therefore reports a syntax error.

3.2.4   switch Statements

The `if` statement in Example 3.1 makes selections based on a single `true` or `false` condition. There are four cases for computing taxes, which depend on the value of `status`. To fully account for all the cases, nested `if` statements were used. Overuse of nested `if` statements makes

EXAMPLE 3.2 (CONTINUED)

LISTING 3.2   TestWhile.java (Using while Loop)

```java
 1 import javax.swing.JOptionPane;
 2
 3 public class TestWhile {
 4   /** Main method */
 5   public static void main(String[] args) {
 6     // Read an initial data
 7     String dataString = JOptionPane.showInputDialog(null,
 8       "Enter an int value, \nthe program exits if the input is 0",
 9       "Example 3.2 Input", JOptionPane.QUESTION_MESSAGE);
10     int data = Integer.parseInt(dataString);
11
12     // Keep reading data until the input is 0
13     int sum = 0;
14     while (data != 0) {
15       sum += data;
16
17       // Read the next data
18       dataString = JOptionPane.showInputDialog(null,
19         "Enter an int value, \nthe program exits if the input is 0",
20         "Example 3.2 Input", JOptionPane.QUESTION_MESSAGE);
21       data = Integer.parseInt(dataString);
22     }
23
24     JOptionPane.showMessageDialog(null, "The sum is " + sum,
25       "Example 3.2 Output", JOptionPane.INFORMATION_MESSAGE);
26   }
27 }
```

input dialog (lines 7–9)
convert string to int (line 10)
loop (line 14)
message dialog (lines 24–25)

Review

If data is not 0, it is added to the sum (Line 15) and the next items of input data are read (Lines 18–21). If data is 0, the loop body is not executed and the while loop terminates.

Note that if the first input read is 0, the loop body never executes, and the resulting sum is 0.

NOTE

The program uses the input value 0 as the end of the input. A special input value that signifies the end of the input, such as 0 in this example, is also known as a *sentinel value*.

sentinel value

CAUTION

Don't use floating-point values for equality checking in a loop control. Since floating-point values are approximations, using them could result in imprecise counter values and inaccurate results. This example uses int value for data. If a floating-point type value is used for data, (data != 0) may be true even though data is 0.

numeric error

Here is a good example provided by a reviewer of this book:

```java
// data should be zero
double data = Math.pow(Math.sqrt(2), 2) - 2;

if (data == 0)
  System.out.println("data is zero");
else
  System.out.println("data is not zero");
```

> Like pow, sqrt is a method in the Math class for computing the square root of a number. The variable data in the above code should be zero, but it is not, because of rounding-off errors.

3.3.2 The do-while Loop

do-while loop

The do-while loop is a variation of the while loop. Its syntax is given below:

```
do {
  // Loop body;
  Statement(s);
} while (loop-continuation-condition);
```

Its execution flow chart is shown in Figure 3.8.

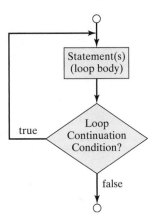

FIGURE 3.8 *The do-while loop executes the loop body first, and then checks the loop-continuation-condition to determine whether to continue or terminate the loop.*

The loop body is executed first. Then the loop-continuation-condition is evaluated. If the evaluation is true, the loop body is executed again; if it is false, the do-while loop terminates. The major difference between a while loop and a do-while loop is the order in which the loop-continuation-condition is evaluated and the loop body executed. The while loop and the do-while loop have equal expressive power. Sometimes one is a more convenient choice than the other. For example, you can rewrite Example 3.2 as shown in Listing 3.3.

LISTING 3.3 TestDo.java (Using do-while Loop)

loop

```
1 import javax.swing.JOptionPane;
2
3 public class TestDoWhile {
4   /** Main method */
5   public static void main(String[] args) {
6     int data;
7     int sum = 0;
8
9     // Keep reading data until the input is 0
10    do {
11      // Read the next data
```

```
12        String dataString = JOptionPane.showInputDialog(null,
13          "Enter an int value, \nthe program exits if the input is 0",
14          "TestDo", JOptionPane.QUESTION_MESSAGE);
15
16        data = Integer.parseInt(dataString);
17
18        sum += data;
19      } while (data != 0);
20
21      JOptionPane.showMessageDialog(null, "The sum is " + sum,
22        "TestDo", JOptionPane.INFORMATION_MESSAGE);
23    }
24 }
```

TIP

Use the `do-while` loop if you have statements inside the loop that must be executed at least once, as in the case of the `do-while` loop in the preceding TestDoWhile program. These statements must appear before the loop as well as inside the loop if you use a `while` loop.

3.3.3 The for Loop

Often you write a loop in the following common form:

```
i = initialValue; // Initialize loop control variable
while (i < endValue) {
  // Loop body
  ...
  i++; // Adjust loop control variable
}
```

A `for` loop can be used to simplify the above loop:

```
for (i = initialValue; i < endValue; i++) {
  // Loop body
  ...
}
```

In general, the syntax of a `for` loop is as shown below:

```
for (initial-action; loop-continuation-condition;
    action-after-each-iteration) {
  // Loop body;
  Statement(s);
}
```

for loop

The flow chart of the `for` loop is shown in Figure 3.9(a).

The `for` loop statement starts with the keyword `for`, followed by a pair of parentheses enclosing `initial-action`, `loop-continuation-condition`, and `action-after-each-iteration`, and the loop body, enclosed inside braces. `initial-action`, `loop-continuation-condition`, and `action-after-each-iteration` are separated by semicolons.

A `for` loop generally uses a variable to control how many times the loop body is executed and when the loop terminates. This variable is referred to as a *control variable*. The `initial-action` often initializes a control variable, the `action-after-each-iteration` usually increments or decrements the control variable, and the `loop-continuation-condition` tests whether the control

control variable

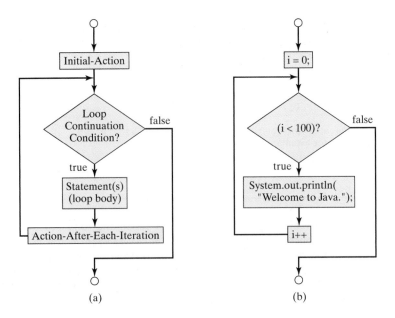

FIGURE 3.9 *A* for *loop performs an initial action once, then repeatedly executes the statements in the loop body, and performs an action after an iteration when the* loop-continuation-condition *evaluates as* true.

variable has reached a termination value. For example, the following for loop prints Welcome to Java! a hundred times:

```java
int i;
for (i = 0; i < 100; i++) {
  System.out.println("Welcome to Java!");
}
```

The flow chart of the statement is shown in Figure 3.9(b). The for loop initializes i to 0, then repeatedly executes the println statement and evaluates i++ if i is less than 100.

The initial-action, i = 0, initializes the control variable, i.

The loop-continuation-condition, i < 100, is a Boolean expression. The expression is evaluated at the beginning of each iteration. If this condition is true, execute the loop body. If it is false, the loop terminates and the program control turns to the line following the loop.

The action-after-each-iteration, i++, is a statement that adjusts the control variable. This statement is executed after each iteration. It increments the control variable. Eventually, the value of the control variable forces the loop-continuation-condition to become false.

The loop control variable can be declared and initialized in the for loop. Here is an example:

```java
for (int i = 0; i < 100; i++) {
  System.out.println("Welcome to Java!");
}
```

If there is only one statement in the loop body, as in this example, the braces can be omitted.

 TIP

The control variable must always be declared inside the control structure of the loop or before the loop. If the loop control variable is used only in the loop, and not elsewhere, it is good programming practice to declare it in the initial-action of the `for` loop. If the variable is declared inside the loop control structure, it cannot be referenced outside the loop. For example, you cannot reference `i` outside the `for` loop in the preceding code, because it is declared inside the `for` loop.

 NOTE

The `initial-action` in a `for` loop can be a list of zero or more comma-separated variable declaration statements or assignment expressions. For example,

```
for (int i = 0, j = 0; (i + j < 10); i++, j++) {
  // Do something
}
```

The `action-after-each-iteration` in a `for` loop can be a list of zero or more comma-separated statements. For example,

```
for (int i = 1; i < 100; System.out.println(i), i++);
```

This example is correct, but it is not a good example, because it makes the code difficult to read. Normally, you declare and initialize a control variable as initial action, and increment or decrement the control variable as an action after each iteration.

 NOTE

If the `loop-continuation-condition` in a `for` loop is omitted, it is implicitly true. Thus the statement given below in (a), which is an infinite loop, is correct. Nevertheless, I recommend that you use the equivalent loop in (b) to avoid confusion:

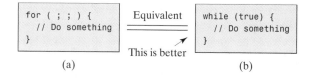

EXAMPLE 3.3 USING for LOOPS

Problem

Write a program that sums a series that starts with 0.01 and ends with 1.0. The numbers in the series will increment by 0.01, as follows: 0.01 + 0.02 + 0.03 and so on.

Solution

Listing 3.4 gives the solution to the problem. The output of the program appears in Figure 3.10.

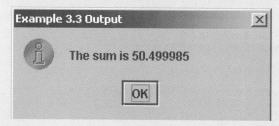

FIGURE 3.10 *Example 3.3 uses a for loop to sum a series from 0.01 to 1 in increments of 0.01.*

EXAMPLE 3.3 (CONTINUED)

LISTING 3.4 TestSum.java (Using for Loop)

loop

```java
1 import javax.swing.JOptionPane;
2
3 public class TestSum {
4   /** Main method */
5   public static void main(String[] args) {
6     // Initialize sum
7     float sum = 0;
8
9     // Add 0.01, 0.02, ..., 0.99, 1 to sum
10    for (float i = 0.01f; i <= 1.0f; i = i + 0.01f)
11      sum += i;
12
13    // Display result
14    JOptionPane.showMessageDialog(null, "The sum is " + sum,
15      "Example 3.3 Output", JOptionPane.INFORMATION_MESSAGE);
16  }
17 }
```

Review

The for loop (Lines 10–11) repeatedly adds the control variable i to the sum. This variable, which begins with 0.01, is incremented by 0.01 after each iteration. The loop terminates when i exceeds 1.0.

The for loop initial action can be any statement, but it is often used to initialize a control variable. From this example, you can see that a control variable can be a float type. In fact, it can be any data type.

numeric error

The exact sum should be 50.50, but the answer is 50.499985. The result is not precise because computers use a fixed number of bits to represent floating-point numbers, and thus cannot represent some floating-point numbers exactly. If you change float in the program to double as follows, you should see a slight improvement in precision because a double variable takes sixty-four bits, whereas a float variable takes thirty-two bits:

```java
// Initialize sum
double sum = 0;

// Add 0.01, 0.02, ..., 0.99, 1 to sum
for (double i = 0.01; i <= 1.0; i = i + 0.01)
  sum += i;
```

However, you will be stunned to see that the result is actually 49.50000000000003. What went wrong? If you print out i for each iteration in the loop, you will see that the last i is slightly larger than 1 (not exactly 1). This causes the last i not to be added in sum. The fundamental problem is that the floating-point numbers are represented by approximation. Errors commonly occur. To ensure that all items are added to sum, use an integer variable to count the items. Here is the new loop:

```java
double item = 0.01;
for (int count = 0; count < 100; count++) {
  sum += item;
  item += 0.01;
}
```

After this loop, sum is 50.50000000000003.

3.3.4 Nested Loops

Nested loops consist of an outer loop and one or more inner loops. Each time the outer loop is repeated, the inner loops are reentered, and all the required iterations are performed.

EXAMPLE 3.4 DISPLAYING THE MULTIPLICATION TABLE

Problem

Write a program that uses nested for loops to print a multiplication table, as shown in Figure 3.11.

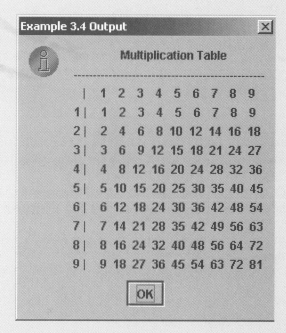

FIGURE 3.11 *Example 3.4 uses nested* for *loops to print a multiplication table.*

Solution

Listing 3.5 gives the solution to the problem.

LISTING 3.5 TestMultiplicationTable.java
(Using Nested for Loop)

```
1 import javax.swing.JOptionPane;
2
3 public class TestMultiplicationTable {
4    /** Main method */
5    public static void main(String[] args) {
6      // Display the table heading
7      String output = " Multiplication Table\n";        table title
8      output += "---------------------------------\n";
9
10     // Display the number title
11     output += "   | ";
12     for (int j = 1; j <= 9; j++)
13        output += "  " + j;
```

EXAMPLE 3.4 (CONTINUED)

```
14
15      output += "\n";
16
17      // Print table body
18      for (int i = 1; i <= 9; i++) {
19        output += i + " | ";
20        for (int j = 1; j <= 9; j++) {
21          // Display the product and align properly
22          if (i * j < 10)
23            output += " " + i * j;
24          else
25            output += " " + i * j;
26        }
27        output += "\n";
28      }
29
30      // Display result
31      JOptionPane.showMessageDialog(null, output,
32        "Example 3.4 Output", JOptionPane.INFORMATION_MESSAGE);
33    }
34 }
```

table body

nested loop

Review

The program displays a title (Line 7) on the first line and dashes (-) (Line 8) on the second line. The first `for` loop (Lines 12–13) displays the numbers 1 through 9 on the third line.

The next loop (Lines 18–28) is a nested `for` loop with the control variable `i` in the outer loop and `j` in the inner loop. For each `i`, the product `i * j` is displayed on a line in the inner loop, with `j` being 1, 2, 3, ..., 9. The `if` statement in the inner loop (Lines 22–25) is used so that the product will be aligned properly. If the product is a single digit, it is displayed with an extra space before it.

3.5 Which Loop to Use?

The three forms of loop statements, `while`, `do-while`, and `for`, are expressively equivalent; that is, you can write a loop in any of these three forms. For example, a `while` loop in (a) in the following figure can always be converted into the `for` loop in (b):

```
while (loop-continuation-condition) {
  // Loop body
}
```
Equivalent
```
for ( ; loop-continuation-condition; )
  // Loop body
}
```
(a)   (b)

A `for` loop in (a) in the next figure can generally be converted into the `while` loop in (b) except in certain special cases (see Review Question 3.20 for such a case):

```
for (initial-action;
     loop-continuation-condition;
     action-after-each-iteration) {
  // Loop body;
}
```
Equivalent
```
initial-action;
while (loop-continuation-condition) {
  // Loop body;
  action-after-each-iteration;
}
```
(a)   (b)

I recommend that you use the loop statement that is most intuitive and comfortable for you. In general, a `for` loop may be used if the number of repetitions is known, as, for example, when you need to print a message a hundred times. A `while` loop may be used if the number of repetitions is not known, as in the case of reading the numbers until the input is 0. A `do-while` loop can be used to replace a `while` loop if the loop body has to be executed before the continuation condition is tested.

 CAUTION

Adding a semicolon at the end of the `for` clause before the loop body is a common mistake, as shown below in (a). Similarly, the loop in (b) is also wrong.

Logic Error   Logic Error

```
for (int i = 0; i < 10; i++);
{
   System.out.println("i is " + i);
}
```

```
int i = 0;
while (i < 10);
{
   System.out.println("i is " + i);
   i++;
}
```

(a)   (b)

In both cases, the semicolon signifies the end of the loop prematurely. These errors often occur when you use the next-line block style.

In the case of the `do-while` loop, the semicolon is needed to end the loop.

```
int i = 0;
do {
   System.out.println("i is " + i);
   i++;
} while (i < 10);  ◄──── Correct
```

3.6   Using the Keywords `break` and `continue`

Two statements, `break` and `continue`, can be used in loop statements to provide the loop with additional control.

✦ **break** immediately ends the innermost loop that contains it. It is generally used with an `if` statement.

break statement

✦ **continue** only ends the current iteration. Program control goes to the end of the loop body. This keyword is generally used with an `if` statement.

continue statement

You have already used the keyword `break` in a `switch` statement. You can also use `break` and `continue` in a loop.

EXAMPLE 3.5 DEMONSTRATING A `break` STATEMENT

Problem

Add the integers from 1 to 20 in this order to sum until sum is greater than or equal to 100.

Solution

Listing 3.6 gives the solution to the problem.

EXAMPLE 3.5 (CONTINUED)

LISTING 3.6 TestBreak.java (Skipping Loop)

break

```
 1 public class TestBreak {
 2   /** Main method */
 3   public static void main(String[] args) {
 4     int sum = 0;
 5     int number = 0;
 6
 7     while (number < 20) {
 8       number++;
 9       sum += number;
10       if (sum >= 100) break;
11     }
12
13     System.out.println("The number is " + number);
14     System.out.println("The sum is " + sum);
15   }
16 }
```

Review

Without the `if` statement (Line 10), this program calculates the sum of the numbers from 1 to 20. But with the `if` statement, the loop terminates when the sum becomes greater than or equal to 100. The output of the program is shown in Figure 3.12(a).

If you changed the `if` statement as shown below, the output would resemble that in Figure 3.12(b).

```
if (sum == 100) break;
```

In this case, the `if` condition will never be `true`. Therefore, the break statement will never be executed.

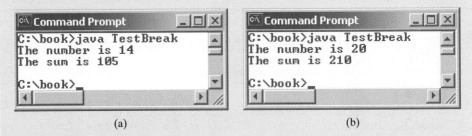

(a)   (b)

FIGURE 3.12 *(a) The* break *statement in the* TestBreak *program forces the* while *loop to exit when* sum *is greater than or equal to 100. (b) The* break *statement is not executed in the modified* TestBreak *program because* sum == 100 *cannot be* true.

EXAMPLE 3.6 DEMONSTRATING A continue STATEMENT

Problem

Add all the integers from 1 to 20 except 10 and 11 to sum.

Solution

Listing 3.7 gives the solution to the problem.

EXAMPLE 3.6 (CONTINUED)

LISTING 3.7   TestContinue.java (Skipping Iteration)

```
1 public class TestContinue {
2   /** Main method */
3   public static void main(String[] args) {
4     int sum = 0;
5     int number = 0;
6
7     while (number < 20) {
8       number++;
9       if (number == 10 || number == 11) continue;
10      sum += number;
11    }
12
13    System.out.println("The sum is " + sum);
14  }
15 }
```

continue

Review

With the `if` statement in the program (Line 9), the `continue` statement is executed when number becomes 10 or 11. The `continue` statement ends the current iteration so that the rest of the statement in the loop body is not executed; therefore, number is not added to sum when it is 10 or 11. The output of the program is shown in Figure 3.13(a).

Without the `if` statement in the program, the output would look like Figure 3.13(b). In this case, all of the numbers are added to sum, including when number is 10 or 11. Therefore, the result is 210, which is 21 more than it was with the `if` statement.

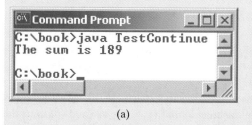
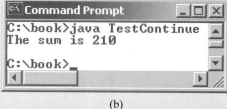

(a)   (b)

FIGURE 3.13   *(a) The* `continue` *statement in the* `TestContinue` *program forces the current iteration to end when* number *equals 10 or 11. (b) Since the modified* `TestContinue` *program has no* `continue` *statement, every number is added to* sum.

NOTE

The `continue` statement is always inside a loop. In the `while` and `do-while` loops, the `loop-continuation-condition` is evaluated immediately after the `continue` statement. In the `for` loop, the `action-after-each-iteration` is performed, then the `loop-continuation-condition` is evaluated, immediately after the `continue` statement.

TIP

You can always write a program without using `break` or `continue` in a loop. See Review Question 3.21. In general, it is appropriate to use `break` and `continue` if their use simplifies coding and makes programs easier to read.

3.6.1   Statement Labels and Breaking with Labels (Optional)

Every statement in Java can have an optional label as an identifier. Labels are often associated with loops. You can use a `break` statement with a label to break out of the labeled loop, and a `continue` statement with a label to break out of the current iteration of the labeled loop.

The `break` statement given below, for example, breaks out of the outer loop if (`i * j > 50`) and transfers control to the statement immediately following the outer loop:

```
outer:
  for (int i = 1; i < 10; i++) {
  inner:
    for (int j = 1; j < 10; j++) {
      if (i * j > 50)
          break outer;

      System.out.println(i * j);
    }
  }
```

If you replace `break outer` with `break` in the preceding statement, the `break` statement would break out of the inner loop and continue to stay inside the outer loop.

The following `continue` statement breaks out of the inner loop if (`i * j > 50`) and starts a new iteration of the outer loop if `i < 10` is true after `i` is incremented by 1:

```
outer:
  for (int i = 1; i < 10; i++) {
  inner:
    for (int j = 1; j < 10; j++) {
      if (i * j > 50)
        continue outer;

      System.out.println(i * j);
    }
  }
```

If you replace `continue outer` with `continue` in the preceding statement, the `continue` statement would break out of the current iteration of the inner loop if (`i * j > 50`) and continue the next iteration of the inner loop if `j < 10` is true after `j` is incremented by 1.

🌸 NOTE

goto

Some programming languages have a `goto` statement, but labeled `break` statements and labeled `continue` statements in Java are completely different from `goto` statements. The `goto label` statement would indiscriminately transfer the control to any labeled statement in the program and execute it. The `break label` statement breaks out of the labeled loop, and the `continue label` statement breaks out of the current iteration in the labeled loop.

3.7   Case Studies

Control statements are fundamental in programming. The ability to write control statements is essential in learning Java programming. *If you can write programs using loops, you know how to program!* For this reason, this section presents four additional examples of how to solve problems using loops.

EXAMPLE 3.7 FINDING THE GREATEST COMMON DIVISOR

Problem

Write a program that prompts the user to enter two positive integers and finds their greatest common divisor.

Solution

The greatest common divisor of the integers 4 and 2, is 2. The greatest common divisor of the integers 16 and 24, is 8. How do you find the greatest common divisor? Let the two input integers be n1 and n2. You know that number 1 is a common divisor, but it may not be the greatest common divisor. So you can check whether k (for k = 2, 3, 4, and so on) is a common divisor for n1 and n2, until k is greater than n1 or n2. Store the common divisor in a variable named gcd. Initially, gcd is 1. Whenever a new common divisor is found, it becomes the new gcd. When you have checked all the possible common divisors from 2 up to n1 or n2, the value in variable gcd is the greatest common divisor. The idea can be translated into the following loop:

GCD

```
int gcd = 1;
int k = 1;
while (k <= n1 && k <= n2) {
  if (n1 % k == 0 && n2 % k == 0)
    gcd = k;
  k++;
}
// After the loop, gcd is the greatest common divisor for n1 and n2
```

The complete program is given in Listing 3.8, and a sample run of the program is shown in Figure 3.14.

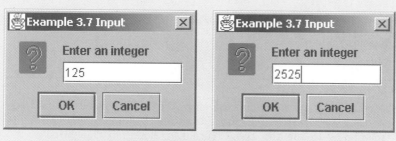

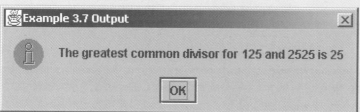

FIGURE 3.14 *The program finds the greatest common divisor for two integers.*

LISTING 3.8 GreatestCommonDivisor.java (Finding GCD)

```
1 import javax.swing.JOptionPane;
2
3 public class GreatestCommonDivisor {
4   /** Main method */
5   public static void main(String[] args) {
```

EXAMPLE 3.7 (CONTINUED)

input

input

gcd

output

```
 6    // Prompt the user to enter two integers
 7    String s1 = JOptionPane.showInputDialog(null, "Enter an integer",
 8      "Example 3.7 Input", JOptionPane.QUESTION_MESSAGE);
 9    int n1 = Integer.parseInt(s1);
10
11    String s2 = JOptionPane.showInputDialog(null, "Enter an integer",
12      "Example 3.7 Input", JOptionPane.QUESTION_MESSAGE);
13    int n2 = Integer.parseInt(s2);
14
15    int gcd = 1;
16    int k = 1;
17    while (k <= n1 && k <= n2) {
18      if (n1 % k == 0 && n2 % k == 0)
19        gcd = k;
20      k++;
21    }
22
23    String output = "The greatest common divisor for " + n1 + " and "
24      + n2 + " is " + gcd;
25    JOptionPane.showMessageDialog(null, output,
26      "Example 3.7 Output", JOptionPane.INFORMATION_MESSAGE);
27  }
28 }
```

Review

think before you type

How did you write this program? Did you immediately begin to write the code? No. It is important to *think before you type*. Thinking enables you to generate a logical solution for the problem without concern about how to write the code. Once you have a logical solution, type the code to translate the solution into a Java program. The translation is not unique. For example, you could use a for loop to rewrite the code as follows:

```
for (int k = 1; k <= n1 && k <= n2; k++) {
  if (n1 % k == 0 && n2 % k == 0)
    gcd = k;
}
```

 NOTE

multiple solutions

A problem often has *multiple solutions*. The GCD problem can be solved in many ways. Exercise 3.20 suggests another solution. A more efficient solution is to use the classic Euclidean algorithm. See http://www.mapleapps.com/maplelinks/html/euclid.html for more information.

EXAMPLE 3.8 FINDING THE SALES AMOUNT

Problem

You have just started a sales job in a department store. Your pay consists of a base salary and a commission. The base salary is $5,000. The scheme shown below is used to determine the commission rate.

Sales Amount	Commission Rate
$0.01–$5,000	8 percent
$5,000.01–$10,000	10 percent
$10,000.01 and above	12 percent

EXAMPLE 3.8 (CONTINUED)

Your goal is to earn $30,000 a year. Write a program that finds out the minimum amount of sales you have to generate in order to make $30,000.

Solution

Since your base salary is $5,000, you have to make $25,000 in commissions to earn $30,000 a year. What is the sales amount for a $25,000 commission? If you know the sales amount, the commission can be computed as follows:

```
if (salesAmount >= 10000.01)
  commission =
    5000 * 0.08 + 5000 * 0.1 + (salesAmount - 10000) * 0.12;
else if (salesAmount >= 5000.01)
  commission = 5000 * 0.08 + (salesAmount - 5000) * 0.10;
else
  commission = salesAmount * 0.08;
```

This suggests that you can try to find the salesAmount to match a given commission through incremental approximation. For salesAmount of $0.01 (1 cent), find commission. If commission is less than $25,000, increment salesAmount by 0.01 and find commission again. If commission is still less than $25,000, repeat the process until the commission is greater than or equal to $25,000. This is a tedious job for humans, but it is exactly what a computer is good for. You can write a loop and let a computer execute it painlessly. The idea can be translated into the following loop:

```
Set COMMISSION_SOUGHT as a constant;
Set an initial salesAmount;

do {
  Increase salesAmount by 1 cent;
  Compute the commission from the current salesAmount;
} while (commission < COMMISSION_SOUGHT);
```

The complete program is given in Listing 3.9, and a sample run of the program is shown in Figure 3.15.

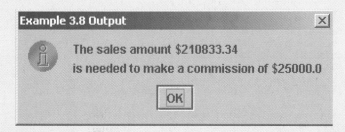

FIGURE 3.15 *The program finds the sales amount for the given commission.*

LISTING 3.9 FindSalesAmount.java (Finding Sales Amount)

```
1 import javax.swing.JOptionPane;
2
3 public class FindSalesAmount {
4   /** Main method */
5   public static void main(String[] args) {
6     // The commission sought
7     final double COMMISSION_SOUGHT = 25000;          constants
8     final double INITIAL_SALES_AMOUNT = 0.01;
9     double commission = 0;
10    double salesAmount = INITIAL_SALES_AMOUNT;
```

EXAMPLE 3.8 (CONTINUED)

loop

```
11
12    do {
13      // Increase salesAmount by 1 cent
14      salesAmount += 0.01;
15
16      // Compute the commission from the current salesAmount;
17      if (salesAmount >= 10000.01)
18        commission =
19          5000 * 0.08 + 5000 * 0.1 + (salesAmount - 10000) * 0.12;
20      else if (salesAmount >= 5000.01)
21        commission = 5000 * 0.08 + (salesAmount - 5000) * 0.10;
22      else
23        commission = salesAmount * 0.08;
24    } while (commission < COMMISSION_SOUGHT);
25
```

prepare output

```
26    // Display the sales amount
27    String output =
28      "The sales amount $" + (int)(salesAmount * 100) / 100.0 +
29      "\nis needed to make a commission of $" + COMMISSION_SOUGHT;
```

output

```
30    JOptionPane.showMessageDialog(null, output,
31      "Example 3.8 Output", JOptionPane.INFORMATION_MESSAGE);
32  }
33 }
```

Review

The do-while loop (Lines 12–24) is used to repeatedly compute commission for an incremental salesAmount. The loop terminates when commission is greater than or equal to a constant COMMISSION_SOUGHT.

In Exercise 3.22, you will rewrite this program to let the user enter COMMISSION_SOUGHT dynamically from an input dialog.

You can improve the performance of this program by estimating a higher INITIAL_SALES_AMOUNT (e.g., 25000).

What is wrong if saleAmount is incremented after the commission is computed as follows?

```
do {
  // Compute the commission from the current salesAmount;
  if (salesAmount >= 10000.01)
    commission =
      5000 * 0.08 + 5000 * 0.1 + (salesAmount - 10000) * 0.12;
  else if (salesAmount >= 5000.01)
    commission = 5000 * 0.08 + (salesAmount - 5000) * 0.10;
  else
    commission = salesAmount * 0.08;

  // Increase salesAmount by 1 cent
  salesAmount += 0.01;
} while (commission < COMMISSION_SOUGHT);
```

off-by-one error

The change is erroneous because saleAmount is 1 cent more than is needed for the commission when the loop ends. This is a common error in loops, known as the *off-by-one* error.

🌿 **TIP**

constants

This example uses *constants* COMMISSION_SOUGHT and INITIAL_SALES_ AMOUNT. Using constants makes programs easy to read and maintain.

EXAMPLE 3.9 DISPLAYING A PYRAMID OF NUMBERS

Problem

Write a program that prompts the user to enter an integer from 1 to 15 and displays a pyramid. If the input integer is 12, for example, the output is shown in Figure 3.16.

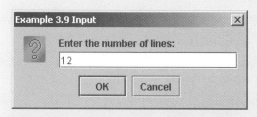

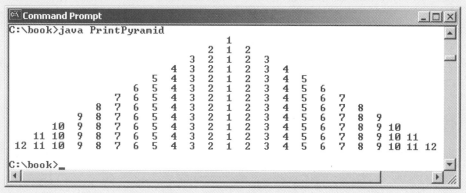

FIGURE 3.16 *The program uses nested loops to print numbers in a triangular pattern.*

Solution

Your program receives the input for an integer (`numberOfLines`) that represents the total number of lines. It displays all the lines one by one. Each line has three parts. The first part comprises the spaces before the numbers; the second part, the leading numbers, such as 3 2 1 on Line 3; and the last part, the ending numbers, such as 2 3 on Line 3.

Each number occupies three spaces. Display an empty space before a double-digit number, and display two empty spaces before a single-digit number.

You can use an outer loop to control the lines. At the nth row, there are (`numberOfLines` − n) * 3 leading spaces, the leading numbers are n, n−1, ..., 1, and the ending numbers are 2, ..., n. You can use three separate inner loops to print each part.

Here is the algorithm for the problem:

```
Input numberOfLines;

for (int row = 1; row <= numberOfLines; row++) {
  Print (numberOfLines - row) * 3 leading spaces;
  Print leading numbers row, row - 1, ..., 1;
  Print ending numbers 2, 3, ..., row - 1, row;
  Start a new line;
}
```

The complete program is given in Listing 3.10.

EXAMPLE 3.9 (CONTINUED)

LISTING 3.10 PrintPyramid.java (Printing Pyramid)

```
 1 import javax.swing.JOptionPane;
 2
 3 public class PrintPyramid {
 4   /** Main method */
 5   public static void main(String[] args) {
 6     // Prompt the user to enter the number of lines
 7     String input = JOptionPane.showInputDialog(null,
 8       "Enter the number of lines:", "Example 3.9 Input",
 9       JOptionPane.QUESTION_MESSAGE);
10     int numberOfLines = Integer.parseInt(input);
11
12     if (numberOfLines < 1 || numberOfLines > 15) {
13       System.out.println("You must enter a number from 1 to 15");
14       System.exit(0);
15     }
16
17     // Print lines
18     for (int row = 1; row <= numberOfLines; row++) {
19       // Print NUMBER_OF_LINES - row) leading spaces
20       for (int column = 1; column <= numberOfLines - row; column++)
21         System.out.print("   ");
22
23       // Print leading numbers row, row - 1, ..., 1
24       for (int num = row; num >= 1; num--)
25         System.out.print((num >= 10) ? " " + num : "  " + num);
26
27       // Print ending numbers 2, 3, ..., row - 1, row
28       for (int num = 2; num <= row; num++)
29         System.out.print((num >= 10) ? " " + num : "  " + num);
30
31       // Start a new line
32       System.out.println();
33     }
34   }
35 }
```

print lines *(line 18)*

print spaces *(line 20)*

print leading numbers *(line 24)*

print ending numbers *(line 28)*

Review

The program uses the print method (Lines 21, 25, and 29) to display a string to the console. This method is identical to the println method except that println moves the cursor to the next line after displaying the string, but print does not advance the cursor to the next line when completed.

The conditional expression (num >= 10) ? " " + num : "   " + num in Lines 25 and 29 returns a string with a single empty space before the number if the number is greater than or equal to 10, and otherwise returns a string with two empty spaces before the number.

Printing patterns like this one and the ones in Exercises 3.23 and 3.24 is my favorite exercise for practicing loop control statements. The key is to understand the pattern and to describe it using loop control variables.

The last line in the outer loop (Line 32), System.out.println(), does not have any argument in the method. This call moves the cursor to the next line.

EXAMPLE 3.10 DISPLAYING PRIME NUMBERS (OPTIONAL)

Problem

Write a program that displays the first fifty *prime numbers* in five lines, each of which contains ten numbers, as shown in Figure 3.17. An integer greater than 1 is *prime* if its only positive divisor is 1 or itself. For example, 2, 3, 5, and 7 are prime numbers, but 4, 6, 8, and 9 are not.

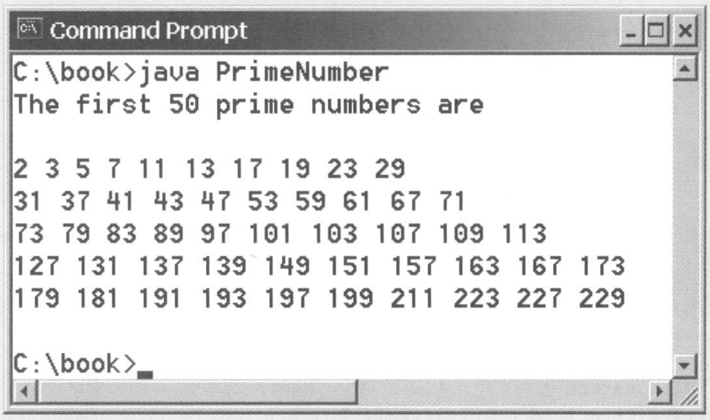

prime number

```
Command Prompt                               _ □ ×
C:\book>java PrimeNumber
The first 50 prime numbers are

2 3 5 7 11 13 17 19 23 29
31 37 41 43 47 53 59 61 67 71
73 79 83 89 97 101 103 107 109 113
127 131 137 139 149 151 157 163 167 173
179 181 191 193 197 199 211 223 227 229

C:\book>
```

FIGURE 3.17 *The program displays the first fifty prime numbers.*

Solution

The problem can be broken into the following tasks:

✦ Determine whether a given number is prime.

✦ For number = 2, 3, 4, 5, 6, ..., test whether the number is prime.

✦ Count the prime numbers.

✦ Print each prime number, and print ten numbers per line.

Obviously, you need to write a loop and repeatedly test whether a new number is prime. If the number is prime, increase the count by 1. The count is 0 initially. When it exceeds 50, the loop terminates.

Here is the algorithm for the problem:

```
Set the number of prime numbers to be printed as
  a constant NUMBER_OF_PRIMES;
Use count to track the number of prime numbers and
  set an initial count to 0;
Set an initial number to 2;

while (count < NUMBER_OF_PRIMES) {
  Test if number is prime;

  if number is prime {
    Print the prime number and increase the count;
  }

  Increment number by 1;
}
```

EXAMPLE 3.10 (CONTINUED)

To test whether a number is prime, check whether the number is divisible by 2, 3, 4, up to number/2. If a divisor is found, the number is not a prime. The algorithm can be described as follows:

```
Use a boolean variable isPrime to denote whether
  the number is prime; Set isPrime to true initially;

for (int divisor = 2; divisor <= number / 2; divisor++) {
  if (number % divisor == 0) {
    Set isPrime to false
    Exit the loop;
  }
}
```

The program is given as shown below.

LISTING 3.11   PrimeNumber.java (Printing Prime Numbers)

```
 1 public class PrimeNumber {
 2   /** Main method */
 3   public static void main(String[] args) {
 4     final int NUMBER_OF_PRIMES = 50; // Number of primes to display
 5     final int NUMBER_OF_PRIMES_PER_LINE = 10; // Display 10 per line
 6     int count = 0; // Count the number of prime numbers
 7     int number = 2; // A number to be tested for primeness
 8     boolean isPrime = true; // Is the current number prime?
 9
10     System.out.println("The first 50 prime numbers are \n");
11
12     // Repeatedly find prime numbers
13     while (count < NUMBER_OF_PRIMES) {
14       // Assume the number is prime
15       isPrime = true;
16
17       // Test if number is prime
18       for (int divisor = 2; divisor <= number / 2; divisor++) {
19         //If true, the number is not prime
20         if (number % divisor == 0) {
21           // Set isPrime to false, if the number is not prime
22           isPrime = false;
23           break; // Exit the for loop
24         }
25       }
26
27       // Print the prime number and increase the count
28       if (isPrime) {
29         count++; // Increase the count
30
31         if (count % NUMBER_OF_PRIMES_PER_LINE == 0) {
32           // Print the number and advance to the new line
33           System.out.println(number);
34         }
35         else
36           System.out.print(number + " ");
37       }
38
39       // Check if the next number is prime
40       number++;
41     }
42   }
43 }
```

count prime numbers

check primeness

exit loop

print if prime

EXAMPLE 3.10 (CONTINUED)

Review

This is a complex example for novice programmers. The key to developing a programmatic solution to this problem, and to many other problems, is to break it into *subproblems* and develop solutions for each of them in turn. Do not attempt to develop a complete solution in the first trial. Instead, begin by writing the code to determine whether a given number is prime, then expand the program to test whether other numbers are prime in a loop.

    To determine whether a number is prime, check whether it is divisible by a number between 2 and `number/2` inclusive. If so, it is not a prime number; otherwise, it is a prime number. For a prime number, display it. If the count is divisible by 10, advance to a new line. The program ends when the count reaches 51.

subproblem

🦋 NOTE

The program uses the `break` statement in Line 23 to exit the `for` loop as soon as the number is found to be a nonprime. You can rewrite the loop (Lines 18–25) without using the `break` statement, as follows:

```
for (int divisor = 2; divisor <= number / 2 && isPrime;
     divisor++) {
  //If true, the number is not prime
  if (number % divisor == 0) {
    // Set isPrime to false, if the number is not prime
    isPrime = false;
  }
}
```

However, using the `break` statement makes the program simpler and easier to read in this case.

KEY TERMS

`break` statement   89, 101
conditional operator   91
`continue` statement   101
fall-through behavior   90
infinite loop   92
iteration   91
labeled `break` statement   104
labled `continue` statement   104

loop   91
`loop-continuation-condition`   91
loop body   91
nested loop   99
off-by-one error   108
selection statement   81
sentinel value   93

CHAPTER SUMMARY

✦ Program control specifies the order in which statements are executed in a program. There are three types of control statements: sequence, selection, and loop.

✦ Selection statements are used for building selection steps into programs. There are several types of selection statements: `if` statements, `if ... else` statements, nested `if` statements, `switch` statements, and conditional expressions.

✦ The various `if` statements all make control decisions based on a Boolean expression. Based on the `true` or `false` evaluation of that expression, these statements take one of two possible courses.

✦ The `switch` statement makes control decisions based on a switch expression of type `char`, `byte`, `short`, `int`, or `boolean`.

✦ The keyword `break` is optional in a switch statement, but it should be used at the end of each case in order to terminate the remainder of the `switch` statement. If the `break` statement is not present, the next `case` statement will be executed.

✦ There are three types of repetition statements: the `while` loop, the `do-while` loop, and the `for` loop. In designing loops, you need to consider both the loop control structure and the loop body.

✦ The `while` loop checks the `loop-continuation-condition` first. If the condition is `true`, the loop body is executed; if it is `false`, the loop terminates. The `do-while` loop is similar to the `while` loop, except that the `do-while` loop executes the loop body first and then checks the `loop-continuation-condition` to decide whether to continue or to terminate.

✦ Since the `while` loop and the `do-while` loop contain the `loop-continuation-condition`, which is dependent on the loop body, the number of repetitions is determined by the loop body. The `while` loop and the `do-while` loop are often used when the number of repetitions is unspecified.

✦ The `for` loop is generally used to execute a loop body a predictable number of times; this number is not determined by the loop body. The loop control has three parts. The first part is an initial action that often initializes a control variable. The second part, the `loop-continuation-condition`, determines whether the loop body is to be executed. The third part is executed after each iteration and is often used to adjust the control variable. Usually, the loop control variables are initialized and changed in the control structure.

✦ Two keywords, `break` and `continue`, can be used in a loop. The `break` keyword immediately ends the innermost loop, which contains the break. The `continue` keyword only ends the current iteration.

REVIEW QUESTIONS

Section 3.2 Selection Statements

3.1 Write a statement to determine whether an integer i is even or odd.

3.2 Suppose x = 3 and y = 2, show the output, if any, of the following code. What is the output if x = 3 and y = 4? What is the output if x = 2 and y = 2?

```
if (x > 2) {
  if (y > 2) {
    int z = x + y;
    System.out.println("z is " + z);
  }
}
else
  System.out.println("x is " + x);
```

3.3 Which of the following statements are equivalent? Which ones are correctly indented?

```
if (i > 0) if
(j > 0)
x = 0; else
if (k > 0) y = 0;
else z = 0;
```

(a)

```
if (i > 0) {
    if (j > 0)
        x = 0;
    else if (k > 0)
        y = 0;
}
else
    z = 0;
```

(b)

```
if (i > 0)
    if (j > 0)
        x = 0;
    else if (k > 0)
        y = 0;
    else
        z = 0;
```

(c)

```
if (i > 0)
    if (j > 0)
        x = 0;
    else if (k > 0)
        y = 0;
    else
        z = 0;
```

(d)

3.4 Suppose x = 2 and y = 3, show the output, if any, of the following code. What is the output if x = 3 and y = 2? What is the output if x = 3 and y = 3? (Hint: indent the statement correctly first.)

```
if (x > 2)
  if (y > 2) {
    int z = x + y;
    System.out.println("z is " + z);
  }
else
  System.out.println("x is " + x);
```

3.5 Are the following two statements equivalent?

```
if (income <= 10000)
    tax = income * 0.1;
else if (income <= 20000)
    tax = 1000 +
        (income - 10000) * 0.15;
```

```
if (income <= 10000)
    tax = income * 0.1;
else if (income > 10000 &&
         income <= 20000)
    tax = 1000 +
        (income - 10000) * 0.15;
```

Section 3.2.4 `switch` Statements

3.6 What data types are required for a `switch` variable? If the keyword `break` is not used after a case is processed, what is the next statement to be executed? Can you convert a `switch` statement to an equivalent `if` statement, or vice versa? What are the advantages of using a `switch` statement?

3.7 What is y after the following `switch` statement is executed?

```
x = 3;
switch (x + 3) {
  case 6: y = 1;
  default: y += 1;
}
```

3.8 Use a `switch` statement to rewrite the following `if` statement:

```
if (a == 1)
  x += 5;
else if (a == 2)
  x += 10;
else if (a == 3)
  x += 16;
else if (a == 4)
  x += 34;
```

Section 3.2.5 Conditional Expressions

3.9   Rewrite the following `if` statement using the conditional operator:

```
if (count % 10 == 0)
  System.out.print(count + "\n");
else
  System.out.print(count + " ");
```

Section 3.3 Loop Statements

3.10   How many times is the following loop body repeated? What is the printout of the loop?

```
int i = 1;
while (i > 10)
  if ((i++) % 2 == 0)
    System.out.println(i);
```

(a)

```
int i = 1;
while (i < 10)
  if ((i++) % 2 == 0)
    System.out.println(i);
```

(b)

3.11   What are the differences between a `while` loop and a `do-while` loop?

3.12   Do the following two loops result in the same value in sum?

```
for (int i = 0; i < 10; ++i) {
  sum += i;
}
```

(a)

```
for (int i = 0; i < 10; i++) {
  sum += i;
}
```

(b)

3.13   What are the three parts of a `for` loop control? Write a `for` loop that prints the numbers from 1 to 100.

3.14   What does the following statement do?

```
for ( ; ; ) {
  do something;
}
```

3.15   If a variable is declared in the `for` loop control, can it be used after the loop exits?

3.16   Can you convert a `for` loop to a `while` loop? List the advantages of using `for` loops.

3.17   Convert the following `for` loop statement to a `while` loop and to a `do-while` loop:

```
long sum = 0;
for (int i = 0; i <= 1000; i++)
  sum = sum + i;
```

Section 3.6 Using the Keywords `break` and `continue`

3.18   What is the keyword `break` for? What is the keyword `continue` for? Will the following program terminate? If so, give the output.

```
int balance = 1000;
while (true) {
  if (balance < 9)
    break;
  balance = balance - 9;
}

System.out.println("Balance is "
  + balance);
```

(a)

```
int balance = 1000;
while (true) {
  if (balance < 9)
    continue;
  balance = balance - 9;
}

System.out.println("Balance is "
  + balance);
```

(b)

3.19   Can you always convert a while loop into a for loop? Convert the following while loop into a for loop:

```
int i = 1;
int sum = 0;
while (sum < 10000) {
  sum = sum + i;
  i++;
}
```

3.20   The for loop on the left is converted into the while loop on the right. What is wrong? Correct it.

```
for (int i = 0; i < 4; i++) {          int i = 0;
    if (i % 3 == 0) continue;          while (i < 4) {
    sum += i;                              if (i % 3 == 0) continue;
}                                          sum += i;
                                           i++;
                                       }
```

Converted

Wrong conversion

3.21   Rewrite the programs TestBreak and TestContinue without using break and continue (see Examples 3.5 and 3.6).

3.22   After the break outer statement is executed in the following loop, which statement is executed?

```
outer:
  for (int i = 1; i < 10; i++) {
  inner:
    for (int j = 1; j < 10; j++) {
      if (i * j > 50)
        break outer;

      System.out.println(i * j);
    }
  }
next:
```

3.23   After the continue outer statement is executed in the following loop, which statement is executed?

```
outer:
  for (int i = 1; i < 10; i++) {
  inner:
    for (int j = 1; j < 10; j++) {
      if (i * j > 50)
        continue outer;

      System.out.println(i * j);
    }
  }
next:
```

Comprehensive

3.24   Identify and fix the errors in the following code:

```
1 public class Test {
2   public void main(String[] args) {
3     for (int i = 0; i < 10; i++);
4       sum += i;
5
6     if (i < j);
7       System.out.println(i)
```

```
7       else
8         System.out.println(j);
9
10      while (j < 10);
11      {
12        j++;
13      };
14
15      do {
16        j++;
17      } while (j < 10)
18    }
19 }
```

3.25. What is wrong with the following program?

```
1 public class ShowErrors {
2   public static void main(String[] args) {
3     int i;
4     int j = 5;
5
6     if (j > 3)
7       System.out.println(i + 4);
8   }
9 }
```

(a)

```
1 public class ShowErrors {
2   public static void main(String[] args) {
3     for (int i = 0; i < 10; i++);
4       System.out.println(i + 4);
5   }
6 }
```

(b)

3.26. Show the output of the following programs:

```
public class Test {
  /** Main method */
  public static void main(String[] args) {
    for (int i = 1; i < 5; i++) {
      int j = 0;
      while (j < i) {
        System.out.print(j + " ");
        j++;
      }
    }
  }
}
```

(a)

```
public class Test {
  /** Main method */
  public static void main(String[] args) {
    int i = 0;
    while (i < 5) {
      for (int j = i; j > 1; j--)
        System.out.print(j + " ");
      System.out.println("****");
      i++;
    }
  }
}
```

(b)

```
public class Test {
  public static void main(String[] args) {
    int i = 5;
    while (i >= 1) {
      int num = 1;
      for (int j = 1; j <= i; j++) {
        System.out.print(num + "xxx");
        num *= 2;
      }

      System.out.println();
      i--;
    }
  }
}
```

(c)

```
public class Test {
  public static void main(String[] args) {
    int i = 1;
    do {
      int num = 1;
      for (int j = 1; j <= i; j++) {
        System.out.print(num + "G");
        num += 2;
      }

      System.out.println();
      i++;
    } while (i <= 5);
  }
}
```

(d)

3.27. Reformat the following programs according to the programming style and documentation guidelines proposed in Section 2.18. Use the next-line brace style.

```java
public class Test {
  public static void main(String[] args) {
    int i = 0;
    if (i>0)
    i++;
    else
    i--;

    char grade;

    if (i >= 90)
     grade = 'A';
    else
      if (i >= 80)
        grade = 'B';
  }
}
```

(a)

```java
public class Test {
  public static void main(String[] args) {
    for (int i = 0; i<10; i++)
      if (i>0)
        i++;
      else
        i--;
  }
}
```

(b)

PROGRAMMING EXERCISES

Section 3.2 Selection Statements

3.1 (*Monetary units*) Modify Example 2.4, "Monetary Units," to display the non-zero denominations only, using singular words for single units like 1 dollar and 1 penny, and plural words for more than one unit like 2 dollars and 3 pennies. (Use 23.67 to test your program.)

3.2* (*Sorting three integers*) Write a program that sorts three integers. The integers are entered from the input dialogs and stored in variables num1, num2, and num3, respectively. The program sorts the numbers so that num1 <= num2 <= num3.

3.3 (*Computing the perimeter of a triangle*) Write a program that reads three edges for a triangle and computes the perimeter if the input is valid. Otherwise, display that the input is invalid. The input is valid if the sum of any two edges is greater than the third edge (also see Exercise 2.9).

3.4 (*Computing taxes*) Example 3.1 gives the partial source code to compute taxes for single filers. Complete Example 3.1 to give the complete source code.

3.5* (*Finding the number of days in a month*) Write a program that prompts the user to enter the month and year, and displays the number of days in the month. For example, if the user entered month 2 and year 2000, the program should display that February 2000 has 29 days. If the user entered month 3 and year 2005, the program should display that March 2005 has 31 days.

3.6 (*Checking a number*) Write a program that prompts the user to enter an integer and checks whether the number is divisible by both 5 and 6, either or just one of them. Here are some sample output for input 10, 30, and 23.

```
10 is divisible by 5 or 6, but not both
30 is divisible by both 5 and 6
23 is not divisible by either 5 or 6
```

Section 3.3 Loop Statements

3.7* (*Counting positive and negative numbers and computing the average of numbers*) Write a program that reads an unspecified number of integers, determines how many positive and negative values have been read, and computes the total and average of the input values, not counting zeros. Your program ends with the input 0. Display the average as a floating-point number. (For example, if you entered 1, 2, and 0, the average should be 1.5.)

3.8 (*Conversion from kilograms to pounds*) Write a program that displays the following table (note that 1 kilogram is 2.2 pound):

Kilograms	Pounds
1	2.2
3	6.6
...	
197	433.4
199	437.8

3.9 (*Conversion from miles to kilometers*) Write a program that displays the following table (note that 1 mile is 1.609 kilometers):

Miles	Kilometers
1	1.609
2	3.218
...	
9	14.481
10	16.09

3.10 (*Conversion from kilograms to pounds*) Write a program that displays the following two tables side-by-side (note that 1 kilogram is 2.2 pounds):

Kilograms	Pounds	Pounds	Kilograms
1	2.2	20	9.09
3	6.6	25	11.36
....			
197	433.4	510	231.82
199	437.8	515	234.09

3.11 (*Conversion from miles to kilometers*) Write a program that displays the following two tables side-by-side (note that 1 mile is 1.609 kilometers):

Miles	Kilometers	Kilometers	Miles
1	1.609	20	12.430
2	3.218	25	15.538
...			
9	14.481	60	37.290
10	16.09	65	40.398

3.12** (*Computing future tuition*) Suppose that the tuition for a university is $10,000 this year and tuition increases 5% every year. Write a program that uses a loop to compute the tuition in ten years.

3.13 (*Finding the highest score*) Write a program that prompts the user to enter the number of students and each student's name and score, and finally displays the student with the highest score.

3.14* (*Finding the two highest scores*) Write a program that prompts the user to enter the number of students and each student's name and score, and finally displays the student with the highest score and the student with the second-highest score.

3.15 (*Finding numbers divisible by 5 and 6*) Write a program that displays all the numbers from 100 to 1000, ten per line, that are divisible by 5 and 6.

3.16 (*Finding numbers divisible by 5 or 6, but not both*) Write a program that displays all the numbers from 100 to 200, ten per line, that are divisible by 5 or 6, but not both.

3.17 (*Finding the smallest* n *such that* n² > 12000) Use a `while` loop to find the smallest integer n such that n² is greater than 12,000.

3.18 (*Finding the largest* n *such that* n³ < 12000) Use a `while` loop to find the largest integer n such that n³ is less than 12,000.

3.19* (*Displaying the ACSII character table*) Write a program that prints the 128 characters in the ASCII character table. Print ten characters per line.

Section 3.7 Case Studies

3.20* (*Computing the greatest common divisor*) Another solution for Example 3.7 to find the greatest common divisor of two integers n1 and n2 is as follows: First find d to be the minimum of n1 and n2, then check whether d, d-1, d-2, ..., 2, or 1 is a divisor for both n1 and n2 in this order. The first such common divisor is the greatest common divisor for n1 and n2.

3.21** (*Finding the factors of an integer*) Write a program that reads an integer and displays all its smallest factors. For example, if the input integer is 120, the output should be as follows: 2, 2, 2, 3, 5.

3.22* (*Finding the sales amount*) Rewrite Example 3.8, "Finding Sales Amount," as follows:

✦ Use a `for` loop instead of a `do-while` loop.
✦ Let the user enter `COMMISSION_SOUGHT` instead of fixing it as a constant.

3.23* (*Printing four patterns using loops*) Use nested loops that print the following patterns in separate programs:

```
Pattern I       Pattern II      Pattern III     Pattern IV
1               1 2 3 4 5 6               1      1 2 3 4 5 6
1 2             1 2 3 4 5              2 1        1 2 3 4 5
1 2 3           1 2 3 4             3 2 1          1 2 3 4
1 2 3 4         1 2 3             4 3 2 1            1 2 3
1 2 3 4 5       1 2             5 4 3 2 1              1 2
1 2 3 4 5 6     1             6 5 4 3 2 1                1
```

3.24** (*Printing numbers in a pyramid pattern*) Write a nested `for` loop that prints the following output:

```
                        1
                    1   2   1
                1   2   4   2   1
            1   2   4   8   4   2   1
        1   2   4   8  16   8   4   2   1
    1   2   4   8  16  32  16   8   4   2   1
  1   2   4   8  16  32  64  32  16   8   4   2   1
1   2   4   8  16  32  64 128  64  32  16   8   4   2   1
```

> ### 🌴 HINT
> Here is the pseudocode solution:
>
> ```
> for the row from 0 to 7 {
>     Pad leading blanks in a row using a loop like this:
>     for the column from 1 to 7-row
>         System.out.print("    ");
>
>     Print left half of the row for numbers 1, 2, 4, up to
>       2^row using a look like this:
>     for the column from 0 to row
>         System.out.print("    " + (int)Math.pow(2, column));
>
>     Print the right half of the row for numbers
>       2^row-1, 2^row-2, ..., 1 using a loop like this:
>     for (int column = row - 1; column >= 0; col--)
>         System.out.print("    " + (int)Math.pow(2, column));
>
>     Start a new line
>     System.out.println();
> }
> ```

You need to figure out how many spaces to print before the number. This is dependent on the number. If a number is a single digit, print four spaces. If a number has two digits, print three spaces. If a number has three digits, print two spaces.

The `Math.pow()` method was introduced in Example 2.3. Can you write this program without using it?

3.25* (*Printing prime numbers between 2 and 1000*) Modify Example 3.10 to print all the prime numbers between 2 and 1000, inclusively. Display eight prime numbers per line.

Comprehensive

3.26** (*Comparing loans with various interest rates*) Write a program that lets the user enter the loan amount and loan period in number of years and displays the monthly and total payments for each interest rate from 5% to 8%, with an increment of 1/8. Suppose you enter the loan amount 10,000 for five years, display a table as follows:

```
Loan Amount: 10000
Number of Years: 5
    Interest Rate       Monthly Payment      Total Payment
    5%                  188.71               11322.74
    5.125%              189.28               11357.13
    5.25%               189.85               11391.59

    ...
    7.85%               202.16               12129.97
    8.0%                202.76               12165.83
```

3.27** (*Displaying the loan amortization schedule*) The monthly payment for a given loan pays the principal and the interest. The monthly interest is computed by multiplying the monthly interest rate and the balance (the remaining principal). The principal paid for the month is therefore the monthly payment minus the monthly interest. Write a program that lets the user enter the loan amount, number of years, and interest rate, and displays the amortization schedule for the loan. Suppose you enter the loan amount 10,000 for one year with an interest rate of 7%, display a table as follows:

```
Loan Amount: 10000
Number of Years: 1
Annual Interest Rate: 7%
```

```
Monthly Payment: 865.26
Total Payment: 10383.21

Payment#        Interest        Principal       Balance
1               58.33           806.93          9193.07
2               53.62           811.64          8381.43

11              10.0            855.26          860.27
12              5.01            860.25          0.01
```

 NOTE

The balance after the last payment may not be zero. If so, the last payment should be the normal monthly payment plus the final balance.

 HINT

Write a loop to print the table. Since monthly payment is the same for each month, it should be computed before the loop. The balance is initially the loan amount. For each iteration in the loop, compute the interest and principal, and update the balance. The loop may look like this:

```java
for (i = 1; i <= numberOfYears * 12; i++) {
   interest = (int)(monthlyInterestRate * balance * 100) / 100.0;
   principal = (int)((monthlyPayment - interest) * 100) / 100.0;
   balance = (int)((balance - principal) * 100) / 100.0;
   System.out.println(i + "\t\t" + interest
   + "\t\t" + principal + "\t\t" + balance);
}
```

3.28* (*Demonstrating cancellation errors*) A cancellation error occurs when you are manipulating a very large number with a very small number. The large number may cancel out the smaller number. For example, the result of 100000000.0 + 0.000000001 is equal to 100000000.0. To avoid cancellation errors and obtain more accurate results, carefully select the order of computation. For example, in computing the following series, you will obtain more accurate results by computing from right to left:

$$1 + \frac{1}{2} + \frac{1}{3} + \cdots + \frac{1}{n}$$

Write a program that compares the results of the summation of the preceding series, computing from left to right and from right to left with $n = 50000$.

3.29* (*Summing a series*) Write a program to sum the following series:

$$\frac{1}{3} + \frac{3}{5} + \frac{5}{7} + \frac{7}{9} + \frac{9}{11} + \frac{11}{13} + \cdots + \frac{95}{97} + \frac{97}{99}$$

3.30** (*Computing π*) You can approximate π by using the following series:

$$\pi = 4\left(1 - \frac{1}{3} + \frac{1}{5} - \frac{1}{7} + \frac{1}{9} - \frac{1}{11} + \frac{1}{13} - \cdots - \frac{1}{2i-1} + \frac{1}{2i+1}\right)$$

Write a program that displays the π value for $i = 10000, 20000, \ldots,$ and 100000.

3.31** (*Computing e*) You can approximate e by using the following series:

$$e = 1 + \frac{1}{1!} + \frac{1}{2!} + \frac{1}{3!} + \frac{1}{4!} + \cdots + \frac{1}{i!}$$

Write a program that displays the e value for i   and 100000. (Hint: Since

$$i! = i \times (i - 1) \times \cdots \times 2 \times 1, \frac{1}{i!} \text{ is } \frac{1}{i(i - 1)!}.$$

Initialize e and item to be 1 and keep adding a new item to e. The new item is the previous item divided by i for $i = 2, 3, 4, \ldots$)

3.32** (*Displaying leap years*) Write a program that displays all the leap years, ten per line, in the twenty-first century (from 2000 to 2100). See page 55 regarding leap year.

3.33** (*Displaying first days of each month*) Write a program that prompts the user to enter the year and first day of the year, and displays the first day of each month in the year on the console. For example, if the user entered year 2005, and 6 for Saturday, January 1, 2005, your program should display the following output:

```
January 1, 2005 is Saturday
...
December 1, 2005 is Thursday
```

3.34** (*Displaying calendars*) Write a program that prompts the user to enter the year and first day of the year, and displays the calendar table for the year on the console. For example, if the user entered year 2005, and 6 for Saturday, January 1, 2005, your program should display the calendar for each month in the year, as follows:

```
              January 2005
      --------------------------
      Sun Mon Tue Wed Thu Fri Sat
                                1
       2   3   4   5   6   7   8
       9  10  11  12  13  14  15
      16  17  18  19  20  21  22
      23  24  25  26  27  28  29
      30  31
      ...
              December 2005
      --------------------------
      Sun Mon Tue Wed Thu Fri Sat
                        1   2   3
       4   5   6   7   8   9  10
      11  12  13  14  15  16  17
      18  19  20  21  22  23  24
      25  26  27  28  29  30  31
```

chapter

4

METHODS

Objectives

+ To create methods, invoke methods, and pass arguments to methods (§§4.2–4.4).

+ To use method overloading and know ambiguous overloading (§4.5).

+ To determine the scope of local variables (§4.6).

+ To learn the concept of method abstraction (§4.7).

+ To know how to use the methods in the Math class (§4.8).

+ To design and implement methods using stepwise refinement (§4.10).

+ To write recursive methods (§4.11 Optional).

+ To group classes into packages (§4.12 Optional).

4.1 Introduction

In the preceding chapters, you learned about such methods as `System.out.println`, `JOptionPane.showMessageDialog`, `JOptionPane.showInputDialog`, `Integer.parseInt`, `Double.parseDouble`, `System.exit`, and `Math.pow`. A method is a collection of statements that are grouped together to perform an operation. When you call the `System.out.println` method, for example, the system actually executes several statements in order to display a message on the console.

This chapter introduces several topics that involve, or are related to, methods. You will learn how to create your own methods with or without return values, invoke a method with or without parameters, overload methods using the same names, write a recursive method that invokes itself, and apply method abstraction in the program design.

4.2 Creating a Method

In general, a method has the following syntax:

```
modifier returnValueType methodName(list of parameters) {
    // Method body;
}
```

Let's take a look at a method created to find which of two integers is bigger. This method, named `max`, has two `int` parameters, `num1` and `num2`, the larger of which is returned by the method. Figure 4.1 illustrates the components of this method.

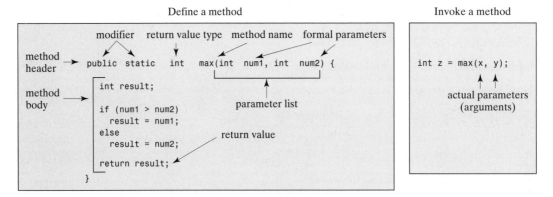

FIGURE 4.1 *A method declaration consists of a method header and a method body.*

The method header specifies the *modifiers, return value type, method name,* and *parameters* of the method. The modifier, which is optional, tells the compiler how to call the method. The static modifier is used for all the methods in this chapter. The reason for using it will be discussed in Chapter 6, "Objects and Classes."

A method may return a value. The `returnValueType` is the data type of the value the method returns. Some methods perform desired operations without returning a value. In this case, the `returnValueType` is the keyword `void`. For example, the `returnValueType` in the main method is `void`, as well as in `System.exit`, `Syste.out.println`, and `JOptionPane.showMessageDialog`.

The *parameter list* refers to the type, order, and number of the parameters of a method. The method name and the parameter list together constitute the *method signature*. Parameters are optional; that is, a method may contain no parameters. The variables defined in the method header are known as *formal parameters* or simply *parameters*. A parameter is like a placeholder. When a

void
parameter list

method signature

formal parameter

method is invoked, you pass a value to the parameter. This value is referred to as *actual parameter or argument*.

argument

The method body contains a collection of statements that define what the method does. The method body of the max method uses an `if` statement to determine which number is larger and return the value of that number. A return statement using the keyword `return` is *required* for a nonvoid method to return a result. The method terminates when a return statement is executed.

 NOTE

In certain other languages, methods are referred to as *procedures* and *functions*. A method with a nonvoid return value type is called a *function*; a method with a `void` return value type is called a *procedure*.

 NOTE

A `return` statement is not needed for a void method, but it can be used for terminating the method and returning to the method's caller. The syntax is simply

return

```
return;
```

This is rare, but sometimes useful for circumventing the normal flow of control in a void method. See Review Question 4.5.

 CAUTION

You need to declare a separate data type for each parameter. For instance, `int num1, num2` should be replaced by `int num1, int num2`.

4.3   Calling a Method

In creating a method, you give a definition of what the method is to do. To use a method, you have to *call* or *invoke* it. There are two ways to call a method; the choice is based on whether the method returns a value or not.

If the method returns a value, a call to the method is usually treated as a value. For example,

```
int larger = max(3, 4);
```

calls `max(3, 4)` and assigns the result of the method to the variable `larger`. Another example of a call that is treated as a value is

```
System.out.println(max(3, 4));
```

which prints the return value of the method call `max(3, 4)`.

If the method returns `void`, a call to the method must be a statement. For example, the method `println` returns `void`. The following call is a statement:

```
System.out.println("Welcome to Java!");
```

 NOTE

A method with a nonvoid return value type can also be invoked as a statement in Java. In this case, the caller simply ignores the return value. In the majority of cases, a call to a method with return value is treated as a value. In some cases, however, the caller is not interested in the return value. For example, many methods in database applications return a Boolean value to indicate whether the operation is successful. You can choose to ignore the return value if you know the operation will always succeed. I recommend, though, that you always treat a call to a method with return value as a value in order to avoid programming errors.

When a program calls a method, program control is transferred to the called method. A called method returns control to the caller when its return statement is executed or when its method-ending closing brace is reached.

The example shown below gives the complete program that is used to test the max method.

EXAMPLE 4.1 TESTING THE max METHOD

Problem

Write a program that demonstrates how to create and invoke the max method.

Solution

Listing 4.1 gives the solution to the problem. The output of the program is shown in Figure 4.2.

FIGURE **4.2** *The program invokes* max(i, j) *in order to get the maximum value between* i *and* j.

LISTING **4.1** TestMax.java (Declaring and Using a Method)

```
 1 public class TestMax {
 2   /** Main method */
 3   public static void main(String[] args) {
 4     int i = 5;
 5     int j = 2;
 6     int k = max(i, j);
 7     System.out.println("The maximum between " + i +
 8       " and " + j + " is " + k);
 9   }
10
11   /** Return the max between two numbers */
12   public static int max(int num1, int num2) {
13     int result;
14
15     if (num1 > num2)
16       result = num1;
17     else
18       result = num2;
19
20     return result;
21   }
22 }
```

main method (line 3)

invoke max (line 6)

declare method (line 12)

Review

This program contains the main method and the max method. The main method is just like any other method except that it is invoked by the Java interpreter.

main method

EXAMPLE 4.1 (CONTINUED)

The main method's header is always the same, like the one in this example, with the modifiers public and static, return value type void, method name main, and a parameter of the String[] type. String[] indicates that the parameter is an array of String, a subject addressed in Chapter 5, "Arrays."

The statements in main may invoke other methods that are defined in the class that contains the main method or in other classes. In this example, the main method invokes max(i, j), which is defined in the same class with the main method.

When the max method is invoked (Line 6), variable i's value 5 is passed to num1, and variable j's value 2 is passed to num2 in the max method. The flow of control transfers to the max method. The max method is executed. When the return statement in the max method is executed, the max method returns the control to its caller (in this case the caller is the main method). This process is illustrated in Figure 4.3.

max method

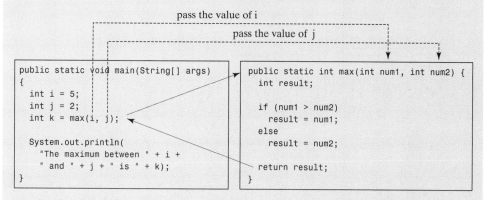

FIGURE 4.3 *When the max method is invoked, the flow of control transfers to the max method. Once the max method is finished, it returns the control back to the caller.*

 CAUTION

A return statement is required for a nonvoid method. The method shown below in (a) is logically correct, but it has a compilation error because the Java compiler thinks it possible that this method does not return any value.

```
public static int sign(int n) {
  if (n > 0) return 1;
  else if (n == 0) return 0;
  else if (n < 0) return -1;
}
```
(a)

Should be →

```
public static int sign(int n) {
  if (n > 0) return 1;
  else if (n == 0) return 0;
  else return -1;
}
```
(b)

To fix this problem, delete if (n < 0) in (a), so that the compiler will see a return statement to be reached regardless of how the if statement is evaluated.

 NOTE

reusing method

One of the benefits of methods is for reuse. The max method can be invoked from any class besides TestMax. If you create a new class, Test, you can invoke the max method using ClassName.methodName (i.e., TestMax.max).

4.3.1   Call Stacks

stack

Each time a method is invoked, the system stores parameters and local variables in an area of memory, known as a *stack*, which stores elements in last-in first-out fashion. When a method calls another method, the caller's stack space is kept intact, and new space is created to handle the new method call. When a method finishes its work and returns to its caller, its associated space is released.

Understanding call stacks helps you to comprehend how methods are invoked. The variables defined in the main method are i, j, and k. The variables defined in the max method are num1, num2, and result. The variables num1 and num2 are defined in the method signature and are parameters of the method. Their values are passed through method invocation. Figure 4.4 illustrates the variables in the stack.

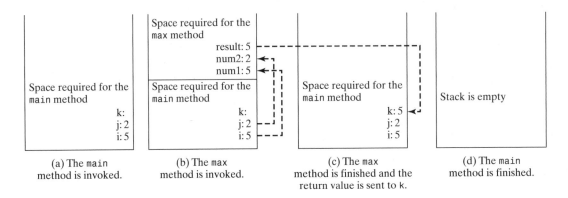

(a) The main method is invoked.

(b) The max method is invoked.

(c) The max method is finished and the return value is sent to k.

(d) The main method is finished.

FIGURE 4.4   *When the* max *method is invoked, the flow of control transfers to the* max *method. Once the* max *method is finished, it returns the control back to the caller.*

4.4   Passing Parameters by Values

The power of a method is its ability to work with parameters. You can use println to print any string and max to find the maximum between any two int values. When calling a method, you need to provide arguments, which must be given in the same order as their respective parameters in the method specification. This is known as *parameter order association*. For example, the following method prints a message n times:

```
public static void nPrintln(String message, int n) {
  for (int i = 0; i < n; i++)
    System.out.println(message);
}
```

You can use nPrintln("Hello", 3) to print "Hello" three times. The nPrintln("Hello", 3) statement passes the actual string parameter, "Hello", to the parameter, message; passes 3 to n; and prints "Hello" three times. However, the statement nPrintln(3, "Hello") would be wrong. The data type of 3 does not match the data type for the first parameter, message, nor does the second parameter, "Hello", match the second parameter, n.

⚜ CAUTION

The arguments must match the parameters in *order*, *number*, and *compatible type*, as defined in the method signature. Compatible type means that you can pass an argument to a parameter without explicit casting, such as passing an int value argument to a double value parameter.

When you invoke a method with a parameter, the value of the argument is passed to the parameter. This is referred to as *pass by value*. If the argument is a variable, the value of the variable is passed to the parameter. The variable is not affected, regardless of the changes made to the parameter inside the method. We will examine an interesting scenario in the following example, in which the parameters are changed in the method but the arguments are not affected.

pass by value

EXAMPLE 4.2 TESTING PASS BY VALUE

Problem

Write a program that demonstrates the effect of passing by value.

Solution

Listing 4.2 creates a method for swapping two variables. The swap method is invoked by passing two arguments. Interestingly, the values of the arguments are not changed after the method is invoked. The output of the program is shown in Figure 4.5.

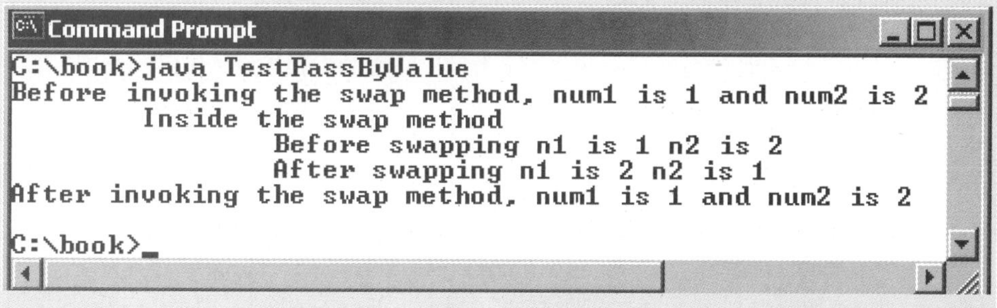

```
Command Prompt                                          _ □ ×
C:\book>java TestPassByValue
Before invoking the swap method, num1 is 1 and num2 is 2
        Inside the swap method
                Before swapping n1 is 1 n2 is 2
                After swapping n1 is 2 n2 is 1
After invoking the swap method, num1 is 1 and num2 is 2

C:\book>_
```

FIGURE 4.5   *The contents of the arguments are not swapped after the swap method is invoked.*

LISTING 4.2   TestPassByValue.java (Passing by Value)

```
1 public class TestPassByValue {
2   /** Main method */
3   public static void main(String[] args) {
4     // Declare and initialize variables
5     int num1 = 1;
6     int num2 = 2;
7
8     System.out.println("Before invoking the swap method, num1 is " +
9       num1 + " and num2 is " + num2);
10
11    // Invoke the swap method to attempt to swap two variables
12    swap(num1, num2);
13
14    System.out.println("After invoking the swap method, num1 is " +
15      num1 + " and num2 is " + num2);
16  }
17
18  /** Swap two variables */
19  public static void swap(int n1, int n2) {
20    System.out.println("\tInside the swap method");
21    System.out.println("\t\tBefore swapping n1 is " + n1
22      + " n2 is " + n2);
```

false swap

EXAMPLE 4.2 (CONTINUED)

```
23
24     // Swap n1 with n2
25     int temp = n1;
26     n1 = n2;
27     n2 = temp;
28
29     System.out.println("\t\tAfter swapping n1 is " + n1
30       + " n2 is " + n2);
31   }
32 }
```

Review

Before the swap method is invoked (Line 12), num1 is 1 and num2 is 2. After the swap method is invoked, num1 is still 1 and num2 is still 2. Their values are not swapped when the swap method is invoked. As shown in Figure 4.6, the values of the arguments num1 and num2 are passed to n1 and n2, but n1 and n2 have their own memory locations independent of num1 and num2. Therefore, changes in n1 and n2 do not affect the contents of num1 and num2.

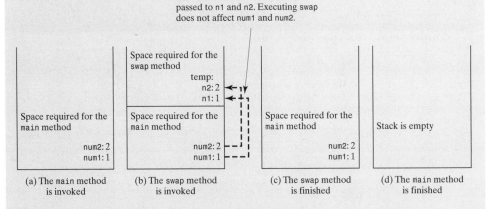

The values of num1 and num2 are passed to n1 and n2. Executing swap does not affect num1 and num2.

| Space required for the main method | Space required for the swap method | | Space required for the main method | Stack is empty |

(a) The main method is invoked   (b) The swap method is invoked   (c) The swap method is finished   (d) The main method is finished

FIGURE 4.6   *The values of the variables are passed to the parameters of the method.*

Another twist is to change the parameter name n1 in swap to num1. What effect does this have? No change occurs, because it makes no difference whether the parameter and the argument have the same name. The parameter is a local variable in the method with its own memory space. The local variable is allocated when the method is invoked, and it disappears when the method is returned to its caller.

NOTE

For simplicity, Java programmers often say *passing an argument* x *to a parameter* y, which actually means *passing the value of* x *to* y.

4.5 Overloading Methods

The max method that was used earlier works only with the int data type. But what if you need to find which of two floating-point numbers has the maximum value? The solution is to create another method with the same name but different parameters, as shown in the following code:

```
public static double max(double num1, double num2) {
  if (num1 > num2)
    return num1;
  else
    return num2;
}
```

If you call max with int parameters, the max method that expects int parameters will be invoked; if you call max with double parameters, the max method that expects double parameters will be invoked. This is referred to as *method overloading*; that is, two methods have the same name but different parameter lists. The Java compiler determines which method is used based on the method signature.

method overloading

EXAMPLE 4.3 OVERLOADING THE **max** METHOD

Problem

Write a program that creates three methods. The first finds the maximum integer, the second finds the maximum double, and the third finds the maximum among three double values. All three methods are named max.

Solution

Listing 4.3 gives the solution to the problem. The output of the program is shown in Figure 4.7.

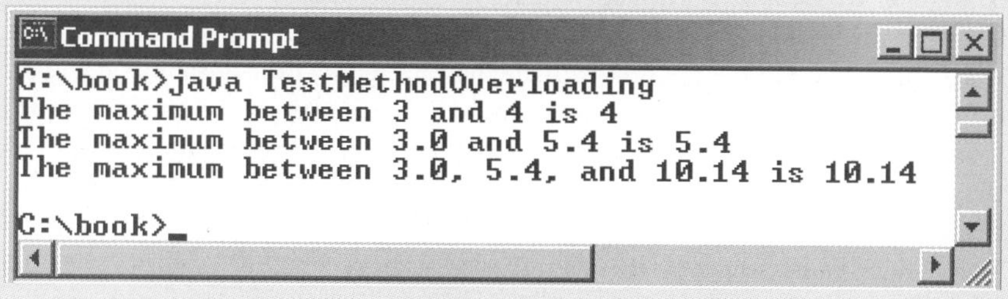

```
C:\book>java TestMethodOverloading
The maximum between 3 and 4 is 4
The maximum between 3.0 and 5.4 is 5.4
The maximum between 3.0, 5.4, and 10.14 is 10.14

C:\book>
```

FIGURE 4.7 *The program invokes three different* max *methods that all have the same name:* max(3, 4), max(3.0, 5.4), *and* max(3.0, 5.4, 10.14).

LISTING 4.3 TestMethodOverloading.java (Overloading Methods)

```
1 public class TestMethodOverloading {
2   /** Main method */
3   public static void main(String[] args) {
4     // Invoke the max method with int parameters
5     System.out.println("The maximum between 3 and 4 is "
6       + max(3, 4));
7
```

EXAMPLE 4.3 (CONTINUED)

```
 8      // Invoke the max method with the double parameters
 9      System.out.println("The maximum between 3.0 and 5.4 is "
10        + max(3.0, 5.4));
11
12      // Invoke the max method with three double parameters
13      System.out.println("The maximum between 3.0, 5.4, and 10.14 is "
14        + max(3.0, 5.4, 10.14));
15    }
16
17    /** Return the max between two int values */
18    public static int max(int num1, int num2) {
19      if (num1 > num2)
20        return num1;
21      else
22        return num2;
23    }
24
25    /** Find the max between two double values */
26    public static double max(double num1, double num2) {
27      if (num1 > num2)
28        return num1;
29      else
30        return num2;
31    }
32
33    /** Return the max among three double values */
34    public static double max(double num1, double num2, double num3) {
35      return max(max(num1, num2), num3);
36    }
37 }
```

Review

When calling max(3, 4) (Line 6), the max method for finding the maximum of two integers is invoked. When calling max(3.0, 5.4) (Line 10), the max method for finding the maximum of two doubles is invoked. When calling max(3.0, 5.4, 10.14) (Line 14), the max method for finding the maximum of three double values is invoked.

Can you invoke the max method with an int value and a double value, such as max(2, 2.5)? If so, which of the max methods is invoked? The answer to the first question is yes. The answer to the second is that the max method for finding the maximum of two double values is invoked. The argument value 2 is automatically converted into a double value and passed to this method.

You may be wondering why the method max(double, double) is not invoked for the call max(3, 4). Both max(double, double) and max(int, int) are possible matches for max(3, 4). The Java compiler finds the most specific method for a method invocation. Since the method max(int, int) is more specific than max(double, double), max(int, int) is used to invoke max(3, 4).

 TIP
Overloading methods can make programs clearer and more readable. Methods that perform closely related tasks should be given the same name.

 NOTE
Overloaded methods must have different parameter lists. You cannot overload methods based on different modifiers or return types.

NOTE

Sometimes there are two or more possible matches for an invocation of a method, but the compiler cannot determine the most specific match. This is referred to as *ambiguous invocation*. Ambiguous invocation is a compilation error. Consider the following code:

ambiguous invocation

```java
public class AmbiguousOverloading {
  public static void main(String[] args) {
    System.out.println(max(1, 2));
  }

  public static double max(int num1, double num2) {
    if (num1 > num2)
      return num1;
    else
      return num2;
  }

  public static double max(double num1, int num2) {
    if (num1 > num2)
      return num1;
    else
      return num2;
  }
}
```

Both `max(int, double)` and `max(double, int)` are possible candidates to match `max(1, 2)`. Since neither of them is more specific than the other, the invocation is ambiguous.

EXAMPLE 4.4 COMPUTING TAXES WITH METHODS

Problem

Example 3.1, "Computing Taxes," uses `if` statements to check the filing status and computes the tax based on the filing status. Simplify Example 3.1 using methods.

Solution

Each filing status has six brackets. The code for computing taxes is nearly the same for each filing status except that each filing status has different bracket ranges. For example, the single filer status has six brackets [0, 6000], (6000, 27950], (27950, 67700], (67700, 141250], (141250, 307050], (307050, ∞), and the married file jointly status has six brackets [0, 12000], (12000, 46700], (46700, 112850], (112850, 171950], (171950, 307050], (307050, ∞). The first bracket of each filing status is taxed at 10%, the second at 15%, the third at 27%, the fourth at 30%, the fifth at 35%, and the sixth at 38.6%. So you can write a method with the brackets as arguments to compute the tax for the filing status. The header of the method is:

```
public static double computeTax(double income, ◄─────────── 400000
      int r1, int r2, int r3, int r4, int r5)
```

`[0, 6000], [6000, 27950], [27950, 67700], [67700, 141250], [141250, 307050], (307050,∞)`

For example, you can invoke `computeTax(400000, 6000, 27950, 67700, 141250, 307050)` to compute the tax for single filers with $400,000 of taxable income.

EXAMPLE 4.4 (CONTINUED)

Listing 4.4 gives the solution to the problem. The output of the program is similar to Figure 3.3.

LISTING 4.4 ComputeTaxWithMethod.java (Computing Tax)

```
 1 import javax.swing.JOptionPane;
 2
 3 public class ComputeTaxWithMethod {
 4   public static void main(String[] args) {
 5     // Prompt the user to enter filing status
 6     String statusString = JOptionPane.showInputDialog(
 7       "Enter the filing status:");
 8     int status = Integer.parseInt(statusString);
 9
10     // Prompt the user to enter taxable income
11     String incomeString = JOptionPane.showInputDialog(
12       "Enter the taxable income:");
13     double income = Double.parseDouble(incomeString);
14
15     // Display the result
16     JOptionPane.showMessageDialog(null, "Tax is " +
17       (int)(computeTax(status, income) * 100) / 100.0);
18   }
19
20   public static double computeTax(double income,
21       int r1, int r2, int r3, int r4, int r5) {
22     double tax = 0;
23
24     if (income <= r1)
25       tax = income * 0.10;
26     else if (income <= r2)
27       tax = r1 * 0.10 + (income - r1) * 0.15;
28     else if (income <= r3)
29       tax = r1 * 0.10 + (r2 - r1) * 0.15 + (income - r2) * 0.27;
30     else if (income <= r4)
31       tax = r1 * 0.10 + (r2 - r1) * 0.15 +
32         (r3 - r2) * 0.27 + (income - r3) * 0.30;
33     else if (income <= r5)
34       tax = r1 * 0.10 + (r2 - r1) * 0.15 + (r3 - r2) * 0.27 +
35         (r4 - r3) * 0.30 + (income - r4) * 0.35;
36     else
37       tax = r1 * 0.10 + (r2 - r1) * 0.15 + (r3 - r2) * 0.27 +
38         (r4 - r3) * 0.30 + (r5 - r4) * 0.35 + (income - r5) * 0.386;
39
40     return tax;
41   }
42
43   public static double computeTax(int status, double income) {
44     switch (status) {
45       case 0: return
46         computeTax(income, 6000, 27950, 67700, 141250, 307050);
47       case 1: return
48         computeTax(income, 12000, 46700, 112850, 171950, 307050);
49       case 2: return
50         computeTax(income, 6000, 23350, 56425, 85975, 153525);
51       case 3: return
52         computeTax(income, 10000, 37450, 96700, 156600, 307050);
53       default: return 0;
54     }
55   }
56 }
```

input status

input income

compute tax

computeTax

overloaded computeTax

EXAMPLE **4.4** (CONTINUED)

Review

This program does the same thing as Example 3.1. Instead of writing the same code for computing taxes for different filing statuses, the new program uses a method for computing taxes. Using the method not only shortens the program, it also makes the program simpler, easy to read, and easy to maintain.

The program uses two overloaded `computeTax` methods (Lines 20, 43). The first `computeTax` method in Line 20 computes the tax for the specified brackets and taxable income. The second `computeTax` method in Line 43 computes the tax for the specified status and taxable income.

4.6   The Scope of Local Variables

The *scope of a variable* is the part of the program where the variable can be referenced. A variable defined inside a method is referred to as a *local variable*.

scope of variable
local variable

The scope of a local variable starts from its declaration and continues to the end of the block that contains the variable. A local variable must be declared before it can be used.

A *parameter* is actually a local variable. The scope of a method parameter covers the entire method.

parameter

A variable declared in the initial action part of a `for` loop header has its scope in the entire loop. But a variable declared inside a `for` loop body has its scope limited in the loop body from its declaration and to the end of the block that contains the variable, as shown in Figure 4.8.

for loop control variable

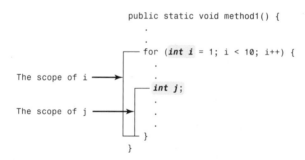

FIGURE 4.8   *A variable declared in the initial action part of a* `for` *loop header has its scope in the entire loop.*

You can declare a local variable with the same name multiple times in different non-nesting blocks in a method, but you cannot declare a local variable twice in nested blocks, as shown in Figure 4.9.

multiple declarations

 CAUTION

Do not declare a variable inside a block and then use it outside the block. Here is an example of a common mistake:

```
for (int i = 0; i < 10; i++) {
}

System.out.println(i);
```

The last statement would cause a syntax error because variable `i` is not defined outside of the `for` loop.

It is fine to declare *i* in two non-nesting blocks

It is wrong to declare *i* in two two nesting blocks

```
public static void method1() {
  int x = 1;
  int y = 1;

  for (int i = 1; i < 10; i++) {
    x += i;
  }

  for (int i = 1; i < 10; i++) {
    y += i;
  }
}
```

```
public static void method2() {
  int i = 1;
  int sum = 0;

  for (int i = 1; i < 10; i++)
    sum += i;
  }

}
```

FIGURE 4.9 *A variable can be declared multiple times in non-nested blocks, but can be declared only once in nesting blocks.*

4.7 Method Abstraction

method abstraction

information hiding

The key to developing software is to apply the concept of abstraction. You will learn many levels of abstraction from this book. *Method abstraction* is achieved by separating the use of a method from its implementation. The client can use a method without knowing how it is implemented. The details of the implementation are encapsulated in the method and hidden from the client who invokes the method. This is known as *information hiding* or *encapsulation*. If you decide to change the implementation, the client program will not be affected, provided that you do not change the method signature. The implementation of the method is hidden from the client in a "black box," as shown in Figure 4.10.

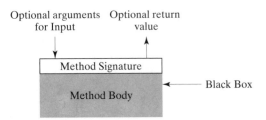

FIGURE 4.10 *The method body can be thought of as a black box that contains the detailed implementation for the method.*

You have already used the `System.out.print` method to display a string, the `JOptionPane.showInputDialog` method to read a string from a dialog box, and the `max` method to find the maximum number. You know how to write the code to invoke these methods in your program, but as a user of these methods, you are not required to know how they are implemented. The next section introduces the use of methods in the `Math` class.

4.8 The `Math` Class

The `Math` class contains the methods needed to perform basic mathematical functions. You have already used the `pow(a, b)` method to compute a^b in Example 2.3, "Computing Loan Payments." This section introduces other useful methods in the `Math` class. They can be categorized as *trigonometric methods*, *exponent methods*, and *service methods*. Besides methods, the `Math` class provides two useful `double` constants, `PI` and `E` (the base of natural logarithms). You can use these constants as `Math.PI` and `Math.E` in any program.

4.8.1 Trigonometric Methods

The Math class contains the following trigonometric methods:

```
public static double sin(double radians)
public static double cos(double radians)
public static double tan(double radians)
public static double asin(double radians)
public static double acos(double radians)
public static double atan(double radians)
public static double toRadians(double degree)
public static double toDegrees(double radians)
```

Each method has a single double parameter, and its return type is double. The parameter represents an angle in radians. One degree is equal to $\pi/180$ in radians. For example, Math.sin(Math.PI) returns the trigonometric sine of π. Since JDK 1.2, the Math class has also provided the method toRadians(double angdeg) for converting an angle in degrees to radians, and the method toDegrees(double angrad) for converting an angle in radians to degrees.

For example,

```
Math.sin(0) returns 0.0
Math.sin(Math.toRadians(270)) returns -1.0
Math.sin(Math.PI / 6) returns 0.5
Math.sin(Math.PI / 2) returns 1.0
Math.cos(0) returns 1.0
Math.cos(Math.PI / 6) returns 0.866
Math.cos(Math.PI / 2) returns 0
```

4.8.2 Exponent Methods

There are four methods related to exponents in the Math class:

```
/** Return e raised to the power of a (eª) */
public static double exp(double a)

/** Return the natural logarithm of a (ln(a) = logₑ(a)) */
public static double log(double a)

/** Return a raised to the power of b (aᵇ) */
public static double pow(double a, double b)

/** Return the square root of a (√a) */
public static double sqrt(double a)
```

Note that the parameter in the sqrt method must not be negative.

For example,

```
Math.pow(2, 3) returns 8.0
Math.pow(3, 2) returns 9.0
Math.pow(3.5, 2.5) returns 22.91765
Math.sqrt(4) returns 2.0
Math.sqrt(10.5) returns 3.24
```

4.8.3 The Rounding Methods

The Math class contains five rounding methods:

```
/** x rounded up to its nearest integer. This integer is
  * returned as a double value. */
public static double ceil(double x)

/** x is rounded down to its nearest integer. This integer is
  * returned as a double value. */
public static double floor(double x)

/** x is rounded to its nearest integer. If x is equally close
  * to two integers, the even one is returned as a double. */
public static double rint(double x)
```

```
/** Return (int)Math.floor(x + 0.5). */
public static int round(float x)

/** Return (long)Math.floor(x + 0.5). */
public static long round(double x)
```

For example,

```
Math.ceil(2.1) returns 3.0
Math.ceil(2.0) returns 2.0
Math.ceil(-2.0) returns -2.0
Math.ceil(-2.1) returns -2.0
Math.floor(2.1) returns 2.0
Math.floor(2.0) returns 2.0
Math.floor(-2.0) returns -2.0
Math.floor(-2.1) returns -3.0
Math.rint(2.1) returns 2.0
Math.rint(2.0) returns 2.0
Math.rint(-2.0) returns -2.0
Math.rint(-2.1) returns -2.0
Math.rint(2.5) returns 2.0
Math.rint(-2.5) returns -2.0
Math.round(2.6f) returns 3 // Returns int
Math.round(2.0) returns 2 //  Returns long
Math.round(-2.0f) returns -2
Math.round(-2.6) returns -3
```

4.8.4   The min, max, and abs Methods

The min and max methods are overloaded to return the minimum and maximum numbers between two numbers (int, long, float, or double). For example, max(3.4, 5.0) returns 5.0, and min(3, 2) returns 2.

The abs method is overloaded to return the absolute value of the number (int, long, float, and double).

For example,

```
Math.max(2, 3) returns 3
Math.max(2.5, 3) returns 3.0
Math.min(2.5, 3.6) returns 2.5
Math.abs(-2) returns 2
Math.abs(-2.1) returns 2.1
```

4.8.5   The random Methods

The Math class also has a powerful method, random, which generates a random double value greater than or equal to 0.0 and less than 1.0 (0 <= Math.random() < 1.0). This method is very useful. You can use it to write a simple expression to generate random numbers in any range. For example,

```
(int) (Math.random() * 10)
```
⟶ Returns a random integer between 0 and 9.

```
50 + (int) (Math.random() * 50)
```
⟶ Returns a random integer between 50 and 99.

In general,

```
a + Math.random() * b
```
⟶ Returns a random number between a and a + b, excluding a + b.

🌿 **TIP**

view documentation online   You can view the complete documentation for the Math class online from http://java.sun.com/j2se/1.5.0/docs/api/index.html, as shown in Figure 4.11.

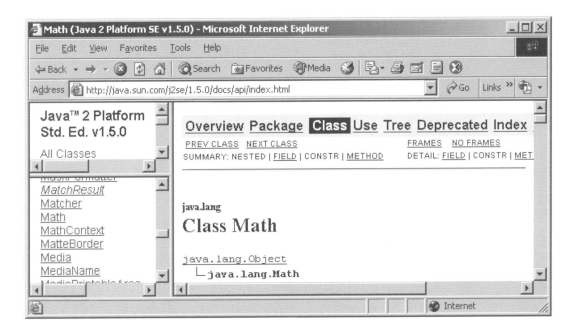

FIGURE 4.11 *You can view the documentation for Java API online at* http://java.sun.com/j2se/1.5.0/docs/api/ index.html.

You can also download j2sdk-1_5_0-doc.zip from http://java.sun.com/j2se/ 1.5.0/download.jsp#docs and install it on your PC so that you can browse the documents locally.

 NOTE

Not all classes need a main method. The Math class and JOptionPane class do not have main methods. These classes contain methods for other classes to use.

4.9 Case Study: Generating Random Characters

Computer programs process numerical data and characters. You have seen many examples that involve numerical data. It is also important to understand characters and how to process them. This section presents an example for generating random characters.

As introduced in Section 2.9, every character has a unique Unicode between 0 and FFFF in hexadecimal (65535 in decimal). To generate a random character is to generate a random integer between 0 and 65535 using the following expression (note that since 0 <= Math.random() < 1.0, you have to add 1 to 65535):

```
(int)(Math.random() * (65535 + 1))
```

Now let us consider how to generate a random lowercase letter. The Unicodes for lowercase letters are consecutive integers starting from the Unicode for 'a', then for 'b', 'c', ..., and 'z'. The Unicode for 'a' is

```
(int)'a'
```

So a random integer between `(int)'a'` and `(int)'z'` is

```
(int)((int)'a' + Math.random() * ((int)'z' - (int)'a' + 1)
```

As discussed in Section 2.9.4, all numeric operators can be applied to the `char` operands. The `char` operand is cast into a number if the other operand is a number or a character. Thus the preceding expression can be simplified as follows:

```
'a' + Math.random() * ('z' - 'a' + 1)
```

and a random lowercase letter is

```
(char)('a' + Math.random() * ('z' - 'a' + 1))
```

To generalize the foregoing discussion, a random character between any two characters `ch1` and `ch2` with `ch1 < ch2` can be generated as follows:

```
(char)(ch1 + Math.random() * (ch2 - ch1 + 1))
```

This is a simple but useful discovery. Let us create a class named `RandomCharacter` in Listing 4.5 with five overloaded methods to get a certain type of character randomly. You can use these methods in your future projects.

LISTING 4.5   RandomCharacter.java (Generating Random Characters)

```
 1 public class RandomCharacter {
 2   /** Generate a random character between ch1 and ch2 */
 3   public static char getRandomCharacter(char ch1, char ch2) {
 4     return (char)(ch1 + Math.random() * (ch2 - ch1 + 1));
 5   }
 6
 7   /** Generate a random lowercase letter */
 8   public static char getRandomLowerCaseLetter() {
 9     return getRandomCharacter('a', 'z');
10   }
11
12   /** Generate a random uppercase letter */
13   public static char getRandomUpperCaseLetter() {
14     return getRandomCharacter('A', 'Z');
15   }
16
17   /** Generate a random digit character */
18   public static char getRandomDigitCharacter() {
19     return getRandomCharacter('0', '9');
20   }
21
22   /** Generate a random character */
23   public static char getRandomCharacter() {
24     return getRandomCharacter('\u0000', '\uFFFF');
25   }
26 }
```

Listing 4.6 gives a test program that displays one hundred lowercase letters.

LISTING 4.6   TestRandomCharacter.java (Using RandomCharacter)

constants

```
 1 public class TestRandomCharacter {
 2   /** Main method */
 3   public static void main(String args[]) {
 4     final int NUMBER_OF_CHARS = 175;
 5     final int CHARS_PER_LINE = 25;
 6
```

```
 7       // Print random characters between '!' and '~', 25 chars per line
 8       for (int i = 0; i < NUMBER_OF_CHARS; i++) {
 9         char ch = RandomCharacter.getRandomLowerCaseLetter();
10         if ((i + 1) % CHARS_PER_LINE == 0)
11           System.out.println(ch);
12         else
13           System.out.print(ch);
14       }
15     }
16 }
```

lowercase letter

4.10   Stepwise Refinement (Optional)

The concept of method abstraction can be applied to the process of developing programs. When writing a large program, you can use the "divide and conquer" strategy, also known as *stepwise refinement*, to decompose it into subproblems. The subproblems can be further decomposed into smaller, more manageable problems.

divide and conquer

stepwise refinement

Suppose you write a program that displays the calendar for a given month of the year. The program prompts the user to enter the year and the month, and then displays the entire calendar for the month, as shown in Figure 4.12.

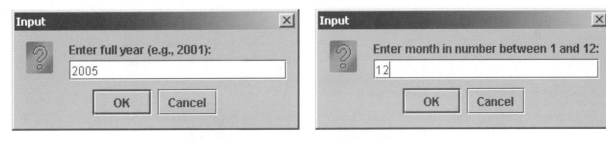

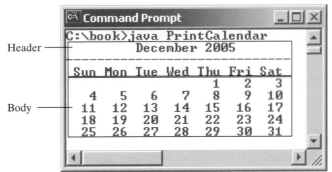

FIGURE 4.12   *After prompting the user to enter the year and the month, the program displays the calendar for that month.*

Let us use this example demonstrate the divide-and-conquer approach.

4.10.1   Top-Down Design

How would you get started on such a program? Would you immediately start coding? Beginning programmers often start by trying to work out the solution to every detail. Although details are important in the final program, concern for detail in the early stages may block the problem-solving process. To make problem-solving flow as smoothly as possible, this example begins by using method abstraction to isolate details from design and only later implements the details.

For this example, the problem is first broken into two subproblems: get input from the user, and print the calendar for the month. At this stage, the creator of the program should be concerned with what the subproblems will achieve, not with how to get input and print the calendar for the month. You can draw a structure chart to help visualize the decomposition of the problem (see Figure 4.13(a)).

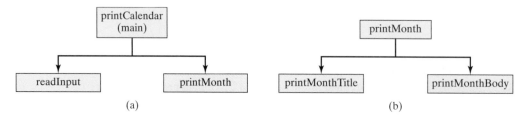

(a)   (b)

FIGURE 4.13 *The structure chart shows that the* printCalendar *problem is divided into two subproblems,* readInput *and* printMonth, *and that* printMonth *is divided into two smaller subproblems,* printMonthTitle *and* printMonthBody.

Use the JOptionPane.showInputDialog method to display input dialog boxes that prompt the user to enter the year and the month.

The problem of printing the calendar for a given month can be broken into two subproblems: print the month title, and print the month body, as shown in Figure 4.13(b). The month title consists of three lines: month and year, a dash line, and the names of the seven days of the week. You need to get the month name (e.g., January) from the numeric month (e.g., 1). This is accomplished in getMonthName (see Figure 4.14(a)).

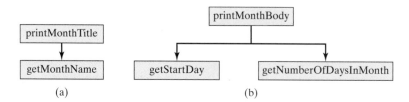

(a)   (b)

FIGURE 4.14 *(a) To* printMonthTitle, *you need* getMonthName. *(b) The* printMonthBody *problem is refined into several smaller problems.*

In order to print the month body, you need to know which day of the week is the first day of the month (getStartDay) and how many days the month has (getNumberOfDaysInMonth), as shown in Figure 4.14(b). For example, December 2005 has thirty-one days, and the first of the month is Thursday, as shown in Figure 4.12.

How would you get the start day for the first date in a month? There are several ways to find the start day. The simplest approach is to use the Calendar class in Section 9.3, "The Calendar and GregorianCalendar classes." For now, an alternative approach is used. Assume that you know that the start day (startDay1800 = 3) for January 1, 1800 was Wednesday. You could compute the total number of days (totalNumberOfDays) between January 1, 1800 and the first date of the calendar month. The start day for the calendar month is (totalNumberOfDays + startDay1800) % 7, since every week has seven days. So the getStartDay problem can be further refined as getTotalNumberOfDays, as shown in Figure 4.15(a).

To get the total number of days, you need to know whether a year is a leap year and the number of days in each month. So the getTotalNumberOfDays is further refined into two subproblems: isLeapYear and getNumberOfDaysInMonth, as shown in Figure 4.15(b). The complete structure chart is shown in Figure 4.16.

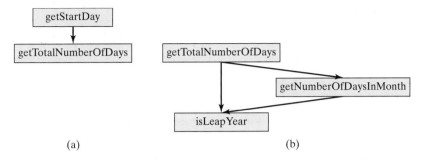

(a)   (b)

FIGURE 4.15   *(a) To* getStartDay, *you need* getTotalNumberOfDays. *(b) The* getTotalNumberOfDays *problem is refined into two smaller problems.*

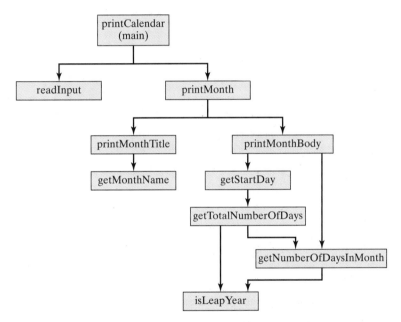

FIGURE 4.16   *The structure chart shows the hierarchical relationship of the subproblems in the program.*

4.10.2   Top-Down or Bottom-Up Implementation

Now we turn our attention to implementation. In general, a subproblem corresponds to a method in the implementation, although some are so simple that this is unnecessary. You would need to decide which modules to implement as methods and which to combine in other methods. Decisions of this kind should be based on whether the overall program will be easier to read as a result of your choice. In this example, the subproblem readInput can be simply implemented in the main method.

You can use either a "top-down" approach or a "bottom-up" approach. The *top-down approach* implements one method in the structure chart at a time from the top to the bottom. Stubs can be used for the methods waiting to be implemented. A *stub* is a simple but incomplete version of a method. The use of stubs enables you to test invoking the method from a caller. Implement the main method first, and then use a stub for the printMonth method. For

top-down approach

stub

example, let `printMonth` display the year and the month in the stub. Thus, your program may begin like this:

```java
public class PrintCalendar {
  /** Main method */
  public static void main(String[] args) {
    // Prompt the user to enter year
    String yearString = JOptionPane.showInputDialog(
      "Enter full year (e.g., 2001):");

    // Convert string into integer
    int year = Integer.parseInt(yearString);

    // Prompt the user to enter month
    String monthString = JOptionPane.showInputDialog(
      "Enter month in number between 1 and 12:");

    // Convert string into integer
    int month = Integer.parseInt(monthString);

    // Print calendar for the month of the year
    printMonth(year, month);
  }

  /** A stub for printMonth may look like this */
  public static void printMonth(int year, int month) {
    System.out.print(month + " " + year);
  }

  /** A stub for printMonthTitle may look like this */
  public static void printMonthTitle(int year, int month) {
  }

  /** A stub for getMonthName may look like this */
  public static String getMonthName(int month) {
    return "January"; // a dummy value
  }

  /** A stub for getMonthName may look like this */
  public static int getStartDay(int year, int month) {
    return 1; // a dummy value
  }

  /** A stub for getNumberOfDaysInMonth may look like this */
  public static int getNumberOfDaysInMonth(int year, int month) {
    return 31; // a dummy value
  }

  /** A stub for getTotalNumberOfDays may look like this */
  public static int getTotalNumberOfDays(int year, int month) {
    return 10000; // a dummy value
  }

  /** A stub for getTotalNumberOfDays may look like this */
  public static boolean isLeapYear(int year) {
    return true; // a dummy value
  }
}
```

Compile and test the program, and fix any errors. You can now implement the `printMonth` method. For methods invoked from the `printMonth` method, you can again use stubs.

bottom-up approach

The *bottom-up approach* implements one method in the structure chart at a time from the bottom to the top. For each method implemented, write a test program to test it. The top-down and bottom-up approaches are both fine. Both approaches implement methods incrementally, help to isolate programming errors, and make debugging easy. Sometimes they can be used together.

4.10.3   Implementation Details

The `isLeapYear(int year)` method can be implemented using the following code:

```
return (year % 400 == 0 || (year % 4 == 0 && year % 100 != 0));
```

Use the following fact to implement `getTotalNumberOfDaysInMonth(int year, int month)`:

✦ January, March, May, July, August, October, and December have thirty-one days.

✦ April, June, September, and November have thirty days.

✦ February has twenty-eight days during a regular year and twenty-nine days during a leap year. A regular year, therefore, has 365 days, whereas a leap year has 366 days.

To implement `getTotalNumberOfDays(int year, int month)`, you need to compute the total number of days (`totalNumberOfDays`) between Jan 1, 1800 and the first day of the calendar month. You could find the total number of days between the year 1800 and the calendar year and then figure out the total number of days prior to the calendar month in the calendar year. The sum of these two totals is `totalNumberOfDays`.

To print a body, first pad some space before the start day and then print the lines for every week, as shown for December 2005 (see Figure 4.12).

The complete program is given in Listing 4.7.

LISTING 4.7   **PrintCalendar.java (Printing Calendar)**

```
 1 import javax.swing.JOptionPane;
 2
 3 public class PrintCalendar {
 4   /** Main method */
 5   public static void main(String[] args) {
 6     // Prompt the user to enter year
 7     String yearString = JOptionPane.showInputDialog(
 8       "Enter full year (e.g., 2001):");
 9
10     // Convert string into integer
11     int year = Integer.parseInt(yearString);
12
13     // Prompt the user to enter month
14     String monthString = JOptionPane.showInputDialog(
15       "Enter month in number between 1 and 12:");
16
17     // Convert string into integer
18     int month = Integer.parseInt(monthString);
19
20     // Print calendar for the month of the year
21     printMonth(year, month);
22   }
23
24   /** Print the calendar for a month in a year */
25   static void printMonth(int year, int month) {
26     // Print the headings of the calendar
27     printMonthTitle(year, month);
28
29     // Print the body of the calendar
30     printMonthBody(year, month);
31   }
32
33   /** Print the month title, e.g., May, 1999 */
34   static void printMonthTitle(int year, int month) {
35     System.out.println("     " + getMonthName(month)
36       + " " + year);
37     System.out.println("-----------------------------");
38     System.out.println(" Sun Mon Tue Wed Thu Fri Sat");
39   }
```

```
40
41    /** Get the English name for the month */
42    static String getMonthName(int month) {
43      String monthName = null;
44      switch (month) {
45        case 1: monthName = "January"; break;
46        case 2: monthName = "February"; break;
47        case 3: monthName = "March"; break;
48        case 4: monthName = "April"; break;
49        case 5: monthName = "May"; break;
50        case 6: monthName = "June"; break;
51        case 7: monthName = "July"; break;
52        case 8: monthName = "August"; break;
53        case 9: monthName = "September"; break;
54        case 10: monthName = "October"; break;
55        case 11: monthName = "November"; break;
56        case 12: monthName = "December";
57      }
58
59      return monthName;
60    }
61
62    /** Print month body */
63    static void printMonthBody(int year, int month) {
64      // Get start day of the week for the first date in the month
65      int startDay = getStartDay(year, month);
66
67      // Get number of days in the month
68      int numberOfDaysInMonth = getNumberOfDaysInMonth(year, month);
69
70      // Pad space before the first day of the month
71      int i = 0;
72      for (i = 0; i < startDay; i++)
73        System.out.print("    ");
74
75      for (i = 1; i <= numberOfDaysInMonth; i++) {
76        if (i < 10)
77          System.out.print("    " + i);
78        else
79          System.out.print("   " + i);
80
81        if ((i + startDay) % 7 == 0)
82          System.out.println();
83      }
84
85      System.out.println();
86    }
87
88    /** Get the start day of the first day in a month */
89    static int getStartDay(int year, int month) {
90      // Get total number of days since 1/1/1800
91      int startDay1800 = 3;
92      int totalNumberOfDays = getTotalNumberOfDays(year, month);
93
94      // Return the start day
95      return (totalNumberOfDays + startDay1800) % 7;
96    }
97
98    /** Get the total number of days since Jan 1, 1800 */
99    static int getTotalNumberOfDays(int year, int month) {
100     int total = 0;
101
102     // Get the total days from 1800 to year - 1
103     for (int i = 1800; i < year; i++)
104     if (isLeapYear(i))
105       total = total + 366;
106     else
107       total = total + 365;
108
```

```
109    // Add days from Jan to the month prior to the calendar month
110    for (int i = 1; i < month; i++)
111      total = total + getNumberOfDaysInMonth(year, i);
112
113    return total;
114  }
115
116  /** Get the number of days in a month */
117  static int getNumberOfDaysInMonth(int year, int month) {
118    if (month == 1 || month == 3 || month == 5 || month == 7 ||
119      month == 8 || month == 10 || month == 12)
120      return 31;
121
122    if (month == 4 || month == 6 || month == 9 || month == 11)
123      return 30;
124
125    if (month == 2) return isLeapYear(year) ? 29 : 28;
126
127    return 0; // If month is incorrect
128  }
129
130  /** Determine if it is a leap year */
131  static boolean isLeapYear(int year) {
132    return year % 400 == 0 || (year % 4 == 0 && year % 100 137 != 0);
133  }
134 }
```

The program does not validate user input. For instance, if the user enters a month not in the range between 1 and 12, or a year before 1800, the program would display an erroneous calendar. To avoid this error, add an if statement to check the input before printing the calendar.

This program prints calendars for a month but could easily be modified to print calendars for a whole year. Although it can only print months after January 1800, it could be modified to trace the day of a month before 1800.

 NOTE

Method abstraction modularizes programs in a neat, hierarchical manner. Programs written as collections of concise methods are easier to write, debug, maintain, and modify than would otherwise be the case. This writing style also promotes method reusability.

 TIP

When implementing a large program, use the top-down or bottom-up coding approach. Do not write the entire program at once. This approach seems to take more time for coding (because you are repeatedly compiling and running the program), but it actually saves time and makes debugging easier.

4.11   Recursion (Optional)

You have seen a method calling another method; that is, a statement contained in a method body calling another method. Can a method call itself? And what happens if it does? This section examines these questions and uses three classic examples to demonstrate recursive programming.

4.11.1   Computing Factorials

recursion

Recursion, a powerful mathematical concept, is the process of a function calling itself, directly or indirectly. Many mathematical functions are defined using recursion. The factorial of a number n can be recursively defined as follows:

```
0! = 1;
n! = n × (n - 1)!; n > 0
```

How do you find n! for a given n? It is easy to find 1! because you know 0! and 1! is 1 × 0!. Assuming that you know (n-1)!, n! can be obtained immediately using n × (n-1)!. Thus, the problem of computing n! is reduced to computing (n-1)!. When computing (n-1)!, you can apply the same idea recursively until n is reduced to 0.

Let factorial(n) be the method for computing n!. If you call the method with n=0, it immediately returns the result. The method knows how to solve the simplest case, which is referred to as the *base case* or the *stopping condition*. If you call the method with n>0, it reduces the problem into a subproblem for computing the factorial of n-1. The subproblem is essentially the same as the original problem, but is slightly simpler or smaller than the original. Because the subproblem has the same property as the original, you can call the method with a different argument, which is referred to as a *recursive call*.

stopping condition

recursive call

The recursive algorithm for computing factorial(n) can be simply described as follows:

```
if (n == 0)
  return 1;
else
  return n * factorial(n - 1);
```

A recursive call can result in many more recursive calls because the method is dividing a subproblem into new subproblems. For a recursive method to terminate, the problem must eventually be reduced to a stopping case. When it reaches a stopping case, the method returns a result to its caller. The caller then performs a computation and returns the result to its own caller. This process continues until the result is passed back to the original caller. The original problem can now be solved by multiplying n with the result of factorial(n - 1).

EXAMPLE 4.5 COMPUTING FACTORIALS

Problem

Write a recursive method for computing a factorial factorial(n), given n. The test program prompts the user to enter n.

Solution

Listing 4.8 gives the solution to the problem. A sample run of the program is shown in Figure 4.17.

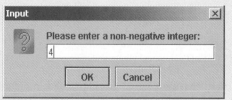
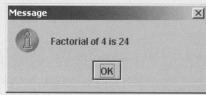

FIGURE **4.17**   *The program prompts the user to enter a non-negative integer and then displays the factorial for the number.*

Chapter 4 Methods **151**

EXAMPLE 4.5 (CONTINUED)

LISTING 4.8   ComputeFactorial.java (Computing Factorial)

```java
1 import javax.swing.JOptionPane;
2
3 public class ComputeFactorial {
4   /** Main method */
5   public static void main(String[] args) {
6     // Prompt the user to enter an integer
7     String intString = JOptionPane.showInputDialog(
8       "Please enter a non-negative integer:");
9
10    // Convert string into integer
11    int n = Integer.parseInt(intString);
12
13    // Display factorial
14    JOptionPane.showMessageDialog(null,
15      "Factorial of " + n + " is " + factorial(n));
16  }
17
18  /** Return the factorial for a specified index */
19  static long factorial(int n) {
20    if (n == 0) // Stopping condition
21      return 1;
22    else
23      return n * factorial(n - 1); // Call factorial recursively
24  }
25 }
```
recursion

Review

The factorial method (Lines 19–24) is essentially a direct translation of the recursive mathematical definition for the factorial into Java code. The call to factorial is recursive because it calls itself. The parameter passed to factorial is decremented until it reaches the base case of 0.

Figure 4.18 illustrates the execution of the recursive calls, starting with n = 4. The use of stack space for recursive calls is shown in Figure 4.19.

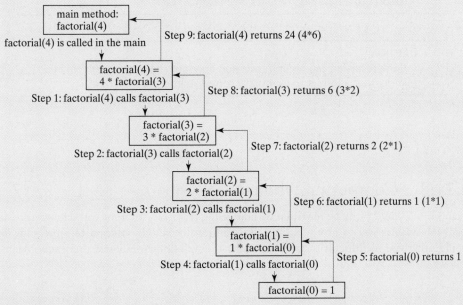

FIGURE 4.18 *Invoking* factorial(4) *spawns recursive calls to* factorial.

EXAMPLE 4.5 (CONTINUED)

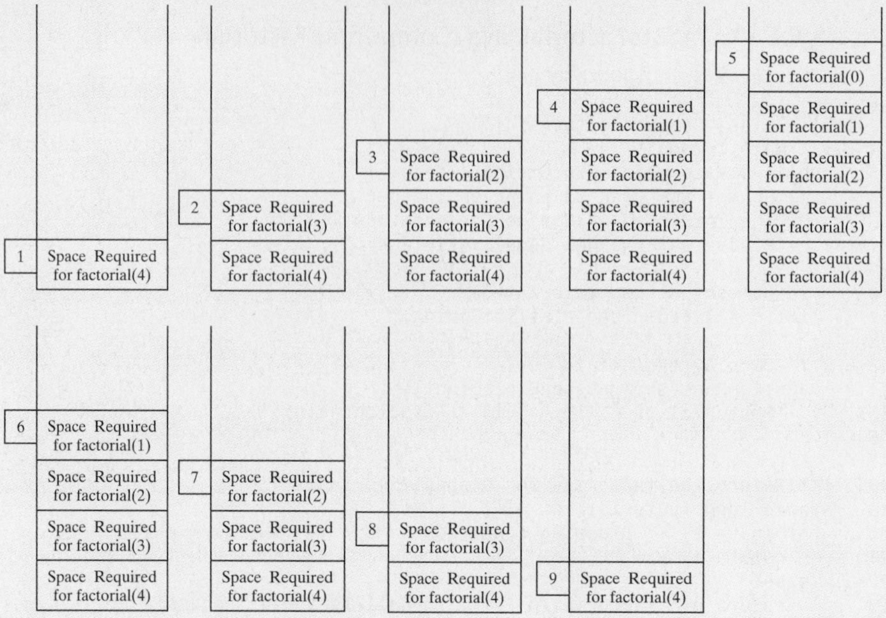

FIGURE 4.19   *When* `factorial(4)` *is being executed, the* `factorial` *method is called recursively, causing memory space to dynamically change.*

NOTE

All recursive methods have the following characteristics:

◆ One or more base cases (the simplest case) are used to stop recursion.

◆ Every recursive call reduces the original problem, bringing it increasingly closer to a base case until it becomes that case.

CAUTION

Infinite recursion can occur if recursion does not reduce the problem in a manner that allows it to eventually converge into the base case.

4.11.2   Computing Fibonacci Numbers

Example 4.5 could easily be rewritten without using recursion. In some cases, however, using recursion enables you to give a natural, straightforward, simple solution to a program that would otherwise be difficult to solve. Consider the well-known Fibonacci series problem, as follows:

The series:	0	1	1	2	3	5	6	8	13	21	34	55	89	...

The series: 0   1   1   2   3   5   8   13   21   34   55   89   ...
indices: 0   1   2   3   4   5   6   7   8   9   10   11

Example 4.7 (Continued)

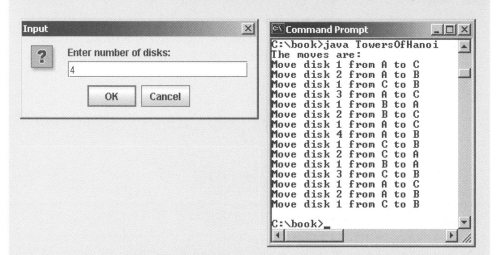

Figure 4.23 *The program prompts the user to enter the number of disks and then displays the steps that must be followed to solve the Towers of Hanoi problem.*

Listing 4.10   TowersOfHanoi.java (Towers of Hanoi Problem)

```
1 import javax.swing.JOptionPane;
2
3 public class TowersOfHanoi {
4   /** Main method */
5   public static void main(String[] args) {
6     // Read number of disks, n
7     String intString = JOptionPane.showInputDialog(
8       "Enter number of disks:");
9
10    // Convert string into integer
11    int n = Integer.parseInt(intString);
12
13    // Find the solution recursively
14    System.out.println("The moves are:");
15    moveDisks(n, 'A', 'B', 'C');
16  }
17
18  /** The method for finding the solution to move n disks
19      from fromTower to toTower with auxTower */
20  public static void moveDisks(int n, char fromTower,
21      char toTower, char auxTower) {
22    if (n == 1) // Stopping condition
23      System.out.println("Move disk " + n + " from " +
24        fromTower + " to " + toTower);
25    else {
26      moveDisks(n - 1, fromTower, auxTower, toTower);          recursion
27      System.out.println("Move disk " + n + " from " +
28        fromTower + " to " + toTower);
29      moveDisks(n - 1, auxTower, toTower, fromTower);          recursion
30    }
31  }
32 }
```

EXAMPLE 4.7 (CONTINUED)

Review

This problem is inherently recursive. Using recursion makes it possible to find a natural, simple solution. It would be difficult to solve the problem without using recursion.

Consider tracing the program for `n = 3`. The successive recursive calls are shown in Figure 4.24. As you can see, writing the program is easier than tracing the recursive calls. The system uses stacks to trace the calls behind the scenes. To some extent, recursion provides a level of abstraction that hides iterations and other details from the user.

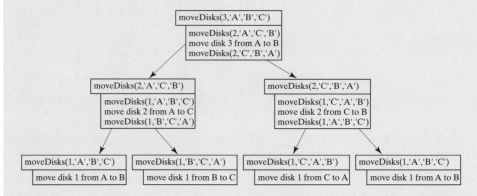

FIGURE 4.24 *Invoking* `moveDisks(3, 'A', 'B', 'C')` *spawns calls to* `moveDisks` *recursively.*

The `fib` method in the preceding example returns a value to its caller, but the `moveDisks` method in this example does not return a value to its caller.

4.11.4   Recursion versus Iteration

Recursion is an alternative form of program control. It is essentially repetition without a loop control. When you use loops, you specify a loop body. The repetition of the loop body is controlled by the loop-control structure. In recursion, the method itself is called repeatedly. A selection statement must be used to control whether to call the method recursively or not.

Recursion bears substantial overhead. Each time the program calls a method, the system must assign space for all of the method's local variables and parameters. This can consume considerable memory and requires extra time to manage the additional space.

Any problem that can be solved recursively can be solved nonrecursively with iterations. Recursion has many negative aspects: it uses up too much time and too much memory. Why, then, should you use it? In some cases, using recursion enables you to specify a clear, simple solution that would otherwise be difficult to obtain.

The decision whether to use recursion or iteration should be based on the nature of the problem you are trying to solve and your understanding of the problem. The rule of thumb is to use whichever of the two approaches can best develop an intuitive solution that naturally mirrors the problem. If an iterative solution is obvious, use it. It will generally be more efficient than the recursive option.

 NOTE

Your recursive program could run out of memory, causing a runtime error. In Chapter 15, "Exceptions and Assertions," you will learn how to handle errors so that the program terminates gracefully when there is a stack overflow.

> **TIP**
>
> If you are concerned about your program's performance, avoid using recursion, because it takes more time and consumes more memory than iteration. Commercial software generally do not use recursion.

4.12 Packages (Optional)

Packages are used to group classes. So far, all the classes in this book are grouped into a default package. You can explicitly specify a package for each class. There are four reasons for using packages.

why packages?

♦ **To locate classes.** Classes with similar functions can be placed in the same package so they can be easily located.

♦ **To avoid naming conflicts.** When you develop reusable classes to be shared by other programmers, naming conflicts often occur. To prevent this, put your classes into packages so that they can be referenced through package names.

♦ **To distribute software conveniently.** Packages group related classes so that they can be easily distributed.

♦ **To protect classes.** Packages provide protection so that the protected members of the classes are accessible to the classes in the same package, but not to the external classes.

4.12.1 Package-Naming Conventions

Packages are hierarchical, and you can have packages within packages. For example, `java.lang.Math` indicates that `Math` is a class in the package `lang` and that `lang` is a package in the package `java`. Levels of nesting can be used to ensure the uniqueness of package names.

Choosing a unique name is important because your package may be used on the Internet by other programs. Java designers recommend that you use your Internet domain name in reverse order as a package prefix. Since Internet domain names are unique, this prevents naming conflicts. Suppose you want to create a package named `mypackage` on a host machine with the Internet domain name `prenhall.com`. To follow the naming convention, you would name the entire package `com.prenhall.mypackage`. By convention, package names are all in lowercase.

4.12.2 Package Directories

Java expects one-to-one mapping of the package name and the file system directory structure. For the package named `com.prenhall.mypackage`, you must create a directory, as shown in Figure 4.25(a). In other words, a package is actually a directory that contains the bytecode of the classes.

(a)   (b)

FIGURE 4.25 *The package* `com.prenhall.mypackage` *is mapped to a directory structure in the file system.*

classpath
class directory

current directory

The com directory does not have to be the root directory. In order for Java to know where your package is in the file system, you must modify the environment variable classpath so that it points to the directory in which your package resides. Such a directory is known as the *class directory* for the class. Suppose the com directory is under c:\book, as shown in Figure 4.25(b). The following line adds c:\book into the classpath:

```
classpath=.;c:\book;
```

The period (.) indicating the *current directory* is always in classpath. The directory c:\book is in classpath so that you can use the package com.prenhall.mypackage in the program.

You can add as many directories as necessary in classpath. The order in which the directories are specified is the order in which the classes are searched. If you have two classes of the same name in different directories, Java uses the first one it finds.

The classpath variable is set differently in Windows and Unix, as outlined below.

✦ **Windows 98:** Edit autoexec.bat using a text editor, such as Microsoft Notepad.

✦ **Windows NT/2000/XP:** Go to the start button and choose control panel, select the system icon, then modify classpath in the Environment Variables.

✦ **UNIX:** Use the setenv command to set classpath, such as

```
setenv classpath .:/home/book
```

If you insert this line into the .cshrc file, the classpath variable will be set automatically when you log on.

 NOTE

On Windows 95 and Windows 98, you must restart the system in order for the classpath variable to take effect. On Windows NT and Windows 2000, however, the settings are effective immediately. They affect any new command-line windows, but not the existing command-line windows.

4.12.3 Putting Classes into Packages

Every class in Java belongs to a package. The class is added to a package when it is compiled. All the classes that you have used so far in this book were placed in the current directory (a default package) when the Java source programs were compiled. To put a class in a specific package, you need to add the following line as the first noncomment and nonblank statement in the program:

```
package packagename;
```

EXAMPLE 4.8 PUTTING CLASSES INTO PACKAGES

Problem

This example creates a class named Format and places it in the package com. prenhall.mypackage. The Format class contains the format(number, numberOfDecimal-Digits) method, which returns a new number with the specified number of digits after the decimal point. For example, format(10.3422345, 2) returns 10.34, and format (−0.343434, 3) returns −0.343.

Example 4.8 (Continued)

Solution

1. Create Format.java in Listing 4.11 and save it into c:\book\com\prenhall\
   mypackage.

Listing 4.11   Format.java (Formatting Numbers)

```
1 package com.prenhall.mypackage;
2
3 public class Format {
4   public static double format(
5       double number, int numberOfDecimalDigits) {
6     return Math.round(number * Math.pow(10, numberOfDecimalDigits)) /
7       Math.pow(10, numberOfDecimalDigits);
8   }
9 }
```

specify a package

2. Compile Format.java. Make sure Format.class is in c:\book\com\prenhall\mypackage.

Review

A class must be defined as public in order to be accessed by other programs. If you want to put several classes into the package, you have to create separate source files for them because one file can have only one public class.

Format.java can be placed under anyDir\com\prenhall\mypackage and Format.class in anyOtherDir\com\prenhall\mypackage, and anyDir and anyOtherDir may be the same or different. To make the class available, add anyOtherDir in the classpath using the command:

```
set classpath=%classpath%;anyOtherDir
```

Note

Class files can be archived into a single file for convenience. For instance, you may compress all the class files in the folder mypackage into a single zip file named mypackage.zip with subfolder information kept as shown in Figure 4.26. To make the classes in the zip file available for use, add the zip file to the classpath like this:

```
classpath=%classpath%;c:\mypackage.zip
```

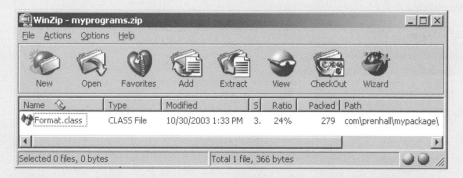

Figure 4.26   *Class files can be archived into a single compressed file.*

EXAMPLE 4.8 (CONTINUED)

 NOTE

An IDE such as JBuilder and NetBeans uses the *source directory path* to specify where the source files are stored and uses the *class directory path* to specify where the compiled class files are stored.

A source file must be stored in a package directory under the source directory path. For example, if the source directory is c:\mysource and the package statement in the source code is package com.prenhall. mypackage, then the source code file must be stored in c:\mysource\com\ prenhall\mypackage.

A class file must be stored in a package directory under the class directory path. For example, if the class directory is c:\myclass and the package statement in the source code is package com.prenhall.my- package, then the class file must be stored in c:\myclass\com\prenhall\ mypackage.

4.12.4 Using Classes from Packages

There are two ways to use classes from a package. One way is to use the fully qualified name of the class. For example, the fully qualified name for JOptionPane is javax.swing.JOptionPane. For Format in the preceding example, it is com.prenhall.mypackage.Format. This is convenient if the class is used only a few times in the program. The other way is to use the import statement. For example, to import all the classes in the javax.swing package, you can use

```
import javax.swing.*;
```

An import that uses an * is called *an import on demand* declaration . You can also import a specific class. For example, this statement imports javax.swing.JOptionPane:

```
import javax.swing.JOptionPane;
```

The information for the classes in an imported package is not read in at compile time or runtime unless the class is used in the program. The import statement simply tells the compiler where to locate the classes. There is no performance difference between an import on demand declaration and a specific class import declaration.

EXAMPLE 4.9 USING PACKAGES

Problem

This example shows a program that uses the Format class in the com.prenhall. mypackage.mypackage package.

Solution

1. Create TestFormatClass.java in Listing 4.12 and save it into c:\book.

LISTING 4.12 **TestFormatClass.java (Using the Format Class)**

import class

```
1 import com.prenhall.mypackage.Format;
2
3 public class TestFormatClass {
4   /** Main method */
```

EXAMPLE 4.9 (CONTINUED)

```
5    public static void main(String[] args) {
6      System.out.println(Format.format(10.3422345, 2));
7      System.out.println(Format.format(-0.343434, 3));
8    }
9  }
```

2. Run TestFormatClass, as shown in Figure 4.27.

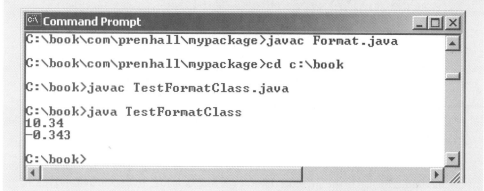

FIGURE 4.27 *TestFormatClass uses Format defined in com.prenhall.mypackage.*

Review

TestFormatClass.java can be placed anywhere as long as c:\book is in the classpath so that the Format class can be found. Please note that Format is defined as public so that it can be used by classes in other packages.

The program uses an import statement to get the class Format. You cannot import entire packages, such as com.prenhall.*.*. Only one asterisk (*) can be used in an import statement.

 NOTE

The format method can be invoked from any class. If you create a new class in the same package with Format, you can invoke the format method using ClassName.methodName (e.g., Format.format). If you create a new class in a different package, you can invoke the format method using packagename.ClassName.method (e.g., com.prenhall.mypackage. Format.format).

KEY TERMS

actual parameter   127
ambiguous invocation   135
divide and conquer   143
formal parameter (i.e., parameter)   126
information hiding   138
method abstraction   138
method overloading   133
method signature   126
modifier   126

package   159
pass by value   131
recursion   149
return type   126
return value   126
scope of variable   137
stub   145

KEY CLASSES AND METHODS

✦ `java.lang.Math` is a class that contains methods to perform trigonometric functions (`sin`, `cos`, `tan`, `acos`, `asin`, `atan`), exponent functions (`exp`, `log`, `pow`, `sqrt`), and some service functions (`min`, `max`, `abs`, `round`, `random`). All of these methods operate on `double` values; `min`, `max`, and `abs` can also operate on `int`, `long`, `float`, and `double`.

CHAPTER SUMMARY

✦ Making programs modular and reusable is one of the central goals in software engineering. Java provides many powerful constructs that help to achieve this goal. The methods are one such construct.

✦ The method header specifies the *modifiers, return value type, method name,* and *parameters* of the method. The modifier, which is optional, tells the compiler how to call the method. The static modifier is used for all the methods in this chapter.

✦ A method may return a value. The `returnValueType` is the data type of the value the method returns. If the method does not return a value, the `returnValueType` is the keyword `void`.

✦ The *parameter list* refers to the type, order, and number of the parameters of a method. The method name and the parameter list together constitute the *method signature.* Parameters are optional; that is, a method may contain no parameters.

✦ A return statement can also be used in a void method for terminating the method and returning to the method's caller. This is occasionally useful for circumventing the normal flow of control in a method.

✦ The arguments that are passed to a method should have the same number, type, and order as the parameters in the method definition.

✦ When a program calls a method, program control is transferred to the called method. A called method returns control to the caller when its return statement is executed or when its method-ending closing brace is reached.

✦ A method with a nonvoid return value type can also be invoked as a statement in Java. In this case, the caller simply ignores the return value. In the majority of cases, a call to a method with return value is treated as a value. In some cases, however, the caller is not interested in the return value.

✦ Each time a method is invoked, the system stores parameters, local variables, and system registers in a space known as a *stack.* When a method calls another method, the caller's stack space is kept intact, and new space is created to handle the new method call. When a method finishes its work and returns to its caller, its associated space is released.

✦ A method can be overloaded. This means that two methods can have the same name as long as their method parameter lists differ.

✦ The scope of a local variable is limited locally to a method. The scope of a local variable starts from its declaration and continues to the end of the block that contains the variable.

A local variable must be declared before it can be used, and it must be initialized before it is referenced.

◆ *Method abstraction* is achieved by separating the use of a method from its implementation. The client can use a method without knowing how it is implemented. The details of the implementation are encapsulated in the method and hidden from the client who invokes the method. This is known as *information hiding* or *encapsulation*.

◆ Method abstraction modularizes programs in a neat, hierarchical manner. Programs written as collections of concise methods are easier to write, debug, maintain, and modify than would otherwise be the case. This writing style also promotes method reusability.

◆ When implementing a large program, use the top-down or bottom-up coding approach. Do not write the entire program at once. This approach seems to take more time for coding (because you are repeatedly compiling and running the program), but it actually saves time and makes debugging easier.

◆ Recursion is an alternative form of program control. It is essentially repetition without a loop control. It can be used to specify simple, clear solutions for inherently recursive problems that would otherwise be difficult to solve.

◆ Recursion bears substantial overhead. Each time the program calls a method, the system must assign space for all of the method's local variables and parameters. This can consume considerable memory and requires extra time to manage the additional space.

REVIEW QUESTIONS

Sections 4.2–4.3

4.1   What are the benefits of using a method? How do you declare a method? How do you invoke a method?

4.2   What is the `return` type of a `main` method?

4.3   Can you simplify the `max` method in Example 4.1 using the conditional operator?

4.4   True or false? A call to a method with a `void` return type is always a statement, but a call to a method with a nonvoid return type is always a component of an expression.

4.5   What would be wrong with not writing a `return` statement in a nonvoid method? Can you have a `return` statement in a `void` method, such as the following?

```java
public static void main(String[] args) {
  int i;
  while (true) {
    // Prompt the user to enter an integer
    String intString = JOptionPane.showInputDialog(
      "Enter an integer:");

    // Convert a string into int
    int i = Integer.parseInt(intString);
    if (i == 0)
      return;
    System.out.println("i = " + i);
  }
}
```

Does the `return` statement in the following method cause syntax errors?

```java
public static void xMethod(double x, double y) {
  System.out.println(x + y);
  return x + y;
}
```

4.6 In some languages, you can define methods inside a method. Can you define a method inside a method in Java?

4.7 For each of the following, decide whether a `void` method or a nonvoid method is the most appropriate implementation:

✦ Computing a sales commission, given the sales amount and the commission rate.

✦ Printing the calendar for a month.

✦ Computing a square root.

✦ Testing whether a number is even, and returning `true` if it is.

✦ Printing a message a specified number of times.

✦ Computing the monthly payment, given the loan amount, number of years, and annual interest rate.

✦ Finding the corresponding uppercase letter, given a lowercase letter.

4.8 Identify and correct the errors in the following program:

```java
1 public class Test {
2   public static method1(int n, m) {
3     n += m;
4     xMethod(3.4);
5   }
6
7   public static int xMethod(int n) {
8     if (n > 0) return 1;
9     else if (n == 0) return 0;
10    else if (n < 0) return -1;
11  }
12 }
```

4.9 Reformat the following program according to the programming style and documentation guidelines proposed in Section 2.18, "Programming Style and Documentation." Use the next-line brace style.

```java
public class Test {
  public static double xMethod(double i,double j)
  {
  while (i<j) {
    j--;
  }
  return j;
  }
}
```

Section 4.4 Passing Parameters

4.10 How is an argument passed to a method? Can the argument have the same name as its parameter?

4.11   What is pass by value? Show the result of the following programs:

```java
public class Test {
  public static void main(String[] args) {
    int max = 0;
    max(1, 2, max);
    System.out.println(max);
  }

  public static void max(
    int value1, int value2, int max) {
    if (value1 > value2)
      max = value1;
    else
      max = value2;
  }
}
```

(a)

```java
public class Test {
  public static void main(String[] args) {
    // Initialize times
    int times = 3;
    System.out.println("Before the call,"
      + " variable times is " + times);

    // Invoke nPrintln and display times
    nPrintln("Welcome to Java!", times);
    System.out.println("After the call,"
      + "variable times is " + times);
  }

  // Print the message n times
  public static void nPrintln(
    String message, int n) {
    while (n > 0) {
      System.out.println("n = " + n);
      System.out.println(message);
      n--;
    }
  }
}
```

(b)

```java
public class Test {
  public static void main(String[] args) {
    int i = 1;
    while (i <= 6) {
      xMethod(i, 2);
      i++;
    }
  }

  public static void xMethod(
    int i, int num) {
    for (int j = 1; j <= i; j++) {
      System.out.print(num + " ");
      num *= 2;
    }

    System.out.println();
  }
}
```

(c)

```java
public class Test {
  public static void main(String[] args) {
    int i = 0;
    while (i <= 4) {
      xMethod(i);
      i++;
    }

    System.out.println("i is " + i);
  }

  public static void xMethod(int i) {
    do {
      if (i % 3 != 0)
        System.out.print(i + " ");
      i--;
    }
    while (i >= 1);

    System.out.println();
  }
}
```

(d)

4.12   For (a) in the preceding question, show the contents of the stack just before the method max is invoked, just entering max, just before max is returned, and right after max is returned.

Section 4.5 Overloading Methods

4.13   What is method overloading? Is it possible to define two methods that have the same name but different parameter types? Is it possible to define two methods in a class that have identical method names and parameter lists with different return value types or different modifiers?

4.14 What is wrong in the following program?

```java
public class Test {
  public static void method(int x) {
  }

  public static int method(int y) {
    return y;
  }
}
```

Section 4.6 The Scope of Local Variables

4.15 Identify and correct the errors in the following program:

```java
1 public class Test {
2   public static void main(String[] args) {
3     nPrintln("Welcome to Java!", 5);
4   }
5
6   public static void nPrintln(String message, int n) {
7     int n = 1;
8     for (int i = 0; i < n; i++)
9       System.out.println(message);
10  }
11 }
```

Section 4.8 The Math Class

4.16 Which of the following is a possible output from invoking Math.random()?

323.4, 0.5, 34, 1.0, 0.0, 0.234

4.17 Write an expression that returns a random integer between 34 and 55. Write an expression that returns a random integer between 0 and 999. Write an expression that returns a random number between 5.5 and 55.5. Write an expression that returns a random lowercase letter.

4.18 Evaluate the following method calls:

```
A. Math.sqrt(4)                 J. Math.floor(-2.5)
B. Math.sin(2 * Math.PI)        K. Math.round(-2.5f)
C. Math.cos(2 * Math.PI)        L. Math.round(-2.5)
D. Math.pow(2, 2)               M. Math.rint(2.5)
E. Math.log(Math.E)             N. Math.ceil(2.5)
F. Math.exp(1)                  O. Math.floor(2.5)
G. Math.max(2, Math.min(3, 4))  P. Math.round(2.5f)
H. Math.rint(-2.5)              Q. Math.round(2.5)
I. Math.ceil(-2.5)              R. Math.round(Math.abs(-2.5))
```

Section 4.11 Recursion (Optional)

4.19 What is a recursive method? Describe the characteristics of recursive methods.

4.20 Show the output of the following program:

```java
public class Test {
  public static void main(String[] args) {
    System.out.println("Sum is " + xMethod(5));
  }

  public static int xMethod(int n) {
    if (n == 1)
      return 1;
    else
      return n + xMethod(n - 1);
  }
}
```

4.21   Show the output of the following two programs:

```
public class Test {
  public static void main(String[] args) {
    xMethod(5);
  }

  public static void xMethod(int n) {
    if (n > 0) {
      System.out.print(n + " ");
      xMethod(n - 1);
    }
  }
}
```

```
public class Test {
  public static void main(String[] args) {
    xMethod(5);
  }

  public static void xMethod(int n) {
    if (n > 0) {
      xMethod(n - 1);
      System.out.print(n + " ");
    }
  }
}
```

Section 4.12 Packages (Optional)

4.22   What are the benefits of using packages?

4.23   If a class uses the package statement "package java.chapter4", where should the source code be stored, and where should the .class files be stored? How do you make the class available for use by other programs?

4.24   Why do you have to import JOptionPane not the Math class?

PROGRAMMING EXERCISES

Sections 4.2–4.3

4.1   (*Converting an uppercase letter to lowercase*) Write a method that converts an uppercase letter to a lowercase letter. Use the following method header:

```
public static char upperCaseToLowerCase(char ch)
```

For example, upperCaseToLowerCase('B') returns b.

4.2   (*Summing the digits in an integer*) Write a method that computes the sum of the digits in an integer. Use the following method header:

```
public static int sumDigits(long n)
```

For example, sumDigits(234) returns $2 + 3 + 4 = 9$.

> **HINT**
> Use the % operator to extract digits, and use the / operator to remove the extracted digit. For instance, $234 \% 10 = 4$ and $234 / 10 = 23$. Use a loop to repeatedly extract and remove the digit until all the digits are extracted.

4.3   (*Computing the future investment value*) Write a method that computes future investment value at a given interest rate for a specified number of years. The future investment is determined using the formula in Exercise 2.11.

Use the following method header:

```
public static double futureInvestmentValue(
  double investmentAmount, double monthlyInterestRate, int years)
```

For example, futureInvestmentValue(10000, 0.05 / 12, 5) returns 12833.59.

Write a test program that prompts the user to enter the investment amount (e.g., 1000) and the interest rate (e.g., 9%), and print a table that displays future value for the years from 1 to 30, as shown below:

```
The amount invested: 1000
Annual interest rate: 9%
Years           Future Value
1               1093.8
2               1196.41
...

29              13467.25
30              14730.57
```

4.4 (*Conversions between Celsius and Fahrenheit*) Write a class that contains the following two methods:

```
/** Converts from Celsius to Fahrenheit */
public static double celsiusToFahrenheit(double celsius)

/** Converts from Fahrenheit to Celsius */
public static double fahrenheitToCelsius(double fahrenheit)
```

The formula for the conversion is:

```
fahrenheit = (9.0 / 5) * celsius + 32
```

Write a test program that invokes these methods to display the following tables:

Celsius	Fahrenheit		Fahrenheit	Celsius
40.0	104.0		120.0	48.89
39.0	102.2		110.0	43.33
...				
32.0	89.6		40.0	4.44
31.0	87.8		30.0	-1.11

4.5 (*Conversions between feet and meters*) Write a class that contains the following two methods:

```
/** Converts from feet to meters */
public static double footToMeter(double foot)

/** Converts from meters to feet */
public static double meterToFoot(double meter)
```

The formula for the conversion is:

```
meter = 0.305 * foot
```

Write a test program that invokes these methods to display the following tables:

Feet	Meters		Meters	Feet
1.0	0.305		20.0	65.574
2.0	0.61		25.0	81.967
...				
9.0	2.745		60.0	195.721
10.0	3.05		65.0	213.115

4.6 (*Computing GCD*) Write a method that returns the greatest common divisor between two positive integers using the following header:

```
public static int gcd(int m, int n)
```

Write a test program that computes gcd(24, 16) and gcd(255, 25).

4.7 (*Computing commissions*) Write a method that computes the commission using the scheme in Example 3.8. The header of the method is as follows:

```
public static double computeCommission(double salesAmount)
```

Write a test program that displays the following tables:

```
SalesAmount     Commission
10000           900.0
15000           1500.0
...
95000           11100.0
100000          11700.0
```

4.8   (*Displaying characters*) Write a method that prints characters using the following header:

```
public static void printChars(char ch1, char ch2, int numberPerLine)
```

This method prints the characters between ch1 and ch2 with the specified numbers per line. Write a test program that prints ten characters per line from '1' and 'Z'.

4.9*   (*Printing a tax table*) Use the computeTax methods in Example 4.4 to write a program that prints a 2002 tax table for taxable income from $50,000 to $60,000 with intervals of $50 for all four statuses, as follows:

Taxable Income	Single	Married Joint	Married Separate	Head of a House
50000	9846	7296	10398	8506
50050	9859	7309	10411	8519
...				
59950	12532	9982	13190	11192
60000	12546	9996	13205	11206

4.10*   (*Revising Example 3.9 "Displaying Prime Numbers"*) Write a program that meets the following requirements:

✦ Declare a method to determine whether an integer is a prime number. Use the following method header:

```
public static boolean isPrime(int num)
```

An integer greater than 1 is a *prime number* if its only divisor is 1 or itself. For example, isPrime(11) returns true, and isPrime(9) returns false.

✦ Use the isPrime method to find the first thousand prime numbers and display every ten prime numbers in a row, as follows:

```
2  3  5  7  11  13  17  19  23  29
31  37  41  43  47  53  59  61  67  71
73  79  83  89  97  ...
...
```

Section 4.8 The Math Class

4.11*   (*Displaying matrix of 0s and 1s*) Write a method that displays an *n* by *n* matrix using the following header:

```
public static void printMatrix(int n)
```

Each element is 0 or 1, which is generated randomly. Write a test program that prints a 3 by 3 matrix that may look like this:

```
0  1  0
0  0  0
1  1  1
```

4.12   (*Using the* `Math.sqrt` *method*) Write a program that prints the following table using the `sqrt` method in the `Math` class:

Number	SquareRoot
0	0.0000
2	1.4142
...	
18	4.2426
20	4.4721

4.13*   (*The* `MyTriangle` *class*) Create a class named `MyTriangle` that contains the following two methods:

```
public static boolean isValid(
   double side1, double side2, double side3)
```

Returns `true` if the sum of any two sides is greater than the third side.

```
public static double area(
   double side1, double side2, double side3)
```

Returns the area of the triangle.

The formula for computing the area is

$$s = (side1 + side2 + side3)/2;$$
$$area = \sqrt{s(s - side1)(s - side2)(s - side3)}$$

Write a test program that reads three sides for a triangle and computes the area if the input is valid. Otherwise, display that the input is invalid.

4.14   (*Using trigonometric methods*) Print the following table to display the `sin` value and `cos` value of degrees from 0 to 360 with increments of 10 degrees. Round the value to keep four digits after the decimal point.

Degree	Sin	Cos
0	0.0	1.0
10	0.1736	0.9848
...		
350	-0.1736	0.9848
360	0.0	1.0

4.15**   (*Computing mean and standard deviation*) In business applications, you are often asked to compute the mean and standard deviation of data. The mean is simply the average of the numbers. The standard deviation is a statistic that tells you how tightly all the various data are clustered around the mean in a set of data. For example, what is the average age of the students in a class? How close are the ages? If all the students are the same age, the deviation is 0. Write a program that generates ten random numbers between 0 and 1000, and computes the mean and standard deviations of these numbers using the following formula:

$$mean = \frac{\sum_{i=1}^{n} x_i}{n} = \frac{x_1 + x_2 + \cdots + x_n}{n} \qquad deviation = \sqrt{\frac{\sum_{i=1}^{n} x_i^2 - \frac{\left(\sum_{i=1}^{n} x_i\right)^2}{n}}{n - 1}}$$

4.16**   (*Approximating the square root*) implement the `sqrt` method. The square root of a number, `num`, can be approximated by repeatedly performing a calculation using the following formula:

```
nextGuess = (lastGuess + (num / lastGuess)) / 2
```

When nextGuess and lastGuess are almost identical, nextGuess is the approximated square root. The initial guess will be the starting value of lastGuess. If the difference between nextGuess and lastGuess is less than a very small number, such as 0.0001, you can claim that nextGuess is the approximated square root of num.

Sections 4.9–4.10

4.17* (*Generating random characters*) Use the methods in RandomCharacter in Listing 4.5 to print one hundred uppercase letters and then one hundred single digits, and print ten per line.

4.18* (*Displaying current date and time*) Example 2.5, "Displaying Current Time," displays the current time. Improve this example to display the current date and time. The calendar example in Section 4.10, "Stepwise Refinement," should give you some ideas on how to find year, month, and day.

Section 4.11 Recursion (Optional)

4.19 (*Computing factorials*) Rewrite Example 4.5, "Computing Factorials," using iterations.

4.20* (*Fibonacci numbers*) Revise Example 4.6, "Computing Fibonacci Numbers," using a nonrecursive method that computes Fibonacci numbers.

🌼 HINT

To compute fib(n) without recursion, you need to obtain fib(n - 2) and fib(n - 1) first. Let f0 and f1 denote the two previous Fibonacci numbers. The current Fibonacci number would then be f0 + f1. The algorithm can be described as follows:

```
f0 = 0; // For fib(0)
f1 = 1; // For fib(1)
for (int i = 1; i <= n; i++) {
  currentFib = f0 + f1;
  f0 = f1;
  f1 = currentFib;
}
// After the loop, currentFib is fib(n)
```

4.21* (*Towers of Hanoi*) Modify Example 4.7, "Solving the Towers of Hanoi Problem," so that the program finds the number of moves needed to move n disks from tower A to tower B.

4.22* (*Computing greatest common divisor using recursion*) The gcd(m, n) can also be defined recursively as follows:

◆ If m % n is 0, gcd (m, n) is n.

◆ Otherwise, gcd(m, n) is gcd(n, m % n).

Write a recursive method to find the GCD. Write a test program that computes gcd(24, 16) and gcd(255, 25).

4.23* (*Printing message using recursion*) Write a method with the following header that displays a message n times using recursion.

```
public static void displayMessage(String message, int times)
```

4.24** (*Summing the digits in an integer using recursion*) Rewrite Exercise 4.2 using recursion.

4.25** (*Summing the series*) Write a recursive method and a nonrecursive method to compute the following function (for $i > 1$):

$$m(i) = \frac{1}{2} + \frac{2}{3} + \cdots + \frac{i}{i + 1}$$

Write a test program that displays the following table:

```
i          m(i)

2          0.5
3          1.1667
...
19         15.4523
20         16.4023
```

chapter

5

ARRAYS

Objectives

- ✦ To describe why an array is necessary in programming (§5.1).
- ✦ To learn the steps involved in using arrays: declaring array reference variables and creating arrays (§§5.2.1-5.2.2).
- ✦ To initialize the values in an array (§5.2.3).
- ✦ To access array elements using indexed variables (§5.2.4).
- ✦ To simplify programming using the JDK 1.5 enhanced for loop (§5.2.5).
- ✦ To declare, create, and initialize an array using an array initializer (§5.2.6).
- ✦ To copy contents from one array to another (§5.3).
- ✦ To develop and invoke methods with array arguments and return value (§§5.4–5.5).
- ✦ To sort an array using the selection sort algorithm (§5.6).
- ✦ To search elements using the linear or binary search algorithm (§5.7).
- ✦ To declare and create multidimensional arrays (§5.8.1).
- ✦ To obtain the lengths of multidimensional arrays (§5.8.2).
- ✦ To create ragged arrays (§5.8.3).

5.1 Introduction

Often you will have to store a large number of values during the execution of a program. Suppose, for instance, that you want to read one hundred numbers, compute their average, and find out how many numbers are above the average. Your program first reads the numbers and computes their average, and then compares each number with the average to determine whether it is above the average. The numbers must all be stored in variables in order to accomplish this task. You have to declare one hundred variables and repetitively write almost identical code one hundred times. From the standpoint of practicality, it is impossible to write a program this way. An efficient, organized approach is needed. Java and all other high-level languages provide a data structure, the *array*, which stores a fixed-size sequential collection of elements of identical types.

5.2 Array Basics

This section introduces how to declare array variables, create arrays, and process arrays.

5.2.1 Declaring Array Variables

To use an array in a program, you must declare a variable to reference the array and specify the type of array the variable can reference. Here is the syntax for declaring an array variable:

```
dataType[] arrayRefVar;
```

or

```
dataType arrayRefVar[]; // This style is correct, but not preferred
```

The following code snippets are examples of this syntax:

```
double[] myList;
```

or

```
double myList[]; // This style is correct, but not preferred
```

> ### 🌱 NOTE
>
> The style `dataType[] arrayRefVar` is preferred. The style `dataType arrayRefVar[]` comes from the C language and was adopted in Java to accommodate C programmers.

5.2.2 Creating Arrays

Unlike declarations for primitive data type variables, the declaration of an array variable does not allocate any space in memory for the array. Only a storage location for the reference to an array is created. If a variable does not reference to an array, the value of the variable is `null`. You cannot assign elements to an array unless it has already been created. After an array variable is declared, you can create an array by using the `new` operator with the following syntax:

```
arrayRefVar = new dataType[arraySize];
```

This statement does two things: (1) it creates an array using new `dataType[arraySize]`; (2) it assigns the reference of the newly created array to the variable `arrayRefVar`.

Declaring an array variable, creating an array, and assigning the reference of the array to the variable can be combined in one statement, as shown below:

```
dataType[] arrayRefVar = new dataType[arraySize];
```

or

```
dataType arrayRefVar[] = new dataType[arraySize];
```

Here is an example of such a statement:

```
double[] myList = new double[10];
```

This statement declares an array variable, `myList`, creates an array of ten elements of `double` type, and assigns its reference to `myList`, as shown in Figure 5.1.

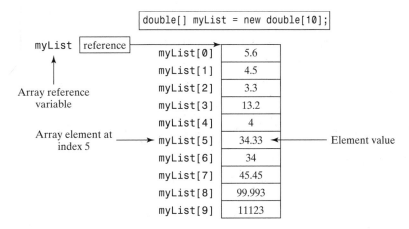

FIGURE **5.1**   *The array* `myList` *has ten elements of* `double` *type and* `int` *indices from 0 to 9.*

> 🌿 **NOTE**
>
> An array variable that appears to hold an array actually contains a reference to that array. Strictly speaking, an array variable and an array are different, but most of the time the distinction between them can be ignored. Thus it is all right to say, for simplicity, that `myList` is an array, instead of stating, at greater length, that `myList` is a variable that contains a reference to an array of ten double elements. When the distinction makes a subtle difference, the longer phrase should be used.

array vs. array variable

5.2.3   Array Size and Default Values

When space for an array is allocated, the array size must be given, to specify the number of elements that can be stored in it. The size of an array cannot be changed after the array is created. Size can be obtained using `arrayRefVar.length`. For example, `myList.length` is 10.

array length

When an array is created, its elements are assigned the *default value* of 0 for the numeric primitive data types, `'\u0000'` for char types, and `false` for `boolean` types.

default values

5.2.4   Array Indexed Variables

The array elements are accessed through the index. Array indices are *0-based*; that is, they start from 0 to `arrayRefVar.length-1`. In the example in Figure 5.1, `myList` holds ten `double` values and the indices are from 0 to 9.

array index
0-based

index variables

Each element in the array is represented using the following syntax, known as an *indexed variable*:

```
arrayRefVar[index];
```

For example, myList[9] represents the last element in the array myList.

 NOTE

In Java, an array index must be an integer or an integer expression. In many other languages, such as Ada and Pascal, the index can be either an integer or another type of value.

 CAUTION

Some languages use parentheses to reference an array element, as in myList(9). But Java uses brackets, as in myList[9].

After an array is created, an indexed variable can be used in the same way as a regular variable. For example, the following code adds the value in myList[0] and myList[1] to myList[2]:

```
myList[2] = myList[0] + myList[1];
```

The following loop assigns 0 to myList[0], 1 to myList[1], ..., and 9 to myList[9]:

```
for (int i = 0; i < myList.length; i++)
  myList[i] = i;
```

5.2.5   Enhanced for Loop (JDK 1.5 Feature)

JDK 1.5 introduced a new for loop that enables you to traverse the complete array sequentially without using an index variable. For example, the following code displays all the elements in the array myList:

```
for (double value: myList)
  System.out.println(value);
```

In general, the syntax is

```
for (elementType value: arrayRefVar) {
  // Process the value
}
```

You still have to use an index variable if you wish to traverse the array in a different order or change the elements in the array.

5.2.6   Array Initializers

array initializer

Java has a shorthand notation, known as the *array initializer*, which combines declaring an array, creating an array, and initializing in one statement using the following syntax:

```
dataType[] arrayRefVar = {literal0, literal1, ..., literalk};
```

For example,

```
double[] myList = {1.9, 2.9, 3.4, 3.5};
```

This statement declares, creates, and initializes the array `myList` with four elements, which is equivalent to the statements shown below:

```
double[] myList = new double[4];
myList[0] = 1.9;
myList[1] = 2.9;
myList[2] = 3.4;
myList[3] = 3.5;
```

CAUTION

The `new` operator is not used in the array initializer syntax. Using an array initializer, you have to declare, create, and initialize the array all in one statement. Splitting it would cause a syntax error. Thus the next statement is wrong:

```
double[] myList;
myList = {1.9, 2.9, 3.4, 3.5};
```

NOTE

You can also create and initialize an array using the following syntax:

```
new dataType[]{literal0, literal1, ..., literalk};
```

For example, these statements are correct:

```
double[] myList = {1, 2, 3};
// Some time later you need assign a new array to myList
myList = new double[]{1.9, 2.9, 3.4, 3.5};
```

When processing array elements, you will often use a `for` loop. Here are the reasons why:

◆ All of the elements in an array are of the same type. They are evenly processed in the same fashion by repeatedly using a loop.

◆ Since the size of the array is known, it is natural to use a `for` loop.

EXAMPLE 5.1 TESTING ARRAYS

Problem

Write a program that reads six integers, finds the largest of them, and counts its occurrences. Suppose that you entered 3, 5, 2, 5, 5, 5, as shown in Figure 5.2; the program finds that the largest is 5 and the occurrence count for 5 is 4.

Solution

An intuitive solution is to first read the numbers and store them in an array, then find the largest number in the array, and finally count the occurrences of the largest number in the array.

EXAMPLE 5.1 (CONTINUED)

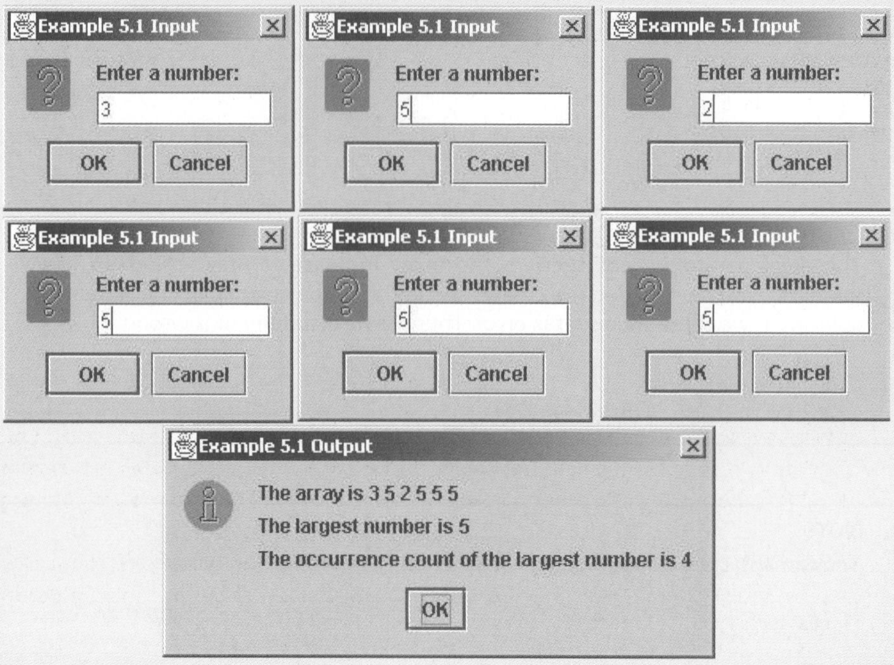

FIGURE 5.2   *The program finds the largest number and counts its occurrences.*

LISTING 5.1   **TestArray.java (Using Arrays)**

```
 1 import javax.swing.JOptionPane;
 2
 3 public class TestArray {
 4   /** Main method */
 5   public static void main(String[] args) {
 6     final int TOTAL_NUMBERS = 6;
 7     int[] numbers = new int[TOTAL_NUMBERS];
 8
 9     // Read all numbers
10     for (int i = 0; i < numbers.length; i++) {
11       String numString = JOptionPane.showInputDialog(null,
12         "Enter a number:",
13         "Example 5.1 Input", JOptionPane.QUESTION_MESSAGE);
14
15       // Convert string into integer
16       numbers[i] = Integer.parseInt(numString);
17     }
18
19     // Find the largest
20     int max = numbers[0];
21     for (int i = 1; i < numbers.length; i++) {
22       if (max < numbers[i])
23         max = numbers[i];
24     }
25
26     // Find the occurrence of the largest number
27     int count = 0;
28     for (int i = 0; i < numbers.length; i++) {
29       if (numbers[i] == max) count++;
30     }
31
```

create array

store numbers

update max

count occurrence

EXAMPLE 5.1 (CONTINUED)

```
32      // Prepare the result
33      String output = "The array is ";
34      for (int i = 0; i < numbers.length; i++) {
35        output += numbers[i] + " ";
36      }
37
38      output += "\nThe largest number is " + max;
39      output += "\nThe occurrence count of the largest number "
40        + "is " + count;
41
42      // Display the result
43      JOptionPane.showMessageDialog(null, output,
44        "Example 5.1 Output", JOptionPane.INFORMATION_MESSAGE);
45    }
46 }
```

prepare output

output

Review

The program declares and creates an array of six integers (Line 7). It finds the largest number in the array (Lines 20–24), counts its occurrences (Lines 27–30), and displays the result (Lines 32–44). To display the array, you need to display each element in the array using a loop.

Without using the numbers array, you would have to declare a variable for each number entered, because all the numbers are compared to the largest number to count its occurrences after it is found.

✿ CAUTION

Accessing an array out of bounds is a common programming error, which throws a runtime ArrayIndexOutOfBoundsException. To avoid it, make sure that you do not use an index beyond arrayRefVar.length - 1.

Programmers often mistakenly reference the first element in an array with index 1, so that the index of the tenth element becomes 10. This is called the *off-by-one error*.

ArrayIndexOutOfBounds
Exception

off-by-one error

EXAMPLE 5.2 ASSIGNING GRADES

Problem

Write a program that reads student scores, gets the best score, and then assigns grades based on the following scheme:

Grade is A if score is $>=$ best -10;

Grade is B if score is $>=$ best -20;

Grade is C if score is $>=$ best -30;

Grade is D if score is $>=$ best -40;

Grade is F otherwise.

The program prompts the user to enter the total number of students, then prompts the user to enter all of the scores, and concludes by displaying the grades.

EXAMPLE 5.2 (CONTINUED)

Solution

The program reads the scores, then finds the best score, and finally assigns grades to the students based on the preceding scheme. Listing 5.2 gives the solution to the problem. The output of a sample run of the program is shown in Figure 5.3.

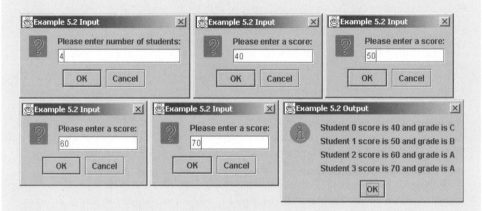

FIGURE 5.3 *The program receives the number of students and their scores, and then assigns grades.*

LISTING 5.2 AssignGrade.java (Assigning Grades)

```java
 1 import javax.swing.JOptionPane;
 2
 3 public class AssignGrade {
 4   /** Main method */
 5   public static void main(String[] args) {
 6     int numberOfStudents = 0; // The number of students
 7     int[] scores; // Array scores
 8     int best = 0; // The best score
 9     char grade; // The grade
10
11     // Get number of students
12     String numberOfStudentsString = JOptionPane.showInputDialog(
13       null, "Please enter number of students:",
14       "Example 5.2 Input", JOptionPane.QUESTION_MESSAGE);
15
16     // Convert string into integer
17     numberOfStudents = Integer.parseInt(numberOfStudentsString);
18
19     // Create array scores
20     scores = new int[numberOfStudents];
21
22     // Read scores and find the best score
23     for (int i = 0; i < scores.length; i++) {
24       String scoreString = JOptionPane.showInputDialog(null,
25         "Please enter a score:",
26         "Example 5.2 Input", JOptionPane.QUESTION_MESSAGE);
27
28       // Convert string into integer
29       scores[i] = Integer.parseInt(scoreString);
30       if (scores[i] > best)
31         best = scores[i];
32     }
33
```

declare array — (line 7)

create array — (line 20)

get a score — (line 24)

update best — (line 30)

EXAMPLE 5.2 (CONTINUED)

```
34     // Declare and initialize output string
35     String output = "";
36
37     // Assign and display grades
38     for (int i = 0; i < scores.length; i++) {
39       if (scores[i] >= best - 10)
40         grade = 'A';
41       else if (scores[i] >= best - 20)
42         grade = 'B';
43       else if (scores[i] >= best - 30)
44         grade = 'C';
45       else if (scores[i] >= best - 40)
46         grade = 'D';
47       else
48         grade = 'F';
49
50       output += "Student " + i + " score is " +
51         scores[i] + " and grade is " + grade + "\n";
52     }
53
54     // Display the result
55     JOptionPane.showMessageDialog(null, output,
56       "Example 5.2 Output", JOptionPane.INFORMATION_MESSAGE);
57   }
58 }
```

assign grade

Review

The program declares scores as an array of int type in order to store the students' scores (Line 7). After the user enters the number of students into numberOfStudents in Lines 12–17, an array with the size numberOfStudents is created in Line 20. The size of the array is set at runtime; it cannot be changed once the array is created.

The array is not needed to find the best score, but it is needed to keep all of the scores so that grades can be assigned later on, and it is needed when scores are printed along with the students' grades.

5.3   Copying Arrays

Often, in a program, you need to duplicate an array or a part of an array. In such cases you could attempt to use the assignment statement (=), as follows:

```
list2 = list1;
```

This statement does not copy the contents of the array referenced by list1 to list2, but merely copies the reference value from list1 to list2. After this statement, list1 and list2 reference to the same array, as shown in Figure 5.4. The array previously referenced by list2 is no longer referenced; it becomes garbage, which will be automatically collected by the Java Virtual Machine.

copy reference

In Java, you can use assignment statements to copy primitive data type variables, but not arrays. Assigning one array variable to another array variable actually copies one reference to another and makes both variables point to the same memory location.

There are three ways to copy arrays:

✦ Use a loop to copy individual elements.

✦ Use the static arraycopy method in the System class.

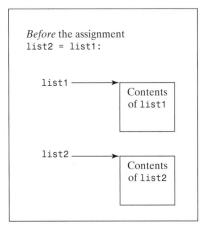
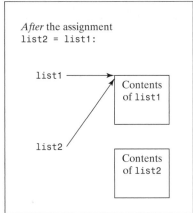

FIGURE 5.4 *Before the assignment statement,* `list1` *and* `list2` *point to separate memory locations. After the assignment, the reference of the* `list1` *array is passed to* `list2`.

✦ Use the `clone` method to copy arrays; this will be introduced in Chapter 8, "Inheritance and Polymorphism."

You can write a loop to copy every element from the source array to the corresponding element in the target array. The following code, for instance, copies `sourceArray` to `targetArray` using a `for` loop:

```
int[] sourceArray = {2, 3, 1, 5, 10};
int[] targetArray = new int[sourceArray.length];
for (int i = 0; i < sourceArray.length; i++)
  targetArray[i] = sourceArray[i];
```

arraycopy method

Another approach is to use the `arraycopy` method in the `java.lang.System` class to copy arrays instead of using a loop. The syntax for `arraycopy` is as follows:

```
arraycopy(sourceArray, src_pos, targetArray, tar_pos, length);
```

The parameters `src_pos` and `tar_pos` indicate the starting positions in `sourceArray` and `targetArray`, respectively. The number of elements copied from `sourceArray` to `target-Array` is indicated by `length`. For example, you can rewrite the loop using the following statement:

```
System.arraycopy(sourceArray, 0, targetArray, 0, sourceArray.length);
```

The `arraycopy` method does not allocate memory space for the target array. The target array must have already been created with its memory space allocated. After the copying takes place, `targetArray` and `sourceArray` have the same content but independent memory locations.

 NOTE

The `arraycopy` method violates the Java naming convention. By convention, this method should be named `arrayCopy`.

5.4 Passing Arrays to Methods

Just as you can pass the primitive type values to methods, you can also pass the arrays to methods. For example, the following method displays the elements in an `int` array:

```
public static void printArray(int[] array) {
  for (int i = 0; i < array.length; i++) {
    System.out.print(array[i] + " ");
  }
}
```

You can invoke it by passing an array. For example, the next statement invokes the `printArray` method to display 3, 1, 2, 6, 4, and 2:

```
printArray(new int[]{3, 1, 2, 6, 4, 2});
```

 NOTE

The preceding statement creates an array using the following syntax:

```
new dataType[]{literal0, literal1, . . . , literalk};
```

There is no explicit reference variable for the array. Such array is called an anonymous array.

anonymous array

Java uses *pass by value* to pass arguments to a method. There are important differences between passing the values of variables of primitive data types and passing arrays.

pass by value

✦ For an argument of a primitive type, the argument's value is passed.

✦ For an argument of an array type, the value of the argument contains a reference to an array; this reference is passed to the method.

Take the following code for example:

```
public class Test {
  public static void main(String[] args) {
    int x = 1; // x represents an int value
    int[] y = new int[10]; // y represents an array of int values

    m(x, y); // Invoke m with arguments x and y

    System.out.println("x is " + x);
    System.out.println("y[0] is " + y[0]);
  }

  public static void m(int number, int[] numbers) {
    number = 1001; // Assign a new value to number
    numbers[0] = 5555; // Assign a new value to numbers[0]
  }
}
```

You will see that after m is invoked, x remains 1, but y[0] is 5555. This is because y and numbers reference to the same array, although y and numbers are independent variables, as illustrated in Figure 5.5. When invoking m(x, y), the values of x and y are passed to number and numbers. Since y contains the reference value to the array, numbers now contains the same reference value to the same array.

 NOTE

The JVM stores the array in an area of memory called *heap*, which is used for dynamic memory allocation where blocks of memory are allocated and freed in an arbitrary order.

heap

The following is another example that shows the difference between passing a primitive data type value and an array reference variable to a method.

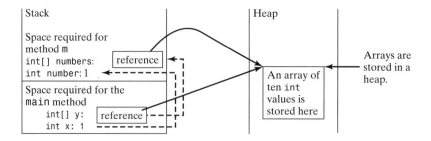

FIGURE 5.5   *The primitive type value in* x *is passed to* number, *and the reference value in* y *is passed to* numbers.

EXAMPLE 5.3 PASSING ARRAYS AS ARGUMENTS

Problem

Write two methods for swapping elements in an array. The first method, named swap, fails to swap two int arguments. The second method, named swapFirstTwoInArray, successfully swaps the first two elements in the array argument.

Solution

Listing 5.3 gives the program. Figure 5.6 shows a sample run of the program.

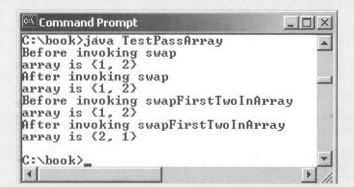

FIGURE 5.6   *The program attempts to swap two elements using the* swap *method and the* swapFirstTwoInArray *method.*

LISTING 5.3   TestPassArray.java (Passing Array Arguments)

```
1 public class TestPassArray {
2   /** Main method */
3   public static void main(String[] args) {
4     int[] a = {1, 2};
5
6     // Swap elements using the swap method
7     System.out.println("Before invoking swap");
8     System.out.println("array is {" + a[0] + ", " + a[1] + "}");
9     swap(a[0], a[1]);
10    System.out.println("After invoking swap");
11    System.out.println("array is {" + a[0] + ", " + a[1] + "}");
12
```

false swap

EXAMPLE 5.3 (CONTINUED)

```
13    // Swap elements using the swapFirstTwoInArray method
14    System.out.println("Before invoking swapFirstTwoInArray");
15    System.out.println("array is {" + a[0] + ", " + a[1] + "}");
16    swapFirstTwoInArray(a);
17    System.out.println("After invoking swapFirstTwoInArray");
18    System.out.println("array is {" + a[0] + ", " + a[1] + "}");
19  }
20
21  /** Swap two variables */
22  public static void swap(int n1, int n2) {
23    int temp = n1;
24    n1 = n2;
25    n2 = temp;
26  }
27
28  /** Swap the first two elements in the array */
29  public static void swapFirstTwoInArray(int[] array) {
30    int temp = array[0];
31    array[0] = array[1];
32    array[1] = temp;
33  }
34 }
```

swap array elements

Review

As shown in Figure 5.6, the two elements are not swapped using the swap method. However, they are swapped using the swapFirstTwoInArray method. Since the parameters in the swap method are primitive type, the values of a[0] and a[1] are passed to n1 and n2 inside the method when invoking swap(a[0], a[1]). The memory locations for n1 and n2 are independent of the ones for a[0] and a[1]. The contents of the array are not affected by this call. This is pictured in Figure 5.7.

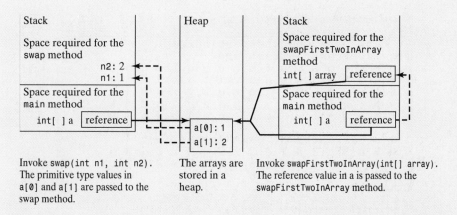

FIGURE 5.7   *When passing an array to a method, the reference of the array is passed to the method.*

The parameter in the swapFirstTwoInArray method is an array. As shown in Figure 5.7, the reference of the array is passed to the method. Thus the variables a (outside the method) and array (inside the method) both refer to the same array in the same memory location. Therefore, swapping array[0] with array[1] inside the method swapFirst TwoInArray is the same as swapping a[0] with a[1] outside of the method.

5.5 Returning an Array from a Method

You can pass arrays to invoke a method. A method may also return an array. For example, the method shown below returns an array that is the reversal of another array:

create array

return array

```
1 public static int[] reverse(int[] list) {
2   int[] result = new int[list.length];
3
4   for (int i = 0, j = result.length - 1;
5        i < list.length; i++, j--) {
6     result[j] = list[i];
7   }
8
9   return result;
10 }
```

Line 2 creates a new array result. Lines 4–7 copies elements from array list to array result. Line 9 returns the array. For example, the following statement returns a new array list2 with elements 6, 5, 4, 3, 2, 1:

```
int[] list1 = {1, 2, 3, 4, 5, 6};
int[] list2 = reverse(list1);
```

EXAMPLE 5.4 COUNTING THE OCCURRENCES OF EACH LETTER

Problem

Write a program that does the following:

1. Generate one hundred lowercase letters randomly and assign them to an array of characters.

2. Count the occurrences of each letter in the array.

   Figure 5.8 shows a sample run of the program.

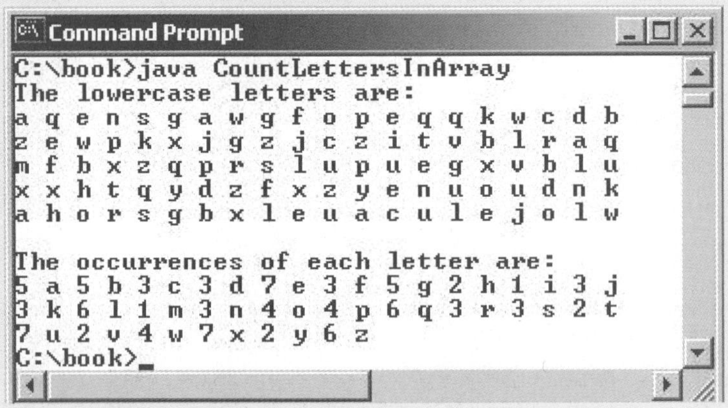

FIGURE 5.8 *The program generates one hundred lowercase letters randomly and counts the occurrences of each letter.*

Solution

1. You can obtain a random letter by using the getRandomLowerCaseLetter() method in the RandomCharacter class on page 142.

2. To count the occurrences of each letter in the array, create an array, say counts of twenty-six int values, each of which counts the occurrences of a letter. That is, counts[0] counts the number of a's, counts[1] counts the number of b's, and so on.

5.7   Searching Arrays

Searching is the process of looking for a specific element in an array; for example, discovering whether a certain score is included in a list of scores. Searching, like sorting, is a common task in computer programming. There are many algorithms and data structures devoted to searching. In this section, two commonly used approaches are discussed, *linear search* and *binary search*.

5.7.1   The Linear Search Approach

The *linear search* approach compares the key element key with each element in the array. The method continues to do so until the key matches an element in the array or the array is exhausted without a match being found. If a match is made, the linear search returns the index of the element in the array that matches the key. If no match is found, the search returns - 1. The linearSearch method in Listing 5.6 gives the solution.

linear search

LISTING 5.6   LinearSearch.java (Linear Search)

```
1 public class LinearSearch {
2   /** The method for finding a key in the list */
3   public static int linearSearch(int[] list, int key) {
4     for (int i = 0; i < list.length; i++)
5       if (key == list[i])
6         return i;
7     return - 1;
8   }
9 }
```

Please trace the method using the following statements:

```
int[] list = {1, 4, 4, 2, 5, -3, 6, 2};
int i = linearSearch(list, 4);  //  returns 1
int j = linearSearch(list, -4); // returns - 1
int k = linearSearch(list, -3); // returns 5
```

The linear search method compares the key with each element in the array. The elements in the array can be in any order. On average, the algorithm will have to compare half of the elements in an array. Since the execution time of a linear search increases linearly as the number of array elements increases, linear search is inefficient for a large array.

5.7.2   The Binary Search Approach

Binary search is the other common search approach. For binary search to work, the elements in the array must already be ordered. Without loss of generality, assume that the array is in ascending order. The binary search first compares the key with the element in the middle of the array. Consider the following three cases:

binary search

✦ If the key is less than the middle element, you only need to search the key in the first half of the array.

✦ If the key is equal to the middle element, the search ends with a match.

✦ If the key is greater than the middle element, you only need to search the key in the second half of the array.

Clearly, the binary search method eliminates half of the array after each comparison. Suppose that the array has n elements. For convenience, let n be a power of 2. After the first comparison, there are $n/2$ elements left for further search; after the second comparison, there are $(n/2)/2$ elements left for further search. After the kth comparison, there are $n/2^k$ elements left for further search. When k = log$_2$n, only one element is left in the array, and you only need one more comparison. Therefore, in the worst case, you need $\log_2 n + 1$ comparisons to find an element in the sorted array when using the binary search approach. For a list of 1024 (2^{10}) elements, binary search requires only eleven comparisons in the worst case, whereas a linear search would take 1024 comparisons in the worst case.

The portion of the array being searched shrinks by half after each comparison. Let low and high denote, respectively, the first index and last index of the array that is currently being searched. Initially, low is 0 and high is list.length - 1. Let mid denote the index of the middle element. So mid is (low + high)/2. Figure 5.11 shows how to find key 11 in the list {2, 4, 7, 10, 11, 45, 50, 59, 60, 66, 69, 70, 79} using binary search.

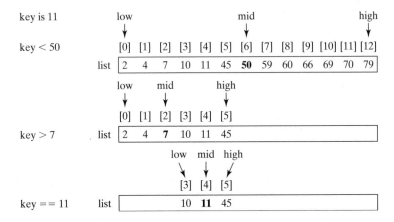

FIGURE 5.11 *Binary search eliminates half of the list from further consideration after each comparison.*

The binary search returns the index of the search key if it is contained in the list. Otherwise, it returns –insertion point −1. The insertion point is the point at which the key would be inserted into the list. For example, the insertion point for key 5 is 2, so the binary search returns −3; the insertion point for key 51 is 7, so the binary search returns −8.

You know how the binary approach works. The task now is to implement it in Java, as shown in Listing 5.7.

LISTING 5.7 **BinarySearch.java (Binary Search)**

```
 1 public class BinarySearch {
 2   /** Use binary search to find the key in the list */
 3   public static int binarySearch(int[] list, int key) {
 4     int low = 0;
 5     int high = list.length - 1;
 6
 7     while (high >= low) {
 8       int mid = (low + high) / 2;
 9       if (key < list[mid])
10         high = mid - 1;
11       else if (key == list[mid])
12         return mid;
13       else
14         low = mid + 1;
15     }
16
17     return -low - 1;
18   }
19 }
```

You start to compare the key with the middle element in the list whose low index is 0 and high index is list.length - 1. If key < list[mid], set the high index to mid - 1; if key == list[mid], a match is found and return mid; if key > list[mid], set the low index to mid + 1.

Continue the search until `low > high` or a match is found. If `low > high`, return `–1 – low`, where `low` is the insertion point.

What happens if `(high >= low)` in Line 7 is replaced by `(high > low)`? The search would miss a possible matching element. Consider a list with just one element. The search would miss the element.

Does the method still work if there are duplicate elements in the list? Yes, as long as the elements are sorted in increasing order in the list. The method returns the index of one of the matching element if the element is in the list.

Please trace the program using the following statements:

```
int[] list = {2, 4, 7, 10, 11, 45, 50, 59, 60, 66, 69, 70, 79};
int i = binarySearch(list, 2); // returns 0
int j = binarySearch(list, 11); // returns 4
int k = binarySearch(list, 12); // returns - 6
```

 NOTE

Linear search is useful for finding an element in a small array or an unsorted array, but it is inefficient for large arrays. Binary search is more efficient, but requires that the array be pre-sorted.

 TIP

Since binary search is frequently used in programming, Java provides several overloaded `binarySearch` methods for searching a key in an array of `int`, `double`, `char`, `short`, `long`, and `float` in the `java.util.Arrays` class. For example, the following code searches the keys in an array of numbers and an array of characters:

```
int[] list = {2, 4, 7, 10, 11, 45, 50, 59, 60, 66, 69, 70, 79};
System.out.println("Index is " +
  java.util.Arrays.binarySearch(list, 11));

char[] chars = {'a', 'c', 'g', 'x', 'y', 'z'};
System.out.println("Index is " +
  java.util.Arrays.binarySearch(chars, 't'));
```

For the `binarySearch` method to work, the array must be pre-sorted in increasing order.

5.7.3 Recursive Implementation of Binary Search (Optional)

The preceding section implements binary search using iteration. You can also implement it using recursion in two overloaded methods, as follows:

```
/** Use binary search to find the key in the list */
public static int recursiveBinarySearch(int[] list, int key) {
  int low = 0;
  int high = list.length - 1;
  return recursiveBinarySearch(list, key, low, high);
}

/** Use binary search to find the key in the list between
    list[low] and list[high] */
public static int recursiveBinarySearch(int[] list, int key,
    int low, int high) {
  if (low > high) // The list has been exhausted without a match
    return -low - 1;
```

```
    int mid = (low + high) / 2;
    if (key < list[mid])
      return recursiveBinarySearch(list, key, low, mid - 1);
    else if (key == list[mid])
      return mid;
    else
      return recursiveBinarySearch(list, key, mid + 1, high);
  }
```

The first method finds a key in the whole list. The second method finds a key in the list with index from low to high.

The first binarySearch method passes the initial array with low = 0 and high = list.length - 1 to the second binarySearch method. The second method is invoked recursively to find the key in an ever-shrinking subarray. It is a common design technique in recursive programming to choose a second method that can be called recursively.

There are two reasons why this is a good example of using recursion. First, using recursion enables you to specify a clear, simple solution for the binary search problem. Second, the number of recursive calls is less than the size of the list. So the solution is reasonably efficient.

5.8 Multidimensional Arrays

Thus far, you have used one-dimensional arrays to model linear collections of elements. You can use a two-dimensional array to represent a matrix or a table. Occasionally, you will need to represent *n*-dimensional data structures. In Java, you can create *n*-dimensional arrays for any integer *n*.

5.8.1 Declaring Variables of Multidimensional Arrays and Creating Multidimensional Arrays

Here is the syntax for declaring a two-dimensional array:

```
dataType[][] arrayRefVar;
```

or

```
dataType arrayRefVar[][]; // This style is correct, but not preferred
```

As an example, here is how you would declare a two-dimensional array variable matrix of int values:

```
int[][] matrix;
```

or

```
int matrix[][]; // This style is correct, but not preferred
```

You can create a two-dimensional array of 5 by 5 int values and assign it to matrix using this syntax:

```
matrix = new int[5][5];
```

Two subscripts are used in a two-dimensional array, one for the row, and the other for the column. As in a one-dimensional array, the index for each subscript is of the int type and starts from 0, as shown in Figure 5.12(a).

To assign the value 7 to a specific element at row 2 and column 1, as shown in Figure 5.12(b), you can use the following:

```
matrix[2][1] = 7;
```

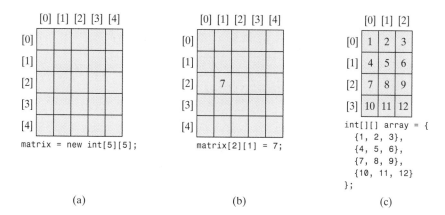

FIGURE 5.12 *The index of each subscript of a multidimensional array is an* `int` *value starting from 0.*

 CAUTION

It is a common mistake to use `matrix[2, 1]` to access the element at row 2 and column 1. In Java, each subscript must be enclosed in a pair of square brackets.

You can also use an array initializer to declare, create, and initialize a two-dimensional array. For example, the following code in (a) creates an array with the specified initial values, as shown in Figure 5.12(c). This is equivalent to the code in (a).

```
int[][] array = {
  {1, 2, 3},
  {4, 5, 6},
  {7, 8, 9},
  {10, 11, 12}
};
```

Equivalent

```
int[][] array = new int[4][3];
array[0][0] = 1; array[0][1] = 2; array[0][2] = 3;
array[1][0] = 4; array[1][1] = 5; array[1][2] = 6;
array[2][0] = 7; array[2][1] = 8; array[2][2] = 9;
array[3][0] = 10; array[3][1] = 11; array[3][2] = 12;
```

(a)   (b)

The way to declare two-dimensional array variables and create two-dimensional arrays can be generalized to declare *n*-dimensional array variables and create *n*-dimensional arrays for $n >= 3$. For example, the following syntax declares a three-dimensional array variable `scores`, creates an array, and assigns its reference to `scores`:

```
double[][][] scores = new double[10][5][2];
```

5.8.2 Obtaining the Lengths of Multidimensional Arrays

A multidimensional array is actually an array in which each element is another array. A two-dimensional array consists of an array of elements, each of which is a one-dimensional array. A three-dimensional array consists of an array of two-dimensional arrays, each of which is an array of one-dimensional arrays. The length of an array x is the number of elements in the array, which can be obtained using `x.length`. `x[0]`, `x[1]`, . . . , and `x[x.length - 1]` are arrays. Their lengths can be obtained using `x[0].length`, `x[1].length`, . . . , and `x[x.length - 1].length`.

For example, suppose `x = new int[3][4]`, `x[0]`, `x[1]`, and `x[2]` are one-dimensional arrays and each contains four elements, as shown in Figure 5.13. `x.length` is 3, and `x[0].length`, `x[1].length` and `x[2].length` are 4.

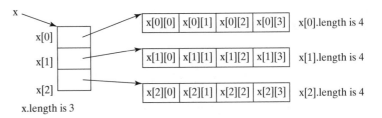

FIGURE 5.13   *A two-dimensional array is a one-dimensional array in which each element is another one-dimensional array.*

Suppose x = new int[2][2][5], x[0] and x[1] are two-dimensional arrays. X[0][0], x[0][1], x[1][0], and x[1][1] are one-dimensional arrays and each contains five elements. x.length is 2, x[0].length and x[1].length are 2, and X[0][0].length, x[0][1].length, x[1][0].length, and x[1][1].length are 5.

5.8.3   Ragged Arrays

ragged array

Each row in a two-dimensional array is itself an array. Thus the rows can have different lengths. An array of this kind is known as a *ragged array*. Here is an example of creating a ragged array:

```
int[][] triangleArray = {
  {1, 2, 3, 4, 5},
  {2, 3, 4, 5},
  {3, 4, 5},
  {4, 5},
  {5}
};
```

As can be seen triangleArray[0].length is 5, triangleArray[1].length is 4, triangle Array[2].length is 3, triangleArray[3].length is 2, and triangleArray[4].length is 1.

If you don't know the values in a ragged array in advance, but know the sizes, say the same as before, you can create a ragged array using the syntax that follows:

```
int[][] triangleArray = new int[5][];
triangleArray[0] = new int[5];
triangleArray[1] = new int[4];
triangleArray[2] = new int[3];
triangleArray[3] = new int[2];
triangleArray[4] = new int[1];
```

You can now assign random values to the array using the following loop:

```
for (int row = 0; row < triangleArray.length; row++)
  for (int column = 0; column < triangleArray[row].length; column++)
    triangleArray[row][column] = (int)(Math.random() * 1000);
```

 NOTE

The syntax new int[5][] for creating an array requires the first index to be specified. The syntax new int[][] would be wrong.

EXAMPLE 5.5 GRADING A MULTIPLE-CHOICE TEST

Problem

Write a program that grades multiple-choice tests. Suppose there are eight students and ten questions, and the answers are stored in a two-dimensional array. Each row records a student's answers to the questions. For example, the following array stores the test:

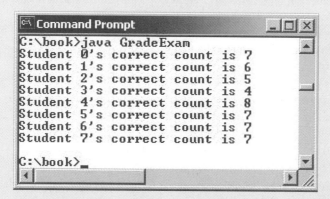

The key is stored in a one-dimensional array, as follows:

Key to the Questions:

	0	1	2	3	4	5	6	7	8	9
Key	D	B	D	C	C	D	A	E	A	D

Your program grades the test and displays the result, as shown in Figure 5.14.

```
C:\book>java GradeExam
Student 0's correct count is 7
Student 1's correct count is 6
Student 2's correct count is 5
Student 3's correct count is 4
Student 4's correct count is 8
Student 5's correct count is 7
Student 6's correct count is 7
Student 7's correct count is 7

C:\book>
```

FIGURE 5.14 *The program grades students' answers to the multiple-choice questions.*

Solution

The program compares each student's answers with the key, counts the number of correct answers, and displays it. Listing 5.8 for the program is shown below.

LISTING 5.8 **GradeExam.java (Grading Exams)**

```
1 public class GradeExam {
2   /** Main method */
3   public static void main(String args[]) {
4     // Students' answers to the questions
```

EXAMPLE 5.5 (CONTINUED)

```
5    char[][] answers = {
6      {'A', 'B', 'A', 'C', 'C', 'D', 'E', 'E', 'A', 'D'},
7      {'D', 'B', 'A', 'B', 'C', 'A', 'E', 'E', 'A', 'D'},
8      {'E', 'D', 'D', 'A', 'C', 'B', 'E', 'E', 'A', 'D'},
9      {'C', 'B', 'A', 'E', 'D', 'C', 'E', 'E', 'A', 'D'},
10     {'A', 'B', 'D', 'C', 'C', 'D', 'E', 'E', 'A', 'D'},
11     {'B', 'B', 'E', 'C', 'C', 'D', 'E', 'E', 'A', 'D'},
12     {'B', 'B', 'A', 'C', 'C', 'D', 'E', 'E', 'A', 'D'},
13     {'E', 'B', 'E', 'C', 'C', 'D', 'E', 'E', 'A', 'D'}};
14
15     // Key to the questions
16     char[] keys = {'D', 'B', 'D', 'C', 'C', 'D', 'A', 'E', 'A', 'D'};
17
18     // Grade all answers
19     for (int i = 0; i < answers.length; i++) {
20       // Grade one student
21       int correctCount = 0;
22       for (int j = 0; j < answers[i].length; j++) {
23         if (answers[i][j] == keys[j])
24           correctCount++;
25       }
26
27       System.out.println("Student " + i + "'s correct count is " +
28         correctCount);
29     }
30   }
31 }
```

Review

The statement in Lines 5–13 declares, creates, and initializes a two-dimensional array of characters and assigns the reference to answers of the char[][] type.

The statement in Line 16 declares, creates, and initializes an array of char values and assigns the reference to keys of the char[][] type.

Each row in the array answers stores a student's answer, which is graded by comparing it with the key in the array keys. The result is displayed immediately after a student's answer is graded.

EXAMPLE 5.6 COMPUTING TAXES USING ARRAYS

Problem

Example 4.4, "Computing Taxes with Methods," simplified Example 3.1, "Computing Taxes." Example 4.4 can be further improved using arrays. Rewrite Example 3.1 using arrays to store tax rates and brackets.

Solution

For each filing status, there are six tax rates. Each rate is applied to a certain amount of taxable income. For example, from the taxable income of $400,000 for a single filer, $6,000 is taxed at 10%, (27950 − 6000) at 15%, (67700 − 27950) at 27%, (141250 − 67700) at 35%, and (400000 − 307050) at 38.6%. The six rates are the same for all filing statuses, which can be represented in the following array:

```
double[] rates = {0.10, 0.15, 0.27, 0.30, 0.35, 0.386};
```

EXAMPLE 5.6 (CONTINUED)

The brackets for each rate for all the filing statuses can be represented in a two-dimensional array as follows:

```
int[][] brackets = {
  {6000, 27950, 67700, 141250, 307050}, // Single filer
  {12000, 46700, 112850, 171950, 307050}, // married jointly
  {6000, 23350, 56425, 85975, 153525}, // married separately
  {10000, 37450, 96700, 156600, 307050} // head of household
};
```

Suppose the taxable income is $400,000 for single filers, the tax can be computed as follows:

```
brackets[0][0] * rates[0] +
(brackets[0][1] - brackets[0][0]) * rates[1] +
(brackets[0][2] - brackets[0][1]) * rates[2] +
(brackets[0][3] - brackets[0][2]) * rates[3] +
(brackets[0][4] - brackets[0][3]) * rates[4] +
(400000 - brackets[0][4]) * rates[5]
```

Listing 5.9 gives the solution to the program.

LISTING 5.9 ComputeTax.java (Computing Tax)

```
1 import javax.swing.JOptionPane;
2
3 public class ComputeTax {
4   public static void main(String[] args) {
5     // Prompt the user to enter filing status
6     String statusString = JOptionPane.showInputDialog(
7       "Enter the filing status:\n" +
8       "(0-single filer, 1-married jointly,\n" +
9       "2-married separately, 3-head of household)");
10    int status = Integer.parseInt(statusString);
11
12    // Prompt the user to enter taxable income
13    String incomeString = JOptionPane.showInputDialog(
14      "Enter the taxable income:");
15    double income = Double.parseDouble(incomeString);
16
17    // Compute and display the result
18    JOptionPane.showMessageDialog(null, "Tax is " +
19      (int)(computeTax(status, income) * 100) / 100.0);
20  }
21
22  public static double computeTax(int status, double income) {
23    double[] rates = {0.10, 0.15, 0.27, 0.30, 0.35, 0.386};
24
25    int[][] brackets = {
26      {6000, 27950, 67700, 141250, 307050}, // Single filer
27      {12000, 46700, 112850, 171950, 307050}, // Married jointly
28      {6000, 23350, 56425, 85975, 153525}, // Married separately
29      {10000, 37450, 96700, 156600, 307050} // Head of household
30    };
31
32    double tax = 0; // Tax to be computed
33
34    // Compute tax in the first bracket
35    if (income <= brackets[status][0])
36      return tax = income * rates[0]; // Done
37    else
38      tax = brackets[status][0] * rates[0];
```

EXAMPLE 5.6 (CONTINUED)

```
39
40     // Compute tax in the 2nd, 3rd, 4th, and 5th brackets, if needed
41     for (int i = 1; i < brackets[0].length; i++) {
42       if (income > brackets[status][i])
43         tax += (brackets[status][i] - brackets[status][i - 1]) *
44           rates[i];
45       else {
46         tax += (income - brackets[status][i - 1]) * rates[i];
47         return tax; // Done
48       }
49     }
50
51     // Compute tax in the last (i.e., 6th) bracket
52     return tax += (income - brackets[status][4]) * rates[5];
53   }
54 }
```

Review

The computeTax method computes the tax for the taxable income of a given filing status. The tax for the first bracket (0 to brackets[status][0]) is computed in Lines 35–38. The taxes for the second, third, fourth, and fifth brackets are computed in the loop in Lines 41–49. The tax for the last bracket is computed in Line 52.

EXAMPLE 5.7 CALCULATING TOTAL SCORES

Problem

Write a program that calculates the total score for the students in a class. Suppose the scores are stored in a three-dimensional array named scores. The first index in scores refers to a student, the second refers to an exam, and the third refers to a part of the exam. Suppose there are seven students, five exams, and each exam has two parts: a multiple-choice part and a programming part. scores[i][j][0] represents the score on the multiple-choice part for the i's student on the j's exam. scores[i][j][1] represents the score on the programming part for the i's student on the j's exam. Your program displays the total score for each student, as shown in Figure 5.15.

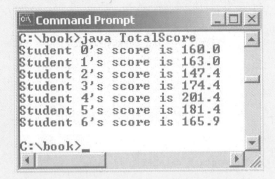

FIGURE 5.15   *The program displays the total score for each student.*

EXAMPLE 5.7 (CONTINUED)

Solution

The program in Listing 5.10 processes the `scores` array for all the students. For each student, it adds the two scores from all exams to `totalScore` and displays `totalScore`.

LISTING 5.10 TotalScore.java (Computing Student Scores)

```
 1 public class TotalScore {
 2   /** Main method */
 3   public static void main(String args[]) {    scores[0][3][1]   scores[0][4][1]
 4     double[][][] scores = {
 5       {{7.5, 20.5}, {9.0, 22.5}, {15, 33.5}, {13, 21.5}, {15, 2.5}},
 6       {{4.5, 21.5}, {9.0, 22.5}, {15, 34.5}, {12, 20.5}, {14, 9.5}},
 7       {{5.5, 30.5}, {9.4, 10.5}, {11, 33.5}, {11, 23.5}, {10, 2.5}},
 8       {{6.5, 23.5}, {9.4, 32.5}, {13, 34.5}, {11, 20.5}, {16, 7.5}},
 9       {{8.5, 25.5}, {9.4, 52.5}, {13, 36.5}, {13, 24.5}, {16, 2.5}},
10       {{9.5, 20.5}, {9.4, 42.5}, {13, 31.5}, {12, 20.5}, {16, 6.5}},
11       {{1.5, 29.5}, {6.4, 22.5}, {14, 30.5}, {10, 30.5}, {16, 5.0}}};
12
13     // Calculate and display total score for each student
14     for (int i = 0; i < scores.length; i++) {              scores[6][4][1]
15       double totalScore = 0;
16       for (int j = 0; j < scores[i].length; j++)
17         for (int k = 0; k < scores[i][j].length; k++)
18           totalScore += scores[i][j][k];
19
20       System.out.println("Student " + i + "'s score is " +
21         totalScore);
22     }
23   }
24 }
```

Review

To understand this example, it is essential to know how data in the three-dimensional array are interpreted. `scores[0]` is a two-dimensional array that stores all the exam scores for the first student. `scores[0][0]` is {7.5, 20.5}, a one-dimensional array, which stores two scores for two parts of the first student's first exam. `scores[0][0][0]` is 7.5, which is the score for the first part of the first student's first exam. `scores[5]` is a two-dimensional array that stores all the exam scores for the sixth student. `scores[5][4]` is {16, 6.5}, a one-dimensional array, which stores two scores for two parts of the sixth student's fifth exam. `scores[5][4][1]` is 6.5, which is the score for the second part of the sixth student's fifth exam.

The statement in Lines 4–11 declares, creates, and initializes a three-dimensional array of `double` values and assigns the reference to `scores` of the `double[][][]` type.

The scores for each student are added in Lines 16–18, and the result is displayed in Lines 20–21. The `for` loop in Line 14 process the scores for all the students.

KEY TERMS

KEY CLASSES AND METHODS

◆ `System.arraycopy(…)` copies the contents from a source array to a target array.

◆ `java.util.Arrays` is a class that contains static methods for manipulating arrays.

◆ `Arrays.sort(array)` sorts an array of `short`, `int`, `long`, `float`, `double`, and `char`.

◆ `Arrays.binarySearch(array, key)` uses the binary search method to search a key in the array of `short`, `int`, `long`, `float`, `double`, and `char`.

CHAPTER SUMMARY

◆ A variable is declared as an array type using the syntax `dataType[] arrayRefVar` or `dataType arrayRefVar[]`. The style `dataType[] arrayRefVar` is preferred, although `dataType arrayRefVar[]` is `legal`.

◆ Unlike declarations for primitive data type variables, the declaration of an array variable does not allocate any space in memory for the array. An array variable is not a primitive data type variable. An array variable contains a reference to an array.

◆ You cannot assign elements to an array unless it has already been created. You can create an array by using the `new` operator with the following syntax: `new dataType[arraySize]`.

◆ Each element in the array is represented using the syntax `arrayRefVar[index]`. An index must be an integer or an integer expression.

◆ After an array is created, its size becomes permanent and can be obtained using `arrayRefVar.length`. Since the index of an array always begins with 0, the last index is always `arrayRefVar.length - 1`. An out-of-bounds error will occur if you attempt to reference elements beyond the bounds of an array.

◆ Programmers often mistakenly reference the first element in an array with index 1, so that the index of the tenth element becomes 10. This is called the *index off-by-one error*.

◆ Java has a shorthand notation, known as the *array initializer*, which combines declaring an array, creating an array, and initializing in one statement using the syntax: `dataType[] arrayRefVar = {literal0, literal1, ..., literalk}`.

◆ When you pass an array argument to a method, you are actually passing the reference of the array; that is, the called method can modify the elements in the caller's original arrays.

◆ You can use arrays of arrays to form multidimensional arrays. For example, a two-dimensional array is declared as an array of arrays using the syntax `dataType[][] arrayRefVar` or `dataType arrayRefVar[][]`.

REVIEW QUESTIONS

Section 5.2 Array Basics

5.1 How do you declare and create an array?

5.2 How do you access elements of an array?

5.3 Is memory allocated when an array is declared? When is the memory allocated for an array? What is the printout of the following code?

```
int x = 30;
int[] numbers = new int[x];
x = 60;
System.out.println("x is " + x);
System.out.println("The size of numbers is " + numbers.length);
```

5.4 Indicate true or false for the following statements:

- ✦ Every element in an array has the same type.

- ✦ The array size is fixed after it is declared.

- ✦ The array size is fixed after it is created.

- ✦ The elements in an array must be of primitive data type.

5.5 Which of the following statements are valid array declarations?

```
int i = new int(30);
double d[] = new double[30];
char[] r = new char(1..30);
int i[] = (3, 4, 3, 2);
float f[] = {2.3, 4.5, 5.6};
char[] c = new char();
int[][] r = new int[2];
```

5.6 What is the array index type? What is the lowest index?

5.7 What is the representation of the third element in an array named a?

5.8 What happens when your program attempts to access an array element with an invalid index?

5.9 Identify and fix the errors in the following code:

```
1 public class Test {
2   public static void main(String[] args) {
3     double[100] r;
4
5     for (int i = 0; i < r.length(); i++);
6       r(i) = Math.random * 100;
7   }
8 }
```

Section 5.3 Copying Arrays

5.10 Use the arraycopy() method to copy the following array to a target array t:

```
int[] source = {3, 4, 5};
```

5.11 Once an array is created, its size cannot be changed. Does the following code resize the array?

```
int[] myList;
myList = new int[10];
// Some time later you want to assign a new array to myList
myList = new int[20];
```

Sections 5.4–5.5

5.12 When an array is passed to a method, a new array is created and passed to the method. Is this true?

5.13   Show the output of the following program:

```
1 public class Test {
2   public static void main(String[] args) {
3     int number = 0;
4     int[] numbers = new int[1];
5
6     m(number, numbers);
7     System.out.println("numbers is " + number +
8       " and numbers[0] is " + numbers[0]);
9   }
10
11   public static void m(int x, int[] y) {
12     x = 3;
13     y[0] = 3;
14   }
15 }
```

5.14   Where are the arrays stored during execution? Show the contents of the stack and heap during and after executing createArray, displayArray, countLetters, displayCounts in Example 5.4,

Section 5.6–5.7

5.15   Use Figure 5.10 as an example to show how to apply the selection sort approach to sort {3.4, 5, 3, 3.5, 2.2, 1.9, 2}.

5.16   What types of array can be sorted using the java.util.Arrays.sort method? Does this sort method create a new array?

5.17   Use Figure 5.11 as an example to show how to apply the binary search approach to search for key 10 and key 12 in list {2, 4, 7, 10, 11, 45, 50, 59, 60, 66, 69, 70, 79}.

5.18   To apply java.util.Arrays.binarySearch(array, key), should the array be sorted in increasing order, in decreasing order, or either?

Section 5.8 Multidimensional Arrays

5.19   Declare and create a 4 × 5 int matrix.

5.20   Can the rows in a two-dimensional array have different lengths?

5.21   What is the output of the following code?

```
int[][] array = new int[5][6];
int[] x = {1, 2};
array[0] = x;
System.out.println("array[0][1] is " + array[0][1]);
```

PROGRAMMING EXERCISES

Section 5.2 Array Basics

5.1   *(Analyzing input)* Write a program that reads ten numbers, computes their average, and finds out how many numbers are above the average.

5.2   *(Alternative solution to Example 5.1, "Testing Arrays")* The solution of Example 5.1 counts the occurrences of the largest number by comparing *each number* with the largest. So you have to use an array to store all the numbers. Another way to solve the problem is to maintain two variables, max and count. max stores the current max number, and count stores its occurrences. Initially, assign the first number to max and 1 to count. Compare each subsequent number with max. If the number is greater than max, assign it to max and reset count to 1. If the number is equal to max, increment count by 1. Use this approach to rewrite Example 5.1.

5.3   *(Reversing the numbers entered)* Write a program that reads ten integers and displays them in reverse order.

5.4   *(Analyzing scores)* Write a program that reads an unspecified number of scores and determines how many scores are above or equal to the average and how many scores are below the average. Enter a negative number to signify the end of the input. Assume that the maximum number of scores is 100.

5.5**   *(Printing unique numbers)* Write a program that reads in ten numbers and display unique numbers. *Hint:* Read a number and store it to an array if it is new. If the number is already in the array, discard it. After the input, the numbers in the array contains all the unique numbers.

5.6*   *(Revising Example 3.10 "Displaying Prime Numbers")* Example 3.10 determines whether a number n is prime by checking whether 2, 3, 4, 5, 6, ..., n/2 is a divisor. If a divisor is found, n is not prime. A more efficient approach to determine whether n is prime is to check whether any of the prime numbers less than or equal to $\sqrt{n}$ can divide n evenly. If not, n is prime. Rewrite Example 3.10 to display the first fifty prime numbers using this approach. You need to use an array to store the prime numbers and later use them to check whether they are possible divisors for n.

5.7*   *(Counting single digits)* Write a program that generates one hundred random integers between 0 and 9 and displays the count for each number. *Hint:* Use `(int)(Math.random() * 10)` to generate a random integer between 0 and 9. Use an array of ten integers, say counts, to store the counts for the number of 0's, 1's, ..., 9's.

Sections 5.4–5.5

5.8   *(Averaging an array)* Write two overloaded methods that return the average of an array with the following headers:

```
public static int average(int[] array);
public static double average(double[] array);
```

Use {1, 2, 3, 4, 5, 6} and {5.0, 4.4, 1.9, 2.9, 3.4, 3.5} to test the methods.

5.9   *(Finding the smallest element)* Write a method that finds the smallest element in an array of integers. Use {1, 2, 4, 5, 10, 100, 2, −22} to test the method.

5.10   *(Finding the index of the smallest element)* Write a method that returns the index of the smallest element in an array of integers. If there are more than one such elements, return the smallest index. Use {1, 2, 4, 5, 10, 100, 2, −22} to test the method.

5.11*   *(Computing deviation)* Exercise 4.15 computes the standard deviation of numbers. This exercise uses a different but equivalent formula to compute the standard deviation of n numbers.

$$mean = \frac{\sum_{i=1}^{n} x_i}{n} = \frac{x_1 + x_2 + \cdots + x_n}{n} \qquad deviation = \sqrt{\frac{\sum_{i=1}^{n} (x_i - mean)^2}{n - 1}}$$

To compute deviation with this formula, you have to store the individual numbers using an array, so that they can be used after the mean is obtained. Use {1, 2, 3, 4, 5, 6, 7, 8, 9, 10} to test the method.

Sections 5.6–5.7

5.12**   *(Recursive selection sort)* Use recursion to rewrite the selection sort in Section 5.6.

5.13* *(Revising selection sort)* In Section 5.6, you used selection sort to sort an array. The selection sort method repeatedly finds the largest number in the current array and swaps it with the last number in the array. Rewrite this example by finding the smallest number and swapping it with the first number in the array.

5.14* *(Bubble sort)* Write a sort method that uses the bubble-sort algorithm. The bubble-sort algorithm makes several passes through the array. On each pass, successive neighboring pairs are compared. If a pair is in decreasing order, its values are swapped; otherwise, the values remain unchanged. The technique is called a *bubble sort* or *sinking sort* because the smaller values gradually "bubble" their way to the top and the larger values sink to the bottom.

The algorithm can be described as follows:

```
boolean changed = true;
do {
  changed = false;
  for (int j = 0; j < list.length - 1; j++)
    if (list[j] > list[j + 1]) {
      swap list[j] with list[j + 1];
      changed = true;
    }
}
while (changed);
```

Clearly, the list is in increasing order when the loop terminates. It is easy to show that the do loop executes at most list.length −1 times.

Use {5.0, 4.4, 1.9, 2.9, 3.4, 2.9, 3.5} to test the method.

5.15** *(Insertion sort)* Write a sort method that uses the insertion-sort algorithm. The insertion-sort algorithm sorts a list of values by repeatedly inserting an unsorted element into a sorted sublist until the whole list is sorted. The algorithm can be described as follows:

```
for (int i = 1; i < list.length; i++) {
  /** The elements in list[0..i - 1] are already sorted. To insert
    * the element list[i] into list[0..i - 1] is to move list[k] into
    * list[k + 1] for k <= i - 1 such that list[k] > list[i] */
  double currentElement = list[i];
  int k = i - 1;
  while (k >= 0 && list[k] > currentElement) {
    list[k + 1] = list[k];
    k--;
  }

  // Insert the current element into list[k + 1]
  list[k + 1] = currentElement;
}
```

Use {5.0, 4.4, 1.9, 2.9, 3.4, 2.9, 3.5} to test the method.

5.16** *(Sorting students)* Write a program that prompts the user to enter the number of students, and student names and their scores, and prints student names in decreasing order of their scores.

5.17** *(Finding the sales amount)* Rewrite Example 3.8, "Finding the Sales Amount," using the binary search approach. Since the sales amount is between 1 and COMMISSION_SOUGHT/0.08, you can use a binary search to improve Example 3.8.

Section 5.8 Multidimensional Arrays

5.18* *(Summing all the numbers in a matrix)* Write a method that sums all the integers in a matrix of integers. Use {{1, 2, 4, 5}, {6, 7, 8, 9}, {10, 11, 12, 13}, {14, 15, 16, 17}} to test the method.

5.19* *(Summing the major diagonal in a matrix)* Write a method that sums all the integers in the major diagonal in a matrix of integers. Use $\{\{1, 2, 4, 5\}, \{6, 7, 8, 9\}, \{10, 11, 12, 13\}, \{14, 15, 16, 17\}\}$ to test the method.

5.20* *(Sorting students on grades)* Rewrite Example 5.5, "Grading a Multiple-Choice Test," to display the students in increasing order of the number of correct answers.

5.21* *(Computing the weekly hours for each employee)* Suppose the weekly hours for all employees are stored in a two-dimensional array. Each row records an employee's seven-day work hours with seven columns. For example, the following array stores the work hours for eight employees. Write a program that displays employees and their total hours in decreasing order of the total hours.

	Su	M	T	W	H	F	Sa
Employee 0	2	4	3	4	5	8	8
Employee 1	7	3	4	3	3	4	4
Employee 2	3	3	4	3	3	2	2
Employee 3	9	3	4	7	3	4	1
Employee 4	3	5	4	3	6	3	8
Employee 5	3	4	4	6	3	4	4
Employee 6	3	7	4	8	3	8	4
Employee 7	6	3	5	9	2	7	9

5.22 *(Adding two matrices)* Write a method to add two matrices. The header of the method is as follows:

```
public static int[][] addMatrix(int[][] a, int[][] b)
```

In order to be added, two matrices must have the same dimensions and the same or compatible types of elements. As shown below, two matrices are added by adding the two elements of the arrays with the same index:

$$\begin{pmatrix} a_{11}\ a_{12}\ a_{13}\ a_{14}\ a_{15} \\ a_{21}\ a_{22}\ a_{23}\ a_{24}\ a_{25} \\ a_{31}\ a_{32}\ a_{33}\ a_{34}\ a_{35} \\ a_{41}\ a_{42}\ a_{43}\ a_{44}\ a_{45} \\ a_{51}\ a_{52}\ a_{53}\ a_{54}\ a_{55} \end{pmatrix} + \begin{pmatrix} b_{11}\ b_{12}\ b_{13}\ b_{14}\ b_{15} \\ b_{21}\ b_{22}\ b_{23}\ b_{24}\ b_{25} \\ b_{31}\ b_{32}\ b_{33}\ b_{34}\ b_{35} \\ b_{41}\ b_{42}\ b_{43}\ b_{44}\ b_{45} \\ b_{51}\ b_{52}\ b_{53}\ b_{54}\ b_{55} \end{pmatrix}$$

$$= \begin{pmatrix} a_{11} + b_{11}\ a_{12} + b_{12}\ a_{13} + b_{13}\ a_{14} + b_{14}\ a_{15} + b_{15} \\ a_{21} + b_{21}\ a_{22} + b_{22}\ a_{23} + b_{23}\ a_{24} + b_{24}\ a_{25} + b_{25} \\ a_{31} + b_{31}\ a_{32} + b_{32}\ a_{33} + b_{33}\ a_{34} + b_{34}\ a_{35} + b_{35} \\ a_{41} + b_{41}\ a_{42} + b_{42}\ a_{43} + b_{43}\ a_{44} + b_{44}\ a_{45} + b_{45} \\ a_{51} + b_{51}\ a_{52} + b_{52}\ a_{53} + b_{53}\ a_{54} + b_{54}\ a_{55} + b_{55} \end{pmatrix}$$

5.23** *(Multiplying two matrices)* Write a method to multiply two matrices. The header of the method is as follows:

```
public static int[][] multiplyMatrix(int[][] a, int[][] b)
```

To multiply matrix a by matrix b, the number of columns in a must be the same as the number of rows in b, and the two matrices must have elements of the same or compatible types. Let c be the result of the multiplication, and a, b, and c are denoted as follows:

$$
\begin{pmatrix}
a_{11}\,a_{12}\,a_{13}\,a_{14}\,a_{15} \\
a_{21}\,a_{22}\,a_{23}\,a_{24}\,a_{25} \\
a_{31}\,a_{32}\,a_{33}\,a_{34}\,a_{35} \\
a_{41}\,a_{42}\,a_{43}\,a_{44}\,a_{45} \\
a_{51}\,a_{52}\,a_{53}\,a_{54}\,a_{55}
\end{pmatrix}
\times
\begin{pmatrix}
b_{11}\,b_{12}\,b_{13}\,b_{14}\,b_{15} \\
b_{21}\,b_{22}\,b_{23}\,b_{24}\,b_{25} \\
b_{31}\,b_{32}\,b_{33}\,b_{34}\,b_{35} \\
b_{41}\,b_{42}\,b_{43}\,b_{44}\,b_{45} \\
b_{51}\,b_{52}\,b_{53}\,b_{54}\,b_{55}
\end{pmatrix}
=
\begin{pmatrix}
c_{11}\,c_{12}\,c_{13}\,c_{14}\,c_{15} \\
c_{21}\,c_{22}\,c_{23}\,c_{24}\,c_{25} \\
c_{31}\,c_{32}\,c_{33}\,c_{34}\,c_{35} \\
c_{41}\,c_{42}\,c_{43}\,c_{44}\,c_{45} \\
c_{51}\,c_{52}\,c_{53}\,c_{54}\,c_{55}
\end{pmatrix}
$$

where

$$c_{ij} = a_{i1} \times b_{1j} + a_{i2} \times b_{2j} + a_{i3} \times b_{3j} + a_{i4} \times b_{4j} + a_{i5} \times b_{5j}$$

5.24* *(TicTacToe board)* Write a program that randomly fills in 0s and 1s into a TicTacToc board, prints the board, and finds the rows, columns, or diagonals with all 0s or 1s. Use a two-dimensional array to represent a TicTacToe board. Here is a sample run of the program:

```
001
001
111
All 0's on row 0
All 1's on row 2
All 1's on column 2
```

5.25** *(Checker board)* Write a program that randomly fills in 0s and 1s into an 8 × 8 checker board, prints the board, and finds the rows, columns, or diagonals with all 0s or 1s. Use a two-dimensional array to represent a checker board. Here is a sample run of the program:

```
10101000
10100001
11100011
10100001
11100111
10000001
10100111
00100001
All 0's on subdiagonal
```

5.26*** *(Playing a TicTacToe game)* In a game of TicTacToe, two players take turns marking an available cell in a 3 × 3 grid with their respective tokens (either X or O). When one player has placed three tokens in a horizontal, vertical, or diagonal row on the grid, the game is over and that player has won. A draw (no winner) occurs when all the cells on the grid have been filled with tokens and neither player has achieved a win. Create a program for playing TicTacToe, as follows:

✦ The program prompts the first player to enter an X token, and then prompts the second player to enter an O token. Whenever a token is entered, the program redisplays the board and determines the status of the game (win, draw, or unfinished).

✦ To place a token, display two dialog boxes to prompt the user to enter the row and the column for the token.

PART II

OBJECT-ORIENTED PROGRAMMING

In Part I, "Fundamentals of Programming," you learned how to write simple Java applications using primitive data types, control statements, methods, and arrays, all of which are features commonly available in procedural programming languages. Java, however, is an object-oriented programming language that uses abstraction, encapsulation, inheritance, and polymorphism to provide great flexibility, modularity, and reusability for developing software. In this part of the book you will learn how to define, extend, and work with classes and their objects.

Chapter 6
Objects and Classes

Chapter 7
Strings

Chapter 8
Inheritance and Polymorphism

Chapter 9
Abstract Classes and Interfaces

Chapter 10
Object-Oriented Modeling

Prerequisites for Part II

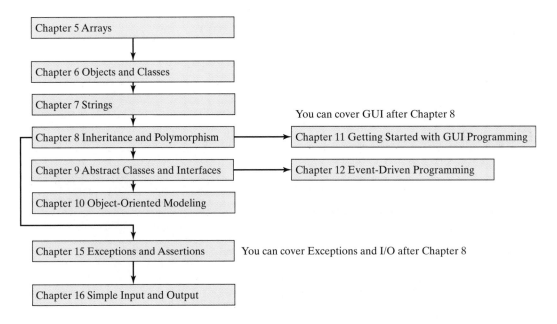

A class defines a type, known as a *reference type*. Any variable of the class type can reference to an instance of the class. The following statement declares the variable `myCircle` to be of the `Circle` type:

reference type

```
Circle myCircle;
```

The variable `myCircle` can reference a `Circle` object. The next statement creates an object and assigns its reference to `myCircle`:

```
myCircle = new Circle();
```

Using the syntax shown below, you can write one statement that combines the declaration of an object reference variable, the creation of an object, and the assigning of an object reference to the variable:

```
ClassName objectRefVar = new ClassName();
```

Here is an example:

```
Circle myCircle = new Circle();
```

The variable `myCircle` holds a reference to a `Circle` object.

 NOTE

An object reference variable that appears to hold an object actually contains a reference to that object. Strictly speaking, an object reference variable and an object are different, but most of the time the distinction between them can be ignored. So it is fine, for simplicity, to say that `myCircle` is a `Circle` object rather than a more long-winded phrase stating that `myCircle` is a variable that contains a reference to a `Circle` object. When the distinction makes a subtle difference, the long phrase should be used.

object vs. object reference variable

 NOTE

Arrays are treated as objects in Java. Arrays are created using the `new` operator. An array variable is actually a variable that contains a reference to an array.

array object

6.4.2 Accessing an Object's Data and Methods

After an object is created, its data can be accessed and its methods invoked using the following dot notation:

◆ `objectRefVar.data` references an object's data.

◆ `objectRefVar.method(arguments)` invokes an object's method.

For example, `myCircle.radius` references the radius of `myCircle`, and `myCircle.findArea()` invokes the `findArea` method of `myCircle`. Methods are invoked as operations on objects.

The data field `radius` is referred to as an *instance variable* because it is dependent on a specific instance. For the same reason, the method `findArea` is referred to as an *instance method*, because you can only invoke it on a specific instance.

instance variable
instance method

 NOTE

Most of the time, you create an object and assign it to a variable. Later you can use the variable to reference the object. Occasionally, an object does not need to be referenced later. In this case, you can create an object without explicitly assigning it to a variable, as shown below:

```
new Circle();
```

or

```
System.out.println("Area is " + new Circle().findArea());
```

The former statement creates a `Circle` object. The latter statement creates a `Circle` object and invokes its `findArea` method to return its area. An object created in this way is known as an *anonymous object*.

anonymous object

EXAMPLE 6.1 DECLARING CLASSES AND CREATING OBJECTS

Problem

Write a program that constructs an object with radius 5 and an object with radius 1 and displays the radius and area of each of the two circles. Change the radius of the second object to 100 and display its new radius and area, as shown in Figure 6.4.

Solution

To avoid a naming conflict with several improved versions of the `Circle` class introduced later in this chapter, the `Circle` class in this example is named `SimpleCircle` and given in Listing 6.1.

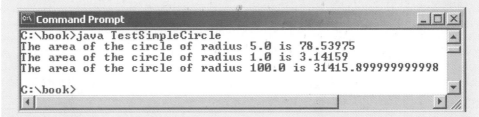

```
Command Prompt
C:\book>java TestSimpleCircle
The area of the circle of radius 5.0 is 78.53975
The area of the circle of radius 1.0 is 3.14159
The area of the circle of radius 100.0 is 31415.899999999998

C:\book>
```

FIGURE **6.4** *The program constructs two circles with radii of 5 and 1, and displays their radii and areas.*

LISTING 6.1 TestSimpleCircle.java (A Simple Circle Class)

```
 1 public class TestSimpleCircle {
 2   /** Main method */
 3   public static void main(String[] args) {
 4     // Create a circle with radius 5.0
 5     SimpleCircle myCircle = new SimpleCircle(5.0);
 6     System.out.println("The area of the circle of radius "
 7       + myCircle.radius + " is " + myCircle.findArea());
 8
 9     // Create a circle with radius 1
10     SimpleCircle yourCircle = new SimpleCircle();
11     System.out.println("The area of the circle of radius "
12       + yourCircle.radius + " is " + yourCircle.findArea());
13
14     // Modify circle radius
15     yourCircle.radius = 100;
16     System.out.println("The area of the circle of radius "
17       + yourCircle.radius + " is " + yourCircle.findArea());
18   }
19 }
20
```

EXAMPLE 6.1 (CONTINUED)

```
21 // Define the circle class with two constructors
22 class SimpleCircle {
23   double radius;
24
25   /** Construct a circle with radius 1 */
26   SimpleCircle() {
27     radius = 1.0;
28   }
29
30   /** Construct a circle with a specified radius */
31   SimpleCircle(double newRadius) {
32     radius = newRadius;
33   }
34
35   /** Return the area of this circle */
36   double findArea() {
37     return radius * radius * 3.14159;
38   }
39 }
```

no-arg constructor

second constructor

Review

The program contains two classes. The first class, TestSimpleCircle, is the main class. Its sole purpose is to test the second class, SimpleCircle. Every time you run the program, the Java runtime system invokes the main method in the main class.

You can put the two classes into one file, but only one class in the file can be a public class. Furthermore, the public class must have the same name as the file name. Therefore, the file name is TestSimpleCircle.java if the TestSimpleCircle and SimpleCircle classes are both in the same file.

The main class contains the main method (Line 3) that creates two objects. The constructor SimpleCircle(5.0) was used to create myCircle with a radius of 5.0 (Line 5), and the constructor SimpleCircle() was used to create yourCircle with a radius of 1.0 (Line 10).

These two objects (referenced by myCircle and yourCircle) have different data but share the same methods. Therefore, you can compute their respective areas by using the findArea() method.

To write the findArea method in a procedural programming language like Pascal, you would pass radius as an argument to the method. But in object-oriented programming, radius and findArea are defined in the same class. The radius is a data member in the SimpleCircle class, which is accessible by the findArea method. In procedural programming languages, data and methods are separated, but in an object-oriented programming language, data and methods are defined together in a class.

The findArea method is an instance method that is always invoked by an instance in which the radius is specified.

There are many ways to write Java programs. For instance, you can combine the two classes in the example into one, as shown below:

```
public class SimpleCircle {
  /** Main method */
  public static void main(String[] args) {
    // Create a circle with radius 5.0
    SimpleCircle myCircle = new SimpleCircle(5.0);
    System.out.println("The area of the circle of radius "
      + myCircle.radius + " is " + myCircle.findArea());

    // Create a circle with radius 1
    SimpleCircle yourCircle = new SimpleCircle();
    System.out.println("The area of the circle of radius "
      + yourCircle.radius + " is " + yourCircle.findArea());
```

EXAMPLE 6.1 (CONTINUED)

```
    // Modify circle radius
    yourCircle.radius = 100;
    System.out.println("The area of the circle of radius "
      + yourCircle.radius + " is " + yourCircle.findArea());
  }

  double radius;

  /** Construct a circle with radius 1 */
  SimpleCircle() {
    radius = 1.0;
  }

  /** Construct a circle with a specified radius */
  SimpleCircle(double newRadius) {
    radius = newRadius;
  }

  /** Return the area of this circle */
  double findArea() {
    return radius * radius * 3.14159;
  }
}
```

Since the combined class has a main method, it can be executed by the Java interpreter. The main method creates myCircle as a SimpleCircle object and then displays radius and finds area in myCircle. This demonstrates that you can test a class by simply adding a main method in the same class.

> **CAUTION**
>
> Recall that you use Math.methodName(arguments) (e.g., Math.pow(3, 2.5)) to invoke a method in the Math class. Can you invoke findArea() using SimpleCircle.findArea()? The answer is no. All the methods used before this chapter are static methods, which are defined using the static keyword. However, findArea() is non-static. It must be invoked from an object using objectRefVar.methodName(arguments) (e.g., myCircle.findArea()). More explanations will be given in Section 6.10, "Static Variables, Constants, and Methods."

invoking methods

6.4.3 The null Value

If a variable of a reference type does not reference any object, the variable holds a special Java value, null. null is a literal just like true and false. While true and false are literals for boolean type variables, null is for reference type variables.

default field values

The default value of a data field is null for a reference type, 0 for a numeric type, false for a boolean type, and '\u0000' for a char type. However, Java assigns no default value to a local variable inside a method. The following code displays the default values of data fields name, age, isScienceMajor, and gender for a Student object:

```
class Student {
  String name; // name has default value null
  int age; // age has default value 0
  boolean isScienceMajor; // isScienceMajor has default value false
  char gender; // c has default value '\u0000'

  public static void main(String[] args) {
    Student student = new Student();
    System.out.println("name? " + student.name);
```

Visibility modifiers are used for the members of the class, not local variables inside the methods. Using a visibility modifier inside a method body would cause a compilation error.

 NOTE

In most cases, the constructor should be public. However, if you want to prohibit the user from creating an instance of a class, you can use a private constructor. For example, there is no reason to create an instance from the Math class because all of the data and methods are static. One solution is to define a dummy private constructor in the class. The Math class cannot be instantiated because it has a private constructor, as follows:

```
private Math() {
}
```

The Math class that comes with the Java system was introduced in Section 4.8, "The Math Class."

6.7   Data Field Encapsulation

Example 6.1 works fine, but it is not a good practice to allow the fields to be modified directly through the object reference (e.g., myCircle.radius = 5). Doing so makes the class difficult to maintain and vulnerable to bugs. Suppose you want to modify the Circle class to ensure that the radius is non-negative after other programs have already used the class. You have to change not only the Circle class, but also the programs that use the Circle class. Such programs are often referred to as *clients*. This is because the clients may have modified the radius directly (e.g., myCircle.radius = -5). To prevent direct modifications of properties through the object reference, you should declare the field private, using the private modifier. This is known as *data field encapsulation*.

client

data field encapsulation

A private data field cannot be accessed by an object through a direct reference outside the class that defines the private field. But often a client needs to retrieve and modify a data field. To make a private data field accessible, provide a *get* method to return the value of the data. To enable a private data field to be updated, provide a *set* method to set a new value.

 NOTE

Colloquially, a get method is referred to as a *getter* (or *accessor*), and a set method is referred to as a *setter* (or *mutator*).

accessor

mutator

A get method has the following signature:

```
public returnType getPropertyName()
```

If the returnType is boolean, the get method should be defined as follows by convention:

```
public boolean isPropertyName()
```

A set method has the following signature:

```
public void setPropertyName(dataType propertyValue)
```

Let us create a new Circle class with a private data field radius and its associated accessor and mutator methods, as follows:

LISTING 6.3   Circle.java (A Circle Class with Private Fields)

```
1 public class Circle {
2   /** The radius of the circle */
3   private double radius;
4
```

encapsulate radius

```
 5   /** Construct a circle with radius 1 */
 6   public Circle() {
 7     radius = 1.0;
 8   }
 9
10   /** Construct a circle with a specified radius */
11   public Circle(double newRadius) {
12     radius = newRadius;
13   }
14
15   /** Return radius */
16   public double getRadius() {
17     return radius;
18   }
19
20   /** Set a new radius */
21   public void setRadius(double newRadius) {
22     radius = (newRadius >= 0) ? newRadius : 0;
23   }
24
25   /** Return the area of this circle */
26   public double findArea() {
27     return radius * radius * 3.14159;
28   }
29 }
```

access method

mutator method

The getRadius() method (Lines 16–18) returns the radius, and the setRadius(newRadius) method (Line 21–23) sets a new radius into the object. If the new radius is negative, 0 is set to the radius in the object. Since these methods are the only ways to read and modify radius, you have total control over how the radius property is accessed. If you have to change the implementation of these methods, you need not change the client programs that use them. This makes the class easy to maintain. For this reason, most of the data fields in this book will be private.

Here is a client program that uses the Circle class to create a Circle object and modifies the radius using the setRadius method.

```
 1 // TestCircle.java : Demonstrate private modifier
 2 public class TestCircle {
 3   /** Main method */
 4   public static void main(String[] args) {
 5     // Create a Circle with radius 5.0
 6     Circle myCircle = new Circle(5.0);
 7     System.out.println("The area of the circle of radius "
 8       + myCircle.getRadius() + " is " + myCircle.findArea());
 9
10     // Increase myCircle's radius by 10%
11     myCircle.setRadius(myCircle.getRadius() * 1.1);
12     System.out.println("The area of the circle of radius "
13       + myCircle.getRadius() + " is " + myCircle.findArea());
14   }
15 }
```

The data field radius is declared private. Private data can only be accessed within their defining class. You cannot use myCircle.radius in the client program. A compilation error would occur if you attempted to access private data from a client.

Suppose you combined TestCircle and Circle into one class by moving the main method in TestCircle into Circle. Could you use myCircle.radius in the main method? See Review Question 6.12 for the answer.

 NOTE

When you compile TestCircle.java, the Java compiler automatically compiles Circle.java if it has not been compiled since the last change.

6.8 Immutable Objects and Classes

If the contents of an object cannot be changed once the object is created, the object is called an *immutable object* and its class is called an *immutable class*. If you delete the set method in the Circle class in the preceding example, the class would be immutable because radius is private and cannot be changed without a set method.

immutable class
immutable object

A class with all private data fields and no mutators is not necessarily immutable. For example, the following class Student has all private data fields and no mutators, but it is mutable:

```java
public class Student {
  private int id;
  private BirthDate birthDate;

  public Student(int ssn, int year, int month, int day) {
    id = ssn;
    birthDate = new BirthDate(year, month, day);
  }

  public int getId() {
    return id;
  }

  public BirthDate getBirthDate() {
    return birthDate;
  }
}

public class BirthDate {
  private int year;
  private int month;
  private int day;

  public BirthDate(int newYear, int newMonth, int newDay) {
    year = newYear;
    month = newMonth;
    day = newDay;
  }

  public void setYear(int newYear) {
    year = newYear;
  }
}
```

As shown in the following code, the data field birthDate is returned using the getBirthDate() method. This is a reference to a BirthDate object. Through this reference, the year of the birth date is changed, which effectively changes the contents of the Student object.

```java
public class Test {
  public static void main(String[] args) {
    Student student = new Student(111223333, 1970, 5, 3);
    BirthDate date = student.getBirthDate();
    date.setYear(2010); // Now the student birth year is changed!
  }
}
```

For a class to be immutable, it must mark all data fields private and provide no mutator methods and no accessor methods that would return a reference to a mutable data field object.

6.9 Passing Objects to Methods

So far, you have learned how to pass arguments of primitive types and array types to methods. You can also pass objects to methods. Like passing an array, passing an object is actually passing the reference of the object. The following code passes the myCircle object as an argument to the printCircle method:

```
public class TestPassObject {
  public static void main(String[] args) {
    Circle myCircle = new Circle(5.0);
    printCircle(myCircle);
  }

  public static void printCircle(Circle c) {
    System.out.println("The area of the circle of radius "
      + c.getRadius() + " is " + c.findArea());
  }
}
```

pass by value

Java uses exactly one mode of passing arguments: *pass by value*. In the preceding code, the value of myCircle is passed to the printCircle method. This value is a reference to a Circle object.

Let us demonstrate the difference between passing a primitive type value and passing a reference value with the program in Listing 6.4:

LISTING 6.4 TestPassObject.java (Object Arguments)

```
1 public class TestPassObject {
2   /** Main method */
3   public static void main(String[] args) {
4     // Create a Circle object with radius 1
5     Circle myCircle = new Circle();
6
7     // Print areas for radius 1, 2, 3, 4, and 5.
8     int n = 5;
9     printAreas(myCircle, n);
10
11    // See myCircle.radius and times
12    System.out.println("\n" + "Radius is " + myCircle.getRadius());
13    System.out.println("n is " + n);
14  }
15
16  /** Print a table of areas for radius */
17  public static void printAreas(Circle c, int times) {
18    System.out.println("Radius \t\tArea");
19    while (times >= 1) {
20      System.out.println(c.getRadius() + "\t\t" + c.findArea());
21      c.setRadius(c.getRadius() + 1);
22      times--;
23    }
24  }
25 }
```

The program passes a Circle object myCircle and an integer value from n to invoke printAreas(myCircle, n) (Line 9), which prints a table of areas for radii 1, 2, 3, 4, and 5, as shown in Figure 6.11.

Figure 6.12 shows the call stack for executing the methods in the program. Note that the objects are stored in a heap.

When passing an argument of a primitive data type, the value of the argument is passed. In this case, the value of n (5) is passed to times. Inside the printAreas method, the content of times is changed; this does not affect the content of n. When passing an argument of a reference type, the reference of the object is passed. In this case, c contains a reference for the object that is also referenced via myCircle. Therefore, changing the properties of the object through c inside

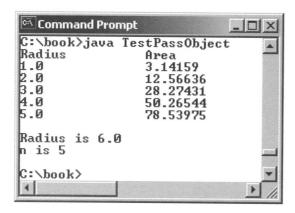

FIGURE 6.11   *The program passes a* `Circle` *object* `myCircle` *and an integer value* `n` *as arguments to the* `printAreas` *method, which displays a table of the areas for radii 1, 2, 3, 4, and 5.*

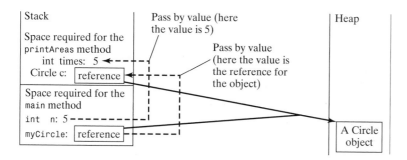

FIGURE 6.12   *The value of* `n` *is passed to* `times`, *and the reference of* `myCircle` *is passed to* `c` *in the* `printAreas` *method.*

the `printAreas` method has the same effect as doing so outside the method through the variable `myCircle`.

6.10   Static Variables, Constants, and Methods

The variable `radius` in the circle classes in the preceding examples is known as an *instance variable*. An instance variable is tied to a specific instance of the class; it is not shared among objects of the same class. For example, suppose that you create the following objects:

```
Circle circle1 = new Circle();
Circle circle2 = new Circle(5);
```

The `radius` in `circle1` is independent of the `radius` in `circle2`, and is stored in a different memory location. Changes made to `circle1`'s `radius` do not affect `circle2`'s `radius`, and vice versa.

If you want all the instances of a class to share data, use *static variables*. Static variables store values for the variables in a common memory location. Because of this common location, all objects of the same class are affected if one object changes the value of a static variable. Java supports static methods as well as static variables. *Static methods* can be called without creating an instance of the class.

Let us modify the `Circle` class by adding a static variable `numberOfObjects` to track the number of circle objects created. The UML of the new circle class named `CircleWithStatic`

instance variable

static variable

static method

UML Notation:
+: public variables or methods
−: private variables or methods
underline: static variables or methods

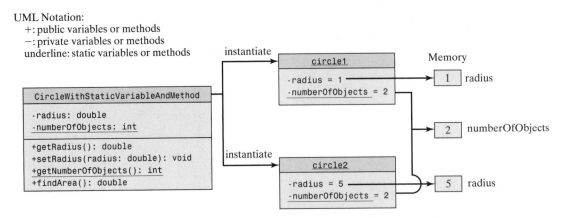

FIGURE **6.13** *The instance variables, which belong to the instances, have memory storage independent of one another. The static variables are shared by all the instances of the same class.*

VariableAndMethod is shown in Figure 6.13. The CircleWithStaticVariableAndMethod class defines the instance variable radius and the static variable numberOfObjects, the instance methods getRadius, setRadius, and findArea, and the static method getNumberOfObjects.

To declare a static variable or a static method, put the modifier static in the variable or method declaration. The static variable numberOfObjects and the static method getNumberOfObjects() can be declared as follows:

declare static variable

```
private static int numberOfObjects;
```

declare static method

```
public static int getNumberObjects() {
  return numberOfObjects;
}
```

When the first object of this class is created, numberOfObjects is 1. When the second object is created, numberOfObjects becomes 2, as shown in Figure 6.13.

To declare a class constant, add the final keyword in the static variable declaration. For example, the constant PI in the Math class is defined as:

declare constant

```
public final static double PI = 3.14159265358979323846;
```

The CircleWithStaticVariableAndMethod class can be declared as follows:

LISTING 6.5 CircleWithStaticVariableAndMethod.java (Static Fields and Methods)

```
 1 public class CircleWithStaticVariableAndMethod {
 2   /** The radius of the circle */
 3   private double radius;
 4
 5   /** The number of the objects created */
 6   private static int numberOfObjects = 0;
 7
 8   /** Construct a circle with radius 1 */
 9   public CircleWithStaticVariableAndMethod() {
10     radius = 1.0;
11     numberOfObjects++;
12   }
13
14   /** Construct a circle with a specified radius */
15   public CircleWithStaticVariableAndMethod(double newRadius) {
16     radius = newRadius;
17     numberOfObjects++;
18   }
19
```

```
20    /** Return radius */
21    public double getRadius() {
22      return radius;
23    }
24
25    /** Set a new radius */
26    public void setRadius(double newRadius) {
27      radius = newRadius;
28    }
29
30    /** Return numberOfObjects */
31    public static int getNumberOfObjects() {
32      return numberOfObjects;
33    }
34
35    /** Return the area of this circle */
36    public double findArea() {
37      return radius * radius * Math.PI;
38    }
39  }
```

Method getNumberOfObjects() in CircleWithStaticVariableAndMethod is a static method. Other examples of static methods are showMessageDialog and showInputDialog in the JOptionPane class, and all the methods in the Math class. In fact, so are all the methods used in Part I of this book, including the main method.

Instance methods (e.g., getRadius, setRadius, and findArea) belong to instances and can only be applied after the instances are created. They are called by the following:

```
objectRefVar.methodName();
```

Static methods (e.g., getNumberOfObjects()) are called by one of these syntaxes:

```
ClassRefVar.methodName(arguments); // Invoked from a class name
objectRefVar.methodName(arguments); // Invoked from a calling object
```

For example, method getNumberOfObjects can be invoked using CircleWithStatic VariableAndMethod.getNumberOfObjects() or circle1.getNumberOfObjects(), where circle1 is a variable declared as CircleWithStaticVariableAndMethod.

TIP

I recommend that you invoke a static method using ClassName.method-Name(arguments). This improves readability because the user can easily recognize the static method invoked with the class name.

The program in Listing 6.6 demonstrates how to use instance and static variables and methods, and illustrates the effects of using them. Its output is shown in Figure 6.14.

```
Command Prompt                                           _ □ ×
C:\book>java TestCircleWithStaticVariableAndMethod
Before creating circle2
circle1 is : radius (1.0) and number of Circle objects (1)

After creating circle2 and modifying circle1's radius to 9
circle1 is : radius (9.0) and number of Circle objects (2)
circle2 is : radius (5.0) and number of Circle objects (2)

C:\book>_
```

FIGURE 6.14 *The program uses the instance variable* radius *as well as the static variable* numberOfObjects. *All of the objects share the same* numberOfObjects.

LISTING 6.6 TestCircleWithStaticVariableAndMethod.java

```java
1 public class TestCircleWithStaticVariableAndMethod {
2   /** Main method */
3   public static void main(String[] args) {
4     // Create circle1
5     CircleWithStaticVariableAndMethod circle1 =
6       new CircleWithStaticVariableAndMethod();
7
8     // Display circle1 BEFORE circle2 is created
9     System.out.println("Before creating circle2");
10    System.out.print("circle1 is : ");
11    printCircle(circle1);
12
13    // Create circle2
14    CircleWithStaticVariableAndMethod circle2 =
15      new CircleWithStaticVariableAndMethod(5);
16
17    // Change the radius in circle1
18    circle1.setRadius(9);
19
20    // Display circle1 and circle2 AFTER circle2 was created
21    System.out.println("\nAfter creating circle2 and modifying " +
22      "circle1's radius to 9");
23    System.out.print("circle1 is : ");
24    printCircle(circle1);
25    System.out.print("circle2 is : ");
26    printCircle(circle2);
27  }
28
29  /** Print circle information */
30  public static void printCircle(
31      CircleWithStaticVariableAndMethod c) {
32    System.out.println("radius (" + c.getRadius() +
33      ") and number of Circle objects (" +
34      c.getNumberOfObjects() + ")");
35  }
36 }
```

The main method creates two circles, circle1 and circle2 (Lines 5, 14). The instance variable radius in circle1 is modified to become 9 (Line 18). This change does not affect the instance variable radius in circle2, since these two instance variables are independent. The static variable numberOfObjects becomes 1 after circle1 is created (Lines 5–6), and it becomes 2 after circle2 is created (Lines 14–15). This change affects all the instances of the CircleWithStaticVariableAndMethod class, since the static variable numberOfObjects is shared by all the instances of the CircleWithStaticVariableAndMethod class.

Since numberOfObjects is private, it cannot be modified. This prevents tampering. For example, the user cannot set numberOfObjects to 100. The only way to make it 100 is to create one hundred objects of the CircleWithStaticVariableAndMethod class.

Note that Math.PI is used to access PI, and that c.numberOfObjects in the printCircle method (Line 34) is used to access numberOfObjects. Math is the class name, and c is an object of the Circle class. To access a constant like PI, you can use either the ClassName.CONSTANTNAME or the objectName.CONSTANTNAME. To access an instance variable like radius, you need to use objectRefVar.variableName.

I recommend that you invoke static variables and methods using ClassName.variable and ClassName.method. This improves readability because the user can easily recognize the static variables and methods. In this example you should replace c.getNumberOfObjects() in Line 34 by CircleWithStaticVariableAndMethod.getNumberOfObjects().

 CAUTION

Static variables and methods can be used from either instance or static methods in the class. However, instance variables and methods can only be used from instance methods, not from static methods, since static variables and methods belong to the class as a whole and not to particular objects. Thus the code given below would be wrong.

```java
public class Foo {
  int i = 5;
  static int k = 2;

  public static void main(String[] args) {
    int j = i; // Wrong because i is an instance variable
    m1(); // Wrong because m1() is an instance method
  }

  public void m1() {
    // Correct since instance and static variables and methods
    // can be used in an instance method
    i = i + k + m2(i, k);
  }

  public static int m2(int i, int j) {
    return (int)(Math.pow(i, j));
  }
}
```

TIP

How do you decide whether a variable or method should be an instance one or a static one? A variable or method that is dependent on a specific instance of the class should be an instance variable or method. A variable or method that is not dependent on a specific instance of the class should be a static variable or method. For example, every circle has its own radius. Radius is dependent on a specific circle. Therefore, `radius` is an instance variable of the `Circle` class. Since the `findArea` method is dependent on a specific circle, it is an instance method. None of the methods in the `Math` class, such as `random`, `pow`, `sin`, and `cos`, is dependent on a specific instance. Therefore, these methods are static methods. The `main` method is static, and can be invoked directly from a class.

instance or static?

6.11   The Scope of Variables

Chapter 4, "Methods," discussed local variables and their scope rules. Local variables are declared and used inside a method locally. This section discusses the scope rules of all the variables in the context of a class.

Instance and static variables in a class are referred to as the *class's variables or data fields*. A variable defined inside a method is referred to as a local variable. The scope of a class's variables is the entire class, regardless of where the variables are declared. A class's variables and methods can be declared in any order in the class, as shown in Figure 6.15(a). The exception is when a data field

```java
public class Circle {
  public double findArea() {
    return radius * radius * Math.PI;
  }

  private double radius = 1;
}
```

```java
public class Foo {
  private int i;
  private int j = i + 1;
}
```

(a) variable radius and method `findArea()`   (b) `i` has to be declared before `j` because
    can be declared in any order   `j`'s initial value is dependent on `i`.

FIGURE 6.15 *Members of a class can be declared in any order, with one exception.*

is initialized based on a reference to another data field. In such cases, the other data field must be declared first, as shown in Figure 6.15(b).

You can declare a class's variable only once, but you can declare the same variable in a method many times in different non-nesting blocks.

If a local variable has the same name as a class's variable, the local variable takes precedence and the class's variable with the same name is hidden. For example, in the following program, x is defined as an instance variable and as a local variable in the method:

```
class Foo {
  int x = 0; // instance variable
  int y = 0;

  Foo() {
  }

  void p() {
    int x = 1; // local variable
    System.out.println("x = " + x);
    System.out.println("y = " + y);
  }
}
```

What is the printout for f.p(), where f is an instance of Foo? The printout for f.p() is 1 for x and 0 for y. Here is why:

✦ x is declared as a data field with the initial value of 0 in the class, but is also defined in the method p() with an initial value of 1. The latter x is referenced in the System.out.println statement.

✦ y is declared outside the method p(), but is accessible inside it.

TIP
As demonstrated in the example, it is easy to make mistakes. To avoid confusion, do not declare a variable twice in a class, except for method parameters and loop control variables in a for loop.

6.12 The this Keyword

hidden variable

Sometimes you need to reference a class's *hidden variable* in a method. For example, a property name is often used as the parameter name in a set method for the property. In this case, you need to reference the hidden property name in the method in order to set a new value to

```
class Foo {
  int i = 5;
  static double k = 0;

  void setI(int i) {
    this.i = i;
  }

  static void setK(double k) {
    Foo.k = k;
  }
}
```

Suppose that f1 and f2 are two objects of Foo.

Invoking f1.setI(10) is to execute
➤f1.i = 10, where *this* is replaced by f1

Invoking f2.setI(45) is to execute
➤f2.i = 45, where *this* is replaced by f2

(a)   (b)

FIGURE 6.16 *The this keyword serves as the proxy for the object that invokes the method.*

it. A hidden static variable can be accessed simply by using the `ClassName.StaticVariable` reference. A hidden instance variable can be accessed by using the keyword `this`, as shown in Figure 6.16(a).

The line `this.i = i` means "assign the value of parameter `i` to the data field `i` of the calling object." The keyword `this` serves as a proxy for the object that invokes the instance method `setI`, as shown in Figure 6.16(b). The line `Foo.k = k` means that the value in parameter `k` is assigned to the static data field `k` of the class, which is shared by all the objects of the class.

The keyword `this` can also be used inside a constructor to invoke another constructor of the same class. For example, you can redefine the `Circle` class as follows:

```
public class Circle {
  private double radius;

  public Circle(double radius) {
    this.radius = radius;        this must be explicitly used to reference the data
  }                              field radius of the object being constructed
  public Circle() {
    this(1.0);
  }                              this is used to invoke another constructor
  public double findArea() {
    return this.radius * this.radius * Math.PI;
  }                    ↓              ↓
}           Every instance variable belongs to an instance represented by this,
            which is normally omitted
```

The line `this(1.0)` invokes the constructor with a `double` value argument in the class.

TIP

If a class has multiple constructors, I recommend that you implement them using `this(arg-list)` as much as possible. In general, a constructor with no or fewer arguments can invoke the constructor with more arguments using `this(arg-list)`. This often simplifies coding and makes the class easier to read and to maintain.

NOTE

Java requires that the `this(arg-list)` statement appear first in the constructor before any other statements.

6.13   Array of Objects

In Chapter 5, "Arrays," arrays of primitive type elements were created. You can also create arrays of objects. For example, the following statement declares and creates an array of ten `Circle` objects:

```
Circle[] circleArray = new Circle[10];
```

To initialize the `circleArray`, you can use a `for` loop like this one:

```
for (int i = 0; i < circleArray.length; i++) {
  circleArray[i] = new Circle();
}
```

An array of objects is actually an *array of reference variables*. So invoking `circleArray[1].findArea()` involves two levels of referencing, as shown in Figure 6.17. `circleArray` references the entire array. `circleArray[1]` references a `Circle` object.

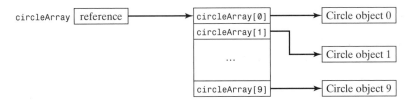

FIGURE 6.17   *In an array of objects, an element of the array contains a reference to an object.*

 NOTE

When an array of objects is created using the new operator, each element is a reference variable with a default value of null.

The example given below demonstrates how to use an array of objects.

EXAMPLE 6.2 SUMMARIZING THE AREAS OF THE CIRCLES

Problem

Write a program that summarizes the areas of an array of circles. The program creates circleArray, an array composed of ten Circle objects; it then initializes circle radii with random values, and displays the total area of the circles in the array.

Solution

Listing 6.7 gives the solution to the problem. The output of a sample run of the program is shown in Figure 6.18.

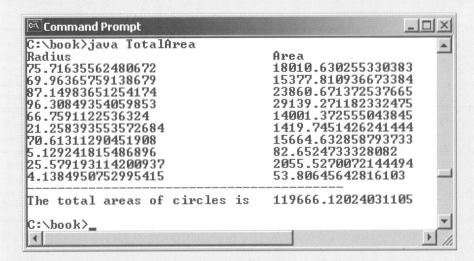

FIGURE 6.18   *The program creates an array of Circle objects, then displays their total area.*

LISTING 6.7   TotalArea.java (Array of Objects)

```
1 public class TotalArea {
2   /** Main method */
3   public static void main(String[] args) {
4     // Declare circleArray
5     Circle[] circleArray;
6
```

EXAMPLE 6.2 (CONTINUED)

```
7       // Create circleArray
8       circleArray = createCircleArray();
9
10      // Print circleArray and total areas of the circles
11      printCircleArray(circleArray);
12    }
13
14    /** Create an array of Circle objects */
15    public static Circle[] createCircleArray() {
16      Circle[] circleArray = new Circle[10];
17
18      for (int i = 0; i < circleArray.length; i++) {
19        circleArray[i] = new Circle(Math.random() * 100);
20      }
21
22      // Return Circle array
23      return circleArray;
24    }
25
26    /** Print an array of circles and their total area */
27    public static void printCircleArray
28        (Circle[] circleArray) {
29      System.out.println("Radius\t\t\t\t" + "Area");
30      for (int i = 0; i < circleArray.length; i++) {
31        System.out.print(circleArray[i].getRadius() + "\t\t" +
32          circleArray[i].findArea() + '\n');
33      }
34
35      System.out.println("----------------");
36
37      // Compute and display the result
38      System.out.println("The total areas of circles is \t" +
39        sum(circleArray));
40    }
41
42    /** Add circle areas */
43    public static double sum(Circle[] circleArray) {
44      // Initialize sum
45      double sum = 0;
46
47      // Add areas to sum
48      for (int i = 0; i < circleArray.length; i++)
49        sum += circleArray[i].findArea();
50
51      return sum;
52    }
53 }
```

Review

The program invokes createCircleArray() (Line 8) to create an array of ten Circle objects. Several Circle classes were introduced in this chapter. This example uses the Circle class introduced in Section 6.7, "Data Field Encapsulation."

The circle radii are randomly generated using the Math.random() method (Line 19). The createCircleObject method returns an array of Circle objects (Line 23). The array is passed to the printCircleArray method, which displays the radii of the total area of the circles.

The sum of the areas of the circle is computed using the sum method (Line 39), which takes the array of Circle objects as the argument and returns a double value for the total area.

6.14 Class Abstraction and Encapsulation

class abstraction

In Chapter 4, "Methods," you learned about method abstraction and used it in program development. Java provides many levels of abstraction. *Class abstraction* is the separation of class implementation from the use of a class. The creator of a class provides a description of the class and lets the user know how the class can be used. The collection of methods and fields that are accessible from outside the class, together with the description of how these members are expected to behave, serves as the *class's contract*. As shown in Figure 6.19, the user of the class does not need to know how the class is implemented. The details of implementation are encapsulated and hidden from the user. This is known as *class encapsulation*. For example, you can create a `Circle` object and find the area of the circle without knowing how the area is computed.

class encapsulation

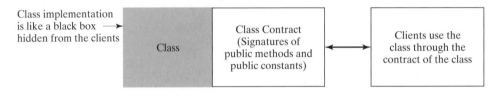

FIGURE 6.19 *Class abstraction separates class implementation from the use of the class.*

Class abstraction and encapsulation are two sides of the same coin. There are many real-life examples that illustrate the concept of class abstraction. Consider building a computer system, for instance. Your personal computer is made up of many components, such as a CPU, CD-ROM, floppy disk, motherboard, fan, and so on. Each component can be viewed as an object that has properties and methods. To get the components to work together, all you need to know is how each component is used and how it interacts with the others. You don't need to know how it works internally. The internal implementation is encapsulated and hidden from you. You can build a computer without knowing how a component is implemented.

The computer-system analogy precisely mirrors the object-oriented approach. Each component can be viewed as an object of the class for the component. For example, you might have a class that models all kinds of fans for use in a computer, with properties like fan size and speed, and methods like start, stop, and so on. A specific fan is an instance of this class with specific property values.

Consider getting a loan, for another example. A specific loan can be viewed as an object of a `Loan` class. Interest rate, loan amount, and loan period are its data properties, and computing monthly payment and total payment are its methods. When you buy a car, a loan object is created by instantiating the class with your loan interest rate, loan amount, and loan period. You can then use the methods to find the monthly payment and total payment of your loan. As a user of the `Loan` class, you don't need to know how these methods are implemented.

6.15 CASE STUDY: The `Loan` Class

Let us use the `Loan` class as an example to demonstrate the creation and use of classes. `Loan` has the data fields `annualInterestRate`, `numberOfYears`, `loanAmount`, and `loanDate`, and the methods `getAnnualInterestRate`, `getNumberOfYears`, `getLoanAmount`, `getLoanDate`, `setAnnualInterestRate`, `setNumberOfYears`, `setLoanAmount`, `monthlyPayment`, and `totalPayment`, as shown in Figure 6.20.

The UML diagram in Figure 6.20 serves as the contract for the `Loan` class. Throughout the book, you will play the role of both class user and class writer. The user can use the class without knowing how the class is implemented. Assume that the `Loan` class is available. Let us begin by writing a test program that uses the `Loan` class in Listing 6.8.

Loan	
-annualInterestRate: double	The annual interest rate of the loan (default: 2.5).
-numberOfYears: int	The number of years for the loan (default: 1).
-loanAmount: double	The loan amount (default: 1000).
-loanDate: Date	The date this loan was created.
+Loan()	Constructs a default loan object.

+Loan(annualInterestRate: double,
  numberOfYears: int,
  loanAmount: double)
	Constructs a loan with specified interest rate, years, and
	  loan amount.

+getAnnualInterestRate(): double	Returns the annual interest rate of this loan.
+getNumberOfYears(): int	Returns the number of the years of this loan.
+getLoanAmount(): double	Returns the amount of this loan.
+getLoanDate(): Date	Returns the date of the creation of this loan.
+setAnnualInterestRate(annualInterestRate: double): void	Sets a new annual interest rate for this loan.
+setNumberOfYears(numberOfYears: int): void	Sets a new number of years for this loan.
+setLoanAmount(loanAmount: double): void	Sets a new amount for this loan.
+monthlyPayment(): double	Returns the monthly payment of this loan.
+totalPayment(): double	Returns the total payment of this loan.

FIGURE 6.20   *The Loan class models the properties and behaviors of loans.*

LISTING 6.8   TestLoanClass.java (Using the Loan Class)

```
1 import javax.swing.JOptionPane;
2
3 public class TestLoanClass {
4   /** Main method */
5   public static void main(String[] args) {
6     // Enter yearly interest rate
7     String annualInterestRateString = JOptionPane.showInputDialog(
8       "Enter yearly interest rate, for example 8.25:");
9
10    // Convert string to double
11    double annualInterestRate =
12      Double.parseDouble(annualInterestRateString);
13
14    // Enter number of years
15    String numberOfYearsString = JOptionPane.showInputDialog(
16      "Enter number of years as an integer, \nfor example 5:");
17
18    // Convert string to int
19    int numberOfYears = Integer.parseInt(numberOfYearsString);
20
21    // Enter loan amount
22    String loanString = JOptionPane.showInputDialog(
23      "Enter loan amount, for example 120000.95:");
24
25    // Convert string to double
26    double loanAmount =  Double.parseDouble(loanString);
27
28    // Create Loan object
29    Loan loan =
30      new Loan(annualInterestRate, numberOfYears, loanAmount);
31
32    // Format to keep two digits after the decimal point
33    double monthlyPayment =
34      (int)(loan.monthlyPayment() * 100) / 100.0;
35    double totalPayment =
36      (int)(loan.totalPayment() * 100) / 100.0;
37
```

```
38     // Display results
39     String output = "The loan was created on " +
40       loan.getLoanDate().toString() + "\nThe monthly payment is " +
41       monthlyPayment + "\nThe total payment is " + totalPayment;
42     JOptionPane.showMessageDialog(null, output);
43   }
44 }
```

The main method reads interest rate, payment period (in years), and loan amount; creates a Loan object; and then obtains the monthly payment (Lines 33–34) and total payment (Lines 35-36) using the instance methods in the Loan class. Figure 6.21 shows the output of a sample run of the program.

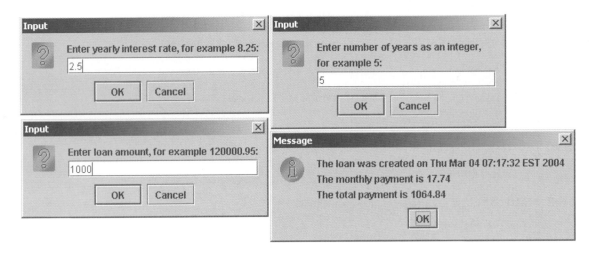

FIGURE **6.21**   *The program creates a Loan instance with the annual interest rate, number of years, and loan amount, and displays the loan date, monthly payment, and total payment by invoking the methods of the instance.*

The Loan class is implemented in Listing 6.9.

LISTING 6.9   **Loan.java (The Loan Class)**

```
 1 public class Loan {
 2   private double annualInterestRate;
 3   private int numberOfYears;
 4   private double loanAmount;
 5   private java.util.Date loanDate;
 6
 7   /** Construct a loan with interest rate 2.5, 1 year, and $1000 */
 8   public Loan() {
 9     this(2.5, 1, 1000);
10   }
11
12   /** Construct a loan with specified annual interest rate,
13       number of years and loan amount
14   */
15   public Loan(double annualInterestRate, int numberOfYears,
16       double loanAmount) {
17     this.annualInterestRate = annualInterestRate;
18     this.numberOfYears = numberOfYears;
19     this.loanAmount = loanAmount;
20     loanDate = new java.util.Date();
21   }
22
```

no-arg constructor

second constructor

```
23    /** Return annualInterestRate */
24    public double getAnnualInterestRate() {
25      return annualInterestRate;
26    }
27
28    /** Set a new annualInterestRate */
29    public void setAnnualInterestRate(double annualInterestRate) {
30      this.annualInterestRate = annualInterestRate;
31    }
32
33    /** Return numberOfYears */
34    public int getNumberOfYears() {
35      return numberOfYears;
36    }
37
38    /** Set a new numberOfYears */
39    public void setNumberOfYears(int numberOfYears) {
40      this.numberOfYears = numberOfYears;
41    }
42
43    /** Return loanAmount */
44    public double getLoanAmount() {
45      return loanAmount;
46    }
47
48    /** Set a newloanAmount */
49    public void setLoanAmount(double loanAmount) {
50      this.loanAmount = loanAmount;
51    }
52
53    /** Find monthly payment */
54    public double monthlyPayment() {
55      double monthlyInterestRate = annualInterestRate / 1200;
56      return loanAmount * monthlyInterestRate / (1 -
57        (Math.pow(1 / (1 + monthlyInterestRate), numberOfYears * 12)));
58    }
59
60    /** Find total payment */
61    public double totalPayment() {
62      return monthlyPayment() * numberOfYears * 12;
63    }
64
65    /** Return loan date */
66    public java.util.Date getLoanDate() {
67      return loanDate;
68    }
69 }
```

From a writer's perspective, a class is designed for use by many different customers. In order to be useful in a wide range of applications, a class should provide a variety of ways for customization through constructors, properties, and methods.

The Loan class contains two constructors, four get methods, three set methods, and the methods for finding monthly payment and total payment. You can construct a Loan object by using the no-arg constructor or the one with three parameters: annual interest rate, number of years, and loan amount. When a loan object is created, its date is stored in the loanDate field. The getLoanDate method returns the date. The three get methods, getAnnualInterest, getNumberOfYears, and getLoanAmount, return annual interest rate, payment years, and loan amount, respectively. All the data properties and methods in this class are tied to a specific instance of the Loan class. Therefore, they are instance variables or methods.

Recall that the java.util.Date can be used to create an instance to represent current date and time (see page 222). The Loan class contains the accessor method for loanDate, but no mutator method for it. Does this mean that the contents of loanDate cannot be changed? See Review Question 6.24.

IMPORTANT PEDAGOGICAL TIP

The UML diagram for the Loan class is shown in Figure 6.20. Students should begin by writing a test program that uses the Loan class even though they do not know how the Loan class is implemented. This has three benefits:

✦ It demonstrates that developing a class and using a class are two separate tasks.

✦ It makes it possible to skip the complex implementation of certain classes without interrupting the sequence of the book.

✦ It is easier to learn how to implement a class if you are familiar with the class through using it.

For all the examples from now on, I recommend that you first create an object from the class and try to use its methods and then turn your attention to its implementation.

 # 6.16 CASE STUDY: The **StackOfIntegers** Class (Optional)

This section gives another example to demonstrate the creation and use of classes. Let us create a class for stacks.

stack

A *stack* is a data structure that holds objects in a last-in first-out fashion. It has many applications. For example, the compiler uses a stack to process method invocations. When a method is invoked, the parameters and local variables of the method are pushed into a stack. When a method calls another method, the new method's parameters and local variables are pushed into the stack. When a method finishes its work and returns to its caller, its associated space is released from the stack.

The UML diagram for the class is shown in Figure 6.22. Suppose that the class is available. Let us write a test program in Listing 6.10 that uses the class to create a stack, stores ten integers, and displays them in reverse order, as shown in Figure 6.23.

StackOfIntegers	
-elements: int[]	An array to store integers in the stack.
-size: int	The number of integers in the stack.
+StackOfIntegers()	Constructs an empty stack with a default capacity of 16.
+StackOfIntegers(capacity: int)	Constructs an empty stack with a specified capacity.
+empty(): boolean	Returns true if the stack is empty.
+peek(): int	Returns the integer at the top of the stack without removing it from the stack.
+push(value: int): int	Stores an integer in the top of the stack.
+pop(): int	Removes the integer at the top of the stack and returns it.
+getSize(): int	Returns the number of elements in the stack.

FIGURE 6.22 *The StackOfIntegers class encapsulates the stack storage and provides the operations for manipulating the stack.*

FIGURE 6.23   *You can store and retrieve integers from* StackOfIntegers.

LISTING 6.10   TestStackOfIntegers.java

```
public class TestStackOfIntegers {
  public static void main(String[] args) {
    StackOfIntegers stack = new StackOfIntegers();

    for (int i = 0; i < 10; i++)
      stack.push(i);

    while (!stack.empty())
      System.out.print(stack.pop() + " ");
  }
}
```

How do you implement the StackOfIntegers class? The elements in the stack are stored in an array named elements. When you create a stack, the array is also created. The no-arg constructor creates an array with the default capacity of 16. The variable size counts the number of elements in the stack, and size – 1 is the index of the element at the top of the stack, as shown in Figure 6.24. For an empty stack, size is 0.

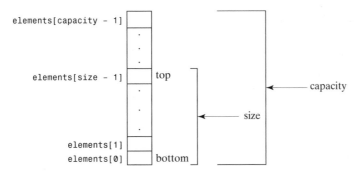

FIGURE 6.24   *The* StackOfIntegers *class encapsulates the stack storage and provides the operations for manipulating the stack.*

The StackOfIntegers class is implemented in Listing 6.11. The methods empty(), peek(), pop(), and getSize() are easy to implement. To implement push(int value), assign value to elements[size] if size < capacity (Line 23). If the stack is full (i.e., size >= capacity), create a new array of twice the current capacity (Line 18), copy the contents of the current array to the new array (Line 19), and assign the reference of the new array to the current array in the stack (Line 20). Now you can add the new value to the array (Line 23).

LISTING 6.11   StackOfIntegers.java (The StackOfIntegers Class)

```
1 public class StackOfIntegers {
2   private int[] elements;
3   private int size;
4
5   /** Construct a stack with the default capacity 16 */
6   public StackOfIntegers() {
7     this(16);
8   }
```

default capacity 16

double the capacity

add to stack

```
 9
10    /** Construct a stack with the specified maximum capacity */
11    public StackOfIntegers(int capacity) {
12      elements = new int[capacity];
13    }
14
15    /** Push a new integer into the top of the stack */
16    public int push(int value) {
17      if (size >= elements.length) {
18        int[] temp = new int[elements.length * 2];
19        System.arraycopy(elements, 0, temp, 0, elements.length);
20        elements = temp;
21      }
22
23      return elements[size++] = value;
24    }
25
26    /** Return and remove the top element from the stack */
27    public int pop() {
28      return elements[--size];
29    }
30
31    /** Return the top element from the stack */
32    public int peek() {
33      return elements[size - 1];
34    }
35
36    /** Test whether the stack is empty */
37    public boolean empty() {
38      return size == 0;
39    }
40
41    /** Return the number of elements in the stack */
42    public int getSize() {
43      return size;
44    }
45  }
```

 NOTE

When you create a StackOfIntegers object, an array object is created. A StackOfIntegers object contains a reference to the array. For simplicity, you can say that the StackOfIntegers object contains the array.

 NOTE

The user can create a stack and manipulate it through the public methods push, pop, peek, empty, and getSize. However, the user doesn't need to know how these methods are implemented. The StackOfIntegers class encapsulates the internal implementation of the stack. This example uses an array to implement a stack. You may use something other than an array to implement a stack. The program that uses StackOfIntegers does not need to change, since the contract of the public methods remains unchanged.

NOTE

Stacks are frequently used in programming. Java provides the Stack class in the java.util package, which will be introduced in Chapter 18, "Java Collections Framework."

6.17 Inner Classes

An *inner class,* or *nested class,* is a class defined within the scope of another class. Here is an example of an inner class:

```java
// ShowInnerClass.java: Demonstrate using inner classes
public class ShowInnerClass {
  private int data;

  /** A method in the outer class */
  public void m() {
    // Do something
    InnerClass instance = new InnerClass();
  }

  // An inner class
  class InnerClass {
    /** A method in the inner class */
    public void mi() {
      // Directly reference data and method defined in its outer class
      data++;
      m();
    }
  }
}
```

The class `InnerClass` is defined inside `ShowInnerClass`. An inner class is just like any regular class, with the following features:

✦ An inner class can reference the data and methods defined in the outer class in which it nests, so you do not need to pass the reference of an object of the outer class to the constructor of the inner class. For this reason, inner classes can make programs simple and concise.

✦ An inner class supports the work of its containing outer class and is compiled into a class named *OuterClassName$InnerClassName*.class. For example, the inner class `InnerClass` in `ShowInnerClass` is compiled into *ShowInnerClass$InnerClass*.class.

✦ An inner class can be declared `public`, `protected`, or `private` subject to the same visibility rules applied to a member of the class.

✦ An inner class can be declared `static`. A `static` inner class can be accessed using the outer class name. A `static` inner class cannot access nonstatic members of the outer class.

✦ Objects of an inner class are often created in the outer class. But you can also create an object of an inner class from another class. If the inner class is non-static, you must first create an instance of the outer class, then use the following syntax to create an object for the inner class:

```java
OuterClass.InnerClass innerObject = outerObject.new InnerClass();
```

✦ If the inner class is static, use the following syntax to create an object for it:

```java
OuterClass.InnerClass innerObject = new OuterClass.InnerClass();
```

KEY TERMS

accessor method (getter)   225
class   214
class abstraction   238
class encapsulation   238
class's contract   238
constant   230
constructor   215
data field encapsulation   225
default constructor   215
dot operator (.)   217
immutable class   227
inner class   245
instance   216
instance method   217
instance variable   217
instantiation   216

mutator method (setter)   225
null   220
no-arg constructor   215
object-oriented programming (OOP)   214
package-private (or package-access)   223
private   223
public   223
reference variable   216
reference type   217
static method   229
static variable   229
this keyword   234
Unified Modeling Language (UML)   216

KEY CLASSES AND METHODS

✦ **java.util.Date** is a class that encapsulates date and time. The no-arg constructor of Date creates an instance for the current date and time. Its toString() method returns the date and time as a string.

CHAPTER SUMMARY

✦ A class is a template for objects. It defines the generic properties of objects, and provides constructors for creating objects and methods for manipulating them.

✦ A class is also a data type. You can use it to declare object reference variables. An object reference variable that appears to hold an object actually contains a reference to that object. Strictly speaking, an object reference variable and an object are different, but most of the time the distinction between them can be ignored.

✦ An object is an instance of a class. You use the new operator to create an object, and the dot (.) operator to access members of that object through its reference variable.

✦ Modifiers specify how the class, method, and data are accessed. A public class, method, or data is accessible to all clients. A private method or data is only accessible inside the class. A static variable or a static method is defined using the keyword static.

✦ You can provide a get method or a set method to enable clients to see or modify the data. Colloquially, a get method is referred to as a *getter* (or *accessor*), and a set method is referred to as a *setter* (or *mutator*).

✦ A get method has the signature public returnType getPropertyName(). If the returnType is boolean, the get method should be defined as public boolean isPropertyName(). A set method has the signature public void setPropertyName- (dataType propertyValue).

✦ All parameters are passed to methods using pass by value. For a parameter of a primitive type, the actual value is passed; for a parameter of a reference type, the reference for the object is passed.

✦ An instance variable is a variable that belongs to an instance of a class. Its use is associated with individual instances. A static variable is a variable shared by all instances of the same class.

✦ An instance method is a method that belongs to an instance of a class. Its use is associated with individual instances. A static method is a method that can be invoked without using instances.

✦ Every instance of a class can access the class's static variables and methods. However, I recommend that you invoke static variables and methods using `ClassName.variable` and `ClassName.method`.

✦ The scope of instance and static variables is the entire class, regardless of where the variables are declared. The instance and static variables can be declared anywhere in the class.

✦ The object reference `this` inside an instance method serves as a pointer to the current instance of the class that invokes the instance method. The keyword `this` can also be used inside a constructor to invoke another constructor of the same class.

✦ A Java array is an object that can contain primitive type values or object type values. When an array is created, its elements are assigned the default value of `0` for the numeric primitive data types, `'\u0000'` for char types, `false` for `boolean` types, and `null` for object types.

✦ An *inner class*, or *nested class*, is a class defined within the scope of another class. An inner class can reference the data and methods defined in the outer class in which it nests, so you do not need to pass the reference of the outer class to the constructor of the inner class.

REVIEW QUESTIONS

Sections 6.2–6.4

6.1 Describe the relationship between an object and its defining class. How do you declare a class? How do you declare an object reference variable? How do you create an object? How do you declare and create an object in one statement?

6.2 What are the differences between constructors and methods?

6.3 What is wrong with the following program?

```
1 public class ShowErrors {
2   public static void main(String[] args) {
3     ShowErrors t = new ShowErrors(5);
4   }
5 }
```

6.4 Is an array an object or a primitive type value? Can an array contain elements of a primitive type as well as an object type? Describe the default value for the elements of an array.

6.5 What is wrong in the following code?

```
1 public class Foo {
2   public void method1() {
3     Circle c;
4     System.out.println("What is radius " + c.getRadius());
5     c = new Circle();
6   }
7 }
```

6.6 What is wrong in the following code?

```
1 class Test {
2   public static void main(String[] args) {
3     A a = new A();
4     a.print();
5   }
6 }
7
8 class A {
9   String s;
10
11   A(String s) {
12     this.s = s;
13   }
14
15   public void print() {
16     System.out.print(s);
17   }
18 }
```

6.7 What is wrong in the following code?

```
1 class Test {
2   public static void main(String[] args) {
3     C c = new C(5.0);
4     System.out.println(c.value);
5   }
6 }
7
8 class C {
9   int value = 2;
10 }
```

6.8 What is the printout of the following code?

```
public class Foo {
  private boolean x;

  public static void main(String[] args) {
    Foo foo = new Foo();
    System.out.println(foo.x);
  }
}
```

6.9 What is wrong with the following program?

```
1 public class ShowErrors {
2   public static void main(String[] args) {
3     ShowErrors t = new ShowErrors();
4     t.x();
5   }
6 }
```

Sections 6.6-6.8

6.10 What is an accessor method? What is a mutator method? What are the naming conventions for accessor methods and mutator methods?

6.11 What are the benefits of data field encapsulation?

6.12 In the following code, radius is private in the Circle class, and myCircle is an object of the Circle class. Can the following code compile and run? Explain why.

```
public class Circle {
  private double radius = 1.0;

  /** Find the area of this circle */
  double findArea() {
    return radius * radius * 3.14159;
  }

  public static void main(String[] args) {
    Circle myCircle = new Circle();
    System.out.println("Radius is " + myCircle.radius);
  }
}
```

6.13 If a class contains only private data fields and no set methods, is the class immutable?

6.14 If all the data fields in a class are private and primitive, and the class contains no set methods, is the class immutable?

Section 6.9 Passing Objects to Methods

6.15 Describe the difference between passing a parameter of a primitive type and passing a parameter of a reference type. Show the output of the following program:

```
public class Test {
  public static void main(String[] args) {
    Count myCount = new Count();
    int times = 0;

    for (int i = 0; i < 100; i++)
      increment(myCount, times);

    System.out.println("count is " + myCount.count);
    System.out.println("times is " + times);
  }

  public static void increment (Count c, int times) {
    c.count++;
    times++;
  }
}
```

```
class Count {
  public int count;

  Count(int c) {
    count = c;
  }

  Count() {
    count = 1;
  }
}
```

6.16 Show the output of the following program:

```
public class Test {
  public static void main(String[] args) {
    Circle circle1 = new Circle(1);
    Circle circle2 = new Circle(2);

    swap1(circle1, circle2);
    System.out.println("After swap1: circle1 = " +
      circle1.radius + " circle2 = " + circle2.radius);
    swap2(circle1, circle2);
    System.out.println("After swap2: circle1 = " +
      circle1.radius + " circle2 = " + circle2.radius);
  }

  public static void swap1(Circle x, Circle y) {
    Circle temp = x;
    x = y;
```

```
        y = temp;
    }

    public static void swap2(Circle x, Circle y) {
        double temp = x.radius;
        x.radius = y.radius;
        y.radius = temp;
    }
}

class Circle {
    double radius;

    Circle(double newRadius) {
        radius = newRadius;
    }
}
```

6.17 Show the printout of the following code:

```
public class Test {
    public static void main(String[] args) {
        int[] a = {1, 2};
        swap(a[0], a[1]);
        System.out.println("a[0] = " + a[0]
            + " a[1] = " + a[1]);
    }

    public static void swap(int n1, int n2) {
        int temp = n1;
        n1 = n2;
        n2 = temp;
    }
}
```

(a)

```
public class Test {
    public static void main(String[] args) {
        int[] a = {1, 2};
        swap(a);
        System.out.println("a[0] = " + a[0]
            + " a[1] = " + a[1]);
    }

    public static void swap (int[] a) {
        int temp = a[0];
        a[0] = a[1];
        a[1] = temp;
    }
}
```

(b)

```
public class Test {
    public static void main(String[] args) {
        T t = new T();
        swap(t);
        System.out.println("e1 = " + t.e1
            + " e2 = " + t.e2);
    }

    public static void swap(T t) {
        int temp = t.e1;
        t.e1 = t.e2;
        t.e2 = temp;
    }
}

class T {
    int e1 = 1;
    int e2 = 2;
}
```

(c)

```
public class Test {
    public static void main(String[] args) {
        T t1 = new T();
        T t2 = new T();
        System.out.println("t1's i = " +
            t1.i + " and j = " + t1.j);
        System.out.println("t2's i = " +
            t2.i + " and j = " + t2.j);
    }
}

class T {
    static int i = 0;
    int j = 0;

    T() {
        i++;
        j = 1;
    }
}
```

(d)

Section 6.10 Static Variables, Constants, and Methods

6.18 Suppose that the class Foo is defined in (a). Let f be an instance of Foo. Which of the statements in (b) are correct?

```
public class Foo {
    int i;
    static String s;

    void imethod() {
    }

    static void smethod() {
    }
}
```
(a)

```
System.out.println(f.i);
System.out.println(f.s);
f.imethod();
f.smethod();
System.out.println(Foo.i);
System.out.println(Foo.s);
Foo.imethod();
Foo.smethod();
```
(b)

6.19 What is the output of the following program?

```
public class Foo {
  static int i = 0;
  static int j = 0;

  public static void main(String[] args) {
    int i = 2;
    int k = 3;

    {
      int j = 3;
      System.out.println("i + j is " + i + j);
    }

    k = i + j;
    System.out.println("k is " + k);
    System.out.println("j is " + j);
  }
}
```

6.20 Can you invoke an instance method or reference an instance variable from a static method? Can you invoke a static method or reference a static variable from an instance method? What is wrong in the following code?

```
1 public class Foo {
2   public static void main(String[] args) {
3     method1();
4   }
5
6   public void method1() {
7     method2();
8   }
9
10  public static void method2() {
11    System.out.println("What is radius " + c.getRadius());
12  }
13
14  Circle c = new Circle();
15 }
```

Sections 6.11–6.12

6.21 Describe the role of the this keyword.

6.22 What is wrong in the following code?

```
1 public class C {
2   int p;
3
4   public void setP(int p) {
5     p = p;
6   }
7 }
```

Sections 6.13–6.17

6.23   What is wrong in the following code?

```
1 public class Test {
2   public static void main(String[] args) {
3     java.util.Date[] dates = new java.util.Date[10];
4     System.out.println(dates[0]);
5     System.out.println(dates[0].toString());
6   }
7 }
```

6.24   The Loan class contains a private data field loanDate with a get method, but no set method. Is the Loan class immutable?

6.25   Is the StackOfIntegers class immutable?

6.26   Can an inner class be used in a class other than the class in which it nests?

6.27   Can the modifiers public, private, and static be used on inner classes?

PROGRAMMING EXERCISES

Sections 6.2–6.11

6.1   (*The* Rectangle *class*) Write a class named Rectangle to represent rectangles. The UML diagram for the class is shown in Figure 6.25. Suppose that all the rectangles are the same color. Use a static variable for color.

Write a client program to test the class Rectangle. In the client program, create two Rectangle objects. Assign width 4 and height 40 to each of the two objects. Assign color yellow. Display the properties of both objects and find their areas.

6.2   (*The* Fan *class*) Write a class named Fan to model fans. The properties, as shown in Figure 6.26, are speed, on, radius, and color. You need to provide the accessor and mutator methods for the properties, and the toString method for returning a string consisting of all the values of all the properties in this class. Suppose the fan has three fixed speeds. Use constants 1, 2, and 3 to denote slow, medium, and fast speed.

Rectangle	
-width: double	The width of this rectangle.
-height: double	The height of this rectangle.
-color: String	The color of this rectangle.
+Rectangle()	Constructs a rectangle with width 1 and height 1.
+Rectangle(width: double, height: double, color: String)	Constructs a rectangle with the specified width and height.
+getWidth(): double	Returns the width of this rectangle.
+setWidth(width: double): void	Sets a new width for this rectangle.
+getHeight(): double	Returns the height of this rectangle.
+setHeight(height: double): void	Sets a new height for this rectangle.
+getColor(): String	Returns the color of all rectangles.
+setColor(color: String): void	Sets a new color for all rectangles.
+findArea(): double	Returns the area of this rectangle.
+findPerimeter(): double	Returns the perimeter of this rectangle.

FIGURE 6.25   *The* Rectangle *class contains the properties* width, height, *and* color, *accessor and mutator methods, and the methods for computing area and perimeter.*

Fan	
-speed: int	The speed of this fan (default 1).
-on: boolean	Indicates whether the fan is on (default false).
-radius: double	The radius of this fan (default 5).
-color: String	The color of this fan (default white).
+Fan()	Constructs a fan with default values.
+getSpeed(): int	Returns the speed of this fan.
+setSpeed(speed: int): void	Sets a new speed for this fan.
+isOn(): boolean	Returns true if this fan is on.
+setOn(on: boolean): void	Sets this fan on to true or false.
+getRadius(): double	Returns the radius of this fan.
+setRadius(radius: double): void	Sets a new radius for this fan.
+getColor(): String	Returns the color of this fan.
+setColor(color: String): void	Sets a new color for this fan.
+toString(): String	Returns a string representation for this fan.

FIGURE 6.26   *The* Fan *class contains the properties* speed, on, radius, *and* color, *accessor and mutator methods, and the* toString *method for returning the values of the properties.*

Write a client program to test the Fan class. In the client program, create a Fan object. Assign maximum speed, radius 10, color yellow, and turn it on. Display the object by invoking its toString method.

6.3   (*The* Account *class*) Write a class named Account to model accounts. The UML diagram for the class is shown in Figure 6.27.

Write a client program to test the Account class. In the client program, create an Account object with an account ID of 1122, a balance of 20000, and an annual interest rate of 4.5%. Use the withdraw method to withdraw $2500, use the deposit method to deposit $3000, and print the balance and the monthly interest.

Account	
-id: int	The ID of this account.
-balance: double	The balance of this account.
-annualInterestRate: double	The interest rate of this account.
+Account()	Constructs a default account.
+Account(id: int, balance: double, annualInterestRate: double)	Constructs an account with the specified ID, balance, and interest rate.
+getId(): int	Returns the ID of this account.
+getBalance(): double	Returns the balance of this account.
+getAnnualInterestRate():double	Returns the interest rate of this account.
+setId(id: int): void	Sets a new ID for this account.
+setBalance(balance: double): void	Sets a new balance for this account.
+setAnnualInterestRate(annualInterestRate: double): void	Sets a new interest rate for this account.
+getMonthlyInterestRate(): double	Returns the monthly interest rate of this account.
+withdraw(amount: double): void	Withdraws the specified amount from this account.
+deposit(amount: double): void	Deposits the specified amount to this account.

FIGURE 6.27   *The* Account *class contains the properties ID, balance, annual interest rate, accessor and mutator methods, and the methods for computing interest, withdrawing money, and depositing money.*

Stock
-symbol: String
-name: String
-previousClosingPrice: double
-currentPrice: double
+Stock(symbol: String, name: String)
+getSymbol(): String
+getName(): String
+getPreviousClosingPrice(): double
+getCurrentPrice(): double
+setPreviousClosingPrice(price: double): void
+setCurrentPrice(price: double): void
+changePercent(): double

The symbol of this stock.

The name of this stock.

The previous closing price of this stock.

The current price of this stock.

Constructs a stock with a specified symbol and a name.

Returns the symbol of this stock.

Returns the name of this stock.

Returns the previous closing price of this stock.

Returns the current price of this stock.

Sets the previous closing price of this stock.

Sets the current price of this stock.

Returns the percentage of change of this stock.

FIGURE 6.28   *The* Stock *class contains the properties symbol, name, previous closing price, and current price, accessor and mutator methods, and the methods for computing price changes.*

6.4   (*The* Stock *class*) Write a class named Stock to model a stock. The UML diagram for the class is shown in Figure 6.28. The method changePercent computes the percentage of the change between the current price and the previous closing price.

Write a client program to test the Stock class. In the client program, create a Stock object with the stock symbol SUNW, the name Sun Microsystems Inc., and the previous closing price of 100. Set a new current price to 90 and display the price-change percentage.

6.5*   (*Using the* GregorianCalendar *class*) Java API has the GregorianCalendar class in the java.util package that can be used to obtain the year, month, and day of a date. The no-arg constructor constructs an instance for the current date, and the methods get(GregorianCalendar.YEAR), get(GregorianCalendar.MONTH), and get(GregorianCalendar.DAY) return the year, month, and day. Write a program to test this class to display the current year, month, and day.

6.6**   (*Displaying calendars*) Rewrite the PrintCalendar class in Section 4.10, "Stepwise Refinement," to display calendars in a message dialog box. Since the output is generated from several static methods in the class, you may define a static String variable output for storing the output and display it in a message dialog box.

6.7*   (*The* Time *class*) Write a class named Time. The Time class contains the data fields hour, minute, and second with their respective get methods. The no-arg constructor sets the hour, minute, and second for the current time in GMT. The current time can be obtained using System.currentTime(), as shown in Example 2.5, "Displaying Current Time."

Write a client program to test the Time class. In the client program, create a Time object and display hour, minute, and second using the get methods.

6.8*   (*The* Vote *and* Candidate *Classes*) Create two classes, Vote and Candidate. The Vote class has the data field count to count votes, and the methods getCount, setCount, clear, increment, and decrement for reading and handling the votes, as shown in Figure 6.29. The clear method sets the count to 0. The increment and decrement methods increase and decrease the count. The Candidate class has the data fields name (name of the candidate), vote (track the votes received by the candidate), and numberOfCandidates (track the total number of candidates), and the methods getName,

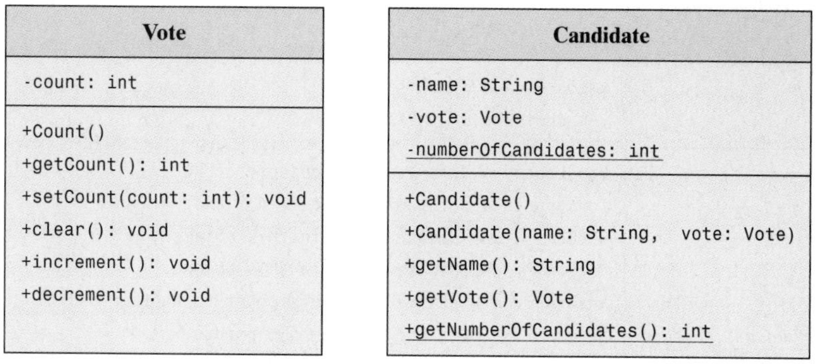

Vote
-count: int
+Count()
+getCount(): int
+setCount(count: int): void
+clear(): void
+increment(): void
+decrement(): void

Candidate
-name: String
-vote: Vote
-numberOfCandidates: int
+Candidate()
+Candidate(name: String, vote: Vote)
+getName(): String
+getVote(): Vote
+getNumberOfCandidates(): int

FIGURE 6.29 *The* Vote *class encapsulates the vote count, and the* Candidate *class encapsulates the candidates.*

getVote, and getNumberOfCandidates for reading the name, vote, and numberOf Candidates, as shown in Figure 6.29.

Write a test program that counts votes for two candidates for student body president. The votes are entered from the keyboard. Number 1 is a vote for Candidate 1, and number 2 is a vote for Candidate 2. Number −1 deducts a vote from Candidate 1, and −2 deducts a vote from Candidate 2. Number 0 signifies the end of the count.

Sections 6.12-6.16

6.9 (*The* Int *class*) Write a class named Int to represent an int value as an object. The UML diagram for the class is shown in Figure 6.30. Write a client program to test all the methods in the Int class.

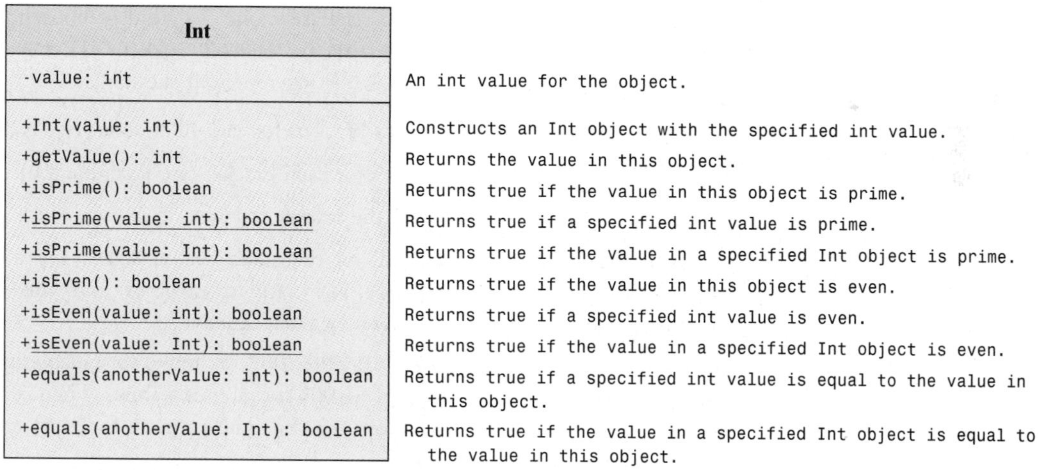

Int	
-value: int	An int value for the object.
+Int(value: int)	Constructs an Int object with the specified int value.
+getValue(): int	Returns the value in this object.
+isPrime(): boolean	Returns true if the value in this object is prime.
+isPrime(value: int): boolean	Returns true if a specified int value is prime.
+isPrime(value: Int): boolean	Returns true if the value in a specified Int object is prime.
+isEven(): boolean	Returns true if the value in this object is even.
+isEven(value: int): boolean	Returns true if a specified int value is even.
+isEven(value: Int): boolean	Returns true if the value in a specified Int object is even.
+equals(anotherValue: int): boolean	Returns true if a specified int value is equal to the value in this object.
+equals(anotherValue: Int): boolean	Returns true if the value in a specified Int object is equal to the value in this object.

FIGURE 6.30 *The* Int *class represents an* int *value.*

6.10 (*Modifying the* Loan *class*) Rewrite the Loan class to add two static methods for computing monthly payment and total payment, as follows:

```
public static double monthlyPayment(double annualInterestRate,
  int numOfYears, double loanAmount)

public static double totalPayment(double annualInterestRate,
  int numOfYears, double loanAmount)
```

Write a client program to test these two methods.

MyPoint	
-x: double	x-coordinate of this point.
-y: double	y-coordinate of this point.
+MyPoint()	Constructs a default point object.
+MyPoint(double x, double y)	Constructs a point with specified x and y values.
+getX(): double	Returns x-coordinate value in this object.
+getY():double	Returns y-coordinate value in this object.
+distance(secondPoint: MyPoint): double	Returns the distance from this point to another point.
+distance(p1: Point, p2: MyPoint): double	Returns the distance between two points.

FIGURE 6.31   *The MyPoint class models a point.*

6.11   (*The MyPoint class*) Write a class named MyPoint to represent a point, as shown in Figure 6.31.

6.12*   (*Displaying the prime factors*) Write a program that receives a positive integer and displays all its smallest factors in decreasing order. For example, if the integer is 120, the smallest factors are displayed as 5, 3, 2, 2, 2. Use the StackOfIntegers class to store the factors (e.g., 2, 2, 2, 3, 5) and retrieve and display the factors in reverse order.

6.13**   (*Displaying the prime numbers*) Write a program that displays all the prime numbers less than 120 in decreasing order. Use the StackOfIntegers class to store the prime numbers (e.g., 2, 3, 5, . . .) and retrieve and display them in reverse order.

6.14***   (*The Tax class*) Write a class named Tax. The Tax class contains the following instance data fields:

◆   **int filingStatus**: One of the four tax filing statuses: 0 - single filer, 1 - married filing jointly, 2 - married filing separately, and 3 - head of household. Use the public static constants SINGLE_FILER (0), MARRIED_JOINTLY (1), MARRIED_SEPARATELY (2), and HEAD_OF_HOUSEHOLD (3) to represent the status.

◆   **int[][] brackets**: Stores the tax brackets for each filing status (see Example 5.6).

◆   **double[] rates**: Stores tax rates for each bracket (see Example 5.6).

◆   **double taxableIncome**: Stores the taxable income.

Provide the get and set methods for each data field and the findTax() method that returns the tax. Also provide a no-arg constructor and the constructor Tax(filingStatus, brackets, rates, taxableIncome).

Use the Tax class to print the 2001 and 2002 tax tables for taxable income from $50,000 to $60,000 with intervals of $1,000 for all four statuses. The tax rates for the year 2002 were given in Table 3.1 on page 86. The tax rates for 2001 are shown in Table 6.1.

TABLE 6.1   **2001 United States Federal Personal Tax Rates**

Tax rate	Single filers	Married filing jointly or qualifying widow(er)	Married filing separately	Head of household
15%	Up to $27,050	Up to $45,200	Up to $22,600	Up to $36,250
27.5%	$27,051–$65,550	$45,201–$109,250	$22,601–$54,625	$36,251–$93,650
30.5%	$65,551–$136,750	$109,251–166,500	$54,626–$83,250	$93,651–$151,650
35.5%	$136,751–$297,350	$166,501–$297,350	$83,251–$148,675	$151,651–$297,350
39.1%	$297,351 or more	$297,351 or more	$148,676 or more	$297,351 or more

chapter

7

Strings

Objectives

- ✦ To use the String class to process fixed strings (§7.2).

- ✦ To use the Character class to process a single character (§7.3).

- ✦ To use the StringBuffer class to process flexible strings (§7.4).

- ✦ To use the StringTokenizer class to extract tokens from a string (§7.5).

- ✦ To know the differences between the String, StringBuffer, and StringTokenizer classes (§§7.2–7.5).

- ✦ To use the JDK 1.5 Scanner class to scan tokens using words as delimiters (§7.6).

- ✦ To input primitive values and strings from the keyboard using the Scanner class (§7.7).

- ✦ To learn how to pass strings to the main method from the command line (§7.8).

7.1 Introduction

Strings are used often in programming. A *string* is sequence of characters. In many languages, strings are treated as arrays of characters, but in Java a string is an object. Java provides the String class, the StringBuffer class, and the StringTokenizer class for storing and processing strings.

In most cases, you use the String class to create strings. The String class is efficient for storing and processing strings, but strings created with the String class cannot be modified. The StringBuffer class enables you to create flexible strings that can be modified. StringTokenizer is a utility class that can be used to extract tokens from a string.

7.2 The String Class

The java.lang.String class models a sequence of characters as a string. You have already used string literals, such as the parameter in the println(String s) method. The Java compiler converts the string literal into a string object and passes it to println.

The String class has eleven constructors and more than forty methods for examining individual characters in a sequence, comparing strings, searching substrings, extracting substrings, and creating a copy of a string with all the characters translated to uppercase or lowercase. The most frequently used methods are listed in Figure 7.1.

7.2.1 Constructing a String

You can create a string from a string value or from an array of characters. To create a string from a string literal, use a syntax like this one:

```
String newString = new String(stringLiteral);
```

The argument stringLiteral is a sequence of characters enclosed inside double quotes. The following statement creates a String object message for the string literal "Welcome to Java":

```
String message = new String("Welcome to Java");
```

shorthand initializer

Since strings are used frequently, Java provides a *shorthand initializer* for creating a string:

```
String message = "Welcome to Java";
```

You can also create a string from an array of characters. For example, the following statements create the string "Good Day".

```
char[] charArray = {'G', 'o', 'o', 'd', ' ', 'D', 'a', 'y'};
String message = new String(charArray);
```

 NOTE

string, string variable, string value

A String variable holds a reference to a String object that stores a string value. Strictly speaking, the terms *String variable*, *String object*, and *string value* are different, but the distinctions between them can be ignored most of the time. For simplicity, the term *string* will often be used to refer to String variable, String object, and string value.

---

java.lang.String	
+String()	Constructs an empty string.
+String(value: String)	Constructs a string with the specified string literal value.
+String(value: char[])	Constructs a string with the specified character array.
+charAt(index: int): char	Returns the character at the specified index from this string.
+compareTo(anotherString: String): int	Compares this string with another string.
+compareToIgnoreCase(anotherString: String): int	Compares this string with another string ignoring case.
+concat(anotherString: String): String	Concatenate this string with another string.
+endsWith(suffix: String): boolean	Returns true if this string ends with the specified suffix.
+equals(anotherString: String): boolean	Returns true if this string is equal to another string.
+equalsIgnoreCase(anotherString: String): boolean	Checks whether this string equals another string ignoring case.
+getChars(int srcBegin, int srcEnd, char[] dst, int dstBegin): void	Copies characters from this string into the destination character array.
+indexOf(ch: int): int	Returns the index of the first occurrence of ch.
+indexOf(ch: int, fromIndex: int): int	Returns the index of the first occurrence of ch after fromIndex.
+indexOf(str: String): int	Returns the index of the first occurrence of str.
+indexOf(str: String, fromIndex: int): int	Returns the index of the first occurrence of str after fromIndex.
+lastIndexOf(ch: int): int	Returns the index of the last occurrence of ch.
+lastIndexOf(ch: int, fromIndex: int): int	Returns the index of the last occurrence of ch before fromIndex.
+lastIndexOf(str: String): int	Returns the index of the last occurrence of str.
+lastIndexOf(str: String, fromIndex: int): int	Returns the index of the last occurrence of str before fromIndex.
+regionMatches(toffset: int, other: String, offset: int, len: int): boolean	Returns true if the specified subregion of this string exactly. matches the specified subregion of the string argument.
+length(): int	Returns the number of characters in this string.
+replace(oldChar: char, newChar: char): String	Returns a new string with oldChar replaced by newChar.
+startsWith(prefix: String): boolean	Returns true if this string starts with the specified prefix.
+subString(beginIndex: int): String	Returns the substring from beginIndex.
+subString(beginIndex: int, endIndex: int): String	Returns the substring from beginIndex to endIndex −1.
+toCharArray(): char[]	Returns a char array consisting of characters from this string.
+toLowerCase(): String	Returns a new string with all characters converted to lowercase.
+toString(): String	Returns a new string with itself.
+toUpperCase(): String	Returns a new string with all characters converted to uppercase.
+trim(): String	Returns a string with blank characters trimmed on both sides.
+copyValueOf(data: char[]): String	Returns a new string consisting of the char array data.
+valueOf(c: char): String	Returns a string consisting of the character c.
+valueOf(data: char[]): String	Same as copyValueOf(data: char[]): String.
+valueOf(d: double): String	Returns a string representing the double value.
+valueOf(f: float): String	Returns a string representing the float value.
+valueOf(i: int): String	Returns a string representing the int value.
+valueOf(l: long): String	Returns a string representing the long value.

FIGURE 7.1 *The String class provides the methods for processing a string.*

7.2.2 Immutable Strings and Canonical Strings

A String object is immutable; its contents cannot be changed. Does the following code change the contents of the string?   immutable

```
String s = "Java";
s = "HTML";
```

The answer is no. The first statement creates a String object with the content "Java" and assigns its reference to s. The second statement creates a new String object with the content "HTML" and

After executing

`String s = "Java";`

s ⟶ | **s: String** |
| `String object for "Java"` |

Contents cannot be changed

After executing   s

`s = "HTML";`

| **:String** |
| `String object for "Java"` |

This string object is
now unreferenced

| **s: String** |
| `String object for "HTML"` |

FIGURE 7.2   *Strings are immutable; their contents cannot be changed once created.*

assigns its reference to s. The first `String` object still exists after the assignment, but it can no longer be accessed because variable s now points to the new object, as shown in Figure 7.2.

Since strings are immutable and are frequently used, JVM improves efficiency and saves memory by storing two `String` objects in the same object if they were created with the same string literal using the shorthand initializer. Such a string is called a *canonical string*. You can also use a `String` object's `intern` method to return a canonical string. A string of this kind is the same string that is created using the shorthand initializer. For example, the following statements:

canonical string

```
String s = "Welcome to Java";

String s1 = new String("Welcome to Java");

String s2 = s1.intern();

String s3 = "Welcome to Java";

System.out.println("s1 == s is " + (s1 == s));
System.out.println("s2 == s is " + (s2 == s));
System.out.println("s == s3 is " + (s == s3));
```

| **:String** |
| `Canonical string object`
`for "Welcome to Java"` |

| **:String** |
| `A string object for`
`"Welcome to Java"` |

display

```
s1 == s is false
s2 == s is true
s == s3 is true
```

In the preceding statements, s, s2, and s3 refer to the same canonical string `"Welcome to Java"`; therefore s2 == s and s == s3 are true. However, s1 == s is false, because s and s1 are two different string objects even though they have the same contents.

7.2.3   String Length and Retrieving Individual Characters

length()

You can get the length of a string by invoking its `length()` method. For example, `message.length()` returns the length of the string `message`.

charAt(index)

The `s.charAt(index)` method can be used to retrieve a specific character in a string s, where the index is between 0 and `s.length()-1`. For example, `message.charAt(0)` returns the character W, as shown in Figure 7.3.

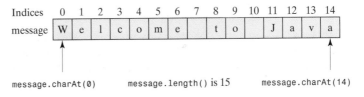

FIGURE 7.3   *A* String *object is represented using an array internally.*

NOTE

When you use a string, you often know its literal value. For convenience, Java allows you to use the string literal to refer directly to strings without creating new variables. Thus, `"Welcome to Java".charAt(0)` is correct and returns `W`.

NOTE

A string value is represented using a private array variable internally. The array cannot be accessed outside of the `String` class. The `String` class provides many public methods, such as `length()` and `charAt(index)`, to retrieve the array information. This is a good example of encapsulation: the detailed data structure of the class is hidden from the user through the private modifier, and thus the user cannot directly manipulate the internal data structure. If the array were not private, the user would be able to change the string content by modifying the array. This would violate the tenet that the `String` class is immutable.

CAUTION

Accessing characters in a string s out of bounds is a common programming error. To avoid it, make sure that you do not use an index beyond `s.length() - 1`. For example, `s.charAt(s.length())` would cause a `StringIndexOutOfBoundsException`.

CAUTION

`length` is a method in the `String` class, but `length` is a property in an array object. So you have to use `s.length()` to get the number of characters in string s, and `a.length` to get the number of elements in array a.

7.2.4   String Concatenation

You can use the `concat` method to concatenate two strings. The statement shown below, for example, concatenates strings s1 and s2 into s3:

```
String s3 = s1.concat(s2);
```

Since string concatenation is heavily used in programming, Java provides a convenient way to concatenate strings. You can use the plus (+) sign to concatenate two or more strings. The following code combines the strings `message`, `" and "`, and `"HTML"` into one string:

s1 + s2

```
String myString = message + " and " + "HTML";
```

Recall that you used the + sign to concatenate a number with a string in the `println` method. A number is converted into a string and then concatenated.

7.2.5   Extracting Substrings

`String` is an immutable class. After a string is created, its value cannot be modified. For example, you cannot change `"Java"` in `message` to `"HTML"`. So what can you do if you need to change the `message` string? You assign a completely new string to `message`. The following code illustrates this:

```
message = "Welcome to HTML";
```

As an alternative, you can use the substring method. You extract a substring from a string by using the substring method in the String class. The substring method has two versions:

substring(int, int)

◆ `public String substring(int beginIndex, int endIndex)`

Returns a new string that is a substring of the string. The substring begins at the specified beginIndex and extends to the character at index endIndex - 1, as shown in Figure 7.4. Thus the length of the substring is endIndex-beginIndex.

substring(int)

◆ `public String substring(int beginIndex)`

Returns a new string that is a substring of the string. The substring begins with the character at the specified index and extends to the end of the string, as shown in Figure 7.4.

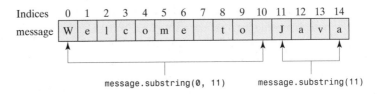

FIGURE 7.4 *The substring method extracts a substring from a string.*

For example,

```
String message = "Welcome to Java".substring(0, 11) + "HTML";
```

The string message now becomes "Welcome to HTML".

7.2.6 String Comparisons

Often, in a program, you need to compare the contents of two strings. You might attempt to use the == operator, as follows:

==

```
if (string1 == string2)
   System.out.println("string1 and string2 are the same object");
else
   System.out.println("string1 and string2 are different objects");
```

However, the == operator only checks whether string1 and string2 refer to the same object; it does not tell you whether string1 and string2 contain the same contents when they are different objects. Therefore, you cannot use the == operator to find out whether two string variables have the same contents. Instead, you should use the equals() method for an equality comparison of the contents of objects. The code given below, for instance, can be used to compare two strings:

s1.equals(s2)

```
if (string1.equals(string2))
   System.out.println("string1 and string2 have the same contents");
else
   System.out.println("string1 and string2 are not equal");
```

🌸 **NOTE**

Two String references are the same if they are created with the same literal value using the shorthand initializer. But strings with the same contents do not always share the same object. For example, the following two variables, s1 and s2, are different even though their contents are identical:

```
String s0 = " Java";
String s1 = "Welcome to" + s0;
String s2 = "Welcome to Java";

System.out.println("s1 == s2 is " + (s1 == s2));
System.out.println("s1.equals(s2) is " + (s1.equals(s2)));
```

In this case, s1 == s2 is false since they point to two different objects, but s1.equals(s2) is true since the objects have the same contents. For safety and clarity, you should always use the equals method to test whether two strings have the same contents, and the == operator to test whether the two strings have the same references (i.e., point to the same memory location).

 NOTE

For two strings x and y, x.equals(y) if and only if x.intern() == y.intern().

The compareTo method can also be used to compare two strings. For example, consider the following code:

```
s1.compareTo(s2)
```

The method returns the value 0 if s1 is equal to s2, a value less than 0 if s1 is lexicographically less than s2, and a value greater than 0 if s1 is lexicographically greater than s2.

The actual value returned from the compareTo method depends on the offset of the first two distinct characters in s1 and s2 from left to right. For example, suppose s1 is "abc" and s2 is "abg", and s1.compareTo(s2) returns -4. The first two characters (a vs. a) from s1 and s2 are compared. Because they are equal, the second two characters (b vs. b) are compared. Because they are also equal, the third two characters (c vs. g) are compared. Since the character c is 4 less than g, the comparison returns -4.

 CAUTION

Syntax errors will occur if you compare strings by using comparison operators, such as >, >=, <, or <=. Instead, you have to use s1.compareTo(s2).

 NOTE

The equals method returns true if two strings are equal, and false if they are not equal. The compareTo method returns 0, a positive integer, or a negative integer, depending on whether one string is equal to, greater than, or less than the other string.

The String class also provides equalsIgnoreCase and regionMatches methods for comparing strings. The equalsIgnoreCase method ignores the case of the letters when determining whether two strings are equal. The regionMatches method compares portions of two strings for equality. You can also use str.startsWith(prefix) to check whether string str starts with a specified prefix, and str.endsWith(suffix) to check whether string str ends with a specified suffix.

7.2.7   String Conversions

The contents of a string cannot be changed once the string is created. But you can obtain a new string using the toLowerCase, toUpperCase, trim, and replace methods. The toLowerCase and toUpperCase methods return a new string by converting all the characters in the string to lowercase or uppercase. The trim method returns a new string by eliminating blank characters from both ends of the string. The replace(oldChar, newChar) method can be used to replace all occurrences of a character in the string with a new character.

For example,

`toLowerCase()`
`toUpperCase()`
`trim()`
`replace`

`"Welcome".toLowerCase()` returns a new string, welcome.
`"Welcome".toUpperCase()` returns a new string, WELCOME.
`"  Welcome  ".trime()` returns a new string, Welcome.
`"Welcome".replace('e', 'A')` returns a new string, WAlcomA.
`"Welcome".replaceFirst("e", "A")` returns a new string, WAlcome.
`"Welcome".replaceAll("e", "A")` returns a new string, WAlcomA.

7.2.8   Finding a Character or a Substring in a String

You can use the indexOf and lastIndexOf methods to find a character or a substring in a string. Four overloaded indexOf methods and four overloaded lastIndexOf methods are defined in the String class.

✦ `public int indexOf(int ch)`

   (*public int lastIndexOf(int ch)*)

   Returns the index of the first (*last*) character in the string that matches the specified character ch. Returns −1 if the specified character is not in the string. When you pass a character to ch (e.g., indexOf('a')), the character's Unicode value is passed to the parameter ch (e.g., the Unicode value for 'a' is 97 in decimal).

✦ `public int indexOf(int ch, int fromIndex)`

   (*public int lastIndexOf(int ch, int endIndex)*)

   Returns the index of the first (*last*) character in the string starting from (*ending at*) the specified fromIndex (*endIndex*) that matches the specified character ch. Returns −1 if the specified character is not in the substring beginning at position fromIndex (*ending at position endIndex*).

✦ `public int indexOf(String str)`

   (*public int lastIndexOf(String str)*)

   Returns the index of the first (*last*) character of the substring in the string that matches the specified string str. Returns −1 if the str argument is not in the string.

✦ `public int indexOf(String str, int fromIndex)`

   (*public int lastIndexOf(String str, int endIndex)*)

   Returns the index of the first (*last*) character of the substring in the string starting from (*ending at*) the specified fromIndex (*endIndex*) that matches the specified string str. Returns −1 if the str argument is not in the substring.

For example,

`indexOf`

`"Welcome to Java".indexOf('W')` returns 0.
`"Welcome to Java".indexOf('o')` returns 4.
`"Welcome to Java".indexOf('o', 5)` returns 9.

```
"Welcome to Java".indexOf("come") returns 3.
"Welcome to Java".indexOf("Java", 5) returns 11.
"Welcome to Java".indexOf("java", 5) returns -1.
"Welcome to Java".lastIndexOf('W') returns 0.
"Welcome to Java".lastIndexOf('o') returns 9.
"Welcome to Java".lastIndexOf('o', 5) returns 4.
"Welcome to Java".lastIndexOf("come") returns 3.
"Welcome to Java".lastIndexOf("Java", 5) returns -1.
"Welcome to Java".lastIndexOf("java", 5) returns -1.
```

lastIndexOf

7.2.9 Conversion between Strings and Arrays

Strings are not arrays, but a string can be converted into an array, and vice versa. To convert a string to an array of characters, use the `toCharArray` method. For example, the following statement converts the string `"Java"` to an array:

```
char[] chars = "Java".toCharArray();
```

toCharArray

So `chars[0]` is `'J'`, `chars[1]` is `'a'`, `chars[2]` is `'v'`, and `chars[3]` is `'a'`.

You can also use the `getChars(int srcBegin, int srcEnd, char[] dst, int dstBegin)` method to copy a substring of the string from index `srcBegin` to index `srcEnd-1` into a character array `dst` starting from index `dstBegin`. For example, the following code copies a substring `"3720"` in `"CS3720"` from index 2 to index 6-1 into the character array `dst` starting from index 4.

```
char[] dst = {'J', 'A', 'V', 'A', '1', '3', '0', '1'};
"CS3720".getChars(2, 6, dst, 4);
```

getChars

Thus `dst` becomes `{'J', 'A', 'V', 'A', '3', '7', '2', '0'}`.

To convert an array of characters into a string, use the `String(char[])` constructor or the `valueOf(char[])` method. For example, the following statement constructs a string from an array using the `String` constructor:

```
String str = new String(new char[]{'J', 'a', 'v', 'a'});
```

The next statement constructs a string from an array using the `valueOf` method:

```
String str = String.valueOf(new char[]{'J', 'a', 'v', 'a'});
```

valueOf

7.2.10 Converting Characters and Numeric Values to Strings

The `valueOf` method can be used to convert an array of characters into a string. There are several overloaded versions of the `valueOf` method that can be used to convert a character and numeric values to strings with different parameter types, `char`, `double`, `long`, `int`, and `float`. For example, to convert a double value 5.44 to a string, use `String.valueOf(5.44)`. The return value is a string consisting of the characters `'5'`, `'.'`, `'4'`, and `'4'`.

overloaded valueOf

 NOTE

Use `Double.parseDouble(str)` or `Integer.parseInt(str)` to convert a string to a double value or an int value.

EXAMPLE 7.1 CHECKING PALINDROMES

Problem

Write a program that prompts the user to enter a string and reports whether the string is a palindrome, as shown in Figure 7.5. A string is a palindrome if it reads the same forward and backward. The words "mom," "dad," and "noon," for instance, are all palindromes.

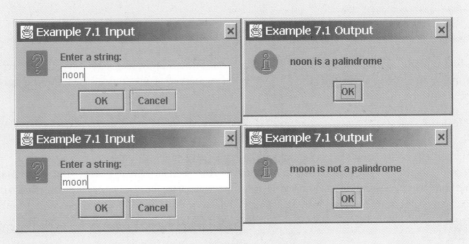

FIGURE 7.5 *The program checks whether a string is a palindrome.*

Solution

One solution is to check whether the first character in the string is the same as the last character. If so, check whether the second character is the same as the second-last character. This process continues until a mismatch is found or all the characters in the string are checked, except for the middle character if the string has an odd number of characters.

To implement this idea, use two variables, say low and high, to denote the position of two characters at the beginning and the end in a string s. Initially, low is 0 and high is s.length() - 1. If the two characters at these positions match, increment low by 1 and decrement high by 1. This process continues until (low >= high) or a mismatch is found.

LISTING 7.1 CheckPalindrome.java (Is a String Palindrome?)

input string

```
1 import javax.swing.JOptionPane;
2
3 public class CheckPalindrome {
4   /** Main method */
5   public static void main(String[] args) {
6     // Prompt the user to enter a string
7     String s = JOptionPane.showInputDialog(null,
8       "Enter a string:", "Example 7.1 Input",
9       JOptionPane.QUESTION_MESSAGE);
10
11    // Declare and initialize output string
12    String output = "";
13
14    if (isPalindrome(s))
15      output = s + " is a palindrome";
16    else
17      output = s + " is not a palindrome";
18
```

EXAMPLE 7.1 (CONTINUED)

```
19     // Display the result
20     JOptionPane.showMessageDialog(null, output,
21       "Example 7.1 Output", JOptionPane.INFORMATION_MESSAGE);
22   }
23
24   /** Check if a string is a palindrome */
25   public static boolean isPalindrome(String s) {
26     // The index of the first character in the string
27     int low = 0;
28
29     // The index of the last character in the string
30     int high = s.length() - 1;
31
32     while (low < high) {
33       if (s.charAt(low) != s.charAt(high))
34         return false; // Not a palindrome
35
36       low++;
37       high--;
38     }
39
40     return true; // The string is a palindrome
41   }
42 }
```

low index

high index

update indices

Review

The isPalindrome method uses a while loop (Lines 32–38) to compare characters and determine whether a string is a palindrome.

Alternatively, you can create a new string that is a reversal of the original string. If both strings have the same contents, the original string is a palindrome. The String class does not have a method for reversing a string. You can create a method of your own to return a reversed string (see Exercise 7.1) or you can use the reverse method provided in the StringBuffer class. Example 7.3 uses StringBuffer and the reverse method to determine whether a string is a palindrome.

7.3 The Character Class

Java provides a wrapper class for every primitive data type. These classes are Character, Boolean, Byte, Short, Integer, Long, Float, and Double for char, boolean, byte, short, int, long, float, and double. All these classes are in the java.lang package. They enable the primitive data values to be treated as objects. They also contain useful methods for processing primitive values. This section introduces the Character class. The other wrapper classes will be introduced in Chapter 9, "Abstract Classes and Interfaces."

The Character class has a constructor and more than thirty methods for manipulating characters. The most frequently used methods are shown in Figure 7.6.

You can create a Character object from a char value. For example, the following statement creates a Character object for the character 'a':

```
Character character = new Character('a');
```

The charValue method returns the character value wrapped in the Character object. The compareTo method compares this character with another character and returns an integer that is the difference between the Unicodes of this character and the other character. The equals method returns true if and only if the two characters are the same. For example, suppose charObject is new Character('b').

java.lang.Character	
+Character(value: char)	Constructs a character object with char value.
+charValue(): char	Returns the char value from this object.
+compareTo(anotherCharacter: Character): int	Compares this character with another.
+equals(anotherCharacter: Character): boolean	Returns true if this character is equal to another.
+isDigit(ch: char): boolean	Returns true if the specified character is a digit.
+isLetter(ch: char): boolean	Returns true if the specified character is a letter.
+isLetterOrDigit(ch: char): boolean	Returns true if the character is a letter or a digit.
+isLowerCase(ch: char): boolean	Returns true if the character is a lowercase letter.
+isUpperCase(ch: char): boolean	Returns true if the character is an uppercase letter.
+toLowerCase(ch: char): char	Returns the lowercase of the specified character.
+toUpperCase(ch: char): char	Returns the uppercase of the specified character.

FIGURE 7.6 *The Character class provides the methods for manipulating a character.*

```
charObject.compareTo(new Character('a')) returns 1
charObject.compareTo(new Character('b')) returns 0
charObject.compareTo(new Character('c')) returns -1
charObject.compareTo(new Character('d') returns -2
charObject.equals(new Character('b')) returns true
charObject.equals(new Character('d')) returns false
```

Most of the methods in the Character class are static methods. The isDigit(char ch) method returns true if the character is a digit. The isLetter(char ch) method returns true if the character is a letter. The isLetterOrDigit(char ch) method is true if the character is a letter or a digit. The isLowerCase(char ch) method is true if the character is a lowercase letter. The isUpperCase(char ch) method is true if the character is an uppercase letter. The toLowerCase(char) method returns the lowercase letter for the character, and the toUpperCase(char ch) method returns the uppercase letter for the character.

EXAMPLE 7.2 COUNTING EACH LETTER IN A STRING

Problem

Write a program that prompts the user to enter a string and counts the number of occurrences of each letter in the string regardless of case, as shown in Figure 7.7.

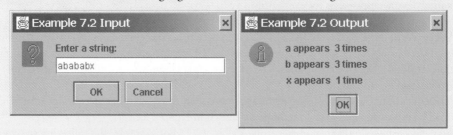

FIGURE 7.7 *The program counts the number of occurrences for each letter in the string.*

Solution

Here are the steps to solve this problem:

1. Convert all the uppercase letters in the string to lowercase using the toLowerCase method in the String class.

EXAMPLE 7.2 (CONTINUED)

2. Create an array, say counts of twenty-six int values, each of which counts the occurrences of a letter. That is, counts[0] counts the number of a's, counts[1] counts the number of b's, and so on.

3. For each character in the string, check whether it is a lowercase letter. If so, increment the corresponding count in the array.

LISTING 7.2 CountEachLetter.java (Counting Letters)

```java
 1 import javax.swing.JOptionPane;
 2
 3 public class CountEachLetter {
 4   /** Main method */
 5   public static void main(String[] args) {
 6     // Prompt the user to enter a string
 7     String s = JOptionPane.showInputDialog(null,
 8       "Enter a string:", "Example 7.2 Input",
 9       JOptionPane.QUESTION_MESSAGE);
10
11     // Invoke the countLetters method to count each letter
12     int[] counts = countLetters(s.toLowerCase());
13
14     // Declare and initialize output string
15     String output = "";
16
17     // Display results
18     for (int i = 0; i < counts.length; i++) {
19       if (counts[i] != 0)
20         output += (char)('a' + i) + " appears " +
21           counts[i] + ((counts[i] == 1) ? " time\n" : " times\n");
22     }
23
24     // Display the result
25     JOptionPane.showMessageDialog(null, output,
26       "Example 7.2 Output", JOptionPane.INFORMATION_MESSAGE);
27   }
28
29   // Count each letter in the string
30   public static int[] countLetters(String s) {
31     int[] counts = new int[26];
32
33     for (int i = 0; i < s.length(); i++) {
34       if (Character.isLetter(s.charAt(i)))
35         counts[s.charAt(i) - 'a']++;
36     }
37
38     return counts;
39   }
40 }
```

input string

count letters

count a letter

Review

The main method reads a string (Lines 7–9) and counts the number of occurrences of each letter in it by invoking the countLetters method (Line 12). Since the case of the letters is ignored, the program uses the toLowerCase method to convert the string into all lowercase and pass the new string to the countLetters method.

EXAMPLE 7.2 (CONTINUED)

The countLetters method (Lines 30–39) returns an array of twenty-six elements. Each element counts the number of occurrences of a letter in the string s. The method processes each character in the string. If the character is a letter, its corresponding count is increased by 1. For example, if the character (s.charAr(i)) is 'a', the corresponding count is counts['a' – 'a'] (i.e., counts[0]). If the character is 'b', the corresponding count is counts['b' – 'a'] (i.e., counts[1]), since the Unicode of 'b' is 1 more than that of 'a'. If the character is 'z', the corresponding count is counts['z' – 'a'] (i.e., counts[25]) since the Unicode of 'z' is 25 more than that of 'a'.

7.4 The **StringBuffer** Class

The StringBuffer class is an alternative to the String class. In general, a string buffer can be used wherever a string is used. StringBuffer is more flexible than String. You can add, insert, or append new contents into a string buffer, whereas the value of a string is fixed once the string is created.

The StringBuffer class has three constructors and more than thirty methods for managing the buffer and modifying strings in the buffer. The most frequently used methods are listed in Figure 7.8.

java.lang.StringBuffer	
+StringBuffer()	Constructs an empty string buffer with capacity 16.
+StringBuffer(capacity: int)	Constructs a string buffer with the specified capacity.
+StringBuffer(str: String)	Constructs a string buffer with the specified string.
+append(data: char[]): StringBuffer	Appends a char array into this string buffer.
+append(data: char[], offset: int, len: int): StringBuffer	Appends a subarray in data into this string buffer.
+append(v: *aPrimitiveType*): StringBuffer	Appends a primitive type value as a string to this buffer.
+append(str: String): StringBuffer	Appends a string to this string buffer.
+capacity(): int	Returns the capacity of this string buffer.
+charAt(index: int): char	Returns the character at the specified index.
+delete(startIndex: int, endIndex: int): StringBuffer	Deletes characters from startIndex to endIndex.
+deleteCharAt(index: int): StringBuffer	Deletes a character at the specified index.
+insert(index: int, data: char[], offset: int, len: int): StringBuffer	Inserts a subarray of the data in the array to the buffer a the specified index.
+insert(offset: int, data: char[]): StringBuffer	Inserts data into this buffer at the position offset.
+insert(offset: int, b: *aPrimitiveType*): StringBuffer	Inserts a value converted to a string into this buffer.
+insert(offset: int, str: String): StringBuffer	Inserts a string into this buffer at the position offset.
+length(): int	Returns the number of characters in this buffer.
+replace(startIndex: int, endIndex: int, str: String): StringBuffer	Replaces the characters in this buffer from startIndex to endIndex with the specified string.
+reverse(): StringBuffer	Reverses the characters in the buffer.
+setCharAt(index: int, ch: char): void	Sets a new character at the specified index in this buffer.
+setLength(newLength: int): void	Sets a new length in this buffer.
+substring(startIndex: int): String	Returns a substring starting at startIndex.
+substring(startIndex: int, endIndex: int): String	Returns a substring from startIndex to endIndex –1.

FIGURE 7.8 *The StringBuffer class provides the methods for processing a string buffer.*

7.4.1 Constructing a String Buffer

The `StringBuffer` class provides three constructors:

✦ `public StringBuffer()`

Constructs a string buffer with no characters in it and an initial capacity of sixteen characters.

✦ `public StringBuffer(int length)`

Constructs a string buffer with no characters in it and an initial capacity specified by the `length` argument.

✦ `public StringBuffer(String string)`

Constructs a string buffer for the string argument with an initial capacity of sixteen plus the length of the string argument.

7.4.2 Modifying Strings in the Buffer

You can append new contents at the end of a string buffer, insert new contents at a specified position in a string buffer, and delete or replace characters in a string buffer.

The `StringBuffer` class provides several overloaded methods to append `boolean`, `char`, `char array`, `double`, `float`, `int`, `long`, and `String` into a string buffer. For example, the following code appends strings and characters into `strBuf` to form a new string, `"Welcome to Java"`:

```
StringBuffer strBuf = new StringBuffer();
strBuf.append("Welcome");
strBuf.append(' ');
strBuf.append("to");
strBuf.append(' ');
strBuf.append("Java");
```

append

The `StringBuffer` class also contains overloaded methods to insert `boolean`, `char`, `char array`, `double`, `float`, `int`, `long`, and `String` into a string buffer. Consider the following code:

```
strBuf.insert(11, "HTML and ");
```

insert

Suppose `strBuf` contains `"Welcome to Java"` before the `insert` method is applied. This code inserts `"HTML and "` at position 11 in `strBuf` (just before J). The new `strBuf` is `"Welcome to HTML and Java"`.

You can also delete characters from a string in the buffer using the two `delete` methods, reverse the string using the `reverse` method, replace characters using the `replace` method, or set a new character in a string using the `setCharAt` method.

For example, suppose `strBuf` contains `"Welcome to Java"` before each of the following methods is applied:

`strBuf.delete(8, 11)` changes the buffer to `Welcome Java`.

delete

`strBuf.deleteCharAt(8)` changes the buffer to `Welcome o Java`.

`strBuf.reverse()` changes the buffer to `avaJ ot emocleW`.

reverse

`strBuf.replace(11, 15, "HTML")` changes the buffer to `Welcome to HTML`.

replace

`strBuf.setCharAt(0, 'w')` sets the buffer to `welcome to Java`.

setCharAt

🌸 NOTE

All these modification methods except `setCharAt` do two things: (1) change the contents of the string buffer, (2) return the reference of the string buffer. A method with nonvoid return value type can also be invoked as a statement in Java, if you are not interested in the return value of the method. In this case, the return value is simply ignored.

Tip

If a string does not require any change, use `String` rather than `StringBuffer`. Java can perform some optimizations for `String`, such as sharing canonical strings.

7.4.3 The `toString`, `capacity`, `length`, `setLength`, and `charAt` Methods

The `StringBuffer` class provides many other methods for manipulating string buffers.

`toString()`

✦ The `toString()` method returns the string from the string buffer.

`capacity()`

✦ The `capacity()` method returns the current capacity of the string buffer. The capacity is the number of new characters it is able to store without having to increase its size.

`length()`

✦ The `length()` method returns the number of characters actually stored in the string buffer.

`setLength(int)`

✦ The `setLength(newLength)` method sets the length of the string buffer. If the `newLength` argument is less than the current length of the string buffer, the string buffer is truncated to contain exactly the number of characters given by the `newLength` argument. If the `newLength` argument is greater than or equal to the current length, sufficient null characters (`'\u0000'`) are appended to the string buffer so that `length` becomes the `newLength` argument. The `newLength` argument must be greater than or equal to 0.

`charAt(int)`

✦ The `charAt(index)` method returns the character at a specific `index` in the string buffer. The first character of a string buffer is at index 0, the next at index 1, and so on. The `index` argument must be greater than or equal to 0, and less than the length of the string buffer.

 Note

The length of the string is always less than or equal to the capacity of the buffer. The length is the actual size of the string stored in the buffer, and the capacity is the current size of the buffer. The buffer is dynamically increased if more characters are added to exceed its capacity. Internally, a string buffer is an array of characters, so the buffer's capacity is the size of the array. If the buffer's capacity is exceeded, the array is replaced by a new array. The new array size is 2 * (the previous array size + 1).

EXAMPLE 7.3 IGNORING NONALPHANUMERIC CHARACTERS WHEN CHECKING PALINDROMES

Problem

Example 7.1, "Checking Palindromes," considered all the characters in a string to check whether it was a palindrome. Write a new program that ignores nonalphanumeric characters in checking whether a string is a palindrome. A sample run of the program is shown in Figure 7.9.

EXAMPLE 7.3 (CONTINUED)

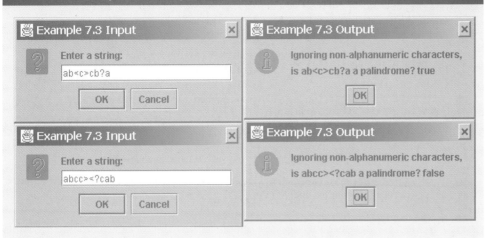

FIGURE 7.9 *The program checks whether a string is a palindrome, ignoring nonalphanumeric characters.*

Solution

Here are the steps to solve the problem:

1. Filter the string by removing the nonalphanumeric characters. This can be done by creating an empty string buffer, adding each alphanumeric character in the string to a string buffer, and returning the string from the string buffer. You can use the isLetterOrDigit(ch) method in the Character class to check whether character ch is a letter or a digit.

2. Obtain a new string that is the reversal of the filtered string. Compare the reversed string with the filtered string using the equals method.

LISTING 7.3 **PalindromeIgnoreNonAlphanumeric.java**

```
 1 import javax.swing.JOptionPane;
 2
 3 public class PalindromeIgnoreNonAlphanumeric {
 4   /** Main method */
 5   public static void main(String[] args) {
 6     // Prompt the user to enter a string
 7     String s = JOptionPane.showInputDialog(null,
 8       "Enter a string:", "Example 7.3 Input",
 9       JOptionPane.QUESTION_MESSAGE);
10
11     // Declare and initialize output string
12     String output = "Ignoring non-alphanumeric characters, \nis "
13       + s + " a palindrome? " + isPalindrome(s);
14
15     // Display the result
16     JOptionPane.showMessageDialog(null, output,
17       "Example 7.3 Output", JOptionPane.INFORMATION_MESSAGE);
18   }
19
20   /** Return true if a string is a palindrome */
21   public static boolean isPalindrome(String s) {
22     // Create a new string by eliminating non-alphanumeric chars
23     String s1 = filter(s);
24
```

EXAMPLE 7.3 (CONTINUED)

```
25      // Create a new string that is the reversal of s1
26      String s2 = reverse(s1);
27
28      // Compare if the reversal is the same as the original string
29      return s2.equals(s1);
30    }
31
32    /** Create a new string by eliminating non-alphanumeric chars */
33    public static String filter(String s) {
34      // Create a string buffer
35      StringBuffer strBuf = new StringBuffer();
36
37      // Examine each char in the string to skip alphanumeric char
38      for (int i = 0; i < s.length(); i++) {
39        if (Character.isLetterOrDigit(s.charAt(i))) {
40          strBuf.append(s.charAt(i));
41        }
42      }
43
44      // Return a new filtered string
45      return strBuf.toString();
46    }
47
48    /** Create a new string by reversing a specified string */
49    public static String reverse(String s) {
50      StringBuffer strBuf = new StringBuffer(s);
51      strBuf.reverse(); // Use the reverse method for StringBuffer object
52      return strBuf.toString();
53    }
54 }
```

add letter or digit

Review

The `filter(String s)` method (Lines 33–46) examines each character in string s and copies it to a string buffer if the character is a letter or a numeric character. The `filter` method returns the string in the buffer. The `reverse(String s)` method (Lines 49–53) creates a new string that reverses the specified string s. The `filter` and `reverse` methods both return a new string. The original string is not changed.

The program in Example 7.1 checks whether a string is a palindrome by comparing pairs of characters from both ends of the string. Example 7.3 uses the `reverse` method in the `StringBuffer` class to reverse the string, then compares whether the two strings are equal to determine whether the original string is a palindrome.

7.5   The `StringTokenizer` Class

Another useful class related to processing strings is the `java.util.StringTokenizer` class. This class is used to break a string into pieces so that information contained in it can be retrieved and processed. For example, to get all of the words in a string like `"I am learning Java now"`, you create an instance of the `StringTokenizer` class for the string and then retrieve individual words in the string by using the methods in the `StringTokenizer` class, as shown in Figure 7.10.

How does the `StringTokenizer` class recognize individual words? You can specify a set of characters as delimiters when constructing a `StringTokenizer` object. Each delimiters is a character. The delimiters break a string into pieces known as *tokens*. You can specify delimiters in the `StringTokenizer` constructors:

✦ `public StringTokenizer(String s, String delim, boolean returnDelims)`

   Constructs a `StringTokenizer` for string s with specified delimiters. Each character in the string `delim` is a delimiter. If `returnDelims` is true, the delimiters are counted as tokens.

java.util.StringTokenizer	
+StringTokenizer(s: String)	Constructs a string tokenizer for the string
+StringTokenizer(s: String, delimiters: String)	Constructs a string tokenizer for the string with the specified delimiters.
+StringTokenizer (s: String, delimiters: String, returnDelimiters: boolean)	Constructs a string tokenizer for the string with the delimiters and returnDelims.
+countTokens(): int	Returns the number of remaining tokens.
+hasMoreTokens(): boolean	Returns true if there are more tokens left.
+nextToken(): String	Returns the next token.
+nextToken(delimiters: String): String	Returns the next token using new delimiters.

FIGURE 7.10   *The StringTokenizer class provides the methods for processing tokens in a string.*

◆ public StringTokenizer(String s, String delim)

Constructs a StringTokenizer for string s with specified delimiters delim, and the delimiters are not counted as tokens.

◆ public StringTokenizer(String s)

Constructs a StringTokenizer for string s with default delimiters " \t\n\r" (a space, tab, new line, and carriage return), and the delimiters are not counted as tokens.

The following code creates a string tokenizer for a string using space as delimiters and extracts all the tokens:

```
1 String s = "Java is cool.";
2 StringTokenizer tokenizer = new StringTokenizer(s);
3
4 System.out.println("The total number of tokens is " +
5   tokenizer.countTokens());
6
7 while (tokenizer.hasMoreTokens())
8   System.out.println(tokenizer.nextToken());
```

create a tokenizer

The code displays

```
The total number of tokens is 3
Java
is
cool.
```

Line 2 creates a string tokenizer using the default delimiters. If you create it using delimiters "a" or "c" (new StringTokenizer(s, "ac")), the output would be

```
The total number of tokens is 4
J
v
 is
ool.
```

If you want the delimiters to be counted as tokens, create a string tokenizer using new StringTokenizer(s, "ac", ture), the output would be

```
The total number of tokens is 7
J
a
v
a
 is
c
ool.
```

no no-arg constructor

 NOTE

The StringTokenizer class does not have a no-arg constructor. Normally it is good programming practice to provide a no-arg constructor for each class. On rare occasions, however, a no-arg constructor does not make sense. StringTokenizer is such an example. A StringTokenizer object must be created for a string that is to be passed as an argument from a constructor.

7.6 The Scanner Class (JDK 1.5 Feature)

The delimiters are single characters in StringTokenizer. You can use the new JDK 1.5 java.util.Scanner class to specify a word as a delimiter. Here is an example that uses the word *Java* as a delimiter to scan tokens in a string:

create a scanner

```
1 String s = "Welcome to Java! Java is fun! Java is cool!";
2 Scanner scanner = new Scanner(s);
3 scanner.useDelimiter("Java");
4
5 while (scanner.hasNext())
6   System.out.println(scanner.next());
```

Line 2 creates an instance of Scanner for the string. Line 3 sets "Java" as a delimiter. Line 5, hasNext() returns true if there are still any tokens left. Line 6, the next() method returns a token as a string. So the output from this code is

```
Welcome to
!
 is fun!
 is cool!
```

If a token is a primitive data type value, you can use the methods nextByte(), nextShort(), nextInt(), nextLong(), nextFloat(), nextDouble(), or nextBoolean() to obtain it. For example, the following code adds all the numbers in the string. Note that the delimiter is space by default.

```
String s = "1 2 3 4";
Scanner scanner = new Scanner(s);

int sum = 0;
while (scanner.hasNext())
  sum += scanner.nextInt();

System.out.println("Sum is " + sum);
```

StringTokenizer vs. Scanner

 NOTE

StringTokenizer can specify several single characters as delimiters. Scanner can use a single character or a word as the delimiter. If you need to scan a string with multiple single characters as delimiters, use StringTokenizer. If you need to use a word as the delimiter, use Scanner.

7.7 Implementing MyInput Using Scanner

Java uses System.out to refer to a standard output device and System.in to refer to a standard input device. By default the output device is the console and the input device is the keyboard. To perform console output, you simply use the print or println method to display a primitive value or a string to the console. Keyboard input is not directly supported in Java, but you can use the Scanner class to create an object to read input from System.in as follows:

```
Scanner scanner = new Scanner(System.in);
```

Now you can use next(), nextByte(), nextShort(), nextInt(), nextLong(), nextFloat(), nextDouble(), or nextBoolean() to obtain a string, byte, short, int, long, float, double, or boolean value. For convenience, let us create a class named MyInput for reading primitive data type values and strings from the keyboard, as shown in Figure 7.11.

MyInput	
+readByte(): byte	Reads an integer in the byte type from the keyboard.
+readShort(): short	Reads an integer in the short type from the keyboard.
+readInt(): int	Reads an integer in the int type from the keyboard.
+readLong(): int	Reads an integer in the long type from the keyboard.
+readFloat(): float	Reads a decimal value in the float type from the keyboard.
+readDouble(): double	Reads a decimal value in the double type from the keyboard.
+readChar(): char	Reads a character from the keyboard.
+readBoolean(): boolean	Reads a boolean value from the keyboard.
+readString(): String	Reads a string from the keyboard.

FIGURE 7.11 *MyInput provides static methods for reading primitive values and strings from the keyboard.*

This class was introduced in Section 2.16, "Getting Input from the Console." TestMyInput, a test program that uses MyInput, was also given in that section. Listing 7.4 implements MyInput.

LISTING 7.4 MyInput.java (Console Input)

```java
1  import java.util.*;
2
3  public class MyInput {
4    static Scanner scanner = new Scanner(System.in);
5
6    /** Read a string from the keyboard */
7    public static String readString() {
8      return scanner.next();
9    }
10
11   /** Read an int value from the keyboard */
12   public static int readInt() {
13     return scanner.nextInt();
14   }
15
16   /** Read a double value from the keyboard */
17   public static double readDouble() {
18     return scanner.nextDouble();
19   }
20
21   /** Read a byte value from the keyboard */
22   public static byte readByte() {
23     return scanner.nextByte();
24   }
25
26   /** Read a short value from the keyboard */
27   public static short readShort() {
28     return scanner.nextShort();
29   }
30
```

```
31   /** Read a long value from the keyboard */
32   public static long readLong() {
33     return scanner.nextLong();
34   }
35
36   /** Read a float value from the keyboard */
37   public static float readFloat() {
38     return scanner.nextFloat();
39   }
40
41   /** Read a character from the keyboard */
42   public static char readChar() {
43     return (scanner.next()).charAt(0);
44   }
45
46   /** Read a boolean value from the keyboard */
47   public static boolean readBoolean() {
48     return scanner.nextBoolean();
49   }
50 }
```

7.8   Command-Line Arguments

Perhaps you have already noticed the unusual declarations for the main method, which has parameter args of String[] type. It is clear that args is an array of strings. The main method is just like a regular method with a parameter. You can call a regular method by passing actual parameters. Can you pass arguments to main? This section will discuss how to pass and process arguments from the command line.

7.8.1   Passing Strings to the main Method

You can pass strings to a main method from the command line when you run the program. The following command line, for example, starts the program TestMain with three strings: arg0, arg1, and arg2:

```
java TestMain arg0 arg1 arg2
```

arg0, arg1, and arg2 are strings, but they don't have to appear in double quotes on the command line. The strings are separated by a space. A string that contains a space must be enclosed in double quotes. Consider the following command line:

```
java TestMain "First num" alpha 53
```

It starts the program with three strings: "First num" and alpha, and 53, a numeric string. Note that 53 is actually treated as a string. You can use "53" instead of 53 in the command line.

When the main method is invoked, the Java interpreter creates an array to hold the command-line arguments and pass the array reference to args. For example, if you invoke a program with n arguments, the Java interpreter creates an array like this:

```
args = new String[n];
```

The Java interpreter then passes args to invoke the main method.

 NOTE

If you run the program with no strings passed, the array is created with new String[0]. In this case, the array is empty with length 0. args references to this empty array. Therefore, args is not null, but args.length is 0.

7.8.2   Processing Command-Line Arguments

The strings passed to the main program are stored in args, which is an array of strings. The first string is stored in args[0], and args.length is the number of strings passed.

EXAMPLE 7.4 PASSING COMMAND-LINE ARGUMENTS

Problem

Write a program that performs binary operations on integers. The program receives three arguments: an integer followed by an operator and another integer. For example, to add two integers, use this command:

```
java Calculator 2 + 3
```

The program will display the following output:

```
2 + 3 = 5
```

Figure 7.12 shows sample runs of the program.

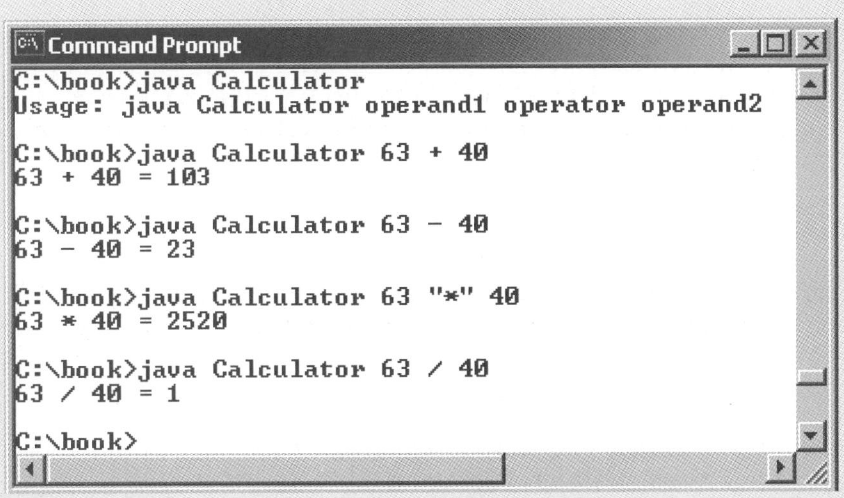

```
Command Prompt                                        _ □ ×
C:\book>java Calculator
Usage: java Calculator operand1 operator operand2

C:\book>java Calculator 63 + 40
63 + 40 = 103

C:\book>java Calculator 63 - 40
63 - 40 = 23

C:\book>java Calculator 63 "*" 40
63 * 40 = 2520

C:\book>java Calculator 63 / 40
63 / 40 = 1

C:\book>
```

FIGURE **7.12**   *The program takes three arguments (operand1, operator, operand2) from the command line and displays the expression and the result of the arithmetic operation.*

Solution

Here are the steps in the program:

1. Use args.length to determine whether three arguments have been provided in the command line. If not, terminate the program using System.exit(0).

2. Perform a binary arithmetic operation on the operands args[0] and args[2] using the operator specified in args[1].

LISTING 7.5   Calculator.java (Command-Line Arguments)

```
1 public class Calculator {
2   /** Main method */
3   public static void main(String[] args) {
```

check operator

EXAMPLE 7.4 (CONTINUED)

```
 4    // Check number of strings passed
 5    if (args.length != 3) {
 6      System.out.println(
 7        "Usage: java Calculator operand1 operator operand2");
 8      System.exit(0);
 9    }
10
11    // The result of the operation
12    int result = 0;
13
14    // Determine the operator
15    switch (args[1].charAt(0)) {
16      case '+': result = Integer.parseInt(args[0]) +
17                        Integer.parseInt(args[2]);
18              break;
19      case '-': result = Integer.parseInt(args[0]) -
20                        Integer.parseInt(args[2]);
21              break;
22      case '*': result = Integer.parseInt(args[0]) *
23                        Integer.parseInt(args[2]);
24              break;
25      case '/': result = Integer.parseInt(args[0]) /
26                        Integer.parseInt(args[2]);
27    }
28
29    // Display result
30    System.out.println(args[0] + ' ' + args[1] + ' ' + args[2]
31      + " = " + result);
32  }
33 }
```

Review

`Integer.parseInt(args[0])` (Line 16) converts a digital string into an integer. The string must consist of digits. If not, the program will terminate abnormally.

In the sample run, `"*"` had to be used instead of * for the command

```
java Calculator 63 "*" 40
```

In JDK 1.1 and above, the * symbol refers to all the files in the current directory when it is used on a command line. Therefore, in order to specify the multiplication operator, the * must be enclosed in quote marks in the command line. The following program displays all the files in the current directory when issuing the command `java Test *`:

```
public class Test {
  public static void main(String[] args) {
    for (int i = 0; i < args.length; i++)
      System.out.println(args[i]);
  }
}
```

KEY CLASSES AND METHODS

✦ **java.lang.String**   is a class for creating an immutable string.

✦ **java.lang.Character**   is a class for wrapping a character into an object.

✦ **java.lang.StringBuffer**   is a class for creating a buffer to hold a modifiable string.

✦ **java.util.StringTokenizer**   is a class for extracting tokens from a string.

✦ **java.util.Scanner**   is a new JDK 1.5 class for scanning tokens.

CHAPTER SUMMARY

✦ Strings are objects encapsulated in the String class. A string can be constructed using one of the eleven constructors or using a string literal shorthand initializer.

✦ A String object is immutable; its contents cannot be changed. To improve efficiency and save memory, Java Virtual Machine stores two String objects in the same object if they were created with the same string literal using the shorthand initializer. Therefore, the shorthand initializer is preferred in creating strings.

✦ You can get the length of a string by invoking its length() method, and retrieve a character at the specified index in the string using the charAt(index) method.

✦ You can use the concat method to concatenate two strings, or the plus (+) sign to concatenate two or more strings.

✦ You can use the substring method to extract a substring from the string.

✦ You can use the equals and compareTo methods to compare strings. The equals method returns true if two strings are equal, and false if they are not equal. The compareTo method returns 0, a positive integer, or a negative integer, depending on whether one string is equal to, greater than, or less than the other string.

✦ The Character class is a wrapper class for a single character. The Character class provides useful static methods to determine whether a character is a letter (isLetter(char)), a digit (isDigit(char)), uppercase (isUpperCase(char)), or lowercase (isLowerCase(char)).

✦ The StringBuffer class can be used to replace the String class. The String object is immutable, but you can add, insert, or append new contents into a StringBuffer object. Use String if the string contents do not require any change, and use StringBuffer if they change.

✦ The StringTokenizer class is used to retrieve and process tokens in a string. You learned the role of delimiters, how to create a StringTokenizer from a string, and how to use the countTokens, hasMoreTokens, and nextToken methods to process a string tokenizer.

✦ You can pass strings to the main method from the command line. Strings passed to the main program are stored in args, which is an array of strings. The first string is represented by args[0], and args.length is the number of strings passed.

REVIEW QUESTIONS

Section 7.2 The String Class

7.1 Suppose that s1, s2, s3, and s4 are four strings, given as follows:

```
String s1 = "Welcome to Java";
String s2 = s1;
String s3 = new String("Welcome to Java");
String s4 = s3.intern();
```

What are the results of the following expressions?

```
(1)  s1 == s2
(2)  s2 == s3
(3)  s1.equals(s2)
(7)  s1 == s4
(8)  s1.charAt(0)
(9)  s1.indexOf('j')
(10) s1.indexOf("to")
(11) s1.lastIndexOf('a')
(12) s1.lastIndexOf("o", 15)
(13) s1.length()
(14) s1.substring(5)
(15) s1.substring(5, 11)
```

```
(4)  s2.equals(s3)
(5)  s1.compareTo(s2)
(6)  s2.compareTo(s3)
(16) s1.startsWith("Wel")
(17) s1.endsWith("Java")
(18) s1.toLowerCase()
(19) s1.toUpperCase()
(20) "  Welcome ".trim()
(21) s1.replace('o', "T")
(22) s1.replaceAll("o", "T")
(23) s1.replaceFirst("o", "T")
(24) s1.toCharArray()
```

7.2 Suppose that s1 and s2 are two strings. Which of the following statements or expressions are incorrect?

```
String s = new String("new string");
String s3 = s1 + s2;
String s3 = s1 - s2;
s1 == s2;
s1 >= s2;
s1.compareTo(s2);
int i = s1.length();
char c = s1(0);
char c = s1.charAt(s1.length());
```

7.3 How do you compare whether two strings are equal without considering cases?

7.4 How do you convert all the letters in a string to uppercase? How do you convert all the letters in a string to lowercase? Do the conversion methods (toLowerCase, toUpperCase, trim, replace) change the contents of the string that invokes these methods?

7.5 Suppose string s is created using new String(); what is s.length()?

7.6 How do you convert a char, an array of characters, or a number to a string?

7.7 Why does the following code cause a NullPointerException?

```
1 public class Test {
2   private String text;
3
4   public Test(String s) {
5     String text = s;
6   }
7
8   public static void main(String[] args) {
9     Test test = new Test("ABC");
10    System.out.println(test.text.toLowerCase());
11  }
12 }
```

7.8 What is wrong in the following program?

```
1 public class Test {
2   String text;
3
4   public void Test(String s) {
5     this.text = s;
6   }
7
8   public static void main(String[] args) {
9     Test test = new Test("ABC");
10    System.out.println(test);
11  }
12 }
```

Section 7.3 The `Character` Class

7.9   How do you determine whether a character is in lowercase or uppercase?

7.10   How do you determine whether a character is alphanumeric?

Section 7.4 The `StringBuffer` Class

7.11   How do you create a string buffer for a string? How do you get the string from a string buffer?

7.12   Write three statements to reverse a string `s` using the `reverse` method in the `StringBuffer` class.

7.13   Write three statements to delete a substring from a string `s` of twenty characters, starting at index 4 and ending with index 10. Use the `delete` method in the `StringBuffer` class.

7.14   What is the internal structure of a string and a string buffer?

7.15   Suppose that s1 and s2 are given as follows:

```
StringBuffer s1 = new StringBuffer("Java");
StringBuffer s2 = new StringBuffer("HTML");
```

Show the results of the following expressions of s1 after each statement. Assume that the expressions are independent.

```
(1)  s1.append(" is fun");       (7)  s1.deleteCharAt(3);
(2)  s1.append(s2);              (8)  s1.delete(1, 3);
(3)  s1.insert(2, "is fun");     (9)  s1.reverse();
(4)  s1.insert(1, s2);           (10) s1.replace(1, 3, "Computer");
(5)  s1charAt(2);                (11) s1.substring(1, 3);
(6)  s1.length();                (12) s1.substring(2);
```

Section 7.5 The `StringTokenizer` Class

7.16   Declare a `StringTokenizer` for a string s with delimiters `"%$#"`.

7.17   What is the output of the following program?

```
 1 import java.util.StringTokenizer;
 2
 3 public class TestStringTokenizer {
 4   public static void main(String[] args) {
 5     String s = "Java is cool.";
 6     StringTokenizer tokenizer = new StringTokenizer(s, "v.");
 7
 8     System.out.println("The total number of tokens is " +
 9       tokenizer.countTokens());
10
11     while (tokenizer.hasMoreTokens())
12         System.out.println(tokenizer.nextToken());
13
14     System.out.println("Any tokens left? " + tokenizer.countTokens());
15   }
16 }
```

What would be the output if Line 6 is replaced by the following code?

```
StringTokenizer tokenizer = new StringTokenizer(s, "v.", ture);
```

Section 7.6 The Scanner Class

7.18 Write the code to display all the tokens in a strings using the word `"to"` as the delimiter.

7.19 Write the code to read an `int` value from the console.

Section 7.7 Command-Line Arguments

7.19 Show the output of the following program when invoked using

1. java Test I have a dream
2. java Test "1 2 3"
3. java Test
4. java Test "*"
5. java Test *

```
public class Test {
  public static void main(String[] args) {
    System.out.println("Number of strings is " + args.length);
    for (int i = 0; i < args.length; i++)
      System.out.println(args[i]);
  }
}
```

PROGRAMMING EXERCISES

Section 7.2 The String Class

7.1* (*Revising Example 7.1 "Checking Palindromes"*) Rewrite Example 7.1 by creating a new string that is a reversal of the string and compare the two to determine whether the string is a palindrome. Write your own `reverse` method using the following header:

```
public static String reverse(String s)
```

7.2* (*Revising Example 7.1 "Checking Palindromes"*) Rewrite Example 7.1 to ignore cases.

7.3** (*Checking substrings*) You can check whether a string is a substring of another string by using the `indexOf` method in the `String` class. Write your own method for this function. Write a program that prompts the user to enter two strings, and check whether the first string is a substring of the second.

7.4* (*Occurrence of a specified character*) Write a method that finds the number of occurrences of a specified letter in the string using the following header:

```
public static int count(String str, char a)
```

For example, `count("Welcome", 'e')` returns 2.

Section 7.3 The Character Class

7.5** (*Occurrences of each digit in a string*) Write a method that counts the occurrences of each digit in a string using the following header:

```
public static int[] count(String s)
```

The method counts how many times a digit appears in the string. The return value is an array of ten elements, each of which holds the count for a digit.

Write a `main` method to display the count for `"SSN is 343 32 4545 and ID is 434 34 4323"`.

7.6* (*Counting the letters in a string*) Write a method that counts the number of letters in the string using the following header:

```
public static int countLetters(String s)
```

Write a main method to invoke countLetters("Java in 2008") and display its return value.

7.7* (*Hex to decimal*) Write a method that parses a hex number as a string into a decimal integer. The method header is as follows:

```
public static int parseHex(String hexString)
```

For example, hexString A5 is $10 \times 16 + 5$ and FAA is $15 \times 16^2 + 10 \times 16 + 10$. Use hex strings ABC and 10A to test the method.

7.8* (*Binary to decimal*) Write a method that parses a binary number as a string into a decimal integer. The method header is as follows:

```
public static int parseBinary(String binaryString)
```

For example, binaryString 10001 is $1 \times 2^4 + 0 \times 2^3 + 0 \times 2^2 + 0 \times 2 + 1$. Use binary string 11111111 to test the method.

Section 7.4 The `StringBuffer` Class

7.9** (*Decimal to hex*) Write a method that parses a decimal number into a hex number as a string. The method header is as follows:

```
public static String convertDecimalToHex(int value)
```

See Section 1.5, "Number Systems," for converting a decimal into a hex. Use decimal 298 and 9123 to test the method.

7.10** (*Decimal to binary*) Write a method that parses a decimal number into a binary number as a string. The method header is as follows:

```
public static String convertDecimalToBinary(int value)
```

See Section 1.5, "Number Systems," for converting a decimal into a binary. Use decimal 298 and 9123 to test the method.

7.11** (*Sorting characters in a string*) Write a method that returns a sorted string using the following header:

```
public static String sort(String s)
```

For example, sort("acb") returns abc.

7.12** (*Anagrams*) Write a method that checks whether two words are anagrams. Two words are anagrams if they contain the same letters in any order. For example, "silent" and "listen" are anagrams. The header of the method is as follows:

```
public static boolean isAnagram(String s1, String s2)
```

Write a main method to invoke isAnagram("silent", "listen"), isAnagram("garden", "ranged"), and isAnagram("split", "lisp").

Section 7.5 The `StringTokenizer` Class

7.13* (*Monetary units*) Rewrite Example 2.3, "Monetary Units," to receive the input as a string, and extract the dollars and cents using the StringTokenizer class.

7.14* (*Extracting words*) Write a program that extracts words from a string using the spaces and punctuation marks as delimiters. Enter the string from an input dialog box.

Section 7.6 The Scanner Class

7.15* (*Revising Exercise 7.13 using* Scanner) Write a program that reads a string from an input dialog box. The string consists of double values separated by spaces. Display the sum of the values.

7.16* (*Console input*) Use the Scanner class to read numbers separated by spaces from the keyboard and displays their sum and average. Press CTRL+C to end the input.

Section 7.7 Command-Line Arguments

7.17* (*Passing a string to check palindromes*) Rewrite Example 7.1, "Checking Palindromes," by passing the string as a command-line argument.

7.18* (*Summing integers*) Write two programs. The first program passes an unspecified number of integers as separate strings to the main method and displays their total. The second program passes an unspecified number of integers in one string to the main method and displays their total. Name the two programs Exercise7_18a and Exercise7_18b, as shown in Figure 7.13.

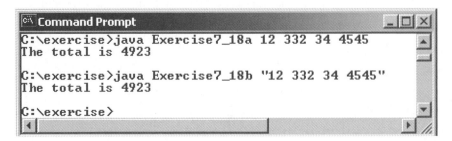

FIGURE 7.13 *The program adds all the numbers passed from the command line.*

7.19* (*Finding the number of uppercase letters in a string*) Write a program that passes a string to the main method and displays the number of uppercase letters in a string.

chapter

8

INHERITANCE AND POLYMORPHISM

Objectives

- ✦ To develop a subclass from a superclass through inheritance (§8.2).

- ✦ To invoke the superclass's constructors and methods using the super keyword (§8.3).

- ✦ To override methods in the subclass (§8.4).

- ✦ To explore the useful methods (equals(Object), hashCode(), toString(), finalize(), clone(), and getClass()) in the Object class (§8.5, §8.11 Optional).

- ✦ To comprehend polymorphism, dynamic binding, and generic programming (§8.6).

- ✦ To describe casting and explain why explicit downcasting is necessary (§8.7).

- ✦ To understand the effect of hiding data fields and static methods (§8.8 Optional).

- ✦ To restrict access to data and methods using the protected visibility modifier (§8.9).

- ✦ To declare constants, unmodifiable methods, and nonextendable classes using the final modifier (§8.10).

- ✦ To initialize data using initialization blocks and to distinguish between instance initialization and static initialization blocks (§8.12 Optional).

8.1 Introduction

inheritance

Object-oriented programming allows you to derive new classes from existing classes. This is called *inheritance*. Inheritance is an important and powerful concept in Java. In fact, every class you define in Java is inherited from an existing class, either explicitly or implicitly. The classes you created in the preceding chapters were all derived implicitly from the `java.lang.Object` class.

This chapter introduces the concept of inheritance. Specifically, it discusses superclasses and subclasses, the use of the keyword `super`, and the `Object` class, explores polymorphism and dynamic binding, generic programming, and casting objects, and introduces the modifiers `protected` and `final`.

8.2 Superclasses and Subclasses

subclass
superclass

In OOP terminology, a class C1 derived from another class C2 is called a *subclass*, and C2 is called a *superclass*. A superclass is also referred to as a *parent class* or a *base class*, and a subclass as a *child class*, an *extended class*, or a *derived class*. A subclass inherits accessible data fields and methods from its superclass, and may also add new data fields and methods.

NOTE
Contrary to the conventional interpretation, a subclass is not a subset of its superclass. In fact, a subclass is usually extended to contain more functions and more detailed information than its superclass.

Let us demonstrate inheritance by creating a new class, `Cylinder`, derived from the `Circle` class defined in Listing 6.3 on page 225. The `Cylinder` class inherits all accessible data fields and methods from the `Circle` class. In addition, it has a new data field, `length`, and a new method, `findVolume`. The relationship of these two classes is shown in Figure 8.1. An arrow pointing to the superclass is used to denote the inheritance relationship between the two classes involved. The `Cylinder` class is defined in Listing 8.1.

LISTING 8.1   First Version of the `Cylinder` Class

```
1 // Cylinder.java: Class definition for describing Cylinder
2 public class Cylinder extends Circle {
3   private double length = 1;
4
5   /** Return length */
6   public double getLength() {
7     return length;
8   }
9
10   /** Set length */
11   public void setLength(double length) {
12     this.length = length;
13   }
14
15   /** Return the volume of this cylinder */
16   public double findVolume() {
17     return findArea() * length;
18   }
19 }
```

The reserved word `extends` (Line 2) tells the compiler that the `Cylinder` class is derived from the `Circle` class, thus inheriting the methods `getRadius`, `setRadius`, and `findArea` from `Circle`.

8.9   The `protected` Data and Methods

The modifier `protected` can be applied to data and methods in a class. A protected datum or a protected method in a public class can be accessed *by any class in the same package or its subclasses*, even if the subclasses are in different packages.

8.9.1   Using the Visibility Modifiers

The modifiers `private`, `protected`, and `public` are known as *visibility* or *accessibility modifiers* because they specify how class and class members are accessed. The visibility of these modifiers increases in this order:

Visibility increases

private, none (if no modifier is used), protected, public

Figure 8.4 illustrates how a public, protected, default, and private data or method in class `C1` can be accessed from a class `C2` in the same package, from a subclass `C3` in the same package, from a subclass `C4` in a different package, and from a class `C5` in a different package.

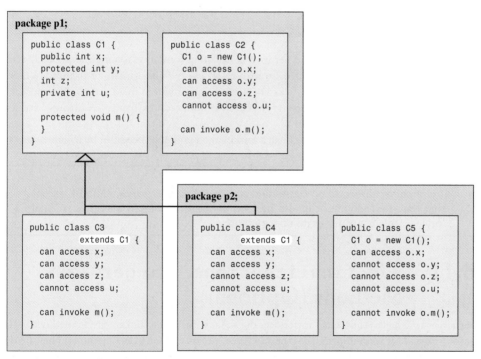

FIGURE 8.4   *Visibility modifiers are used to control how data and methods are accessed.*

Use the `private` modifier to hide the members of the class completely so that they cannot be accessed directly from outside the class. Use no modifiers to allow the members of the class to be accessed directly from any class within the same package but not from other packages. Use the `protected` modifier to enable the members of the class to be accessed by the subclasses in any package or classes in the same package. Use the `public` modifier to enable the members of the class to be accessed by any class.

Your class can be used in two ways: for creating instances of the class, and for creating subclasses by extending the class. Make the members `private` if they are not intended for use from outside the class. Make the members `public` if they are intended for the users of the class. Make the fields or methods `protected` if they are intended for the extenders of the class but not the users of the class.

The `private` and `protected` modifiers can only be used for members of the class. The `public` modifier and the default modifier (i.e., no modifier) can be used on members of the class as well on the class. A class with no modifier (i.e., not a public class) is not accessible by classes from other packages.

NOTE
In UML, the symbols –, #, and +, respectively, are used to denote `private`, `protected`, and `public` modifiers.

NOTE
A subclass may override a protected method in its superclass and change its visibility to public. However, a subclass cannot weaken the accessibility of a method defined in the superclass. For example, if a method is defined as public in the superclass, it must be defined as public in the subclass.

8.10   The `final` Classes, Methods, and Variables

You have already seen the `final` modifier used in declaring constants. You may occasionally want to prevent classes from being extended. In such cases, use the `final` modifier to indicate that a class is final and cannot be a parent class. The `Math` class, introduced in Chapter 4, "Methods," is a final class. The `String` and `StringBuffer` classes, introduced in Chapter 7, "Strings," are also final classes.

You also can define a method to be final; a final method cannot be overriden by its subclasses.

NOTE
The modifiers are used on classes and class members (data and methods), except that the `final` modifier can also be used on local variables in a method. A final local variable is a constant inside a method.

8.11   The `finalize`, `clone`, and `getClass` Methods (Optional)

Section 8.5, "The `Object` Class," introduces the `equals`, `hashCode`, and `toString` methods in the `Object` class. This section introduces the `finalize`, `clone`, and `getClass` methods. They are defined in the `Object` class as follows:

✦ `protected void finalize() throws Throwable`

✦ `protected native Object clone()`
   `throws CloneNotSupportedException`

✦ `public final native Class getClass()`

NOTE
The `native` modifier indicates that the method is implemented using a programming language other than Java. Some methods, such as `clone`, need to access hardware using the native machine language or the C language. These methods are marked `native`. A native method can be final, public, private, protected, overloaded, or overridden.

NOTE

The `finalize` method may throw `Throwable`, and the `clone` method may throw `CloneNotSupportedException`. Exception handling will be introduced in Chapter 15, "Exceptions and Assertions." (*Chapter 15 can be covered after Chapter 8.*) For now, you need to know that `throws Throwable` and `throws CloneNotSupported-Exception` are part of the method declarations for the `finalize` and `clone` methods.

8.11.1 The `finalize` Method

The `finalize` method is invoked by the garbage collector on an object when the object becomes garbage. An object becomes garbage if it is no longer accessed. By default, the `finalize` method does nothing. A subclass should override the `finalize` method to dispose of system resources or to perform other cleanup, if necessary.

 NOTE

The `finalize` method is invoked by the JVM. You should never write the code to invoke it in your program.

For an illustration, see the following code:

```
1 public class Test {
2   public static void main(String[] args) {
3     Cake a1 = new Cake(1);
4     Cake a2 = new Cake(2);
5     Cake a3 = new Cake(3);
6
7     // To dispose the objects a2 and a3
8     a2 = a3 = null;
9     System.gc(); // Invoke the Java garbage collector
10  }
11 }
12
13 class Cake extends Object {
14   int id;
15
16   public Cake(int id) {
17     this.id = id;
18     System.out.println("Cake object " + id + " is created");
19   }
20
21   public void finalize() throws java.lang.Throwable {
22     System.out.println("Cake object " + id + " is disposed");
23   }
24 }
```

Here is the output of this program:

```
Cake object 1 is created
Cake object 2 is created
Cake object 3 is created
Cake object 2 is disposed
Cake object 3 is disposed
```

Line 8 assigns `null` to a2 and a3. The objects previously referenced by a2 and a3 are no longer accessible. Therefore, they are garbage. `System.gc()` in Line 9 requests the garbage collector to be invoked to reclaim space from all discarded objects. Normally you don't need to invoke this method explicitly, because the JVM automatically invokes it whenever the JVM determines it is necessary. The `finalize` method on the objects a2 and a3 are invoked by the garbage collector. When the program terminates, a1 also becomes garbage, and a1's `finalize` method is then invoked. Since the program has already exited, no message is displayed on the console.

8.11.2 The `clone` Method

Sometimes you need to make a copy of an object. Mistakenly, you might use the assignment statement, as follows:

```
newObject = someObject;
```

This statement does not create a duplicate object. It simply assigns the reference of someObject to newObject. To create a new object with separate memory space, use the clone() method:

```
newObject = someObject.clone();
```

This statement copies someObject to a new memory location and assigns the reference of the new object to newObject. For example,

```
java.util.Date date = new java.util.Date();
java.util.Date date1 = (java.util.Date)(date.clone());
```

creates a new Date object, date, and its clone, date1.

NOTE

Not all objects can be cloned. For an object to be cloneable, its class must implement the java.lang.Cloneable interface, which is introduced in Section 9.4.4, "The Cloneable Interface."

TIP

An array is treated as an object in Java and is an instance of the Object class. The clone method can also be used to copy arrays. The following statement uses the clone method to copy the sourceArray of the int[] type to the targetArray:

```
int[] targetArray = (int[])sourceArray.clone();
```

Since the return type of the clone method is Object, (int[]) is used to cast it to the int[] type.

8.11.3 The `getClass` Method

meta-object

A class must be loaded in order to be used. When the JVM loads the class, it creates an object that contains the information about the class, such as class name, constructors, and methods. This object is an instance of java.lang.Class. It is referred to as a *meta-object* in this book because it describes the information about the class. Through the meta-object, you can discover the information about the class at runtime. Every object can use the getClass() method to return its meta-object. For example, the following code

```
Object obj = new Object();
Class metaObject = obj.getClass();

System.out.println("Object obj's class is "
  + metaObject.getName());
```

displays

```
Object obj's class is java.lang.Object
```

NOTE

There is only one meta-object for a class. Every object has a meta-object. If two objects were created from the same class, their meta-objects are the same.

8.12 Initialization Blocks (Optional)

Initialization blocks can be used to initialize objects along with the constructors. An *initialization block* is a block of statements enclosed inside a pair of braces. An initialization block appears within the class declaration, but not inside methods or constructors. It is executed as if it were placed at the beginning of every constructor in the class.

Initialization blocks can simplify the classes if you have multiple constructors sharing a common code and none of the constructors can invoke other constructors. The common code can be placed in an initialization block, as shown in the example in Figure 8.5(a). In this example, none of the constructors can invoke any of the others using the syntax this(...). When an instance is created using a constructor of the Book class, the initialization block is executed to increase the object count by 1. The program is equivalent to Figure 8.5(b):

```
public class Book {
  private static int numOfObjects;
  private String title
  private int id;

  public Book(String title) {
    this.title = title;
  }

  public Book(int id) {
    this.id = id;
  }

  {
    numOfObjects++;
  }
}
```

Equivalent

```
public class Book {
  private static int numOfObjects;
  private String title;
  private int id;

  public Book(String title) {
    numOfObjects++;
    this.title = title;
  }

  public Book(int id) {
    numOfObjects++;
    this.id = id;
  }
}
```

(a) A class with initialization blocks   (b) An equivalent class

FIGURE 8.5 *An initialization block can simplify coding for constructors.*

 NOTE
A class may have multiple initialization blocks. In such cases, the blocks are executed in the order they appear in the class.

The initialization block in Figure 8.5(a) is referred to as an *instance initialization block* because it is invoked whenever an instance of the class is created. A *static initialization block* is much like an instance initialization block except that it is declared static, can only refer to static members of the class, and is invoked when the class is loaded. The JVM loads the class dynamically when it is needed. A superclass is loaded before its subclasses. The order of execution can be summarized as follows:

1. When a class is used for the first time, load the class, initialize static data fields, and execute the static initialization block of the class.

2. When an object of a class is created, a constructor of the class is invoked. The construction has three phases:
   2.1. Invoke a constructor of the superclass.
   2.2. Initialize instance data fields and execute instance initialization blocks.
   2.3. Execute the body of the constructor.

instatic initialization block
static initialization block

For an illustration, see the following code:

```
 1 public class Test {
 2   public static void main(String[] args) {
 3     new Test();
 4   }
 5
 6   public Test() {
 7     new Parrot();
 8   }
 9
10   { // instance initialization block
11     System.out.println("(2) Test's instance initialization " +
12       "block is invoked");
13   }
14
15   static { // static initialization block
16     System.out.println("(1) Test's static initialization block " +
17       "is invoked");
18   }
19 }
20
21 class Parrot extends Bird {
22   Parrot() {
23     System.out.println("(8) Parrot's constructor is invoked");
24   }
25
26   { // instance initialization block
27     System.out.println("(7) Parrot's instance initialization block "
28       + "is invoked");
29   }
30
31   static { // static initialization block
32     System.out.println("(4) Parrot's static initialization block " +
33       "is invoked");
34   }
35 }
36
37 class Bird {
38   Bird() {
39     System.out.println("(6) Bird's constructor is invoked");
40   }
41
42   { // instance initialization block
43     System.out.println("(5) Bird's instance initialization block " +
44       "is invoked");
45   }
46
47   static { // static initialization block
48     System.out.println("(3) Bird's static initialization block " +
49       "is invoked");
50   }
51 }
```

instance initialization block

static initialization block

instance initialization block

static initialization block

instance initialization block

static initialization block

The output of this program is:

```
(1) Test's static initialization block is invoked
(2) Test's instance initialization block is invoked
(3) Bird's static initialization block is invoked
(4) Parrot's static initialization block is invoked
(5) Bird's instance initialization block is invoked
(6) Bird's constructor is invoked
(7) Parrot's instance initialization block is invoked
(8) Parrot's constructor is invoked
```

The program is executed in the following order:

1. Class Test is loaded first, so Test's static initialization block is invoked.

2. Test's constructor is invoked (Line 3), so Test's instance initialization block is invoked.

3. When executing new Parrot() (Line 7), class Parrot needs to be loaded, which causes class Parrot's superclass (i.e., Bird) to be loaded first. So Bird's static instance initialization block is invoked.

4. Class Parrot is now loaded, so Parrot's static initialization block is invoked.

5. When invoking Parrot's constructor, the no-arg constructor of Parrot's superclass is invoked first; therefore, Bird's instance initialization block is invoked.

6. The regular code in Bird's no-arg constructor is invoked after Bird's instance initialization block is invoked.

7. After Bird's no-arg constructor is invoked, Parrot's no-arg constructor is invoked, which causes Parrot's instance initialization block to be invoked first.

8. The regular code in Parrot's no-arg constructor is invoked after Parrot's instance initialization block is invoked.

 NOTE

If an instance variable is declared with an initial value (e.g., double radius = 5), the variable is initialized just like in an initialization block. That is, it is initialized when the constructor of the class is executed.

If a static variable is declared with an initial value (e.g., static double radius = 5), the variable is initialized just like in a static initialization block. That is, it is initialized when the class is loaded.

KEY TERMS

casting objects   296
constructor chaining   290
dynamic binding   295
final   302
generic programming   296
inheritance   288
initialization block   305

instanceof   297
meta-object   304
override   291
polymorphism   295
protected   301
subclass   288
superclass   288

KEY CLASSES AND METHODS

✦ **java.lang.Object**   is the root class of all Java classes. The Object class contains the useful methods toString, equals, hashCode, clone, finalize, and getClass. The toString() method returns a string that represents the object. The equals method tests whether two objects are equal. The hashCode method returns the hash code of the object. The hash code is an integer that can be used to store the object in a hash set so that it can be located quickly. The clone() method copies an object. The getClass method returns an instance of the java.lang.Class class, which contains the information about the class for the object. The finalize method is invoked by the garbage collector on an object when the object becomes garbage. An object becomes garbage if it is no longer accessed.

CHAPTER SUMMARY

✦ You can derive a new class from an existing class. This is known as *class inheritance*. The new class is called a *subclass*, *child class*, or *derived class*. The existing class is called a *superclass*, *parent class*, or *base class*.

✦ A constructor is used to construct an instance of a class. Unlike properties and methods, the constructors of a superclass are not inherited in the subclass. They can only be invoked from the constructors of the subclasses, using the keyword `super`.

✦ A constructor may invoke an overloaded constructor or its superclass's constructor. If none of them is invoked explicitly, the compiler puts `super()` as the first statement in the constructor.

✦ To override a method, the method must be defined in the subclass using the same signature as in its superclass.

✦ An instance method can be overridden only if it is accessible. Thus a private method cannot be overridden, because it is not accessible outside its own class. If a method defined in a subclass is private in its superclass, the two methods are completely unrelated.

✦ Like an instance method, a static method can be inherited. However, a static method cannot be overridden. If a static method defined in the superclass is redefined in a subclass, the method defined in the superclass is hidden.

✦ Every class in Java is descended from the `java.lang.Object` class. If no inheritance is specified when a class is defined, the superclass of the class is `Object`.

✦ If a method's parameter type is a superclass (e.g., `Object`), you may pass an object to this method of any of the parameter's subclasses (e.g., `Circle` or `String`). When an object (e.g., a `Circle` object or a `String` object) is used in the method, the particular implementation of the method of the object that is invoked (e.g., `toString`) is determined dynamically.

✦ It is always possible to cast an instance of a subclass to a variable of a superclass, because an instance of a subclass is *always* an instance of its superclass. When casting an instance of a superclass to a variable of its subclass, explicit casting must be used to confirm your intention to the compiler with the `(SubclassName)` cast notation.

✦ You can override an instance method, but you cannot override a field (instance or static) or a static method. If you declare a field or a static method in a subclass with the same name as one in the superclass, the one in the superclass is hidden, but it still exists. The two fields or static methods are independent. You can reference the hidden field or static method using the `super` keyword in the subclass. The hidden field or method can also be accessed via a reference variable of the superclass's type.

✦ When invoking an instance method from a reference variable, the *actual class of the object* referenced by the variable decides which implementation of the method is used *at runtime*. When accessing a field or a static method, the *declared type* of the reference variable decides which method is used *at compile time*.

✦ You can use `obj instanceof AClass` to check whether an object is an instance of a class.

✦ You can use the `protected` modifier to prevent the data and methods from being accessed by non-subclasses from a different package.

✦ You can use the `final` modifier to indicate that a class is final and cannot be a parent class.

REVIEW QUESTIONS

Sections 8.2–8.4

8.1 What is the printout of running the class C?

```
1 class A {
2   public A() {
3     System.out.println(
4       "The no-arg constructor of A is invoked");
5   }
6 }
7
8 class B extends A {
9   public B() {
10   }
11 }
12
13 public class C {
14   public static void main(String[] args) {
15     B b = new B();
16   }
17 }
```

8.2 What problem arises in compiling the following program?

```
1 class A {
2   public A(int x) {
3   }
4 }
5
6 class B extends A {
7   public B() {
8   }
9 }
10
11 public class C {
12   public static void main(String[] args) {
13     B b = new B();
14   }
15 }
```

8.3 Identify the problems in the following classes:

```
1 public class Circle {
2   private double radius;
3
4   public Circle(double radius) {
5     radius = radius;
6   }
7
8   public double getRadius() {
9     return radius;
10   }
11
12   public double findArea() {
13     return radius * radius * Math.PI;
14   }
15 }
16
17 class Cylinder extends Circle {
18   private double length;
19
20   Cylinder(double radius, double length) {
21     Circle(radius);
22     length = length;
23   }
24
```

```
25   /** Return the surface area for the cylinder */
26   public double findArea() {
27     return findArea() * length;
28   }
29 }
```

8.4   Explain the difference between method overloading and method overriding.

Section 8.5 The `Object` class

8.5   Does every class have a `toString` method and an `equals` method? Where do they come from? How are they used?

8.6   Show the output of the following program:

```
1 public class Test {
2   public static void main(String[] args) {
3     A a = new A(3);
4   }
5 }
6
7 class A extends B {
8   public A(int t) {
9     System.out.println("A's constructor is invoked");
10   }
11 }
12
13 class B {
14   public B() {
15     System.out.println("B's constructor is invoked");
16   }
17 }
```

Is the no-arg constructor of `Object` invoked when new `A(3)` is invoked?

Sections 8.6–8.7

8.7   When overriding the `equals` method, a common mistake is mistyping its signature in the subclass. For example, the `equals` method is incorrectly written as `equals(Circle circle)`, as shown in (a) in the following code; instead, it should be `equals(Object circle)`, as shown in (b). Show the output of running class `Test` with the `Circle` class in (a) and in (b).

```
public class Test {
  public static void main(String[] args) {
    Object circle1 = new Circle();
    Object circle2 = new Circle();
    System.out.println(circle1.equals(circle2));
  }
}
```

```
class Circle {
  double radius;

  public boolean equals(Circle circle) {
    return this.radius == circle.radius;
  }
}
```

```
class Circle {
  double radius;

  public boolean equals(Object circle) {
    return this.radius ==
      ((Circle)circle).radius;
  }
}
```

(a)   (b)

8.8   For the `Circle` and `Cylinder` class in Listing 8.2 on page 292 answer the following questions:

(a) Are the following Boolean expressions true or false?

chapter

9

ABSTRACT CLASSES AND INTERFACES

Objectives

- ✦ To design and use abstract classes (§9.2).

- ✦ To process a calendar using the `Calendar` and `GregorianCalendar` classes (§9.3).

- ✦ To declare interfaces to model weak inheritance relationships (§9.4).

- ✦ To define a natural order using the `Comparable` interface (§9.4.1).

- ✦ To know the similarities and differences between an abstract class and an interface (§9.4.2).

- ✦ To declare custom interfaces (§9.4.3).

- ✦ To enable objects cloneable using the `Cloneable` interface (§9.4.4 Optional).

- ✦ To use wrapper classes (`Byte`, `Short`, `Integer`, `Long`, `Float`, `Double`, `Character`, and `Boolean`) to wrap primitive data values into objects (§9.5).

- ✦ To create a generic sort method (§9.5).

- ✦ To simplify programming using JDK 1.5 automatic conversion between primitive types and wrapper class types (§9.6).

9.1 Introduction

In the inheritance hierarchy, classes become more specific and concrete *with each new subclass*. If you move from a subclass back up to a superclass, the classes become more general and less specific. Class design should ensure that a superclass contains common features of its subclasses. Sometimes a superclass is so abstract that it cannot have any specific instances. Such a class is referred to as an *abstract class*.

abstract class

multiple inheritance
single inheritance

Sometimes it is necessary to derive a subclass from several classes. This capability is known as *multiple inheritance*. Java, however, does not allow multiple inheritance. Each Java class may inherit directly from one superclass. This restriction is known as *single inheritance*. If you use the `extends` keyword to define a subclass, it allows only one parent class. With interfaces, you can obtain the effect of multiple inheritance.

This chapter introduces abstract classes and interfaces, and discusses how to use wrapper classes for primitive data type values.

9.2 Abstract Classes

Consider geometric objects. Suppose you want to design the classes to model geometric objects like circles, cylinders, and rectangles. Geometric objects have many common properties and behaviors. They can be drawn in a certain color, filled or unfilled. Color and filled are examples of common properties. Common behaviors include the fact that the areas and perimeters of geometric objects can be computed. Thus a general class `GeometricObject` can be used to model all geometric objects. This class contains the properties `color` and `filled`, and the methods `findArea` and `findPerimeter`. Since a circle is a special type of geometric object, it shares common properties and methods with other geometric objects. Further, since a cylinder is a special type of circle, it shares common properties and behaviors with a circle. Thus it makes sense to define the `Circle` class that extends the `GeometricObject` class and the `Cylinder` class that extends the `Circle` class. Figure 9.1 illustrates the relationship of the classes for geometric objects.

The methods `findArea` and `findPerimeter` cannot be implemented in the `GeometricObject` class because their implementation is dependent on the specific type of geometric object. Such

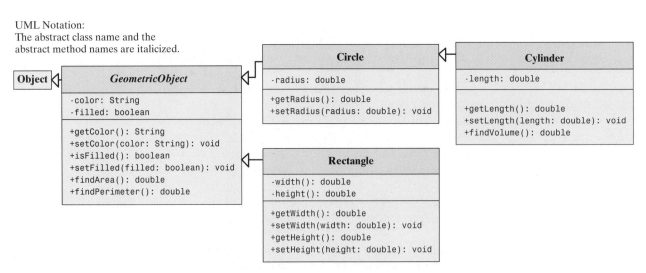

FIGURE 9.1 *The `GeometricObject` class models the common features of geometric objects.*

methods are referred to as *abstract methods*. In UML graphic notation, the names of abstract class-   abstract method
es and their abstract methods are italicized. The GeometricObject class is shown in Listing 9.1.

LISTING 9.1   GeometricObject.java (The GeometricObject Class)

```
 1  public abstract class GeometricObject {
 2    private String color = "white";
 3    private boolean filled;
 4
 5    /** Construct a default geometric object */
 6    protected GeometricObject() {
 7    }
 8
 9    /** Construct a geometric object with specified properties */
10    protected GeometricObject(String color, boolean filled) {
11      this.color = color;
12      this.filled = filled;
13    }
14
15    /** Return color */
16    public String getColor() {
17      return color;
18    }
19
20    /** Set a new color */
21    public void setColor(String color) {
22      this.color = color;
23    }
24
25    /** Return filled. Since filled is boolean,
26       so, the get method name is isFilled */
27    public boolean isFilled() {
28      return filled;
29    }
30
31    /** Set a new filled */
32    public void setFilled(boolean filled) {
33      this.filled = filled;
34    }
35
36    /** Abstract method findArea */
37    public abstract double findArea();
38
39    /** Abstract method findPerimeter */
40    public abstract double findPerimeter();
41  }
```

(Margin notes: abstract class; abstract method; abstract method)

Abstract classes are like regular classes with data and methods, but you cannot create instances of abstract classes using the new operator. An abstract method is a method signature without im-plementation. Its implementation is provided by the subclasses. A class that contains abstract methods must be declared abstract.

The GeometricObject abstract class provides the common features (data and methods) for geometric objects. Because you don't know how to compute areas and perimeters of geometric objects, findArea and findPerimeter are defined as abstract methods. These methods are imple-mented in the subclasses. Listings 9.2, 9.3, and 9.4 give the implementation of the classes Circle, Rectangle, and Cylinder.

NOTE

To avoid naming conflicts with the Circle and Cylinder classes in the preceding chapter, the Circle and Cylinder classes are named Circle9 and Cylinder9. For convenience, they are still referred to as Circle and Cylinder classes.

LISTING 9.2 Circle9.java (The Circle Class)

```java
 1  public class Circle9 extends GeometricObject {
 2    private double radius;
 3
 4    /** Construct a circle with default properties */
 5    public Circle9() {
 6      this(1.0);
 7    }
 8
 9    /** Construct a circle with a specified radius */
10    public Circle9(double radius) {
11      this(radius, "white", false);
12    }
13
14    /** Construct a circle with specified radius, filled, and color */
15    public Circle9(double radius, String color, boolean filled) {
16      super(color, filled);
17      this.radius = radius;
18    }
19
20    /** Return radius */
21    public double getRadius() {
22      return radius;
23    }
24
25    /** Set a new radius */
26    public void setRadius(double radius) {
27      this.radius = radius;
28    }
29
30    /** Implement the findArea method defined in GeometricObject */
31    public double findArea() {
32      return radius * radius * Math.PI;
33    }
34
35    /** Implement the findPerimeter method defined in GeometricObject*/
36    public double findPerimeter() {
37      return 2 * radius * Math.PI;
38    }
39
40    /** Override the toString() method defined in the Object class */
41    public String toString() {
42      return "[Circle] radius = " + radius;
43    }
44  }
```

override findArea — line 31
override findPerimeter — line 36
override toString — line 41

LISTING 9.3 Rectangle.java (The Rectangle Class)

```java
 1  public class Rectangle extends GeometricObject {
 2    private double width;
 3    private double height;
 4
 5    /** Construct a rectangle with default properties */
 6    public Rectangle() {
 7      this(1.0, 1.0);
 8    }
 9
10    /** Construct a rectangle with specified width and height */
11    public Rectangle(double width, double height) {
12      this(width, height, "white", false);
13    }
14
15    /** Construct a rectangle with specified width, height,
16        filled, and color */
17    public Rectangle(double width, double height,
18        String color, boolean filled) {
19      super(color, filled);
20      this.width = width;
```

```
21        this.height = height;
22      }
23
24      /** Return width */
25      public double getWidth() {
26        return width;
27      }
28
29      /** Set a new width */
30      public void setWidth(double width) {
31        this.width = width;
32      }
33
34      /** Return height */
35      public double getHeight() {
36        return height;
37      }
38
39      /** Set a new height */
40      public void setHeight(double height) {
41        this.height = height;
42      }
43
44      /** Implement the findArea method in GeometricObject */
45      public double findArea() {                                    override findArea
46        return width * height;
47      }
48
49      /** Implement the findPerimeter method in GeometricObject */
50      public double findPerimeter() {                               override findPerimeter
51        return 2 * (width + height);
52      }
53
54      /** Override the toString method defined in the Object class */
55      public String toString() {                                    override toString
56        return "[Rectangle] width = " + width +
57          " and height = " + height;
58      }
59    }
60
```

LISTING 9.4   Cylinder9.java (The `Cylinder9` Class)

```
1   public class Cylinder9 extends Circle9 {
2     private double length;
3
4     /** Construct a cylinder with default properties */
5     public Cylinder9() {
6       this(1.0, 1.0);
7     }
8
9     /** Construct a cylinder with specified radius, and length */
10    public Cylinder9(double radius, double length) {
11      this(radius, "white", false, length);
12    }
13
14    /** Construct a cylinder with specified radius, filled, color, and
15       length
16     */
17    public Cylinder9(double radius,
18        String color, boolean filled, double length) {
19      super(radius, color, filled);
20      this.length = length;
21    }
22
23    /** Return length */
24    public double getLength() {
25      return length;
26    }
```

```
27
28     /** Set a new length */
29     public void setLength(double length) {
30       this.length = length;
31     }
32
33     /** Return the surface area of this cylinder */
34     public double findArea() {
35       return 2 * super.findArea() + 2 * getRadius() * Math.PI * length;
36     }
37
38     /** Return the volume of this cylinder */
39     public double findVolume() {
40       return super.findArea() * length;
41     }
42
43     /** Override the toString method defined in the Object class */
44     public String toString() {
45       return "[Cylinder] radius = " + getRadius() + " and length "
46         + length;
47     }
48   }
```

override findArea

override toString

The method `toString` is defined in the `Object` class and modified in the `Circle`, `Rectangle`, and `Cylinder` classes. The abstract methods `findArea` and `findPerimeter` defined in the `GeometricObject` class are implemented in the `Circle` and `Rectangle` classes.

abstract method in abstract class

NOTE

An abstract method cannot be contained in a nonabstract class. If a subclass of an abstract superclass does not implement all the abstract methods, the subclass must be declared abstract. In other words, in a nonabstract subclass extended from an abstract class, all the abstract methods must be implemented, even if they are not used in the subclass.

object cannot be created from abstract class

NOTE

An abstract class cannot be instantiated using the `new` operator, but you can still define its constructors, which are invoked in the constructors of its subclasses. For instance, the constructors of `GeometricObject` are invoked in the `Circle` class and the `Rectangle` class.

abstract class without abstract method

NOTE

A class that contains abstract methods must be abstract. However, it is possible to declare an abstract class that contains no abstract methods. In this case, you cannot create instances of the class using the `new` operator. This class is used as a base class for defining a new subclass.

superclass of abstract class may be concrete

NOTE

A subclass can be abstract even if its superclass is concrete. For example, the `Object` class is concrete, but its subclasses, such as `GeometricObject`, may be abstract.

concrete method overridden to be abstract

NOTE

A subclass can override a method from its superclass to declare it `abstract`. This is *very unusual*, but is useful when the implementation of the method in the superclass becomes invalid in the subclass. In this case, the subclass must be declared abstract.

abstract class as type

NOTE

You cannot create an instance from an abstract class using the new operator, but an abstract class can be used as a data type. Therefore, the following statement, which creates an array whose elements are of GeometricObject type, is correct:

```
GeometricObject[] geo = new GeometricObject[10];
```

NOTE

Cylinder inherits the findPerimeter method from Circle. If you invoke this method on a Cylinder object, the perimeter of a circle is returned. This method is not useful for Cylinder objects. Removing or disabling it from Cylinder would be helpful, but there is no good way to get rid of this method in a subclass once it is defined as public in its superclass. If you define the findPerimeter method as abstract in the Cylinder class, then the Cylinder class must be declared abstract.

You may be wondering whether the abstract methods findArea and findPerimeter should be removed from the GeometricObject class. The following example shows the benefits of retaining them in the GeometricObject class.

EXAMPLE 9.1 USING THE `GeometricObject` CLASS

Problem

Write a program that creates two geometric objects, a circle and a rectangle, invokes the equalArea method to check whether the two objects have equal areas, and invokes the displayGeometricObject method to display the objects.

Solution

Listing 9.5 gives the solution to the problem. A sample run of the program is shown in Figure 9.2.

```
C:\book>java TestGeometricObject
The two objects have the same area? false

[Circle] radius = 5.0
The area is 78.53981633974483
The perimeter is 31.41592653589793

[Rectangle] width = 5.0 and height = 3.0
The area is 15.0
The perimeter is 16.0

C:\book>
```

FIGURE 9.2 *The program compares the areas of the objects and displays their properties.*

LISTING 9.5 TestGeometricObject.java

```
1 public class TestGeometricObject {
2   /** Main method */
```

EXAMPLE 9.1 (CONTINUED)

```
3  public static void main(String[] args) {
4    // Declare and initialize two geometric objects
5    GeometricObject geoObject1 = new Circle9(5);
6    GeometricObject geoObject2 = new Rectangle(5, 3);
7
8    System.out.println("The two objects have the same area? " +
9      equalArea(geoObject1, geoObject2));
10
11    // Display circle
12    displayGeometricObject(geoObject1);
13
14    // Display rectangle
15    displayGeometricObject(geoObject2);
16  }
17
18  /** A method for comparing the areas of two geometric objects */
19  static boolean equalArea(GeometricObject object1,
20      GeometricObject object2) {
21    return object1.findArea() == object2.findArea();
22  }
23
24  /** A method for displaying a geometric object */
25  static void displayGeometricObject(GeometricObject object) {
26    System.out.println();
27    System.out.println(object.toString());
28    System.out.println("The area is " + object.findArea());
29    System.out.println("The perimeter is " + object.findPerimeter());
30  }
31 }
```

Review

The methods findArea() and findPerimeter() defined in the GeometricObject class are overridden in the Circle9 class and the Rectangle class. The statements (Lines 5–6)

```
GeometricObject geoObject1 = new Circle9(5);
GeometricObject geoObject2 = new Rectangle(5, 3);
```

create a new circle and rectangle, and assign them to the variables geoObject1 and geoObject2. These two variables are of the GeometricObject type.

When invoking equalArea(geoObject1, geoObject2) (Line 9), the findArea method defined in the Circle9 class is used for object1.findArea(), since geoObject1 is a circle, and the findArea method defined in the Rectangle class is used for object2.findArea(), since geoObject2 is a rectangle.

Similarly, when invoking displayGeometricObject(geoObject1) (Line 12), the methods findArea, findPerimeter, and toString defined in the Circle class are used, and when invoking displayGeometricObject(geoObject2) (Line 15), the methods findArea, findPerimeter, and toString defined in the Rectangle class are used. Which of these methods is invoked is dynamically determined at runtime, depending on the type of object.

9.3   The Calendar and GregorianCalendar classes

An instance of java.util.Date represents a specific instant in time with millisecond precision. java.util.Calendar is an abstract base class for extracting detailed calendar information, such as year, month, date, hour, minute, and second. Subclasses of Calendar can implement specific calendar systems, such as the Gregorian calendar, the lunar calendar, and the Jewish calendar. Currently, `java.util.GregorianCalendar` for the Gregorian calendar is supported in Java.

You can use new `GregorianCalendar()` to construct a default `GregorianCalendar` with the current time and new `GregorianCalendar(year, month, date)` to construct a `GregorianCalendar` with the specified year, month, and date. The month parameter is 0-based, that is, 0 is for January.

The `get(int field)` method defined in the `Calendar` class is useful to extract the value for a given time field. The time fields are defined as constants, such as YEAR, MONTH, DATE, HOUR (for the twelve-hour clock), HOUR_OF_DAY (for the twenty-four-hour clock), MINUTE, SECOND, DAY_OF_WEEK (the day number within the current week, with 1 for Sunday), DAY_OF_MONTH (the day in the current month), DAY_OF_YEAR (the day number in the current year, with 1 for the first day of the year), WEEK_OF_MONTH (the week number within the current month), and WEEK_OF_YEAR (the week number within the current year). For example, the following code

```
// Construct a Gregorian calendar for the current date and time
java.util.Calendar calendar = new java.util.GregorianCalendar();
System.out.println("Year\tMonth\tDate\tHour\tHour24\tMinute\tSecond");
System.out.println(calendar.get(Calendar.YEAR) + "\t" +
  calendar.get(Calendar.MONTH) + "\t" + calendar.get(Calendar.DATE)
  + "\t" + calendar.get(Calendar.HOUR) + "\t" +
  calendar.get(Calendar.MINUTE) + "\t" +
  calendar.get(Calendar.SECOND));
System.out.print("Day of week: " +
  calendar.get(Calendar.DAY_OF_WEEK) + "\t");
System.out.print("Day of month: " +
  calendar.get(Calendar.DAY_OF_MONTH) + "\t");
System.out.println("Day of year: " +
  calendar.get(Calendar.DAY_OF_YEAR));
System.out.print("Week of month: " +
  calendar.get(Calendar.WEEK_OF_MONTH) + "\t");
System.out.print("Week of year: " +
  calendar.get(Calendar.WEEK_OF_YEAR));
```

displays the information for the current date and time, as follows:

```
Year Month  Date   Hour  Hour24     Minute   Second
2003 2      9      8     20         17       39
Day of week: 1     Day of month: 9          Day of year: 68
Week of month: 3   Week of year: 11
```

To obtain the number of days in a month, use `calendar.getActualMaximum(Calendar.DAY_OF_MONTH)`. For example, if the `calendar` were for March, this method would return 31.

The `set(int field, value)` method defined in the `Calendar` class can be used to set a field. For example, you can use `calendar.set(Calendar.DAY_OF_MONTH, 1)` to set the `calendar` to the first day of the month.

9.4 Interfaces

An *interface* is a classlike construct that contains only constants and abstract methods. In many ways, an interface is similar to an abstract class, but an abstract class can contain variables and concrete methods as well as constants and abstract methods.

interface

To distinguish an interface from a class, Java uses the following syntax to declare an interface:

```
modifier interface InterfaceName {
  /** Constant declarations */
  /** Method signatures */
}
```

An interface is treated like a special class in Java. Each interface is compiled into a separate byte-code file, just like a regular class. As with an abstract class, you cannot create an instance from an interface using the new operator, but in most cases you can use an interface more or less the same way you use an abstract class. For example, you can use an interface as a data type for a variable, as the result of casting, and so on.

Suppose you want to design a generic method to find the larger of two objects. The objects can be students, circles, or cylinders. Since compare methods are different for different types of objects, you need to define a generic compare method to determine the order of the two objects. Then you can tailor the method to compare students, circles, or cylinders. For example, you can use student ID as the key for comparing students, radius as the key for comparing circles, and volume as the key for comparing cylinders. You can use an interface to define a generic compareTo method, as follows:

java.lang.Comparable

```
// Interface for comparing objects, defined in java.lang
package java.lang;

public interface Comparable {
  public int compareTo(Object o);
}
```

The compareTo method determines the order of this object with the specified object o, and returns a negative integer, zero, or a positive integer if this object is less than, equal to, or greater than the specified object o.

 NOTE

The Comparable interface has been available since JDK 1.2, and is included in the java.lang package.

A generic max method for finding the larger of two objects can be declared in a class named Max, as follows:

```
// Max.java: Find a maximum object
public class Max {
  /** Return the maximum between two objects */
  public static Object max(Object o1, Object o2) {
    if (((Comparable)o1).compareTo(o2) > 0)
      return o1;
    else
      return o2;
  }
}
```

The Max class contains a static method named max. To use the max method to find the larger of two objects, implement the Comparable interface for the class of these objects. Since o1 is declared as Object, (Comparable)o1 tells the compiler to cast o1 into Comparable so that the compareTo method can be invoked from o1.

Many classes (e.g., String and Date) in the Java library implement Comparable to define a natural order for the objects. So you can use the max method in the Max class to find the larger of two instances of String or Date. Here is an example:

```
String s1 = "abcdef";
String s2 = "abcdee";
String s3 = (String)Max.max(s1, s2);
```

Since every object is automatically an instance of Object, s1 and s2 can be passed to the max method without explicit casting. However, an instance of Object is not necessarily an instance of String. Therefore, to assign the return value from the max method to a String type variable, you need to cast it to String explicitly. The string in s1 is larger than that in s2. So s3 is "abcdef".

9.4.1 Implementing Interfaces

You cannot use the max method to find the larger of two instances of Rectangle, because Rectangle does not implement Comparable. However, you can declare a new rectangle class that implements Comparable. The instances of this new class are comparable. Let this new class be named ComparableRectangle, as shown in Listing 9.6.

LISTING 9.6   ComparableRectangle.java (Comparable)

```
 1 public class ComparableRectangle extends Rectangle
 2     implements Comparable {
 3   /** Construct a ComparableRectangle with specified properties */
 4   public ComparableRectangle(double width, double height) {
 5     super(width, height);
 6   }
 7
 8   /** Implement the compareTo method defined in Comparable */
 9   public int compareTo(Object o) {
10     if (findArea() > ((ComparableRectangle)o).findArea())
11       return 1;
12     else if (findArea() < ((ComparableRectangle)o).findArea())
13       return -1;
14     else
15       return 0;
16   }
17 }
```

ComparableRectangle extends Rectangle and implements Comparable, as shown in Figure 9.3. The keyword implements indicates that ComparableRectangle inherits all the constant from the Comparable interface and implements the methods in the interface. The compareTo method compares the areas of two rectangles. An instance of CompareRectangle is also an instance of Rectangle, GeometricObject, Object, and Comparable.

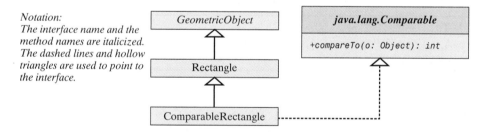

Notation:
The interface name and the method names are italicized. The dashed lines and hollow triangles are used to point to the interface.

FIGURE 9.3   *ComparableRectangle extends Rectangle and implements Comparable.*

You can now use the max method to find the larger of two objects of CompareRectangle. Here is an example:

```
ComparableRectangle rectangle1 = new ComparableRectangle(4, 5);
ComparableRectangle rectangle2 = new ComparableRectangle(3, 6);
System.out.println(Max.max(rectangle1, rectangle2));
```

An interface provides another form of generic programming. It would be difficult to use a generic max method to find the maximum of the objects without using an interface in this example, because multiple inheritance would be necessary to inherit Comparable and another class, such as Rectangle, at the same time.

The Object class contains the equals method, which is intended for the subclasses of the Object class to override in order to compare whether the contents of the objects are the same. Suppose that the Object class contains the compareTo method, as defined in the Comparable interface; the new max method can be used to compare a list of *any* objects. Whether a compareTo method should be included in the `Object` class is debatable. Since the `compareTo` method is not defined in the `Object` class, the `Comparable` interface is created in Java 2 to enable objects to be compared if they are instances of the `Comparable` interface. It is strongly recommended (though not required) that `compareTo` should be consistent with `equals`. That is, for two objects o1 and o2, o1.compareTo(o2) == 0 if and only if o1.equals(o2) is true.

9.4.2 Interfaces vs. Abstract Classes

An interface can be used the same way as an abstract class, but defining an interface is different from defining an abstract class.

✦ In an interface, the data must be constants; an abstract class can have non-constant data fields.

✦ Each method in an interface has only a signature without implementation; an abstract class can have concrete methods.

omitting modifiers

 NOTE
All data fields are `public final static` and all methods are `public abstract` in an interface. For this reason, these modifiers can be omitted, as shown below:

```public interface T1 { public static final int k = 1; public abstract void p ();}```	Equivalent	```public interface T1 { int k = 1; void p ();}```

accessing constants

 TIP
A constant defined in an interface can be accessed using syntax `InterfaceName.CONSTANT_NAME` (e.g., `T1.K`).

Java allows only single inheritance for class extension, but multiple extensions for interfaces. For example,

```
public class NewClass extends BaseClass
    implements Interface1, ..., InterfaceN {
    ...
}
```

An interface can inherit other interfaces using the extends keyword. Such an interface is called a *subinterface*. For example, `NewInterface` in the following code is a subinterface of `Interface1`, ..., and `InterfaceN`:

subinterface

```
public interface NewInterface extends Interface1, ..., InterfaceN {
    // constants and abstract methods
}
```

A class implementing `NewInterface` must implement the abstract methods defined in `NewInterface`, `Interface1`, ..., and `InterfaceN`. An interface can only extend other interfaces, not classes. A class can extend its superclass and implement multiple interfaces.

All classes share a single root, the `Object` class, but there is no single root for interfaces. Like a class, an interface also defines a type. A variable of an interface type can reference any instance of the class that implements the interface. If a class implements an interface, the interface is like a superclass for the class. You can use an interface as a data type and cast a variable of an interface type to its subclass, and vice versa. For example, suppose that c is an instance of Class2 in Figure 9.4. c is also an instance of Object, Class1, Interface1, Interface1_1, Interface1_2, Interface2_1, and Interface2_2.

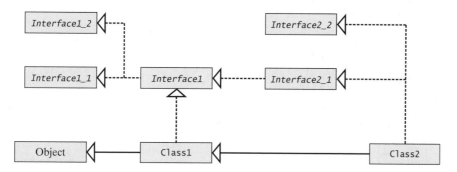

FIGURE 9.4 *Abstract class* Class1 *implements* Interface1. Interface1 *extends* Interface1_1 *and* Interface1_2. Class2 *extends* Class1 *and implements* Interface2_1 *and* Interface2_2.

Abstract classes and interfaces can both be used to model common features. How do you decide whether to use an interface or a class? In general, a *strong is-a relationship* that clearly describes a parent–child relationship should be modeled using classes. For example, a staff member is a person. So the relationship between them should be modeled using class inheritance. A *weak is-a relationship*, also known as an *is-kind-of relationship*, indicates that an object possesses a certain property. A weak is-a relationship can be modeled using interfaces. For example, all strings are comparable, so the String class implements the Comparable interface. You can also use interfaces to circumvent single inheritance restriction if multiple inheritance is desired. In the case of multiple inheritance, you have to design one as a superclass, and others as interfaces. See Chapter 10, "Object-Oriented Modeling," for more discussions.

strong is-a relationship

is-kind-of relationship

> **NOTE**
> Class names are nouns. Interface names may be adjectives or nouns. For example, both java.lang.Comparable and java.awt.event.ActionListener are interfaces. Comparable is an adjective, and ActionListener is a noun. ActionListener will be introduced in Chapter 12, "Event-Driven Programming."

9.4.3 Creating Custom Interfaces

Section 9.4.1, "Implementing Interfaces," gives an example of implementing an interface defined in the Java API. This section creates a custom interface. Suppose you want to describe whether an object is edible. You can declare the Edible interface as:

```
public interface Edible {
  /** Describe how to eat */
  public String howToEat();
}
```

To denote that an object is edible, the class for the object must implement Edible. Let us create the following two sets of classes:

◆ Create a class named Animal and its subclasses Tiger, Chicken, and Elephant. Since chicken is edible, implement the Edible interface for the Chicken class, as follows:

```
class Animal {
}

class Chicken extends Animal implements Edible {
  public String howToEat() {
```

```
      return "Fry it";
    }
  }

  class Tiger extends Animal {
  }
```

✦ Create a class named `Fruit` and its subclasses `Apple` and `Orange`. Since all fruits are edible, implement the `Edible` interface for the `Fruit` class. In the `Fruit` class, give a generic implementation of the `howToEat` method. In the `Apple` class and the `Orange` class, give a specific implementation of the `howToEat` method, as follows:

```java
class Fruit implements Edible {
  public String howToEat() {
    return "Eat it fresh";
  }
}

class Apple extends Fruit {
  public String howToEat() {
    return "Make apple cider";
  }
}

class Orange extends Fruit {
  public String howToEat() {
    return "Make orange juice";
  }
}
```

To demonstrate how the `Edible` interface may be used, create the following program that creates an array with three objects. The `showObject` method invokes the `howToEat()` method if the object is edible.

```java
public class TestEdible {
  public static void main(String[] args) {
    Object[] objects = {new Tiger(), new Chicken(), new Apple()};
    for (int i = 0; i < objects.length; i++)
      showObject(objects[i]);
  }

  public static void showObject(Object object) {
    if (object instanceof Edible)
      System.out.println(((Edible)object).howToEat());
  }
}
```

The program displays

```
Fry it
Make apple cider
```

9.4.4   The `Cloneable` Interface (Optional)

An interface contains constants and abstract methods, but the `Cloneable` interface is a special case. The `Cloneable` interface in the `java.lang` package is defined as follows:

java.lang.Cloneable

```java
package java.lang;

public interface Cloneable {
}
```

marker interface

This interface is empty. An interface with an empty body is referred to as a *marker interface*. A marker interface does not contain constants or methods. It is used to denote that a class possesses certain desirable properties. A class that implements the `Cloneable` interface is marked cloneable, and its objects can be cloned using the `clone()` method defined in the `Object` class.

Many classes (e.g., Date and Calendar) in the Java library implement Cloneable. Thus, the instances of these classes can be cloned. For example, the following code

```
Calendar calendar = new GregorianCalendar(2003, 2, 1);
Calendar calendarCopy = (Calendar)calendar.clone();
System.out.println("calendar == calendarCopy is " +
  (calendar == calendarCopy));
System.out.println("calendar.equals(calendarCopy) is " +
  calendar.equals(calendarCopy));
```

displays

```
calendar == calendarCopy is false
calendar.equals(calendarCopy) is true
```

To declare a custom class that implements the Cloneable interface, the class must override the clone() method in the Object class. Listing 9.7 declares a class named House that implements Cloneable and Comparable.

how to implement Cloneable

LISTING 9.7 House.java (Cloneable and Comparable)

```
 1  public class House implements Cloneable, Comparable {
 2    private int id;
 3    private double area;
 4    private java.util.Date whenBuilt;
 5
 6    public House(int id, double area) {
 7      this.id = id;
 8      this.area = area;
 9      whenBuilt = new java.util.Date();
10    }
11
12    public double getId() {
13      return id;
14    }
15
16    public double getArea() {
17      return area;
18    }
19
20    public java.util.Date getWhenBuilt() {
21      return whenBuilt;
22    }
23
24    /** Override the protected clone method defined in the Object
25      class, and strengthen its accessibility */
26    public Object clone() {
27      try {
28        return super.clone();
29      }
30      catch (CloneNotSupportedException ex) {
31        return null;
32      }
33    }
34
35    /** Implement the compareTo method defined in Comparable */
36    public int compareTo(Object o) {
37      if (area > ((House)o).area)
38        return 1;
39      else if (area < ((House)o).area)
40        return -1;
41      else
42        return 0;
43    }
44  }
```

The House class overrides the clone method (Lines 26–33) defined in the Object class. The clone method in the Object class is defined as follows:

```
protected native Object clone() throws CloneNotSupportedException;
```

The keyword `native` indicates that this method is not written in Java, but is implemented in the JVM for the native platform. The keyword `protected` restricts the method to be accessed in the same package or in a subclass. For this reason, the `Cloneable` class must override the method and change the visibility modifier to `public` so that the method can be used in any package. Since the `clone` method implemented for the native platform in the `Object` class performs the task of cloning objects, the `clone` method in the `House` class simply invokes `super.clone()`. The `clone` method defined in the `Object` class may throw `CloneNotSupportedException`. Thus, `super.clone()` must be placed in a `try-catch` block. Exceptions and the `try-catch` block are introduced in Chapter 15, "Exceptions and Assertions."

The `House` class overrides the `compareTo` method (Lines 36–43) defined in the `Comparable` interface. The method compares the areas of two houses.

You can now create an object of the `House` class and create an identical copy from it, as follows:

```
House house1 = new House(1, 1750.50);
House house2 = (House)house1.clone();
```

`house1` and `house2` are two different objects with identical contents. The `clone` method in the `Object` class copies each field from the original object to the target object. If the field is of a primitive type, its value is copied. For example, the value of `area` (double type) is copied from `house1` to `house2`. If the field is of an object, the reference of the field is copied. For example, the field `whenBuilt` is of the `Date` class, so its reference is copied into `house2`, as shown in Figure 9.5. Therefore, `house1.whenBuilt == house2.whenBuilt` is true, although `house1 == house2` is false. This is referred to as a *shallow copy* rather than a *deep copy*, meaning that if the field is of an object, the reference of the field is copied rather than its contents.

shallow copy
deep copy

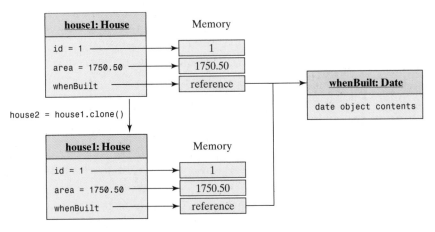

FIGURE 9.5 *The `clone` method copies the values of primitive type fields and the references of object type fields.*

If you want to perform a deep copy, you can override the `clone` method with custom cloning operations instead of invoking `super.clone()`. See Exercise 9.4.

 NOTE
You learned how to use the `arraycopy` method to copy arrays in Chapter 5, "Arrays." This method provides shallow copies. It works fine for arrays of primitive data type elements, but not for arrays of object type elements. To support a deep copy, you have to deal with how to copy individual object elements in the array.

CAUTION

If the House class does not override the clone() method, the program will receive a syntax error because clone() is protected in java.lang.Object. If House does not implement java.lang.Cloneable, invoking super.clone() (Line 28) in House.java would cause a CloneNotSupportedException. Thus, to enable cloning an object, the class for the object must override the clone() method and implement Cloneable.

9.5   Processing Primitive Data Type Values as Objects

Primitive data types are not used as objects in Java due to performance considerations. Because of the overhead of processing objects, the language's performance would be adversely affected if primitive data types were treated as objects. However, many Java methods require the use of objects as arguments. Java offers a convenient way to incorporate, or wrap, a primitive data type into an object (e.g., wrapping int into the Integer class, and wrapping double into the Double class). The corresponding class is called a *wrapper class*. By using a wrapper object instead of a primitive data type variable, you can take advantage of generic programming.

wrapper class

Java provides Boolean, Character, Double, Float, Byte, Short, Integer, and Long wrapper classes for primitive data types. These classes are grouped in the java.lang package. Their inheritance hierarchy is shown in Figure 9.6.

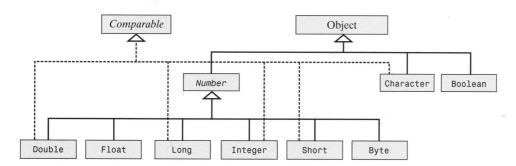

FIGURE 9.6   *The Number class is an abstract superclass for* Double, Float, Long, Integer, Short, *and* Byte.

 NOTE

The wrapper class name for a primitive type is the same as the primitive data type name with the first letter capitalized. The exceptions are Integer and Character.

Each numeric wrapper class extends the abstract Number class, which contains the methods doubleValue(), floatValue(), intValue(), longValue(), shortValue(), and byteValue(). These methods "convert" objects into primitive type values. The methods doubleValue(), floatValue(), intValue(), and longValue() are abstract. The methods byteValue() and shortValue() are not abstract; they simply return (byte)intValue() and (short)intValue(), respectively.

Each wrapper class overrides the toString, equals, and hashCode methods defined in the Object class. Since all the numeric wrapper classes and the Character class implement the Comparable interface, the compareTo method is implemented in these classes.

Wrapper classes are very similar. The `Character` class was introduced in Chapter 7, "Strings." The `Boolean` class is rarely used. The following sections use `Integer` and `Double` as examples to introduce the numeric wrapper classes. The key features of `Integer` and `Double` are shown in Figure 9.7.

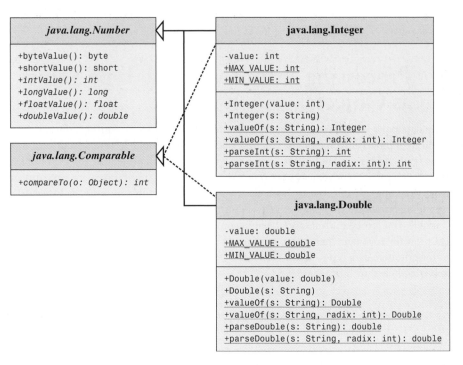

FIGURE 9.7   *The wrapper classes provide constructors, constants, and conversion methods for manipulating various data types.*

9.5.1   Numeric Wrapper Class Constructors

You can construct a wrapper object either from a primitive data type value or from a string representing the numeric value. The constructors for `Integer` and `Double` are:

```
public Integer(int value)
public Integer(String s)
public Double(double value)
public Double(String s)
```

For example, you can construct a wrapper object for `double` value `5.0` using either

```
Double doubleObject = new Double(5.0);
```

or

```
Double doubleObject = new Double("5.0");
```

You can construct a wrapper object for `int` value `5` using either

```
Integer integerObject = new Integer(5);
```

or

```
Integer integerObject = new Integer("5");
```

9.17 Describe the boxing and unboxing features in JDK 1.5. Are the following statements correct in JDK 1.5?

```
Number x = 3;
Integer x = 3;
Double x = 3;
Double x = 3.0;
int x = new Integer(3);
int x = new Integer(3) + new Integer(4);
double y = 3.4;
y.intValue();
```

Comprehensive

9.18 Define the following terms: abstract classes, interfaces. What are the similarities and differences between abstract classes and interfaces?

9.19 Indicate true or false for the following statements:

✦ An abstract class can have instances created using the constructor of the abstract class.
✦ An abstract class can be extended.
✦ You can always successfully cast an instance of a subclass to a superclass.
✦ You can always successfully cast an instance of a superclass to a subclass.
✦ An interface is compiled into a separate bytecode file.
✦ A subclass of a nonabstract superclass cannot be abstract.
✦ A subclass cannot override a concrete method in a superclass to declare it abstract.

PROGRAMMING EXERCISES

Comprehensive

9.1* (*Enabling* GeometricObject *comparable*) Modify the GeometricObject class to implement the Comparable interface, and define the max method in the GeometricObject class. Write a test program that uses the max method to find the larger of two circles and the larger of two cylinders.

9.2* (*The* ComparableCylinder *class*) Create a class named ComparableCylinder that extends Cylinder and implements Comparable. Implement the compareTo method to compare the cylinders on the basis of volume. Write a test class to find the larger of two instances of ComparableCylinder objects.

9.3* (*The* Colorable *interface*) Create an interface named Colorable, as follows:

```
public interface Colorable {
  public void howToColor();
}
```

Every class of a colorable object must implement the Colorable interface. Create a class named Square that extends GeometricObject and implements Colorable. Implement howToColor to display a message on how to color the square.

9.4* (*Revising the* House *class*) Rewrite the House class in Listing 9.7 to perform a deep copy on the whenBuilt field.

9.5* (*Enabling* Circle *comparable*) Rewrite the Circle class on page 318 to extend GeometricObject and implement the Comparable interface. Override the equals and hashCode methods in the Object class. Two Circle objects are equal if their radii are the same.

9.6* (*Enabling* Rectangle *comparable*) Rewrite the Rectangle class on page 318 to extend GeometricObject and implement the Comparable interface. Override the equals and hashCode methods in the Object class. Two Rectangle objects are equal if their areas are the same.

9.7* (*The* Octagon *class*) Write a class named Octagon that extends GeometricObject and implements the Comparable and Cloneable interfaces. Assume that all eight sides of the octagon are of equal size. The area can be computed using the following formula:

$$area = (2 + 4/\sqrt{2})\ side * side$$

Write a test program that creates an Octagon object with side value 5 and displays its area and perimeter. Create a new object using the clone method and compare the two objects using the compareTo method.

9.8* (*Summing the areas of geometric objects*) Write a method that sums the areas of all the geometric objects in an array. The method header is:

```
public static double sumArea(GeometricObject[] a)
```

Write a test program that creates an array of three objects (a circle, a cylinder, and a rectangle) and computes their total area using the sumArea method.

9.9* (*Finding the largest object*) Write a method that returns the largest object in an array of objects. The method header is:

```
public static Object max(Object[] a)
```

All the objects are instances of the Comparable interface. The order of the objects in the array is determined using the compareTo method.

Write a test program that creates an array of ten strings, an array of ten integers, and an array of ten dates, and finds the largest string, integer, and date in the arrays.

9.10** (*Displaying calendars*) Rewrite the PrintCalendar class in Listing 4.7 on page 147 to display a calendar for a specified month using the Calendar and Gregorian Calendar classes. Your program receives the month and year from the command line. For example:

```
java Exercise9_10 3 2003
```

This displays the calendar shown in Figure 9.9.

You also can run the program without the year. In this case, the year is the current year. If you run the program without specifying a month and a year, the month is the current month.

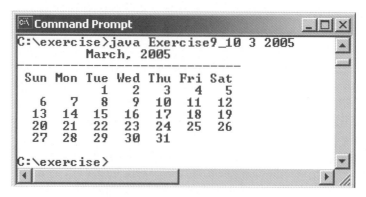

FIGURE 9.9 *The program displays a calendar for March 2005.*

OBJECT-ORIENTED MODELING

Objectives

- ✦ To become familiar with the process of program development (§10.2).

- ✦ To learn the relationship types: association, aggregation, composition, strong inheritance, and weak inheritance (§10.3).

- ✦ To declare classes to represent the relationships among the classes (§10.3).

- ✦ To design systems by identifying the classes and discovering the relationships among them (§10.4).

- ✦ To implement the `Rational` class and process rational numbers using this class (§10.5).

- ✦ To design classes that follow the class-design guidelines (§10.6).

- ✦ To model dynamic behavior using sequence diagrams and statechart diagrams (§10.7 Optional)

- ✦ To know the concept of framework-based programming using Java API (§10.8).

10.1   Introduction

The preceding chapters introduced objects, classes, class inheritance, and interfaces. You learned the concepts of object-oriented programming. This chapter focuses on the development of software systems using the object-oriented approach, and introduces class modeling using the Unified Modeling Language (UML). You will learn class-design guidelines, and the techniques for designing reusable classes through the `Rational` class.

10.2   The Software Development Process

Developing a software project is an engineering process. Software products, no matter how large or how small, have the same developmental phases: requirements specification, analysis, design, implementation, testing, deployment, and maintenance, as shown in Figure 10.1.

requirements specification

Requirements specification is a formal process that seeks to understand the problem and document in detail what the software system needs to do. This phase involves close interaction between users and designers. Most of the examples in this book are simple, and their requirements are clearly stated. In the real world, however, problems are not well defined. You need to study a problem carefully to identify its requirements.

system analysis

System analysis seeks to analyze the business process in terms of data flow, and to identify the system's input and output. Part of the analysis entails modeling the system's behavior. The model is intended to capture the essential elements of the system and to define services to the system.

system design

System design is the process of designing the system's components. This phase involves the use of many levels of abstraction to decompose the problem into manageable components, identify classes and interfaces, and establish relationships among the classes and interfaces.

implementation

Implementation is the process of translating the system design into programs. Separate programs are written for each component and put to work together. This phase requires the use of a programming language like Java. The implementation involves coding, testing, and debugging.

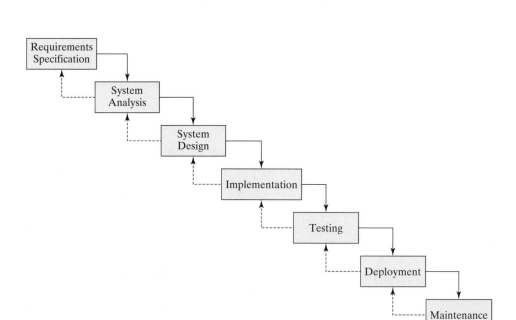

FIGURE 10.1 *Developing a project involves requirements specification, system analysis, system design, implementation, testing, deployment, and maintenance.*

Testing ensures that the code meets the requirements specification and weeds out bugs. An independent team of software engineers not involved in the design and implementation of the project usually conducts such testing.

Deployment makes the project available for use. For a Java applet, this means installing it on a Web server; for a Java application, installing it on the client's computer. A project usually consists of many classes. An effective approach for deployment is to package all the classes into a Java archive file, as will be introduced in Section 14.13, "Packaging and Deploying Java Projects."

Maintenance is concerned with changing and improving the product. A software product must continue to perform and improve in a changing environment. This requires periodic upgrades of the product to fix newly discovered bugs and incorporate changes.

The central task in object-oriented system development is to design classes to model the system. While there are many object-oriented methodologies, UML has become the industry-standard notation for object-oriented modeling, and itself leads to a methodology. The process of designing classes calls for identifying the classes and discovering the relationships among them. Class relationships are introduced in the next section.

(margin notes: testing, deployment, maintenance)

10.3 Discovering Relationships Among Classes

The relationships among classes can be classified into three types: *association*, *aggregation*, and *inheritance*.

10.3.1 Association

Association is a general binary relationship that describes an activity between two classes. For example, a student taking a course is an association between the `Student` class and the `Course` class, and a faculty member teaching a course is an association between the `Faculty` class and the `Course` class. These associations can be represented in UML graphical notations, as shown in Figure 10.2.

(margin note: association)

FIGURE 10.2 *A student may take any number of courses, and a faculty member teaches at most three courses. A course may have from five to sixty students and is taught by only one faculty member.*

An association is illustrated using a solid line between two classes with an optional label that describes the relationship. In Figure 10.2, the labels are *Take* and *Teach*. Each relationship may have an optional small black triangle that indicates the direction of the relationship. In Figure 10.2, the direction indicates that a student takes a course, as opposed to a course taking a student.

Each class involved in the relationship may have a role name that describes the role played by the class in the relationship. In Figure 10.2, *teacher* is the role name for `Faculty`.

Each class involved in an association may specify a *multiplicity*. A multiplicity could be a number or an interval that specifies how many objects of the class are involved in the relationship. The character * means unlimited number of objects, and the interval m..n means that the number of objects should be between m and n, inclusive. In Figure 10.2, each student may take any number of courses, and each course must have at least five students and at most sixty students. Each course is taught by only one faculty member, and a faculty member may teach from zero to three courses per semester.

Association may exist between objects of the same class. For example, a person may have a supervisor. This is illustrated in Figure 10.3.

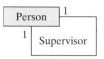

FIGURE 10.3   *A person may have a supervisor.*

An association is usually represented as a data field in the class. For example, the relationships in Figure 10.2 can be represented in the following classes:

```
public class Student {
  /** Data fields omitted */
  private Course[]
    courseList;

  /** Constructors omitted */
  /** Methods omitted */
}
```

```
public class Course {
  /** Data fields omitted */
  private Student[]
    classList;
  private Faculty faculty;

  /** Constructors */
  /** Methods */
}
```

```
public class Faculty {
  /** Data fields omitted */
  private Course[]
    courseList;

  /** Constructors omitted */
  /** Methods omitted */
}
```

> **NOTE**
>
> If you don't need to know the courses a student takes or a faculty member teaches, the data field `courseList` in `Student` or `Faculty` can be omitted.

In the association "a person has a supervisor," as shown in Figure 10.3, a supervisor can be represented as a data field in the `Person` class, as follows:

```
public class Person {
  /** Data fields omitted*/
  private Person supervisor;

  /** Constructors omitted*/
  /** Methods omitted*/
}
```

10.3.2   Aggregation and Composition

aggregation

Aggregation is a special form of association that represents an ownership relationship between two classes. Aggregation models *has-a* relationships. An object may be owned by several other aggregated objects. If an object is exclusively owned by an aggregated object, the relationship between the object and its aggregated object is referred to as *composition*. For example, "a person

composition

has a name" is a composition relationship between the `Person` class and the `Name` class, whereas "a person has an address" is an aggregation relationship between the `Person` class and the `Address` class, since an address may be shared by several persons. In UML, a filled diamond is attached to the `Person` class to denote the composition relationship with the `Name` class, and an empty diamond is attached to the `Person` class to denote the aggregation relationship with the `Address` class, as shown in Figure 10.4.

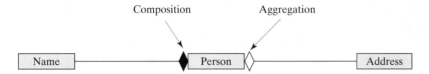

FIGURE 10.4   *A person has a name and an address.*

An aggregation relationship is usually represented as a data field in the aggregated class. For example, the relationship in Figure 10.4 can be represented as follows:

```
public class Name {
  /** Data fields omitted */
  /** Constructors omitted */
  /** Methods omitted */
}
```

```
public class Person {
  /** Data fields omitted */
  private Name name;
  private Address address;

  /** Constructors omitted */
  /** Methods omitted */
}
```

```
public class Address {
  /** Data fields omitted */
  /** Constructors omitted */
  /** Methods omitted */
}
```

🌿 **NOTE**

If `Name` or `Address` is used only in the `Person` class, it can be declared as an inner class in `Person`. For example,

```
public class Person {
  private Name name;
  private Address address;
  ...

  class Name {
  ...
  }

  class Address {
  ...
  }
}
```

10.3.3   Inheritance

Inheritance models the *is-a* relationship between two classes. A *strong is-a* relationship describes a direct inheritance relationship between two classes. A *weak is-a* relationship describes that a class has certain properties. A strong is-a relationship can be represented using class inheritance. For example, the relationship "a faculty member is a person," shown in Figure 10.5(a), is a strong is-a relationship and can be represented using the class in Figure 10.5(b).

strong is-a

weak is-a

```
public class Faculty extends Person {
  /** Data fields omitted */
  /** Constructors omitted */
  /** Methods omitted */
}
```

Person ◁── Faculty

(a)   (b)

FIGURE 10.5   `Faculty` *extends* `Person`.

A weak is-a relationship can be represented using interfaces. For example, the weak is-a relationship "students are comparable based on their grades," shown in Figure 10.6(a), can be represented by implementing the `Comparable` interface, as shown in Figure 10.6(b).

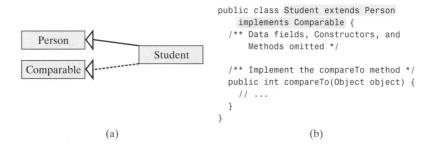

(a)   (b)

FIGURE 10.6 `Student` *extends* `Person` *and implements* `Comparable`.

✦ 10.4 CASE STUDY: A Class Design Example

The key to object-oriented programming is to model the application in terms of cooperative objects. Carefully designed classes are critical when a project is being developed. There are many levels of abstraction in system design. You have learned method abstraction and have applied it to the development of large programs. Methods are a means to group statements. Classes extend abstraction to a higher level and provide a means of grouping methods. Classes do more than just group methods, however; they also contain data fields. Methods and data fields together describe the properties and behaviors of classes.

The power of classes is further extended by inheritance. Inheritance enables a class to extend the contract and the implementation of an existing class without knowing the details of the existing class. In the development of a Java program, class abstraction is applied to decompose the problem into a set of related classes, and method abstraction is applied to design individual classes.

This case study models borrowing loans to demonstrate how to identify classes, discover the relationships between classes, and apply class abstraction in object-oriented program development.

For simplicity, the example does not attempt to build a complete system for storing, processing, and manipulating loans for borrowers; instead it focuses on modeling borrowers and the loans for the borrowers. The following steps are usually involved in building an object-oriented system:

1. Identify classes for the system.

2. Describe the attributes and methods in each class.

3. Establish relationships among classes.

4. Create classes.

identify classes

The first step is to *identify classes* for the system. There are many strategies for identifying classes in a system, one of which is to study how the system works and select a number of use cases, or scenarios. Since a borrower is a person who obtains a loan, and a person has a name and an address, you can identify the following classes: `Person`, `Name`, `Address`, `Borrower`, and `Loan`.

Identifying objects is not easy for novice programmers. How do you find the right objects? There is no unique solution even for simple problems. Software development is more an art than a science. The quality of a program ultimately depends on the programmer's intuition, experience, and knowledge. This example identifies five classes: `Name`, `Address`, `Person`, `Borrower`, and `Loan`. There are several alternatives. One would combine `Name`, `Address`, `Person`, and `Borrower` into one class. This design is not clear because it puts too many entities into one class.

The second step is to *describe the attributes* and methods in each of the classes you have identified. The attributes and methods can be illustrated using UML, as shown in Figure 10.7. The `Name` class has the properties `firstName`, `mi`, and `lastName`, their associated `get` and `set` methods, and the `getFullName` method for returning the full name. The `Address` class has the properties `street`, `city`, `state`, and `zip`, their associated `get` and `set` methods, and the `getAddress` method for returning the full address. The `Loan` class, presented in Section 6.15, "Case Study: The Loan Class," has the properties `annualInterestRate`, `numberOfYears`, and `loanAmount`, property `get` and `set` methods, and `monthlyPayment` and `totalPayment` methods. The `Person` class has the properties `name` and `address`, their associated `get` and `set` methods, and the `toString` method for displaying complete information about the person. `Borrower` is a subclass of `Person`. Additionally, `Borrower` has the `loan` property and its associated `get` and `set` methods, and the `toString` method for displaying the person and the loan payments.

describe attributes

The third step is to *establish relationships* among the classes. The relationship is derived from the analysis in the preceding two steps. The first three steps are intertwined. When you identify classes, you also think about the relationships among them. Establishing relationships among objects helps you understand the interactions among objects. An object-oriented system consists of a collection of interrelated cooperative objects. The relationships for the classes in this example are illustrated in Figure 10.7.

establish relationships

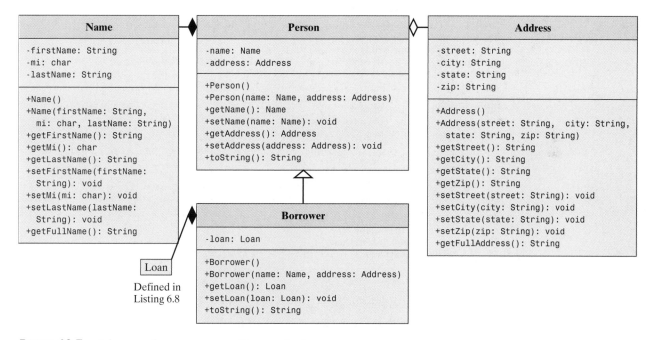

FIGURE 10.7 *A borrower has a name, an address, and a loan.*

The fourth step is to write the code for the classes. The program is long, but most of the *coding* is for the `get` and `set` methods. Once an object is identified, its properties and methods can be defined by analyzing the requirements and scenarios of the system. It is a good practice to provide complete `get` and `set` methods. These may not be needed for your current project, but will be useful in other projects, because your classes are designed for reuse in future projects. Listings 10.1, 10.2, 10.3, and 10.4 give the `Name`, `Address`, `Person`, and `Borrower` classes.

coding

LISTING 10.1   Name.java (The Name Class)

```
1 public class Name implements Cloneable {
2   private String firstName;
3   private char mi;
4   private String lastName;
5
6   /** Construct a name with default properties */
7   public Name() {
8     this("Jill", 'S', "Barr");
9   }
10
11   /** Construct a name with firstName, mi, and lastName */
12   public Name(String firstName, char mi, String lastName) {
13     this.firstName = firstName;
14     this.mi = mi;
15     this.lastName = lastName;
16   }
17
18   /** Return firstName */
19   public String getFirstName() {
20     return firstName;
21   }
22
23   /** Set a new firstName */
24   public void setFirstName(String firstName) {
25     this.firstName = firstName;
26   }
27
28   /** Return middle name initial */
29   public char getMi() {
30     return mi;
31   }
32
33   /** Set a new middlename initial */
34   public void setMi(char mi) {
35     this.mi = mi;
36   }
37
38   /** Return lastName */
39   public String getLastname() {
40     return lastName;
41   }
42
43   /** Set a new lastName */
44   public void setLastName(String lastName) {
45     this.lastName = lastName;
46   }
47
48   /** Obtain full name */
49   public String getFullName() {
50     return firstName + ' ' + mi + ' ' + lastName;
51   }
52 }
```

LISTING 10.2   Address.java (The Address Class)

```
1 public class Address {
2   private String street;
3   private String city;
4   private String state;
5   private String zip;
6
7   /** Construct an address with default properties */
8   public Address() {
9     this("100 Main", "Savannah", "GA", "31411");
10   }
11
```

```
12    /** Create an address with street, city, state, and zip */
13    public Address(String street, String city,
14      String state, String zip) {
15      this.street = street;
16      this.city = city;
17      this.state = state;
18      this.zip = zip;
19    }
20
21    /** Return street */
22    public String getStreet() {
23      return street;
24    }
25
26    /** Set a new street */
27    public void setStreet(String street) {
28      this.street = street;
29    }
30
31    /** Return city */
32    public String getCity() {
33      return city;
34    }
35
36    /** Set a new city */
37    public void setCity(String city) {
38      this.city = city;
39    }
40
41    /** Return state */
42    public String getState() {
43      return state;
44    }
45
46    /** Set a new state */
47    public void setState(String state) {
48      this.state = state;
49    }
50
51    /** Return zip */
52    public String getZip() {
53      return zip;
54    }
55
56    /** Set a new zip */
57    public void setZip(String zip) {
58      this.zip = zip;
59    }
60
61    /** Get full address */
62    public String getFullAddress() {
63      return street + '\n' + city + ", " + state + ' ' + zip + '\n';
64    }
65  }
```

LISTING 10.3   Person.java (The Person Class)

```
1  public class Person {
2    private Name name;
3    private Address address;
4
5    /** Construct a person with default properties */
6    public Person() {
7      this(new Name("Jill", 'S', "Barr"),
8        new Address("100 Main", "Savannah", "GA", "31411"));
9    }
10
```

```
11    /** Construct a person with specified name and address */
12    public Person(Name name, Address address) {
13      this.name = name;
14      this.address = address;
15    }
16
17    /** Return name */
18    public Name getName() {
19      return name;
20    }
21
22    /** Set a new name */
23    public void setName(Name name) {
24      this.name = name;
25    }
26
27    /** Return address */
28    public Address getAddress() {
29      return address;
30    }
31
32    /** Set a new address */
33    public void setAddress(Address address) {
34      this.address = address;
35    }
36
37    /** Override the toString method */
38    public String toString() {
39      return '\n' + name.getFullName() + '\n' +
40        address.getFullAddress() + '\n';
41    }
42 }
```

LISTING 10.4   Borrower.java (The Borrower Class)

```
 1 public class Borrower extends Person {
 2   private Loan loan;
 3
 4   /** Construct a borrower with default properties */
 5   public Borrower() {
 6     super();
 7   }
 8
 9   /** Create a borrower with specified name and address */
10   public Borrower(Name name, Address address) {
11     super(name, address);
12   }
13
14   /** Return loan */
15   public Loan getLoan() {
16     return loan;
17   }
18
19   /** Set a new loan */
20   public void setLoan(Loan loan) {
21     this.loan = loan;
22   }
23
24   /** String representation for borrower */
25   public String toString() {
26     return super.toString() +
27       "Monthly payment is " + loan.monthlyPayment() + '\n' +
28       "Total payment is " + loan.totalPayment();
29   }
30 }
```

Listing 10.5 is a test program that uses the classes Name, Address, Borrower, and Loan. The output of the program is shown in Figure 10.8.

LISTING 10.5   BorrowLoan.java

```
 1 import javax.swing.JOptionPane;
 2
 3 public class BorrowLoan {
 4   /** Main method */
 5   public static void main(String[] args) {
 6     // Create a name
 7     Name name = new Name("John", 'D', "Smith");
 8
 9     // Create an address
10     Address address = new Address("100 Main Street", "Savannah",
11       "GA", "31419");
12
13     // Create a loan
14     Loan loan = new Loan(5.5, 15, 250000);
15
16     // Create a borrower
17     Borrower borrower = new Borrower(name, address);
18
19     borrower.setLoan(loan);
20
21     // Display loan information
22     JOptionPane.showMessageDialog(null, borrower.toString());
23   }
24 }
```

FIGURE 10.8   *The program creates name, address, and loan, stores the information in a* Borrower *object, and displays the information with the loan payment.*

10.5   CASE STUDY: The Rational Class

A rational number is a number with a numerator and a denominator in the form a/b, where a is the numerator and b is the denominator. For example, 1/3, 3/4, and 10/4.

A rational number cannot have a denominator of 0, but a numerator of 0 is fine. Every integer a is equivalent to a rational number a/1. Rational numbers are used in exact computations involving fractions; for example, 1/3 = 0.33333. ... This number cannot be precisely represented in floating-point format using data type double or float. To obtain the exact result, it is necessary to use rational numbers.

Java provides data types for integers and floating-point numbers, but not for rational numbers. This section shows how to design a class to represent rational numbers.

Since rational numbers share many common features with integers and floating-point numbers, and Number is the root class for numeric wrapper classes, it is appropriate to define Rational as a subclass of Number. Since rational numbers are comparable, the Rational class should also implement the Comparable interface. Figure 10.9 illustrates the Rational class and its relationship to the Number class and the Comparable interface.

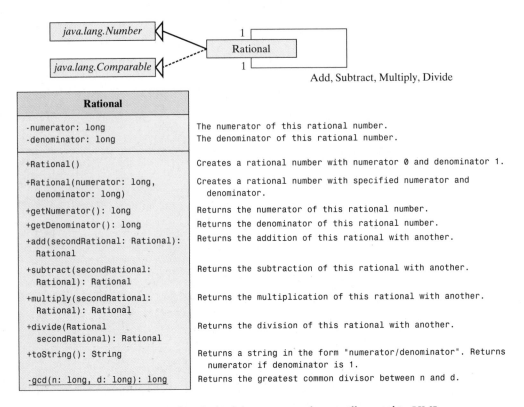

Figure 10.9 *The properties, constructors, and methods of the Rational class are illustrated in UML.*

A rational number consists of a numerator and a denominator. There are many equivalent rational numbers; for example, $1/3 = 2/6 = 3/9 = 4/12$. For convenience, $1/3$ is used in this example to represent all rational numbers that are equivalent to $1/3$. The numerator and the denominator of $1/3$ have no common divisor except 1, so $1/3$ is said to be in lowest terms.

To reduce a rational number to its lowest terms, you need to find the greatest common divisor (GCD) of the absolute values of its numerator and denominator, and then divide both numerator and denominator by this value. You can use the method for computing the GCD of two integers n and d, as suggested in Example 3.7, "Finding Greatest Common Divisor". The numerator and denominator in a Rational object are reduced to their lowest terms.

As usual, I recommend that you first write a test program to create two Rational objects and test its methods (see the Important Pedagogical Tip on page 242). Listing 10.6 is a test program. Its output is shown in Figure 10.10.

LISTING 10.6 TestRationalClass.java

```
1 public class TestRationalClass {
2   /** Main method */
3   public static void main(String[] args) {
4     // Create and initialize two rational numbers r1 and r2.
5     Rational r1 = new Rational(4, 2);
6     Rational r2 = new Rational(2, 3);
7
```

```
8      // Display results
9      System.out.println(r1 + " + " + r2 + " = " + r1.add(r2));
10     System.out.println(r1 + " - " + r2 + " = " + r1.subtract(r2));
11     System.out.println(r1 + " * " + r2 + " = " + r1.multiply(r2));
12     System.out.println(r1 + " / " + r2 + " = " + r1.divide(r2));
13     System.out.println(r2 + " is " + r2.doubleValue());
14   }
15 }
```

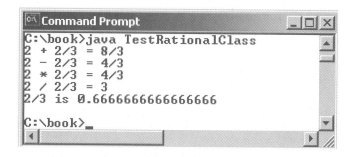

FIGURE 10.10   *The program creates two* Rational *objects and displays their addition, subtraction, multiplication, and division.*

The main method creates two rational numbers, r1 and r2 (Lines 5–6), and displays the results of r1 + r2, r1 - r2, r1 x r2, and r1 / r2 (Lines 9–12). To perform r1 + r2, invoke r1.add(r2) to return a new Rational object. Similarly, r1.subtract(r2) is for r1 - r2, r1.multiply(r2) for r1 x r2, and r1.divide(r2) for r1 / r2.

The doubleValue() method displays the double value of r2 (Line 13). The doubleValue() method is defined in java.lang.Number and overridden in Rational.

Note that when a string is concatenated with an object using the plus sign (+), the object's string representation from the toString() method is used to concatenate with the string. So r1 + " + " + r2 + " = " + r1.add(r2) is equivalent to r1.toString() + " + " + r2.toString() + " = " + r1.add(r2).toString().

The Rational class is implemented in Listing 10.7.

LISTING 10.7   Rational.java (The Rational Class)

```java
1  public class Rational extends Number implements Comparable {
2    // Data fields for numerator and denominator
3    private long numerator = 0;
4    private long denominator = 1;
5
6    /** Construct a rational with default properties */
7    public Rational() {
8      this(0, 1);
9    }
10
11   /** Construct a rational with specified numerator and denominator */
12   public Rational(long numerator, long denominator) {
13     long gcd = gcd(numerator, denominator);
14     this.numerator = ((denominator > 0) ? 1 : -1) * numerator / gcd;
15     this.denominator = Math.abs(denominator) / gcd;
16   }
17
18   /** Find GCD of two numbers */
19   private static long gcd(long n, long d) {
20     long n1 = Math.abs(n);
21     long n2 = Math.abs(d);
22     int gcd = 1;
```

```
23
24       for (int k = 1; k <= n1 && k <= n2; k++) {
25         if (n1 % k == 0 && n2 % k == 0)
26           gcd = k;
27       }
28
29       return gcd;
30     }
31
32     /** Return numerator */
33     public long getNumerator() {
34       return numerator;
35     }
36
37     /** Return denominator */
38     public long getDenominator() {
39       return denominator;
40     }
41
42     /** Add a rational number to this rational */
43     public Rational add(Rational secondRational) {
44       long n = numerator * secondRational.getDenominator() +
45         denominator * secondRational.getNumerator();
46       long d = denominator * secondRational.getDenominator();
47       return new Rational(n, d);
48     }
49
50     /** Subtract a rational number from this rational */
51     public Rational subtract(Rational secondRational) {
52       long n = numerator * secondRational.getDenominator()
53         - denominator * secondRational.getNumerator();
54       long d = denominator * secondRational.getDenominator();
55       return new Rational(n, d);
56     }
57
58     /** Multiply a rational number to this rational */
59     public Rational multiply(Rational secondRational) {
60       long n = numerator * secondRational.getNumerator();
61       long d = denominator * secondRational.getDenominator();
62       return new Rational(n, d);
63     }
64
65     /** Divide a rational number from this rational */
66     public Rational divide(Rational secondRational) {
67       long n = numerator * secondRational.getDenominator();
68       long d = denominator * secondRational.numerator;
69       return new Rational(n, d);
70     }
71
72     /** Override the toString() method */
73     public String toString() {
74       if (denominator == 1)
75         return numerator + "";
76       else
77         return numerator + "/" + denominator;
78     }
79
80     /** Override the equals method in the Object class */
81     public boolean equals(Object parm1) {
82       if ((this.subtract((Rational)(parm1))).getNumerator() == 0)
83         return true;
84       else
85         return false;
86     }
87
88     /** Override the hashCode method in the Object class */
89     public int hashCode() {
90       return new Double(this.doubleValue()).hashCode();
91     }
92
```

$$\frac{a}{b} + \frac{c}{d} = \frac{ad + bc}{bd}$$

$$\frac{a}{b} - \frac{c}{d} = \frac{ad - cb}{bd}$$

$$\frac{a}{b} \times \frac{c}{d} = \frac{ac}{bd}$$

$$\frac{a}{b} \div \frac{c}{d} = \frac{ad}{bc}$$

PROGRAMMING EXERCISES

Section 10.5 The Rational Class

10.1 (*Using the Rational class*) Write a program that will compute the following summation series using the Rational class:

$$\frac{1}{2} + \frac{2}{3} + \frac{3}{4} + \cdots + \frac{98}{99} + \frac{99}{100}$$

10.2* (*Demonstrating the benefits of encapsulation*) Rewrite the Rational class in Section 10.5 using a new internal representation for numerator and denominator. Declare an array of two integers as follows:

```
private long[] r = new long[2];
```

Use r[0] to represent the numerator and r[1] to represent the denominator. The signatures of the methods in the Rational class are not changed, so a client application that uses the previous Rational class can continue to use this new Rational class without being recompiled.

10.3* (*Creating a rational number calculator*) Write a program similar to the Calculator class on page 279. Instead of using integers, use rationals, as shown in Figure 10.15. You will need to use the StringTokenizer class, introduced in Chapter 7, "Strings," to retrieve the numerator string and denominator string, and convert strings into integers using the Integer.parseInt method.

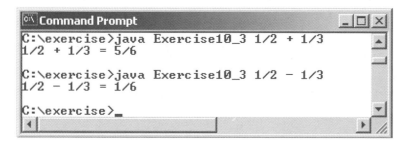

FIGURE 10.15 *The program takes three arguments (operand1, operator, and operand2) from the command line and displays the expression and the result of the arithmetic operation.*

Comprehensive

10.4** (*The Person and Student classes*) Create the classes as shown in Figure 10.16. Implement the compareTo method in the Person class to compare persons in alphabetical order of their last name, first name, and middle initial. Implement the compareTo method to compare students in alphabetical order of their major, last name, first name, and middle initial.

Write a test program with the following three methods:

```
/** Sort an array of comparable objects   */
public static void sort(Object[] list)

/** Return the max object in an array of comparable objects */
public static Object max(Object[] list)
```

main method: Test the sort and max methods using an array of four students, an array of four strings, an array of one hundred random rationals, and an array of one hundred random integers.

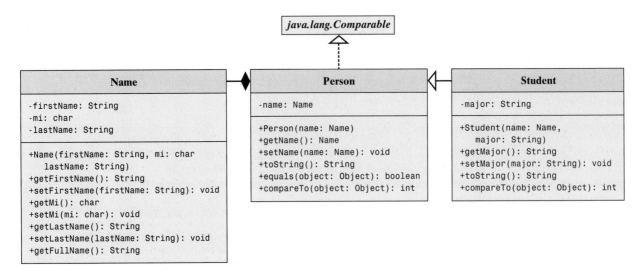

FIGURE **10.16** *A person has a name, a student is a person, and students are comparable.*

PART III

GUI PROGRAMMING

Part I, "Fundamentals of Programming," introduced basic programming concepts that are supported in all programming languages. Part II, "Object-Oriented Programming," introduced object-oriented programming concepts, principles, and practices that are common in the object-oriented programming languages. Java is not simply a programming language. It is also a development and deployment platform with an extensive set of classes and interfaces in the API. You have to use the classes and interfaces in the API and follow their conventions and rules to develop your own projects. The design of the API for Java GUI programming is an excellent example of how the object-oriented principle is applied. In the chapters that follow, you will learn the framework of Java GUI API and use the GUI components to develop user-friendly interfaces for applications and applets.

Chapter 11
Getting Started with GUI Programming

Chapter 12
Event-Driven Programming

Chapter 13
Creating User Interfaces

Chapter 14
Applets, Images, and Audio

Prerequisites for Part III

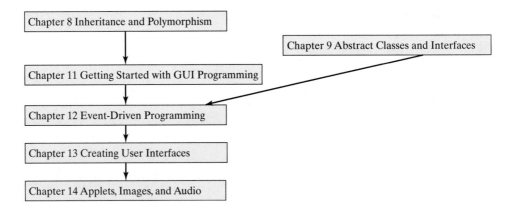

GETTING STARTED WITH GUI PROGRAMMING

Objectives

- ✦ To get a glimpse of simple GUI components (§11.2).

- ✦ To describe the Java GUI API hierarchy (§11.3).

- ✦ To create user interfaces using frames, panels, and simple GUI components (§11.4).

- ✦ To understand the role of layout managers (§11.5).

- ✦ To use the FlowLayout, GridLayout, and BorderLayout managers to layout components in a container (§11.5).

- ✦ To specify colors and fonts using the Color and Font classes (§§11.6–11.7).

- ✦ To use JPanels as subcontainers (§11.8).

- ✦ To paint graphics using the paintComponent method on a panel (§11.9).

- ✦ To draw strings, lines, rectangles, ovals, arcs, and polygons using the drawing methods in the Graphics class (§11.9).

- ✦ To center display using the FontMetrics Class (§11.10).

- ✦ To develop a reusable component, MessagePanel, to display a message on a panel (§11.11).

- ✦ To develop a reusable component, StillClock, to emulate an analog clock (§11.12 Optional).

11.1 Introduction

Until now, you have only used dialog boxes and the command window for input and output. You used `JOptionPane.showInputDialog` to obtain input, and `JOptionPane.showMessage-Dialog` and `System.out.println` to display results. These approaches have limitations and are inconvenient. For example, to read ten numbers, you have to open ten input dialog boxes. Starting with this chapter, you will learn Java GUI programming. You will create custom graphical user interfaces (GUI, pronounced *goo-ee*) to obtain input and display output in the same user interface.

This chapter introduces the basics of Java GUI programming. Specifically, it discusses GUI components and their relationships, containers and layout managers, colors, fonts, and drawing geometric figures, such as lines, rectangles, ovals, arcs, polygons, and polylines.

11.2 GUI Components

You create graphical user interfaces using GUI objects, such as buttons, labels, text fields, check boxes, radio buttons, and combo boxes. Each type of GUI object is defined in a class, such as `JButton`, `JLabel`, `JTextField`, `JCheckBox`, `JRadioButton`, and `JComboBox`. Each GUI component class provides several constructors that you can use to create GUI component objects. The following are the examples to create buttons, labels, text fields, check boxes, radio buttons, and combo boxes.

```
// Create a button with text OK
JButton jbtOK = new JButton("OK");

// Create a label with text "Enter your name: "
JLabel jlblName = new JLabel("Enter your name: ");

// Create a text field with text "Type Name Here"
JTextField jtfName = new JTextField("Type Name Here");

// Create a check box with text bold
JCheckBox jchkBold = new JCheckBox("Bold");

// Create a radio button with text red
JRadioButton jrbRed = new JRadioButton("Red");

// Create a combo box with choices red, green, and blue
JComboBox jcboColor = new JComboBox(new String[]{"Red",
  "Green", "Blue"});
```

Figure 11.1 shows these objects displayed in a frame. How to add the components into a frame will be introduced in Section 11.3.

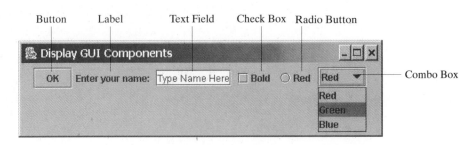

FIGURE 11.1 *The GUI component objects can be displayed.*

11.2.1 Swing vs. AWT

Why do the GUI component classes have the prefix *J*? Instead of JButton, why not name it simply Button? In fact, there is a class already named Button in the java.awt package.

When Java was introduced, the GUI classes were bundled in a library known as the Abstract Windows Toolkit (AWT). For every platform on which Java runs, the AWT components are automatically mapped to the platform-specific components through their respective agents, known as *peers*. AWT is fine for developing simple graphical user interfaces, but not for developing comprehensive GUI projects. Besides, AWT is prone to platform-specific bugs because its peer-based approach relies heavily on the underlying platform. With the release of Java 2, the AWT user-interface components were replaced by a more robust, versatile, and flexible library known as *Swing components*. Swing components are painted directly on canvases using Java code, except for components that are subclasses of java.awt.Window or java.awt.Panel, which must be drawn using native GUI on a specific platform. Swing components are less dependent on the target platform and use less of the native GUI resource. For this reason, Swing components that don't rely on native GUI are referred to as *lightweight components,* and AWT components are referred to as *heavyweight components.*

lightweight
heavyweight

To distinguish new Swing component classes from their AWT counterparts, the names of Swing GUI component classes begin with a prefixed *J*. Although AWT components are still supported in Java 2, it is better to learn how to program using Swing components, because the AWT user-interface components will eventually fade away. This book uses Swing GUI components exclusively.

11.3 The Java GUI API

The design of the Java API for GUI programming is an excellent example of the use of classes, inheritance, and interfaces. The API contains the essential classes listed below. Their hierarchical relationships are shown in Figures 11.2 and 11.3.

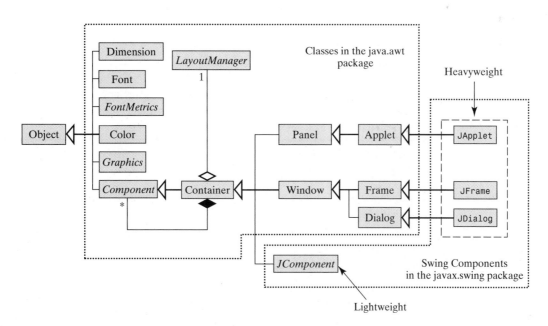

FIGURE 11.2 *Java GUI programming utilizes the classes shown in this hierarchical diagram.*

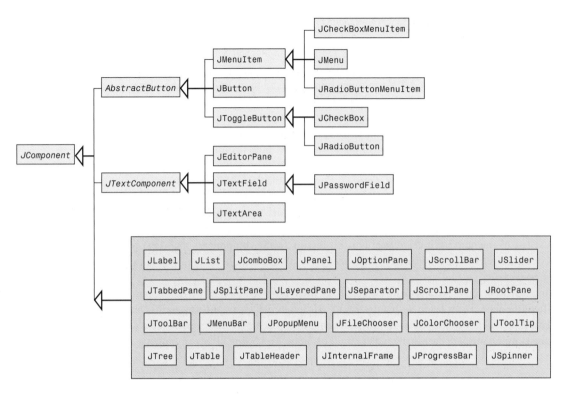

FIGURE 11.3 *JComponent and its subclasses are the basic elements for building graphical user interfaces.*

The GUI classes can be classified into three groups: *container classes*, *helper classes*, and *component classes*. The container classes, such as JFrame, JPanel, and JApplet, are used to contain other components. The helper classes, such as Graphics, Color, Font, FontMetrics, and Dimension, are used by components and containers to draw and place objects. The GUI component classes, such as JButton, JTextField, JTextArea, JComboBox, JList, JRadioButton, and JMenu, are subclasses of JComponent.

> **NOTE**
>
> The JFrame, JApplet, JDialog, and JComponent classes and their subclasses are grouped in the javax.swing package. All the other classes in Figures 11.2 are grouped in the java.awt package.

11.3.1 Swing GUI Components

Component is a superclass of all the user-interface classes, and JComponent is a superclass of all the lightweight Swing components. Since JComponent is an abstract class, you cannot use new JComponent() to create an instance of JComponent. However, you can use the constructors of concrete subclasses of JComponent to create JComponent instances. It is important to become familiar with the class inheritance hierarchy. For example, the following statements all display true:

```
JButton jbtOK = new JButton("OK");
System.out.println(jbtOK instanceof JButton);
System.out.println(jbtOK instanceof AbstractButton);
System.out.println(jbtOK instanceof JComponent);
System.out.println(jbtOK instanceof Container);
```

```
System.out.println(jbtOK instanceof Component);
System.out.println(jbtOK instanceof Object);
```

An instance of a subclass can invoke the accessible method defined in its superclass. For example, the getWidth() and getHeight() methods are defined in the Component class to return the component width and height. You can invoke the methods to find the width and height of a button.

11.3.2 Container Classes

Container classes are GUI components that are used as containers to contain other GUI components. Window, Panel, Applet, Frame, and Dialog are the container classes for AWT components. To work with Swing components, use Component, Container, JFrame, JDialog, JApplet, and JDialog.

◆ **Container** is used to group components. A layout manager is used to position and place components in a container in the desired location and style. Frames, panels, and applets are examples of containers.

◆ **JFrame** is a window not contained inside another window. It is the container that holds other Swing user-interface components in Java GUI applications.

◆ **JDialog** is a popup window or message box generally used as a temporary window to receive additional information from the user or to provide notification that an event has occurred.

◆ **JApplet** is a subclass of Applet. You must extend JApplet to create a Swing-based Java applet.

◆ **JPanel** is an invisible container that holds user-interface components. Panels can be nested. You can place panels inside a container that includes a panel. JPanel can also be used as a canvas to draw graphics.

11.3.3 GUI Helper Classes

The helper classes, such as Graphics, Color, Font, FontMetrics, Dimension, and LayoutManager, are not subclasses of Component. They are used to describe the properties of GUI components, such as graphics context, colors, fonts, and dimension.

◆ **Graphics** is an abstract class that provides a graphical context for drawing strings, lines, and simple shapes.

◆ **Color** deals with the colors of GUI components. For example, you can specify background or foreground colors in components like JFrame and JPanel, or you can specify colors of lines, shapes, and strings in drawings.

◆ **Font** specifies fonts for the text and drawings on GUI components. For example, you can specify the font type (e.g., SansSerif), style (e.g., bold), and size (e.g., 24 points) for the text on a button.

◆ **FontMetrics** is an abstract class used to get the properties of the fonts.

◆ **Dimension** encapsulates the width and height of a component (in integer precision) in a single object.

◆ **LayoutManager** is an interface, whose instances specify how components are arranged in a container.

NOTE

The helper classes are in the `java.awt` package. The Swing components do not re-place all the classes in AWT, only the AWT GUI component classes (e.g., `Button`, `TextField`, `TextArea`). The AWT helper classes remain unchanged.

11.4   Frames

To create a user interface, you need to create either a frame or an applet to hold the user-interface components. Creating Java applets will be introduced in Chapter 14, "Applets, Images, and Audio." This section introduces the procedure for creating frames.

11.4.1   Creating a Frame

The following program creates a frame:

LISTING 11.1   MyFrame.java (Creating a Frame)

```
 1 import javax.swing.*;
 2
 3 public class MyFrame {
 4   public static void main(String[] args) {
 5     JFrame frame = new JFrame("MyFrame");
 6     frame.setSize(400, 300);
 7     frame.setVisible(true);
 8     frame.setDefaultCloseOperation(JFrame.EXIT_ON_CLOSE);
 9   }
10 }
```

Because `JFrame` is in the `javax.swing` package, the statement `import javax.swing.*` (Line 1) makes available all the classes from the `javax.swing` package, including `JFrame`, so that they can be used in the `MyFrame` class.

The following two constructors are used to create a `JFrame` object:

✦   `public JFrame()`

Constructs an untitled `JFrame` object.

✦   `public JFrame(String title)`

Constructs a `JFrame` object with a specified title. The title appears in the title bar of the frame.

The frame is not displayed *until* the `frame.setVisible(true)` method is applied. `frame.setSize(400, 300)` specifies that the frame is 400 pixels wide and 300 pixels high. If the `setSize` method is not used, the frame will be sized to display just the title bar. Since the `setSize` and `setVisible` methods are both defined in the `Component` class, they are inherited by the `JFrame` class. Later you will see that these methods are also useful in many other subclasses of `Component`.

When you run the `MyFrame` program, a window will be displayed on-screen (see Figure 11.4).

`frame.setDefaultCloseOperation(JFrame.EXIT_ON_CLOSE)` (Line 8) tells the program to ter-minate when the frame is closed. If this statement is not used, the program does not terminate when the frame is closed. In that case, you have to stop the program by pressing `Ctrl+C` at the DOS prompt window in Windows or use the kill command to stop the process in Unix.

11.4.2   Adding Components to a Frame

The frame shown in Figure 11.4 is empty. Using the `add` method, you can add components into the frame's content pane, as in Listing 11.2.

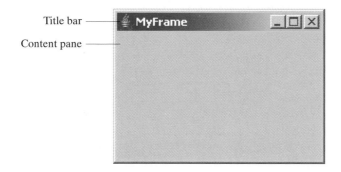

Title bar

Content pane

FIGURE **11.4**   *The program creates and displays a frame with the title* `MyFrame`.

LISTING **11.2**   `MyFrameWithComponents.java` (Adding Components to a Frame)

```
 1 import javax.swing.*;
 2
 3 public class MyFrameWithComponents {
 4   public static void main(String[] args) {
 5     JFrame frame = new JFrame("Adding Components into the Frame");
 6
 7     // Add a button into the frame
 8     java.awt.Container container = frame.getContentPane();
 9     JButton jbtOK = new JButton("OK");
10     container.add(jbtOK);
11
12     frame.setSize(400, 300);
13     frame.setVisible(true);
14     frame.setDefaultCloseOperation(JFrame.EXIT_ON_CLOSE);
15   }
16 }
```

The `getContentPane` method (Line 8) in the `JFrame` class returns the content pane of the frame, which is an instance of `java.awt.Container`. The GUI components such as buttons are placed in the content pane. An object of `JButton` was created using `new JButton("OK")`, and this object was added to the content pane of the frame (Line 10).

You may be wondering how the content pane (a `Container` object) is created. The `getContentPane` method does not produce it. The content pane is created when a `JFrame` object is created. The `getContentPane` method simply returns a reference to the content pane, and you can use it to reference the content pane.

The `add(Componentcomp)` method defined in the `Container` class adds an instance of `Component` to the container. Since `JButton` is a subclass of `Component`, an instance of `JButton` is also an instance of `Component`. To remove a component from a container, use the `remove` method. The following statement removes the button from the container:

```
container.remove(jbtOK);
```

When you run the program `MyFrameWithComponents`, the following window will be displayed in Figure 11.5. The button is always centered in the frame and occupies the entire frame no matter how you resize it. This is because components are put in the frame by the content pane's layout manager, and the default layout manager for the content pane places the button in the center. In the next section, you will use several different layout managers to place components in other locations as desired.

11.4.3   Centering a Frame (Optional)

By default, a frame is displayed in the upper-left corner of the screen. The coordinates at the upper-left corner of the screen are (0, 0). The *x* coordinate increases rightward, and the

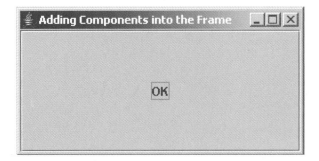

FIGURE 11.5   *An OK button is added to the frame.*

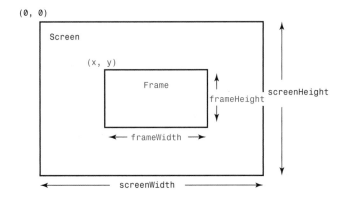

FIGURE 11.6   *The frame is centered on the screen.*

y coordinate increases downward. To display a frame at a specified location, use the setLocation(x, y) method in the JFrame class. This method places the upper-left corner of the frame at location (x, y) on the screen.

To center a frame on the screen, you need to know the width and height of the screen and the frame in order to determine the frame's upper-left coordinates. The screen's width and height can be obtained using the java.awt.Toolkit class:

```
Dimension screenSize = Toolkit.getDefaultToolkit().getScreenSize();
int screenWidth = screenSize.width;
int screenHeight = screenSize.height;
```

Therefore, as shown in Figure 11.6, the upper-left x and y coordinates of the centered frame frame are:

```
// Locate the upper-left corner (x, y) of the centered frame
int x = (screenWidth - frame.getWidth()) / 2;
int y = (screenHeight - frame.getHeight()) / 2;
```

The java.awt.Dimension class encapsulates the width and height of a component (in integer precision) in a single object. The methods getWidth() and getHeight() are defined in the Component class. You can apply these methods to get the width and height of any component.

Listing 11.3 displays a frame centered on the screen.

LISTING 11.3   CenterFrame.java (Centering a Frame)

```
1 import javax.swing.*;
2 import java.awt.*;
3
```

```
 4 public class CenterFrame {
 5   public static void main(String[] args) {
 6     JFrame frame = new JFrame("CenterFrame");
 7     frame.setSize(400, 300);
 8     frame.setDefaultCloseOperation(JFrame.EXIT_ON_CLOSE);
 9
10     // Get the dimension of the screen
11     Dimension screenSize =
12       Toolkit.getDefaultToolkit().getScreenSize();
13     int screenWidth = screenSize.width;
14     int screenHeight = screenSize.height;
15
16     // Locate the upper-left corner (x, y) of the centered frame
17     int x = (screenWidth - frame.getWidth()) / 2;
18     int y = (screenHeight - frame.getHeight()) / 2;
19
20     // Set the location of the frame
21     frame.setLocation(x, y);
22     frame.setVisible(true);
23   }
24 }
```

11.5   Layout Managers

In many other window systems, the user-interface components are arranged by using hard-coded pixel measurements. For example, put a button at location (10, 10) in the window. Using hard-coded pixel measurements, the user interface might look fine on one system but be unusable on another. Java's layout managers provide a level of abstraction that automatically maps your user interface on all window systems.

 NOTE

Java also supports hard-coded fixed layout, which will be covered in Chapter 22, "Containers, Layout Managers, and Borders." Since it is platform-dependent, it is rarely used in practice.

The Java GUI components are placed in containers, where they are arranged by the container's layout manager. In the preceding program, you did not specify where to place the OK button in the frame, but Java knows where to place it because the layout manager works behind the scenes to place components in the correct locations. A layout manager is created using a layout manager class. Every layout manager class implements the LayoutManager interface.

Layout managers are set in containers using the setLayout(LayoutManager) method. For example, you can use the following statements to create an instance of XLayout and set it in a container:

```
LayoutManager layoutManager = new XLayout();
container.setLayout(layoutManager);
```

This section introduces three basic layout managers: FlowLayout, GridLayout, and BorderLayout. More layout managers will be introduced in Chapter 22, "Containers, Layout Managers, and Borders."

11.5.1   FlowLayout

FlowLayout is the simplest layout manager. The components are arranged in the container from left to right in the order in which they were added. When one row is filled, a new row is started. You can specify the way the components are aligned by using one of three constants:

FlowLayout.RIGHT, FlowLayout.CENTER, or FlowLayout.LEFT. You can also specify the gap between components in pixels. FlowLayout has three constructors:

◆ `public FlowLayout(int align, int hGap, int vGap)`

Constructs a new FlowLayout with the specified alignment, horizontal gap, and vertical gap. The gaps are the distances in pixels between components.

◆ `public FlowLayout(int alignment)`

Constructs a new FlowLayout with a specified alignment and a default gap of 5 pixels horizontally and vertically.

◆ `public FlowLayout()`

Constructs a new FlowLayout with a default center alignment and a default gap of 5 pixels horizontally and vertically.

EXAMPLE 11.1 TESTING THE **FlowLayout** MANAGER

Problem

Write a program that adds ten buttons labeled Component 1, ..., and Component 10 into the content pane of a frame with a FlowLayout manager, as shown in Figure 11.7.

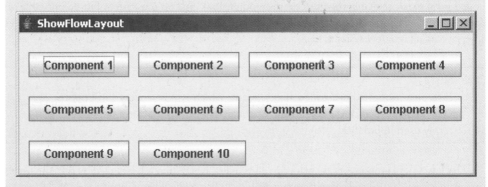

FIGURE 11.7 *The components are added with the* FlowLayout *manager to fill in the rows in the container one after another.*

Solution

Create a subclass of JFrame, set the layout manager of the content pane to a FlowLayout, and add ten buttons into the content pane using a loop.

LISTING 11.4 ShowFlowLayout.java (Using FlowLayout)

```java
1 import javax.swing.JButton;
2 import javax.swing.JFrame;
3 import java.awt.Container;
4 import java.awt.FlowLayout;
5
6 public class ShowFlowLayout extends JFrame {
7   public ShowFlowLayout() {
```

EXAMPLE 11.1 (CONTINUED)

```
 8      // Get the content pane of the frame
 9      Container container = getContentPane();
10
11      // Set FlowLayout, aligned left with horizontal gap 10
12      // and vertical gap 20 between components
13      container.setLayout(new FlowLayout(FlowLayout.LEFT, 10, 20));
14
15      // Add buttons to the frame
16      for (int i = 1; i <= 10; i++)
17        container.add(new JButton("Component " + i));
18    }
19
20    /** Main method */
21    public static void main(String[] args) {
22      ShowFlowLayout frame = new ShowFlowLayout();
23      frame.setTitle("ShowFlowLayout");
24      frame.setDefaultCloseOperation(JFrame.EXIT_ON_CLOSE);
25      frame.setSize(200, 200);
26      frame.setVisible(true);
27    }
28  }
```

contentPane

set layout

add buttons

create frame

set visible

Review

This example creates a program using a style different from the programs in the preceding section, where frames were created using the JFrame class. This example creates a class named ShowFlowLayout that extends the JFrame class (Line 6). The main method in this program creates an instance of ShowFlowLayout (Line 22). The constructor of ShowFlowLayout constructs and places the components in the frame. This is the preferred style of creating GUI applications for two reasons: (1) creating a GUI application means creating a frame, so it is natural to define a frame to extend JFrame; (2) the new class can be reused if desirable. Using one style consistently makes programs easy to read. From now on, all the GUI main classes will extend the JFrame class. The constructor of the main class constructs the user interface. The main method creates an instance of the main class and then displays the frame.

In this example, the FlowLayout manager is used to place components in a frame. If you resize the frame, the components are automatically rearranged to fit in it.

If you replace the setLayout statement (Line 13) with setLayout(newFlowLayout (FlowLayout.RIGHT, 0, 0)), all the rows of buttons will be right-aligned with no gaps.

An anonymous FlowLayout object was created in the statement (Line 13):

```
container.setLayout(new FlowLayout(FlowLayout.LEFT, 10, 20));
```

which is equivalent to:

```
FlowLayout layout = new FlowLayout(FlowLayout.LEFT, 10, 20);
container.setLayout(layout);
```

This code creates an explicit reference to the object layout of the FlowLayout class. The explicit reference is not necessary, because the object is not directly referenced in the ShowFlowLayout class.

The setTitle method (Line 23) is defined in the java.awt.Frame class. Since JFrame is a subclass of Frame, you can use it to set a title for an object of JFrame.

Suppose you add the same button into the container ten times, will ten buttons appear in the container? No, only the last one will be displayed.

CAUTION

Do not forget to put the `new` operator before a layout manager class when setting a layout style; for example, `setLayout(new FlowLayout())`.

 NOTE

The constructor `ShowFlowLayout()` does not explicitly invoke the constructor `JFrame()`, but the constructor `JFrame()` is invoked implicitly. See Section 8.3.2, "Constructor Chaining".

11.5.2 `GridLayout`

The `GridLayout` manager arranges components in a grid (matrix) formation with the number of rows and columns defined by the constructor. The components are placed in the grid from left to right, starting with the first row, then the second, and so on, in the order in which they are added. The `GridLayout` manager has three constructors:

✦ `public GridLayout(int rows, int columns, int hGap, int vGap)`

   Constructs a new `GridLayout` with the specified number of rows and columns, along with specified horizontal and vertical gaps between components in the container.

✦ `public GridLayout(int rows, int columns)`

   Constructs a new `GridLayout` with the specified number of rows and columns. The horizontal and vertical gaps are zero.

✦ `public GridLayout()`

   Constructs a new `GridLayout` with one row.

You can specify the number of rows and columns in the grid. The basic rule is as follows:

✦ The number of rows or the number of columns can be zero, but not both. If one is zero and the other is nonzero, the nonzero dimension is fixed, while the zero dimension is determined dynamically by the layout manager. For example, if you specify zero rows and three columns for a grid that has ten components, `GridLayout` creates three fixed columns of four rows, with the last row containing one component. If you specify three rows and zero columns for a grid that has ten components, `GridLayout` creates three fixed rows of four columns, with the last row containing two components.

✦ If both the number of rows and the number of columns are nonzero, the number of rows is the dominating parameter; that is, the number of rows is fixed, and the layout manager dynamically calculates the number of columns. For example, if you specify three rows and three columns for a grid that has ten components, `GridLayout` creates three fixed rows of four columns, with the last row containing two components.

EXAMPLE 11.2 TESTING THE `GridLayout` MANAGER

Problem

Write a program that adds ten buttons labeled `Component 1`, ..., and `Component 10` into the content pane of a frame with a `GridLayout` manager, as shown in Figure 11.8.

EXAMPLE 11.2 (CONTINUED)

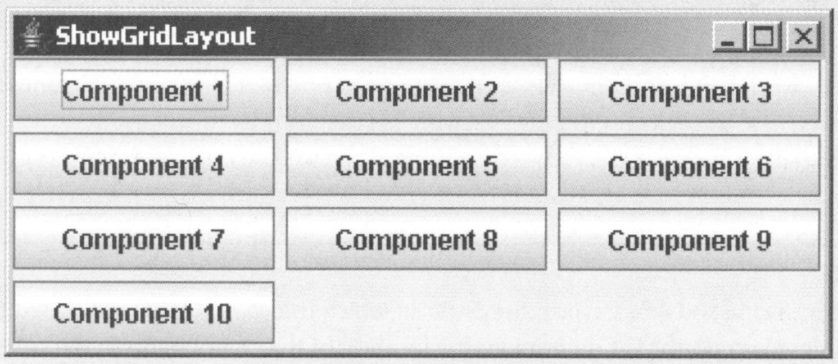

FIGURE 11.8 *The* GridLayout *manager divides the container into grids, then the components are added to fill in the cells row by row.*

Solution

Create a subclass of JFrame, set the layout manager of the content pane to a GridLayout with four rows and three columns, and add ten buttons into the content pane using a loop.

LISTING 11.5 **ShowGridLayout.java (Using** GridLayout**)**

```
1 import javax.swing.JButton;
2 import javax.swing.JFrame;
3 import java.awt.GridLayout;
4 import java.awt.Container;
5
6 public class ShowGridLayout extends JFrame {
7   public ShowGridLayout() {
8     // Get the content pane of the frame
9     Container container = getContentPane();                    contentPane
10
11    // Set GridLayout, 4 rows, 3 columns, and gaps 5 between
12    // components horizontally and vertically
13    container.setLayout(new GridLayout(4, 3, 5, 5));           set layout
14
15    // Add buttons to the frame
16    for (int i = 1; i <= 10; i++)
17      container.add(new JButton("Component " + i));            add buttons
18  }
19
20  /** Main method */
21  public static void main(String[] args) {
22    ShowGridLayout frame = new ShowGridLayout();
23    frame.setTitle("ShowGridLayout");
24    frame.setDefaultCloseOperation(JFrame.EXIT_ON_CLOSE);
25    frame.setSize(200, 200);
26    frame.setVisible(true);
27  }
28 }
```

Review

If you resize the frame, the layout of the buttons remains unchanged (i.e., the number of rows and columns does not change, and the gaps don't change either).

All components are given equal size in the container of GridLayout.

Replacing the setLayout statement (Line 13) with setLayout(new GridLayout(3, 10)) would yield three rows and *four* columns, with the last row containing two

EXAMPLE **11.2** (CONTINUED)

components. The columns parameter is ignored because the rows parameter is nonzero. The actual number of columns is calculated by the layout manager.

What would happen if the `setLayout` statement (Line 13) is replaced with `setLayout(new GridLayout(3, 2))` or with `setLayout(new GridLayout(2, 2))`? Please try it yourself.

 NOTE

In `FlowLayout` and `GridLayout`, the order in which the components are added to the container is important. It determines the location of the components in the container.

11.5.3 `BorderLayout`

The `BorderLayout` manager divides the window into five areas: East, South, West, North, and Center. Components are added to a `BorderLayout` by using `add(Component, index)`, where `index` is a constant `BorderLayout.EAST`, `BorderLayout.SOUTH`, `BorderLayout.WEST`, `BorderLayout.NORTH`, or `BorderLayout.CENTER`. You can use one of the following two constructors to create a new `BorderLayout`:

◆ `public BorderLayout(int hGap, int vGap)`

Constructs a new `BorderLayout` with the specified horizontal and vertical gaps between the components.

◆ `public BorderLayout()`

Constructs a new `BorderLayout` without horizontal or vertical gaps.

The components are laid out according to their preferred sizes and where they are placed in the container. The North and South components can stretch horizontally; the East and West components can stretch vertically; the Center component can stretch both horizontally and vertically to fill any empty space.

EXAMPLE **11.3** TESTING THE `BorderLayout` MANAGER

Problem

Write a program that adds five buttons labeled `East`, `South`, `West`, `North`, and `Center` into the content pane of a frame with a `BorderLayout` manager, as shown in Figure 11.9.

FIGURE 11.9 *BorderLayout divides the container into five areas, each of which can hold a component.*

EXAMPLE 11.3 (CONTINUED)

Solution

Create a subclass of JFrame, set the layout manager of the content pane to a BorderLayout, and add five buttons into the content pane.

LISTING 11.6 ShowBorderLayout.java (Using BorderLayout)

```
1 import javax.swing.JButton;
2 import javax.swing.JFrame;
3 import java.awt.Container;
4 import java.awt.BorderLayout;
5
6 public class ShowBorderLayout extends JFrame {
7   public ShowBorderLayout() {
8     // Get the content pane of the frame
9     Container container = getContentPane();                              contentPane
10
11    // Set BorderLayout with horizontal gap 5 and vertical gap 10
12    container.setLayout(new BorderLayout(5, 10));                        set layout
13
14    // Add buttons to the frame
15    container.add(new JButton("East"), BorderLayout.EAST);              add buttons
16    container.add(new JButton("South"), BorderLayout.SOUTH);
17    container.add(new JButton("West"), BorderLayout.WEST);
18    container.add(new JButton("North"), BorderLayout.NORTH);
19    container.add(new JButton("Center"), BorderLayout.CENTER);
20  }
21
22  /** Main method */
23  public static void main(String[] args) {
24    ShowBorderLayout frame = new ShowBorderLayout();
25    frame.setTitle("ShowBorderLayout");
26    frame.setDefaultCloseOperation(JFrame.EXIT_ON_CLOSE);
27    frame.setSize(300, 200);
28    frame.setVisible(true);
29  }
30 }
```

Review

The buttons are added to the frame (Lines 15-19). Note that the add method for BorderLayout is different from the one for FlowLayout and GridLayout. With BorderLayout you specify where to put the components.

It is unnecessary to place components to occupy all the areas. If you remove the East button from the program and rerun it, you will see that the center stretches rightward to occupy the East area.

❀ **NOTE**

For convenience, BorderLayout interprets the absence of an index specification as BorderLayout.CENTER. For example, add(component) is the same as add(Component, BorderLayout.CENTER). If you add two components into a container of BorderLayout, as follows,

```
container.add(component1);
container.add(component2);
```

only the last component is displayed.

TIP
You can use a new JDK 1.5 feature to directly import static constants from a class. The imported constants can be referenced without specifying a class. For example, you can use EAST, instead of BorderLayout.EAST, if you have the following import statement in the class:

```
import static java.awt.BorderLayout.*;
```

11.5.4 Properties of Layout Managers (Optional)

Layout managers have properties that can be changed dynamically. FlowLayout has alignment, hGap, and vGap properties. You can use the setAlignment, setHGap, and setVGap methods to specify the alignment and the horizontal and vertical gaps. GridLayout has the rows, columns, hGap, and vGap properties. You can use the setRows, setColumns, setHGap, and setVGap methods to specify the number of rows, the number of columns, and the horizontal and vertical gaps. BorderLayout has the hGap and vGap properties. You can use the setHGap and setVGap methods to specify the horizontal and vertical gaps.

In the preceding sections, an anonymous layout manager is used because the properties of a layout manager do not change once it is created. If you have to change the properties of a layout manager dynamically, the layout manager must be explicitly referenced by a variable. You can then change the properties of the layout manager through the variable. For example, the following code creates a layout manager and sets its properties:

```
// Create a layout manager
FlowLayout flowLayout = new FlowLayout();

// Set layout properties
flowLayout.setAlignment(FlowLayout.RIGHT);
flowLayout.setHGap(10);
flowLayout.setVGap(20);
```

11.5.5 The validate and doLayout Methods (Optional)

A container can have only one layout manager at a time. You can change its layout manager by using the setLayout(aNewLayout) method and then use the validate() method to force the container to again layout the components in the container using the new layout manager.

If you use the same layout manager but change its properties, you need to use the doLayout() method to force the container to re-layout the components using the new properties of the layout manager.

validate()

doLayout()

11.6 The Color Class

You can set colors for GUI components by using the java.awt.Color class. Colors are made of red, green, and blue components, each of which is represented by a byte value that describes its intensity, ranging from 0 (darkest shade) to 255 (lightest shade). This is known as the *RGB model*.

You can create a color using the following constructor:

```
public Color(int r, int g, int b);
```

in which r, g, and b specify a color by its red, green, and blue components. For example,

```
Color color = new Color(128, 100, 100);
```

You can use the setBackground(Color c) and setForeground(Color c) methods defined in the java.awt.Component class to set a component's background and foreground colors. Here is an example of setting the background of a panel using a color:

```
JButton jbtOK = new JButton();
jbtOK.setBackground(color);
jbtOK.setForeground(new Color(100, 1, 1));
```

Alternatively, you can use one of the thirteen standard colors (black, blue, cyan, darkGray, gray, green, lightGray, magenta, orange, pink, red, white, yellow) defined as constants in java.awt.Color. The following code, for instance, sets the background color of a panel to yellow:

```
jbtOK.setForeground(Color.red);
```

 NOTE

The standard color names are constants, but they are named as variables with low-ercase for the first word and uppercase for the first letters of subsequent words. Thus the color names violate the Java naming convention. Since JDK 1.4, you can also use the new constants BLACK, BLUE, CYAN, DARK_GRAY, GRAY, GREEN, LIGHT_GRAY, MAGENTA, ORANGE, PINK, RED, WHITE, and YELLOW.

color constants

11.7 The **Font** Class

You can create a font using the java.awt.Font class and set fonts for the components using the setFont method in the Component class.

The constructor for Font is:

```
public Font(String name, int style, int size);
```

You can choose a font name from SansSerif, Serif, Monospaced, Dialog, or DialogInput, choose a style from Font.PLAIN (0), Font.BOLD (1), Font.ITALIC (2), and Font.BOLD + Font.ITALIC (3), and specify a font size of any positive integer. For example, the following statements create two fonts and set one font to a button:

```
Font font1 = new Font("SansSerif", Font.BOLD, 16);
Font font2 = new Font("Serif", Font.BOLD + Font.ITALIC, 12);

JButton jbtOK = new JButton("OK");
jbtOK.setFont(font1);
```

 TIP (OPTIONAL)

If your system supports other fonts, such as "Times New Roman," you can use it to create a Font object. To find the fonts available on your system, you need to create an instance of java.awt.GraphicsEnvironment using its static method getLocalGraphicsEnvironment(). GraphicsEnvironment is an abstract class that describes the graphics environment on a particular system. You can use its getAllFonts() method to obtain all the available fonts on the system, and its getAvailableFontFamilyNames() method to obtain the names of all the available fonts. For example, the following statements print all the available font names in the system:

```
GraphicsEnvironment e =
  GraphicsEnvironment.getLocalGraphicsEnvironment();
String[] fontnames = e.getAvailableFontFamilyNames();

for (int i = 0; i < fontnames.length; i++)
  System.out.println(fontnames[i]);
```

find available fonts

11.8   Using Panels as Subcontainers

Suppose that you want to place ten buttons and a text field on a frame. The buttons are placed in grid formation, but the text field is placed on a separate row. It is difficult to achieve the desired look by placing all the components in a single container. With Java GUI programming, you can divide a window into panels. Panels act as subcontainers to group user-interface components. You add the buttons in one panel, and then add the panel into the frame.

The Swing version of panel is JPanel. You can use new JPanel() to create a panel with a default FlowLayout manager or new JPanel(LayoutManager) to create a panel with the specified layout manager. Use the add(Component) method to add a component to the panel. For example, the following code creates a panel and adds a button to it:

```
JPanel p = new JPanel();
p.add(new JButton("OK"));
```

Panels can be placed inside a frame or inside another panel. The following statement places panel p into frame f:

```
f.getContentPane().add(p);
```

NOTE

To add a component to JFrame, you actually add it to the content pane of JFrame. To add a component to a panel, you add it directly to the panel using the add method.

EXAMPLE 11.4 TESTING PANELS

Problem

Write a program that uses panels to organize components. The program creates a user interface for a microwave oven, as shown in Figure 11.10.

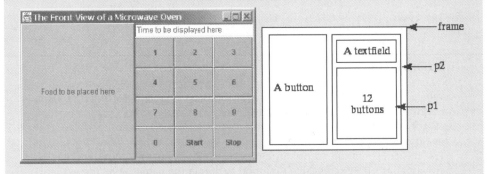

FIGURE 11.10   *The program uses panels to organize components.*

Solution

The program is given in Listing 11.7.

EXAMPLE 11.4 (CONTINUED)

LISTING 11.7   TestPanels.java (Using Panels as Subcontainers)

```
1 import java.awt.*;
2 import javax.swing.*;
3
4 public class TestPanels extends JFrame {
5   public TestPanels() {
6     // Get the content pane of the frame
7     Container container = getContentPane();
8
9     // Set BorderLayout for the frame
10    container.setLayout(new BorderLayout());
11
12    // Create panel p1 for the buttons and set GridLayout
13    JPanel p1 = new JPanel();                                     panel p1
14    p1.setLayout(new GridLayout(4, 3));
15
16    // Add buttons to the panel
17    for (int i = 1; i <= 9; i++) {
18      p1.add(new JButton("" + i));
19    }
20
21    p1.add(new JButton("" + 0));
22    p1.add(new JButton("Start"));
23    p1.add(new JButton("Stop"));
24
25    // Create panel p2 to hold a text field and p1
26    JPanel p2 = new JPanel(new BorderLayout());                   panel p2
27    p2.add(new JTextField("Time to be displayed here"),
28      BorderLayout.NORTH);
29    p2.add(p1, BorderLayout.CENTER);
30
31    // Add p2 and a button to the frame
32    container.add(p2, BorderLayout.EAST);
33    container.add(new JButton("Food to be placed here"),
34      BorderLayout.CENTER);
35  }
36
37  /** Main method */
38  public static void main(String[] args) {
39    TestPanels frame = new TestPanels();
40    frame.setTitle("The Front View of a Microwave Oven");
41    frame.setDefaultCloseOperation(JFrame.EXIT_ON_CLOSE);
42    frame.setSize(400, 250);
43    frame.setVisible(true);
44  }
45 }
```

Review

The setLayout method is defined in java.awt.Container. Since JPanel is a subclass of Container, you can use setLayout to set a new layout manager in the panel (Line 14). Lines 13–14 can be replaced by JPanel p1 = new JPanel(new GridLayout(4, 3)).

To achieve the desired layout, the program uses panel p1 of GridLayout to group the number buttons, the Stop button, and the Start button, and panel p2 of BorderLayout to hold a text field in the north and p1 in the center. The button representing the food is placed in the center of the frame, and p2 is placed in the east of the frame.

The statement (Lines 27–28)

```
p2.add(new JTextField("Time to be displayed here"),
  BorderLayout.NORTH);
```

creates an instance of JTextField and adds it to p2.

EXAMPLE 11.4 (CONTINUED)

Text field is a GUI component that can be used for user input as well as to display values. More detail on using text fields will be introduced in Chapter 13, "Creating User Interfaces."

11.9 Drawing Graphics on Panels

Panels are invisible and are used as small containers that group components to achieve a desired layout. Another important use of JPanel is for drawing.

To draw in a JPanel, you create a new class that extends JPanel and overrides the paintComponent method to tell the panel how to draw things. Although you can draw things directly in a frame or an applet using the paint method, it is better to use JPanel to draw strings and shapes and to show images; this way your drawing will not interfere with other components.

The paintComponent method is defined in JComponent, and its signature is as follows:

```
protected void paintComponent(Graphics g)
```

The Graphics object g is created automatically by the JVM for every visible GUI component. This object controls how information is drawn. You can use various drawing methods defined in the Graphics class to draw strings and geometric figures. For example, you can draw a string using the following method in the Graphics class:

```
public void drawString(String string, int x, int y)
```

The program given in Listing 11.8 draws the message "Welcome to Java" on the panel, as shown in Figure 11.11.

LISTING 11.8 DrawMessage.java (Using Panels as Canvases)

```
 1 import javax.swing.*;
 2 import java.awt.*;
 3
 4 public class DrawMessage extends JPanel {
 5   /** Main method */
 6   public static void main(String[] args) {
 7     JFrame frame = new JFrame("DrawMessage");
 8     frame.getContentPane().add(new DrawMessage());
 9     frame.setDefaultCloseOperation(JFrame.EXIT_ON_CLOSE);
10     frame.setSize(300, 200);
11     frame.setVisible(true);
12   }
13
14   /** Paint the message */
15   protected void paintComponent(Graphics g) {
16     super.paintComponent(g);
17
18     g.drawString("Welcome to Java!", 40, 40);
19   }
20 }
```

override paintComponent

draw string

All the drawing methods have parameters that specify the locations of the subjects to be drawn. All measurements in Java are made in pixels. Each component has its own coordinate system with the origin (0, 0) at the upper-left corner of the component. The x coordinate increases to the right, and the y coordinate increases downward. Note that the Java coordinate system is different from the traditional coordinate system, as shown in Figure 11.12.

FIGURE 11.11 *The message is drawn on a panel, and the panel is placed inside the frame.*

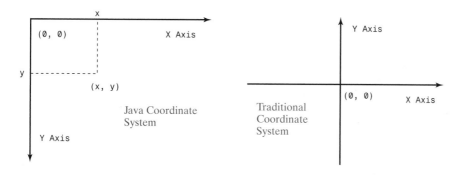

FIGURE 11.12 *The Java graphics coordinate system is measured in pixels, with (0, 0) at its upper-left corner.*

 NOTE

The Graphics class is an abstract class that provides a device-independent graphics interface for displaying figures and images on the screen on different platforms. The Graphics class is implemented on the native platform in the JVM. When you use the paintComponent method to draw things in a graphics context g, this g is an instance of a concrete subclass of the abstract Graphics class for the specific platform. The Graphics class encapsulates the platform details and enables you to draw things uniformly without having to be concerned about the specific platform.

Graphics class

 NOTE

Whenever a component is displayed, a Graphics object is created for it. The Swing components use the paintComponent method to draw things. The paintComponent method is automatically invoked to paint the graphics context when the component is first displayed or whenever the component needs to be redisplayed. Invoking super.paintComponent(g) is necessary to ensure that the viewing area is cleared before a new drawing is displayed. The user can request the component to be redisplayed by invoking the repaint() method defined in the Component class. Invoking repaint() causes paintComponent to be invoked by the JVM. The user should never invoke paintComponent directly. For this reason, the protected visibility is sufficient for paintComponent.

repaint()

 NOTE

To draw things, normally you create a subclass of JPanel and override its paintComponent method to tell the system how to draw. In fact, you can draw things on any GUI component. See Exercise 11.6 for a custom button class that displays a figure instead of a text in the button.

You can not only draw strings, but also lines, rectangles, ovals, arcs, polygons, and polylines.

11.9.1 Drawing Lines

You can use the method shown below to draw a straight line:

```
drawLine(int x1, int y1, int x2, int y2);
```

The parameters x1, y1, x2, and y2 represent the starting point (x1, y1) and the ending point (x2, y2) of the line, as shown in Figure 11.13.

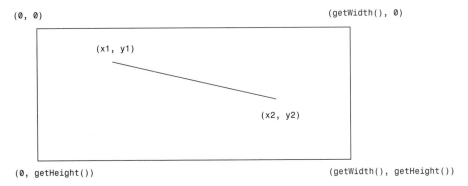

FIGURE 11.13 *The drawLine method draws a line between two specified points.*

11.9.2 Drawing Rectangles

Java provides six methods for drawing rectangles in outline or filled with color. You can draw plain rectangles, rounded rectangles, or three-dimensional rectangles.

To draw a plain rectangle, use the following code:

```
drawRect(int x, int y, int w, int h);
```

To draw a rectangle filled with color, use:

```
fillRect(int x, int y, int w, int h);
```

The parameters x and y represent the upper-left corner of the rectangle, and w and h are its width and height (see Figure 11.14).

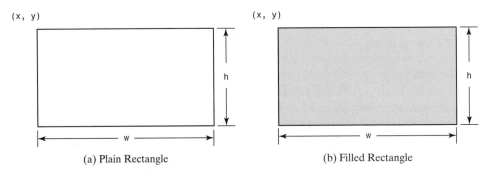

(a) Plain Rectangle   (b) Filled Rectangle

FIGURE 11.14 *The drawRect method draws a rectangle with specified upper-left corner (x, y), width, and height.*

To draw a rounded rectangle, use the following method:

```
drawRoundRect(int x, int y, int w, int h, int aw, int ah);
```

To draw a rounded rectangle filled with color, use this method:

```
fillRoundRect(int x, int y, int w, int h, int aw, int ah);
```

Parameters x, y, w, and h are the same as in the drawRect method, parameter aw is the horizontal diameter of the arcs at the corner, and ah is the vertical diameter of the arcs at the corner (see Figure 11.15). In other words, aw and ah are the width and the height of the oval that produces a quarter-circle at each corner.

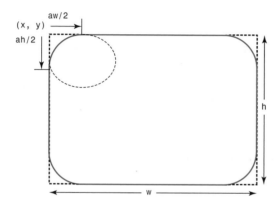

FIGURE 11.15   *The drawRoundRect method draws a rounded rectangle.*

To draw a 3D rectangle, use

```
draw3DRect(int x, int y, int w, int h, int raised);
```

in which x, y, w, and h are the same as in the drawRect method. The last parameter, a Boolean value, indicates whether the rectangle is raised above the surface or etched into the surface.

The example given in Listing 11.9 demonstrates these methods. The output is shown in Figure 11.16.

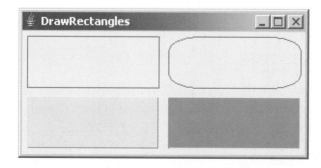

FIGURE 11.16   *The program draws a rectangle, a rounded rectangle, a raised 3D rectangle, and a plain 3D rectangle.*

LISTING 11.9 DrawRectangles.java (Drawing Rectangles)

add a panel

```
 1 import java.awt.Graphics;
 2 import java.awt.Color;
 3 import javax.swing.JPanel;
 4 import javax.swing.JFrame;
 5
 6 public class DrawRectangles extends JFrame {
 7   public DrawRectangles() {
 8     setTitle("DrawRectangles");
 9     getContentPane().add(new RectPanel());
10   }
11
12   /** Main method */
13   public static void main(String[] args) {
14     DrawRectangles frame = new DrawRectangles();
15     frame.setDefaultCloseOperation(JFrame.EXIT_ON_CLOSE);
16     frame.setSize(300, 250);
17     frame.setVisible(true);
18   }
19 }
20
21 class RectPanel extends JPanel {
22   protected void paintComponent(Graphics g) {
23     super.paintComponent(g);
24
25     // Set new color
26     g.setColor(Color.red);
27
28     // Draw a rectangle
29     g.drawRect(5, 5, getWidth() / 2 - 10, getHeight() / 2 - 10);
30
31     // Draw a rounded rectangle
32     g.drawRoundRect(getWidth() / 2 + 5, 5,
33       getWidth() / 2 - 10, getHeight() / 2 - 10, 60, 30);
34
35     // Change the color to cyan
36     g.setColor(Color.cyan);
37
38     // Draw a 3D rectangle
39     g.fill3DRect(5, getHeight() / 2 + 5, getWidth() / 2 - 10,
40       getHeight() / 2 - 10, true);
41
42     // Draw a raised 3D rectangle
43     g.fill3DRect(getWidth() / 2 + 5, getHeight() / 2 + 5,
44       getWidth() / 2 - 10, getHeight() / 2 - 10, false);
45   }
46 }
```

override paintComponent

 NOTE

You can draw things using appropriate colors and fonts using the setColor method and setFont method in the Graphics class.

11.9.3 Drawing Ovals

Depending on whether you wish to draw an oval in outline or filled solid, you can use either the drawOval method or the fillOval method. Since an oval in Java is drawn based on its bounding rectangle, give the parameters as if you were drawing a rectangle.

Here is the method for drawing an oval:

```
drawOval(int x, int y, int w, int h);
```

To draw a filled oval, use the following method:

```
fillOval(int x, int y, int w, int h);
```

Parameters x and y indicate the top-left corner of the bounding rectangle, and w and h indicate the width and height, respectively, of the bounding rectangle, as shown in Figure 11.17(a).

Listing 11.10 is an example of how to draw ovals, with the output in Figure 11.17(b).

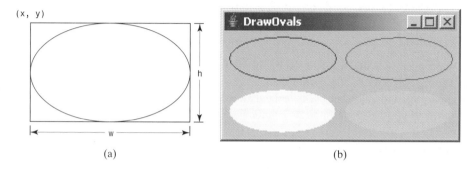

(a)   (b)

FIGURE 11.17 *(a) The* drawOval *method draws an oval based on its bounding rectangle. (b) The DrawOvals program draws four ovals.*

LISTING 11.10   DrawOvals.java (Drawing Ovals)

```
 1 import javax.swing.JFrame;
 2 import javax.swing.JPanel;
 3 import java.awt.Color;
 4 import java.awt.Graphics;
 5
 6 public class DrawOvals extends JFrame {
 7   public DrawOvals() {
 8     setTitle("DrawOvals");
 9     getContentPane().add(new OvalsPanel());          add a panel
10   }
11
12   /** Main method */
13   public static void main(String[] args) {
14     DrawOvals frame = new DrawOvals();
15     frame.setDefaultCloseOperation(JFrame.EXIT_ON_CLOSE);
16     frame.setSize(250, 250);
17     frame.setVisible(true);
18   }
19 }
20
21 // The class for drawing the ovals on a panel
22 class OvalsPanel extends JPanel {
23   protected void paintComponent(Graphics g) {          override paintComponent
24     super.paintComponent(g);
25
26     g.drawOval(5, 5, getWidth() / 2 - 10, getHeight() / 2 - 10);
27     g.setColor(Color.red);
28     g.drawOval(getWidth() / 2 + 5, 5, getWidth() / 2 - 10,
29       getHeight() / 2 - 10);
30     g.setColor(Color.yellow);
31     g.fillOval(5, getHeight() / 2 + 5, getWidth() / 2 - 10,
32       getHeight() / 2 - 10);
33     g.setColor(Color.orange);
```

```
34      g.fillOval(getWidth() / 2 + 5, getHeight() / 2 + 5,
35        getWidth() / 2 - 10, getHeight() / 2 - 10);
36    }
37 }
```

11.9.4 Drawing Arcs

An arc is conceived as part of an oval. Like an oval, an arc is drawn based on its bounding rectangle. The methods to draw or fill an arc are as follows:

```
drawArc(int x, int y, int w, int h, int startAngle, int arcAngle);
fillArc(int x, int y, int w, int h, int startAngle, int arcAngle);
```

Parameters x, y, w, and h are the same as in the drawOval method; parameter startAngle is the starting angle; arcAngle is the spanning angle (i.e., the angle covered by the arc). Angles are measured in degrees and follow the usual mathematical conventions (i.e., 0 degrees is in the easterly direction), and positive angles indicate counterclockwise rotation from the easterly direction; see Figure 11.18.

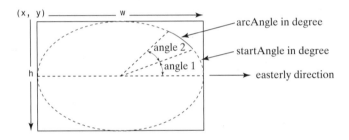

FIGURE 11.18 *The drawArc method draws an arc based on an oval with specified angles.*

Listing 11.11 is an example of how to draw arcs; the output is shown in Figure 11.19.

LISTING 11.11 DrawArcs.java (Drawing Arcs)

```
 1 import javax.swing.JFrame;
 2 import javax.swing.JPanel;
 3 import java.awt.Graphics;
 4
 5 public class DrawArcs extends JFrame {
 6   public DrawArcs() {
 7     setTitle("DrawArcs");
 8     getContentPane().add(new ArcsPanel());
 9   }
10
11   /** Main method */
12   public static void main(String[] args) {
13     DrawArcs frame = new DrawArcs();
14     frame.setDefaultCloseOperation(JFrame.EXIT_ON_CLOSE);
15     frame.setSize(250, 300);
16     frame.setVisible(true);
17   }
18 }
19
20 // The class for drawing arcs on a panel
21 class ArcsPanel extends JPanel {
22   // Draw four blazes of a fan
23   protected void paintComponent(Graphics g) {
24     super.paintComponent(g);
25
```

add a panel (margin note for line 8)

override paintComponent (margin note for line 23)

```
26     int xCenter = getWidth() / 2;
27     int yCenter = getHeight() / 2;
28     int radius =
29       (int)(Math.min(getWidth(), getHeight()) * 0.4);
30
31     int x = xCenter - radius;
32     int y = yCenter - radius;
33
34     g.fillArc(x, y, 2 * radius, 2 * radius, 0, 30);
35     g.fillArc(x, y, 2 * radius, 2 * radius, 90, 30);
36     g.fillArc(x, y, 2 * radius, 2 * radius, 180, 30);
37     g.fillArc(x, y, 2 * radius, 2 * radius, 270, 30);
38   }
39 }
```

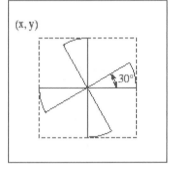

FIGURE 11.19   *The program draws four filled arcs.*

11.9.5   The Polygon class and Drawing Polygons and Polylines

The Polygon class encapsulates a description of a closed two-dimensional region within a coordinate space. This region is bounded by an arbitrary number of line segments, each of which is one side (or edge) of the polygon. Internally, a polygon comprises a list of (x, y) coordinate pairs in which each pair defines a vertex of the polygon, and two successive pairs are the endpoints of a line that is a side of the polygon. The first and final pairs of (x, y) points are joined by a line segment that closes the polygon.

The two constructors given below are used to create a Polygon object.

◆   public Polygon()

Constructs an empty polygon.

◆   Polygon(int[] xpoints, int[] ypoints, int npoints)

Constructs and initializes a Polygon with specified points. Parameters xpoints and ypoints are arrays representing x-coordinates and y-coordinates, and npoints indicates the number of points.

To append a point to the polygon, use the addPoint(int x, int y) method. The Polygon class has the public data fields xpoints, ypoints, and npoints, which represent the array of x-coordinates and y-coordinates, and the total number of points.

Here is an example of creating a polygon and adding points into it:

```
Polygon polygon = new Polygon();
polygon.addPoint(40, 20);
polygon.addPoint(70, 40);
polygon.addPoint(60, 80);
polygon.addPoint(45, 45);
polygon.addPoint(20, 60);
```

To draw or fill a polygon, use one of the following methods:

```
drawPolygon(Polygon polygon);

fillPolygon(Polygon polygon);

drawPolygon(int[] xpoints, int[] ypoints, int npoints);

fillPolygon(int[] xpoints, int[] ypoints, int npoints);
```

For example:

```
int x[] = {40, 70, 60, 45, 20};
int y[] = {20, 40, 80, 45, 60};
g.drawPolygon(x, y, x.length);
```

The drawing method opens the polygon by drawing lines between point (x[i], y[i]) and point (x[i+1], y[i+1]) for i = 0, ... , x.length - 1; it closes the polygon by drawing a line between the first and last points (see Figure 11.20(a)).

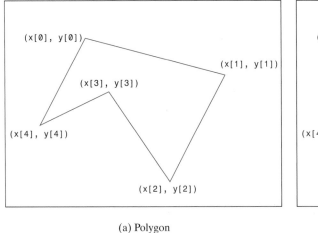
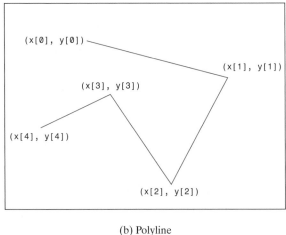

(a) Polygon   (b) Polyline

FIGURE 11.20 *The drawPolygon method draws a polygon, and the polyLine method draws a polyline.*

To draw a polyline, use the drawPolyline(int[] x, int[] y, int nPoints) method, which draws a sequence of connected lines defined by arrays of x and y coordinates. For example, the following code draws the polyline shown in Figure 11.20(b):

```
int x[] = {40, 70, 60, 45, 20};
int y[] = {20, 40, 80, 45, 60};
g.drawPolygon(x, y, x.length);
```

Listing 11.12 is an example of how to draw a hexagon, with the output shown in Figure 11.21.

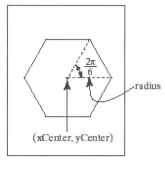

FIGURE 11.21   *The program uses the `drawPolygon` method to draw a polygon.*

LISTING 11.12   DrawPolygon.java (Drawing Polygons)

```
1 import javax.swing.JFrame;
2 import javax.swing.JPanel;
3 import java.awt.Graphics;
4 import java.awt.Polygon;
5
6 public class DrawPolygon extends JFrame {
7   public DrawPolygon() {
8     setTitle("DrawPolygon");
9     getContentPane().add(new PolygonsPanel());          add a panel
10   }
11
12   /** Main method */
13   public static void main(String[] args) {
14     DrawPolygon frame = new DrawPolygon();
15     frame.setDefaultCloseOperation(JFrame.EXIT_ON_CLOSE);
16     frame.setSize(200, 250);
17     frame.setVisible(true);
18   }
19 }
20
21 // Draw a polygon in the panel
22 class PolygonsPanel extends JPanel {
23   protected void paintComponent(Graphics g) {          override paintComponent
24     super.paintComponent(g);
25
26     int xCenter = getWidth() / 2;
27     int yCenter = getHeight() / 2;
28     int radius =
29       (int)(Math.min(getWidth(), getHeight()) * 0.4);
30
31     // Create a Polygon object
32     Polygon polygon = new Polygon();
33
34     // Add points to the polygon
35     polygon.addPoint(xCenter + radius, yCenter);
36     polygon.addPoint((int)(xCenter + radius *
37       Math.cos(2 * Math.PI / 6)), (int)(yCenter - radius *
38       Math.sin(2 * Math.PI / 6)));
39     polygon.addPoint((int)(xCenter + radius *
40       Math.cos(2 * 2 * Math.PI / 6)), (int)(yCenter - radius *
41       Math.sin(2 * 2 * Math.PI / 6)));
42     polygon.addPoint((int)(xCenter + radius *
43       Math.cos(3 * 2 * Math.PI / 6)), (int)(yCenter - radius *
44       Math.sin(3 * 2 * Math.PI / 6)));
45     polygon.addPoint((int)(xCenter + radius *
46       Math.cos(4 * 2 * Math.PI / 6)), (int)(yCenter - radius *
47       Math.sin(4 * 2 * Math.PI / 6)));
```

```
48    polygon.addPoint((int)(xCenter + radius *
49      Math.cos(5 * 2 * Math.PI / 6)), (int)(yCenter - radius *
50      Math.sin(5 * 2 * Math.PI / 6)));
51
52    // Draw the polygon
53    g.drawPolygon(polygon);
54  }
55 }
```

11.10 Centering a Display Using the FontMetrics Class

You can display a string at any location in a panel. Can you display it centered? To do so, you need to use the FontMetrics class to measure the exact width and height of the string for a particular font. FontMetrics can measure the following attributes (see Figure 11.22):

✦ **Leading,** pronounced *ledding*, is the amount of space between lines of text.

✦ **Ascent** is the height of a character, from the baseline to the top.

✦ **Descent** is the distance from the baseline to the bottom of a descending character, such as *j*, *y*, and *g*.

✦ **Height** is the sum of leading, ascent, and descent.

FIGURE 11.22 *The FontMetrics class can be used to determine the font properties of characters.*

FontMetrics is an abstract class. To get a FontMetrics object for a specific font, use the following getFontMetrics methods defined in the Graphics class:

✦ public FontMetrics getFontMetrics(Font font)

Returns the font metrics of the specified font.

✦ public FontMetrics getFontMetrics()

Returns the font metrics of the current font.

You can use the following instance methods in the FontMetrics class to obtain the attributes of a font and the width of a string when it is drawn using the font:

```
public int getAscent() // Return the ascent
public int getDescent() // Return the descent
public int getLeading() // Return the leading
public int getHeight() // Return the hight
public int stringWidth(String str) // Return the width of the sting
```

Now you can modify the DrawMessage class to display a message in the center of the panel, as shown in Figure 11.23.

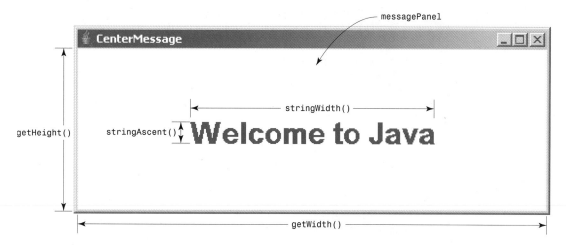

FIGURE 11.23 *The program uses the* FontMetrics *class to measure the string width and height, and displays it at the center of the frame.*

LISTING 11.13 CenterMessage.java (Centering a Message)

```
1  import javax.swing.*;
2  import java.awt.*;
3
4  public class CenterMessage extends JPanel {
5    /** Main method */
6    public static void main(String[] args) {
7      JFrame frame = new JFrame("CenterMessage");
8      CenterMessage m = new CenterMessage();              a message panel
9      m.setBackground(Color.white);                       set background
10     m.setFont(new Font("Californian FB", Font.BOLD, 30)); set font
11     frame.getContentPane().add(m);
12     frame.setDefaultCloseOperation(JFrame.EXIT_ON_CLOSE);
13     frame.setSize(300, 200);
14     frame.setVisible(true);
15   }
16
17   /** Paint the message */
18   protected void paintComponent(Graphics g) {            override paintComponent
19     super.paintComponent(g);
20
21     // Get font metrics for the current font
22     FontMetrics fm = g.getFontMetrics();                 get FontMetrics
23
24     // Find the center location to display
25     int stringWidth = fm.stringWidth("Welcome to Java");
26     int stringAscent = fm.getAscent();
27
28     // Get the position of the leftmost character in the baseline
29     int xCoordinate = getWidth() / 2 - stringWidth / 2;
30     int yCoordinate = getHeight() / 2 + stringAscent / 2;
31
32     g.drawString("Welcome to Java", xCoordinate, yCoordinate);
33   }
34 }
```

The methods getWidth() and getHeight(), defined in the Component class, return the component's width and height, respectively.

yCoordinate is the height of the baseline for the first character of the string to be displayed. When centered is true, yCoordinate should be getHeight() / 2 + stringAscent / 2.

xCoordinate is the width of the baseline for the first character of the string to be displayed. When centered is true, xCoordinate should be getWidth() / 2 - stringWidth / 2.

11.11 CASE STUDY: The `MessagePanel` Class

This case study develops a useful class that displays a message in a panel. The class enables the user to set the location of the message, center the message, and move the message with the specified interval. The UML diagram for the class is shown in Figure 11.24.

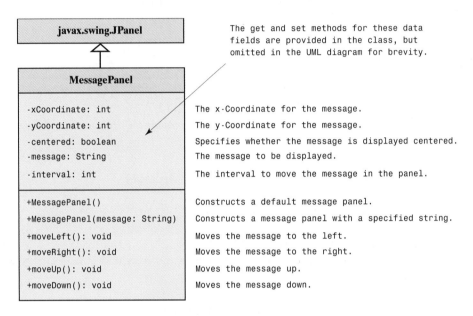

The get and set methods for these data fields are provided in the class, but omitted in the UML diagram for brevity.

-xCoordinate: int	The x-Coordinate for the message.
-yCoordinate: int	The y-Coordinate for the message.
-centered: boolean	Specifies whether the message is displayed centered.
-message: String	The message to be displayed.
-interval: int	The interval to move the message in the panel.
+MessagePanel()	Constructs a default message panel.
+MessagePanel(message: String)	Constructs a message panel with a specified string.
+moveLeft(): void	Moves the message to the left.
+moveRight(): void	Moves the message to the right.
+moveUp(): void	Moves the message up.
+moveDown(): void	Moves the message down.

FIGURE 11.24 `MessagePanel` *displays a message on the panel.*

The UML diagram serves as the contract for the `MessagePanel` class. The user can use the class without knowing how the class is implemented. Let us begin by writing a program in Listing 11.14 that uses the class to display four message panels, as shown in Figure 11.25.

LISTING 11.14 TestMessagePanel.java (Using `MessagePanel`)

```
1 import java.awt.*;
2 import javax.swing.*;
3
4 public class TestMessagePanel extends JFrame {
5   public TestMessagePanel() {
6     MessagePanel messagePanel1 = new MessagePanel("Wecome to Java");
7     MessagePanel messagePanel2 = new MessagePanel("Java is fun");
8     MessagePanel messagePanel3 = new MessagePanel("Java is cool");
9     MessagePanel messagePanel4 = new MessagePanel("I love Java");
10    messagePanel1.setFont(new Font("SansSerif", Font.ITALIC, 20));
11    messagePanel2.setFont(new Font("Courier", Font.BOLD, 20));
12    messagePanel3.setFont(new Font("Times", Font.ITALIC, 20));
13    messagePanel4.setFont(new Font("Californian FB", Font.PLAIN, 20));
14    messagePanel1.setBackground(Color.red);
15    messagePanel2.setBackground(Color.cyan);
16    messagePanel3.setBackground(Color.green);
17    messagePanel4.setBackground(Color.white);
18    messagePanel1.setCentered(true);
19
20    getContentPane().setLayout(new GridLayout(2, 2));
21    getContentPane().add(messagePanel1);
22    getContentPane().add(messagePanel2);
```

create message panel

set font

set background

add message panel

```
23      getContentPane().add(messagePanel3);
24      getContentPane().add(messagePanel4);
25    }
26
27    public static void main(String[] args) {
28      TestMessagePanel frame = new TestMessagePanel();
29      frame.setSize(300, 200);
30      frame.setTitle("TestMessagePanel");
31      frame.setDefaultCloseOperation(JFrame.EXIT_ON_CLOSE);
32      frame.setVisible(true);
33    }
34  }
```

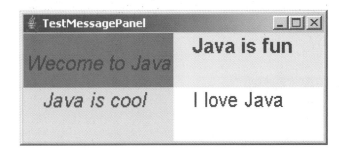

FIGURE 11.25   *TestMessagePanel uses* MessagePanel *to display four message panels.*

The MessagePanel class is implemented in Listing 11.15. The program seems long but is actually simple, because most of the methods are get and set methods, and each method is relatively short and easy to read.

LISTING 11.15   MessagePanel.java (The MessagePanel Class)

```
1 import java.awt.Font;
2 import java.awt.FontMetrics;
3 import java.awt.Dimension;
4 import java.awt.Graphics;
5 import javax.swing.JPanel;
6
7 public class MessagePanel extends JPanel {
8   /** The message to be displayed */
9   private String message = "Welcome to Java";
10
11  /** The x coordinate where the message is displayed */
12  private int xCoordinate = 20;
13
14  /** The y coordinate where the message is displayed */
15  private int yCoordinate = 20;
16
17  /** Indicate whether the message is displayed in the center */
18  private boolean centered;
19
20  /** The interval for moving the message horizontally and vertically */
21  private int interval = 10;
22
23  /** Construct with default properties */
24  public MessagePanel() {
25  }
26
27  /** Construct a message panel with a specified message */
28  public MessagePanel(String message) {
29    this.message = message;
30  }
31
32  /** Return message */
33  public String getMessage() {
```

```
34      return message;
35    }
36
37    /** Set a new message */
38    public void setMessage(String message) {
39      this.message = message;
40      repaint();
41    }
42
43    /** Return xCoordinator */
44    public int getXCoordinate() {
45      return xCoordinate;
46    }
47
48    /** Set a new xCoordinator */
49    public void setXCoordinate(int x) {
50      this.xCoordinate = x;
51      repaint();
52    }
53
54    /** Return yCoordinator */
55    public int getYCoordinate() {
56      return yCoordinate;
57    }
58
59    /** Set a new yCoordinator */
60    public void setYCoordinate(int y) {
61      this.yCoordinate = y;
62      repaint();
63    }
64
65    /** Return centered */
66    public boolean isCentered() {
67      return centered;
68    }
69
70    /** Set a new centered */
71    public void setCentered(boolean centered) {
72      this.centered = centered;
73      repaint();
74    }
75
76    /** Return interval */
77    public int getInterval() {
78      return interval;
79    }
80
81    /** Set a new interval */
82    public void setInterval(int interval) {
83      this.interval = interval;
84      repaint();
85    }
86
87    /** Paint the message */
88    protected void paintComponent(Graphics g) {
89      super.paintComponent(g);
90
91      if (centered) {
92        // Get font metrics for the current font
93        FontMetrics fm = g.getFontMetrics();
94
95        // Find the center location to display
96        int stringWidth = fm.stringWidth(message);
97        int stringAscent = fm.getAscent();
98        // Get the position of the leftmost character in the baseline
99        xCoordinate = getWidth() / 2 - stringWidth / 2;
100       yCoordinate = getHeight() / 2 + stringAscent / 2;
101     }
102
```

override paintComponent

```
103        g.drawString(message, xCoordinate, yCoordinate);
104    }
105
106    /** Move the message left */
107    public void moveLeft() {
108      xCoordinate -= interval;
109      repaint();
110    }
111
112    /** Move the message right */
113    public void moveRight() {
114      xCoordinate += interval;
115      repaint();
116    }
117
118    /** Move the message up */
119    public void moveUp() {
120      yCoordinate -= interval;
121      repaint();
122    }
123
124    /** Move the message down */
125    public void moveDown() {
126      yCoordinate += interval;
127      repaint();
128    }
129
130    /** Override get method for preferredSize */
131    public Dimension getPreferredSize() {
132      return new Dimension(200, 30);
133    }
134 }
```

override getPreferredSize

The getPreferredSize() method (Lines 131–133), defined in Component, is overridden in MessagePanel to specify the preferred size for the layout manager to consider when laying out a MessagePanel object. This property may or may not be considered by the layout manager, depending on its rules. For example, a component uses its preferred size in a container with a FlowLayout manager, but its preferred size may be ignored if it is placed in a container with a GridLayout manager.

The repaint method is defined in the Component class. Invoking repaint causes the paintComponent method to be called. The repaint method is invoked to refresh the viewing area. Typically, you call it if you have new things to display.

CAUTION

The paintComponent method should never be invoked directly. It is invoked either by the JVM whenever the viewing area changes or by the repaint method. You should override the paintComponent method to tell the system how to paint the viewing area, but never override the repaint method.

don't invoke
paintComponent

NOTE

The repaint method lodges a request to update the viewing area and returns immediately. Its effect is asynchronous, and if several requests are outstanding, it is likely that only the last paintComponent will be done.

request repaint using
repaint()

CAUTION

The MessagePanel class uses the properties xCoordinate and yCoordinate to specify the position of the message displayed on the panel. Do not use the property names x and y, because they are already defined in the Component class to specify the position of the component in the parent's coordinate system.

 NOTE

The Component class has the setBackground, setForeground, and setFont methods. These methods are for setting colors and fonts for the entire component. Suppose you want to draw several messages in a panel with different colors and fonts; you have to use the setColor and setFont methods in the Graphics class to set the color and font for the current drawing.

---

design classes for reuse

 NOTE

One of the key features of Java programming is the reuse of classes. Throughout the book, you will develop reusable classes and later reuse them. MessagePanel is an example of this. It can be reused whenever you need to display a message on a panel. To make your class reusable in a wide range of applications, you should provide a variety of ways to use it. MessagePanel provides many properties and methods that will be used in several examples in the book.

 ## 11.12 CASE STUDY: The **StillClock** Class (Optional)

This case study develops a class that displays a clock in a panel. The contract of the class is shown in Figure 11.26.

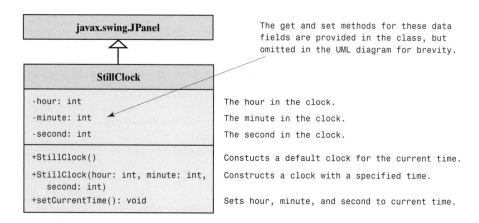

FIGURE 11.26 *StillClock displays an analog clock.*

Let us first write a test program in Listing 11.16 that uses the StillClock class to display an analog clock and the MessagePanel class to display the hour, minute, and second in a panel, as shown in Figure 11.26.

LISTING 11.16   DisplayClock.java (Using `StillClock`)

```
1 import java.awt.*;
2 import javax.swing.*;
3 import java.util.*;
4
5 public class DisplayClock extends JFrame {
6   public DisplayClock() {
7     // Create an analog clock for the current time
8     StillClock clock = new StillClock();                          create a clock
9
10    // Display hour, minute, and hour in the message panel
11    MessagePanel messagePanel = new MessagePanel(clock.getHour() +    create a message panel
12      ":" + clock.getMinute() + ":" + clock.getSecond());
13    messagePanel.setCentered(true);
14    messagePanel.setForeground(Color.blue);
15    messagePanel.setFont(new Font("Courier", Font.BOLD, 16));
16
17    // Add the clock and message panel to the frame
18    getContentPane().add(clock);                                   add a clock
19    getContentPane().add(messagePanel, BorderLayout.SOUTH);        add a message panel
20  }
21
22  public static void main(String[] args) {
23    DisplayClock frame = new DisplayClock();
24    frame.setTitle("DisplayClock");
25    frame.setDefaultCloseOperation(JFrame.EXIT_ON_CLOSE);
26    frame.setSize(300, 350);
27    frame.setVisible(true);
28  }
29 }
```

Now we turn our attention to implementing the `StillClock` class. To draw a clock, you need to draw a circle and three hands for second, minute, and hour. To draw a hand, you need to specify the two ends of the line. As shown in Figure 11.27(a), one end is the center of the clock at (`xCenter`, `yCenter`); the other end, at (`xEnd`, `yEnd`), is determined by the following formula:

```
xEnd = xCenter + handLength × sin(θ)
yEnd = yCenter - handLength × cos(θ)
```

Since there are sixty seconds in one minute, the angle for the second hand is

```
second × (2π/60)
```

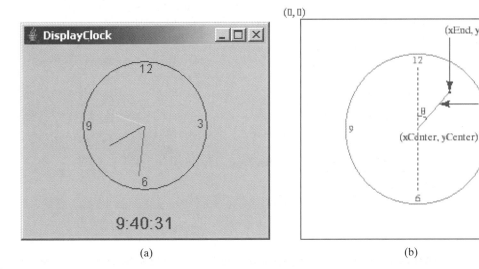

(a)   (b)

FIGURE **11.27**   *(a) The DisplayClock program displays a clock that shows the current time. (b) The end point of a clock hand can be determined given the spanning angle, the hand length, and the center point.*

The position of the minute hand is determined by the minute and second. The exact minute value combined with seconds is `minute + second/60`. For example, if the time is 3 minutes and 30 seconds, the total minutes are 3.5. Since there are sixty minutes in one hour, the angle for the minute hand is

```
(minute + second/60) × (2π/60)
```

Since one circle is divided into twelve hours, the angle for the hour hand is

```
(hour + minute/60 + second/(60 × 60))) × (2π/12)
```

For simplicity, you can omit the seconds in computing the angles of the minute hand and the hour hand, because they are very small and can be neglected. Therefore, the end points for the second hand, minute hand, and hour hand can be computed as:

```
xSecond = xCenter + secondHandLength × sin(second × (2π/60))
ySecond = yCenter - secondHandLength × cos(second × (2π/60))
xMinute = xCenter + minuteHandLength × sin(minute × (2π/60))
yMinute = yCenter - minuteHandLength × cos(minute × (2π/60))
xHour = xCenter + hourHandLength × sin((hour + minute/60) × (2π/60)))
yHour = yCenter - hourHandLength × cos((hour + minute/60) × (2π/60)))
```

The `StillClock` class is implemented in Listing 11.17.

LISTING 11.17 StillClock.java (Displaying a Still Clock)

```java
 1 import java.awt.*;
 2 import javax.swing.*;
 3 import java.util.*;
 4
 5 public class StillClock extends JPanel {
 6   private int hour;
 7   private int minute;
 8   private int second;
 9
10   /** Construct a default clock with the current time*/
11   public StillClock() {
12     setCurrentTime();
13   }
14
15   /** Construct a clock with specified hour, minute, and second */
16   public StillClock(int hour, int minute, int second) {
17     this.hour = hour;
18     this.minute = minute;
19     this.second = second;
20   }
21
22   /** Return hour */
23   public int getHour() {
24     return hour;
25   }
26
27   /** Set a new hour */
28   public void setHour(int hour) {
29     this.hour = hour;
30     repaint();
31   }
32
33   /** Return minute */
34   public int getMinute() {
35     return minute;
36   }
37
38   /** Set a new minute */
39   public void setMinute(int minute) {
40     this.minute = minute;
```

```
41      repaint();
42    }
43
44    /** Return second */
45    public int getSecond() {
46      return second;
47    }
48
49    /** Set a new second */
50    public void setSecond(int second) {
51      this.second = second;
52      repaint();
53    }
54
55    /** Draw the clock */
56    protected void paintComponent(Graphics g) {                          override paintComponent
57      super.paintComponent(g);
58
59      // Initialize clock parameters
60      int clockRadius =
61        (int)(Math.min(getWidth(), getHeight()) * 0.8 * 0.5);
62      int xCenter = getWidth() / 2;
63      int yCenter = getHeight() / 2;
64
65      // Draw circle
66      g.setColor(Color.black);
67      g.drawOval(xCenter - clockRadius, yCenter - clockRadius,
68        2 * clockRadius, 2 * clockRadius);
69      g.drawString("12", xCenter - 5, yCenter - clockRadius + 12);
70      g.drawString("9", xCenter - clockRadius + 3, yCenter + 5);
71      g.drawString("3", xCenter + clockRadius - 10, yCenter + 3);
72      g.drawString("6", xCenter - 3, yCenter + clockRadius - 3);
73
74      // Draw second hand
75      int sLength = (int)(clockRadius * 0.8);
76      int xSecond = (int)(xCenter + sLength *
77        Math.sin(second * (2 * Math.PI / 60)));
78      int ySecond = (int)(yCenter - sLength *
79        Math.cos(second * (2 * Math.PI / 60)));
80      g.setColor(Color.red);
81      g.drawLine(xCenter, yCenter, xSecond, ySecond);
82
83      // Draw minute hand
84      int mLength = (int)(clockRadius * 0.65);
85      int xMinute = (int)(xCenter + mLength *
86        Math.sin(minute * (2 * Math.PI / 60)));
87      int yMinute = (int)(yCenter - mLength *
88        Math.cos(minute * (2 * Math.PI / 60)));
89      g.setColor(Color.blue);
90      g.drawLine(xCenter, yCenter, xMinute, yMinute);
91
92      // Draw hour hand
93      int hLength = (int)(clockRadius * 0.5);
94      int xHour = (int)(xCenter + hLength *
95        Math.sin((hour % 12 + minute / 60.0) * (2 * Math.PI / 12)));
96      int yHour = (int)(yCenter - hLength *
97        Math.cos((hour % 12 + minute / 60.0) * (2 * Math.PI / 12)));
98      g.setColor(Color.green);
99      g.drawLine(xCenter, yCenter, xHour, yHour);
100   }
101
102   public void setCurrentTime() {
103     // Construct a calendar for the current date and time
104     Calendar calendar = new GregorianCalendar();                       get current time
105
106     // Set current hour, minute and second
107     this.hour = calendar.get(Calendar.HOUR_OF_DAY);
108     this.minute = calendar.get(Calendar.MINUTE);
109     this.second = calendar.get(Calendar.SECOND);
110   }
111
```

override getPreferredSize
```
112    public Dimension getPreferredSize() {
113      return new Dimension(200, 200);
114    }
115  }
```

The program enables the clock size to adjust as the frame resizes. Every time you resize the frame, the `paintComponent` method is automatically invoked to paint the new frame. The `paintComponent` method displays the clock in proportion to the panel width (`getWidth()`) and height (`getHeight()`) (Lines 60–63 in `StillClock`).

 NOTE

Like the `MessagePanel` class, the `StillClock` class is an example of a reusable class. `StillClock` will be used throughout the book. `StillClock` provides many properties and methods that enable it to be used in a wide range of applications.

KEY CLASSES AND METHODS

✦ **java.awt.Component** is the root class for GUI components.

✦ **java.awt.Container** is the root class for all container classes. The container classes (e.g., `JFrame`, `JPanel`, `JApplet`) are used to contain other GUI components.

✦ **javax.swing.JFrame** is a class for creating a frame as a top-level container.

✦ **javax.swing.JComponent** is the root class for Swing GUI components such as `JButton`, `JLabel`, `JTextField`, and `JPanel`.

✦ **java.awt.FlowLayout** is the flow layout manager for a container. In a container with `FlowLayout`, the components are arranged from left to right in the order in which they were added. When one row is filled, a new row is started.

✦ **java.awt.GridLayout** is the grid layout manager for a container. The `GridLayout` manager arranges components in a grid (matrix) formation with the number of rows and columns defined by the constructor. The components are placed in the grid from left to right, starting with the first row, then the second, and so on, in the order in which they are added.

✦ **java.awt.BorderLayout** is the border layout manager for a container. The `BorderLayout` manager divides the window into five areas: East, South, West, North, and Center. Components are added to a `BorderLayout` by using `add(Component, index)`, where index is a constant `BorderLayout.EAST`, `BorderLayout.SOUTH`, `BorderLayout.WEST`, `BorderLayout.NORTH`, or `BorderLayout.CENTER`.

✦ **javax.swing.JPanel** is a class for holding components or for displaying drawings.

✦ **java.awt.Color** is a class for specifying a color.

✦ **java.awt.Font** is a class for specifying a font. To set a font, you need to create a `Font` object from the `Font` class. The syntax is `Font myFont = new Font(name, style, size)`.

✦ **java.awt.FontMetrics** is a class for measuring font properties: leading, ascent, descent, and height. Leading is the amount of space between lines of text. Ascent is the height of a character, from the baseline to the top. Descent is the distance from the baseline to the bottom of a descending character, such as *j*, *y*, and *g*. Height is the sum of leading, ascent, and descent.

✦ **java.awt.Dimension** is a class for measuring the dimensions of a GUI component.

✦ **java.awt.Graphics** is a class for drawing strings and geometrical figures.

CHAPTER SUMMARY

✦ Each container uses a layout manager to position and place components in a container in the desired location. Three simple and useful layout managers are FlowLayout, GridLayout, and BorderLayout.

✦ Panels are invisible and are used as small containers that group components to achieve a desired layout. Another important use of JPanel is for drawing. To draw in a JPanel, you create a new class that extends JPanel and overrides the paintComponent method to tell the panel how to draw things.

✦ To add components to a JFrame, you need to add them into the JFrame's content pane. You can add components directly into a JPanel. By default, the content pane's layout is BorderLayout, and the JPanel's layout is FlowLayout.

✦ The paintComponent method is defined in JComponent, and its signature is protected void paintComponent(Graphics g). The Graphics object g is created automatically by the JVM for every visible GUI component. This object controls how information is drawn. You can use various drawing methods defined in the Graphics class to draw figures.

✦ The Graphics class is an abstract class for displaying figures and images on the screen on different platforms. The Graphics class is implemented on the native platform in the JVM. When you use the paintComponent method to draw things on a graphics context g, this g is an instance of a concrete subclass of the abstract Graphics class for the specific platform. The Graphics class encapsulates the platform details and enables you to draw things uniformly without concern for the specific platform.

✦ Invoking super.paintComponent(g) is necessary to ensure that the viewing area is cleared before a new drawing is displayed. The user can request the component to be redisplayed by invoking the repaint() method defined in the Component class. Invoking repaint() causes paintComponent to be invoked by the JVM. The user should never invoke paintComponent directly. For this reason, the protected visibility is sufficient for paint-Component.

✦ Each component has its own coordinate system with the origin (0, 0) at the upper-left corner of the window. The x coordinate increases to the right, and the y coordinate increases downward.

✦ You can set colors for GUI components by using the java.awt.Color class. Colors are made of red, green, and blue components, each of which is represented by a byte value that describes its intensity, ranging from 0 (darkest shade) to 255 (lightest shade). This is known as the *RGB model*.

✦ The syntax to create a Color object is Color color = new Color(r, g, b), in which r, g, and b specify a color by its red, green, and blue components. Alternatively, you can use one of the thirteen standard colors (black, blue, cyan, darkGray, gray, green, lightGray, magenta, orange, pink, red, white, yellow) defined as constants in java.awt.Color.

✦ You can use the setBackground(Color c) and setForeground(Color c) methods defined in the Component class to set a component's background and foreground colors.

✦ You can set fonts for the components or subjects you draw, and use font metrics to measure font size. Fonts and font metrics are encapsulated in the classes Font and FontMetrics. FontMetrics can be used to compute the exact length and width of a string, which is helpful for measuring the size of a string in order to display it in the right position.

✦ The Component class has the setBackground, setForeground, and setFont methods. These methods are used to set colors and fonts for the entire component. Suppose you want to draw several messages in a panel with different colors and fonts; you have to use the setColor and setFont methods in the Graphics class to set the color and font for the current drawing.

✦ The method for drawing a string is drawString(string, x, y). To draw a line, use drawLine(x1, y1, x2, y2). To draw a plain rectangle, use drawRect(x, y, w, h). To draw a filled rectangle, use fillRect(x, y, w, h). To draw a rounded rectangle, use drawRoundRect(x, y, w, h, aw, ah). To draw a 3D rectangle, use draw3DRect(x, y, w, h, raised). To draw an oval, use drawOval(x, y, w, h). To draw a filled oval, use fillOval(x, y, w, h). To draw an arc, use drawArc(x, y, w, h, startAngle, arcAngle). To draw a filled arc, use fillArc(x, y, w, h, startAngle, arcAngle). To draw a polygon, use drawPolygon(Polygon polygon) or drawPolygon(int[] xpoints, int[] ypoints, int npoints). To draw a filled polygon, use fillPolygon(Polygon polygon) or fillPolygon(int[] xpoints, int[] ypoints, int npoints).

REVIEW QUESTIONS

Sections 11.3–11.4

11.1 Which class is the root of the Java GUI component classes? Is a container class a subclass of Component? Which class is the root of the Swing GUI component classes? Since a GUI component class such as JButton is a subclass of Container, can you add components into a button?

11.2 Explain the difference between AWT GUI components, such as java.awt.Button, and Swing GUI components, such as javax.swing.JButton.

11.3 How do you create a frame? How do you set the size for a frame? How do you get the size of a frame? How do you add components to a frame? What would happen if the statements frame.setSize(400, 300) and frame.setVisible(true) were swapped in the MyFrameWithComponents class in Section 11.4.2, "Adding Components to a Frame"?

11.4 Determine whether the following statements are true or false:

✦ You can add a button to a frame.

✦ You can add a frame to a panel.

✦ You can add a panel to a frame.

✦ You can add any number of components to a panel, a frame, or an applet.

✦ You can derive a class from JPanel, JFrame, or JApplet.

11.5 The following program is supposed to display a button in a frame, but nothing is displayed. What is the problem?

```
 1 public class Test extends javax.swing.JFrame {
 2   public Test() {
 3     getContentPane().add(new javax.swing.JButton("OK"));
 4   }
 5
 6   public static void main(String[] args) {
 7     javax.swing.JFrame frame = new javax.swing.JFrame();
 8     frame.setSize(100, 200);
 9     frame.setVisible(true);
10   }
11 }
```

11.6   The following program is supposed to display a message on the panel, but nothing is displayed. There are problems in Lines 2 and 14. Identify them.

```
1 public class TestDrawMessage extends javax.swing.JFrame {
2   public void TestDrawMessage() {
3     getContentPane().add(new DrawMessage());
4   }
5
6   public static void main(String[] args) {
7     javax.swing.JFrame frame = new TestDrawMessage();
8     frame.setSize(100, 200);
9     frame.setVisible(true);
10   }
11 }
12
13 class DrawMessage extends javax.swing.JPanel {
14   protected void PaintComponent(java.awt.Graphics g) {
15     super.paintComponent(g);
16     g.drawString("Welcome to Java", 20, 20);
17   }
18 }
```

Section 11.5 Layout Managers

11.7   Why do you need to use layout managers? What is the default layout manager for the content pane of a frame? How do you add a component to a frame?

11.8   Describe FlowLayout. How do you create a FlowLayout manager? How do you add a component to a FlowLayout container? Is there a limit to the number of components that can be added to a FlowLayout container?

11.9   Describe GridLayout. How do you create a GridLayout manager? How do you add a component to a GridLayout container? Is there a limit to the number of components that can be added to a GridLayout container?

11.10   Describe BorderLayout. How do you create a BorderLayout manager? How do you add a component to a BorderLayout container? Can you add multiple components in the same section?

Sections 11.6–11.7

11.11   How do you get and set background color, foreground color, and font for a component? How do you get and set colors and fonts in a graphics context?

11.12   How do you create a color? How do you create a font?

Section 11.8 Using Panels as Subcontainers

11.13   How do you create a panel with a specified layout manager?

11.14   What is the default layout manager for a JPanel? How do you add a component to a JPanel?

11.15   Can you use the setTitle method in a panel? What is the purpose of using a panel?

Section 11.9 Drawing Graphics on Panels

11.16   Suppose that you want to draw a new message below an existing message. Should the x, y coordinate increase or decrease?

11.17   Describe the paintComponent method. Where is it defined? How is it invoked? Can you use the paintComponent method to draw things directly on a frame?

11.18   Describe the methods for drawing lines, rectangles, ovals, arcs, and polygons.

11.19   Write a statement to draw the following shapes:

   ✦ Draw a thick line from (10, 10) to (70, 30). You can draw several lines next to each other to create the effect of one thick line.

✦ Draw a rectangle of width 100 and height 50 with the upper-left corner at (10, 10).

✦ Draw a rounded rectangle with width 100, height 200, corner horizontal diameter 40, and corner vertical diameter 20.

✦ Draw a circle with radius 30.

✦ Draw an oval with width 50 and height 100.

✦ Draw the upper half of a circle with radius 50.

✦ Draw a polygon connecting the following points: (20, 40), (30, 50), (40, 90), (90, 10), (10, 30).

✦ Draw a 3D cube like the one in Figure 11.28.

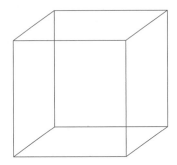

FIGURE 11.28 *Use the* drawLine *method to draw a 3D cube.*

PROGRAMMING EXERCISES

Section 11.5 Layout Managers

11.1 (*Using the* FlowLayout *manager*) Write a program that meets the following requirements (see Figure 11.29):

✦ Create a frame and set its content pane's layout to FlowLayout.
✦ Create two panels and add them to the frame.
✦ Each panel contains three buttons. The panel uses FlowLayout.

FIGURE 11.29 *Exercise 11.1 places the first three buttons in one panel and the remaining three buttons in another panel.*

11.2 (*Using the* BorderLayout *manager*) Rewrite the preceding program to create the same user interface, but instead of using FlowLayout for the frame's content pane, use BorderLayout. Place one panel in the south of the content pane, and the other panel in the center of the content pane.

11.3 (*Using the* GridLayout *manager*) Rewrite the preceding program to create the same user interface. Instead of using FlowLayout for the panels, use a GridLayout of two rows and three columns.

11.4 (*Creating a subclass of* JPanel *to group buttons*) Rewrite the preceding program to create the same user interface. Instead of creating buttons and panels separately, define a class that extends the JPanel class. Place three buttons in your panel class, and create two panels from the user-defined panel class.

Sections 11.6–11.9

11.5* (*Displaying a 3 by 3 grid*) Write a program that displays a 3 by 3 grid, as shown in Figure 11.30(a). Use red color for vertical lines and blue color for horizontal lines.

11.6** (*Creating a custom button class*) Develop a custom button class named OvalButton that extends JButton and displays the button text inside an oval. Figure 11.30(b) shows two buttons created using the OvalButton class.

11.7* (*Displaying a checker board*) Write a program that displays a checkerboard, as shown in Figure 11.30(c).

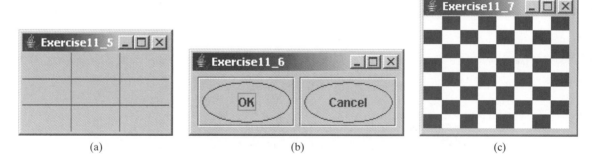

(a) (b) (c)

FIGURE 11.30 (*a*) *Exercise 11.5 displays a grid.* (*b*) *Exercise 11.6 displays two objects of* OvalButton. (*c*) *Exercise 11.7 displays a checkerboard.*

11.8* (*Displaying a multiplication table*) Write a program that displays a multiplication table in a panel using the drawing methods, as shown in Figure 11.31(a).

11.9** (*Displaying numbers in a triangular pattern*) Write a program that displays numbers in a triangular pattern, as shown in Figure 11.31(b). The number of lines in the display changes to fit the window as the window resizes.

11.10** (*Creating four panels of various shapes*) Write a program that creates four panels using the classes RectPanel, OvalsPanel, ArcsPanel, and PolygonsPanel presented in Section 11.9, "Drawing Graphics on Panels," and places the panels in the content pane of the frame using a GridLayout, as shown in Figure 11.32.

11.11** (*Displaying a pie chart*) Write a program that uses a pie chart to display the percentages of the overall grade represented by projects, quizzes, midterm exams, and the final exam, as shown in Figure 11.33(a). Suppose that projects take 20 percent and are displayed in red, quizzes take 10 percent and are displayed in blue, midterm exams take 30 percent and are displayed in green, and the final exam takes 40 percent and is displayed in orange.

11.12** (*Drawing an octagon*) Write a program that draws an octagon, as shown in Figure 11.33(b).

11.13* (*Creating four fans*) Write a program that places four fans in a frame of GridLayout with two rows and two columns, as shown in Figure 11.34(a).

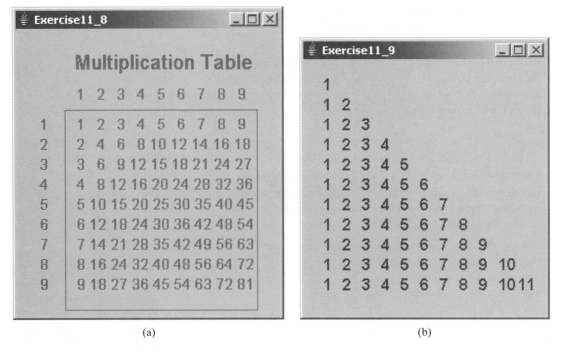

FIGURE **11.31** *(a) Exercise 11.8 displays a multiplication table. (b) Exercise 11.9 displays numbers in a triangular formation.*

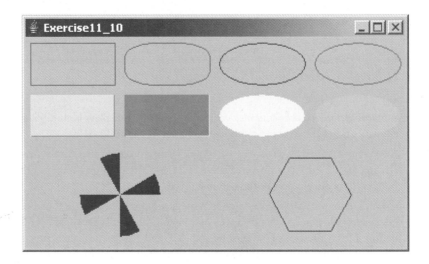

FIGURE **11.32** *Four panels of geometric figures are displayed in a frame of* GridLayout.

Comprehensive

11.14 (*Drawing a detailed clock*) Modify the StillClock class in Section 11.12, "Case Study: The StillClock class," to draw the clock with more details on the hours and minutes, as shown in Figure 11.34(b).

11.15** (*Plotting the square function*) Write a program that draws a diagram for the function $f(x) = x^2$ (see Figure 11.35).

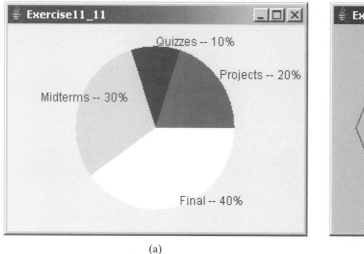

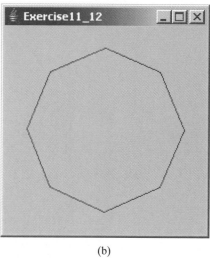

(a)   (b)

FIGURE 11.33 *(a) Exercise 11.11 uses a pie chart to show the percentages of projects, quizzes, midterm exams, and the final exam in the overall grade. (b) Exercise 11.12 draws an octagon.*

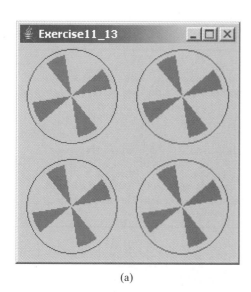

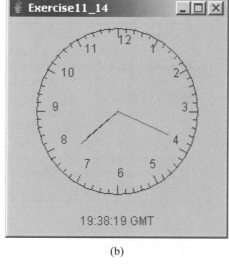

(a)   (b)

FIGURE 11.34 *(a) Exercise 11.13 draws four fans. (b) Exercise 11.14 displays a detailed clock.*

🌸 HINT

Add points to a polygon p using the following loop:

```
double scaleFactor = 0.1;
for (int x = -100; x <= 100; x++) {
  p.addPoint(x + 200, 200 - (int)(scaleFactor * x * x));
}
```

Connect the points using g.drawPolyline(p.xpoints,p.ypoints, p.npoints) for a Graphics object g. p.xpoints returns an array of x coordinates, p.ypoints returns an array of y coordinates, and p.npoints returns the number of points in Polygon object p.

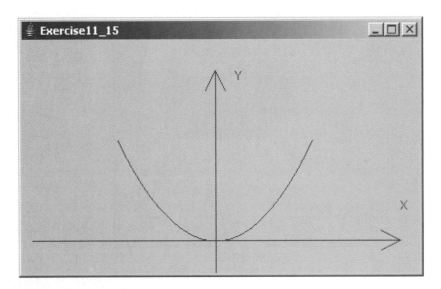

FIGURE 11.35 *Exercise 11.15 draws a diagram for function f(x) = x²*

11.16** (*Plotting the sine function*) Write a program that draws a diagram for the sine function, as shown in Figure 11.36.

🌺 **HINT**

The Unicode for π is \u03c0. To display -2π, use g.drawString ("-2\u03c0", x, y). For a trigonometric function like sin(x), x is in radians. Use the following loop to add the points to a polygon p:

```
for (int x = -100; x <= 100; x++) {
  p.addPoint(x + 200,
    100 - (int)(50 * Math.sin((x / 100.0) * 2 * Math.PI)));
}
```

-2π is at (100, 100), the center of the axis is at (200, 100), and 2π is at (300, 100). Use the drawPolyline method in the Graphics class to connect the points.

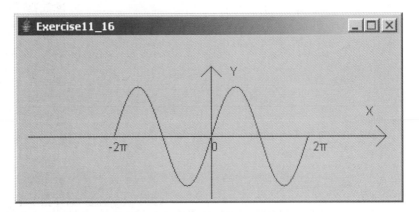

FIGURE 11.36 *Exercise 11.16 draws a diagram for function f(x) = sin(x)*

11.17** (*Plotting functions using generic methods*) Write a generic class that draws the diagram for a function. The class is defined as follows:

```java
public abstract class AbstractDrawFunction extends JPanel {
  /** Polygon to hold the points */
  private Polygon p = new Polygon();

  protected AbstractDrawFunction () {
    drawFunction();
  }

  /** Return the y coordinate */
  abstract double f(double x);

  /** Obtain points for x coordinates 100, 101, ..., 300 */
  public void drawFunction() {
    for (int x = -100; x <= 100; x++) {
      p.addPoint(x + 200, 200 - (int)f(x));
    }
  }

  /** Implement paintComponent to draw axes, labels, and
   *  connecting points
   */
  protected void paintComponent(Graphics g) {
    // To be completed by you
  }
}
```

Test the class with the following functions:

```java
f(x) = x²;
f(x) = sin(x);
f(x) = cos(x);
f(x) = tan(x);
f(x) = cos(x) + 5sin(x);
f(x) = cos(x) + 5sin(x);
f(x) = log(x) + x²;
```

For each function, create a class that extends the AbstractDrawFunction class and implements the f method. Figure 11.37 displays the drawings for the sine function and the cosine function.

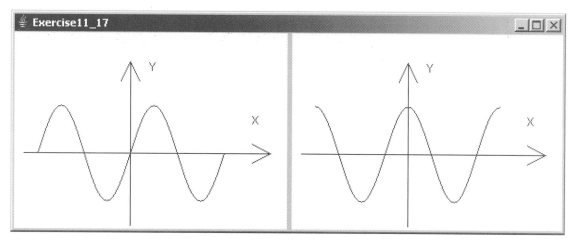

FIGURE **11.37** *Exercise 11.17 draws the sine and cosine functions.*

11.18** (*Displaying a bar chart*) Write a program that uses a bar chart to display the percentages of the overall grade represented by projects, quizzes, midterm exams, and the final exam, as shown in Figure 11.38. Suppose that projects take 20 percent and are displayed in red, quizzes take 10 percent and are displayed in blue, midterm exams take 30 percent and are displayed in green, and the final exam takes 40 percent and is displayed in orange.

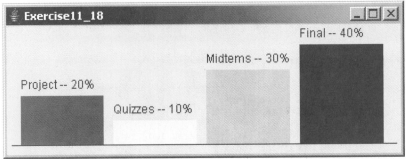

FIGURE 11.38 *Exercise 11.18 uses a bar chart to show the percentages of projects, quizzes, midterm exams, and the final exam in the overall grade.*

11.19 (*Using the* MessagePanel *class*) Write a program that displays four messages, as shown in Figure 11.39(a).

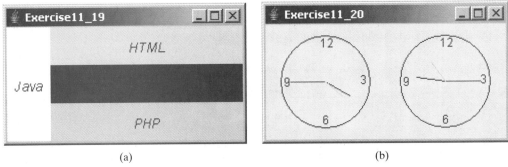

         (a)   (b)

FIGURE 11.39 *(a) Exercise 11.19 uses* MessagePanel *to display four strings. (b) Exercise 11.20 displays two clocks.*

11.20 (*Using the* StillClock *class*) Write a program that displays two clocks. The hour, minute, and second values are 4, 20, 45 for the first clock, and 22, 46, 15 for the second clock, as shown in Figure11.39(b).

11.21** (*Displaying a TicTacToe board*) Create a custom panel that displays X, O, or nothing. What to display is randomly decided whenever a panel is repainted. Use the Math.random() method to generate an integer 0, 1, or 2, which corresponds to displaying X, O, or nothing. Create a frame that contains nine custom panels, as shown in Figure 11.40.

FIGURE 11.40 *TicTacToe cells display X, O, or nothing randomly.*

chapter

12

EVENT-DRIVEN PROGRAMMING

Objectives

✦ To explain the concept of event-driven programming (§12.2).

✦ To understand events, event sources, and event classes (§12.2).

✦ To declare listener classes and write the code to handle events (§12.3).

✦ To register listener objects in the source object (§12.3).

✦ To understand how an event is handled (§12.3).

✦ To write programs to deal with `ActionEvent` (§12.3).

✦ To write programs to deal with `MouseEvent` (§12.4).

✦ To write programs to deal with `KeyEvent` (§12.5).

✦ To use the `Timer` class to control animations (§12.6 Optional).

12.1   Introduction

event-driven programming

All non-GUI programs execute in a procedural order. Java GUI programming is event-driven. In *event-driven programming*, code is executed when an event occurs—a button click, perhaps, or a mouse movement. This chapter introduces the concepts and techniques for Java event-driven programming

12.2   Event and Event Source

event

When you run Java GUI programs, the program interacts with the user and the events drive its execution. An *event* can be defined as a signal to the program that something has happened. Events are triggered either by external user actions, such as mouse movements, button clicks, and keystrokes, or by the operating system, such as a timer. The program can choose to respond to or ignore an event.

source object

The component on which an event is generated is called the *source object*. For example, a button is the source object for a button-clicking action event. An event is an instance of an event class. The root class of the event classes is `java.util.EventObject`. The hierarchical relationships of some event classes are shown in Figure 12.1.

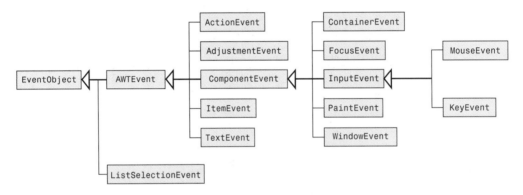

FIGURE 12.1   *An event is an object of the `EventObject` class.*

getSource()

An event object contains whatever properties are pertinent to the event. You can identify the source object of an event using the `getSource()` instance method in the `EventObject` class. The subclasses of `EventObject` deal with special types of events, such as action events, window events, component events, mouse movements, and keystrokes. Table 12.1 lists external user actions, source objects, and event types generated.

 NOTE
If a component can generate an event, any subclass of the component can generate the same type of event. For example, every GUI component can generate `MouseEvent`, `KeyEvent`, `FocusEvent`, and `ComponentEvent`, since `Component` is the superclass of all GUI components.

 NOTE
All the event classes in Figure 12.1 are included in the `java.awt.event` package except `ListSelectionEvent`, which is in the `javax.swing.event` package. The AWT events were originally designed for AWT components, but many Swing components fire them.

TABLE 12.1   User Action, Source Object, and Event Type

User action	Source object	Event type generated
Click a button	JButton	ActionEvent
Press return on a text field	JTextField	ActionEvent
Select a new item	JComboBox	ItemEvent, ActionEvent
Select item(s)	JList	ListSelectionEvent
Click a check box	JCheckBox	ItemEvent, ActionEvent
Click a radio button	JRadioButton	ItemEvent, ActionEvent
Select a menu item	JMenuItem	ActionEvent
Move the scroll bar	JScrollBar	AdjustmentEvent
Window opened, closed, iconified, deiconified, or closing	Window	WindowEvent
Component added or removed from the container	Container	ContainerEvent
Component moved, resized, hidden, or shown	Component	ComponentEvent
Component gained or lost focus	Component	FocusEvent
Key released or pressed	Component	KeyEvent
Mouse pressed, released, clicked, entered, or exited	Component	MouseEvent
Mouse moved or dragged	Component	MouseEvent

12.3   Listeners, Registrations, and Handling Events

Java uses a delegation-based model for event handling: an external user action on a source object triggers an event, and an object interested in the event receives the event. The latter object is called a *listener*. Two things are needed for an object to be a listener for an event on a source object:

listener

✦ The listener object's class must implement the corresponding event-listener interface. Java provides a listener interface for every type of GUI event. The listener interface is usually named *X*Listener for *X*Event, with the exception of MouseMotionListener. For example, the corresponding listener interface for ActionEvent is ActionListener; each listener for ActionEvent should implement the ActionListener interface. Table 12.2 lists event types, the corresponding listener interfaces, and the methods defined in the listener interfaces. The listener interface contains the method(s), known as the *handler(s)*, which process the events.

listener interface

handler

✦ The listener object must be registered by the source object. Registration methods are dependent on the event type. For ActionEvent, the method is addActionListener. In

TABLE 12.2 Events, Event Listeners, and Listener Methods

Event class	Listener interface	Listener methods (Handlers)
ActionEvent	ActionListener	actionPerformed(ActionEvent)
ItemEvent	ItemListener	itemStateChanged(ItemEvent)
WindowEvent	WindowListener	windowClosing(WindowEvent)
		windowOpened(WindowEvent)
		windowIconified(WindowEvent)
		windowDeiconified(WindowEvent)
		windowClosed(WindowEvent)
		windowActivated(WindowEvent)
		windowDeactivated(WindowEvent)
ContainerEvent	ContainerListener	componentAdded(ContainerEvent)
		componentRemoved(ContainerEvent)
ComponentEvent	ComponentListener	componentMoved(ComponentEvent)
		componentHidden(ComponentEvent)
		componentResized(ComponentEvent)
		componentShown(ComponentEvent)
FocusEvent	FocusListener	focusGained(FocusEvent)
		focusLost(FocusEvent)
KeyEvent	KeyListener	keyPressed(KeyEvent)
		keyReleased(KeyEvent)
		keyTyped(KeyEvent)
MouseEvent	MouseListener	mousePressed(MouseEvent)
		mouseReleased(MouseEvent)
		mouseEntered(MouseEvent)
		mouseExited(MouseEvent)
		mouseClicked(MouseEvent)
	MouseMotionListener	mouseDragged(MouseEvent)
		mouseMoved(MouseEvent)
AdjustmentEvent	AdjustmentListener	adjustmentValueChanged(AdjustmentEvent)

general, the method is named addXListener for XEvent. A source object may fire several types of events. For each event, the source object maintains a list of listeners and notifies all the *registered listeners* by invoking the *handler* on the listener object to respond to the event, as shown in Figure 12.2.

register listener

For example, if an object is interested in listening to an action event on a JButton source object, its defining class must implement the ActionListener interface and the actionPerformed method, as shown in Figure 12.3.

The listener object must also register with the JButton object. The registration is done by invoking the addActionListener method in the JButton object, as follows:

create listener object
create source object
register listener

```
ListenerClass listener = new ListenerClass();
JButton jbt = new JButton("OK");
jbt.addActionListener(listener);
```

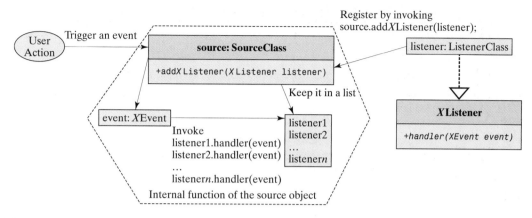

FIGURE 12.2 *An event is triggered by user actions on the source object; the source object generates the event object and invokes the handler of the listener object to process the event.*

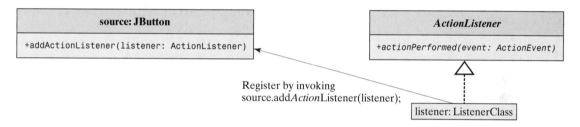

FIGURE 12.3 *An* ActionListener *is registered with a* JButton.

When you click the button, the JButton object generates an ActionEvent and passes it to invoke the actionPerformed method to handle the event.

The event object contains information pertinent to the event type, which can be obtained using the methods, as shown in Figure 12.4. For example, you can use e.getSource() to obtain the source object in order to determine whether it is a button, a check box, or a radio button. For an action event, you can use the e.getWhen() to obtain the time when the event occurs.

Three examples of the use of event handling are given below. The first is for ActionEvent, the second for WindowEvent, and the third involves multiple listeners for a source.

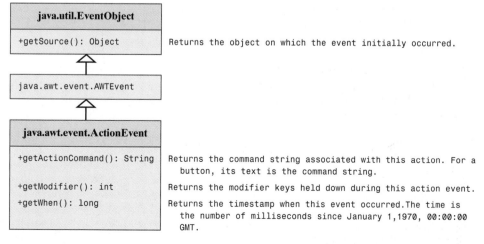

FIGURE 12.4 *You can obtain useful information from an event object.*

EXAMPLE **12.1** HANDLING SIMPLE ACTION EVENTS

Problem

Write a program that displays two buttons, OK and Cancel, in the window. A message is displayed on the console to indicate which button and when it is clicked, as shown in Figure 12.5.

FIGURE **12.5** *The program responds to the button action events.*

Solution

Here are the steps in the program:

1. Create a listener class named `ButtonListener` for handling `ActionEvent` on the buttons. This class implements the `ActionListener` interface.

2. Create a test program named `TestActionEvent` that extends `JFrame`. Add two buttons to the frame, and create a listener object from `ButtonListener`. Register the listener with the buttons.

LISTING **12.1** TestActionEvent.java (Handling an `ActionEvent`)

```
1 import javax.swing.*;
2 import java.awt.*;
3 import java.awt.event.*;
4
5 public class TestActionEvent extends JFrame {
6   // Create two buttons
7   private JButton jbtOk = new JButton("OK");
8   private JButton jbtCancel = new JButton("Cancel");
9
10   public TestActionEvent() {
11     // Set the window title
12     setTitle("TestActionEvent");
13
14     // Set FlowLayout manager to arrange the components
15     // inside the frame
16     getContentPane().setLayout(new FlowLayout());
17
18     // Add buttons to the frame
19     getContentPane().add(jbtOk);
20     getContentPane().add(jbtCancel);
21
22     // Create a listener object
23     ButtonListener btListener = new ButtonListener();
24
25     // Register listeners
26     jbtOk.addActionListener(btListener);
27     jbtCancel.addActionListener(btListener);
28   }
29
30   /** Main method */
31   public static void main(String[] args) {
```

listener

register

EXAMPLE 12.1 (CONTINUED)

```
32     TestActionEvent frame = new TestActionEvent();
33     frame.setDefaultCloseOperation(JFrame.EXIT_ON_CLOSE);
34     frame.setSize(100, 80);
35     frame.setVisible(true);
36   }
37 }
38
39 class ButtonListener implements ActionListener {
40   /** This method will be invoked when a button is clicked */
41   public void actionPerformed(ActionEvent e) {
42     System.out.println("The " + e.getActionCommand() + " button is "
43       + "clicked at\n  " + new java.util.Date(e.getWhen()));
44   }
45 }
```

listener class

Review

The button objects jbtOk and jbtCancel are the source of ActionEvent. The ButtonListener class defines the listeners for the buttons, and its instance btListener is registered with the buttons (Lines 26–27).

Clicking a button causes the actionPerformed method in btListener to be invoked. The e.getActionCommand() method returns the action command from the button (Line 42). By default, a button's action command is the text of the button.

The e.getWhen() method returns the time in milliseconds since January 1, 1970, 00:00:00 GMT. The Date class converts the time to year, month, date, hours, minutes, and seconds (Line 43).

The TestActionEvent class itself can be a listener class if you rewrite the program as follows:

```
1 import javax.swing.*;
2 import java.awt.*;
3 import java.awt.event.*;
4
5 public class TestActionEvent extends JFrame
6     implements ActionListener {
7   // Create two buttons
8   private JButton jbtOk = new JButton("OK");
9   private JButton jbtCancel = new JButton("Cancel");
10
11   public TestActionEvent() {
12     // Set the window title
13     setTitle("TestActionEvent");
14
15     // Set FlowLayout manager to arrange the components
16     // inside the frame
17     getContentPane().setLayout(new FlowLayout());
18
19     // Add buttons to the frame
20     getContentPane().add(jbtOk);
21     getContentPane().add(jbtCancel);
22
23     // Register listeners
24     jbtOk.addActionListener(this);
25     jbtCancel.addActionListener(this);
26   }
27
28   /** Main method */
29   public static void main(String[] args) {
30     TestActionEvent frame = new TestActionEvent();
31     frame.setDefaultCloseOperation(JFrame.EXIT_ON_CLOSE);
32     frame.setSize(100, 80);
33     frame.setVisible(true);
34   }
```

EXAMPLE 12.1 (CONTINUED)

```
35
36   /** This method will be invoked when a button is clicked */
37   public void actionPerformed(ActionEvent e) {
38     System.out.println("The " + e.getActionCommand() + " button is "
39       + "clicked at\n  " + new java.util.Date(e.getWhen()));
40   }
41 }
```

The statements (Lines 24–25)

```
jbtOk.addActionListener(this);
jbtCancel.addActionListener(this);
```

register this (referring to the object of TestActionEvent, which is being constructed. See Section 6.12, "The this Keyword,") to listen to ActionEvent on jbtOk and jbtCancel.

 CAUTION

listener registration

Missing *listener registration* is a common mistake in event handling. If the source object doesn't notify the listener, the listener cannot act on the event.

 NOTE

If a listener is registered with a source twice, the handler of the listener will be invoked twice when an event occurs.

EXAMPLE 12.2 HANDLING WINDOW EVENTS

Problem

Write a program that demonstrates handling window events.

Solution

Any subclass of the Window class can generate the following window events: window opened, closing, closed, activated, deactivated, iconified, and deiconified. The program in Listing 12.2 creates a frame, listens to the window events, and displays a message to indicate the occurring event. Figure 12.6 shows a sample run of the program.

FIGURE 12.6 *The window events are displayed on the console when you run the program from a DOS prompt.*

LISTING 12.2 TestWindowEvent.java (Handling a WindowEvent)

```
1 import java.awt.*;
2 import java.awt.event.*;
3 import javax.swing.JFrame;
```

EXAMPLE 12.2 (CONTINUED)

```
4
5 public class TestWindowEvent extends JFrame
6     implements WindowListener {
7   // Main method
8   public static void main(String[] args) {
9     TestWindowEvent frame = new TestWindowEvent();
10    frame.setDefaultCloseOperation(JFrame.EXIT_ON_CLOSE);
11    frame.setTitle("TestWindowEvent");
12    frame.setSize(100, 80);
13    frame.setVisible(true);
14  }
15
16  public TestWindowEvent() {
17    addWindowListener(this);  // Register listener
18  }
19
20  /**
21   * Handler for window deiconified event
22   * Invoked when a window is changed from a minimized
23   * to a normal state.
24   */
25  public void windowDeiconified(WindowEvent event) {
26    System.out.println("Window deiconified");
27  }
28
29  /**
30   * Handler for window iconified event
31   * Invoked when a window is changed from a normal to a
32   * minimized state. For many platforms, a minimized window
33   * is displayed as the icon specified in the window's
34   * iconImage property.
35   */
36  public void windowIconified(WindowEvent event) {
37    System.out.println("Window iconified");
38  }
39
40  /**
41   * Handler for window activated event
42   * Invoked when the window is set to be the user's
43   * active window, which means the window (or one of its
44   * subcomponents) will receive keyboard events.
45   */
46  public void windowActivated(WindowEvent event) {
47    System.out.println("Window activated");
48  }
49
50  /**
51   * Handler for window deactivated event
52   * Invoked when a window is no longer the user's active
53   * window, which means that keyboard events will no longer
54   * be delivered to the window or its subcomponents.
55   */
56  public void windowDeactivated(WindowEvent event) {
57    System.out.println("Window deactivated");
58  }
59
60  /**
61   * Handler for window opened event
62   * Invoked the first time a window is made visible.
63   */
64  public void windowOpened(WindowEvent event) {
65    System.out.println("Window opened");
66  }
67
68  /**
69   * Handler for window closing event
70   * Invoked when the user attempts to close the window
```

override handler (lines 25, 36, 46, 56, 64)

EXAMPLE 12.2 (CONTINUED)

```
71      * from the window's system menu.  If the program does not
72      * explicitly hide or dispose the window while processing
73      * this event, the window close operation will be cancelled.
74      */
75     public void windowClosing(WindowEvent event) {
76       System.out.println("Window closing");
77     }
78
79     /**
80      * Handler for window closed event
81      * Invoked when a window has been closed as the result
82      * of calling dispose on the window.
83      */
84     public void windowClosed(WindowEvent event) {
85       System.out.println("Window closed");
86     }
87   }
```

override handler *(line 75)*

override handler *(line 84)*

Review

The WindowEvent can be generated by the Window class or any subclass of Window. Since JFrame is a subclass of Window, it can generate WindowEvent.

TestWindowEvent extends JFrame and implements WindowListener. The WindowListener interface defines several abstract methods (windowActivated, windowClosed, windowClosing, windowDeactivated, windowDeiconified, windowIconified, windowOpened) for handling window events when the window is activated, closed, closing, deactivated, deiconified, iconified, or opened.

When a window event, such as activation, occurs, the windowActivated method is triggered. Implement the windowActivated method with a concrete response if you want the event to be processed.

Because the methods in the WindowListener interface are abstract, you must implement all of them even if your program does not care about some of the events.

For an object to receive event notification, it must register as an event listener. addWindowListener(this) (Line 17) registers the object of TestWindowEvent as a window-event listener so that it can receive notification about the window event. TestWindowEvent is both a listener and a source object.

> **NOTE**
> As demonstrated in this example, a source object and a listener object may be the same.

EXAMPLE 12.3 MULTIPLE LISTENERS FOR A SINGLE SOURCE

Problem

Write a program that modifies Example 12.1, "Handling Simple Action Events," to add a new listener for the OK and Cancel buttons. This example creates a new listener class as an additional listener for the action events on the buttons. When a button is clicked, both listeners respond to the action event.

Solution

Listing 12.3 gives the solution to the problem. Figure 12.7 shows a sample run of the program.

EXAMPLE 12.2 (CONTINUED)

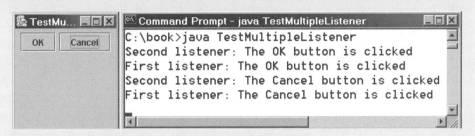

FIGURE **12.7** *Both listeners respond to the button action events.*

LISTING 12.3 TestMultipleListener.java (Multiple Listeners on a Source)

```
1 import javax.swing.*;
2 import java.awt.*;
3 import java.awt.event.*;
4
5 public class TestMultipleListener extends JFrame
6    implements ActionListener {
7   // Create two buttons
8   private JButton jbtOk = new JButton("OK");
9   private JButton jbtCancel = new JButton("Cancel");
10
11  public TestMultipleListener() {
12    // Set the window title
13    setTitle("TestMultipleListener");
14
15    // Set FlowLayout manager to arrange the components
16    // inside the frame
17    getContentPane().setLayout(new FlowLayout());
18
19    // Add buttons to the frame
20    getContentPane().add(jbtOk);
21    getContentPane().add(jbtCancel);
22
23    // Register the frame as listeners
24    jbtOk.addActionListener(this);                           register listener
25    jbtCancel.addActionListener(this);
26
27    // Register a second listener for buttons
28    SecondListener secondListener = new SecondListener();    create listener
29    jbtOk.addActionListener(secondListener);                 register listener
30    jbtCancel.addActionListener(secondListener);
31  }
32
33  /** Main method */
34  public static void main(String[] args) {
35    TestMultipleListener frame = new TestMultipleListener();
36    frame.setDefaultCloseOperation(JFrame.EXIT_ON_CLOSE);
37    frame.setSize(100, 80);
38    frame.setVisible(true);
39  }
40
41  /** This method will be invoked when a button is clicked */
42  public void actionPerformed(ActionEvent e) {              override handler
43    System.out.print("First listener: ");
44
45    if (e.getSource() == jbtOk) {
46      System.out.println("The OK button is clicked");
47    }
48    else if (e.getSource() == jbtCancel) {
49      System.out.println("The Cancel button is clicked");
50    }
```

EXAMPLE 12.3 (CONTINUED)

```
51   }
52 }
53
54 /** The class for the second listener */
55 class SecondListener implements ActionListener {
56   /** Handle ActionEvent */
57   public void actionPerformed(ActionEvent e) {
58     System.out.print("Second listener: ");
59
60     // A button has an actionCommand property, which is same as the
61     // text of the button by default.
62     if (e.getActionCommand().equals("OK")) {
63       System.out.println("The OK button is clicked");
64     }
65     else if (e.getActionCommand().equals("Cancel")) {
66       System.out.println("The Cancel button is clicked");
67     }
68   }
69 }
```

Review

Each source object in the preceding two examples has a single listener. Each button in this example has two listeners: one is an instance of `TestMultipleListener`, and the other is an instance of `SecondListener`.

When a button is clicked, both listeners are notified and their respective `actionPerformed` methods are invoked. Using this method can detect which button is clicked. If you want to use the `getSource` method to detect which button is clicked, see Exercise 12.2.

The source object maintains a list of all its listeners. When a listener is registered with the source object, it is added at the top of the list. When an event occurs, the source object notifies the listener objects on the list by invoking each listener's handler. In this case, the handler is the `actionPerformed` method.

What would happen if you replaced Lines 27-30 in the example with the following code?

```
// Register a second listener for buttons
jbtOk.addActionListener(new SecondListener());
jbtCancel.addActionListener(new SecondListener());
```

Two instances of `SecondListener` would be created. The program would run just as before the change, but the change is obviously not good.

12.4 Mouse Events

A mouse event is generated whenever a mouse is pressed, released, clicked, moved, or dragged on a component. The mouse event object captures the event, such as the number of clicks associated with it or the location (x and y coordinates) of the mouse, as shown in Figure 12.8.

Since the `MouseEvent` class inherits `InputEvent`, you can use the methods defined in the `InputEvent` class on a `MouseEvent` object.

The `java.awt.Point` class encapsulates a point in a plane. The class contains two instance variables, x and y, for coordinates. To create a point object, use the following constructor:

```
Point(int x, int y)
```

This constructs a `Point` object with the specified x-and y-coordinates.

java.awt.event.InputEvent	
+getWhen(): long	Returns the timestamp when this event occurred.
+isAltDown(): boolean	Returns whether or not the Alt modifier is down on this event.
+isControlDown(): boolean	Returns whether or not the Control modifier is down on this event.
+isMetaDown(): boolean	Returns whether or not the Meta modifier is down on this event
+isShiftDown(): boolean	Returns whether or not the Shift modifier is down on this event.

java.awt.event.MouseEvent	
+getButton(): int	Indicates which mouse button has been clicked.
+getClickCount(): int	Returns the number of mouse clicks associated with this event.
+getPoint():java.awt.Point	Returns a Point object containing the x and y coordinates.
+getX(): int	Returns the x-coordinate of the mouse point.
+getY(): int	Returns the y-coordinate of the mouse point.

FIGURE 12.8   *The MouseEvent class encapsulates information for mouse events.*

java.awt.event.MouseListener	
+mousePressed(e: MouseEvent): void	Invoked when the mouse button has been pressed on the source component.
+mouseReleased(e: MouseEvent): void	Invoked when the mouse button has been released on the source component.
+mouseClicked(e: MouseEvent): void	Invoked when the mouse button has been clicked (pressed and released) on the source component.
+mouseEntered(e: MouseEvent): void	Invoked when the mouse enters the source component.
+mouseExited(e: MouseEvent): void	Invoked when the mouse exits the source component.

java.awt.event.MouseMotionListener	
+mouseDragged(e: MouseEvent): void	Invoked when a mouse button is moved with a button pressed.
+mouseMoved(e: MouseEvent): void	Invoked when a mouse button is moved without a button pressed.

FIGURE 12.9   *The MouseListener interface handles mouse pressed, released, clicked, entered, and exited events. The MouseMotionListener interface handles mouse dragged and moved events.*

Java provides two listener interfaces, MouseListener and MouseMotionListener, to handle mouse events, as shown in Figure 12.9. Implement the MouseListener interface to listen for such actions as pressing, releasing, entering, exiting, or clicking the mouse, and implement the MouseMotionListener interface to listen for such actions as dragging or moving the mouse.

EXAMPLE 12.4 MOVING A MESSAGE ON A PANEL USING A MOUSE

Problem

Write a program that displays a message in a panel. You can use the mouse to move the message. The message moves as the mouse drags and is always displayed at the mouse point. A sample run of the program is shown in Figure 12.10.

EXAMPLE 12.4 (CONTINUED)

FIGURE **12.10** *You can move the message by dragging the mouse.*

Solution

Listing 12.4 gives the solution to the problem.

LISTING 12.4 MoveMessageDemo.java (Handling a MouseEvent)

```
1 import java.awt.*;
2 import java.awt.event.*;
3 import javax.swing.*;
4
5 public class MoveMessageDemo extends JFrame {
6   public MoveMessageDemo() {
7     // Create a MoveMessagePanel instance for drawing a message
8     MoveMessagePanel p = new MoveMessagePanel("Welcome to Java");
9
10    // Place the message panel in the frame
11    getContentPane().setLayout(new BorderLayout());
12    getContentPane().add(p);
13  }
14
15  /** Main method */
16  public static void main(String[] args) {
17    MoveMessageDemo frame = new MoveMessageDemo();
18    frame.setTitle("MoveMessageDemo");
19    frame.setDefaultCloseOperation(JFrame.EXIT_ON_CLOSE);
20    frame.setSize(100, 80);
21    frame.setVisible(true);
22  }
23 }
24
25 // MoveMessagePanel draws a message
26  class MoveMessagePanel extends MessagePanel
27    implements MouseMotionListener {
28    /** Construct a panel to draw string s */
29    public MoveMessagePanel(String s) {
30      super(s); // What if this line is omitted?
31      this.addMouseMotionListener(this);
32    }
33
34    /** Handle mouse moved event */
35    public void mouseMoved(MouseEvent e) {
36    }
37
38    /** Handle mouse dragged event */
39    public void mouseDragged(MouseEvent e) {
40      // Get the new location and repaint the screen
41      setXCoordinate(e.getX());
42      setYCoordinate(e.getY());
43    }
44  }
```

listener class

register listener

override handler

override handler

EXAMPLE 12.4 (CONTINUED)

Review

The class `MoveMessagePanel` extends `MessagePanel` and implements `MouseMotionListener`. The `MessagePanel` class was presented Section 11.11, "Case Study: The `MessagePanel` Class" to display a message in a panel. The `MoveMessagePanel` class inherits all the features from `MessagePanel`. Additionally, it handles redisplaying the message when the mouse is dragged.

The `MouseMotionListener` interface contains two handlers, `mouseMoved` and `mouseDragged`, for handling mouse-motion events. When you move the mouse with the button pressed, the `mouseDragged` method is invoked to repaint the viewing area and display the message at the mouse point. When you move the mouse without pressing the button, the `mouseMoved` method is invoked.

Because the methods in the `MouseMotionListener` interface are abstract, you must implement all of them even if your program does not care about some of the events. In `MoveMessagePanel`, the mouseMoved and mouseDragged event handlers are both implemented, although only the mouseDragged handler is needed.

For an object to receive event notification, it must register as an event listener. `addMouseMotionListener(this)` (Line 31) registers the object of `MoveMessagePanel` as a mouse motion event listener so that the object can receive notification about the mouse-motion event. `MoveMessagePanel` is both a listener and a source object.

The `mouseDragged` method is invoked when you move the mouse with a button pressed. This method obtains the mouse location using `getX` and `getY` methods (Lines 41–42) in the `MouseEvent` class. This becomes the new location for the message, which is set using the `MessagePanel`'s `setXCoordinate` and `setYCoordinate` methods.

EXAMPLE 12.5 SCRIBBLING WITH A MOUSE (OPTIONAL)

Problem

Write a program that uses a mouse for scribbling. It can be used to draw things on a panel by dragging with the left mouse button pressed. The drawing can be erased by dragging with the right button pressed. A sample run of the program is shown in Figure 12.11.

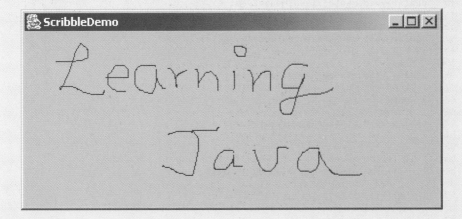

FIGURE 12.11   *The program enables you to scribble using the mouse.*

EXAMPLE 12.5 (CONTINUED)

Solution

Listing 12.5 gives the solution to the problem.

LISTING 12.5 ScribbleDemo.java (Scribble Using Mouse)

```
1  import java.awt.*;
2  import javax.swing.*;
3  import java.awt.event.*;
4
5  public class ScribbleDemo extends JFrame {
6    public ScribbleDemo() {
7      // Create a ScribblePanel and add it to the content pane
8      getContentPane().add(new ScribblePanel(), BorderLayout.CENTER);
9    }
10
11   /** Main method */
12   public static void main(String[] args) {
13     ScribbleDemo frame = new ScribbleDemo();
14     frame.setTitle("ScribbleDemo");
15     frame.setDefaultCloseOperation(JFrame.EXIT_ON_CLOSE);
16     frame.setSize(300, 300);
17     frame.setVisible(true);
18   }
19 }
20
21 // ScribblePanel for scribbling using the mouse
22 class ScribblePanel extends JPanel
23     implements MouseListener, MouseMotionListener {
24   final int CIRCLESIZE = 20; // Circle diameter used for erasing
25   private Point lineStart = new Point(0, 0); // Line start point
26   private Graphics g; // Create a Graphics object for drawing
27
28   public ScribblePanel() {
29     // Register listener for the mouse event
30     addMouseListener(this);
31     addMouseMotionListener(this);
32   }
33
34   public void mouseClicked(MouseEvent e) {
35   }
36
37   public void mouseEntered(MouseEvent e) {
38   }
39
40   public void mouseExited(MouseEvent e) {
41   }
42
43   public void mouseReleased(MouseEvent e) {
44   }
45
46   public void mousePressed(MouseEvent e) {
47     lineStart.move(e.getX(), e.getY());
48   }
49
50   public void mouseDragged(MouseEvent e) {
51     g = getGraphics(); // Get graphics context
52
53     if (e.isMetaDown()) { // Detect right button pressed
54       // Erase the drawing using an oval
55       g.setColor(getBackground());
56       g.fillOval(e.getX() - (CIRCLESIZE / 2),
57         e.getY() - (CIRCLESIZE / 2), CIRCLESIZE, CIRCLESIZE);
58     }
59     else {
60       g.setColor(Color.black);
```

listener class

add mouse listener
add mouse motion listener

override handler

override handler

EXAMPLE 12.5 (CONTINUED)

```
61        g.drawLine(lineStart.x, lineStart.y,
62          e.getX(), e.getY());
63      }
64
65      lineStart.move(e.getX(), e.getY());
66
67      // Dispose this graphics context
68      g.dispose();
69    }
70
71    public void mouseMoved(MouseEvent e) {
72    }
73 }
```

Review

The program creates a `ScribblePanel` instance to capture mouse movements on the panel. Lines are created or erased by dragging the mouse with the left or right button pressed.

When a button is pressed, the `mousePressed` handler is invoked. This handler sets the `lineStart` to the current mouse point as the starting point. Drawing begins when the mouse is dragged with the left button pressed. In this case, the `mouseDragged` handler sets the foreground color to black, and draws a line along the path of the mouse movement.

When the mouse is dragged with the right button pressed, erasing occurs. In this case, the `mouseDragged` handler sets the foreground color to the background color and draws an oval filled with the background color at the mouse pointer to erase the area covered by the oval.

The program does not use the `paintComponent(Graphics g)` method. Instead, it uses `getGraphics()` to obtain a `Graphics` instance and draws on this.

Because the `mousePressed` handler is defined in the `MouseListener` interface, and the `mouseDragged` handler is defined in the `MouseMotionListener` interface, the program implements both interfaces (Line 23).

The `dispose` method (Line 68) disposes of this graphics context and releases any system resources it is using. Although the finalization process of the JVM automatically disposes of an object after it is no longer in use, it is better to manually free the associated resources by calling this method rather than rely on a finalization process that may take a long time to run to completion. In this program, a large number of `Graphics` objects can be created within a short time. The program would run fine if these objects were not disposed of manually, but they would consume a lot of memory.

12.5 Keyboard Events

Keyboard events enable the use of the keys to control and perform actions or get input from the keyboard. A key event is generated whenever a key is pressed, released, or typed on a component. The keyboard event object describes the nature of the event (namely, that a key has been pressed, released, or typed) and the value of the key, as shown in Figure 12.12.

The keys captured in an event are integers representing Unicode character values, which include alphanumeric characters, function keys, the Tab key, the Enter key, and so on. Every keyboard event has an associated key character or key code that is returned by the `getKeyChar()` or `getKeyCode()` method in `KeyEvent`.

Java defines many constants for keys, including function keys in the `KeyEvent` class. Table 12.3 shows the most commonly used ones.

Java provides the `KeyListener` to handle key events, as shown in Figure 12.13.

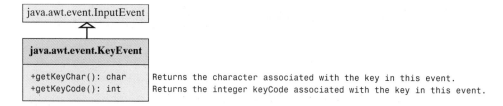

FIGURE 12.12 *The KeyEvent class encapsulates information about key events.*

java.awt.event.KeyListener	
+keyPressed(e: KeyEvent): void	Invoked when a key is pressed on a component.
+keyReleased(e: KeyEvent): void	Invoked when a key is released on a component.
+keyTyped(e: KeyEvent): void	Invoked when a key is pressed and then released on a component.

FIGURE 12.13 *The KeyListener handles key pressed, released, and typed events.*

TABLE 12.3 Key Constants

Constant	Description
VK_HOME	The Home key
VK_End	The End key
VK_PGUP	The Page Up key
VK_PGDN	The Page Down key
VK_UP	The up-arrow key
VK_DOWN	The down-arrow key
VK_LEFT	The left-arrow key
VK_RIGHT	The right-arrow key
VK_ESCAPE	The Esc key
VK_TAB	The Tab key
VK_CONTROL	The Control key
VK_SHIFT	The Shift key
VK_BACK_SPACE	The Backspace key
VK_CAPS_LOCK	The Caps Lock key
VK_NUM_LOCK	The Num Lock key
VK_ENTER	The Enter key
VK_F1 to VK_F12	The function keys from F1 to F12
VK_0 to VK_9	The number keys from 0 to 9
VK_A to VK_Z	The letter keys from A to Z

The keyPressed handler is invoked when a key is pressed, the keyReleased handler is invoked when a key is released, and the keyTyped handler is invoked when a Unicode character is entered. If a key does not have a Unicode (e.g., function keys, modifier keys, action keys, and control keys), the keyTyped handler will be not be invoked.

EXAMPLE 12.6 HANDLING KEY EVENTS

Problem

Write a program that displays a user-input character. The user can move the character up, down, left, and right, using the arrow keys VK_UP, VK_DOWN, VK_LEFT, and VK_RIGHT. Figure 12.14 contains a sample run of the program.

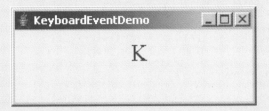

FIGURE 12.14 *The program responds to keyboard events by displaying a character and moving it up, down, left, or right.*

Solution

The following code gives the solution to the problem.

LISTING 12.6   KeyboardEventDemo.java (Handling a KeyEvent)

```
1 import java.awt.*;
2 import java.awt.event.*;
3 import javax.swing.*;
4
5 public class KeyboardEventDemo extends JFrame {
6   private KeyboardPanel keyboardPanel = new KeyboardPanel();
7
8   /** Initialize UI */
9   public KeyboardEventDemo() {
10     // Add the keyboard panel to accept and display user input
11     getContentPane().add(keyboardPanel);
12
13     // Set focus
14     keyboardPanel.setFocusable(true);
15   }
16
17   /** Main method */
18   public static void main(String[] args) {
19     KeyboardEventDemo frame = new KeyboardEventDemo();
20     frame.setTitle("KeyboardEventDemo");
21     frame.setDefaultCloseOperation(JFrame.EXIT_ON_CLOSE);
22     frame.setSize(300, 300);
23     frame.setVisible(true);
24   }
25 }
26
27 // KeyboardPanel for receiving key input
28 class KeyboardPanel extends JPanel implements KeyListener {
29   private int x = 100;
30   private int y = 100;
31   private char keyChar = 'A'; // Default key
32
33   public KeyboardPanel() {
34     addKeyListener(this); // Register listener
35   }
```

listener class

register listener

EXAMPLE 12.6 (CONTINUED)

```
36
37    public void keyReleased(KeyEvent e) {
38    }
39
40    public void keyTyped(KeyEvent e) {
41    }
42
43    public void keyPressed(KeyEvent e) {
44      switch (e.getKeyCode()) {
45        case KeyEvent.VK_DOWN: y += 10; break;
46        case KeyEvent.VK_UP: y -= 10; break;
47        case KeyEvent.VK_LEFT: x -= 10; break;
48        case KeyEvent.VK_RIGHT: x += 10; break;
49        default: keyChar = e.getKeyChar();
50      }
51
52      repaint();
53    }
54
55    /** Draw the character */
56    protected void paintComponent(Graphics g) {
57      super.paintComponent(g);
58
59      g.setFont(new Font("TimesRoman", Font.PLAIN, 24));
60      g.drawString(String.valueOf(keyChar), x, y);
61    }
62  }
```

override handler

Review

When a non-arrow key is pressed, the key is displayed. When an arrow key is pressed, the character moves in the direction indicated by the arrow key.

Because the program gets input from the keyboard, it listens for KeyEvent and implements KeyListener to handle key input.

When a key is pressed, the keyPressed handler is invoked. The program uses e.getKeyCode() to obtain the int value for the key and e.getKeyChar() to get the character for the key. In fact, (int)e.getKeyChar() is the same as e.getKeyCode().

Only a focused component can receive KeyEvent. To make a component focusable, set its isFocusable property to true (Line 14). This new property was introduced in JDK 1.4.

12.6 The Timer Class (Optional)

Not all source objects are GUI components. The javax.swing.Timer class is a source component that fires an ActionEvent at a predefined rate. Figure 12.15 lists some of the methods in the class.

A Timer object serves as the source of an ActionEvent. The listeners must be instances of ActionListener and registered with the Timer object. You create a Timer object using its sole constructor with a delay and a listener, where delay specifies the number of milliseconds between two action events. You can add additional listeners using the addActionListener method, and adjust the delay using the setDelay method. To start the timer, invoke the start() method. To stop the timer, invoke the stop() method.

javax.swing.Timer	
+Timer(delay: int,listener: ActionListener)	Creates a Timer with a specified delay in milliseconds and an ActionListener.
+addActionListener(listener: ActionListener): void	Adds an ActionListener to the timer.
+start(): void	Starts this timer.
+stop(): void	Stops this timer.
+setDelay(delay: int): void	Sets a new delay value for this timer.

FIGURE 12.15 *A Timer object fires an ActionEvent at a fixed rate.*

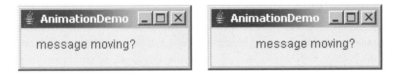

FIGURE 12.16 *A message moves in the panel.*

The Timer class can be used to control animations. For example, you can use it to display a moving message with the code in Listing 12.7.

LISTING 12.7 AnimationDemo.java (Moving a Message)

```
1 import java.awt.*;
2 import java.awt.event.*;
3 import javax.swing.*;
4
5 public class AnimationDemo extends JFrame {
6   public AnimationDemo() {
7     // Create a MovingMessagePanel for displaying a moving message
8     MovingMessagePanel p = new MovingMessagePanel("message moving?");
9     getContentPane().add(p);
10
11    // Create a timer for the listener p
12    Timer timer = new Timer(1000, p);                                        create timer
13    timer.start();                                                           start timer
14  }
15
16  /** Main method */
17  public static void main(String[] args) {
18    AnimationDemo frame = new AnimationDemo();
19    frame.setTitle("AnimationDemo");
20    frame.setDefaultCloseOperation(JFrame.EXIT_ON_CLOSE);
21    frame.setSize(100, 80);
22    frame.setVisible(true);
23  }
24 }
25
26 // Displaying a moving message
27 class MovingMessagePanel extends JPanel implements ActionListener {
28   private String message = "Welcome to Java";
29   private int xCoordinate = 20;
30   private int yCoordinate = 20;
31
32   public MovingMessagePanel(String message) {
33     this.message = message;                                                 set message
34   }
```

handler
repaint

```
35
36   /** Handle ActionEvent */
37   public void actionPerformed(ActionEvent e) {
38     repaint();
39   }
40
41   /** Paint message */
42   public void paintComponent(Graphics g) {
43     super.paintComponent(g);
44
45     if (xCoordinate > getWidth()) xCoordinate = -20;
46     xCoordinate += 5;
47     g.drawString(message, xCoordinate, yCoordinate);
48   }
49 }
```

move message

The program displays a moving message, as shown in Figure 12.16. MovingMessagePanel implements ActionListener (Line 27) so that it can listen for ActionEvent. Line 12 creates a Timer for a MovingMessagePanel. The timer is started in Line 13. The timer fires an ActionEvent, every second, and the listener responds in Line 38 to repaint the panel. When a panel is painted, its *x* coordinate is increased (Line 46), so the message is displayed to the right.

In Section 11.12, "Case Study: The StillClock Class", you drew a StillClock to show the current time. The clock does not tick after it is displayed. What can you do to make the clock display a new current time every second? The key to making the clock tick is to repaint it every second with a new current time. You can use a timer to control the repainting of the clock with the code in listing 12.8.

LISTING 12.8   ClockAnimation.java (Animating a Clock)

```
 1 import java.awt.*;
 2 import java.awt.event.*;
 3 import javax.swing.*;
 4
 5 public class ClockAnimation extends StillClock
 6     implements ActionListener {
 7   // Create a timer with delay 1000 ms
 8   protected Timer timer = new Timer(1000, this);
 9
10   public ClockAnimation() {
11     timer.start();
12   }
13
14   /** Handle the action event */
15   public void actionPerformed(ActionEvent e) {
16     // Set new time and repaint the clock to display current time
17     setCurrentTime();
18     repaint();
19   }
20
21   /** Main method */
22   public static void main(String[] args) {
23     JFrame frame = new JFrame("ClockAnimation");
24     ClockAnimation clock = new ClockAnimation();
25     frame.getContentPane().add(clock);
26     frame.setDefaultCloseOperation(JFrame.EXIT_ON_CLOSE);
27     frame.setSize(200, 200);
28     frame.setVisible(true);
29   }
30 }
```

create timer

set new time

repaint
start timer

Figure 12.17   *A clock is displayed in the panel.*

The program displays a running clock, as shown in Figure 12.17. ClockAnimation extends StillClock and implements ActionListener (Line 6) so that it can listen for ActionEvent. Line 8 creates a Timer for a ClockAnimation. The timer is started in Line 11 when a ClockAnimation is constructed. The timer fires an ActionEvent every second, and the listener responds in Line 15 to set a new time and repaint the clock. The setCurrentTime() method defined in StillClock sets the current time in the clock.

KEY TERMS

event   420
event delegation   421
event-driven programming   420
event handler   421
event listener   421

event listener interface   421
event object   420
event registration   421
event source (source object)   420

KEY CLASSES AND METHODS

◆ **java.util.EventObject**   is the root class for all event classes. The getSource() method returns the source object for the event.

◆ **java.awt.ActionEvent**   is the action event class. The getActionCommand() method returns the action command for the event, and getWhen() returns the timestamp for the event.

◆ **java.awt.ActionListener**   is the action event listener interface that contains the actionPerformed(ActionEvent) handler.

◆ **java.awt.InputEvent**   is the base class for MouseEvent and KeyEvent. The key methods are getWhen(), isAltDown(), isControlDown(), isMetaDown(), and isShiftDown().

◆ **java.awt.MouseEvent**   is the mouse event class. The getButton() method indicates which button has been clicked, getClickCount() returns the click count, getX() returns the x-coordinate of the mouse, and getY() returns the y-coordinate of the mouse.

◆ **java.awt.MouseListener**   is the mouse event listener interface that contains the mousePressed(MouseEvent), mouseReleased(MouseEvent), mouseClicked(MouseEvent), mouseEntered(MouseEvent), and mouseExited(MouseEvent) handlers.

✦ **java.awt.MouseMotionListener** is the mouse motion event listener interface that contains the mouseMoved(MouseEvent) and mouseDragged(MouseEvent) handlers.

✦ **java.awt.KeyEvent** is the mouse event class. The getKeyChar() method returns the character, and getKeyCode() returns the code for the character.

✦ **java.awt.KeyListener** is the key event listener interface that contains the keyPressed (KeyEvent), keyReleased(KeyEvent), and keyTyped(KeyEvent) handlers.

✦ **javax.swing.Timer** sets a timer that fires one or more action events after a specified delay.

CHAPTER SUMMARY

✦ The root class of the event classes is java.util.EventObject. The subclasses of EventObject deal with special types of events, such as button actions, window events, component events, mouse movements, and keystrokes. You can identify the source object of an event using the getSource() instance method in the EventObject class. If a component can generate an event, any subclass of the component can generate the same type of event.

✦ The listener object's class must implement the corresponding event-listener interface. Java provides a listener interface for every type of GUI event. The listener interface is usually named XListener for XEvent, with the exception of MouseMotionListener. For example, the corresponding listener interface for ActionEvent is ActionListener; each listener for ActionEvent should implement the ActionListener interface. The listener interface contains the method(s), known as the *handler(s)*, which process the events.

✦ The listener object must be registered by the source object. Registration methods are dependent on the event type. For ActionEvent, the method is addActionListener. In general, the method is named addXListener for XEvent.

✦ A source object may fire several types of events. For each event, the source object maintains a list of listeners and notifies all the registered listeners by invoking the *handler* on the listener object to respond to the event.

✦ A mouse event is generated whenever a mouse is clicked, released, moved, or dragged on a component. The mouse event object captures the event, such as the number of clicks associated with it or the location (x-and y-coordinates) of the mouse.

✦ Java provides two listener interfaces, MouseListener and MouseMotionListener, to handle mouse events, implement the MouseListener interface to listen for such actions as pressing, releasing, entering, exiting, or clicking the mouse, and implement the MouseMotionListener interface to listen for such actions as dragging or moving the mouse.

✦ The Point class is often used for handling mouse events. The Point class encapsulates a point on a plane. The class contains two instance variables, x and y, for coordinates.

✦ The keyboard event object describes the nature of the event (namely, that a key has been pressed, released, or typed) and the value of the key.

✦ The keyPressed handler is invoked when a key is pressed, the keyReleased handler is invoked when a key is released, and the keyTyped handler is invoked when a Unicode character is entered. If a key does not have a Unicode (e.g., function keys, modifier keys, action keys, and control keys), the keyTyped handler will not be involved.

✦ Java defines many constants for keys, including function keys in the KeyEvent class. For example, the number keys from 0 to 9 are VK_0 to VK_9. The letter keys from A to Z are VK_A to VK_Z, and the up-arrow key is VK_UP.

✦ You can use the Timer class to control Java animations. The timer fires an ActionEvent at a fixed rate. The listener updates the painting to simulate an animation.

REVIEW QUESTIONS

Sections 12.2–12.3

12.1 Can a button generate a WindowEvent? Can a button generate a MouseEvent? Can a button generate an ActionEvent?

12.2 Explain how to register a listener object and how to implement a listener interface.

12.3 What information is contained in an AWTEvent object and the objects of its subclasses? Find the variables, constants, and methods defined in these event classes.

12.4 How do you override a method defined in the listener interface? Do you need to override all the methods defined in the listener interface?

12.5 What is wrong in the following code?

```
1  import java.awt.*;
2  import java.swing.*;
3
4  public class Test extends JFrame implements ActionListener {
5    public Test() {
6      JButton jbtOK = new JButton("OK");
7      getContentPane().add(jbtOK);
8    }
9
10   public void actionPerform(ActionEvent e) {
11     if (e.getSource() == jbtOK)
12       System.out.println("OK button is clicked");
13   }
14 }
```

Sections 12.4–12.5

12.6 What is the event type for a mouse movement? What is the event type for getting key input?

12.7 What is the listener interface for mouse pressed, released, clicked, entered, and exited? What is the listener interface for mouse moved and dragged?

12.8 What method is used to process a key event?

12.9 What methods are used in responding to a mouse-motion event?

12.10 How do you use the Timer class to control Java animations?

PROGRAMMING EXERCISES

Sections 12.2–12.3

12.1   (*Displaying which button is clicked on the console*) Add the code to Exercise 11.1 that will display a message on the console indicating which button has been clicked.

12.2   (*Multiple listeners*) Rewrite Example 12.3 "Multiple Listeners for a Single Source," as follows:

◆ Create a method in `TestMultipleListener`:

```
public void processButtons(ActionEvent e) {
  if (e.getSource() == jbtOk) {
    System.out.println("The OK button is clicked");
  }
  else if (e.getSource() == jbtCancel) {
    System.out.println("The Cancel button is clicked");
  }
}
```

◆ Invoke `processButtons(e)` from the `actionPerformed(e)` method in `TestMultipleListener`.

◆ Modify `SecondListener` to invoke `processButtons(e)` defined in `TestMultipleListener` from the `actionPerformed` method in `SecondListener`. For the action `Performed` method in the `SecondListener` class to invoke the `processButtons(e)` method in the `TestMultipleListener` class, you may pass a reference of a `TestMultipleListener` object to `SecondListener` through the constructor of `SecondListener`.

12.3*   (*Displaying which button is clicked on a message panel*) Write a program that creates a user interface with two buttons named OK and Cancel and a message panel for displaying a message. When you click the OK button, a message "OK button is clicked" is displayed. When you click the Cancel button, a message "Cancel button is clicked" is displayed, as shown in Figure 12.18(a).

(a)   (b)

FIGURE 12.18   *(a) Exercise 12.3 displays which button is clicked on a message panel. (b) Exercise 12.4 displays the mouse position.*

Section 12.4

12.4*   (*Displaying the mouse position*) Write a program that displays the mouse position when the mouse is pressed (see Figure 12.18(b)).

12.5*   (*Setting background color using a mouse*) Write a program that displays the background color of a panel as black when the mouse is pressed and as white when the mouse is released. You need to create a custom panel class that implements `MouseListener`.

Section 12.5

12.6*   (*Using* KeyboardEvent) Write a program to get character input from the keyboard and put the characters where the mouse points.

12.7*   (*Drawing lines using the arrow keys*) Write a program that draws line segments using the arrow keys. The line starts from the center of the frame and draws toward east, north, west, or south when the right-arrow key, up-arrow key, left-arrow key, or down-arrow key is clicked, as shown in Figure 12.19.

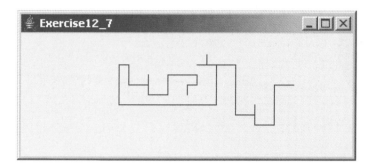

FIGURE 12.19   *You use the arrow keys to draw the lines.*

Section 12.6

12.8*   (*Displaying a flashing label*) Write a program that displays a flashing label. Enable it to run standalone.

 HINT

To make the label flash, you need to repaint the panel alternately with the label and without the label (blank screen) at a fixed rate. Use a boolean variable to control the alternation.

12.9*   (*Controlling a moving label*) Modify Listing 12.7 to control a moving label using the mouse. The label freezes when the mouse is pressed, and moves again when the button is released.

12.10**   (*Displaying a running fan*) Listing 11.11 on page 394 displays a motionless fan. Write a program that displays a running fan.

chapter

13

CREATING USER INTERFACES

Objectives

✦ To create graphical user interfaces with various user-interface
   components: JButton, JCheckBox, JRadioButton, JLabel,
   JTextField, JTextArea, JComboBox, JList, JScrollBar, and
   JSlider (§§13.2–13.12).

✦ To create listeners for various types of events (§§13.2–13.12).

✦ To use borders to visually group user-interface components
   (§13.2).

✦ To create image icons using the ImageIcon class (§13.3).

✦ To display multiple windows in an application (§13.13).

13.1   Introduction

A *graphical user interface* (GUI) makes a system user-friendly and easy to use. Creating a GUI requires creativity and knowledge of how GUI components work. Since the GUI components in
Java are very flexible and versatile, you can create a wide assortment of useful user interfaces.

GUI

Many Java IDEs provide tools for visually designing and programming Java classes. This enables you to rapidly assemble the elements of a user interface (UI) for a Java application or applet
with minimum coding. Tools, however, cannot do everything. You have to modify the programs
they produce. Consequently, before you begin to use the visual tools, it is imperative that you understand the basic concepts of Java GUI programming.

This chapter introduces the frequently used GUI components highlighted in Figure 13.1.

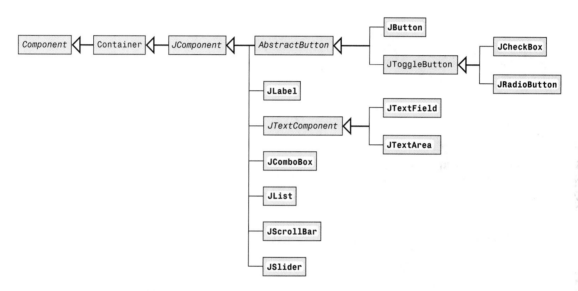

FIGURE 13.1   *The highlighted Swing GUI components are frequently used to create user interfaces.*

13.2   Common Features of Swing GUI Components

Once you understand the basics of Java GUI programming, such as containers, layout managers,
and event handling, you will be able to learn new components and explore their properties. The
`Component` class is the root for all UI components and containers. All but a few Swing components, such as `JFrame`, `JApplet`, and `JDialog`, are subclasses of `JComponent`. Figure 13.2 lists some
frequently used methods in `Component`, `Container`, and `JComponent` for manipulating properties
like font, color, size, tool tip text, and border.

Component
Container
JComponent

You can set a border on any object of the `JComponent` class. Swing has several types of borders.
To create a titled border, use new `TitleBorder(String title)`. To create a line border, use new
`LineBorder(Color color, int width)`, where `width` specifies the thickness of the line. For example, Listing 13.1 displays a titled border on a message panel, as shown in Figure 13.3:

LISTING 13.1   TestSwingCommonFeatures.java (Swing Common Features)

```
1 import java.awt.*;
2 import javax.swing.*;
3 import javax.swing.border.*;
4
5 public class TestSwingCommonFeatures {
6   public static void main(String[] args) {
```

```
            7    // Create a message panel and set its properties
            8    MessagePanel messagePanel = new MessagePanel();
            9    messagePanel.setFont(new Font("timesRoman", Font.BOLD, 20));
           10    messagePanel.setBackground(Color.white);
           11    messagePanel.setForeground(Color.red);
           12    messagePanel.setBorder(new TitledBorder("Display Message"));
           13    messagePanel.setCentered(true);
           14
           15    // Create a frame and set its properties
           16    JFrame frame = new JFrame("TestSwingCommonFeatures");
           17    frame.getContentPane().add(messagePanel);
           18    frame.setSize(300, 200);
           19    frame.setDefaultCloseOperation(JFrame.EXIT_ON_CLOSE);
           20    frame.setVisible(true);
           21
           22    // Set message panel width and height as its tool tip text
           23    messagePanel.setToolTipText("Width " +
           24      messagePanel.getWidth() + " and height " +
           25      messagePanel.getHeight());
           26  }
           27 }
```

message panel
set properties

frame
add panel

---

java.awt.Component

+getFont(): java.awt.Font	Returns the font of this component.
+setFont(f: java.awt.Font): void	Sets the font of this component.
+getBackground(): java.awt.Color	Returns the background color of this component.
+setBackground(c: Color): void	Sets the background color of this component.
+getForeground(): java.awt.Color	Returns the foreground color of this component.
+setForeground(c: Color): void	Sets the foreground color of this component.
+getWidth(): int	Returns the width of this component.
+getHeight(): int	Returns the height of this component.
+getPreferredSize(): Dimension	Returns the preferred size of this component.
+setPreferredSize(d: Dimension): void	Sets the preferred size of this component.
+isVisible(): boolean	Indicates whether this component is visible.
+setVisible(b: boolean): void	Shows or hides this component.

java.awt.Container

+add(comp: Component): Component	Adds a component to the container.
+add(comp: Component, index: int): Component	Adds a component to the container with the specified index.
+remove(comp: Component): void	Removes the component from the container.
+getLayout(): LayoutManager	Returns the layout manager for this container.
+setLayout(l: LayoutManager): void	Sets the layout manager for this container.
+paintComponents(g: Graphics): void	Paints each of the components in this container.

javax.swing.JComponent

+getToolTipText(): String	Returns the tool tip text for this component. Tool tip text is displayed when the mouse points on the component without clicking.
+setToolTipText(text: String): void	Sets a new tool tip text for this component.
+getBorder(): javax.swing.border.Border	Returns the border for this component.
+setBorder(border: Border): void	Sets a new border for this component.

FIGURE 13.2 *All the Swing GUI components inherit the public methods from* Component, Container, *and* JComponent.

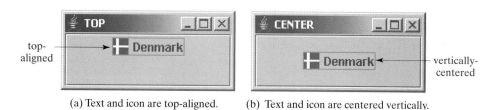

top-
aligned

(a) Text and icon are top-aligned.

vertically-
centered

(b) Text and icon are centered vertically.

bottom-aligned

(c) Text and icon are bottom-aligned.

FIGURE 13.8 *You can specify how the icon and text are placed on a button vertically.*

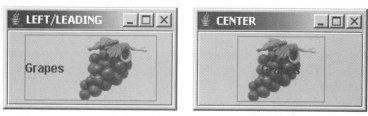

(a) Text is on the left of the icon.

(b) Text is centered on the icon.

(c) Text is on the right of the icon.

FIGURE 13.9 *You can specify the horizontal position of the text relative to the icon.*

TOP, CENTER, BOTTOM, as shown in Figure 13.10. The default vertical text position is SwingConstants.CENTER.

 NOTE

The constants LEFT, CENTER, RIGHT, LEADING, TRAILING, TOP, BOTTOM used in AbstractButton are also used in many other Swing components. These constants are centrally defined in the javax.swing.SwingConstants interface. Since all Swing GUI components implement SwingConstants, you can reference the constants through SwingConstants or a GUI component. For example, SwingConstants.CENTER is the same as JButton.CENTER.

JButton can generate many types of events, but often you need to respond to an ActionEvent. When a button is pressed, it generates an ActionEvent.

(a) Text appears top relative to the icon.   (b) Text appears centered relative to the icon.

(c) Text appears bottom relative to the icon.

FIGURE 13.10 *You can specify the vertical position of the text relative to the icon.*

EXAMPLE 13.1 USING BUTTONS

Problem

Write a program that displays a message on a panel and uses two buttons, $<=$ and $=>$, to move the message on the panel to the left or right. The layout of the UI and the output of the program are shown in Figure 13.11.

FIGURE 13.11 *Clicking the $<=$ and $=>$ buttons causes the message on the panel to move to the left and right, respectively.*

Solution

Here are the major steps in the program:

1. Create the user interface.
   Create a MessagePanel object to display the message. The MessagePanel class was created in Listing 11.15. Place it in the center of the frame. Create two buttons, $<=$ and $=>$, on a panel. Place the panel in the south of the frame.

EXAMPLE 13.1 (CONTINUED)

2. Process the event.

Implement the actionPerformed handler to move the message left or right according to whether the left or right button was clicked.

LISTING 13.3   ButtonDemo.java (Using Buttons)

```java
1 import java.awt.*;
2 import java.awt.event.ActionListener;
3 import java.awt.event.ActionEvent;
4 import javax.swing.*;
5
6 public class ButtonDemo extends JFrame implements ActionListener {
7   // Create a panel for displaying message
8   protected MessagePanel messagePanel
9     = new MessagePanel("Welcome to Java");
10
11   // Declare two buttons to move the message left and right
12   private JButton jbtLeft = new JButton("Left");
13   private JButton jbtRight = new JButton("Right");
14
15   public static void main(String[] args) {
16     ButtonDemo frame = new ButtonDemo();
17     frame.setTitle("ButtonDemo");
18     frame.setDefaultCloseOperation(JFrame.EXIT_ON_CLOSE);
19     frame.setSize(500, 200);
20     frame.setVisible(true);
21   }
22
23   public ButtonDemo() {
24     // Set the background color of messagePanel
25     messagePanel.setBackground(Color.yellow);
26
27     // Create Panel jpButtons to hold two Buttons "<=" and "right =>"
28     JPanel jpButtons = new JPanel();
29     jpButtons.setLayout(new FlowLayout());
30     jpButtons.add(jbtLeft);
31     jpButtons.add(jbtRight);
32
33     // Set keyboard mnemonics
34     jbtLeft.setMnemonic('L');
35     jbtRight.setMnemonic('R');
36
37     // Set icons and remove text
38 //      jbtLeft.setIcon(new ImageIcon("image/left.gif"));
39 //      jbtRight.setIcon(new ImageIcon("image/right.gif"));
40 //      jbtLeft.setText(null);
41 //      jbtRight.setText(null);
42
43     // Set tool tip text on the buttons
44     jbtLeft.setToolTipText("Move message to left");
45     jbtRight.setToolTipText("Move message to right");
46
47     // Place panels in the frame
48     getContentPane().setLayout(new BorderLayout());
49     getContentPane().add(messagePanel, BorderLayout.CENTER);
50     getContentPane().add(jpButtons, BorderLayout.SOUTH);
51
52     // Register listeners with the buttons
53     jbtLeft.addActionListener(this);
54     jbtRight.addActionListener(this);
55   }
```

create frame

create UI

mnemonic

tool tip

register listener

handler

Example 13.1 (Continued)

```
56
57  /** Handle ActionEvent */
58  public void actionPerformed(ActionEvent e) {
59    if (e.getSource() == jbtLeft) {
60      messagePanel.moveLeft();
61    }
62    else if (e.getSource() == jbtRight) {
63      messagePanel.moveRight();
64    }
65  }
66 }
```

Review

messagePanel (Line 8) is deliberately declared protected so that it can be referenced by a subclass in future examples.

You can set an icon image on the button by using the setIcon method. If you uncomment the following code in Lines 38–41:

```
//   jbtLeft.setIcon(new ImageIcon("image/left.gif"));
//   jbtRight.setIcon(new ImageIcon("image/right.gif"));
//   jbtLeft.setText(null);
//   jbtRight.setText(null);
```

the texts are replaced by the icons, as shown in Figure 13.12(a) . "image/left.gif" is located in "c:\book\image\left.gif."

(a)   (b)

Figure 13.12 *(a) You can set an icon on a JButton. (b) You can set a text and icon on a button at the same time.*

file path character

 Note

The back slash (\) is the Windows file path notation. On Unix, the forward slash (/) should be used. In Java, you should use the forward slash (/) to denote a relative file path under the Java classpath (e.g., image/left.gif, as in this example).

You can set text and an icon on a button at the same time, if you wish, as shown in Figure 13.12(b) . By default, the text and icon are centered horizontally and vertically.

Each button has a tool-tip text (Lines 44–45), which appears when the mouse is set on the button without clicking, as shown in Figure 13.13(a) .

The button can also be accessed by using the keyboard mnemonics. Pressing ALT+L is equivalent to clicking the <= button, since you set the mnemonic property to 'L' in the left button (Line 34). If you change the left button text to "Left" and the right button to "Right", the L and R in the captions of these buttons will be underlined, as shown in Figure 13.13(b) .

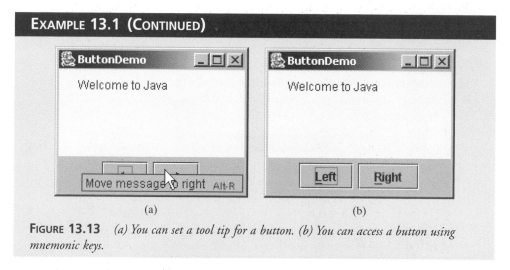

FIGURE 13.13 *(a) You can set a tool tip for a button. (b) You can access a button using mnemonic keys.*

13.4 Check Boxes

A *toggle button* is a two-state button like a light switch. JToggleButton inherits AbstractButton and implements a toggle button. Often JToggleButton's subclasses JCheckBox and JRadioButton are used to enable the user to toggle a choice on or off. This section introduces JCheckBox. JRadioButton will be introduced in the next section.

toggle button

JCheckBox inherits all the properties, such as text, icon, mnemonic, verticalAlignment, horizontalAlignment, horizontalTextPosition, verticalTextPosition, and selected, from AbstractButton, and provides several constructors to create check boxes, as shown in Figure 13.14.

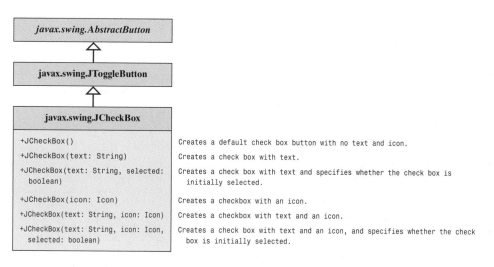

FIGURE 13.14 *JCheckBox defines a check box button.*

Here is an example of a check box with text "Student", red foreground, white background, mnemonic key 'S', and initially selected:

```
JCheckBox jchk = new JCheckBox("Student", true);
jchk.setForeground(Color.red);
jchk.setBackground(Color.white);
jchk.setMnemonic('S');
```

When a check box is clicked (checked or unchecked), it fires an ItemEvent and then an ActionEvent. To see if a check box is selected, use the isSelected() method.

EXAMPLE 13.2 USING CHECK BOXES

Problem

Add three check boxes named *Centered*, *Bold*, and *Italic* into the preceding example to let the user specify whether the message is centered, bold, or italic, as shown in Figure 13.15.

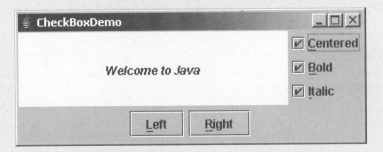

FIGURE 13.15 *Three check boxes are added to specify how the message is displayed.*

Solution

There are at least two approaches to writing this program. The first is to revise the preceding ButtonDemo class to insert the code for adding the check boxes and processing their events. The second is to create a subclass that extends ButtonDemo. Please implement the first approach as an exercise. Below is the code to implement the second approach.

LISTING 13.4 CheckBoxDemo.java (Using Check Boxes)

```
 1 import java.awt.*;
 2 import java.awt.event.ActionEvent;
 3 import javax.swing.*;
 4
 5 public class CheckBoxDemo extends ButtonDemo {
 6   // Create three check boxes to control the display of message
 7   private JCheckBox jchkCentered = new JCheckBox("Centered");
 8   private JCheckBox jchkBold = new JCheckBox("Bold");
 9   private JCheckBox jchkItalic = new JCheckBox("Italic");
10
11   public static void main(String[] args) {
12     CheckBoxDemo frame = new CheckBoxDemo();
13     frame.setTitle("CheckBoxDemo");
14     frame.setDefaultCloseOperation(JFrame.EXIT_ON_CLOSE);
15     frame.setSize(500, 200);
16     frame.setVisible(true);
17   }
18
19   public CheckBoxDemo() {
20     // Set mnemonic keys
21     jchkCentered.setMnemonic('C');
22     jchkBold.setMnemonic('B');
23     jchkItalic.setMnemonic('I');
24
25     // Create a new panel to hold check boxes
26     JPanel jpCheckBoxes = new JPanel();
27     jpCheckBoxes.setLayout(new GridLayout(3, 0));
28     jpCheckBoxes.add(jchkCentered);
29     jpCheckBoxes.add(jchkBold);
30     jpCheckBoxes.add(jchkItalic);
31     getContentPane().add(jpCheckBoxes, BorderLayout.EAST);
32
33     // Register listeners with the check boxes
34     jchkCentered.addActionListener(this);
```

create frame

create UI

register listener

EXAMPLE 13.2 (CONTINUED)

```
35    jchkBold.addActionListener(this);
36    jchkItalic.addActionListener(this);
37  }
38
39  /** Handle ActionEvent */
40  public void actionPerformed(ActionEvent e) {                          handler
41    super.actionPerformed(e); // Invoke the handler for buttons
42
43    if (e.getSource() == jchkCentered) {
44      messagePanel.setCentered(jchkCentered.isSelected());
45    }
46    else if ((e.getSource() == jchkBold) ||
47      (e.getSource() == jchkItalic)) {
48      // Determine a font style
49      int fontStyle = Font.PLAIN;
50      fontStyle += (jchkBold.isSelected() ? Font.BOLD : 0);
51      fontStyle += (jchkItalic.isSelected() ? Font.ITALIC : 0);
52
53      // Set font for the message
54      Font font = messagePanel.getFont();
55      messagePanel.setFont(
56        new Font(font.getName(), fontStyle, font.getSize()));
57    }
58  }
59 }
```

Review

CheckBoxDemo extends ButtonDemo and adds three check boxes to control how the message is displayed. When a CheckBoxDemo is constructed (Line 12), its superclass's no-arg constructor is invoked, so you don't have to rewrite the code that is already in the constructor of ButtonDemo.

Since ButtonDemo implements ActionListener, an instance of CheckBoxDemo can also be a listener for ActionEvent, which is registered with the check boxes in Lines 34–36. An ActionEvent may be fired from a button or a check box. super.actionPerformed(e) (Line 41) invokes the actionPerformed method defined in ButtonDemo class to process ActionEvent fired from the Left or the Right button.

When a check box is checked or unchecked, the actionPerformed method is invoked to process the event. When the Centered check box is checked or unchecked, the centered property of the MessagePanel class is set to true or false.

The current font name and size used in MessagePanel are obtained from messagePanel.getFont() using the getName() and getSize() methods. The font styles (Font.BOLD and Font.ITALIC) are specified in the check boxes. If no font style is selected, the font style is Font.PLAIN. Font styles are combined by adding together the selected integers representing the fonts.

The keyboard mnemonics 'C', 'B', and 'I' are set on the check boxes "Centered", "Bold", and "Italic", respectively (Lines 21–23). You can use a mouse gesture or a shortcut key to select a check box.

The setFont method (Line 55) defined in the Component class is inherited in the MessagePanel class. This method automatically invokes the repaint method. Invoking setFont in messagePanel automatically repaints the message.

A check box fires an ActionEvent or an ItemEvent when it is clicked. You could process either the ActionEvent or the ItemEvent to redisplay the message. The example processes the ActionEvent. If you wish to process the ItemEvent, you could create a listener for ItemEvent and register it with a check box, as shown below:

```
public class CheckBoxDemoUsingItemEvent extends ButtonDemo
    implements ItemListener {
      ... // Same as in CheckBoxDemo.java, so omitted
```

EXAMPLE 13.2 (CONTINUED)

```
public CheckBoxDemoUsingItemEvent() {
    ... // Same as in CheckBoxDemo.java, so omitted

    // TO listen for ItemEvent
    jchkCentered.addItemListener(this);
    jchkBold.addItemListener(this);
    jchkItalic.addItemListener(this);
}

/** Handle ItemEvent */
public void itemStateChanged(ItemEvent e) {
    ... // Same as Lines 46-60 in CheckBoxDemo.java, so omitted
}
}
```

13.5 Radio Buttons

Radio buttons, also known as *option buttons*, enable you to choose a single item from a group of choices. In appearance radio buttons resemble check boxes, but check boxes display a square that is either checked or blank, whereas radio buttons display a circle that is either filled (if selected) or blank (if not selected).

JRadioButton inherits AbstractButton, and provides several constructors to create radio buttons, as shown in Figure 13.16. These constructors are similar to the constructors for JCheckBox.

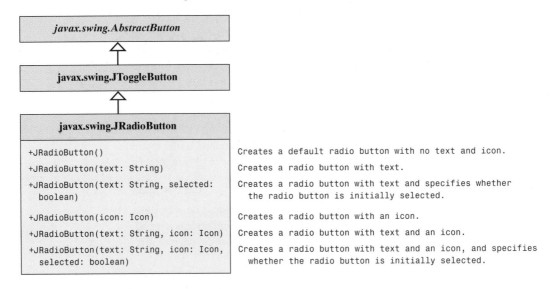

FIGURE 13.16 *JRadioButton defines a radio button.*

Here is an example of a radio button with text "Student", red foreground, white background, mnemonic key 'S', and initially selected:

```
JRadioButton jrb = new JRadioButton("Student", true);
jrb.setForeground(Color.red);
jrb.setBackground(Color.white);
jrb.setMnemonic('S');
```

To group radio buttons, you need to create an instance of java.swing.ButtonGroup and use the add method to add them to it, as follows:

```
ButtonGroup group = new ButtonGroup();
group.add(jrb1);
group.add(jrb2);
```

This code creates a radio button group for radio buttons jrb1 and jrb2 so that jrb1 and jrb2 are selected mutually exclusively. Without grouping, jrb1 and jrb2 would be independent.

 NOTE

ButtonGroup is not a subclass of java.awt.Component, so a ButtonGroup object cannot be added to a container.

When a radio button is clicked (selected or deselected), it fires an ItemEvent and then an ActionEvent. To see if a radio button is selected, use the isSelected() method.

EXAMPLE **13.3** USING RADIO BUTTONS

Problem

Add three radio buttons named *Red*, *Green*, and *Blue* into the preceding example to let the user choose the color of the message, as shown in Figure 13.17.

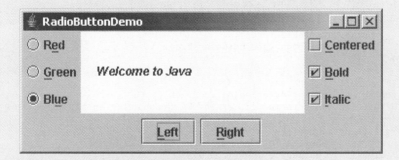

FIGURE **13.17** *Three radio buttons are added to specify the color of the message.*

Solution

Again there are at least two approaches to writing this program. The first is to revise the preceding CheckBoxDemo class to insert the code for adding the radio buttons and processing their events. The second is to create a subclass that extends CheckBoxDemo. Below is the code to implement the second approach.

LISTING **13.5** RadioButtonDemo.java (Using Radio Buttons)

```
 1 import java.awt.*;
 2 import java.awt.event.*;
 3 import javax.swing.*;
 4
 5 public class RadioButtonDemo extends CheckBoxDemo {
 6   // Declare radio buttons
 7   private JRadioButton jrbRed, jrbGreen, jrbBlue;
 8
 9   public static void main(String[] args) {
10     RadioButtonDemo frame = new RadioButtonDemo();                    create frame
11     frame.setDefaultCloseOperation(JFrame.EXIT_ON_CLOSE);
12     frame.setTitle("RadioButtonDemo");
13     frame.setSize(500, 200);
14     frame.setVisible(true);
15   }
16
17   public RadioButtonDemo() {
18     // Create a new panel to hold check boxes                         create UI
```

EXAMPLE 13.3 (CONTINUED)

```
19      JPanel jpRadioButtons = new JPanel();
20      jpRadioButtons.setLayout(new GridLayout(3, 1));
21      jpRadioButtons.add(jrbRed = new JRadioButton("Red"));
22      jpRadioButtons.add(jrbGreen = new JRadioButton("Green"));
23      jpRadioButtons.add(jrbBlue = new JRadioButton("Blue"));
24      getContentPane().add(jpRadioButtons, BorderLayout.WEST);
25
26      // Create a radio button group to group three buttons
27      ButtonGroup group = new ButtonGroup();
28      group.add(jrbRed);
29      group.add(jrbGreen);
30      group.add(jrbBlue);
31
32      // Set keyboard mnemonics
33      jrbRed.setMnemonic('E');
34      jrbGreen.setMnemonic('G');
35      jrbBlue.setMnemonic('U');
36
37      // Register listeners for check boxes
38      jrbRed.addActionListener(this);
39      jrbGreen.addActionListener(this);
40      jrbBlue.addActionListener(this);
41
42      // Set initial message color to blue
43      jrbBlue.setSelected(true);
44      messagePanel.setForeground(Color.blue);
45    }
46
47    /** Handle ActionEvent */
48    public void actionPerformed(ActionEvent e) {
49      super.actionPerformed(e); // Invoke the handler in the superclass
50
51      if (e.getSource() == jrbRed)
52        messagePanel.setForeground(Color.red);
53      else if (e.getSource() == jrbGreen)
54        messagePanel.setForeground(Color.green);
55      else if (e.getSource() == jrbBlue)
56        messagePanel.setForeground(Color.blue);
57    }
58  }
```

group buttons (margin note, line 27)

handler (margin note, line 48)

Review

RadioButtonDemo extends CheckBoxDemo and adds three radio buttons to specify the message color. Since CheckBoxDemo extends ButtonDemo, and ButtonDemo implements ActionListener, an instance of RadioButtonDemo can also be a listener for ActionEvent, which is registered with the radio buttons in Lines 38–40.

When an ActionEvent occurs, the actionPerformed method is invoked to process the event. If it is fired from a button or a check box, it is processed by the actionPerformed method defined in the superclass of RadioButtonDemo (Line 49). When a radio button is clicked, the corresponding foreground color in messagePanel is set.

The keyboard mnemonics 'R' and 'B' are already set for the Right button and Bold check box. To avoid conflict, the keyboard mnemonics 'E', 'G', and 'U' are set on the radio buttons "Red", "Green", and "Blue", respectively (Lines 33–35).

The program creates a ButtonGroup group and puts three JRadioButton instances (jrbRed, jrbGreen, and jrbBlue) in the group (Lines 27–30).

A radio button fires an ActionEvent or an ItemEvent when it is selected or deselected. You could process either the ActionEvent or the ItemEvent to choose a color. The example processes the ActionEvent. Please rewrite the code using the ItemEvent as an exercise.

13.6 Labels

A *label* is a display area for a short text, an image, or both. It is often used to label other components (usually text fields). Figure 13.18 lists the constructors and methods in JLabel.

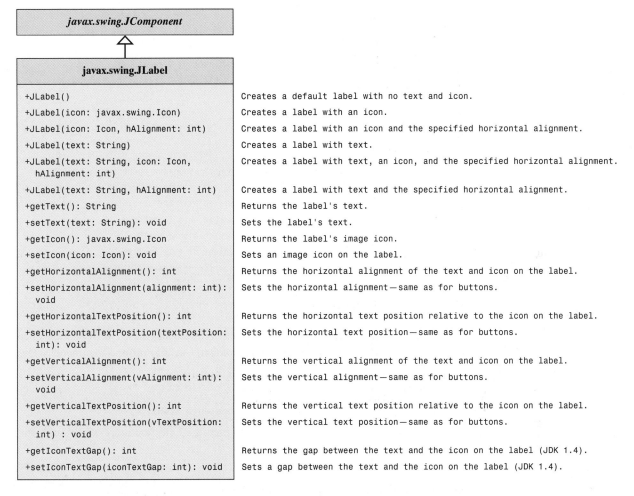

javax.swing.JComponent	
↑	

javax.swing.JLabel	
+JLabel()	Creates a default label with no text and icon.
+JLabel(icon: javax.swing.Icon)	Creates a label with an icon.
+JLabel(icon: Icon, hAlignment: int)	Creates a label with an icon and the specified horizontal alignment.
+JLabel(text: String)	Creates a label with text.
+JLabel(text: String, icon: Icon, hAlignment: int)	Creates a label with text, an icon, and the specified horizontal alignment.
+JLabel(text: String, hAlignment: int)	Creates a label with text and the specified horizontal alignment.
+getText(): String	Returns the label's text.
+setText(text: String): void	Sets the label's text.
+getIcon(): javax.swing.Icon	Returns the label's image icon.
+setIcon(icon: Icon): void	Sets an image icon on the label.
+getHorizontalAlignment(): int	Returns the horizontal alignment of the text and icon on the label.
+setHorizontalAlignment(alignment: int): void	Sets the horizontal alignment—same as for buttons.
+getHorizontalTextPosition(): int	Returns the horizontal text position relative to the icon on the label.
+setHorizontalTextPosition(textPosition: int): void	Sets the horizontal text position—same as for buttons.
+getVerticalAlignment(): int	Returns the vertical alignment of the text and icon on the label.
+setVerticalAlignment(vAlignment: int): void	Sets the vertical alignment—same as for buttons.
+getVerticalTextPosition(): int	Returns the vertical text position relative to the icon on the label.
+setVerticalTextPosition(vTextPosition: int) : void	Sets the vertical text position—same as for buttons.
+getIconTextGap(): int	Returns the gap between the text and the icon on the label (JDK 1.4).
+setIconTextGap(iconTextGap: int): void	Sets a gap between the text and the icon on the label (JDK 1.4).

FIGURE 13.18 *JLabel displays text or an icon, or both.*

JLabel inherits all the properties from JComponent and has many properties similar to the ones in JButton, such as text, icon, horizontalAlignment, verticalAlignment, horizontalTextPosition, verticalTextPosition, and iconTextGap. For example, the following code displays a label with text and an icon:

```
// Create an image icon from an image file
ImageIcon icon = new ImageIcon("image/grapes.gif");

// Create a label with text, an icon,
// with centered horizontal alignment
JLabel jlbl = new JLabel("Grapes", icon, SwingConstants.CENTER);

// Set label's text alignment and gap between text and icon
jlbl.setHorizontalTextPosition(SwingConstants.CENTER);
jlbl.setVerticalTextPosition(SwingConstants.BOTTOM);
jlbl.setIconTextGap(5);
```

13.7 Text Fields

A *text field* can be used to enter or display a string. JTextField is a subclass of JTextComponent. Figure 13.19 lists the constructors and methods in JTextField.

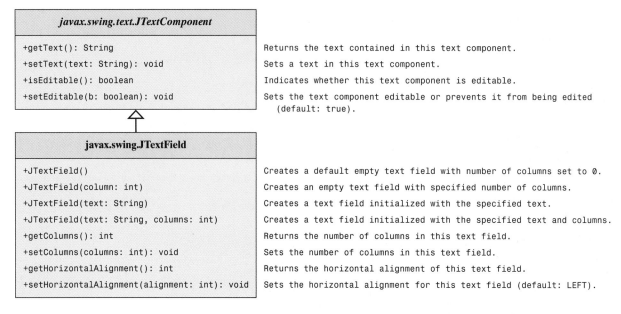

FIGURE 13.19 *JTextField enables you to enter or display a string.*

JTextField inherits JTextComponent, which inherits JComponent. Here is an example of creating a non-editable text field with red foreground color and right horizontal alignment:

```
JTextField jtfMessage = new JTextField("T-Strom");
jtfMessage.setEditable(false);
jtfMessage.setForeground(Color.red);
jtfMessage.setHorizontalAlignment(SwingConstants.RIGHT);
```

When you move the cursor in the text field and press the Enter key, it fires an ActionEvent.

EXAMPLE 13.4 USING TEXT FIELDS

Problem

Add a text field to the preceding example to let the user set a new message, as shown in Figure 13.20.

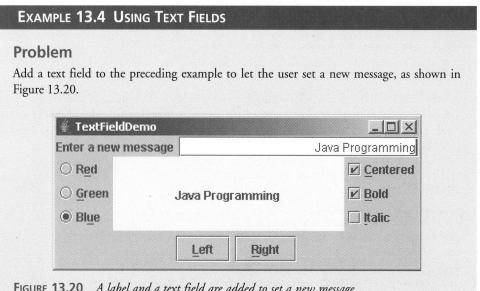

FIGURE 13.20 *A label and a text field are added to set a new message.*

EXAMPLE 13.4 (CONTINUED)

Solution

Listing 13.6 creates a subclass that extends `RadioButtonDemo`.

LISTING 13.6   TextFieldDemo.java (Using Text Fields)

```
 1 import java.awt.*;
 2 import java.awt.event.*;
 3 import javax.swing.*;
 4
 5 public class TextFieldDemo extends RadioButtonDemo {
 6   private JTextField jtfMessage = new JTextField(10);
 7
 8   /** Main method */
 9   public static void main(String[] args) {
10     TextFieldDemo frame = new TextFieldDemo();
11     frame.pack();
12     frame.setTitle("TextFieldDemo");
13     frame.setDefaultCloseOperation(JFrame.EXIT_ON_CLOSE);
14     frame.setVisible(true);
15   }
16
17   public TextFieldDemo() {
18     // Create a new panel to hold label and text field
19     JPanel jpTextField = new JPanel();
20     jpTextField.setLayout(new BorderLayout(5, 0));
21     jpTextField.add(
22       new JLabel("Enter a new message"), BorderLayout.WEST);
23     jpTextField.add(jtfMessage, BorderLayout.CENTER);
24     getContentPane().add(jpTextField, BorderLayout.NORTH);
25
26     jtfMessage.setHorizontalAlignment(JTextField.RIGHT);
27
28     // Register listener
29     jtfMessage.addActionListener(this);
30   }
31
32   /** Handle ActionEvent */
33   public void actionPerformed(ActionEvent e) {
34     super.actionPerformed(e);
35
36     if (e.getSource() == jtfMessage)
37       messagePanel.setMessage(jtfMessage.getText());
38
39     jtfMessage.requestFocusInWindow();
40   }
41 }
```

create frame (line 10)

create UI (line 17)

handler (line 33)

Review

`TextFieldDemo` extends `RadioButtonDemo` and adds a label and a text field to let the user enter a new message. Since `RadioButtonDemo` extends `CheckBoxDemo`, `CheckBoxDemo` extends `ButtonDemo`, and `ButtonDemo` implements `ActionListener`, an instance of `TextFieldDemo` can also be a listener for `ActionEvent`, which is registered with the radio buttons in Line 29, as shown in Figure 13.21.

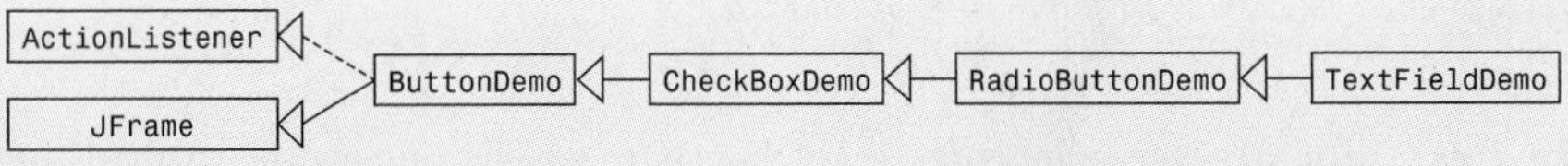

FIGURE 13.21   *TextFieldDemo builds upon* RadioButtonDemo, CheckBoxDemo, *and* ButtonDemo.

When an `ActionEvent` occurs, the `actionPerformed` method is invoked to process the event. If it is fired from a button, a check box, or a radio button, it is processed by

EXAMPLE 13.4 (CONTINUED)

the actionPerformed method defined in the superclass of TextFieldDemo (Line 34). After you set a new message in the text field and press the Enter key, a new message is set in messagePanel (Line 37).

Instead of using the setSize method to set the size for the frame, the program uses the pack() method (Line 11), which automatically sizes up the frame according to the size of the components placed in it.

The requestFocusInWindow() method (Line 39) defined in the Component class requests the component to receive input focus. Thus, jtfMessage.requestFocusInWindow() (Line 39) requests the input focus on jtfMessage. So you will see the cursor on jtfMessage after the actionPerformed method is invoked.

13.8   Text Areas

If you want to let the user enter multiple lines of text, you have to create several instances of JTextField. A better alternative is to use JTextArea, which enables the user to enter multiple lines of text. Figure 13.22 lists the constructors and methods in JTextArea.

javax.swing.text.JTextComponent	

↑

jayax.swing.JTextArea	
+JTextArea()	Creates a default empty text area.
+JTextArea(rows: int, columns: int)	Creates an empty text area with the specified number of rows and columns.
+JTextArea(text: String)	Creates a new text area with the specified text displayed.
+JTextArea(text: String, rows: int, columns: int)	Creates a new text area with the specified text and number of rows and columns.
+append(s: String): void	Appends the string to text in the text area.
+insert(s: String, pos: int): void	Inserts string s in the specified position in the text area.
+replaceRange(s: String, start: int, end: int): void	Replaces partial text in the range from position start to end with string s.
+getColumns(): int	Returns the number of columns in this text area.
+setColumns(columns: int): void	Sets the number of columns in this text area.
+getRows(): int	Returns the number of rows in this text area.
+setRows(rows: int): void	Sets the number of rows in this text area.
+getLineCount(): int	Returns the actual number of lines contained in the text area.
+getTabSize(): int	Returns the number of characters used to expand tabs in this text area.
+setTabSize(size: int): void	Sets the number of characters to expand tabs to (default: 8).
+getLineWrap(): boolean	Indicates whether the line in the text area is automatically wrapped.
+setLineWrap(wrap: boolean): void	Sets the line-wrapping policy of the text area (default: false).
+getWrapStyleWord(): boolean	Indicates whether the line is wrapped on words or characters.
+setWrapStyleWord(word: boolean): void	Sets the style of wrapping used if the text area is wrapping lines. The default value is false, which indicates that the line is wrapped on characters.

FIGURE 13.22 *JTextArea enables you to enter or display multiple lines of character.*

Like JTextField, JTextArea inherits JTextComponent, which contains the methods getText, setText, isEditable, and setEditable. Here is an example of creating a text area with five rows and twenty columns, line-wrapped on words, red foreground color, and courier font, bold, 20 pixels.

```
JTextArea jtaNote = new JTextArea("This is a text area", 5, 20);
jtaNote.setLineWrap(true);
jtaNote.setWrapStyleWord(true);
```

```
jtaNote.setForeground(Color.red);
jtaNote.setFont(new Font("Courier", Font.BOLD, 20));
```

JTextArea does not handle scrolling, but you can create a JScrollPane object to hold an instance of JTextArea and let JScrollPane handle scrolling for JTextArea, as follows:

```
// Create a scroll pane to hold text area
JScrollPane scrollPane = new JScrollPane(jta = new JTextArea());
getContentPane().add(scrollPane, BorderLayout.CENTER);
```

EXAMPLE 13.5 USING TEXT AREAS

Problem

Write a program that displays an image in a label, a title in a label, and a text in a text area. A sample run of the program is shown in Figure 13.23.

FIGURE 13.23   *The program displays an image in a label, a title in a label, and a text in the text area.*

Solution

Here are the major steps in the program:

1. Create a class named DescriptionPanel that extends JPanel. This class contains a text area inside a scroll pane, a label for displaying an image icon, and a label for displaying a title. This class is used in the present example and will be reused in later examples.

2. Create a class named TextAreaDemo that extends JFrame. Create an instance of DescriptionPanel and add it to the center of the frame. The relationship between DescriptionPanel and TextAreaDemo is shown in Figure 13.24.

LISTING 13.7   TextAreaDemo.java (Using Text Area)

```
 1 import java.awt.*;
 2 import javax.swing.*;
 3
 4 public class TextAreaDemo extends JFrame {
 5   // Declare and create a description panel
 6   private DescriptionPanel descriptionPanel = new DescriptionPanel();
 7
 8   public static void main(String[] args) {
 9     TextAreaDemo frame = new TextAreaDemo();
10     frame.pack();
11     frame.setDefaultCloseOperation(JFrame.EXIT_ON_CLOSE);
12     frame.setTitle("TextAreaDemo");
13     frame.setVisible(true);
14   }
```

create frame

EXAMPLE 13.5 (CONTINUED)

```
15
16    public TextAreaDemo() {
17      // Set title, text and image in the description panel
18      descriptionPanel.setTitle("Canada");
19      String description = "The Maple Leaf flag \n\n" +
20        "The Canadian National Flag was adopted by the Canadian " +
21        "Parliament on October 22, 1964 and was proclaimed into law " +
22        "by Her Majesty Queen Elizabeth II (the Queen of Canada) on " +
23        "February 15, 1965. The Canadian Flag (colloquially known " +
24        "as The Maple Leaf Flag) is a red flag of the proportions " +
25        "two by length and one by width, containing in its center a " +
26        "white square, with a single red stylized eleven-point " +
27        "mapleleaf centered in the white square.";
28      descriptionPanel.setDescription(description);
29      descriptionPanel.setImageIcon(new ImageIcon("image/ca.gif"));
30
31      // Add the description panel to the frame
32      getContentPane().setLayout(new BorderLayout());
33      getContentPane().add(descriptionPanel, BorderLayout.CENTER);
34    }
35  }
36
37  // Define a panel for displaying image and text
38  class DescriptionPanel extends JPanel {
39    /** Label for displaying an image icon */
40    private JLabel jlblImage = new JLabel();
41
42    /** Label for displaying a title */
43    private JLabel jlblTitle = new JLabel();
44
45    /** Text area for displaying text */
46    private JTextArea jtaDescription;
47
48    public DescriptionPanel() {
49      // Group image label and title label in a panel
50      JPanel panel = new JPanel();
51      panel.setLayout(new BorderLayout());
52      panel.add(jlblImage, BorderLayout.CENTER);
53      panel.add(jlblTitle, BorderLayout.SOUTH);
54
55      // Create a scroll pane to hold text area
56      JScrollPane scrollPane = new JScrollPane
57        (jtaDescription = new JTextArea());
58
59      // Center the title on the label
60      jlblTitle.setHorizontalAlignment(JLabel.CENTER);
61
62      // Set the font for the title and text
63      jlblTitle.setFont(new Font("SansSerif", Font.BOLD, 16));
64      jtaDescription.setFont(new Font("Serif", Font.PLAIN, 14));
65
66      // Set lineWrap and wrapStyleWord true for text area
67      jtaDescription.setLineWrap(true);
68      jtaDescription.setWrapStyleWord(true);
69      jtaDescription.setEditable(false);
70
71      // Set preferred size for the scroll pane
72      scrollPane.setPreferredSize(new Dimension(200, 100));
73
74      // Set BorderLayout for the whole panel, add panel and scrollpane
75      setLayout(new BorderLayout(5, 5));
76      add(scrollPane, BorderLayout.CENTER);
77      add(panel, BorderLayout.WEST);
78    }
79
```

create UI

create panel

scroll pane
text area

EXAMPLE 13.5 (CONTINUED)

```
80    /** Set the title */
81    public void setTitle(String title) {
82      jlblTitle.setText(title);
83    }
84
85    /** Set the image icon */
86    public void setImageIcon(ImageIcon icon) {
87      jlblImage.setIcon(icon);
88      Dimension dimension = new Dimension(icon.getIconWidth(),
89        icon.getIconHeight());
90      jlblImage.setPreferredSize(dimension);
91    }
92
93    /** Set the text description */
94    public void setDescription(String text) {
95      jtaDescription.setText(text);
96    }
97  }
```

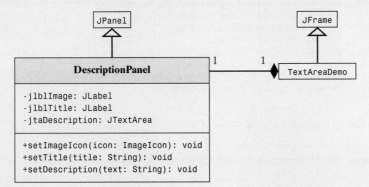

FIGURE **13.24**   *TextAreaDemo uses* DescriptionPanel *to display an image, title, and text description of a national flag.*

Review

TextAreaDemo simply creates an instance of DescriptionPanel (Line 6), and sets the title (Line 18), image (Line 29), and text in the description panel (Line 28). DescriptionPanel is a subclass of JPanel. DescriptionPanel contains a label for displaying the image icon, a label for displaying title, and a text area for displaying a description of the image.

It is not necessary to create a separate class for DescriptionPanel in this example. Nevertheless, this class was created for reuse in the next example, where you will use it to display a description panel for various images.

The text area is inside a JScrollPane, which provides scrolling functions for the text area. Scroll bars automatically appear if there is more text than the physical size of the text area, and disappear if the text is deleted and the remaining text does not exceed the text area size.

The lineWrap property is set to true (Line 67) so that the line is automatically wrapped when the text cannot fit in one line. The wrapStyleWord property is set to true (Line 68) so that the line is wrapped on words rather than characters.

The text area is set non-editable (Line 69), so you cannot edit the description in the text area.

The preferredSize property in jlblImage is set to the size of the image icon (Line 90). The getIconWidth() and getIconHeight() methods (Lines 88–89) obtain the width and height of the icon. The preferredSize property (Line 72) in scrollPane is set to 200 in width and 100 in height. The BorderLayout manager respects the preferred size of the components.

13.9   Combo Boxes

A *combo box*, also known as a *choice list* or *drop-down list*, contains a list of items from which the user can choose. It is useful in limiting a user's range of choices and avoids the cumbersome validation of data input. Figure 13.25 lists several frequently used constructors and methods in JComboBox.

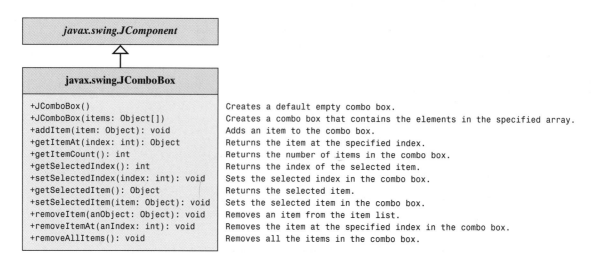

```
javax.swing.JComponent
```
```
javax.swing.JComboBox
```

+JComboBox()	Creates a default empty combo box.
+JComboBox(items: Object[])	Creates a combo box that contains the elements in the specified array.
+addItem(item: Object): void	Adds an item to the combo box.
+getItemAt(index: int): Object	Returns the item at the specified index.
+getItemCount(): int	Returns the number of items in the combo box.
+getSelectedIndex(): int	Returns the index of the selected item.
+setSelectedIndex(index: int): void	Sets the selected index in the combo box.
+getSelectedItem(): Object	Returns the selected item.
+setSelectedItem(item: Object): void	Sets the selected item in the combo box.
+removeItem(anObject: Object): void	Removes an item from the item list.
+removeItemAt(anIndex: int): void	Removes the item at the specified index in the combo box.
+removeAllItems(): void	Removes all the items in the combo box.

FIGURE 13.25   *JComboBox enables you to select an item from a set of items.*

The following statements create a combo box with four items, red foreground, white background, and the second item selected:

```
JComboBox jcb = new JComboBox(new Object[]
  {"Item 1", "Item 2", "Item 3", "Item 4"});
jcb.setForeground(Color.red);
jcb.setBackground(Color.white);
jcb.setSelectedItem("Item 2");
```

JComboBox can generate ActionEvent and ItemEvent, among many other events. Whenever a new item is selected, JComboBox generates ItemEvent twice, once for deselecting the previously selected item, and the other for selecting the currently selected item. JComboBox generates an ActionEvent after generating ItemEvent. To respond to an ItemEvent, you need to implement the itemStateChanged(ItemEvent e) handler for processing a choice. To get data from a JComboBox menu, you can use getSelectedItem() to return the currently selected item, or e.getItem() method to get the item from the itemStateChanged(ItemEvent e) handler.

EXAMPLE 13.6 USING COMBO BOXES

Problem

Write a program that lets users view an image and a description of a country's flag by selecting the country from a combo box. Figure 13.26 shows a sample run of the program.

Solution

Here are the major steps in the program:

1. Create the user interface.
   Create a combo box with country names as its selection values. Create a DescriptionPanel object. The DescriptionPanel class was introduced in the preceding

EXAMPLE **13.6** (CONTINUED)

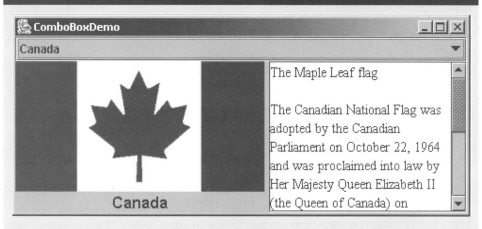

FIGURE **13.26** *A country's info, including a flag image and a description of the flag, is displayed when the country is selected in the combo box.*

example. Place the combo box in the north of the frame and the description panel in the center of the frame.

2. Process the event.
   Implement the `itemStateChanged` handler to set the flag title, image, and text in the description panel for the selected country name.

LISTING **13.8** ComboBoxDemo.java (Using Combo Boxes)

```
1  import java.awt.*;
2  import java.awt.event.*;
3  import javax.swing.*;
4
5  public class ComboBoxDemo extends JFrame implements ItemListener {
6    // Declare an array of Strings for flag titles
7    private String[] flagTitles = {"Canada", "China", "Denmark",
8      "France", "Germany", "India", "Norway", "United Kingdom",
9      "United States of America"};
10
11   // Declare an ImageIcon array for the national flags of 9 countries
12   private ImageIcon[] flagImage = {
13     new ImageIcon("image/ca.gif"),
14     new ImageIcon("image/china.gif"),
15     new ImageIcon("image/denmark.gif"),
16     new ImageIcon("image/fr.gif"),
17     new ImageIcon("image/germany.gif"),
18     new ImageIcon("image/india.gif"),
19     new ImageIcon("image/norway.gif"),
20     new ImageIcon("image/uk.gif"),
21     new ImageIcon("image/us.gif")
22   };
23
24   // Declare an array of strings for flag descriptions
25   private String[] flagDescription = new String[9];
26
27   // Declare and create a description panel
28   private DescriptionPanel descriptionPanel = new DescriptionPanel();
29
30   // Create a combo box for selecting countries
31   private JComboBox jcbo = new JComboBox(flagTitles);
32
33   public static void main(String[] args) {
34     ComboBoxDemo frame = new ComboBoxDemo();
35     frame.pack();
```

country

image icon

description

combo box

create frame

EXAMPLE 13.6 (CONTINUED)

create UI

```
36       frame.setTitle("ComboBoxDemo");
37       frame.setDefaultCloseOperation(JFrame.EXIT_ON_CLOSE);
38       frame.setVisible(true);
39     }
40
41     public ComboBoxDemo() {
42       // Set text description
43       flagDescription[0] = "The Maple Leaf flag \n\n" +
44         "The Canadian National Flag was adopted by the Canadian " +
45         "Parliament on October 22, 1964 and was proclaimed into law " +
46         "by Her Majesty Queen Elizabeth II (the Queen of Canada) on " +
47         "February 15, 1965. The Canadian Flag (colloquially known " +
48         "as The Maple Leaf Flag) is a red flag of the proportions " +
49         "two by length and one by width, containing in its center a " +
50         "white square, with a single red stylized eleven-point " +
51         "mapleleaf centered in the white square.";
52       flagDescription[1] = "Description for China ... ";
53       flagDescription[2] = "Description for Denmark ... ";
54       flagDescription[3] = "Description for France ... ";
55       flagDescription[4] = "Description for Germany ... ";
56       flagDescription[5] = "Description for India ... ";
57       flagDescription[6] = "Description for Norway ... ";
58       flagDescription[7] = "Description for UK ... ";
59       flagDescription[8] = "Description for US ... ";
60
61       // Set the first country (Canada) for display
62       setDisplay(0);
63
64       // Add combo box and description panel to the list
65       getContentPane().add(jcbo, BorderLayout.NORTH);
66       getContentPane().add(descriptionPanel, BorderLayout.CENTER);
67
68       // Register listener
69       jcbo.addItemListener(this);
70     }
71
72     /** Handle item selection */
73     public void itemStateChanged(ItemEvent e) {
74       setDisplay(jcbo.getSelectedIndex());
75     }
76
77     /** Set display information on the description panel */
78     public void setDisplay(int index) {
79       descriptionPanel.setTitle(flagTitles[index]);
80       descriptionPanel.setImageIcon(flagImage[index]);
81       descriptionPanel.setDescription(flagDescription[index]);
82     }
83   }
```

handler

Review

The frame listens to `ItemEvent` from the combo box and implements `ItemListener` (Lines 73–75). Instead of using `ItemEvent`, you may rewrite the program to use `ActionEvent` for handling combo box item selection.

The program stores the flag information in three arrays: `flagTitles`, `flagImage`, and `flagDescription` (Lines 7–25). The array `flagTitles` contains the names of nine countries, the array `flagImage` contains images of the nine countries' flags, and the array `flagDescription` contains descriptions of the flags.

The program creates an instance of `DescriptionPanel` (Line 28), which was presented in Example 13.5, "Using Text Areas." The program creates a combo box with initial values from `flagTitles` (Line 31). When the user selects an item in the combo box, the `ItemStateChanged` handler is executed, finds the selected index, and sets its corresponding flag title, flag image, and flag description on the panel.

13.10   Lists

A *list* is a component that basically performs the same function as a combo box but enables the user to choose a single value or multiple values. The Swing JList is very versatile. Figure 13.27 lists several frequently used constructors and methods in JList.

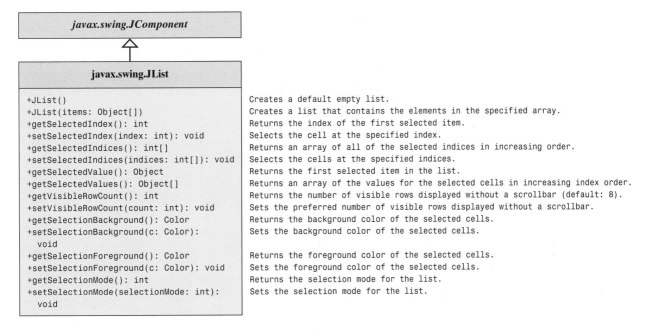

javax.swing.JComponent	

javax.swing.JList	
+JList()	Creates a default empty list.
+JList(items: Object[])	Creates a list that contains the elements in the specified array.
+getSelectedIndex(): int	Returns the index of the first selected item.
+setSelectedIndex(index: int): void	Selects the cell at the specified index.
+getSelectedIndices(): int[]	Returns an array of all of the selected indices in increasing order.
+setSelectedIndices(indices: int[]): void	Selects the cells at the specified indices.
+getSelectedValue(): Object	Returns the first selected item in the list.
+getSelectedValues(): Object[]	Returns an array of the values for the selected cells in increasing index order.
+getVisibleRowCount(): int	Returns the number of visible rows displayed without a scrollbar (default: 8).
+setVisibleRowCount(count: int): void	Sets the preferred number of visible rows displayed without a scrollbar.
+getSelectionBackground(): Color	Returns the background color of the selected cells.
+setSelectionBackground(c: Color): void	Sets the background color of the selected cells.
+getSelectionForeground(): Color	Returns the foreground color of the selected cells.
+setSelectionForeground(c: Color): void	Sets the foreground color of the selected cells.
+getSelectionMode(): int	Returns the selection mode for the list.
+setSelectionMode(selectionMode: int): void	Sets the selection mode for the list.

FIGURE 13.27   *JList enables you to select multiple items from a set of items.*

selectionMode is one of the three values (SINGLE_SELECTION, SINGLE_INTERVAL_SELECTION, MULTIPLE_INTERVAL_SELECTION) defined in javax.swing.SelectionModel that indicate whether a single item, single-interval item, or multiple-interval item can be selected. Single selection allows only one item to be selected. Single-interval selection allows multiple selections, but the selected items must be contiguous. Multiple-interval selection allows selections of multiple contiguous items without restrictions, as shown in Figure 13.28. The default value is MULTIPLE_INTERVAL_SELECTION.

(a) Single selection   (b) Single-interval selection   (c) Multiple-interval selection

FIGURE 13.28   *JList has three selection modes: single selection, single-interval selection, and multiple-interval selection.*

The following statements create a list with six items, red foreground, white background, pink selection foreground, black selection background, and visible row count 4:

```
JList jlst = new JList(new Object[]
  {"Item 1", "Item 2", "Item 3", "Item 4", "Item 5", "Item 6"});
```

```
jlst.setForeground(Color.red);
jlst.setBackground(Color.white);
jlst.setSelectionForeground(Color.pink);
jlst.setSelectionBackground(Color.black);
jlst.setVisibleRowCount(4);
```

Lists do not scroll automatically. To make a list scrollable, create a scroll pane and add the list to it. Text areas are made scrollable in the same way.

JList generates javax.swing.event.ListSelectionEvent to notify the listeners of the selections. The listener must implement the valueChanged handler in the javax.swing.event. ListSelectionListener interface to process the event.

EXAMPLE 13.7 USING LISTS

Problem

Write a program that lets users select countries in a list and display the flags of the selected countries in the labels. Figure 13.29 shows a sample run of the program.

FIGURE 13.29 *When the countries in the list are selected, corresponding images of their flags are displayed in the labels.*

Solution

Here are the major steps in the program:

1. Create the user interface.
   Create a list with nine country names as selection values, and place the list inside a scroll pane. Place the scroll pane in the west of the frame. Create nine labels to be used to display the countries' flag images. Place the labels in the panel, and place the panel in the center of the frame.

2. Process the event.
   Implement the valueChanged method in the ListSelectionListener interface to set the selected countries' flag images in the labels.

LISTING 13.9   ListDemo.java (Using Lists)

```
1 import java.awt.*;
2 import javax.swing.*;
3 import javax.swing.event.*;
4
5 public class ListDemo extends JFrame
6    implements ListSelectionListener {
7   final int NUMBER_OF_FLAGS = 9;
8
```

EXAMPLE 13.7 (CONTINUED)

```
 9    // Declare an array of Strings for flag titles
10    private String[] flagTitles = {"Canada", "China", "Denmark",
11      "France", "Germany", "India", "Norway", "United Kingdom",
12      "United States of America"};
13
14    // The list for selecting countries
15    private JList jlst = new JList(flagTitles);
16
17    // Declare an ImageIcon array for the national flags of 9 countries
18    private ImageIcon[] imageIcons = {
19      new ImageIcon("image/ca.gif"),
20      new ImageIcon("image/china.gif"),
21      new ImageIcon("image/denmark.gif"),
22      new ImageIcon("image/fr.gif"),
23      new ImageIcon("image/germany.gif"),
24      new ImageIcon("image/india.gif"),
25      new ImageIcon("image/norway.gif"),
26      new ImageIcon("image/uk.gif"),
27      new ImageIcon("image/us.gif")
28    };
29
30    // Arrays of labels for displaying images
31    private JLabel[] jlblImageViewer = new JLabel[NUMBER_OF_FLAGS];
32
33    public static void main(String[] args) {
34      ListDemo frame = new ListDemo();                              create frame
35      frame.setSize(650, 500);
36      frame.setTitle("ListDemo");
37      frame.setDefaultCloseOperation(JFrame.EXIT_ON_CLOSE);
38      frame.setVisible(true);
39    }
40
41    public ListDemo() {
42      // Create a panel to hold nine labels                         create UI
43      JPanel p = new JPanel();
44      p.setLayout(new GridLayout(3, 3, 5, 5));
45
46      for (int i = 0; i < NUMBER_OF_FLAGS; i++) {
47        p.add(jlblImageViewer[i] = new JLabel());
48        jlblImageViewer[i].setHorizontalAlignment
49          (SwingConstants.CENTER);
50      }
51
52      // Add p and the list to the frame
53      getContentPane().add(p, BorderLayout.CENTER);
54      getContentPane().add(new JScrollPane(jlst), BorderLayout.WEST);
55
56      // Register listeners
57      jlst.addListSelectionListener(this);
58    }
59
60    /** Handle list selection */                                    handler
61    public void valueChanged(ListSelectionEvent e) {
62      // Get selected indices
63      int[] indices = jlst.getSelectedIndices();
64
65      int i;
66      // Set icons in the labels
67      for (i = 0; i < indices.length; i++) {
68        jlblImageViewer[i].setIcon(imageIcons[indices[i]]);
69      }
70
71      // Remove icons from the rest of the labels
72      for ( ; i < NUMBER_OF_FLAGS; i++) {
73        jlblImageViewer[i].setIcon(null);
74      }
75    }
76  }
```

EXAMPLE 13.7 (CONTINUED)

Review

The frame listens to `ListSelectionEvent` for handling the selection of country names in the list, so it implements `ListSelectionListener` (Line 6). `ListSelectionEvent` and `ListSelectionListener` are defined in the `javax.swing.event` package, so this package is imported in the program (Line 3).

The program creates an array of nine labels for displaying flag images for nine countries. The program loads the images of the nine countries into an image array (Lines 18–28) and creates a list of the nine countries in the same order as in the image array (Lines 10–12). Thus the index 0 of the image array corresponds to the first country in the list.

The list is placed in a scroll pane (Line 54) so that it can be scrolled when the number of items in the list extends beyond the viewing area.

By default, the selection mode of the list is multiple-interval, which allows the user to select multiple items from different blocks in the list. When the user selects countries in the list, the `valueChanged` handler (Lines 61–75) is executed, gets the indices of the selected item, and sets their corresponding image icons in the label to display the flags.

13.11 Scroll Bars

`JScrollBar` is a control that enables the user to select from a range of values. `JScrollBar` has the following properties, as pictured in Figure 13.30:

◆ **orientation** specifies horizontal or vertical style, with `JScrollBar.HORIZONTAL` (0) for horizontal and `JScrollBar.VERTICAL` (1) for vertical.

◆ **maximum** specifies the maximum value the scroll bar represents when the bubble reaches the right end of the scroll bar for horizontal style or the bottom of the scroll bar for vertical style.

◆ **minimum** specifies the minimum value the scroll bar represents when the bubble reaches the left end of the scroll bar for horizontal style or the top of the scroll bar for vertical style.

◆ **visibleAmount** (also called extent) specifies the relative width of the scroll bar's bubble. The actual width appearing on the screen is determined by the maximum value and the value of `visibleAmount`.

◆ **value** represents the current value of the scroll bar. Normally, a program changes a scroll bar's value by calling the `setValue` method. The `setValue` method simultaneously and

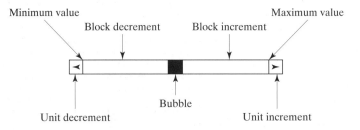

FIGURE 13.30 *A scroll bar represents a range of values graphically.*

synchronously sets the minimum, maximum, visible amount, and value properties of a scroll bar, so that they are mutually consistent.

✦ `blockIncrement` is the value added (subtracted) when the user activates the block-increment (decrement) area of the scroll bar, as shown in Figure 13.30. The `blockIncrement` property, which is new in JDK 1.1, supersedes the `pageIncrement` property used in JDK 1.02.

✦ `unitIncrement` is the value added (subtracted) when the user activates the unit-increment (decrement) area of the scroll bar, as shown in Figure 13.30. The `unitIncrement` property, which is new in JDK 1.1, supersedes the `lineIncrement` property used in JDK 1.02.

🌸 NOTE

The width of the scroll bar's track corresponds to `maximum + visibleAmount`. When a scroll bar is set to its maximum value, the left side of the bubble is at `maximum`, and the right side is at `maximum + visibleAmount`.

Figure 13.31 lists several frequently used constructors and methods in `JScrollBar`.

Normally, the user changes the value of the scroll bar by making a gesture with the mouse. For example, the user can drag the scroll bar's bubble up and down, or click in the scroll bar's unit-increment or block-increment areas. Keyboard gestures can also be mapped to the scroll bar. By convention, the Page Up and Page Down keys are equivalent to clicking in the scroll bar's block-increment and block-decrement areas.

When the user changes the value of the scroll bar, the scroll bar generates an instance of `AdjustmentEvent`, which is passed to every registered listener. An object that wishes to be notified of changes to the scroll bar's value must implement the `adjustmentValueChanged` method in the `AdjustmentListener` interface defined in the package `java.awt.event`.

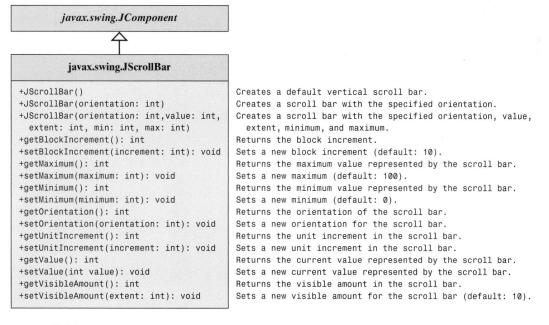

FIGURE 13.31 *JScrollBar enables you to select from a range of values.*

EXAMPLE 13.8 USING SCROLL BARS

Problem

Write a program that uses horizontal and vertical scroll bars to control a message displayed on a panel. The horizontal scroll bar is used to move the message to the left or the right, and the vertical scroll bar to move it up and down. A sample run of the program is shown in Figure 13.32.

FIGURE 13.32 *The scroll bars move the message on a panel horizontally and vertically.*

Solution

Here are the major steps in the program:

1. Create the user interface.
   Create a MessagePanel object and place it in the center of the frame. Create a vertical scroll bar and place it in the east of the frame. Create a horizontal scroll bar and place it in the south of the frame.

2. Process the event.
   Implement the adjustmentValueChanged handler to move the message according to the bar movement in the scroll bars.

LISTING 13.10   ScrollBarDemo.java (Using Scroll Bars)

```
1 import java.awt.*;
2 import java.awt.event.*;
3 import javax.swing.*;
4
5 public class ScrollBarDemo extends JFrame
6     implements AdjustmentListener {
7   // Create horizontal and vertical scroll bars
8   private JScrollBar jscbHort =
9     new JScrollBar(JScrollBar.HORIZONTAL);
10   private JScrollBar jscbVert =
11     new JScrollBar(JScrollBar.VERTICAL);
12
13   // Create a MessagePanel
14   private MessagePanel messagePanel =
15     new MessagePanel("Welcome to Java");
16
17   public static void main(String[] args) {
18     ScrollBarDemo frame = new ScrollBarDemo();
19     frame.setTitle("ScrollBarDemo");
20     frame.setDefaultCloseOperation(JFrame.EXIT_ON_CLOSE);
21     frame.pack();
22     frame.setVisible(true);
23   }
24
25   public ScrollBarDemo() {
26     // Add scroll bars and message panel to the frame
```

scroll bar

create frame

create UI

EXAMPLE 13.8 (CONTINUED)

```
27      getContentPane().setLayout(new BorderLayout());
28      getContentPane().add(messagePanel, BorderLayout.CENTER);
29      getContentPane().add(jscbVert, BorderLayout.EAST);
30      getContentPane().add(jscbHort, BorderLayout.SOUTH);
31
32      // Register listener for the scroll bars
33      jscbHort.addAdjustmentListener(this);
34      jscbVert.addAdjustmentListener(this);
35    }
36
37    /** Handle scroll bar adjustment actions */
38    public void adjustmentValueChanged(AdjustmentEvent e) {
39      if (e.getSource() == jscbHort) {
40        // getValue() and getMaximumValue() return int, but for better
41        // precision, use double
42        double value = jscbHort.getValue();
43        double maximumValue = jscbHort.getMaximum();
44        double newX = (value * messagePanel.getWidth() / maximumValue);
45        messagePanel.setXCoordinate((int)newX);
46      }
47      else if (e.getSource() == jscbVert) {
48        // getValue() and getMaximumValue() return int, but for better
49        // precision, use double
50        double value = jscbVert.getValue();
51        double maximumValue = jscbVert.getMaximum();
52        double newY = (value * messagePanel.getHeight() / maximumValue);
53        messagePanel.setYCoordinate((int)newY);
54      }
55    }
56 }
```

vertical
horizontal

handler

Review

The program creates two scroll bars (jscbVert and jscbHort) (Lines 8–11) and an instance of MessagePanel (messagePanel) (Lines 14–15). messagePanel is placed in the center of the frame; jscbVert and jscbHort are placed in the east and south sections of the frame (Lines 29–30), respectively.

You can specify the orientation of the scroll bar in the constructor or use the setOrientation method. By default, the property value is 100 for maximum, 0 for minimum, 10 for blockIncrement, and 10 for visibleAmount.

When the user drags the bubble, or clicks the increment or decrement unit, the value of the scroll bar changes. An instance of AdjustmentEvent is generated and passed to the listener by invoking the adjustmentValueChanged handler (Lines 38–55). Since there are two scroll bars in the frame, the e.getSource() method is used to determine the source of the event. The vertical scroll bar moves the message up and down, and the horizontal bar moves the message to right and left.

The maximum value of the vertical scroll bar corresponds to the height of the panel, and the maximum value of the horizontal scroll bar corresponds to the width of the panel. The ratio between the current and maximum values of the horizontal scroll bar is the same as the ratio between the x value and the width of the message panel. Similarly, the ratio between the current and maximum values of the vertical scroll bar is the same as the ratio between the y value and the height of the message panel. The x-coordinate and y-coordinate are set in response to the scroll bar adjustments (Lines 45, 53).

13.12 Sliders

JSlider is similar to JScrollBar, but JSlider has more properties and can appear in many forms. Figure 13.33 lists several frequently used constructors and methods in JSlider.

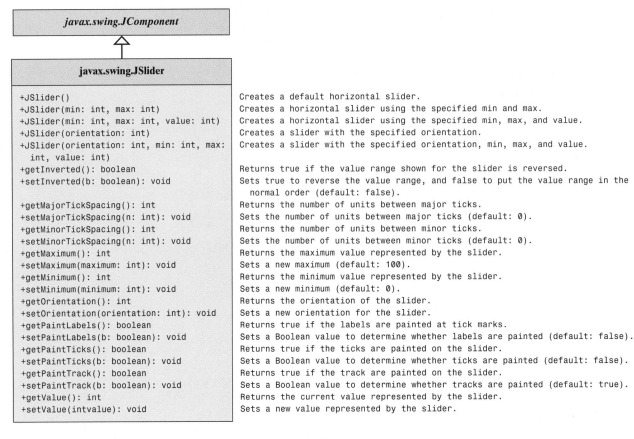

FIGURE 13.33 *JSlider enables you to select from a range of values.*

JSlider lets the user graphically select a value by sliding a knob within a bounded interval. The slider can show both major tick marks and minor tick marks between them. The number of pixels between the tick marks is controlled with setMajorTickSpacing and setMinorTickSpacing. Sliders can be displayed horizontally or vertically, with or without ticks, and with or without labels.

 NOTE

The values of a vertical scroll bar increase from top to bottom, but the values of a vertical slider decrease from top to bottom.

 NOTE

The names of the getPaintLabels(), getPaintTicks(), and getPaintTrack() methods violate the naming pattern. Since paintLabels, paintTicks, and paintTracks are boolean properties, they should be named isPaintLabels(), isPaintTicks(), and isPaintTrack().

When the user changes the value of the slider, the slider generates an instance of javax. swing.event.ChangeEvent, which is passed to any registered listeners. Any object that wishes to be notified of changes to the slider's value must implement stateChanged method in the ChangeListener interface defined in the package javax.swing.event.

EXAMPLE 13.9 USING SLIDERS

Problem

Rewrite the preceding program using the sliders to control a message displayed on a panel instead of using scroll bars, as shown in Figure 13.34.

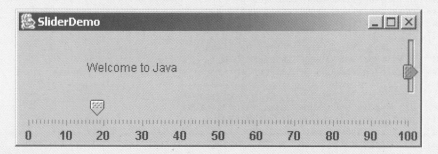

FIGURE **13.34**   *The sliders move the message on a panel horizontally and vertically.*

Solution

Here are the major steps in the program:

1. Create the user interface.
   Create a `MessagePanel` object and place it in the center of the frame. Create a vertical slider and place it in the east of the frame. Create a horizontal slider and place it in the south of the frame.

2. Process the event.
   Implement the `stateChanged` handler in the `ChangeListener` interface to move the message according to the knot movement in the slider.

LISTING 13.11   SliderBarDemo.java (Using Sliders)

```
1  import java.awt.*;
2  import javax.swing.*;
3  import javax.swing.event.*;
4
5  public class SliderDemo extends JFrame implements ChangeListener {
6    // Create horizontal and vertical sliders
7    private JSlider jsldHort = new JSlider(JSlider.HORIZONTAL);           slider
8    private JSlider jsldVert = new JSlider(JSlider.VERTICAL);
9
10   // Create a MessagePanel
11   private MessagePanel messagePanel =
12     new MessagePanel("Welcome to Java");
13
14   public static void main(String[] args) {
15     SliderDemo frame = new SliderDemo();                               create frame
16     frame.setTitle("SliderDemo");
17     frame.setDefaultCloseOperation(JFrame.EXIT_ON_CLOSE);
18     frame.pack();
19     frame.setVisible(true);
20   }
21
22   public SliderDemo() {
23     // Add sliders and message panel to the frame                      create UI
24     getContentPane().setLayout(new BorderLayout());
25     getContentPane().add(messagePanel, BorderLayout.CENTER);
26     getContentPane().add(jsldVert, BorderLayout.EAST);
27     getContentPane().add(jsldHort, BorderLayout.SOUTH);
```

EXAMPLE 13.9 (CONTINUED)

slider properties

handler

```
28
29      // Set properties for sliders
30      jsldHort.setPaintLabels(true);
31      jsldHort.setPaintTicks(true);
32      jsldHort.setMajorTickSpacing(10);
33      jsldHort.setMinorTickSpacing(1);
34      jsldHort.setPaintTrack(false);
35      jsldVert.setInverted(true);
36
37      // Register listener for the sliders
38      jsldHort.addChangeListener(this);
39      jsldVert.addChangeListener(this);
40    }
41
42    /** Handle scroll bar adjustment actions */
43    public void stateChanged(ChangeEvent e) {
44      if (e.getSource() == jsldHort) {
45        // getValue() and getMaximumValue() return int, but for better
46        // precision, use double
47        double value = jsldHort.getValue();
48        double maximumValue = jsldHort.getMaximum();
49        double newX = (value * messagePanel.getWidth() / maximumValue);
50        messagePanel.setXCoordinate((int)newX);
51      }
52      else if (e.getSource() == jsldVert) {
53        // getValue() and getMaximumValue() return int, but for better
54        // precision, use double
55        double value = jsldVert.getValue();
56        double maximumValue = jsldVert.getMaximum();
57        double newY = (value * messagePanel.getHeight() / maximumValue);
58        messagePanel.setYCoordinate((int)newY);
59      }
60    }
61  }
```

Review

JSlider is similar to JScrollBar, but JSlider has more features. As shown in this example, you can specify labels, major ticks, and minor ticks on a JSlider (Lines 30–33). You can also choose to hide the track (Line 34). Since the values of a vertical slider decrease from top to bottom, the setInverted method reverses the order (Line 35).

JSlider fires ChangeEvent when the slider is changed. The listener needs to implement the stateChanged handler in the ChangeListener (Lines 43–60). Note that JScrollBar fires AdjustmentEvent when the scroll bar is adjusted.

13.13   Creating Multiple Windows

Occasionally, you may want to create multiple windows in an application. The application opens a new window to perform the specified task. The new windows are called *subwindows*, and the main frame is called the *main window*.

To create a subwindow from an application, you need to create a subclass of JFrame that defines the task and tells the new window what to do. You can then create an instance of this subclass in the application and launch the new window by setting the frame instance to be visible.

EXAMPLE 13.10 CREATING MULTIPLE WINDOWS

Problem

Write a program that creates a main window with a text area in the scroll pane and a button named "Show Histogram". When the user clicks the button, a new window appears that displays a histogram to show the occurrences of the letters in the text area. Figure 13.35 contains a sample run of the program.

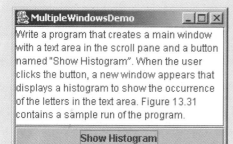
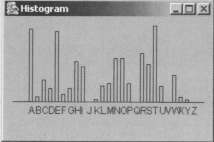

FIGURE **13.35**   *The histogram is displayed in a separate frame.*

Solution

Here are the major steps in the program:

1. Create a main class for the frame named `MultipleWindowsDemo` in Listing 13.12. Add a text area inside a scroll pane, and place the scroll pane in the center of the frame. Create a button "Show Histogram" and place it in the south of the frame.

2. Create a subclass of `JPanel` named `Histogram` in Listing 13.13. The class contains a data field named `count` of the `int[]` type, which counts the occurrences of twenty-six letters. The values in `count` are displayed in the histogram.

3. Implement the `actionPerformed` handler in `MultipleWindowsDemo`, as follows:

   ✦ Create an instance of `Histogram`. Count the letters in the text area and pass the count to the `Histogram` object.

   ✦ Create a new frame and place the `Histogram` object in the center of frame. Display the frame.

LISTING 13.12   MultipleWindowsDemo.java (Creating Multiple Windows)

```
 1  import java.awt.*;
 2  import java.awt.event.*;
 3  import javax.swing.*;
 4
 5  public class MultipleWindowsDemo extends JFrame
 6      implements ActionListener {
 7    private JTextArea jta;
 8    private JButton jbtShowHistogram = new JButton("Show Histogram");
 9    private Histogram histogram = new Histogram();
10
11    // Create a new frame to hold the histogram panel
12    private JFrame histogramFrame = new JFrame();
13
14    public MultipleWindowsDemo() {
15      // Store text area in a scroll pane
```

create subframe

create UI

EXAMPLE 13.10 (CONTINUED)

```
16    JScrollPane scrollPane = new JScrollPane(jta = new JTextArea());
17    scrollPane.setPreferredSize(new Dimension(300, 200));
18    jta.setWrapStyleWord(true);
19    jta.setLineWrap(true);
20
21    // Place scroll pane and button in the frame
22    getContentPane().add(scrollPane, BorderLayout.CENTER);
23    getContentPane().add(jbtShowHistogram, BorderLayout.SOUTH);
24
25    // Register listener
26    jbtShowHistogram.addActionListener(this);
27
28    // Create a new frame to hold the histogram panel
29    histogramFrame.getContentPane().add(histogram);
30    histogramFrame.pack();
31    histogramFrame.setTitle("Histogram");
32  }
33
34  /** Handle the button action */
35  public void actionPerformed(ActionEvent e) {
36    // Count the letters in the text area
37    int[] count = countLetters();
38
39    // Set the letter count to histogram for display
40    histogram.showHistogram(count);
41
42    // Show the frame
43    histogramFrame.setVisible(true);
44  }
45
46  /** Count the letters in the text area */
47  private int[] countLetters() {
48    // Count for 26 letters
49    int[] count = new int[26];
50
51    // Get contents from the text area
52    String text = jta.getText();
53
54    // Count occurrence of each letter (case insensitive)
55    for (int i = 0; i < text.length(); i++) {
56      char character = text.charAt(i);
57
58      if ((character >= 'A') && (character <= 'Z')) {
59        count[(int)character - 65]++; // The ASCII for 'A' is 65
60      }
61      else if ((character >= 'a') && (character <= 'z')) {
62        count[(int)character - 97]++; // The ASCII for 'a' is 97
63      }
64    }
65
66    return count; // Return the count array
67  }
68
69  public static void main(String[] args) {
70    MultipleWindowsDemo frame = new MultipleWindowsDemo();
71    frame.setDefaultCloseOperation(JFrame.EXIT_ON_CLOSE);
72    frame.setTitle("MultipleWindowsDemo");
73    frame.pack();
74    frame.setVisible(true);
75  }
76 }
```

display subframe (margin note, line 40)

create main frame (margin note, line 70)

LISTING 13.13 **Histogram.java (Displaying a Histogram)**

```
1 import javax.swing.*;
2 import java.awt.*;
```

```
        JButton jbt1 = new JButton(usIcon);
        JButton jbt2 = new JButton(usIcon);

        JPanel p1 = new JPanel();
        p1.add(jbt1);

        JPanel p2 = new JPanel();
        p2.add(jbt2);

        JPanel p3 = new JPanel();
        p2.add(jbt1);

        getContentPane().add(p1, BorderLayout.NORTH);
        getContentPane().add(p2, BorderLayout.SOUTH);
        getContentPane().add(p3, BorderLayout.CENTER);
    }
}
```

13.7 Can you share a border or icon for GUI components?

13.8 How do you create a check box? How do you determine whether a check box is selected?

13.9 What is wrong if the statement `super.actionPerformed(e)` in `CheckBoxDemo` in Listing 13.4 is omitted?

13.10 How do you create a radio button? How do you group the radio buttons together? How do you determine whether a radio button is selected?

Sections 13.6–13.10

13.11 How do you create a label named `"Address"`? How do you change the name on a label? How do you set an icon in a label?

13.12 How do you create a text field with ten columns and the default text `"Welcome to Java"`? How do you write the code to check whether a text field is empty?

13.13 How do you create a text area with ten rows and twenty columns? How do you insert three lines into the text area? How do you create a scrollable text area?

13.14 How do you create a combo box, add three items to it, and retrieve a selected item?

13.15 How do you create a list with an array of strings?

Sections 13.11–13.13

13.16 How do you create a horizontal scroll bar? What event can a scroll bar generate?

13.17 How do you create a vertical slider? What event can a slider generate?

13.18 Explain how to create and show multiple frames in an application.

PROGRAMMING EXERCISES

Sections 13.2–13.5

13.1* (*Revising Example 13.1 "Using Buttons"*) Rewrite Example 13.1 to add a group of radio buttons to select background colors. The available colors are red, yellow, white, gray, and green (see Figure 13.37).

13.2* (*Selecting geometric figures*) Write a program that draws various figures on a panel. The user selects a figure from a radio button. The selected figure is then displayed on the panel (see Figure 13.38).

13.3** (*Traffic lights*) Write a program that simulates a traffic light. The program lets the user select one of three lights: red, yellow, or green. When a radio button is selected, the light is turned on, and only one light can be on at a time (see Figure 13.39). No light is on when the program starts.

FIGURE 13.37 *The <= and => buttons move the message on the panel, and you can also set the color for the message.*

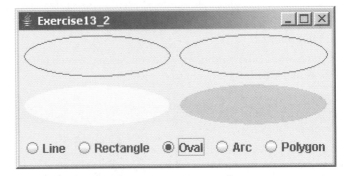

FIGURE 13.38 *The program displays lines, rectangles, ovals, arcs, or polygons when you select a shape type.*

FIGURE 13.39 *The radio buttons are grouped to let you select only one color in the group to control a traffic light.*

Sections 13.6–13.10

13.4* (*Creating a simple calculator*) Write a program to perform add, subtract, multiply, and divide operations (see Figure 13.40).

13.5* (*Creating a miles/kilometers converter*) Write a program that converts miles and kilometers, as shown in Figure 13.41. If you enter a value in the Mile text field and press the Enter key, the corresponding kilometer is displayed in the Kilometer text field.

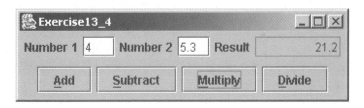

FIGURE 13.40 *The program does addition, subtraction, multiplication, and division on double numbers.*

Exercise13_5	
Mile	0.6241
Kilometer	1

FIGURE 13.41 *The program converts miles to kilometers, and vice versa.*

Likewise, if you enter a value in the Kilometer text field and press the Enter key, the corresponding mile is displayed in the Mile text field.

13.6* (*Creating an investment value calculator*) Write a program that calculates the future value of an investment at a given interest rate for a specified number of years. The formula for the calculation is as follows:

```
futureValue = investmentAmount * (1 + monthlyInterestRate)^years*12
```

Use text fields for interest rate, investment amount, and years. Display the future amount in a text field when the user clicks the Calculate button, as shown in Figure 13.42.

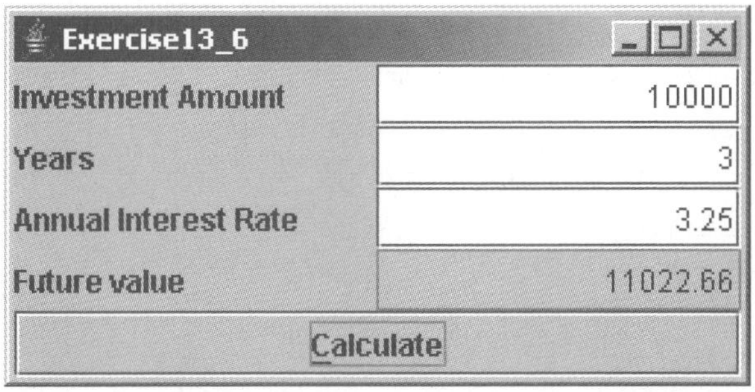

Exercise13_6	
Investment Amount	10000
Years	3
Annual Interest Rate	3.25
Future value	11022.66
Calculate	

FIGURE 13.42 *The user enters the investment amount, years, and interest rate to compute future value.*

13.7* (*Setting clock time*) Write a program that displays a clock time and sets the clock time with three text fields to give the time for the clock, as shown in Figure 13.43. Use the StillClock in Section 11.12, "Case Study: The StillClock Class."

13.8** (*Selecting a font*) Write a program that can dynamically change the font of a message to be displayed on a panel. The message can be displayed in bold and italic at the same time, or can be displayed in the center of the panel. You can select the font name or font size from combo boxes, as shown in Figure 13.44. The available font names can be obtained using getAvailableFontFamilyNames() in GraphicsEnvironment (see page 385). The combo box for font size is initialized with numbers from 1 to 100.

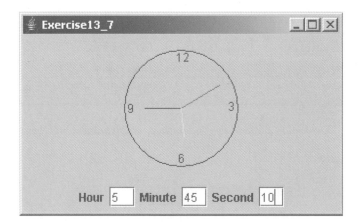

FIGURE 13.43 *The program displays the time specified in the text fields.*

FIGURE 13.44 *You can dynamically set the font for the message.*

13.9** (*Demonstrating* JLabel *properties*) Write a program to let the user dynamically set the properties horizontalAlignment, verticalAlignment, horizontalTextAlignment, and verticalTextAlignment, as shown in Figure 13.45.

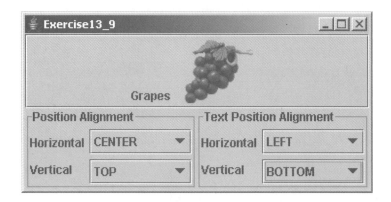

FIGURE 13.45 *You can set the alignment and text-position properties of a button dynamically.*

13.10* (*Adding new features into Example 13.1, "Using Buttons," incrementally*) Improve Example 13.1 incrementally as follows (see Figure 13.46):

1. Add a text field labeled "Enter a new message" in the same panel with the buttons. Upon typing a new message in the text field and pressing the Enter key, the new message is displayed in the message panel.

FIGURE 13.46   *The program uses buttons, labels, text fields, combo boxes, radio buttons, check boxes, and borders.*

2. Add a combo box labeled "Select an interval" in the same panel with the buttons. The combo box enables the user to select a new interval for moving the message. The selection values range from 5 to 100 with interval 5. The user can also type a new interval in the combo box.
3. Add three radio buttons that enable the user to select the foreground color for the message as Red, Green, and Blue. The radio buttons are grouped in a panel, and the panel is placed in the north of the frame's content pane.
4. Add three check boxes that enable the user to center the message and display it in italic or bold. Place the check boxes in the same panel with the radio buttons.
5. Add a border titled "Message Panel" on the message panel, add a border titled "South Panel" on the panel for buttons, and add a border titled "North Panel" on the panel for radio buttons and check boxes.

13.11* (*Demonstrating* `JTextField` *properties*) Write a program that sets the horizontal-alignment and column-size properties of a text field dynamically, as shown in Figure 13.47.

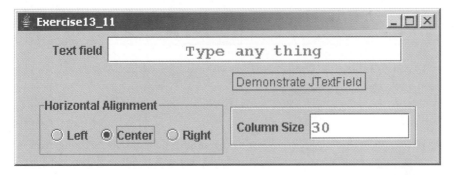

FIGURE 13.47   *You can set the horizontal-alignment and column-size properties of a text field dynamically.*

13.12* (*Demonstrating* `JTextArea` *properties*) Write a program that demonstrates the wrapping styles of the text area. The program uses a check box to indicate whether the text area is wrapped. In the case where the text area is wrapped, you need to specify whether it is wrapped by characters or by words, as shown in Figure 13.48.

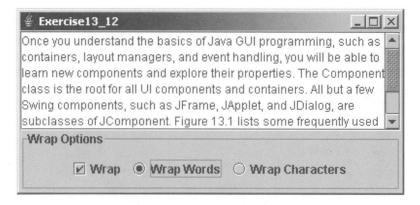

FIGURE **13.48** *You can set the options to wrap a text area by characters or by words dynamically.*

13.13* (*Comparing loans with various interest rates*) Rewrite Exercise 3.26 to create a user interface, as shown in Figure 13.49. Your program should let the user enter the loan amount and loan period in number of years from a text field, and should display the monthly and total payments for each interest rate starting from 5 percent to 8 percent, with increments of one-eighth, in a text area.

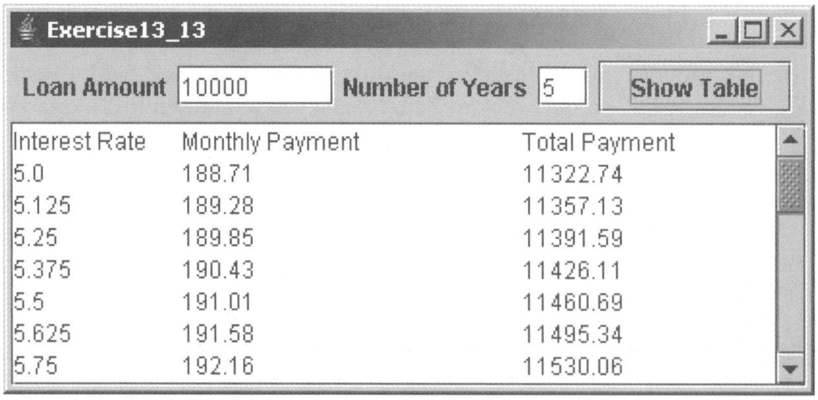

FIGURE **13.49** *The program displays a table for monthly payments and total payments on a given loan based on various interest rates.*

13.14* (*Using* JComboBox *and* JList) Write a program that demonstrates selecting items in a list. The program uses a combo box to specify a selection mode, as shown in Figure 13.50. When you select items, they are displayed in a label below the list.

Sections 13.11–13.13

13.15** (*Creating a color selector*) Write a program that uses scroll bars to select the foreground color for a label, as shown in Figure 13.51. Three horizontal scroll bars are used for selecting the red, green, and blue components of the color. Use a title border on the panel that holds the scroll bars.

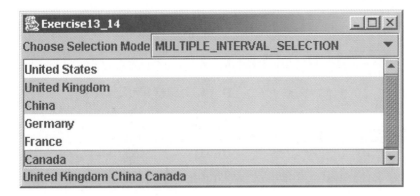

FIGURE **13.50** *You can choose single selection, single-interval selection, or multiple-interval selection in a list.*

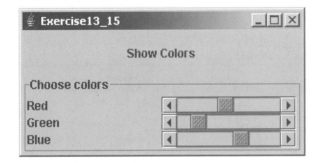

FIGURE **13.51** *The foreground color changes in the label as you adjust the scroll bars.*

13.16* (*Revising Example 13.10, "Creating Multiple Windows"*) Instead of displaying the occurrences of the letters using the Histogram component in Example 13.10, use a bar chart, so that the display is as shown in Figure 13.52.

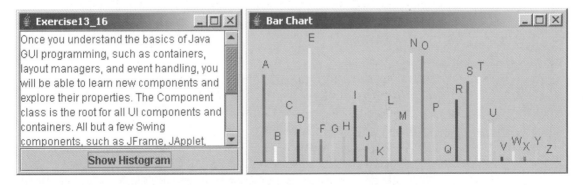

FIGURE **13.52** *The number of occurrences of each letter is displayed in a bar chart.*

13.17★★★ (*Displaying a calendar*) Write a program that displays the calendar for the current month, as shown in Figure 13.53. Use labels, and set texts on the labels to display the calendar. Use the `GregorianCalendar` class on page 322 to obtain the information about month, year, first day of the month, and number of days in the month.

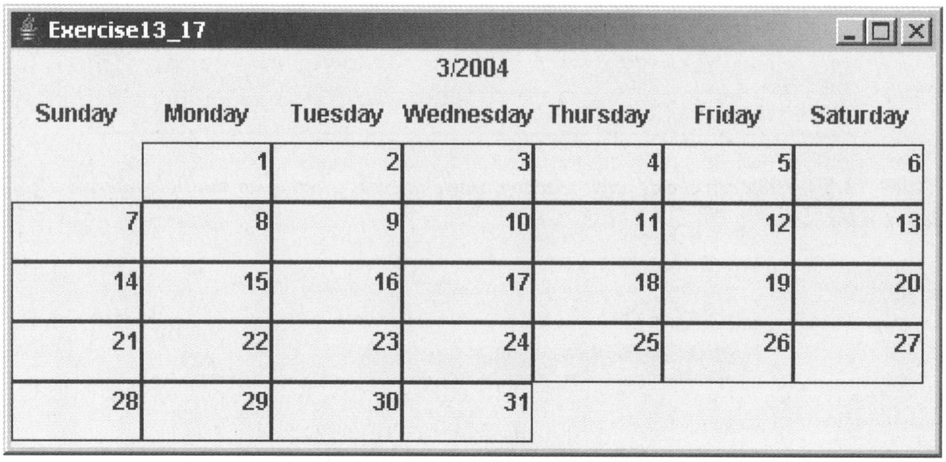

FIGURE 13.53　*The program displays the calendar for the current month.*

14.4   The HTML File and the <applet> Tag

HTML is a markup language that presents static documents on the Web. It uses tags to instruct the Web browser how to render a Web page and contains a tag called <applet> that incorporates applets into a Web page.

The following HTML file named WelcomeApplet.html invokes the **WelcomeApplet.class**:

```
<html>
<head>
<title>Welcome Java Applet</title>
</head>
<body>
<applet
  code = "WelcomeApplet.class"
  width = 350
  height = 200>
</applet>
</body>
</html>
```

A *tag* is an instruction to the Web browser. The browser interprets the tag and decides how to display or otherwise treat the subsequent contents of the HTML document. Tags are enclosed inside brackets. The first word in a tag, called the *tag name*, describes tag functions. Tags can have additional attributes, sometimes with values after an equals sign, which further define the tag's action. For example, in the preceding HTML file, <applet> is the tag name, and code, width, and height are the attributes. The width and height attributes specify the rectangular viewing area of the applet.

Most tags have a *start tag* and a corresponding *end tag*. The tag has a specific effect on the region between the start tag and the end tag. For example, <applet...>...</applet> tells the browser to display an applet. An end tag is always the start tag's name preceded by a slash.

An HTML document begins with the <html> tag, which declares that the document is written in HTML. Each document has two parts, a *head* and a *body*, defined by <head> and <body> tags, respectively. The head part contains the document title, using the <title> tag and other information the browser can use when rendering the document, and the body part contains the actual contents of the document. The header is optional. For more information, refer to Supplement E, "An HTML Tutorial."

The complete syntax of the <applet> tag is as follows:

```
<applet
  [codebase=applet_url]
  code=classfilename.class
  width=applet_viewing_width_in_pixels
  height=applet_viewing_height_in_pixels
  [archive=archivefile]
  [vspace=vertical_margin]
  [hspace=horizontal_margin]
  [align=applet_alignment]
  [alt=alternative_text]
>
<param name=param_name1 value=param_value1>
<param name=param_name2 value=param_value2>
...
<param name=param_name3 value=param_value3>
</applet>
```

The code, width, and height attributes are required; all the others are optional. The <param> tag is introduced in Section 14.5, "Passing Strings to Applets." The meanings of the other attributes are explained below.

◆ **codebase** specifies a base where your classes are loaded. If this attribute is not used, the Web browser loads the applet from the directory in which the HTML page is located. If your applet is located in a different directory from the HTML page, you must specify the applet_url for the browser to load the applet. This attribute enables you to load the class from anywhere on the Internet. The classes used by the applet are dynamically loaded when needed.

◆ **archive** instructs the browser to load an archive file that contains all the class files needed to run the applet. Archiving allows the Web browser to load all the classes from a single compressed file at one time, thus reducing loading time and improving performance. To create archives, see Section 14.13, "Packaging and Deploying Java Projects."

◆ **vspace** and **hspace** specify the size, in pixels, of the blank margin to pad around the applet vertically and horizontally.

◆ **align** specifies how the applet will be aligned in the browser. One of nine values is used: left, right, top, texttop, middle, absmiddle, baseline, bottom, or absbottom.

◆ **alt** attribute specifies the text to be displayed in case the browser cannot run Java.

14.4.1 Viewing Applets Using the Applet Viewer Utility

You can test the applet using the applet viewer utility, which can be invoked from the DOS prompt using the **appletviewer** command from **c:\book**, as shown in Figure 14.2. Its output is shown in Figure 14.3.

```
Command Prompt                                          _ □ ×
C:\book>dir WelcomeApplet.*
 Volume in drive C has no label.
 Volume Serial Number is 9CB6-16F1

 Directory of C:\book

07/25/2003  09:43p                    510 WelcomeApplet.class
10/14/2001  09:39p                    159 WelcomeApplet.html
07/25/2003  09:43p                    264 WelcomeApplet.java
               3 File(s)              933 bytes
               0 Dir(s)   22,434,971,648 bytes free

C:\book>appletviewer WelcomeApplet.html_
```

FIGURE **14.2**   *The appletviewer command runs a Java applet in the applet viewer utility.*

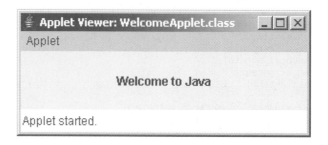

FIGURE **14.3**   *The WelcomeApplet program is running from the applet viewer.*

14.4.2 Viewing Applets from a Web Browser

Applets are eventually displayed in a Web browser. Using the applet viewer, you do not need to start a Web browser. The applet viewer functions as a browser. It is convenient for testing applets during development. However, you should also test the applets from a Web browser before deploying them on a Web site. To display an applet from a Web browser, open the applet's HTML file (e.g., WelcomeApplet.html). Its output is shown in Figure 14.4.

FIGURE 14.4 *The WelcomeApplet program is displayed in Internet Explorer.*

To make your applet accessible on the Web, you need to store the WelcomeApplet.class and WelcomeApplet.html on a Web server. You can view the applet from an appropriate URL. For example, I have uploaded these two files on Web server www.cs.armstrong.edu. As shown in Figure 14.5, you can access the applet from www.cs.armstrong.edu/liang/intro5e/book/ WelcomeApplet.html.

FIGURE 14.5 *The WelcomeApplet program is downloaded from the Web server.*

EXAMPLE 14.1 USING APPLETS

Problem

Write an applet that computes loan payments. The applet enables the user to enter the interest rate, the number of years, and the loan amount. Clicking the Compute Payment button displays the monthly payment and the total payment.

Solution

The applet and the HTML code containing the applet are provided in Listings 14.1 and 14.2. Figure 14.6 contains a sample run of the applet.

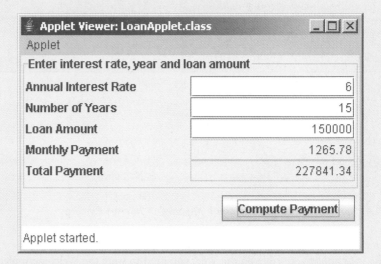

FIGURE 14.6 *The applet computes the monthly payment and the total payment when provided with the interest rate, number of years, and loan amount.*

LISTING 14.1 LoanApplet.java (Computing Loans)

```
1  import java.awt.*;
2  import java.awt.event.*;
3  import javax.swing.*;
4  import javax.swing.border.TitledBorder;
5
6  public class LoanApplet extends JApplet
7      implements ActionListener {
8    // Declare and create text fields for interest rate
9    // year, loan amount, monthly payment, and total payment
10   private JTextField jtfAnnualInterestRate = new JTextField();
11   private JTextField jtfNumberOfYears = new JTextField();
12   private JTextField jtfLoanAmount = new JTextField();
13   private JTextField jtfMonthlyPayment = new JTextField();
14   private JTextField jtfTotalPayment = new JTextField();
15
16   // Declare and create a Compute Payment button
17   private JButton jbtComputeLoan = new JButton("Compute Payment");
18
19   /** Initialize user interface */
20   public void init() {
21     // Set properties on the text fields
22     jtfMonthlyPayment.setEditable(false);
23     jtfTotalPayment.setEditable(false);
24
```

text field

create UI

EXAMPLE 14.1 (CONTINUED)

```
25      // Right align text fields
26      jtfAnnualInterestRate.setHorizontalAlignment(JTextField.RIGHT);
27      jtfNumberOfYears.setHorizontalAlignment(JTextField.RIGHT);
28      jtfLoanAmount.setHorizontalAlignment(JTextField.RIGHT);
29      jtfMonthlyPayment.setHorizontalAlignment(JTextField.RIGHT);
30      jtfTotalPayment.setHorizontalAlignment(JTextField.RIGHT);
31
32      // Panel p1 to hold labels and text fields
33      JPanel p1 = new JPanel();
34      p1.setLayout(new GridLayout(5, 2));
35      p1.add(new JLabel("Annual Interest Rate"));
36      p1.add(jtfAnnualInterestRate);
37      p1.add(new JLabel("Number of Years"));
38      p1.add(jtfNumberOfYears);
39      p1.add(new JLabel("Loan Amount"));
40      p1.add(jtfLoanAmount);
41      p1.add(new JLabel("Monthly Payment"));
42      p1.add(jtfMonthlyPayment);
43      p1.add(new JLabel("Total Payment"));
44      p1.add(jtfTotalPayment);
45      p1.setBorder(new
46        TitledBorder("Enter interest rate, year and loan amount"));
47
48      // Panel p2 to hold the button
49      JPanel p2 = new JPanel();
50      p2.setLayout(new FlowLayout(FlowLayout.RIGHT));
51      p2.add(jbtComputeLoan);
52
53      // Add the components to the applet
54      getContentPane().add(p1, BorderLayout.CENTER);              contentPane
55      getContentPane().add(p2, BorderLayout.SOUTH);
56
57      // Register listener
58      jbtComputeLoan.addActionListener(this);
59    }
60
61    /** Handle the Compute Payment button */
62    public void actionPerformed(ActionEvent e) {                  handler
63      if (e.getSource() == jbtComputeLoan) {
64        // Get values from text fields
65        double interest =
66          Double.parseDouble(jtfAnnualInterestRate.getText());
67        int year =
68          Integer.parseInt(jtfNumberOfYears.getText());
69        double loanAmount =
70          Double.parseDouble(jtfLoanAmount.getText());
71
72        // Create a loan object
73        Loan loan = new Loan(interest, year, loanAmount);          create Loan
74
75        // Display monthly payment and total payment
76        jtfMonthlyPayment.setText("" +
77          (int)(loan.monthlyPayment() * 100) / 100.0);
78        jtfTotalPayment.setText("" +
79          (int)(loan.totalPayment() * 100) / 100.0);
80      }
81    }
82  }
```

LISTING 14.2 LoanApplet.html (HTML File for LOANAPPLET)

```
1  <!--HTML code, this code is separated from the preceding Java code-->
2  <html>
3  <head>
4  <title>Loan Applet</title>
5  </head>
6  <body>
```

```
 7  This is a loan calculator. Enter your input for interest, year, and
 8  loan amount.
 9  Click the "Compute Payment" button, you will get the payment
10  information.<p>
11  <applet
12    code = "LoanApplet.class"
13    width = 300
14    height = 150
15    alt="You must have a Java 2-enabled browser to view the applet">
16  </applet>
17  </body>
18  </html>
```

Review

You need to use the `public` modifier for the `LoanApplet`; otherwise, the Web browser cannot load it.

    `LoanApplet` implements `ActionListener` because it listens for button actions.

    The `init` method initializes the user interface. The program overrides this method to create user-interface components (labels, text fields, and a button), and places them in the applet.

    The only event handled is the Compute Payment button. When this button is clicked, the `actionPerformed` method gets the interest rate, number of years, and loan amount from the text fields. It then creates a `Loan` object (Line 73) to obtain the monthly payment and the total payment. Finally, it displays the monthly and total payments in their respective text fields.

    The `Loan` class is responsible for computing the payments. This class was introduced in Section 6.15, "Case Study: The `Loan` Class."

14.5   Passing Strings to Applets

In Chapter 7, "Strings," you learned how to pass strings to Java applications from a command line. Strings are passed to the `main` method as an array of strings. When the application starts, the `main` method can use these strings. There is no `main` method in an applet, however, and applets are not run from the command line by the Java interpreter.

    How, then, can applets accept arguments? In this section, you will learn how to pass strings to Java applets.

    To be passed to an applet, a parameter must be declared in the HTML file, and must be read by the applet when it is initialized. Parameters are declared using the `<param>` tag. The `<param>` tag must be embedded in the `<applet>` tag and has no end tag. The syntax for the `<param>` tag is given below:

```
<param name=parametername value=stringvalue>
```

This tag specifies a parameter and its corresponding string value.

 NOTE

There is no comma separating the parameter name from the parameter value in the HTML code. The HTML parameter names are not case-sensitive.

Suppose you want to write an applet to display a message. The message is passed as a parameter. In addition, you want the message to be displayed at a specific location with x-coordinate and y-coordinate, which are passed as two parameters. The parameters and their values are listed in Table 14.1.

TABLE 14.1   Parameter Names and Values
for the `DisplayMessage` Applet

Parameter name	Parameter value
MESSAGE	"Welcome to Java"
X	20
Y	30

The HTML source file is given in Listing 14.3:

LISTING 14.3   LoanApplet.html (HTML File for `LoanApplet`)

```
<html>
<head>
<title>Passing Strings to Java Applets</title>
</head>
<body>
This applet gets a message from the HTML page and displays it.
<p>
<applet
  code = "DisplayMessage.class"
  width = 200
  height = 50
  alt="You must have a Java 2-enabled browser to view the applet"
>
<param name = MESSAGE value = "Welcome to Java">
<param name = X value = 20>
<param name = Y value = 30>
</applet>
</body>
</html>
```

To read the parameter from the applet, use the following method defined in the `Applet` class:

```
public String getParameter("parametername");
```

This returns the value of the specified parameter.

EXAMPLE 14.2 PASSING STRINGS TO JAVA APPLETS

Problem

Write an applet that displays a message at a specified location. The message and the location (x, y) are obtained from the HTML source.

Solution

The program creates a Java source file named **DisplayMessage.java**, as shown below. The output of a sample run is shown in Figure 14.7.

LISTING 14.4   DisplayMessage.java (Displaying a Message)

```
1 import javax.swing.*;
2
3 public class DisplayMessage extends JApplet {
4   /** Initialize the applet */
5   public void init() {
6     // Get parameter values from the HTML file
7     String message = getParameter("MESSAGE");
```

getParameter

EXAMPLE 14.2 (CONTINUED)

```
 8      int x = Integer.parseInt(getParameter("X"));
 9      int y = Integer.parseInt(getParameter("Y"));
10
11      // Create a message panel
12      MessagePanel messagePanel = new MessagePanel(message);
13      messagePanel.setXCoordinate(x);
14      messagePanel.setYCoordinate(y);
15
16      // Add the message panel to the applet
17      getContentPane().add(messagePanel);
18    }
19  }
```

contentPane

FIGURE 14.7 *The applet displays the message Welcome to Java passed from the HTML page.*

Review

The program gets the parameter values from the HTML in the init method. The values are strings obtained using the getParameter method (Lines 7–9). Because x and y are int, the program uses Integer.parseInt(string) to parse a digital string into an int value.

If you change *Welcome to Java* in the HTML file to *Welcome to HTML*, and reload the HTML file in the Web browser, you should see *Welcome to HTML* displayed. Similarly, the x and y values can be changed to display the message in a desired location.

 CAUTION

The Applet's getParameter method can be invoked only after an instance of the applet is created. Therefore, this method cannot be invoked in the constructor of the applet class. You should invoke it from the init method.

14.6 Enabling Applets to Run as Applications

The JFrame class and the JApplet class have a lot in common despite some differences. Since they both are subclasses of the Container class, all their user-interface components, layout managers, and event-handling features are the same. Applications, however, are invoked from the static main method by the Java interpreter, and applets are run by the Web browser. The Web browser creates an instance of the applet using the applet's no-arg constructor and controls and executes the applet through the init, start, stop, and destroy methods .

For security reasons, the restrictions listed below are imposed on applets to prevent destructive programs from damaging the system on which the browser is running:

✦ Applets are not allowed to read from, or write to, the file system of the computer. Otherwise, they could damage the files and spread viruses.

✦ Applets are not allowed to run programs on the browser's computer. Otherwise, they might call destructive local programs and damage the local system on the user's computer.

✦ Applets are not allowed to establish connections between the user's computer and any other computer, except for the server where the applets are stored. This restriction prevents the applet from connecting the user's computer to another computer without the user's knowledge.

 NOTE

A new security protocol was introduced in Java 2. You can use a security policy file to grant applets access to local files.

In general, an applet can be converted to an application without loss of functionality. An application can be converted to an applet as long as it does not violate the security restrictions imposed on applets. You can implement a main method in an applet to enable the applet to run as an application. This feature has both theoretical and practical implications. Theoretically, it blurs the difference between applets and applications. You can write a class that is both an applet and an application. From the standpoint of practicality, it is convenient to be able to run a program in two ways.

It is not difficult to write such programs on your own. Suppose you have an applet named TestApplet. To enable it to run as an application, all you need to do is add a main method in the applet with the implementation, as follows:

```
public static void main(String[] args) {
  // Create a frame
  JFrame frame = new JFrame (                               create frame
    "Running a program as applet and frame");

  // Create an instance of TestApplet
  TestApplet applet = new TestApplet();                     create applet

  // Add the applet instance to the frame
  frame.getContentPane().add(applet, BorderLayout.CENTER);  add applet

  // Invoke init and start
  applet.init();                                            init()
  applet.start();                                           start()

  // Display the frame
  frame.setSize(300, 300);
  frame.setVisible(true);                                   show frame
}
```

Since the JApplet class is a subclass of Component, it can be placed in a frame. You can invoke the init and start methods of the applet to run a JApplet object in an application.

EXAMPLE 14.3 RUNNING A PROGRAM AS AN APPLET AND AS AN APPLICATION

Problem

Write a program that modifies the DisplayMessage applet in Example 14.2, "Passing Strings to Java Applets," to enable it to run both as an applet and as an application.

Solution

The program is identical to DisplayMessage except for the addition of a new main method and of a variable named isStandalone to indicate whether it is running as an applet or as an application. Listing 14.5 gives the solution to the problem.

LISTING 14.5 DisplayMessageApp.java (Running Applets Standalone)

```
 1 import javax.swing.*;
 2 import java.awt.Font;
 3 import java.awt.BorderLayout;
 4
 5 public class DisplayMessageApp extends JApplet {
 6   private String message = "A default message"; // Message to display
 7   private int x = 20; // Default x coordinate
 8   private int y = 20; // Default y coordinate
 9
10   /** Determine if it is application */
11   private boolean isStandalone = false;
12
13   /** Initialize the applet */
14   public void init() {
15     if (!isStandalone) {
16       // Get parameter values from the HTML file
17       message = getParameter("MESSAGE");
18       x = Integer.parseInt(getParameter("X"));
19       y = Integer.parseInt(getParameter("Y"));
20     }
21
22     // Create a message panel
23     MessagePanel messagePanel = new MessagePanel(message);
24     messagePanel.setFont(new Font("SansSerif", Font.BOLD, 20));
25     messagePanel.setXCoordinate(x);
26     messagePanel.setYCoordinate(y);
27
28     // Add the message panel to the applet
29     getContentPane().add(messagePanel);
30   }
31
32   /** Main method to display a message
33       @param args[0] x coordinate
34       @param args[1] y coordinate
35       @param args[2] message
36   */
37   public static void main(String[] args) {
38     // Create a frame
39     JFrame frame = new JFrame("DisplayMessageApp");
40
41     // Create an instance of the applet
42     DisplayMessageApp applet = new DisplayMessageApp();
43
44     // It runs as an application
45     applet.isStandalone = true;
46
47     // Get parameters from the command line
48     applet.getCommandLineParameters(args);
49
50     // Add the applet instance to the frame
51     frame.getContentPane().add(applet, BorderLayout.CENTER);
```

isStandalone

applet params

standalone

command params

EXAMPLE 14.3 (CONTINUED)

```
52
53     // Invoke init() and start()
54     applet.init();
55     applet.start();
56
57     // Display the frame
58     frame.setSize(300, 300);
59     frame.setDefaultCloseOperation(JFrame.EXIT_ON_CLOSE);
60     frame.setVisible(true);
61   }
62
63   /** Get command line parameters */
64   private void getCommandLineParameters(String[] args) {
65     // Check usage and get x, y and message
66     if (args.length != 3) {
67       System.out.println(
68         "Usage: java DisplayMessageApp x y message");
69       System.exit(0);
70     }
71     else {
72       x = Integer.parseInt(args[0]);
73       y = Integer.parseInt(args[1]);
74       message = args[2];
75     }
76   }
77 }
```

Review

When you run the program as an applet, the main method is ignored. When you run it as an application, the main method is invoked. A sample run of the program as an application and as an applet is shown in Figure 14.8.

FIGURE **14.8** *The* DisplayMessageApp *class can run as an application and as an applet.*

The main method creates a JFrame object frame and creates a JApplet object applet, then places the applet applet into the frame frame and invokes its init method. The application runs just like an applet.

The main method sets isStandalone true (Line 45) so that it does not attempt to retrieve HTML parameters when the init method is invoked.

The setVisible(true) method (Line 60) is invoked *after* the components are added to the applet, and the applet is added to the frame to ensure that the components will be visible. Otherwise, the components are not shown when the frame starts.

NOTE   omitting main method

From now on, all the GUI examples will be created as applets with a main method. Thus you will be able to run the program either as an applet or as an application. For brevity, the main method is not listed in the text.

✦ 14.7 CASE STUDY: TicTacToe (Optional)

You have learned about objects, classes, arrays, class inheritance, GUI, event-driven programming, and applets from the many examples in this chapter and the preceding chapters. Now it is time to put what you have learned to work in developing comprehensive projects. In this section, you will develop a Java applet with which to play the popular game of TicTacToe.

In a game of TicTacToe, two players take turns marking an available cell in a 3 × 3 grid with their respective tokens (either X or O). When one player has placed three tokens in a horizontal, vertical, or diagonal row on the grid, the game is over and that player has won. A draw (no winner) occurs when all the cells on the grid have been filled with tokens and neither player has achieved a win. Figure 14.9 shows two representative sample runs of the example.

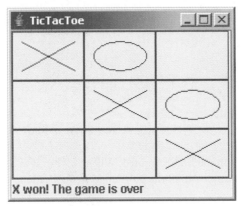
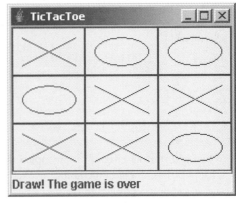

(a) X player won the game   (b) Draw -- No winners

FIGURE **14.9** *Two players play a TicTacToe game.*

All the examples you have seen so far show simple behaviors that are easy to model with classes. The behavior of the TicTacToe game is somewhat more complex. To create classes that model the behavior, you need to study and understand the game.

Assume that all the cells are initially empty, and that the first player takes the X token, and the second player takes the O token. To mark a cell, the player points the mouse to the cell and clicks it. If the cell is empty, the token (X or O) is displayed. If the cell is already filled, the player's action is ignored.

From the preceding description, it is obvious that a cell is a GUI object that handles the mouse-click event and displays tokens. Such an object could be either a button or a panel. Drawing on panels is more flexible than on buttons, because the token (X or O) can be drawn on a panel in any size, but on a button it can only be displayed as a text label. Therefore, a panel should be used to model a cell. How do you know the state of the cell (empty, X, or O)? You use a property named token of char type in the Cell class. The Cell class is responsible for drawing the token when an empty cell is clicked. So you need to write the code for listening to the MouseEvent and for painting the shapes for tokens X and O. The Cell class can be defined as shown in Figure 14.10.

The TicTacToe board consists of nine cells, declared using new Cell[3][3]. To determine which player's turn it is, you can introduce a variable named whoseTurn of char type. whoseTurn is initially X, then changes to O, and subsequently changes between X and O whenever a new cell is occupied. When the game is over, set whoseTurn to ' '.

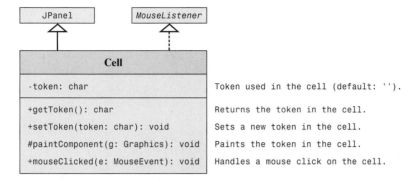

FIGURE 14.10   *The* Cell *class paints the token on a cell.*

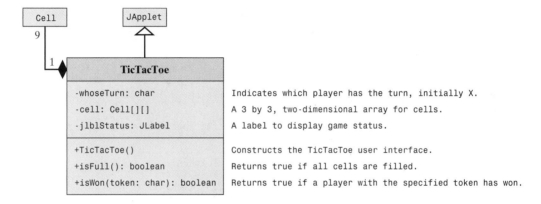

FIGURE 14.11   *The* TicTacToe *class contains nine cells.*

How do you know whether the game is over, whether there is a winner, and who the winner, if any, is? You can create a method named isWon(char token) to check whether a specified token has won and a method named isFull() to check whether all the cells are occupied.

Clearly, two classes emerge from the foregoing analysis. One is the Cell class, which handles operations for a single cell; and the other is the TicTacToe class, which plays the whole game and deals with all the cells. The relationship between these two classes is shown in Figure 14.11.

Since the Cell class is only to support the TicTacToe class, it can be defined as an inner class in TicTacToe. The complete program is given as follows:

LISTING 14.6   TicTacToe.java (TicTacToe Game)

```
1 import java.awt.*;
2 import java.awt.event.*;
3 import javax.swing.*;
4 import javax.swing.border.LineBorder;
5
6 public class TicTacToe extends JApplet {
7   // Indicate which player has a turn, initially it is the X player
8   private char whoseTurn = 'X';
9
10   // Create and initialize cells
11   private Cell[][] cells =  new Cell[3][3];
12
```

```
13    // Create and initialize a status label
14    private JLabel jlblStatus = new JLabel("X's turn to play");
15
16    /** Initialize UI */
17    public TicTacToe() {
18      // Panel p to hold cells
19      JPanel p = new JPanel(new GridLayout(3, 3, 0, 0));
20      for (int i = 0; i < 3; i++)
21        for (int j = 0; j < 3; j++)
22          p.add(cells[i][j] = new Cell());
23
24      // Set line borders on the cells panel and the status label
25      p.setBorder(new LineBorder(Color.red, 1));
26      jlblStatus.setBorder(new LineBorder(Color.yellow, 1));
27
28      // Place the panel and the label to the applet
29      this.getContentPane().add(p, BorderLayout.CENTER);
30      this.getContentPane().add(jlblStatus, BorderLayout.SOUTH);
31    }
32
33    /** Determine if the cells are all occupied */
34    public boolean isFull() {
35      for (int i = 0; i < 3; i++)
36        for (int j = 0; j < 3; j++)
37          if (cells[i][j].getToken() == ' ')
38            return false;
39
40      return true;
41    }
42
43    /** Determine if the player with the specified token wins */
44    public boolean isWon(char token) {
```

check rows

```
45      for (int i = 0; i < 3; i++)
46        if ((cells[i][0].getToken() == token)
47            && (cells[i][1].getToken() == token)
48            && (cells[i][2].getToken() == token)) {
49          return true;
50        }
51
```

check columns

```
52      for (int j = 0; j < 3; j++)
53        if ((cells[0][j].getToken() ==  token)
54            && (cells[1][j].getToken() == token)
55            && (cells[2][j].getToken() == token)) {
56          return true;
57        }
58
```

check major diagonal

```
59      if ((cells[0][0].getToken() == token)
60          && (cells[1][1].getToken() == token)
61          && (cells[2][2].getToken() == token)) {
62        return true;
63      }
64
```

check subdiagonal

```
65      if ((cells[0][2].getToken() == token)
66          && (cells[1][1].getToken() == token)
67          && (cells[2][0].getToken() == token)) {
68        return true;
69      }
70
71      return false;
72    }
73
74    // An inner class for a cell
```

inner class

```
75    public class Cell extends JPanel implements MouseListener {
76      // Token used for this cell
77      private char token = ' ';
78
79      public Cell() {
80        setBorder(new LineBorder(Color.black, 1)); // Set cell's border
81        addMouseListener(this);   // Register listener
82      }
```

```
83
84     /** Return token */
85     public char getToken() {
86       return token;
87     }
88
89     /** Set a new token */
90     public void setToken(char c) {
91       token = c;
92       repaint();
93     }
94
95     /** Paint the cell */
96     protected void paintComponent(Graphics g) {                          paint cell
97       super.paintComponent(g);
98
99       if (token == 'X') {
100        g.drawLine(10, 10, getWidth() - 10, getHeight() - 10);
101        g.drawLine(getWidth() - 10, 10, 10, getHeight() - 10);
102      }
103      else if (token == 'O') {
104        g.drawOval(10, 10, getWidth() - 20, getHeight() - 20);
105      }
106    }
107
108    /** Handle mouse click on a cell */
109    public void mouseClicked(MouseEvent e) {                             handler
110      // If cell is empty and game is not over
111      if (token == ' ' && whoseTurn != ' ') {
112        setToken(whoseTurn); // Set token in the cell
113
114        // Check game status
115        if (isWon(whoseTurn)) {
116          jlblStatus.setText(whoseTurn + " won! The game is over");
117          whoseTurn = ' '; // Game is over
118        }
119        else if (isFull()) {
120          jlblStatus.setText("Draw! The game is over");
121          whoseTurn = ' '; // Game is over
122        }
123        else {
124          whoseTurn = (whoseTurn == 'X') ? 'O': 'X'; // Change the turn
125          jlblStatus.setText(whoseTurn + "'s turn");  // Display whose turn
126        }
127      }
128    }
129
130    public void mousePressed(MouseEvent e) {
131      // TODO: implement this java.awt.event.MouseListener method;
132    }
133
134    public void mouseReleased(MouseEvent e) {
135      // TODO: implement this java.awt.event.MouseListener method;
136    }
137
138    public void mouseEntered(MouseEvent e) {
139      // TODO: implement this java.awt.event.MouseListener method;
140    }
141
142    public void mouseExited(MouseEvent e) {
143      // TODO: implement this java.awt.event.MouseListener method;
144    }
145  }
146 }                                                                main method omitted
```

The TicTacToe class initializes the user interface with nine cells placed in a panel of GridLayout (Lines 19–22). A label named jlblStatus is used to show the status of the game (Line 14). The variable whoseTurn (Line 8) is used to track the next type of token to be placed in a cell. The methods isFull (Lines 34–41) and isWon (Lines 44–72) are for checking the status of the game.

Since Cell is an inner class in TicTacToe, the variable (whoseTurn) and methods (isFull and isWon) defined in TicTacToe can be referenced from the Cell class. The inner class makes programs simple and concise. If Cell were not declared as an inner class of TicTacToe, you would have to pass an object of TicTacToe to Cell in order for the variables and methods in TicTacToe to be used in Cell. You will rewrite the program without using an inner class in Exercise 14.6.

The Cell class implements MouseListener to listen for MouseEvent. If an empty cell is clicked and the game is not over, a token is set in the cell (Line 112). If the game is over, whoseTurn is set to ' ' (Lines 117, 121). Otherwise, whoseTurn is alternated to a new turn (Line 124).

 TIP

Use an incremental approach in developing a Java project of this kind, working one step at a time. The foregoing program can be divided into five steps:

1. Lay out the user interface and display a fixed token X on a cell.

2. Enable the cell to display a fixed token X upon a mouse click.

3. Coordinate between the two players so as to display tokens X and O alternately.

4. Check whether a player wins, or whether all the cells are occupied without a winner.

5. Implement displaying a message on the label upon each move by a player.

 # 14.8 CASE STUDY: Bouncing Ball (Optional)

Write an applet that displays a ball bouncing in a panel. Use two buttons to suspend and resume the movement, and use a scroll bar to control the bouncing speed, as shown in Figure 14.12.

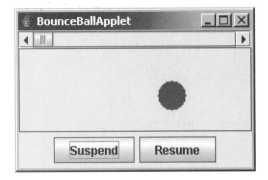 

FIGURE **14.12** *The ball's movement is controlled by the Suspend and Resume buttons and the scroll bar.*

Here are the major steps to complete this example:

1. Create a subclass of JPanel named Ball to display a ball bouncing, as shown in Listing 14.7.

2. Create a subclass of JPanel named BallControl to contain the ball with a scroll bar and two control buttons *Suspend* and *Resume*, as shown in Listing 14.8.

3. Create an applet named BounceBallApp to contain an instance of BallControl and enable the applet to run standalone, as shown in Listing 14.9.

The relationship among these classes is shown in Figure 14.13.

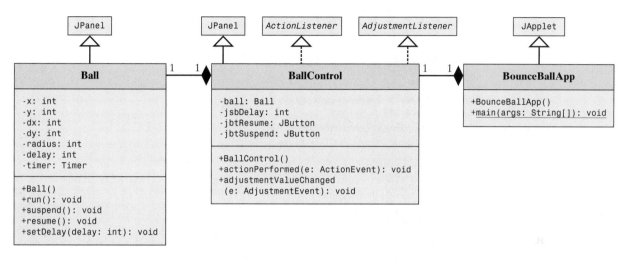

Figure 14.13 *BounceBallApp contains BallControl, and BallControl contains Ball.*

Listing 14.7   Ball.java (Displaying a Moving Ball)

```
1 import java.awt.event.*;
2 import javax.swing.Timer;
3 import java.awt.*;
4 import javax.swing.*;
5
6 public class Ball extends JPanel implements ActionListener {
7   private int delay = 10;
8
9   // Create a timer with delay 1000 ms
10  protected Timer timer = new Timer(delay, this);
11
12  private int x = 0; private int y = 0; // Current ball position
13  private int radius = 15; // Ball radius
14  private int dx = 2; // Increment on ball's x-coordinate
15  private int dy = 2; // Increment on ball's y-coordinate
16
17  public Ball() {
18    timer.start();
19  }
20
21  /** Handle the action event */
22  public void actionPerformed(ActionEvent e) {
23    repaint();
24  }
25
26  protected void paintComponent(Graphics g) {
27    super.paintComponent(g);
28
29    g.setColor(Color.red);
30
31    // Check boundaries
32    if (x < radius) dx = Math.abs(dx);
33    if (x > getWidth() - radius) dx = -Math.abs(dx);
```

timer delay

create timer

start timer

repaint ball

paint ball

```
34        if (y < radius) dy = Math.abs(dy);
35        if (y > getHeight() - radius) dy = -Math.abs(dy);
36
37        // Adjust ball position
38        x += dx;
39        y += dy;
40        g.fillOval(x - radius, y - radius, radius * 2, radius * 2);
41      }
42
43      public void suspend() {
44        timer.stop(); // Suspend clock
45      }
46
47      public void resume() {
48        timer.start(); // Resume clock
49      }
50
51      public void setDelay(int delay) {
52        this.delay = delay;
53        timer.setDelay(delay);
54      }
55  }
```

Using Timer class to control animation was introduced in Section 12.6, "The Timer Class" name. Ball extends JPanel and implements ActionListener (Line 6) so that it can listen for ActionEvent. Line 10 creates a Timer for a Ball. The timer is started in Line 18 when a Ball is constructed. The timer fires an ActionEvent at a fixed rate. The listener responds in Line 23 to repaint the ball to animate ball movement. The center of the ball is at (x, y), which changes to (x + dx, y + dy) on the next display. The suspend and resume methods (Lines 43–49) can be used to stop and start the timer. The setDelay(int) method (Lines 51–54) sets a new delay.

LISTING 14.8 BallControl.java (Controlling Ball Movement)

```
1  import javax.swing.*;
2  import java.awt.event.*;
3  import java.awt.*;
4
5  public class BallControl extends JPanel
6        implements ActionListener, AdjustmentListener {
7    private Ball ball = new Ball();
8    private JButton jbtSuspend = new JButton("Suspend");
9    private JButton jbtResume = new JButton("Resume");
10   private JScrollBar jsbDelay = new JScrollBar();
11
12   public BallControl() {
13     // Group buttons in a panel
14     JPanel panel = new JPanel();
15     panel.add(jbtSuspend);
16     panel.add(jbtResume);
17
18     // Add ball and buttons to the panel
19     ball.setBorder(new javax.swing.border.LineBorder(Color.red));
20     jsbDelay.setOrientation(JScrollBar.HORIZONTAL);
21     ball.setDelay(jsbDelay.getMaximum());
22     setLayout(new BorderLayout());
23     add(jsbDelay, BorderLayout.NORTH);
24     add(ball, BorderLayout.CENTER);
25     add(panel, BorderLayout.SOUTH);
26
27     // Register listeners
28     jbtSuspend.addActionListener(this);
29     jbtResume.addActionListener(this);
30     jsbDelay.addAdjustmentListener(this);
31   }
32
```

button

scroll bar

create UI

register listener

```
33   public void actionPerformed(ActionEvent e) {
34     if (e.getSource() == jbtSuspend)
35       ball.suspend();                                        suspend
36     else if (e.getSource() == jbtResume)
37       ball.resume();                                         resume
38   }
39
40   public void adjustmentValueChanged(AdjustmentEvent e) {
41     ball.setDelay(jsbDelay.getMaximum() - e.getValue());     new delay
42   }
43 }
```

The `BallControl` class extends `JPanel` to display the ball with a scroll bar and two control buttons, implements the `ActionListener` to handle action events from the buttons, and implements the `AdjustmentListener` to handle value change events from the scroll bar. When the *Suspend* button is clicked, the ball's `suspend()` method is invoked to suspend the ball movement (Line 35). When the *Resume* button is clicked, the ball's `resume()` method is invoked to resume the ball movement (Line 37). The bouncing speed can be changed using the scroll bar.

LISTING 14.9   BounceBallApp.java

```
1 import java.awt.*;
2 import java.awt.event.*;
3 import java.applet.*;
4 import javax.swing.*;
5
6 public class BounceBallApp extends JApplet {
7   public BounceBallApp() {
8     getContentPane().add(new BallControl());                  add BallControl
9   }
10 }                                                            main method omitted
```

The `BounceBallApp` class simply places an instance of `BallControl` in the applet's content pane. The `main` method is provided in the applet (not displayed in the listing for brevity) so that you can also run it standalone.

14.8   The URL Class (Optional)

Images and audio are stored in files. The `java.net.URL` class can be used to identify files on the Internet. In general, a URL (Uniform Resource Locator) is a pointer to a "resource" on the World Wide Web. A resource can be something as simple as a file or a directory. You can create a URL object using the following constructor:

```
public URL(String spec) throws MalformedURLException
```

For example, the following statement creates a URL object for `http://www.sun.com`:

```
try {
  URL url = new URL("http://www.sun.com");
}
catch (MalformedURLException ex) {
}
```

A `MalformedURLException` is thrown if the URL string has a syntax error. For example, the URL string `"http:/www.sun.com"` would cause a `MalformedURLException` runtime error because two slashes (`//`) are required.

The following statement creates a URL object for the file c:\book\image\us.gif:

```
try {
  URL url = new URL("c:\\book\\image\\us.gif");
}
catch (MalformedURLException ex) {
}
```

The preceding statement creates a URL for the absolute file name c:\book\image\us.gif on Windows. It has two problems: (1) the file location is fixed; (2) it is platform-dependent. To circumvent these problems, you can create the URL for the file through the meta-object of the class.

As discussed in Section 8.11.3, "The getClass Method," when a class is loaded, the JVM creates a meta-object for the class, which can be obtained using

```
java.lang.Class metaObject = this.getClass();
```

The Class class provides access to useful information about the class, such as the data fields, constructors, and methods. It also contains the getResource(filename) method, which can be used to obtain the URL of a given file name in the class directory. Recall that the class directory is where the class is stored (see page 160). For example, all the classes in this book are stored in c:\book. So the class directory is c:\book.

To obtain the URL of a file in the class directory, use

```
URL url = metaObject.getResource(filename);
```

14.9 Displaying Images (Optional)

You have used the ImageIcon class to create an icon from an image file and the setIcon method or the constructor to place the icon in a GUI component, such as a button or a label. For example, the following statements create an ImageIcon and set it on a JLabel object jlbl:

```
ImageIcon imageIcon = new ImageIcon("c:\\book\\image\\us.gif");
jlbl.setIcon(imageIcon);
```

This approach presents a problem. The file location is fixed, because it uses the absolute file path on Windows. As a result, the program cannot run on other platforms and cannot run as an applet. You can circumvent this problem by creating the URL for the file through the meta-object of the class. For example, suppose the class directory is c:\book, the following statements create a URL for c:\book\image\us.gif:

```
Class metaObject = this.getClass();
URL url = metaObject.getResource("image/us.gif");
```

You can now create an ImageIcon using

```
ImageIcon imageIcon = new ImageIcon(url);
```

An image icon displays a fixed-size image. To display an image in a flexible size, you need to use the java.awt.Image class. An image can be created from an image icon as follows:

```
Image image = imageIcon.getImage();
```

Using a label as an area for displaying images is simple and convenient, but you don't have much control over how the image is displayed. A more flexible way to display images is to use the drawImage method of the Graphics class on a panel.

Here are four versions of the drawImage method:

✦ drawImage(Image img, int x, int y, Color bgcolor, ImageObserver observer)
Draws the image in a specified location. The image's top-left corner is at (x, y) in the graphics context's coordinate space. Transparent pixels in the image are drawn in the specified color bgcolor. The observer is the object on which the image is displayed. The image is cut off if it is larger than the area it is being drawn on.

◆ drawImage(Image img, int x, int y, ImageObserver observer)
This is the same as the preceding method except that it does not specify a background color.

◆ drawImage(Image img, int x, int y, int width, int height, ImageObserver observer)
Draws a scaled version of the image that can fill all of the available space in the specified rectangle.

◆ drawImage(Image img, int x, int y, int width, int height, Color bgcolor, ImageObserver observer)
This is the same as the preceding method except that it provides a solid background color behind the image being drawn.

ImageObserver is an asynchronous update interface that receives notifications of image information as the image is constructed. The Component class implements ImageObserver. Therefore, every GUI component is an instance of ImageObserver. To draw images using the drawImage method in a Swing component, such as JPanel, override the paintComponent method to tell the component how to display the image in the panel.

📖 NOTE

You can also create an ImageIcon from an Image object using new ImageIcon(image).

Listing 14.10 gives the code that displays an image from /image/us.gif in the class directory on a panel.

LISTING 14.10 DisplayImage.java

```java
1  import java.awt.*;
2  import javax.swing.*;
3
4  public class DisplayImage extends Component {
5    public DisplayImage() {
6      getContentPane().add(new ImagePanel());       add panel
7    }
8
9    // Define the panel for showing an image
10   class ImagePanel extends JPanel {                inner class
11     Class metaObject = this.getClass();
12     java.net.URL url = metaObject.getResource("image/us.gif");
13     ImageIcon imageIcon = new ImageIcon(url);
14     Image image = imageIcon.getImage();            get image
15
16     /** Draw image on the panel */
17     public void paintComponent(Graphics g) {
18       super.paintComponent(g);
19
20       if (image != null)
21         g.drawImage(image, 0, 0, getWidth(), getHeight(), this);   show image
22     }
23   }
24 }                                                 main method omitted
```

The file image/us.gif (Line 12) is under the class directory. The Image from the file is created in Lines 11–14. The image is displayed if it exists in Lines 20–22.

✴ 14.10 CASE STUDY: The ImageViewer Component

Displaying an image is a frequent task in Java programming. This case study develops a reusable component named ImageViewer that displays an image in a panel.

The ImageViewer class given in Listing 14.11 contains the properties image, imageFileName, stretched, xCoordinate, and yCoordinate, as shown in Figure 14.14.

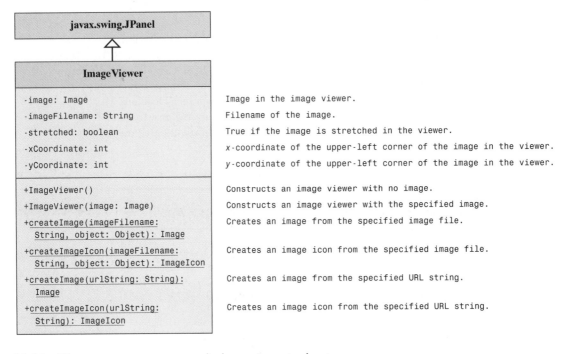

FIGURE **14.14** *The ImageViewer component displays an image in the viewer.*

LISTING **14.11** ImageViewer.java

```
 1 import java.awt.*;
 2 import java.net.URL;
 3 import javax.swing.*;
 4
 5 public class ImageViewer extends JPanel {
 6   /** Hold value of property image. */
 7   private java.awt.Image image;
 8
 9   /** Hold value of property imageFilename. */
10   private String imageFilename = "";
11
12   /** Hold value of property stretched. */
13   private boolean stretched = true;
14
15   /** Hold value of property xCoordinate. */
16   private int xCoordinate;
17
18   /** Hold value of property yCoordinate. */
19   private int yCoordinate;
20
21   /** Construct an empty image viewer */
22   public ImageViewer() {
23   }
24
```

properties

no-arg constructor

```
25    /** Construct an image viewer for a specified Image object */
26    public ImageViewer(Image image) {                                    constructor
27      this.image = image;
28      repaint();
29    }
30
31    /** Create an image icon from a local file name */
32    public static ImageIcon createImageIcon(String imageFilename,        image icon
33        Object object) {
34      URL url = object.getClass().getResource(imageFilename);
35      return new ImageIcon(url);
36    }
37
38    /** Create an image from a local file name */
39    public static Image createImage(String imageFilename,                image
40        Object object) {
41      ImageIcon imageIcon = createImageIcon(imageFilename, object);
42      if (imageIcon != null)
43        return imageIcon.getImage();
44      else
45        return null;
46    }
47
48    /** Create an image icon from an Internet URL string */
49    public static ImageIcon createImageIcon(String urlString) {
50      return new ImageIcon(getURL(urlString));
51    }
52
53    /** Create an image from an URL string */
54    public static Image createImage(String urlString) {
55      return new ImageIcon(getURL(urlString)).getImage();
56    }
57
58    private static URL getURL(String urlString) {
59      URL url = null;
60      try {
61        url = new URL(urlString);
62      }
63      catch (java.net.MalformedURLException ex) {
64        ex.printStackTrace();
65      }
66
67      return url;
68    }
69
70    protected void paintComponent(Graphics g) {
71      super.paintComponent(g);
72
73      if (image != null)
74        if (isStretched())                                               stretched
75          g.drawImage(image, xCoordinate, yCoordinate,
76            getSize().width, getSize().height, this);
77        else
78          g.drawImage(image, xCoordinate, yCoordinate, this);           non-stretched
79    }
80
81    /** Return value of property image */
82    public java.awt.Image getImage() {
83      return image;
84    }
85
86    /** Set a new value for property image */
87    public void setImage(java.awt.Image image) {
88      this.image = image;
89      repaint();
90    }
91
92    /** Return value of property imageFilename */
93    public String getImageFilename() {
94      return imageFilename;
95    }
```

```
96
97    /** Set a new value for property imageFilename */
98    public void setImageFilename(String imageFilename) {
99      this.imageFilename = imageFilename;
109      image = createImage(imageFilename, this);
101      repaint();
102    }
103
104    /** Return value of property stretched */
105    public boolean isStretched() {
106      return stretched;
107    }
108
109    /** Set a new value for property stretched */
110    public void setStretched(boolean stretched) {
111      this.stretched = stretched;
112      repaint();
113    }
114
115    /** Return value of property xCoordinate */
116    public int getXCoordinate() {
117      return xCoordinate;
118    }
119
120    /** Set a new value for property xCoordinate */
121    public void setXCoordinate(int xCoordinate) {
122      this.xCoordinate = xCoordinate;
123      repaint();
124    }
125
126    /** Return value of property yCoordinate */
127    public int getYCoordinate() {
128      return yCoordinate;
129    }
130
131    /** Set a new value for property yCoordinate */
132    public void setYCoordinate(int yCoordinate) {
133      this.yCoordinate = yCoordinate;
134      repaint();
135    }
136 }
```

The `ImageViewer` class provides two overloaded static methods, `createImageIcon (imageFilename, object)` (Lines 32–36) and `createImageIcon(urlString)` (Lines 49–51). The `createImageIcon(imageFilename, object)` method returns an `ImageIcon` from the image file name through the resource of the object, and `createImageIcon(urlString)` returns an `ImageIcon` from the specified URL.

Two other overloaded static methods are `createImage(imageFilename, object)` (Lines 39–46) and `createImage(urlString)` (Lines 54–56). The `createImage(imageFilename, object)` method returns an `Image` from the image file name through the resource of the object, and `createImage (urlString)` returns an `Image` from the specified URL.

The `imageFilename` property enables you to set a filename for the image. The `setImageFilename` method sets the `imageFilename` and creates the image for the file.

The `ImageViewer` component also provides the `image` property. You can set the image directly using the `setImage` method. This is convenient if your program knows the image but not the filename for the image. This is another good example of class design that provides many ways to use the class. You can use the `imageFilename` property or the `image` property to set the image for `ImageViewer`, whichever is convenient.

 NOTE

The `createImageIcon` method and `createImage` method could have been eliminated and combined with the `setImageFilename` method. The purpose of creating these two static methods is for use by other programs. You can now use these two methods as well as other methods to create image icons and images.

 NOTE

You can use images in Swing components like JLabel and JButton, but the images are not stretchable and their filenames cannot be used directly with these components. The ImageViewer component provides better support for displaying images.

Now let us use the ImageViewer class to create six images in Listing 14.12. Figure 14.15 shows a sample run of the program.

LISTING 14.12   SixFlags.java

```
1 import javax.swing.*;
2 import java.awt.*;
3
4 public class SixFlags extends javax.swing.JApplet {
5   public SixFlags() {
6     ImageViewer imageViewer1 = new ImageViewer();
7     ImageViewer imageViewer2 = new ImageViewer();
8     ImageViewer imageViewer3 = new ImageViewer();
9     ImageViewer imageViewer4 = new ImageViewer();
10    ImageViewer imageViewer5 = new ImageViewer();
11    ImageViewer imageViewer6 = new ImageViewer();
12
13    getContentPane().setLayout(new java.awt.GridLayout(2, 0, 5, 5));
14    imageViewer1.setImageFilename("/image/us.gif");
15    getContentPane().add(imageViewer1);
16    imageViewer2.setImageFilename("/image/ca.gif");
17    getContentPane().add(imageViewer2);
18    imageViewer3.setImageFilename("/image/india.gif");
19    getContentPane().add(imageViewer3);
20    imageViewer4.setImageFilename("/image/uk.gif");
21    getContentPane().add(imageViewer4);
22    imageViewer5.setImageFilename("/image/china.gif");
23    getContentPane().add(imageViewer5);
24    imageViewer6.setImageFilename("/image/norway.gif");
25    getContentPane().add(imageViewer6);
26  }
27 }
```

image viewer (line 6)

image file (line 14)

main method omitted

FIGURE 14.15   *Six images are displayed in six ImageViewer components.*

You can use files from your local machine or from any Internet site. For example, you may replace Line 14 with the following statement to use a file from `www.cs.armstrong.edu`:

```
imageViewer1.setImage(ImageViewer.createImage(
  "http://www.cs.armstrong.edu/liang/image/uk.gif"));
```

The image icon in the `createImageIcon(imageFilename, object)` method is created using `new ImageIcon(url)` (Line 35 in ImageViewer.java), where `url` is obtained using the `getResource` method in a `Class` instance of the object. You may create an image icon directly from the absolute path of the image file, as follows:

```
new ImageIcon("c:\\book\image\\someimage.gif");
```

This approach is simple, but it works only with standalone applications. To load images in Java applets, you have to obtain the URL of the image and load the image through it. This approach works for both Java applications and applets.

✴ 14.11   CASE STUDY: Image Animations (Optional)

This case study gives an example of how to display a sequence of images that simulates a movie. You can use a timer to trigger repainting of the viewing area with different images. The `Timer` class was introduced in Section 12.6, "The `Timer` Class."

Let us write a program in Listing 14.13 that displays a sequence of images in order to create a movie. The images are files stored in the **image** directory that are named **L1.gif**, **L2.gif**, and so on, to **L52.gif**. When you run the program, you will see a phrase entitled "Learning Java" rotate, as shown in Figure 14.16.

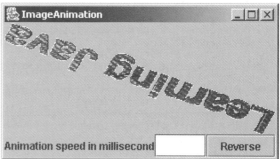

FIGURE **14.16**   *The applet displays a sequence of images.*

LISTING 14.13   ImageAnimation.java

image number

```
 1 import java.awt.*;
 2 import java.awt.event.*;
 3 import javax.swing.*;
 4
 5 public class ImageAnimation extends JApplet
 6     implements ActionListener {
 7   // Total number of images
 8   public final static int NUM_OF_IMAGES = 52;
 9   protected Image[] images = new Image[NUM_OF_IMAGES]; // Hold images
10   protected int currentImageIndex = 0, // Current image subscript
11             sleepTime = 100; // Milliseconds to sleep
12   protected int direction = 1; // Image rotating direction
```

```
13
14    // Image viewer to display an image
15    private ImageViewer imageViewer = new ImageViewer();
16
17    // Text field for setting animation speed
18    protected JTextField jtfSpeed = new JTextField(5);
19
20    // Button for reversing direction
21    private JButton jbtReverse = new JButton("Reverse");
22
23    // Create a timer with delay 1000 ms and listener Clock
24    private Timer timer = new Timer(1000, this);                         create timer
25
26    /** Initialize the applet */
27    public void init() {
28      // Load the image, the image files are named
29      // L1 - L52 in image directory
30      for (int i = 0; i < images.length; i++ ) {
31        images[i] = ImageViewer.createImage(                            create image
32          "image/L" + (i + 1) + ".gif", this );
33      }
34
35      // Panel p to hold animation control                              create UI
36      JPanel p = new JPanel();
37      p.setLayout(new BorderLayout());
38      p.add(new JLabel("Animation speed in millisecond"),
39        BorderLayout.WEST);
40      p.add(jtfSpeed, BorderLayout.CENTER);
41      p.add(jbtReverse, BorderLayout.EAST);
42
43      // Add the image panel and p to the applet
44      getContentPane().add(imageViewer, BorderLayout.CENTER);
45      getContentPane().add(p, BorderLayout.SOUTH);
46
47      // Register listener
48      jtfSpeed.addActionListener(this);
49      jbtReverse.addActionListener(this);
50
51      // Start the timer
52      timer.start();                                                    start timer
53    }
54
55    /** Handle ActionEvent */
56    public void actionPerformed(ActionEvent e) {
57      if (e.getSource() == jtfSpeed) {
58        sleepTime = Integer.parseInt(jtfSpeed.getText());
59        timer.setDelay(sleepTime);
60      }
61      else if (e.getSource() == jbtReverse) {
62        direction = -direction;
63      }
64      else if (e.getSource() == timer) {
65        imageViewer.setImage(                                           change image
66          images[currentImageIndex % NUM_OF_IMAGES]);
67
68        // Make sure currentImageIndex is nonnegative
69        if (currentImageIndex == 0) currentImageIndex = NUM_OF_IMAGES;
70        currentImageIndex = currentImageIndex + direction;
71      }
72    }
73  }                                                                     main method omitted
```

Fifty-two image files are located in the **image** directory, which is a subdirectory of the code base directory. The images in these files are loaded to images (Lines 30–33) and then painted continuously on the applet at a fixed rate using a timer.

The image is drawn to occupy the entire applet viewing area in a rectangle. It is scaled to fill in the area.

The `timer` is created in Line 24 and started in the `init` method in Line 52. You can adjust `sleepTime` to control animation speed by entering a value in milliseconds and pressing the Enter key for the change to take place.

The display sequence can be reversed by clicking the Reverse button.

You can add a simple function to suspend a `timer` when the mouse is pressed. You can resume a suspended `timer` when the mouse is released.

 NOTE

The `JComponent` class has a property named `doubleBuffered`. By default, this property is set to `true`. Double buffering is a technique for reducing animation flickering. It creates a graphics context off-screen and does all the drawings in the off-screen context. When the drawing is complete, it displays the whole context on the real screen. Thus, there is no flickering within an image because all the drawings are displayed at the same time. To see the effect of double buffering, set the `doubleBuffered` property to false. You will be stunned by the difference.

14.12   Playing Audio

There are several formats for audio files. Prior to Java 2, sound files in the AU format used on the UNIX operating system were the only ones Java was able to play. With Java 2, you can play sound files in the WAV, AIFF, MIDI, AU, and RMF formats, with better sound quality.

To play an audio file in an applet, first create an *audio clip object* for the audio file. The audio clip is created once and can be played repeatedly without reloading the file. To create an audio clip, use the static method `newAudioClip()` in the `java.applet.Applet` class:

```
AudioClip audioClip = Applet.newAudioClip(url);
```

Audio was originally used with Java applets. For this reason, the `AudioClip` interface is in the `java.applet` package.

The following statements, for example, create an `AudioClip` for the `beep.au` audio file in the class directory:

```
Class metaObject = this.getClass();
URL url = metaObject.getResource("beep.au");
AudioClip audioClip = Applet.newAudioClip(url);
```

To manipulate a sound for an audio clip, use the `play()`, `loop()`, and `stop()` methods in `java.applet.AudioClip`, as shown in Figure 14.17.

Let us write a program that displays national flags and plays national anthems. The program enables you to select a country from a combo box and then displays the country's flag. You can play the selected country's national anthem by clicking the Play Anthem button, as shown in Figure 14.18. Listing 14.14 gives the solution.

java.applet.AudioClip	
+*play()*	Starts playing this audio clip. Each time this method is called, the clip is restarted from the beginning.
+*loop()*	Plays the clip repeatedly.
+*stop()*	Stops playing the clip.

FIGURE 14.17   *The `AudioClip` interface provides the methods for playing sound.*

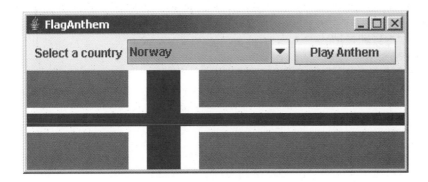

FIGURE 14.18 *The program displays the flag of the selected country and plays its national anthem.*

LISTING 14.14 FlagAnthem.java (Playing Audio)

```java
1 import java.awt.*;
2 import java.awt.event.*;
3 import javax.swing.*;
4 import java.applet.*;
5
6 public class FlagAnthem extends JApplet implements ActionListener {
7   // Image viewer for displaying an image
8   private ImageViewer imageViewer = new ImageViewer();          // image viewer
9
10   // Combo box for selecting a country
11   private JComboBox jcboCountry = new JComboBox(new String[] {
12     "United States of America", "United Kingdom", "Denmark",
13     "Norway", "China", "India", "Germany"});
14
15   // Create flag images
16   private Image[] images = {
17     ImageViewer.createImage("image/us.gif", this),            // images
18     ImageViewer.createImage("image/uk.gif", this),
19     ImageViewer.createImage("image/denmark.gif", this),
20     ImageViewer.createImage("image/norway.gif", this),
21     ImageViewer.createImage("image/china.gif", this),
22     ImageViewer.createImage("image/india.gif", this),
23     ImageViewer.createImage("image/germany.gif", this)};
24
25   // Create audio clips
26   private AudioClip[] audioClips = {
27     Applet.newAudioClip(                                       // audio clips
28       this.getClass().getResource("anthem/us.mid")),
29     Applet.newAudioClip(
30       this.getClass().getResource("anthem/uk.mid")),
31     Applet.newAudioClip(
32       this.getClass().getResource("anthem/denmark.mid")),
33     Applet.newAudioClip(
34       this.getClass().getResource("anthem/norway.mid")),
35     Applet.newAudioClip(
36       this.getClass().getResource("anthem/china.mid")),
37     Applet.newAudioClip(
38       this.getClass().getResource("anthem/india.mid")),
39     Applet.newAudioClip(
40       this.getClass().getResource("anthem/germany.mid"))
41   };
42
43   private int currentIndex = 0; // Denote the current selected index
44
45   // Button to play an audio
46   private JButton jbtPlayAnthem = new JButton("Play Anthem");
```

create UI

```
47
48    /** Initialize the applet */
49    public void init() {
50      // Panel p to hold a label combo box and a button for play audio
51      JPanel p = new JPanel();
52      p.add(new JLabel("Select a country"));
53      p.add(jcboCountry);
54      p.add(jbtPlayAnthem);
55
56      // By default, the US flag is displayed
57      imageViewer.setImage(images[0]);
58
59      // Place p and an image panel in the applet
60      getContentPane().add(p, BorderLayout.NORTH);
61      getContentPane().add(imageViewer, BorderLayout.CENTER);
62
63      // Register listener
64      jbtPlayAnthem.addActionListener(this);
65      jcboCountry.addActionListener(this);
66    }
67
68    /** Handle ActionEvent */
69    public void actionPerformed(ActionEvent e) {
70      if (e.getSource() == jcboCountry)
71        imageViewer.setImage(images[jcboCountry.getSelectedIndex()]);
72      else if (e.getSource() == jbtPlayAnthem) {
73        audioClips[currentIndex].stop(); // Stop current audio clip
74        currentIndex = jcboCountry.getSelectedIndex();
75        audioClips[currentIndex].play();
76      }
77    }
78  }
```

event handler

main method omitted

An image viewer is created in Line 8 to display a flag image. An array of flag images for seven nations is created in Lines 16–23. Each image is created using the static `createImage` method in the `ImageViewer` class.

An array of audio clips is created in Lines 26–41. Each audio clip is created for an audio file through the URL of the current class. The audio files are stored in the same directory with class file `FlagAnthem`.

The combo box for country names is created in Lines 11–13. When a new country name in the combo box is selected, a new image is set in the image viewer (Line 71).

When the *Play Anthem* button is clicked, the current audio is stopped and a new audio for the current selected country is played.

14.13 Packaging and Deploying Java Projects (Optional)

Your project may consist of many classes and supporting files, such as image files and audio files. To make your programs run on the end-user side, you need to provide end-users with all these files. For convenience, Java supports an archive file that can be used to group all the project files in a compressed file.

The Java archive file format (JAR) is based on the popular ZIP file format. Although JAR can be used as a general archiving tool, the primary motivation for its development was to make it possible for Java applications, applets, and their requisite components (.class files, images, and sounds) to be transported in a single file.

This single file can be deployed on an end-user's machine as an application. It also can be downloaded to a browser in a single HTTP transaction, rather than opening a new connection for each piece. This greatly simplifies application deployment and improves the speed with which an applet can be loaded onto a web page and begin functioning. The JAR format also supports compression, which reduces the size of the file and improves download time still further. Additionally, individual entries in a JAR file can be digitally signed by the applet author to authenticate their origin.

You can use the JDK **jar** command to create an archive file. The following command creates an archive file named TicTacToe.jar for classes TicTacToe.class and TicTacToe$Cell.class (inner class):

```
jar -cf TicTacToe.jar TicTacToe.class TicTacToe$Cell.class
```

The **-c** option is for creating a new archive file, and the **-f** option specifies the archive file's name.

> 🌿 **NOTE**
>
> You can view the contents of a .jar file using WinZip, a popular compression utility for Windows, as shown in Figure 14.19.

view .jar contents

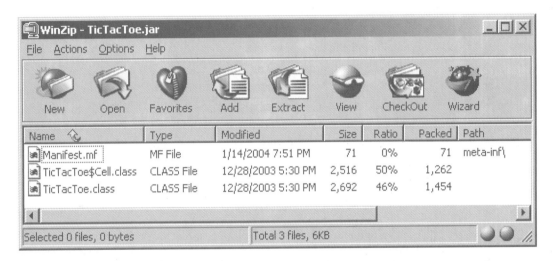

FIGURE 14.19   *You can view the files contained in the archive file using the WinZip utility.*

14.13.1   The Manifest File

As shown in Figure 14.19, a manifest file was created with the path name meta-inf\. The manifest is a special file that contains information about the files packaged in a JAR file. For instance, the manifest file in Figure 14.19 contains the following information:

```
Manifest-Version: 1.0

Name: TicTacToe.class
Java-Bean: True

Name: TioTacToe$Cell.class
Java-Bean: True
```

You can modify the information contained in the manifest file to enable the JAR file to be used for a variety of purposes. For instance, you can add information to specify a main class to run an application using the .jar file.

14.13.2 Running Archived Projects

You can package all the class files and dependent resource files in an archive file for distribution to the end-user. If the project is a Java application, the user should have a Java-running environment already installed. If it is not installed, the user can download the Java Runtime Environment (JRE) from JavaSoft at `http://www.javasoft.com/` and install it.

JRE

 NOTE

The Java Runtime Environment is the minimum standard Java platform for running Java programs. It contains the Java interpreter, Java core classes, and supporting files. The JRE does not contain any development tools (such as Applet Viewer or javac) or classes that pertain only to a development environment. The JRE is a subset of JDK.

To run `TicTacToe` as an application, take the following steps:

1. Update the manifest file to insert an entry for the main class. You need to create a text file containing the following two lines:

```
Main-Class: TicTacToe
Sealed: true
```

The first line specifies the main class. The second line is necessary to ensure that the first line can be inserted into an existing manifest file in a jar. Assume that these two lines are contained in the file temp.mf.

2. Execute the `jar` command to insert the main class line into the manifest file in TicTac-Toe.jar, as follows:

```
jar -uvmf temp.mf TicTacToe.jar
```

The **-u** option is for updating an existing jar file, the **-v** option is for displaying command output, and the **-m** option is for appending the contents in temp.mf to the manifest file in the archive.

3. Run the .jar file using the java command from the directory that contains TicTacToe.jar, as follows:

```
java -jar TicTacToe.jar
```

 NOTE

You can write an installation procedure that creates the necessary directories and subdirectories on the end-user's computer. The installation can also create an icon that the end-user can double-click on to start the program. For information on creating Windows desktop icons, please see Supplement O, "Creating Shortcuts for Java Applications on Windows."

To run `TicTacToe` as an applet, modify the <applet> tag in the HTML file to include an archive attribute. The archive attribute specifies the archive file in which the applet is contained. For example, the HTML file for running `TicTacToe` can be modified as shown below:

```
<applet
  code    = "TicTacToe.class"
```

14.9   Can you place a frame in an applet?

14.10   Can you place an applet in a frame?

14.11   Delete `super.paintComponent(g)` on Line 99 in TicTacToe.java in Listing 14.6 and run the program to see what happens.

Sections 14.8–14.11

14.12   How do you create a `URL` object for the file `www.cs.armstrong.edu/liang/anthem/us.gif` on the Internet? How do you create a `URL` object for the file `image/us.gif` in the class directory?

14.13   How do you create an `ImageIcon` from the file image/us.gif in the class directory? How do you create an `ImageIcon` from `www.cs.armstrong.edu/liang/image/us.gif`?

14.14   How do you create an `Image` object from the `ImageIcon` object?

14.15   How do you create an `ImageIcon` object from an `Image` object?

14.16   Explain the differences between displaying images in a `JLabel` and in a `JPanel`.

14.17   Describe the `drawImage` method in the `Graphics` class.

14.18   Which package contains `ImageIcon` and which contains `Image`?

Section 14.12 Playing Audio

14.19   What types of audio files are used in Java?

14.20   How do you create an audio clip from a file anthem/us.mid in the class directory? How do you create an audio clip from `www.cs.armstrong.edu/liang/anthem/us.mid`?

14.21   How do you play, repeatedly play, and stop an audio clip?

PROGRAMMING EXERCISES

Sections 14.2–14.4

14.1   (*Converting applications to applets*) Convert Example 13.1, "Using Buttons," into an applet.

Sections 14.5–14.6

14.2*   (*Passing strings to applets*) Rewrite Example 14.2, "Passing Strings to Java applets," to display a message with a standard color, font, and size. The `message`, `x`, `y`, `color`, `fontname`, and `fontsize` are parameters in the `<applet>` tag, as shown below:

```
<applet
  code = "Exercise14_2.class"
  width = 200
  height = 50>
  <param name=MESSAGE value="Welcome to Java">
  <param name=X value=40>
  <param name=Y value=50>
  <param name=COLOR value="red">
  <param name=FONTNAME value="Monospaced">
  <param name=FONTSIZE value=20>
You must have a Java-enabled browser to view the applet
</applet>
```

14.3   (*Enabling applets to run standalone*) Rewrite the `LoanApplet` in Example 14.1, "Using Applets," to enable it to run as an application as well as an applet.

14.4*   (*Creating multiple windows from an applet*) Write an applet that contains two buttons called *Investment Calculator* and *Loan Calculator*. When you click Investment Calculator, a frame appears in a new window for calculating future investment values. When you click *Loan Calculator*, a frame appears in a separate new window for computing loan payments (see Figure 14.21).

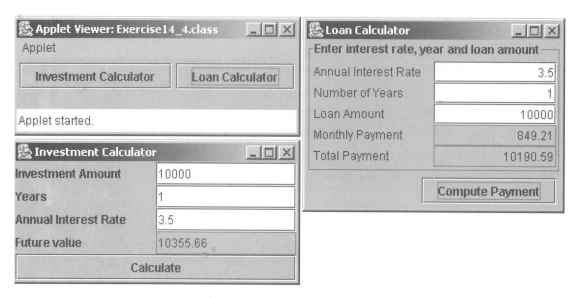

FIGURE 14.21   *You can show frames in the applets.*

14.5**   (*Creating a maze*) Write an applet that will find a path in a maze, as shown in Figure 14.22(a). The applet should also run as an application. The maze is represented by an 8 × 8 board. The path must meet the following conditions:

◆ The path is between the upper-left corner cell and the lower-right corner cell in the maze.

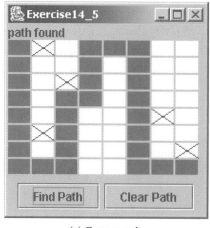

(a) Correct path   (b) Illegal path

FIGURE 14.22   *The program finds a path from the upper-left corner to the bottom-right corner.*

✦ The applet enables the user to insert or remove a mark on a cell. A path consists of adjacent unmarked cells. Two cells are said to be adjacent if they are horizontal or vertical neighbors, but not if they are diagonal neighbors.

✦ The path does not contain cells that form a square. The path in Figure 14.22(b), for example, does not meet this condition. (The condition makes a path easy to identify on the board.)

14.6** (*TicTacToe*) Rewrite the program in Section 14.7, "Case Study: TicTacToe," with the following modifications:

✦ Declare `Cell` as a separate class rather than an inner class.

✦ Add a button named *New Game*, as shown in Figure 14.23. The New Game button starts a new game.

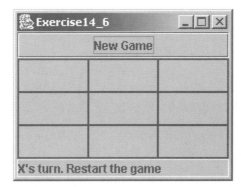

FIGURE 14.23 *The New Game button starts a new game.*

14.7** (*Tax calculator*) Create an applet to compute tax, as shown in Figure 14.24. The applet lets the user select the tax status and enter the taxable income to compute the tax based on the 2001 federal tax rates, as shown in Exercise 6.14 on page 256. Enable it to run standalone.

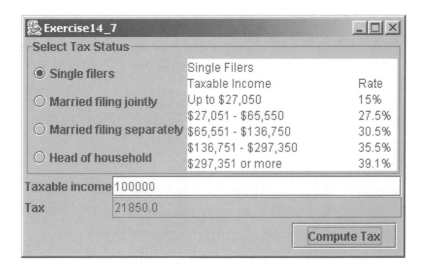

FIGURE 14.24 *The tax calculator computes the tax for the specified taxable income and tax status.*

14.8* *** (*Creating a calculator*) Use various panels of FlowLayout, GridLayout, and BorderLayout to lay out the following calculator and to implement addition (+), subtraction (−), division (/), square root (sqrt), and modulus (%) functions (see Figure 14.25(a)). Enable it to run standalone.

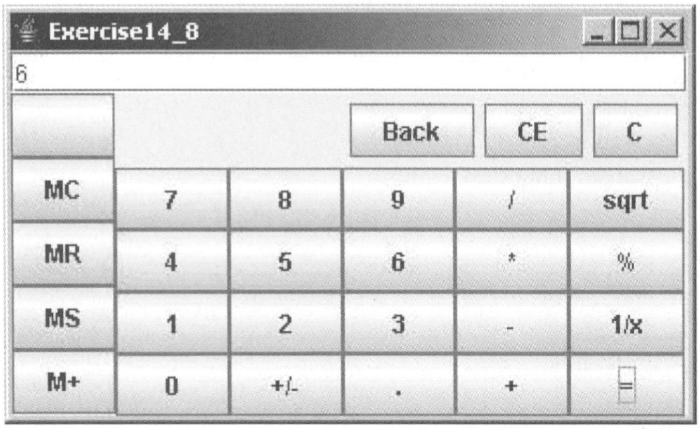

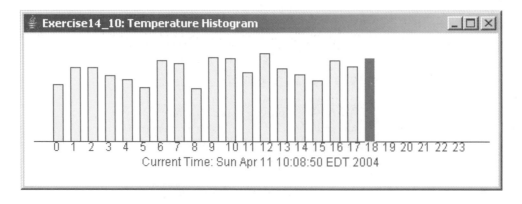

FIGURE **14.25** *(a) Exercise 14.8 is a Java implementation of a popular calculator. (b) Exercise 14.9 converts between decimal, hex, and binary numbers.*

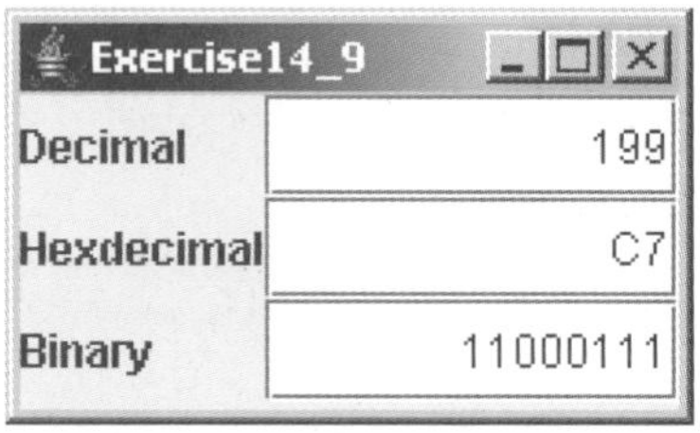

14.9* (*Converting numbers*) Write an applet that converts between decimal, hex, and binary numbers, as shown in Figure 14.25(b). When you enter a decimal value on the decimal value text field and press the Enter key, its corresponding hex and binary numbers are displayed in the other two text fields. Likewise, you can enter values in the other fields and convert them accordingly. Enable it to run standalone.

14.10* (*Repainting a partial area*) When you repaint the entire viewing area of a panel, sometimes only a tiny portion of the viewing area is changed. You can improve the performance by only repainting the affected area, but do not invoke super.paintComponent(g) when repainting the panel, because this will cause the entire viewing area to be cleared. Use this approach to write an applet to display the temperatures of each hour during the last twenty-four hours in a histogram. Suppose that the temperatures between 50 and 90 degrees Fahrenheit are obtained randomly and are updated every hour. The temperature of the current hour needs to be redisplayed, while the others remain unchanged. Use a unique color to highlight the temperature for the current hour (see Figure 14.26).

FIGURE **14.26** *The histogram displays the average temperature of every hour in the last twenty-four hours.*

14.11** (*Showing a running fan*) Write a Java applet that simulates a running fan, as shown in Figure 14.27. The buttons Start, Stop, and Reverse control the fan. The scrollbar controls the fan's speed. Create a class named Fan, a subclass of JPanel, to display the fan. This class also contains the methods to suspend and resume the fan, set its speed, and reverse its direction. Create a class named FanControl that contains a fan, and three buttons and a scroll bar to control the fan. Create a Java applet that contains an instance of FanControl. Enable the applet to run standalone.

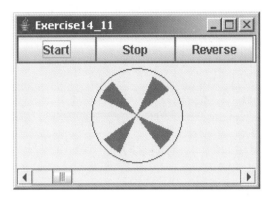

FIGURE **14.27** *The program simulates a running fan.*

14.12** (*Controlling a group of fans*) Write a Java applet that displays three fans in a group, with control buttons to start and stop all of them, as shown in Figure 14.28. Use the FanControl to control and display a single fan. Enable the applet to run standalone.

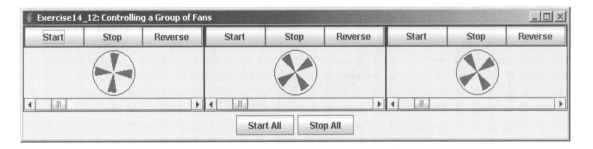

FIGURE **14.28** *The program runs and controls a group of fans.*

14.13*** (*Creating an elevator simulator*) Write an applet that simulates an elevator going up and down (see Figure 14.29). The buttons on the left indicate the floor where the passenger is now located. The passenger must click a button on the left to request that the elevator come to his or her floor. On entering the elevator, the passenger clicks a button on the right to request that it go to the specified floor. Enable the applet to run standalone.

14.14* (*Controlling a group of clocks*) Write a Java applet that displays three clocks in a group, with control buttons to start and stop all of them, as shown in Figure 14.30. Use the ClockControl to control and display a single clock. Enable the applet to run standalone.

Section 14.9 Displaying Images

14.15* (*Enlarging and shrinking an image*) Write an applet that will display a sequence of images from a single image file in different sizes. Initially, the viewing area for this

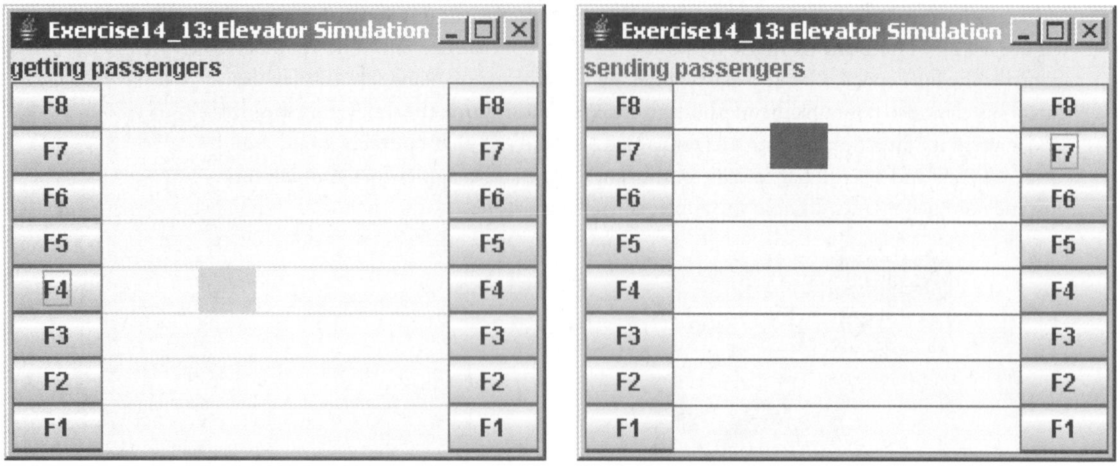

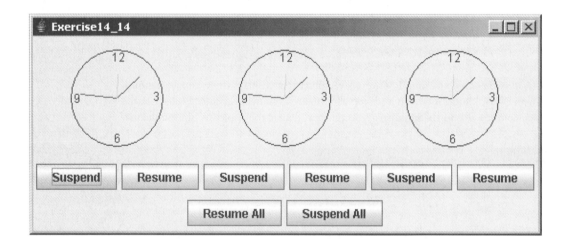

FIGURE 14.29 *The program simulates elevator operations.*

FIGURE 14.30 *Three clocks run independently with individual control and group control.*

image has a width of 300 and a height of 300. Your program should continuously shrink the viewing area by 1 in width and 1 in height until it reaches a width of 50 and a height of 50. At that point, the viewing area should continuously enlarge by 1 in width and 1 in height until it reaches a width of 300 and a height of 300. The viewing area should shrink and enlarge (alternately) to create animation for the single image. Enable the applet to run standalone.

14.16*** (*Simulating a stock ticker*) Write a Java applet that displays a stock index ticker (see Figure 14.31). The stock index information is passed from the <param> tag in the HTML file. Each index has four parameters: Index Name (e.g., S&P 500), Current Time (e.g., 15:54), the index from the previous day (e.g., 919.01), and Change (e.g., 4.54). Enable the applet to run standalone.

Use at least five indexes, such as Dow Jones, S&P 500, NASDAQ, NIKKEI, and Gold & Silver Index. Display positive changes in green, and negative changes in red. The indexes move from right to left in the applet's viewing area. The applet freezes the ticker when the mouse button is pressed; it moves again when the mouse button is released.

FIGURE 14.31 *The program displays a stock index ticker.*

14.17**   (*Showing national flags*) Write an applet that introduces national flags, one after the other, by presenting each one's photo, name, and description (see Figure 14.32) along with audio that reads the description.

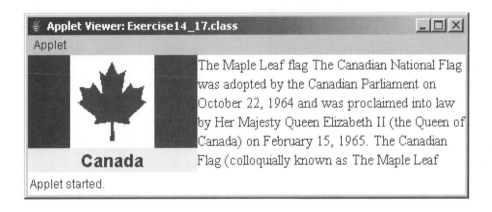

FIGURE 14.32 *This applet shows each country's flag, name, and description, one after another, and reads the description that is currently shown.*

Suppose your applet displays the flags of eight countries. Assume that the photo image files, named **photo0.gif**, **photo1.gif**, and so on, up to **photo7.gif**, are stored in a subdirectory named **photo** in the applet's directory. The length of each audio is less than 10 seconds. Assume that the name and description of each country's flag are passed from the HTML using the parameter name0, name1, ..., name7, and description0, description1, ..., and description7. Pass the number of countries as an HTML parameter using numberOfCountries. Here is an example:

```
<param name="numberOfCountries" value=8>
<param name="name0" value="Canada">
<param name="description0" value=
"The Maple Leaf flag
The Canadian National Flag was adopted by the Canadian
Parliament on October 22, 1964 and was proclaimed into law
by Her Majesty Queen Elizabeth II (the Queen of Canada) on
February 15, 1965. The Canadian Flag (colloquially known
as The Maple Leaf Flag) is a red flag of the proportions
two by length and one by width, containing in its center a
```

```
white square, with a single red stylized eleven-point
mapleleaf centered in the white square.">
```

> **HINT**
> Use the DescriptionPanel class to display the image, name, and text. The
> DescriptionPanel class was introduced in Example 13.5, "Using Text
> Area."

Section 14.12 Playing Audio

14.18* (*Playing, looping, and stopping a sound clip*) Write an applet that meets the following requirements:

◆ Get an audio file. The file is in the class directory.

◆ Place three buttons labeled Play, Loop, and Stop, as shown in Figure 14.33.

FIGURE **14.33** *Click Play to play an audio clip once, click Loop to play an audio repeatedly, and click Stop to terminate playing.*

◆ If you click the Play button, the audio file is played once. If you click the Loop button, the audio file keeps playing repeatedly. If you click the Stop button, the playing stops.

◆ The applet can run as an application.

14.19** (*Creating an alarm clock*) Write an applet that will display a digital clock with a large display panel that shows hour, minute, and second. This clock should allow the user to set an alarm. Figure 14.34(a) shows an example of such a clock. To turn on the alarm, check the Alarm check box. To specify the alarm time, click the "Set alarm" button to display a new frame, as shown in Figure 14.34(b). You can set the alarm time in the frame. Enable the applet to run standalone.

(a)

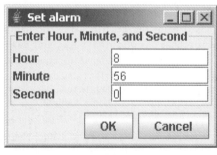

(b)

FIGURE **14.34** *The program displays current hour, minute, and second, and enables you to set an alarm.*

14.20** (*Creating an image animator with audio*) Create animation using the applet (see Figure 14.35) to meet the following requirements:

✦ Allow the user to specify the animation speed. The user can enter the speed in a text field.

✦ Get the number of frames and the image filename prefix from the user. For example, if the user enters **n** for the number of frames and **L** for the image prefix, then the files are **L1**, **L2**, and so on, to **L***n*. Assume that the images are stored in the **image** directory, a subdirectory of the applet's directory.

✦ Allow the user to specify an audio filename. The audio file is stored in the same directory as the applet. The sound is played while the animation runs.

✦ Enable the applet to run standalone.

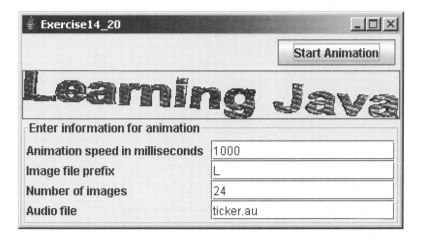

FIGURE **14.35** *This applet lets the user select image files, audio file, and animation speed.*

PART IV

EXCEPTION HANDLING AND IO

This part introduces the use of exception handling and assertions to make programs robust and correct, and the use of input and output to manage and process a large quantity of data.

Chapter 15
Exceptions and Assertions

Chapter 16
Simple Input and Output

Prerequisites for Part IV

Chapter 8 Inheritance and Polymorphism

Chapter 15 Exceptions and Assertions

Chapter 16 Simple Input and Output

chapter

15

EXCEPTIONS AND ASSERTIONS

Objectives

- ✦ To understand exceptions and exception handling (§15.2).
- ✦ To distinguish exception types: Error (fatal) vs. Exception (non-fatal), and checked vs. uncheck exceptions (§§15.2.1–15.2.2).
- ✦ To declare exceptions in the method header (§15.3.1).
- ✦ To throw exceptions out of a method (§15.3.2).
- ✦ To write a try-catch block to handle exceptions (§15.3.3).
- ✦ To explain how an exception is propagated (§15.3.3).
- ✦ To rethrow exceptions in a try-catch block (§15.4).
- ✦ To use the finally clause in a try-catch block (§15.5).
- ✦ To know when to use exceptions (§15.6).
- ✦ To declare custom exception classes (§15.7 Optional).
- ✦ To apply assertions to help ensure program correctness (§15.8 Optional).

15.1 Introduction

Section 2.19, "Programming Errors," introduced three categories of errors: syntax errors, runtime errors, and logic errors. *Syntax errors* arise because the rules of the language have not been followed. They are detected by the compiler. *Runtime errors* occur while the program is running if the environment detects an operation that is impossible to carry out. *Logic errors* occur when a program doesn't perform the way it was intended to. In general, syntax errors are easy to find and easy to correct because the compiler indicates where they came from and why they occurred. You can use the debugging techniques introduced in Section 2.20, "Debugging," to find logic errors. This chapter introduces using exception handling to deal with runtime errors and using assertions to help ensure program correctness.

15.2 Exceptions and Exception Types

Runtime errors cause *exceptions*, which are events that occur during the execution of a program and disrupt the normal flow of control. A program that does not provide code for handling exceptions may terminate abnormally, causing serious problems. For example, if your program attempts to transfer money from a savings account to a checking account, but because of a runtime error is terminated *after* the money is drawn from the savings account and *before* the money is deposited in the checking account, the customer will lose money.

Runtime errors occur for various reasons. The user may enter an invalid input, for example, or the program may attempt to open a file that doesn't exist, or the network connection may hang up, or the program may attempt to access an out-of-bounds array element. When a runtime error occurs, Java raises an exception.

Exceptions are handled differently from the events of GUI programming. (In Chapter 12, "Event-Driven Programming," you learned the events used in GUI programming.) An *event* may be ignored in GUI programming, but an *exception* cannot be ignored. In GUI programming, a listener must register with the source object. External user action on the source object generates an event, and the source object notifies the listener by invoking the handlers implemented by the listener. If no listener is registered with the source object, the event is ignored. When an exception occurs, however, the program will terminate if the exception is not caught by the program.

exception handling

Java provides programmers with the capability to elegantly handle runtime errors. With this capability, referred to as *exception handling*, you can develop robust programs for mission-critical computing.

Here is an example. The following program terminates abnormally if you entered a floating-point value instead of an integer.

```java
import javax.swing.JOptionPane;

public class Test {
  public static void main(String[] args) {
    String input = JOptionPane.showInputDialog(null,
      "Please enter an integer");
    int number = Integer.parseInt(input);

    // Display the result
    JOptionPane.showMessageDialog(null,
      "The number entered is " + number);
  }
}
```

If an exception occurs on this line, the rest of the lines in the method are skipped and the program is terminated.

Terminated.

Java allows the programmer to catch this error when it occurs and perform some specific actions, including choosing whether to halt the program or not. You can handle this error in the following code, using a new construct called the *try-catch block* to enable the program to catch the error and continue to execute:

try-catch block

```
import javax.swing.JOptionPane;

public class Test {
  public static void main(String[] args) {
    try {
      String input = JOptionPane.showInputDialog(null,
        "Please enter an integer");
      int number = Integer.parseInt(input);

      // Display the result
      JOptionPane.showMessageDialog(null,
        "The number entered is " + number);
    }
    catch (Exception ex) {
      JOptionPane.showMessageDialog(null,
        "Incorrect input: an integer is required");
    }

    System.out.println("Execution continues ...");
  }
}
```

If an exception occurs on this line, the rest of the lines in the try clause are skipped and the control is transferred to the catch clause.

After the exception is caught and processed, the control is transferred to the next statement after the try-catch block.

15.2.1 Exception Classes

A Java exception is an instance of a class derived from `Throwable`. The `Throwable` class is contained in the `java.lang` package, and subclasses of `Throwable` are contained in various packages. Errors related to GUI components are included in the `java.awt` package; numeric exceptions are included in the `java.lang` package because they are related to the `java.lang.Number` class . You can create your own exception classes by extending `Throwable` or a subclass of `Throwable`. Figure 15.1 shows some of Java's predefined exception classes.

 NOTE

The class names `Error`, `Exception`, and `RuntimeException` are somewhat confusing. All three of these classes are exceptions, and all of the errors discussed here occur at runtime.

The exception classes can be classified into three major types: system errors, exceptions, and runtime exceptions.

✦ *System errors* are thrown by the JVM and represented in the `Error` class. The `Error` class describes internal system errors. Such errors rarely occur. If one does, there is little you can do beyond notifying the user and trying to terminate the program gracefully. Examples of subclasses of `Error` are listed in Table 15.1.

system error

✦ *Exceptions* are represented in the `Exception` class, which describes errors caused by your program and by external circumstances. These errors can be caught and handled by your program. Examples of subclasses of `Exception` are listed in Table 15.2.

exception

✦ *Runtime exceptions* are represented in the `RuntimeException` class, which describes programming errors, such as bad casting, accessing an out-of-bounds array, and numeric

runtime exception

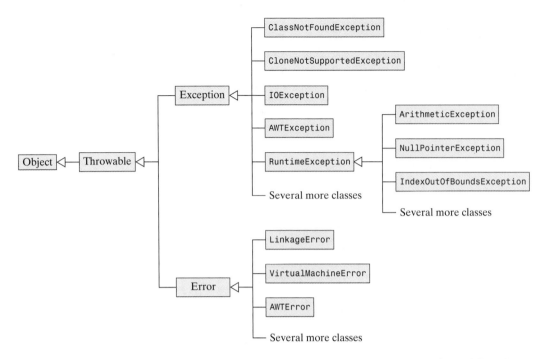

FIGURE 15.1 *Exceptions thrown are instances of the classes shown in this diagram, or of subclasses of one of these classes.*

TABLE 15.1 **Examples of Subclasses of Error**

Class	*Possible Reason for Exception*
LinkageError	A class has some dependency on another class, but the latter class has changed incompatibly after the compilation of the former class.
VirtualMachineError	The JVM is broken or has run out of the resources necessary for it to continue operating.
AWTError	A fatal error in the GUI runtime system.
AssertionError	An assertion has failed. Assertions will be introduced in Section 15.8, "Assertions."

errors. Runtime exceptions are generally thrown by the JVM. Examples of subclasses are listed in Table 15.3.

15.2.2 Checked and Unchecked Exceptions

unchecked exception
checked exception

RuntimeException, Error, and their subclasses are known as *unchecked exceptions*. All other exceptions are known as *checked exceptions*, meaning that the compiler forces the programmer to check and deal with them.

In most cases, unchecked exceptions reflect programming logic errors that are not recoverable. For example, a NullPointerException is thrown if you access an object through a reference variable before an object is assigned to it; an IndexOutOfBoundsException is thrown if you access an element in an array outside the bounds of the array. These are logic errors that should be corrected in the program. Unchecked exceptions can occur anywhere in a program. To avoid

TABLE 15.2 Examples of Subclasses of Exception

Class	Possible reason for exception
ClassNotFoundException	Attempt to use a class that does not exist. This exception would occur, for example, if you tried to run a nonexistent class using the **java** command, or if your program was composed of, say, three class files, only two of which could be found.
CloneNotSupportedException	Attempt to clone an object whose defining class does not implement the `Cloneable` interface. Cloning objects were introduced in Chapter 9, "Abstract Classes and Interfaces."
IOException	Related to input/output operations, such as invalid input, reading past the end of a file, and opening a nonexistent file. Examples of subclasses of `IOException` are `InterruptedIOException`, `EOFException` (EOF is short for End Of File), and `FileNotFoundException`.
AWTException	Exceptions in GUI components.

TABLE 15.3 Examples of Subclasses of RuntimeException

Class	Possible Reason for Exception
ArithmeticException	Dividing an integer by zero. Note that floating-point arithmetic does not throw exceptions.
NullPointerException	Attempt to access an object through a `null` reference variable.
IndexOutOfBoundsException	Index to an array is out of range.
IllegalArgumentException	A method is passed an argument that is illegal or inappropriate.

cumbersome overuse of try-catch blocks, Java does not mandate that you write code to catch or declare unchecked exceptions.

15.3 Understanding Exception Handling

Java's exception-handling model is based on three operations: *declaring an exception*, *throwing an exception*, and *catching an exception*, as shown in Figure 15.2.

15.3.1 Declaring Exceptions

In Java, the statement currently being executed belongs to a method. The Java interpreter invokes the main method for a Java application, and the Web browser invokes the applet's no-arg constructor and then the init method for a Java applet. Every method must state the types of checked exceptions it might throw. This is known as *declaring exceptions*. Because system errors and runtime errors can happen to any code, Java does not require that you declare Error and RuntimeException (unchecked exceptions) explicitly in the method. However, all other exceptions thrown by the

declare exception

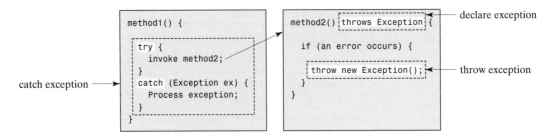

FIGURE 15.2 *Exception handling in Java consists of declaring exceptions, throwing exceptions, and catching and processing exceptions.*

method must be explicitly declared in the method declaration so that the caller of the method is informed of the exception.

To declare an exception in a method, use the `throws` keyword in the method declaration, as in this example:

```
public void myMethod() throws IOException
```

The `throws` keyword indicates that `myMethod` might throw an `IOException`. If the method might throw multiple exceptions, add a list of the exceptions, separated by commas, after `throws`:

```
public void myMethod()
  throws Exception1, Exception2, ..., ExceptionN
```

15.3.2 Throwing Exceptions

throw exception

A program that detects an error can create an instance of an appropriate exception type and throw it. This is known as *throwing an exception*. Here is an example: Suppose the program detected that an argument passed to the method violates the method contract (e.g., the argument must be non-negative, but a negative argument is passed); the program can create an instance of `IllegalArgumentException` and throw it, as follows:

```
IllegalArgumentException ex =
  new IllegalArgumentException("Wrong Argument");
throw ex;
```

Or if you prefer, you can use the following:

```
throw new IllegalArgumentException("Wrong Argument");
```

 NOTE
The keyword to declare an exception is `throws`, and the keyword to throw an exception is `throw`. A method can always throw an unchecked exception. If a method throws a checked exception, the exception must be declared in the method declaration.

15.3.3 Catching Exceptions

catch exception

You now know how to declare an exception and how to throw an exception. When an exception is thrown, it can be caught and handled in a try-catch block, as follows:

```
try {
  statements; // Statements that may throw exceptions
}
```

```
catch (Exception1 exVar1) {
   handler for exception1;
}
catch (Exception2 exVar2) {
   handler for exception2;
}
...
catch (ExceptionN exVar3) {
   handler for exceptionN;
}
```

If no exceptions arise during the execution of the `try` clause, the `catch` clauses are skipped.

If one of the statements inside the `try` block throws an exception, Java skips the remaining statements in the try block and starts the process of finding the code to handle the exception. The code that handles the exception is called the *exception handler*; it is found by propagating the exception backward through a chain of method calls, starting from the current method. Each `catch` clause is examined in turn, from first to last, to see whether the type of the exception object is an instance of the exception class in the `catch` clause. If so, the exception object is assigned to the variable declared and the code in the `catch` clause is executed. If no handler is found, Java exits this method, passes the exception to the method that invoked the method, and continues the same process to find a handler. If no handler is found in the chain of methods being invoked, the program terminates and prints an error message on the console. The process of finding a handler is called *catching an exception.*

exception handler

Suppose the `main` method invokes `method1`, `method1` invokes `method2`, `method2` invokes `method3`, and an exception occurs in `method3`, as shown in Figure 15.3. Consider the following scenario:

◆ If `method3` cannot handle the exception, `method3` is aborted and the control is returned to `method2`. If the exception type is `Exception3`, it is caught by the `catch` clause for handling exception `ex3` in `method2`. `statement5` is skipped, and `statement6` is executed.

◆ If the exception type is `Exception2`, `method2` is aborted, the control is returned to `method1`, and the exception is caught by the `catch` clause for handling exception `ex2` in `method1`. `statement3` is skipped, and `statement4` is executed.

◆ If the exception type is `Exception1`, `method1` is aborted, the control is returned to the `main` method, and the exception is caught by the `catch` clause for handling exception `ex1` in the `main` method. `statement1` is skipped, and `statement2` is executed.

◆ If the exception type is not `Exception1`, `Exception2`, or `Exception3`, the exception is not caught and the program terminates. `statement1` and `statement2` are not executed.

```
main method {                  method1 {                      method2 {                     An exception
   ...                            ...                            ...                          is thrown in
   try {                          try {                          try {                        method3
      ...                            ...                            ...
      invoke method1;                invoke method2;                invoke method3;
      statement1;                    statement3;                    statement5;
   }                              }                              }
   catch (Exception1 ex1) {       catch (Exception2 ex2) {       catch (Exception3 ex3) {
      Process ex1;                   Process ex2;                   Process ex3;
   }                              }                              }
   statement2;                    statement4;                    statement6;
}                              }                              }
```

FIGURE 15.3   *If an exception is not caught in the current method, it is passed to its caller. The process is repeated until the exception is caught or passed to the* `main` *method.*

An exception object contains valuable information about the exception. You may use the following instance methods in the `java.lang.Throwable` class to get information regarding the exception:

✦ `public String getMessage()`
Returns the detailed message of the `Throwable` object.

✦ `public String toString()`
Returns the concatenation of three strings: (1) the full name of the exception class; (2) `": "` (a colon and a space); (3) the `getMessage()` method.

✦ `public void printStackTrace()`
Prints the `Throwable` object and its trace information on the console.

catch clause

 NOTE

Various exception classes can be derived from a common superclass. If a `catch` clause catches exception objects of a superclass, it can catch all the exception objects of the subclasses of that superclass.

order of exception handlers

 NOTE

The order in which exceptions are specified in `catch` clauses is important. A compilation error will result if a catch clause for a superclass type appears before a catch clause for a subclass type. For example, the ordering in (a) is erroneous, because `RuntimeException` is a subclass of `Exception`. The correct ordering should be as shown in (b).

```
try {
   ...
}
catch (Exception ex) {
   ...
}
catch (RuntimeException ex) {
   ...
}
```

(a) Wrong

```
try {
   ...
}
catch (RuntimeException ex) {
   ...
}
catch (Exception ex) {
   ...
}
```

(b) Correct

catch or declare exceptions

 NOTE

Java forces you to deal with checked exceptions. If a method declares a checked exception (i.e., an exception other than `Error` or `RuntimeException`), you must invoke it in a try-catch block or declare to throw the exception in the calling method.

EXAMPLE 15.1 DECLARING, THROWING, AND CATCHING EXCEPTIONS

Problem

This example demonstrates declaring, throwing, and catching exceptions by modifying the `setRadius` method in the `CircleWithStaticVariableAndMethod` class in Section 6.10, "Static Variables, Constants, and Methods." The new `setRadius` method throws an exception if the radius is negative.

EXAMPLE 15.1 (CONTINUED)

Solution

Rename the circle class given in Listing 15.1 as `CircleWithException`, which is the same as `CircleWithStaticVariableAndMethod` except that the `setRadius(double newRadius)` method throws an `IllegalArgumentException` if the argument `newRadius` is negative.

LISTING 15.1   CircleWithException.java (Throwing Exceptions)

```
 1 public class CircleWithException {
 2   /** The radius of the circle */
 3   private double radius;
 4
 5   /** The number of the objects created */
 6   private static int numberOfObjects = 0;
 7
 8   /** Construct a circle with radius 1 */
 9   public CircleWithException() {
10     this(1.0);
11   }
12
13   /** Construct a circle with a specified radius */
14   public CircleWithException(double newRadius) {
15     setRadius(newRadius);
16     numberOfObjects++;
17   }
18
19   /** Return radius */
20   public double getRadius() {
21     return radius;
22   }
23
24   /** Set a new radius */
25   public void setRadius(double newRadius)
26       throws IllegalArgumentException {        declare exception
27     if (newRadius >= 0)
28       radius = newRadius;
29     else
30       throw new IllegalArgumentException(      throw exception
31         "Radius cannot be negative");
32   }
33
34   /** Return numberOfObjects */
35   public static int getNumberOfObjects() {
36     return numberOfObjects;
37   }
38
39   /** Return the area of this circle */
40   public double findArea() {
41     return radius * radius * 3.14159;
42   }
43 }
```

A test program that uses the new `Circle` class is given in Listing 15.2. Figure 15.4 shows a sample run of the test program.

LISTING 15.2   TestCircleWithException.java (Catching Exceptions)

```
 1 public class TestCircleWithException {
 2   /** Main method */
 3   public static void main(String[] args) {
 4     try {                                          try
 5       CircleWithException c1 = new CircleWithException(5);
 6       CircleWithException c2 = new CircleWithException(-5);
```

catch

EXAMPLE 15.1 (CONTINUED)

```
7        CircleWithException c3 = new CircleWithException(0);
8      }
9      catch (IllegalArgumentException ex) {
10        System.out.println(ex);
11      }
12
13      System.out.println("Number of objects created: " +
14        CircleWithException.getNumberOfObjects());
15    }
16 }
```

```
Command Prompt                                              _ □ ×
C:\book>java TestCircleWithException
java.lang.IllegalArgumentException: Radius cannot be negative
Number of objects created: 1

C:\book>
```

FIGURE 15.4 *The exception is thrown when the radius is negative.*

Review

The original CircleWithStaticVariableAndMethod class remains intact except that the class name is changed to CircleWithException, a new constructor CircleWithException-(newRadius) is added, and the setRadius method now declares an exception and throws it if the radius is negative.

The setRadius method declares to throw IllegalArgumentException in the method declaration (Lines 25–26 in CircleWithException.java). The CircleWithException class would still compile if the throws IllegalArgumentException clause were removed from the method declaration, since it is a subclass of RuntimeException and every method can throw RuntimeException (unchecked exception) regardless of whether it is declared in the method header.

The test program creates three CircleWithException objects, c1, c2, and c3, to test how to handle exceptions. Invoking new CircleWithException(-5) (Line 6 in Test CircleWithException) causes the setRadius method to be invoked, which throws an IllegalArgumentException, because the radius is negative. In the catch clause, the type of the object ex is IllegalArgumentException, which matches the exception object thrown by the setRadius method. So this exception is caught by the catch clause.

The exception handler prints a short message, ex.toString() (Line 10), about the exception, using System.out.println(ex).

Note that the execution continues in the event of the exception. If the handlers had not caught the exception, the program would have abruptly terminated.

The test program would still compile if the try statement were not used, because the method throws an instance of IllegalArgumentException, a subclass of Runtime Exception (unchecked exception). If a method throws an exception other than RuntimeException and Error, the method must be invoked within a try-catch block.

Methods are executed on threads. If an exception occurs on a thread, the thread is terminated if the exception is not handled. However, the other threads in the application are not affected. There are several threads running to support a GUI application. A thread is launched to execute an event handler (e.g., the actionPerformed method for the ActionEvent). If an exception occurs during the execution of a GUI event handler, the thread is terminated if the exception is not handled. Interestingly, Java prints the error message on the console, but does not terminate the application. The program goes back to its user-interface-processing loop to run continuously. The next example demonstrates this.

EXAMPLE 15.2 EXCEPTIONS IN GUI APPLICATIONS

Problem

Write a program that creates a user interface to perform integer divisions, as shown in Figure 15.5. The user enters two numbers in the text fields Number 1 and Number 2. The division of Number 1 and Number 2 is displayed in the `Result` field when the Divide button is clicked.

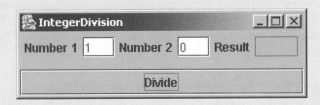

FIGURE 15.5   *Since the divisor is 0 in the Number 2 field, a* `RuntimeException` *is thrown when the Divide button is clicked.*

Solution

Listing 15.3 gives the program.

LISTING 15.3   IntegerDivision.java (Exceptions in GUI Programs)

```
 1  import java.awt.*;
 2  import java.awt.event.*;
 3  import javax.swing.*;
 4
 5  public class IntegerDivision extends JApplet
 6      implements ActionListener {
 7    // Text fields for Number 1, Number 2, and Result
 8    private JTextField jtfNum1, jtfNum2, jtfResult;
 9
10    // Create the "Divide" button
11    private JButton jbtDiv = new JButton("Divide");
12
13    public IntegerDivision() {
14      // Panel p1 to hold text fields and labels
15      JPanel p1 = new JPanel();
16      p1.setLayout(new FlowLayout());
17      p1.add(new JLabel("Number 1"));
18      p1.add(jtfNum1 = new JTextField(3));
19      p1.add(new JLabel("Number 2"));
20      p1.add(jtfNum2 = new JTextField(3));
21      p1.add(new JLabel("Result"));
22      p1.add(jtfResult = new JTextField(4));
23      jtfResult.setEditable(false);
24      jtfResult.setHorizontalAlignment(SwingConstants.RIGHT);
25
26      getContentPane().add(p1, BorderLayout.CENTER);
27      getContentPane().add(jbtDiv, BorderLayout.SOUTH);
28
29      // Register listener
30      jbtDiv.addActionListener(this);
31    }
```

EXAMPLE 15.2 (CONTINUED)

```
32
33    /** Handle ActionEvent from the Divide button */
34    public void actionPerformed(ActionEvent e) {
35      if (e.getSource() == jbtDiv) {
36        // Get numbers
37        int num1 = Integer.parseInt(jtfNum1.getText().trim());
38        int num2 = Integer.parseInt(jtfNum2.getText().trim());
39
40        int result = num1 / num2;
41
42        // Set result in jtfResult
43        jtfResult.setText(String.valueOf(result));
44      }
45    }
46  }
```

main method omitted

Run the program and enter any number in the Number 1 field and 0 in the Number 2 field; then click the Divide button (see Figure 15.5). You will see nothing in the Result field, but an error message will appear in the Output window, as shown in Figure 15.6. The GUI application continues.

```
Command Prompt - java IntegerDivision                         _ | □ | x
C:\book>java IntegerDivision
java.lang.ArithmeticException: / by zero
        at IntegerDivision.actionPerformed(IntegerDivision.java:44)
        at javax.swing.AbstractButton.fireActionPerformed(AbstractButt
64)
        at javax.swing.AbstractButton$ForwardActionEvents.actionPerfor
ctButton.java:1817)
        at javax.swing.DefaultButtonModel.fireActionPerformed(DefaultB
.java:419)
        at javax.swing.DefaultButtonModel.setPressed(DefaultButtonMode
)
        at javax.swing.plaf.basic.BasicButtonListener.mouseReleased(Ba
istener.java:245)
```

FIGURE 15.6 *In GUI programs, if an exception is not caught, an error message appears in the console window.*

Review

An `ArithmeticException` occurred during the execution of the `actionPerformed` method. The thread on which the method is executed is terminated, but the program continues to run.

If you add a try-catch block around the code in Lines 40–43, as shown below, the program will display a message dialog box in the case of a numerical error, as shown in Figure 15.7. No errors are reported because they are handled in the program.

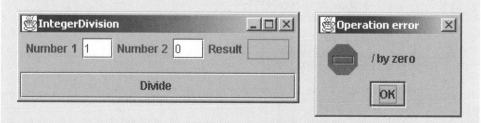

FIGURE 15.7 *When you click the Divide button to divide a number by 0, a numerical exception occurs. The exception is displayed in the message dialog box.*

EXAMPLE 15.2 (CONTINUED)

```
 1 try {
 2   int result = num1 / num2;
 3
 4   // Set result in jtfResult
 5   jtfResult.setText(String.valueOf(result));
 6 }
 7 catch (RuntimeException ex) {
 8   JOptionPane.showMessageDialog(this, ex.getMessage(),
 9     "Operation error", JOptionPane.ERROR_MESSAGE);
10 }
```

15.4 Rethrowing Exceptions

When an exception occurs in a method, the method exits immediately if it does not catch the exception. If the method is required to perform some task before exiting, you can catch the exception in the method and then rethrow it to the calling method in a structure like the one given below:

```
try {
  statements;
}
catch (TheException ex) {
  perform operations before exits;
  throw ex;
}
```

The statement `throw ex` rethrows the exception so that other handlers get a chance to process the exception `ex`.

15.5 The `finally` Clause

Occasionally, you may want some code to be executed regardless of whether an exception occurs or is caught. Java has a `finally` clause that can be used to accomplish this objective. The syntax for the `finally` clause might look like this:

```
try {
  statements;
}
catch (TheException ex) {
  handling ex;
}
finally {
  finalStatements;
}
```

The code in the `finally` block is executed under all circumstances, regardless of whether an exception occurs in the try block or is caught. Consider three possible cases:

✦ If no exception arises in the `try` block, `finalStatements` is executed, and the next statement after the `try` statement is executed.

✦ If one of the statements causes an exception in the `try` block that is caught in a `catch` clause, the other statements in the `try` block are skipped, the `catch` clause is executed, and the `finally` clause is executed. If the `catch` clause does not rethrow an exception, the next statement after the `try` statement is executed. If it does, the exception is passed to the caller of this method.

✦ If one of the statements causes an exception that is not caught in any `catch` clause, the other statements in the `try` block are skipped, the `finally` clause is executed, and the exception is passed to the caller of this method.

omitting catch clause

 NOTE

The catch clause may be omitted when the finally clause is used.

15.6 When to Use Exceptions

Exception handling separates error-handling code from normal programming tasks, thus making programs easier to read and to modify. Be aware, however, that exception handling usually requires more time and resources because it requires instantiating a new exception object, rolling back the call stack, and propagating the exception through the chain of methods invoked to search for the handler.

An exception occurs in a method. If you want the exception to be processed by its caller, you should create an exception object and throw it. If you can handle the exception in the method where it occurs, there is no need to throw it.

In general, common exceptions that may occur in multiple classes in a project are candidates for exception classes. Simple errors that may occur in individual methods are best handled locally without throwing exceptions.

When should you use a try-catch block in the code? Use it when you have to deal with unexpected error conditions. Do not use a try-catch block to deal with simple, expected situations. For example, the following code

```java
try {
  System.out.println(refVar.toString());
}
catch (NullPointerException ex) {
  System.out.println("refVar is null");
}
```

is better replaced by

```java
if (refVar != null)
  System.out.println(refVar.toString());
else
  System.out.println("refVar is null");
```

Which situations are exceptional and which are expected is sometimes difficult to decide. The point is not to abuse exception handling as a way to deal with a simple logic test.

15.7 Creating Custom Exception Classes (Optional)

Java provides quite a few exception classes. Use them whenever possible instead of creating your own exception classes. However, if you run into a problem that cannot be adequately described by the predefined exception classes, you can create your own exception class, derived from Exception or from a subclass of Exception, such as IOException.

In Example 15.1, "Declaring, Throwing, and Catching Exceptions," the setRadius method throws an exception if the radius is negative. Suppose you wish to pass the radius to the handler. In that case you have to create a custom exception class. The class may be created as follows:

```java
// RadiusException.java: An exception class for describing
// invalid radius exception
public class RadiusException extends Exception {
  /** Information to be passed to the handlers */
  private double radius;

  /** Construct an exception */
  public RadiusException(double radius) {
```

```
      this.radius = radius;
   }

   /** Return the radius */
   public double getRadius() {
      return radius;
   }

   /** Override the "toString" method */
   public String toString() {
      return "Radius is " + radius;
   }
}
```

The `java.lang.Exception` class has a no-arg constructor and three other constructors. To create a `RadiusException`, you have to pass a radius. So the `setRadius` method in Example 15.1 can be modified as follows:

```
/** Set a new radius */
public void setRadius(double newRadius)
    throws RadiusException {
   if (newRadius >= 0)
      radius = newRadius;
   else
      throw new RadiusException(newRadius);
}
```

The following code creates a circle object and sets its radius to −5:

```
try {
   CircleWithException1 c = new CircleWithException1(4);
   c.setRadius(-5);
}
catch (RadiusException ex) {
   System.out.println("The invalid radius is " + ex.getRadius());
}
```

Invoking `setRadius(-5)` throws a `RadiusException`, which is caught by the handler. The handler displays the radius in the exception object `ex`.

15.8 Assertions (Optional)

An *assertion* is a Java statement that enables you to assert an assumption about your program. An assertion contains a Boolean expression that should be true during program execution. Assertions can be used to ensure program correctness and avoid logic errors.

assertion

15.8.1 Declaring Assertions

An *assertion* is declared using the new Java keyword `assert` in JDK 1.4, as follows:

```
assert assertion;
```

or

```
assert assertion : detailMessage;
```

where *assertion* is a Boolean expression and *detailMessage* is a primitive-type or an `Object` value.

When an assertion statement is executed, Java evaluates the `assertion`. If it is false, an `AssertionError` will be thrown. The `AssertionError` class has a no-arg constructor and seven overloaded single-parameter constructors of type `int`, `long`, `float`, `double`, `boolean`, `char`, and `Object`. For the first `assert` statement with no detailed message, the no-arg constructor of `AssertionError` is used. For the second `assert` statement with a detailed message, an appropriate `AssertionError` constructor is used to match the data type of the message. AssertionError is a subclass of Error, so when an assertion becomes false, the program displays a message on the console and exits.

Here is an example of using assertions:

```
 1 public class AssertionDemo {
 2   public static void main(String[] args) {
 3     int i; int sum = 0;
 4     for (i = 0; i < 10; i++) {
 5       sum += i;
 6     }
 7     assert i == 10;
 8     assert sum > 10 && sum < 5 * 10 : "sum is " + sum;
 9   }
10 }
```

The statement assert i == 10 asserts that i is 10 when the statement is executed. If i is not 10, an AssertionError is thrown. The statement assert sum > 10 && sum < 5 * 10 : "sum is " + sum asserts that sum > 10 and sum < 5 * 10. If false, an AssertionError with message "sum is " + sum is thrown.

Suppose you typed i < 100 instead of i < 10 by mistake in Line 4, the following AssertionError would be thrown:

```
Exception in thread "main" java.lang.AssertionError
        at AssertionDemo.main(AssertionDemo.java:7)
```

Suppose you typed sum += 1 instead of sum += i by mistake in Line 5, the following AssertionError would be thrown:

```
Exception in thread "main" java.lang.AssertionError: sum is 10
        at AssertionDemo.main(AssertionDemo.java:8)
```

15.8.2   Running Programs with Assertions

By default, assertions are disabled at runtime. To enable them, use the switch -enableassertions, or -ea for short, as follows:

java -ea AssertionDemo

Assertions can be selectively enabled or disabled at the class level or the package level. The disable switch is -disableassertions, or -da for short. For example, the following command enables assertions in package package1 and disables assertions in class Class1.

```
java -ea:package1 -da:Class1 AssertionDemo
```

15.8.3   Using Exception Handling or Assertions

Assertion should not be used to replace exception handling. Exception handling deals with unusual circumstances during program execution. Assertions are intended to ensure the correctness of the program. Exception handling addresses robustness, whereas assertion addresses correctness. Like exception handling, assertions are not used for normal tests, but for internal consistency and validity checks. Assertions are checked at runtime and can be turned on or off at startup time.

Do not use assertions for argument checking in public methods. Valid arguments that may be passed to a public method are considered to be part of the method's contract. The contract must always be obeyed whether assertions are enabled or disabled. For example, the following code should be rewritten using exception handling, as shown in Lines 27–31 in CircleWithException.java in Example 15.1, "Declaring, Throwing, and Catching Exceptions":

```
public void setRadius(double newRadius) {
  assert newRadius >= 0;
  radius = newRadius;
}
```

Use assertions to reaffirm assumptions. This will increase your confidence in the program's correctness. A common use of assertions is to replace assumptions with assertions in the code. For example, the following code in (a) can be replaced by (b):

```
if (even) {
  ...
}
else { // even is false
  ...
}
```

```
if (even) {
  ...
}
else {
  assert !even;
  ...
}
```

(a)   (b)

Similarly, the following code in (a) can also be replaced by (b):

```
if (numberOfDollars > 1) {
  ...
}
else if (numberOfDollars == 1) {
  ...
}
```

```
if (numberOfDollars > 1) {
  ...
}
else if (numberOfDollars == 1) {
  ...
}
else
  assert false : numberOfDollars;
```

(a)   (b)

Another good use of assertions is to place them in a `switch` statement without a default case. For example,

```
switch (month) {
  case 1: ... ; break;
  case 2: ... ; break;
  ...
  case 12: ... ; break;
  default: assert false : "Invalid month: " + month
}
```

KEY TERMS

assertion   563
checked exception   552

exception   551
unchecked exception   552

KEY CLASSES AND METHODS

◆ **java.lang.Throwable** is the root class for exceptions. The `getMessage()` method returns the detailed message of the exception, `toString()` returns the combination of the exception class name, colon (:), and `getMessage()`, and `printStackTrace()` displays track information on the console.

◆ **java.lang.Error** is the base class for internal system errors.

◆ **java.lang.AssertionError** is a subclass of Error thrown when an assertion fails.

◆ **java.lang.Exception** is the base class for errors caused by the program and external circumstances.

◆ **java.lang.ClassNotFoundException** is thrown when a dependent class is not found at runtime.

◆ **java.lang.CloneNotSupportedException** is thrown if the object being cloned is not an instance of java.lang.Cloneable.

◆ **java.lang.RuntimeException** is the base class for programming errors, such as bad casting, array index errors, and numeric errors.

◆ **java.lang.NullPointerException** is a runtime exception thrown when accessing an object through a null reference.

◆ **java.lang.IndexOutOfBoundsException** is a runtime exception thrown when accessing an array object through a null reference.

CHAPTER SUMMARY

◆ When an exception occurs, Java creates an object that contains the information for the exception. You can use the information to handle the exception.

◆ A Java exception is an instance of a class derived from java.lang.Throwable. Java provides a number of predefined exception classes, such as Error, Exception, RuntimeException, ClassNotFoundException, NullPointerException, and ArithmeticException. You can also define your own exception class by extending Exception.

◆ Exceptions occur during the execution of a method. RuntimeException and Error are unchecked exceptions; all other exceptions are checked exceptions.

◆ When declaring a method, you have to declare a checked exception if the method might throw that checked exception, thus telling the compiler what can go wrong.

◆ The keyword for declaring an exception is throws, and the keyword for throwing an exception is throw.

◆ To invoke the method that declares checked exceptions, you must enclose the method call in a try statement. When an exception occurs during the execution of the method, the catch clause catches and handles the exception.

◆ If an exception is not caught in the current method, it is passed to its caller. The process is repeated until the exception is caught or passed to the main method.

◆ If an exception of a subclass of Exception occurs in a GUI component, Java prints the error message on the console, but the program goes back to its user-interface-processing loop to run continuously. The exception is ignored.

◆ Various exception classes can be derived from a common superclass. If a catch clause catches the exception objects of a superclass, it can also catch all the exception objects of the subclasses of that superclass.

◆ The order in which exceptions are specified in a catch clause is important. A compilation error will result if you do not specify an exception object of a class before an exception object of the superclass of that class.

✦ When an exception occurs in a method, the method exits immediately if it does not catch the exception. If the method is required to perform some task before exiting, you can catch the exception in the method and then rethrow it to the caller.

✦ The code in the `finally` block is executed under all circumstances, regardless of whether an exception occurs in the `try` block or is caught.

✦ Exception handling separates error-handling code from normal programming tasks, thus making programs easier to read and to modify.

✦ Exception handling should not be used to replace simple tests. You should test simple exceptions whenever possible, and reserve exception handling for dealing with situations that cannot be handled with `if` statements.

✦ Exceptions address robustness, whereas assertions address correctness. Exceptions and assertions are not meant to substitute for simple tests. Avoid using exception handling if a simple `if` statement is sufficient. Never use assertions to check normal conditions.

REVIEW QUESTIONS

 NOTE

In the following questions, assume that the `divide` method in `Rational` in Section 10.5, "Case Study: The `Rational` Class," is modified as follows:

```
public Rational divide(Rational secondRational) throws Exception {
  if (secondRational.getNumerator() == 0)
    throw new Exception("Divisor cannot be zero");

  long n = numerator * secondRational.getDenominator();
  long d = denominator * secondRational.getNumerator();
  return new Rational(n, d);
}
```

The `divide` method in the `Rational` class throws `Exception` if the divisor is 0.

Sections 15.2–15.3

15.1 Describe the Java `Throwable` class, its subclasses, and the types of exceptions.

15.2 What is the purpose of declaring exceptions? How do you declare an exception, and where? Can you declare multiple exceptions in a method declaration?

15.3 What is a checked exception, and what is an unchecked exception?

15.4 How do you throw an exception? Can you throw multiple exceptions in one `throw` statement?

15.5 What is the keyword `throw` used for? What is the keyword `throws` used for?

15.6 What does the JVM do when an exception occurs?

15.7 How do you catch an exception?

15.8 Suppose that `statement2` causes an exception in the following `try-catch` block:

```
try {
  statement1;
  statement2;
  statement3;
}
catch (Exception1 ex1) {
}
catch (Exception2 ex2) {
}

statement4;
```

Answer the following questions:

◆ Will statement3 be executed?

◆ If the exception is not caught, will statement4 be executed?

◆ If the exception is caught in the catch clause, will statement4 be executed?

◆ If the exception is passed to the caller, will statement4 be executed?

15.9 What is displayed when the following program is run?

```java
public class Test {
  public static void main(String[] args) {
    try {
      Rational r1 = new Rational(3, 4);
      Rational r2 = new Rational(0, 1);
      Rational x = r1.divide(r2);

      int i = 0;
      int y = 2 / i;
      System.out.println("Welcome to Java");
    }
    catch (RuntimeException ex) {
      System.out.println("Integer operation error");
    }
    catch (Exception ex) {
      System.out.println("Rational operation error");
    }
  }
}
```

15.10 What is displayed when the following program is run?

```java
public class Test {
  public static void main(String[] args) {
    try {
      method();
      System.out.println("After the method call");
    }
    catch (RuntimeException ex) {
      System.out.println("Integer operation error");
    }
    catch (Exception e) {
      System.out.println("Rational operation error");
    }
  }

  static void method() throws Exception {
    Rational r1 = new Rational(3, 4);
    Rational r2 = new Rational(0, 1);
    Rational x = r1.divide(r2);
    int i = 0;
    int y = 2 / i;
    System.out.println("Welcome to Java");
  }
}
```

15.11 What is displayed when the following program is run?

```java
public class Test {
  public static void main(String[] args) {
    try {
      method();
      System.out.println("After the method call");
    }
    catch (RuntimeException ex) {
      System.out.println("Integer operation error");
    }
```

```
      catch (Exception ex) {
        System.out.println("Rational operation error");
      }
  }

  static void method() throws Exception {
    try {
      Rational r1 = new Rational(3, 4);
      Rational r2 = new Rational(0, 1);
      Rational x = r1.divide(r2);

      int i = 0;
      int y = 2 / i;
      System.out.println("Welcome to Java");
    }
    catch (RuntimeException ex) {
      System.out.println("Integer operation error");
    }
    catch (Exception ex) {
      System.out.println("Rational operation error");
    }
  }
}
```

15.12 If an exception is not caught in a non-GUI application, what will happen? If an exception is not caught in a GUI application, what will happen?

15.13 What does the method `printStackTrace` do?

15.14 Does the presence of a `try-catch` block impose overhead when no exception occurs?

Sections 15.4–15.5

15.15 Suppose that `statement2` causes an exception in the following statement:

```
try {
  statement1;
  statement2;
  statement3;
}
catch (Exception1 ex1) {
}
catch (Exception2 ex2) {
}
catch (Exception3 ex3) {
  throw ex3;
}
finally {
  statement4;
};
statement5;
```

Answer the following questions:

◆ Will `statement5` be executed if the exception is not caught?

◆ If the exception is of type `Exception3`, will `statement4` be executed, and will `statement5` be executed?

15.16 What is displayed when the following program is run?

```
public class Test {
  public static void main(String[] args) {
    try {
      method();
      System.out.println("After the method call");
    }
    catch (RuntimeException ex) {
      System.out.println("Integer operation error");
    }
```

```
          catch (Exception ex) {
            System.out.println("Rational operation error");
          }
        }

        static void method() throws Exception {
          try {
            Rational r1 = new Rational(3, 4);
            Rational r2 = new Rational(0, 1);
            Rational x = r1.divide(r2);

            int i = 0;
            int y = 2 / i;
            System.out.println("Welcome to Java");
          }
          catch (RuntimeException ex) {
            System.out.println("Integer operation error");
          }
          catch (Exception ex) {
            System.out.println("Rational operation error");
            throw ex;
          }
        }
      }
    }
```

Section 15.8 Assertions

15.17 What is assertion for? How do you declare assertions? How do you compile code with assertions? How do you run programs with assertions?

15.18 What happens when you run the following code?

```
public class Test {
  public static void main(String[] args) {
    int i; int sum = 0;
    for (i = 0; i < 11; i++) {
      sum += i;
    }
    assert i == 10: "i is " + i;
  }
}
```

PROGRAMMING EXERCISES

Sections 15.2–15.3

15.1* (*NumberFormatException*) Example 7.4, "Passing Command-Line Arguments," is a simple command-line calculator. Note that the program terminates if any operand is non-numeric. Write a program with an exception handler that deals with non-numeric operands; then write another program without using an exception handler to achieve the same objective. Your program should display a message that informs the user of the wrong operand type before exiting (see Figure 15.8).

15.2* (*ArithmeticException and NumberFormatException*) Example 15.2, "Exceptions in GUI Applications," is a GUI calculator. Note that if Number 1 or Number 2 were a non-numeric string, the program would report exceptions. Modify the program with an exception handler to catch ArithmeticException (e.g., divided by 0) and NumberFormatException (e.g., input is not an integer), and display the errors in a message dialog box, as shown in Figure 15.9.

15.3* (*ArrayIndexOutBoundsException*) Write a program that meets the following requirements:

✦ Create an array with one hundred randomly chosen integers.

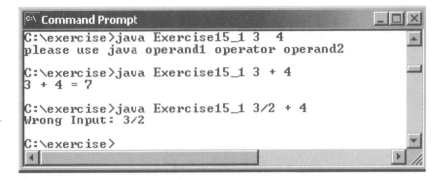

FIGURE 15.8 *The program performs arithmetic operations and detects input errors.*

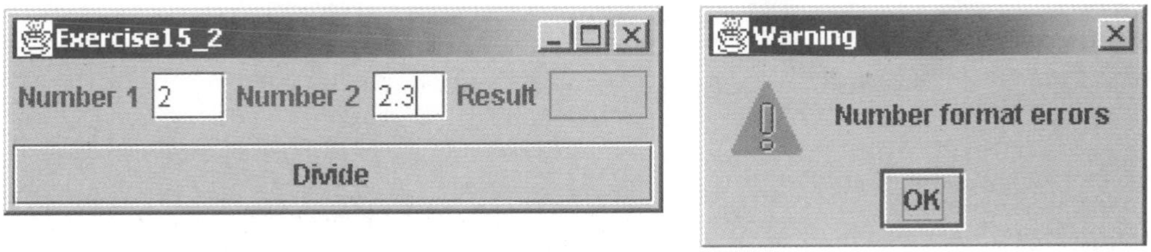

FIGURE 15.9 *The program displays an error message in the dialog box if the number is not well formatted.*

✦ Create a text field to enter an array index and another text field to display the array element at the specified index (see Figure 15.10).

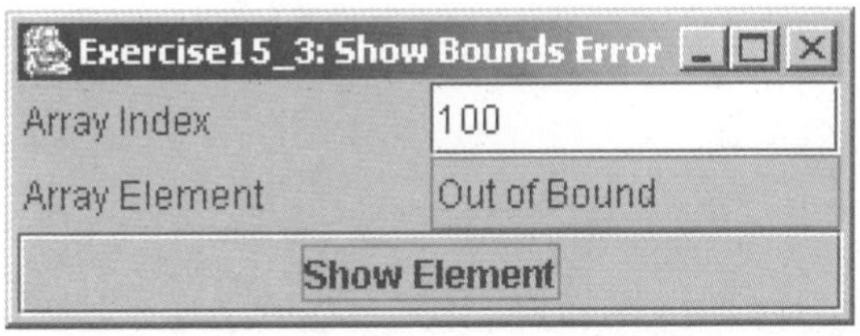

FIGURE 15.10 *The program displays the array element at the specified index or displays the message* Out of Bound *if the index is out of bounds.*

✦ Create a Show Element button to cause the array element to be displayed. If the specified index is out of bounds, display the message Out of Bound.

15.4* (*IllegalArgumentException*) Modify the Loan class in Section 6.15, "Case Study: The Loan Class," to throw IllegalArgumentException if the loan amount, interest rate, or number of years is less than or equal to zero.

15.5* (*IllegalTriangleException*) Exercise 8.1 defined the Triangle class with three sides. In a triangle, the sum of any two sides is greater than the other side. The Triangle class must adhere to this rule. Create the IllegalTriangleException class, and modify the constructor of the Triangle class to throw an IllegalTriangleException object if a triangle is created with sides that violate the rule, as follows:

```
/** Construct a triangle with the specified sides */
public Triangle(double side1, double side2, double side3)
  throws IllegalTriangleException {
  // Implement it
}
```

chapter

16

SIMPLE INPUT AND OUTPUT

Objectives

- ✦ To discover file properties, delete and rename files using the `File` class (§16.2).

- ✦ To understand how I/O is processed in Java (§16.3).

- ✦ To distinguish between text I/O and binary I/O (§16.3.1).

- ✦ To read and write characters using `FileReader` and `FileWriter` (§16.4.1).

- ✦ To improve the performance of text I/O using `BufferedReader` and `BufferedWriter` (§16.4.3).

- ✦ To write primitive values, strings, and objects as text using `PrintWriter` and `PrintStream` (§16.4.4).

- ✦ To read and write bytes using `FileInputStream` and `FileOutputStream` (§16.6.1).

- ✦ To read and write primitive values and strings using `DataInputStream`/`DataOutputStream` (§16.6.3).

- ✦ To store and restore objects using `ObjectOutputStream` and `ObjectInputStream`, and to understand how objects are serialized and what kind of objects can be serialized (§16.9 Optional).

- ✦ To use the `Serializable` interface to enable objects to be serializable (§16.9.1 Optional).

- ✦ To use `RandomAccessFile` for both read and write (§16.10 Optional).

16.1 Introduction

Data stored in variables, arrays, and objects are temporary; they are lost when the program terminates. To permanently store the data created in a program, you need to save them in a file on a disk or a CD. The file can be transported and can be read later by other programs. In this chapter, you will learn how to read/write data from/to a file, and how to store/restore objects to/from a file. Since data are stored in files, the following section introduces how to use the `File` class to obtain file properties and to delete and rename files.

16.2 The `File` Class

Every file is placed in a directory in the file system. The complete file name consists of the directory path and the file name. For example, **c:\book\Welcome.java** is the complete file name for the file **Welcome.java** on the Windows operating system. Here **c:\book** is referred to as the *directory path* for the file. The directory path and complete file name are machine-dependent. On Unix, the complete file name may be **/home/liang/book/Welcome.java**, where **/home/liang/book** is the directory path for the file **Welcome.java.**

directory path

The `File` class is intended to provide an abstraction that deals with most of the machine-dependent complexities of files and path names in a machine-independent fashion. The `File` class contains the methods for obtaining file properties and for renaming and deleting files, as shown in Figure 16.1. However, the `File` class does not contain the methods for reading and writing file contents

The filename is a string. The `File` class is a wrapper class for the file name and its directory path. For example, new `File("c:\\book")` creates a `File` object for the directory **c:\book**, and new `File("c:\\book\\test.dat")` creates a `File` object for the file **c:\\book\\test.dat**, both on Windows. You can use the `File` class's `isDirectory()` method to check whether the object represents a directory, and the `isFile()` method to check whether the object represents a file name.

 CAUTION

The directory separator for Windows is a backslash (\). The backslash is a special character in Java and should be written as \\ (see Table 2.4 on page 46).

directory separator

The `File` class has four constants: `pathSeparator`, `pathSeparatorChar`, `separator`, and `separatorChar`. These constants are platform-dependent path separators and name separators. `separatorChar` is `'\'` on Windows and `'/'` on Unix. `separatorChar` is a char, and `separator` is a string representation of `separatorChar`. Likewise, `pathSeparator` is a string representation for `pathSeparatorChar`. `pathSeparator` is `';'` on Windows and `':'` on Unix.

 NOTE

`pathSeparator`, `pathSeparatorChar`, `separator`, and `separatorChar` are constants, but they are named as variables with lowercase for the first word and uppercase for the first letters of subsequent words. Thus these names violate the Java naming convention.

An *absolute path* name is system-dependent. For example, if you create a `File` object using new `File("c:\\book\\test.dat")`, it is an absolute path name. If you create a `File` object using new `File("test.dat")`, it refers to the file in the current class path directory. This path is not absolute because no system-specific path separators are used.

absolute path

java.io.File	
+File(pathname: String)	Creates a File object for the specified pathname. The pathname may be a directory or a file.
+File(parent: String, child: String)	Creates a File object for the child under the directory parent. The child may be a filename or a subdirectory.
+File(parent: File, child: String)	Creates a File object for the child under the directory parent. The parent is a File object. In the preceding constructor, the parent is a string.
+exists(): boolean	Returns true if the file or the directory represented by the File object exists.
+canRead(): boolean	Returns true if the file represented by the File object exists and can be read.
+canWrite(): boolean	Returns true if the file represented by the File object exists and can be written.
+isDirectory(): boolean	Returns true if the File object represents a directory.
+isFile(): boolean	Returns true if the File object represents a file.
+isAbsolute(): boolean	Returns true if the File object is created using an absolute path name.
+isHidden(): boolean	Returns true if the file represented in the File object is hidden. The exact definition of *hidden* is system-dependent. On Windows, you can mark a file hidden in the File Properties dialog box. On Unix systems, a file is hidden if its name begins with a period character '.'.
+getAbsolutePath(): String	Returns the complete absolute file or directory name represented by the File object.
+getCanonicalPath(): String	Returns the same as getAbsolutePath() except that it removes redundant names, such as "." and "..", from the pathname, resolves symbolic links (on Unix platforms), and converts drive letters to standard uppercase (on Win32 platforms).
+getName(): String	Returns the last name of the complete directory and file name represented by the File object. For example, new File("c:\\book\\test.dat").getName() returns test.dat.
+getPath(): String	Returns the complete directory and file name represented by the File object. For example,new File("c:\\book\\test.dat").getPath() returns c:\book\test.dat.
+getParent(): String	Returns the complete parent directory of the current directory or the file represented by the File object. For example, new File("c:\\book\\test.dat").getParent() returns c:\book.
+lastModified(): long	Returns the time that the file was last modified.
+delete(): boolean	Deletes this file. The method returns true if the deletion succeeds.
+renameTo(dest: File): boolean	Renames this file. The method returns true if the operation succeeds.

FIGURE 16.1 *The File class can be used to obtain file and directory properties and to delete and rename files.*

Do not use the absolute directory and file name literals in your program. If you use a literal such as "c:\\book\\test.dat", it will work on Windows but not on other platforms. To enable the program to run correctly on different platforms, use the following string to replace "c:\\book\\test.dat":

```
new File(".").getCanonicalPath() + "book" + File.separator
  + "test.dat";
```

current directory

Here "." denotes the current directory. If you run the Java program from the command line, the current directory is where the java command is issued. If you run the program from an IDE, the current directory is dependent on the IDE settings.

Listing 16.1 demonstrates how to create a File object in a platform-independent way and use the methods in the File class to obtain its properties. The program creates a File object for the file **us.gif.** This file is stored under the **image** directory in the current directory. The statement in Line 8 creates the object in a platform-independent fashion without using the platform-specific name separator and drive letter.

LISTING 16.1 TestFileClass.java (Using the File Class)

```
 1 import java.io.*;
 2 import java.util.*;
 3
 4 public class TestFileClass {
 5   public static void main(String[] args) {
 6     // Create a File object
 7     File file = new File(".", "image" + File.separator + "us.gif");
 8     System.out.println("Does it exist? " + file.exists());
 9     System.out.println("Can it be read? " + file.canRead());
10     System.out.println("Can it be written? " + file.canWrite());
11     System.out.println("Is it a directory? " + file.isDirectory());
12     System.out.println("Is it a file? " + file.isFile());
13     System.out.println("Is it absolute? " + file.isAbsolute());
14     System.out.println("Is it hidden? " + file.isHidden());
15     System.out.println("What is its absolute path? " +
16       file.getAbsolutePath());
17
18     try {
19       System.out.println("What is its canonical path? " +
20         file.getCanonicalPath());
21     }
22     catch (IOException ex) { }
23
24     System.out.println("What is its name? " + file.getName());
25     System.out.println("What is its path? " + file.getPath());
26     System.out.println("When was it last modified? " +
27       new Date(file.lastModified()));
28
29     System.out.println("What is the path separator? " +
30       File.pathSeparatorChar);
31     System.out.println("What is the name separator? " +
32       File.separatorChar);
33   }
34 }
```

file exist?

All the Java I/O classes introduced in this chapter are in the java.io package, so it is imported in Line 1.

The getCanonicalPath() method can throw an IOException, so it is put in a try-catch block in Lines 18–22.

The lastModified() method returns the date and time when the file was last modified, measured in milliseconds since the epoch (00:00:00 GMT, January 1, 1970). The Date class is used to display it in a readable format in Lines 26–27.

Figure 16.2 shows a sample run of the program on Windows, and Figure 16.3 a sample run on Unix. As shown in the figures, the path name and separator on Windows are different from those on Unix.

 TIP
To develop platform-independent applications, it is imperative not to use absolute directory and file names.

16.3 How is I/O Handled in Java?

A File object encapsulates the properties of a file or a path, but does not contain the methods for reading/writing data from/to a file. In order to perform I/O, you need to create objects using appropriate Java I/O classes. The objects contain the methods for reading/writing data from/to a file. For example, to write text to a file named temp.txt, you may create an object using the java.io.FileWriter class as follows:

```
FileWriter output = new FileWriter("temp.txt");
```

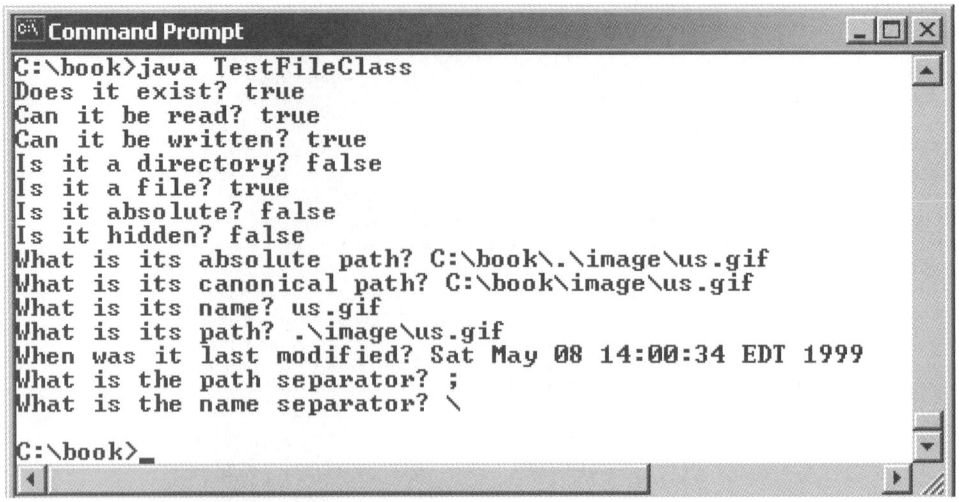

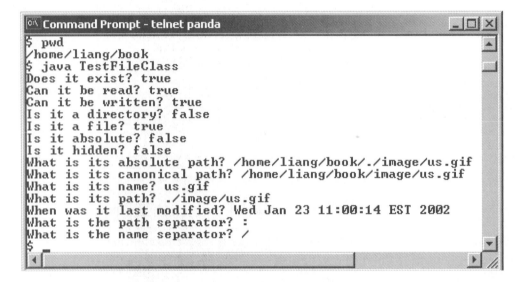

FIGURE 16.2 *The program creates a* File *object and displays file properties on Windows.*

FIGURE 16.3 *The program creates a* File *object and displays file properties on Unix.*

You can now invoke write(String) from the object to write a string into the file. For example, the following statement writes "Java 101" to the file:

```
output.write("Java 101");
```

The next statement closes the file:

```
output.close();
```

There are many I/O classes for various purposes. In general, these can be classified as input classes and output classes. An input class contains the methods to read data, and an output class contains the methods to write data. FileWriter is an example of an output class and FileReader is an example of an input class. The following code shows an example of creating an input object for the file temp.txt and reading data from the file:

```
FileReader input = new FileReader("temp.txt");
int code = input.read();
System.out.println((char)code);
```

If temp.txt contains "Java 101", input.read() returns the Unicode for 'J'. So the printout is J.

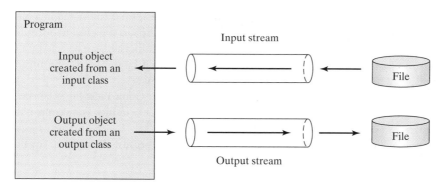

FIGURE 16.4 *The program receives data through an input object and sends data through an output object.*

Figure 16.4 illustrates Java I/O programming. An input object reads a stream of data from a file, and an output object writes a stream of data to a file. You will learn how to use I/O classes to create objects and use the methods in the objects to read/write data from/to files in this chapter.

Almost all the methods in the I/O classes throw java.io.IOException. Therefore you have to declare to throw java.io.IOException in the method or place the code in a try-catch block, as shown below:

IOException

Declaring exception in the method

```
public static void main(String[] args)
    throws IOException {
  FileWriter output =
    new FileWriter("temp.txt");
  output.write("Java 101");
  output.close();

  FileReader input =
    new FileReader("temp.txt");
  int code = input.read();
  System.out.println((char)code);
  input.close();
}
```

Using try-catch block

```
public static void main(String[] args) {
  try {
    FileWriter output =
      new FileWriter("temp.txt");
    output.write("Java 101");
    output.close();

    FileReader input =
      new FileReader("temp.txt");
    int code = input.read();
    System.out.println((char)code);
    input.close();
  }
  catch (IOException ex) {
    ex.printStackTrace();
  }
}
```

 NOTE

An input object reads a stream of data. For convenience, an input object is also called an *input stream*. For the same reason, an output object is called an *output stream*.

input stream
output stream

 TIP

When a stream is no longer needed, always close it using the close() method. Not closing streams may cause programming errors.

close stream

16.3.1 Text Files and Binary Files

Java offers many classes for performing file input and output. These classes can be categorized as *text I/O classes* and *binary I/O classes*.

text I/O
binary I/O

Data stored in a text file are represented in human-readable form. Data stored in a binary file are represented in binary form. You cannot read binary files. They are designed to be read by programs. For example, the Java source programs are stored in text files and can be read by a text editor, but the Java classes are stored in binary files and are read by the JVM. The advantage of binary files is that they are more efficient to process than text files.

Although it is not technically precise and correct, you can envision a text file as consisting of a sequence of characters and a binary file as consisting of a sequence of bits. For example, the decimal integer 199 is stored as the sequence of three characters, '1', '9', '9', in a text file, and the same integer is stored as a `byte`-type value C7 in a binary file, because decimal 199 equals hex C7 ($199 = 12 \times 16^1 + 7$).

16.4 Text I/O

The design of the Java I/O classes is a good example of applying inheritance, where common operations are generalized in superclasses, and subclasses provide specialized operations. Figure 16.5 lists some of the classes for performing text I/O.

`Reader` is the root for text input classes, and `Writer` is the root for text output classes. Figures 16.6 and 16.7 list all the methods in `Reader` and `Writer`.

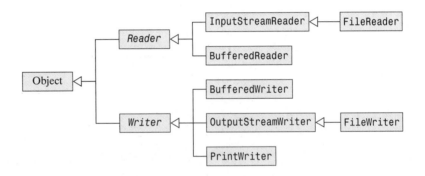

FIGURE 16.5 *`Reader`, `Writer`, and their subclasses are for text I/O.*

java.io.Reader	
+read(): int	Reads the next character from the input stream. The value returned is an int in the range from 0 to 65535, which represents a Unicode character. Returns -1 at the end of the stream.
+read(cbuf: char[]): int	Reads characters from the input stream into an array. Returns the actual number of characters read. Returns -1 at the end of the stream.
+read(cbuf: char[], off: int, len: int): int	Reads characters from the input stream and stores them in cbuf[off], cbuf[off+1], …, cbuf[off+len-1]. The actual number of bytes read is returned. Returns -1 at the end of the stream.
+close(): void	Closes this input stream and releases any system resources associated with it.
+skip(n: long): long	Skips over and discards n characters of data from this input stream. The actual number of characters skipped is returned.
+markSupported(): boolean	Tests whether this input stream supports the mark and reset methods.
+mark(readAheadLimit: int): void	Marks the current position in this input stream.
+ready(): boolean	Returns true if this input stream is ready to be read.
+reset(): void	Repositions this stream to the position at the time the mark method was last called on this input stream.

FIGURE 16.6 *The abstract `Reader` class defines the methods for reading a stream of characters.*

java.io.Writer	
+write(int c): void	Writes the specified character to this output stream. The parameter c is the Unicode for a character
+write(cbuf: byte[]): void	Writes all the characters in array cbuf to the output stream.
+write(cbuf: char[], off: int, len: int): void	Writes cbuf[off], cbuf[off+1], …, cbuf[off+len−1] into the output stream.
+write(str: String): void	Writes the characters from the string into the output stream.
+write(str: String, off: int, len: int): void	Writes a portion of the string characters into the output stream.
+close(): void	Closes this input stream and releases any system resources associated with it.
+flush(): void	Flushes this output stream and forces any buffered output characters to be written out.

FIGURE 16.7 *The abstract* Writer *class defines the methods for writing a stream of characters.*

NOTE

The read() method reads a character. If no data are available, it blocks the thread from executing the next statement. The thread that invokes the read() method is suspended until the data become available.

NOTE

All the methods in the text I/O classes except PrintWriter are declared to throw java.io.IOException.

16.4.1 FileReader/FileWriter

FileReader/FileWriter are convenience classes for reading/writing characters from/to files using the default character encoding on the host computer. FileReader/FileWriter associates an input/output stream with an external file.

All the methods in FileReader/FileWriter are inherited from their superclasses. To construct a FileReader, use the following constructors:

```
public FileReader(String filename)
public FileReader(File file)
```

A java.io.FileNotFoundException would occur if you attempt to create a FileReader with a nonexistent file. For example, Listing 16.2 reads and displays all the characters from the file temp.txt.

FileNotFoundException

LISTING 16.2 TestFileReader.java (Input Using FileReader)

```
 1 import java.io.*;
 2
 3 public class TestFileReader {
 4   public static void main(String[] args) {
 5     FileReader input = null;
 6     try {
 7       // Create an input stream
 8       input = new FileReader("temp.txt");
 9
10       int code;
11       // Repeatedly read a character and display it on the console
12       while ((code = input.read()) != -1)
13         System.out.print((char)code);
14     }
```

import

input object

read character

```
15      catch (FileNotFoundException ex) {
16        System.out.println("File temp.txt does not exist");
17      }
18      catch (IOException ex) {
19        ex.printStackTrace();
20      }
21      finally {
22        try {
23          input.close(); // Close the stream
24        }
25        catch (IOException ex) {
26          ex.printStackTrace();
27        }
28      }
29    }
30 }
```

close file *(margin note, aligned with line 23)*

The constructors and methods in `FileReader` may throw `IOException`, so they are invoked from a try-catch block. Since `java.io.FileNotFoundException` is a subclass of `IOException`, the catch clause for `FileNotFoundException` (Line 15) is put before the `catch` clause for `IOException` (Line 18). Closing files in the `finally` class ensures that the files are always closed in any case (Line 23).

Recall that Java allows the assignment operator in an expression (see page 37). The expression `((code = input.read()) != -1)` (Line 12) reads a byte from `input.read()`, assigns it to `code`, and checks whether it is −1. The input value of −1 signifies the end of a file.

test end of a file *(margin note)*

 NOTE

Attempting to read data after the end of a file is reached would cause `java.io.EOFException`.

EOFException *(margin note)*

To construct a `FileWriter`, use the following constructors:

```
public FileWriter(String filename)
public FileWriter(File file)
public FileWriter(String filename, boolean append)
public FileWriter(File file, boolean append)
```

If the file does not exist, a new file will be created. If the file already exists, the first two constructors will delete the current contents of the file. To retain the current content and append new data into the file, use the last two constructors by passing true to the append parameter. For example, suppose the file temp.txt exists, Listing 16.3 appends a new string, "Introduction to Java," to the file.

LISTING 16.3   TestFileWriter.java (Output Using `FileWriter`)

```
1 import java.io.*;
2
3 public class TestFileWriter {
4   public static void main(String[] args) throws IOException {
5     // Create an output stream to the file
6     FileWriter output = new FileWriter("temp.txt", true);
7
8     // Output a string to the file
9     output.write("Introduction to Java");
10
11    // Close the stream
12    output.close();
13  }
14 }
```

append to file *(margin note, aligned with line 6)*

JDK 1.5 Scanner class

 TIP

You can also use the Scanner class to extract tokens from a file and then use next-Token() to read a string, nextInt() to read an int, nextDouble() to read a double, and so on, as introduced in Section 7.6. "The Scanner Class." To create a Scanner for a file, use

```
Scanner scanner = new Scanner(File file);
```

16.5 Case Study: Text Viewer

This case study writes a program that views a text file in a text area. The user enters a filename in a text field and clicks the View button; the file is then displayed in a text area, as shown in Figure 16.9.

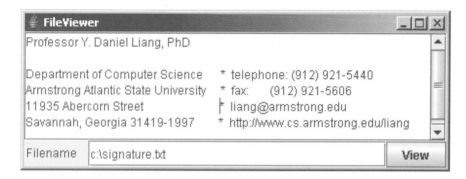

FIGURE **16.9** *The program displays the specified file in the text area.*

Clearly, you need to use text input to read a text file. Normally, you should use BufferedReader wrapped on a FileReader to improve performance. When the View button is pressed, the program gets the input filename from the text field; it then creates a text input stream. The data are read one line at a time and appended to the text area for display. Listing 16.6 displays the source code for the program.

LISTING 16.6 FileViewer.java (View Text Files)

```
1 import java.awt.*;
2 import java.awt.event.*;
3 import java.io.*;
4 import javax.swing.*;
5
6 public class FileViewer extends JFrame implements ActionListener {
7   // Button to view a file
8   private JButton jbtView = new JButton("View");
9
10   // Text field to the receive file name
11   private JTextField jtfFilename = new JTextField(12);
12
13   // Text area to display the file
14   private JTextArea jtaFile = new JTextArea();
15
16   public FileViewer() {
17     // Panel p to hold a label, a text field, and a button
18     Panel p = new Panel();
19     p.setLayout(new BorderLayout());
20     p.add(new Label("Filename"), BorderLayout.WEST);
21     p.add(jtfFilename, BorderLayout.CENTER);
22     p.add(jbtView, BorderLayout.EAST);
```

create UI

```
23
24      // Add jtaFile to a scroll pane
25      JScrollPane jsp = new JScrollPane(jtaFile);
26
27      // Add jsp and p to the frame
28      getContentPane().add(jsp, BorderLayout.CENTER);
29      getContentPane().add(p, BorderLayout.SOUTH);
30
31      // Register listener
32      jbtView.addActionListener(this);
33    }
34
35    /** Handle the View button */
36    public void actionPerformed(ActionEvent e) {
37      if (e.getSource() == jbtView)
38        showFile();
39    }
40
41    /** Display the file in the text area */
42    private void showFile() {
43      // Use a BufferedReader to read text from the file
44      BufferedReader input = null;
45
46      // Get file name from the text field
47      String filename = jtfFilename.getText().trim();
48
49      String inLine;
50
51      try {
52        // Create a buffered stream
53        input = new BufferedReader(new FileReader(filename));
54
55        // Read a line and append the line to the text area
56        while ((inLine = input.readLine()) != null) {
57          jtaFile.append(inLine + '\n');
58        }
59      }
60      catch (FileNotFoundException ex) {
61        System.out.println("File not found: " + filename);
62      }
63      catch (IOException ex) {
64        System.out.println(ex.getMessage());
65      }
66      finally {
67        try {
68          if (input != null) input.close();
69        }
70        catch (IOException ex) {
71          System.out.println(ex.getMessage());
72        }
73      }
74    }
75
76    public static void main(String[] args) {
77      FileViewer frame = new FileViewer();
78      frame.setTitle("FileViewer");
79      frame.setSize(400, 300);
80      frame.setDefaultCloseOperation(JFrame.EXIT_ON_CLOSE);
81      frame.setVisible(true);
82    }
83  }
```

display file (margin note, line 38)

input stream (margin note, line 53)

read line
display line (margin note, lines 56–57)

A BufferedReader is created on top of a FileReader (Line 53). Data from the file are read repeatedly, one line at a time, and appended to the text area (Line 57). If the file does not exist, the catch clause in Lines 60–62 catches and processes it. All other I/O errors are caught and processed in Lines 63–65. Whether the program runs with or without errors, the input stream is closed in Lines 66–73.

16.6 Binary I/O

Text I/O requires encoding and decoding. The JVM converts a Unicode to a file-specific encoding when writing a character and converts a file-specific encoding to a Unicode when reading a character. Binary I/O does not require conversions. When you write a byte to a file, the original byte is copied into the file. When you read a byte from a file, the exact byte in the file is returned, as shown in Figure 16.10.

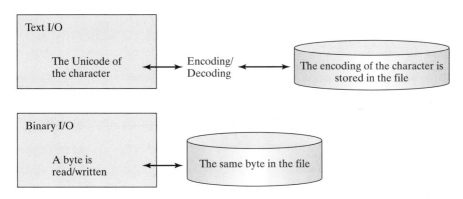

FIGURE 16.10 *Text I/O requires encoding and decoding, whereas binary I/O does not.*

For example, suppose you write character `'9'` using text I/O to a file. Since the Unicode for `'9'` is 0x0039, the Unicode 0x0039 is converted to a code that depends on the encoding scheme for the file. (Note that the prefix **0x** denotes a hex number.) If you write an integer value to a file using binary I/O, the exact integer value in the memory is copied into the file.

Binary I/O is more efficient than text I/O, because binary I/O does not require encoding and decoding. Binary files are independent of the encoding scheme on the host machine and thus are portable. Java programs on any machine can read a binary file created by a Java program. This is why Java class files are binary files. Java class files can run on a JVM on any machine.

Figure 16.11 lists some of the classes for performing binary I/O. InputStream is the root for binary input classes, and OutputStream is the root for binary output classes. Figures 16.12 and 16.13 list all the methods in InputStream and OutputStream. The methods in InputStream/OutputStream are very similar to the methods in Reader/Writer. The difference is that InputStream/OutputStream reads bytes and Reader/Writer reads characters.

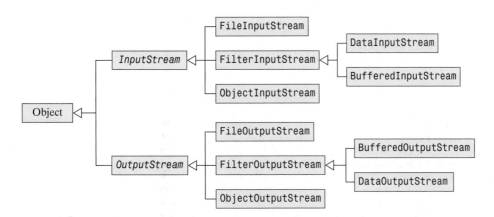

FIGURE 16.11 *InputStream, OutputStream, and their subclasses are for binary I/O.*

java.io.InputStream	
+read(): int	Reads the next byte of data from the input stream. The value byte is returned as an int value in the range 0 to 255. If no byte is available because the end of the stream has been reached, the value –1 is returned.
+read(b: byte[]): int	Reads up to b.length bytes into array b from the input stream and returns the actual number of bytes read. Returns –1 at the end of the stream.
+read(b: byte[], off: int, len: int): int	Reads bytes from the input stream and stores them in b[off], b[off+1], …, b[off+len–1]. The actual number of bytes read is returned. Returns –1 at the end of the stream.
+available(): int	Returns the number of bytes that can be read from the input stream.
+close(): void	Closes this input stream and releases any system resources associated with the stream.
+skip(n: long): long	Skips over and discards n bytes of data from this input stream. The actual number of bytes skipped is returned.
+markSupported(): boolean	Tests whether this input stream supports the mark and reset methods.
+mark(readlimit: int): void	Marks the current position in this input stream.
+reset(): void	Repositions this stream to the position at the time the mark method was last called on this input stream.

FIGURE 16.12 *The abstract* InputStream *class defines the methods for the input stream of bytes.*

java.io.OutputStream	
+write(int b): void	Writes the specified byte to this output stream. The parameter b is an int value. (byte)b is written to the output stream.
+write(b: byte[]): void	Writes all the bytes in array b to the output stream.
+write(b: byte[], off: int, len: int): void	Writes b[off], b[off+1], …, b[off+len–1] into the output stream.
+close(): void	Closes this input stream and releases any system resources associated with the stream.
+flush(): void	Flushes this output stream and forces any buffered output bytes to be written out.

FIGURE 16.13 *The abstract* OutputStream *class defines the methods for the output stream of bytes.*

16.6.1 FileInputStream/FileOutputStream

FileInputStream/FileOutputStream is for reading/writing bytes from/to files. All the methods in these classes are inherited from InputStream and OutputStream. FileInputStream/FileOutputStream does not introduce new methods. To construct a FileInputStream, use the following constructors:

```
public FileInputStream(String filename)
public FileInputStream(File file)
```

A java.io.FileNotFoundException would occur if you attempt to create a FileInputStream with a nonexistent file.

To construct a FileOutputStream, use the following constructors:

```
public FileOutputStream(String filename)
public FileOutputStream(File file)
public FileOutputStream(String filename, boolean append)
public FileOutputStream(File file, boolean append)
```

If the file does not exist, a new file will be created. If the file already exists, the first two constructors will delete the current content of the file. To retain the current content and append new data into the file, use the last two constructors by passing true to the append parameter.

Listing 16.7 uses binary I/O to write ten byte values from 1 to 10 to a file named temp.dat and reads them back from the file.

LISTING **16.7**   TestFileStream.java (Binary I/O)

```
 1 import java.io.*;
 2
 3 public class TestFileStream {
 4   public static void main(String[] args) throws IOException {
 5     // Create an output stream to the file
 6     FileOutputStream output = new FileOutputStream("temp.dat");
 7
 8     // Output values to the file
 9     for (int i = 1; i <= 10; i++)
10       output.write(i);
11
12     // Close the output stream
13     output.close();
14
15     // Create an input stream for the file
16     FileInputStream input = new FileInputStream("temp.dat");
17
18     // Read values from the file
19     int value;
20     while ((value = input.read()) != -1)
21       System.out.print(value + " ");
22
23     // Close the output stream
24     input.close();
25   }
26 }
```

output stream
output
input stream
input

A `FileOutputStream` is created for file temp.dat in Line 6. The `for` loop writes ten byte values into the file (Lines 9–10). Invoking `write(i)` is the same as invoking `write((byte)i)`. Line 13 closes the output stream. Line 16 creates a `FileInputStream` for file temp.dat. Values are read from the file and displayed on the console in Lines 19–21. The expression `((value = input.read()) != -1)` (Line 20) reads a byte from `input.read()`, assigns it to `value`, and checks whether it is −1. The input value of −1 signifies the end of a file.

end of a file

The file temp.dat created in this example is a binary file. It can be read from a Java program but not from a text editor, as shown in Figure 16.14.

binary data ——

FIGURE 16.14   *A binary file cannot be displayed in text mode.*

16.6.2   `FilterInputStream/FilterOutputStream`

Filter streams are streams that filter bytes for some purpose. The basic byte input stream provides a read method that can only be used for reading bytes. If you want to read integers, doubles, or strings, you need a filter class to wrap the byte input stream. Using a filter class enables you to read integers, doubles, and strings instead of bytes and characters. `FilterInputStream` and `FilterOutputStream` are the base classes for filtering data. When you need to process primitive numeric types, use `DataInputStream` and `DataOutputStream` to filter bytes.

16.6.3 DataInputStream/DataOutputStream

DataInputStream reads bytes from the stream and converts them into appropriate primitive type values or strings. DataOutputStream converts primitive type values or strings into bytes and outputs the bytes to the stream.

DataInputStream extends FilterInputStream and implements the DataInput interface, as shown in Figure 16.15. DataOutputStream extends FilterOutputStream and implements the DataOutput interface, as shown in Figure 16.16.

DataInputStream implements the methods defined in the DataInput interface to read primitive data type values and strings. DataOutputStream implements the methods defined in the DataOutput interface to write primitive data type values and strings. Primitive values are copied from memory to the output without any conversions. Characters in a string may be written in several ways, as discussed in the next section.

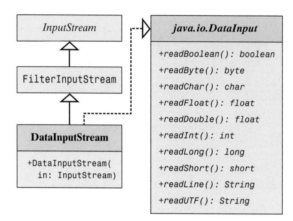

FIGURE 16.15 *DataInputStream filters input stream of bytes into primitive data type values and strings.*

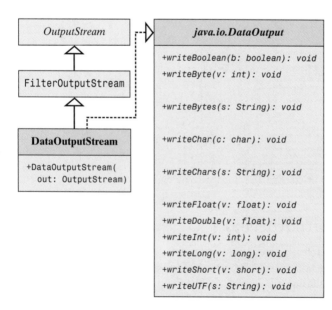

FIGURE 16.16 *DataOutputStream enables you to write primitive data type values and strings into an output stream.*

16.6.3.1   Characters and Strings in Binary I/O

A Unicode consists of two bytes. The writeChar(char c) method writes the Unicode of character c to the output. The writeChars(String s) method writes the Unicode for each character in the string s to the output. The writeBytes(String s) method writes the lower byte of the Unicode for each character in the string s to the output. The high byte of the Unicode is discarded. The writeBytes method is suitable for strings that consist of ASCII characters, since an ASCII code is stored only in the lower byte of a Unicode. If a string consists of non-ASCII characters, you have to use the writeChars method to write the string.

UTF is a coding scheme that allows systems to operate efficiently with both ASCII and Unicode. Most operating systems use ASCII. Java uses Unicode. The ASCII character set is a subset of the Unicode character set. Since most applications need only the ASCII character set, it is a waste to represent an 8-bit ASCII character as a 16-bit Unicode character. The UTF scheme stores a character using one, two, or three bytes. ASCII values less than 0x7F are coded in one byte. Unicode values less than 0x7FF are coded in two bytes. Other Unicode values are coded in three bytes.

The initial bits of a UTF character indicate whether a character is stored in one byte, two bytes, or three bytes. If the first bit is 0, it is a one-byte character. If the first bits are 110, it is the first byte of a two-byte sequence. If the first bits are 1110, it is the first byte of a three-byte sequence. The information that indicates the number of characters in a string is stored in the first two bytes preceding the UTF characters. For example, writeUTF("ABCDEF") actually writes eight bytes to the file because the first two bytes store the number of characters in the string.

The writeUTF(String s) method converts a string into a series of bytes in the UTF format and writes them into a binary stream. The readUTF() method reads a string that has been written using the writeUTF method.

The UTF format has the advantage of saving a byte for each ASCII character, because a Unicode character takes up two bytes and an ASCII character in UTF takes up only one byte. If most characters in a string are regular ASCII characters, using UTF is more efficient.

16.6.3.2   Using `DataInputStream/DataOutputStream`

Data streams are used as wrappers on existing input and output streams to filter data in the original stream. They are created using the following constructors:

```
public DataInputStream(InputStream instream)
public DataOutputStream(OutputStream outstream)
```

The statements given below create data streams. The first statement creates an input stream for file **in.dat**; the second statement creates an output stream for file **out.dat:**

```
DataInputStream infile =
  new DataInputStream(new FileInputStream("in.dat"));
DataOutputStream outfile =
  new DataOutputStream(new FileOutputStream("out.dat"));
```

Listing 16.8 writes student names and scores to a file named temp.dat and reads the data back from the file.

LISTING 16.8   **TestDataStream.java (Binary I/O of Data and Strings)**

```
1 import java.io.*;
2
3 public class TestDataStream {
4   public static void main(String[] args) throws IOException {
5     // Create an output stream for file temp.dat
6     DataOutputStream output =
7       new DataOutputStream(new FileOutputStream("temp.dat"));
```

output stream

output

close stream

input stream

input

```
 8
 9      // Write student test scores to the file
10      output.writeUTF("John");
11      output.writeDouble(85.5);
12      output.writeUTF("Jim");
13      output.writeDouble(185.5);
14      output.writeUTF("George");
15      output.writeDouble(105.25);
16
17      // Close output stream
18      output.close();
19
20      // Create an input stream for file temp.dat
21      DataInputStream input =
22        new DataInputStream(new FileInputStream("temp.dat"));
23
24      // Read student test scores from the file
25      System.out.println(input.readUTF() + " " + input.readDouble());
26      System.out.println(input.readUTF() + " " + input.readDouble());
27      System.out.println(input.readUTF() + " " + input.readDouble());
28    }
29 }
```

A `DataOutputStream` is created for file temp.dat in Lines 6–7. Student names and scores are written to the file in Lines 10–15. Line 18 closes the output stream. A `DataInputStream` is created for the same file in Lines 21–22. Student names and scores are read back from the file and displayed on the console in Lines 25–27.

`DataInputStream` and `DataOutputStream` read and write Java primitive type values and strings in a machine-independent fashion, thereby enabling you to write a data file on one machine and read it on another machine that has a different operating system or file structure. An application uses a data output stream to write data that can later be read by a program using a data input stream.

 CAUTION

You have been reading data in the same order and format in which they are stored. For example, since names are written in UTF using `writeUTF`, you must read names using `readUTF`.

 TIP

If you keep reading data at the end of a `DataInputStream`, an `EOFException` will occur. How, then, do you check the end of a file? Use `input.available()` to check it. `input.available() == 0` indicates the end of a file.

16.6.4   `BufferedInputStream`/`BufferedOutputStream`

`BufferedInputStream`/`BufferedOutputStream` can be used to speed up input and output by reducing the number of reads and writes, just like `BufferedReader`/`BufferedWriter`. `BufferedReader`/`BufferedWriter` is for reading/writing characters, and `BufferedInputStream`/`BufferedOutputStream` is for bytes.

`BufferedInputStream`/`BufferedOutputStream` does not contain new methods. All the methods in `BufferedInputStream`/`BufferedOutputStream` are inherited from the `InputStream`/`OutputStream` classes. `BufferedInputStream`/`BufferedOutputStream` adds a buffer in the stream for storing bytes for efficient processing.

You may wrap a `BufferedInputStream`/`BufferedOutputStream` on any `InputStream`/`OutputStream` using the following constructors:

```
// Create a BufferedInputStream
public BufferedInputStream(InputStream in)
public BufferedInputStream(InputStream in, int bufferSize)
```

```
// Create a BufferedOutputStream
public BufferedOutputStream(OutputStream out)
public BufferedOutputStream(OutputStream out, int bufferSize)
```

If no buffer size is specified, the default size is 512 bytes. A buffered input stream reads as many data as possible into its buffer in a single read call. By contrast, a buffered output stream calls the write method only when its buffer fills up or when the flush() method is called.

You can improve the performance of the TestDataStream program in the preceding example by adding buffers in the stream in Lines 6–7 and 21–22 as follows:

```
DataOutputStream output = new DataOutputStream(
  new BufferedOutputStream(new FileOutputStream("temp.dat")));
```

```
DataInputStream input = new DataInputStream(
  new BufferedInputStream(new FileInputStream("temp.dat")));
```

✦ 16.7 Case Study: Copying Files

This case study develops a program that copies files. The user needs to provide a source file and a target file as command-line arguments using the following command:

java Copy source target

The program copies a source file to a target file and displays the number of bytes in the file. If the source does not exist, tell the user that the file has not been found. If the target file already exists, tell the user that the file exists. A sample run of the program is shown in Figure 16.17.

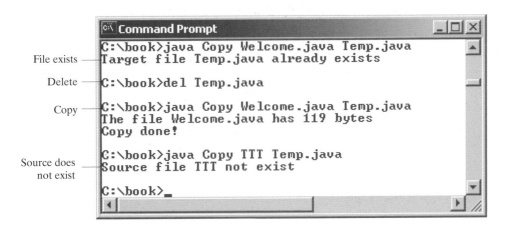

FIGURE 16.17 *The program copies a file.*

To copy the contents from a source to a target file, it is appropriate to use a binary input stream to read bytes from the source file and a binary output stream to send bytes to the target file, regardless of the contents of the file. The source file and the target file are specified from the command line. Create an InputFileStream for the source file and an OutputFileStream for the target file. Use the read() method to read a byte from the input stream, and then use the write(b) method to write the byte to the output stream. Use BufferedInputStream and BufferedOutputStream to improve the performance. Listing 16.9 gives the solution to the problem.

LISTING 16.9 Copy.java (Copy a File)

```
 1 import java.io.*;
 2
 3 public class Copy {
 4   /** Main method
 5      @param args[0] for sourcefile
 6      @param args[1] for target file
 7    */
 8   public static void main(String[] args) throws IOException {
 9     // Check command-line parameter usage
10     if (args.length != 2) {
11       System.out.println(
12         "Usage: java CopyFile sourceFile targetfile");
13       System.exit(0);
14     }
15
16     // Check if source file exists
17     File sourceFile = new File(args[0]);
18     if (!sourceFile.exists()) {
19       System.out.println("Source file " + args[0] + " not exist");
20       System.exit(0);
21     }
22
23     // Check if target file exists
24     File targetFile = new File(args[1]);
25     if (targetFile.exists()) {
26       System.out.println("Target file " + args[1] + " already exists");
27       System.exit(0);
28     }
29
30     // Create an input stream
31     BufferedInputStream input =
32       new BufferedInputStream(new FileInputStream(sourceFile));
33
34     // Create an output stream
35     BufferedOutputStream output =
36       new BufferedOutputStream(new FileOutputStream(targetFile));
37
38     // Display the file size
39     System.out.println("The file " + args[0] + " has "+
40       input.available() + " bytes");
41
42     // Continuously read a byte from input and write it to output
43     int r;
44     while ((r = input.read()) != -1)
45       output.write((byte)r);
46
47     // Close streams
48     input.close();
49     output.close();
50
51     System.out.println("Copy done!");
52   }
53 }
```

(margin notes:) check usage — source file — target file — input stream — output stream — read — write — close stream

✦ The program first checks whether the user has passed two required arguments from the command line in Lines 10–14.

✦ The program uses the File class to check whether the source file and target file exist. If the source file does not exist (Lines 18–21) or if the target file already exists, exit the program.

✦ An input stream is created using BufferedInputStream wrapped on FileInputStream in Lines 31–32, and an output stream is created using BufferedOutputStream wrapped on FileOutputStream in Lines 35–36.

✦ The available() method (Line 40) defined in the InputStream class returns the number of bytes remaining in the input stream.

✦ The expression ((r = input.read()) != -1) (Line 44) reads a byte from input.read(),
assigns it to r, and checks whether it is −1. The input value of −1 signifies the end of a file.
The program continuously reads bytes from the input stream and sends them to the output
stream until all of the bytes have been read.

16.8 More on Text Files and Binary Files

Now it is time to tell the whole story and set the record straight. Computers do not differentiate binary files and text files. All files are stored in binary format, and thus all files are essentially binary
files. Text I/O is built upon binary I/O to provide a level of abstraction for character encoding and
decoding. Encoding and decoding are automatically performed by text I/O. In general, you should
use text input to read a file created by a text editor or a text output program, and use binary input to
read a file created by a Java binary output program. For binary input, you need to know exactly how
data were written in order to read them in correct type and order. Binary I/O also contains methods
to read and write strings.

The example below shows how to write 199 as a numeric value to the file out.dat and read it
back from the same file:

```
1  import java.io.*;
2
3  public class Test {
4    public static void main(String[] args) throws IOException {
5      FileOutputStream output = new FileOutputStream("out.dat");       binary stream
6      output.write(199); // Output byte 199 to the stream
7      output.close();
8
9      FileInputStream input = new FileInputStream("out.dat");
10     System.out.println(input.read()); // Read and display a byte
11     input.close();
12   }
13 }
```

The next example shows how to write 199 as three characters to the file **out.txt** and read it
back from the same file:

```
1  import java.io.*;
2
3  public class Test {
4    public static void main(String[] args) throws IOException {
5      FileWriter output = new FileWriter("out.txt");                   text stream
6      output.write("199"); // Output string "199" to the stream
7      output.close();
8
9      // Read and display three characters
10     FileReader input = new FileReader("out.txt");
11     System.out.print((char)input.read());
12     System.out.print((char)input.read());
13     System.out.println((char)input.read());
14     input.close();
15   }
16 }
```

When you write a byte to a byte stream, the exact byte value is sent to the output, as shown
in Figure 16.18(a). When you write a character to a character stream, the character is converted
to a numeric representation of the character using an encoding scheme. If you don't specify an
encoding scheme, the default encoding scheme of the machine is used. In the United States, the
default encoding for Windows is ASCII. The ASCII code for character 1 is 49 (31 in hex) and
for character 9 is 57 (39 in hex). So to write the characters 199, three bytes, 49, 57, and 57, are
sent to the output, as shown in Figure 16.18(b).

(a) Binary I/O —— Output 199 ——▶ FileOutputStream —— 0xC7 (199 in decimal) ——▶ out.dat

(b) Text I/O —— Output "199" ——▶ FileWriter $\begin{array}{ccc}1 & 9 & 9\\ \text{0x31} & \text{0x39} & \text{0x39}\end{array}$ ——▶ out.txt

FIGURE 16.18 *Binary I/O outputs the exact value, and text I/O outputs the encoding of the characters.*

When you read a byte from a byte stream, one byte value is read from the input. When you read a character from a character stream, how many bytes are read is dependent on the encoding system. On an ASCII system, one byte is read and promoted to a Unicode character. On a Unicode system, two bytes are read to form a Unicode.

 CAUTION

ASCII code uses 8 bits. Java uses the 16-bit Unicode. If a Unicode cannot be converted to an ASCII code, the character '?' is used. For example, if you attempt to write Unicode '\u03b1' to a character stream, the numeric value 63 (representing character '?') would be sent to the stream. Text files are dependent on the encoding used by the host machine. Moving a text file from one computer to another may cause problems if the computers use different encodings.

16.9 Object I/O (Optional)

DataInputStream/DataOutputStream enables you to perform I/O for primitive type values and strings. ObjectInputStream/ObjectOutputStream enables you to perform I/O for objects in addition to primitive type values and strings. Since ObjectInputStream/ObjectOutputStream contains all the functions of DataInputStream/DataOutputStream, you can replace DataInputStream/DataOutputStream completely with ObjectInputStream/ObjectOutputStream.

ObjectInputStream extends InputStream and implements ObjectInput and ObjectStream-Constants, as shown in Figure 16.19. ObjectInput is a subinterface of DataInput. DataInput is shown in Figure 16.15. ObjectStreamConstants contains the constants to support Object InputStream/ObjectOutputStream.

ObjectOutputStream extends OutputStream and implements ObjectOutput and Object-StreamConstants, as shown in Figure 16.20. ObjectOutput is a subinterface of DataOutput. DataOutput is shown in Figure 16.16.

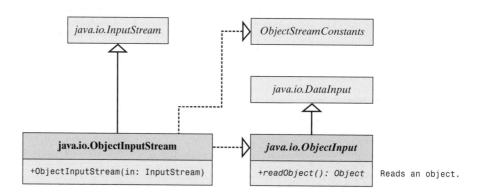

FIGURE 16.19 *ObjectInputStream can read objects, primitive type values, and strings.*

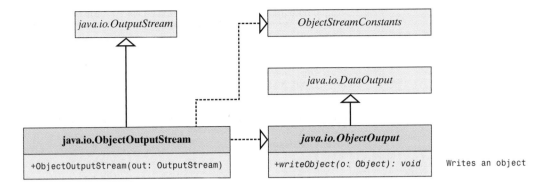

FIGURE 16.20 *ObjectOutputStream can write objects, primitive type values, and strings.*

You may wrap an ObjectInputStream/ObjectOutputStream on any InputStream/OutputStream using the following constructors:

```
// Create an ObjectInputStream
public ObjectInputStream(InputStream in)

// Create an ObjectOutputStream
public ObjectOutputStream(OutputStream out)
```

Listing 16.10 writes student names, scores, and current date to a file named object.dat.

LISTING 16.10 TestObjectOutputStream.java (Object Output)

```
 1 import java.io.*;
 2
 3 public class TestObjectOutputStream {
 4   public static void main(String[] args) throws IOException {
 5     // Create an output stream for file object.dat
 6     ObjectOutputStream output =
 7       new ObjectOutputStream(new FileOutputStream("object.dat"));
 8
 9     // Write a string, double value, and object to the file
10     output.writeUTF("John");
11     output.writeDouble(85.5);
12     output.writeObject(new java.util.Date());
13
14     // Close output stream
15     output.close();
16   }
17 }
```

output stream

output

An ObjectOutputStream is created to write data into file object.dat in Lines 6–7. A string, a double value, and an object are written to the file in Lines 10–12. To improve performance, you may add a buffer in the stream using the following statement to replace Lines 6–7:

```
ObjectOutputStream output = new ObjectOutputStream(
  new BufferedOutputStream(new FileOutputStream("object.dat")));
```

Multiple objects or primitives can be written to the stream. The objects must be read back from the corresponding ObjectInputStream with the same types and in the same order as they were written. Java's safe casting should be used to get the desired type. Listing 16.11 reads data back from object.dat.

LISTING 16.11 TestObjectInputStream.java (Object Input)

```
 1 import java.io.*;
 2
 3 public class TestObjectInputStream {
 4   public static void main(String[] args)
```

input stream

input

```
 5        throws ClassNotFoundException, IOException {
 6      // Create an input stream for file object.dat
 7      ObjectInputStream input =
 8        new ObjectInputStream(new FileInputStream("object.dat"));
 9
10      // Write a string, double value, and object to the file
11      String name = input.readUTF();
12      double score = input.readDouble();
13      java.util.Date date = (java.util.Date)(input.readObject());
14      System.out.println(name + " " + score + " " + date);
15
16      // Close output stream
17      input.close();
18    }
19  }
```

ClassNotFoundException

The readObject() method may throw java.lang.ClassNotFoundException. The reason is that when the JVM restores an object, it first loads the class for the object if the class has not been loaded. Since ClassNotFoundException is a checked exception, the main method declares to throw it in Line 5. An ObjectInputStream is created to read input from object.dat in Lines 7–8. You have to read the data from the file in the same order and format as they were written to the file. A string, a double value, and an object are read in Lines 11–13. Since readObject() returns an Object, it is cast into Date and assigned to a Date variable in Line 13.

16.9.1   The Serializable Interface

Not every object can be written to an output stream. Objects that can be written to an object stream are said to be *serializable*. A serializable object is an instance of the java.io.Serializable interface, so the class of a serializable object must implement Serializable.

serializable

The Serializable interface is a marker interface. Since it has no methods, you don't need to add additional code in your class that implements Serializable. Implementing this interface enables the Java serialization mechanism to automate the process of storing objects and arrays.

To appreciate this automation feature and understand how an object is stored, consider what you need to do in order to store an object without using this feature. Suppose you want to store a JButton object. To do this you need to store all the current values of the properties (e.g., color, font, text, alignment) in the object. Since JButton is a subclass of AbstractButton, the property values of AbstractButton have to be stored as well as the properties of all the superclasses of AbstractButton. If a property is of an object type (e.g., background of the Color type), storing it requires storing all the property values inside this object. As you can see, this is a very tedious process. Fortunately, you don't have to go through it manually. Java provides a built-in mechanism to automate the process of writing objects. This process is referred to as *object serialization*, which is implemented in ObjectOutputStream. In contrast, the process of reading objects is referred to as *object deserialization*, which is implemented in ObjectInputStream.

serialization

deserialization

Many classes in the Java API implement Serializable. The utility classes, such as java.util.Date, and all the Swing GUI component classes implement Serializable. Attempting to store an object that does not support the Serializable interface would cause a NotSerializableException.

NotSerializable-
Exception

When a serializable object is stored, the class of the object is encoded; this includes the class name and the signature of the class, the values of the object's instance variables, and the closure of any other objects referenced from the initial object. The values of the object's static variables are not stored.

🔖 **NOTE**

nonserializable fields

If an object is an instance of Serializable but contains nonserializable instance data fields, can it be serialized? The answer is no. To enable the object to be serialized, mark these data fields with the `transient` keyword to tell the JVM to ignore them when writing the object to an object stream. Consider the following class:

transient

```
public class Foo implements java.io.Serializable {
  private int v1;
  private static double v2;
  private transient A v3 = new A();
}

class A { } // A is not serializable
```

When an object of the `Foo` class is serialized, only variable `v1` is serialized. Variable `v2` is not serialized because it is a static variable, and variable `v3` is not serialized because it is marked `transient`. If `v3` were not marked `transient`, a `java.io.NotSerializableException` would occur.

 NOTE

If an object is written to an object stream more than once, will it be stored in multiple copies? The answer is no. When an object is written for the first time, a serial number is created for it. The JVM writes the complete content of the object along with the serial number into the object stream. After the first time, only the serial number is stored if the same object is written again. When the objects are read back, their references are the same, since only one object is actually created in memory.

duplicate objects

16.9.2   Serializing Arrays

An array is serializable if all its elements are serializable. An entire array can be saved using `writeObject` into a file and later can be restored using `readObject`. Listing 16.12 stores an array of five `int` values, an array of three strings, and an array of two `JButton` objects, and reads them back to display on the console.

LISTING **16.12**   TestObjectStreamForArray.java (Array Object I/O)

```
1 import java.io.*;
2 import javax.swing.*;
3
4 public class TestObjectStreamForArray {
5   public static void main(String[] args)
6       throws ClassNotFoundException, IOException {
7     int[] numbers = {1, 2, 3, 4, 5};
8     String[] strings = {"John", "Jim", "Jake"};
9     JButton[] buttons = {new JButton("OK"), new JButton("Cancel")};
10
11    // Create an output stream for file array.dat
12    ObjectOutputStream output =
13      new ObjectOutputStream(new FileOutputStream("array.dat", true));
14
15    // Write arrays to the object output stream
16    output.writeObject(numbers);
17    output.writeObject(strings);
18    output.writeObject(buttons);
19
20    // Close the stream
21    output.close();
22
23    // Create an input stream for file array.dat
24    ObjectInputStream input =
25      new ObjectInputStream(new FileInputStream("array.dat"));
```

output stream

store array

input stream

restore array

```
26
27    int[] newNumbers = (int[])(input.readObject());
28    String[] newStrings = (String[])(input.readObject());
29    JButton[] newButtons = (JButton[])(input.readObject());
30
31    // Display arrays
32    for (int i = 0; i < newNumbers.length; i++)
33      System.out.print(newNumbers[i] + " ");
34    System.out.println();
35
36    for (int i = 0; i < newStrings.length; i++)
37      System.out.print(newStrings[i] + " ");
38    System.out.println();
39
40    for (int i = 0; i < newButtons.length; i++)
41      System.out.print(newButtons[i].getText() + " ");
42  }
43 }
```

Lines 16–18 write three arrays into file array.dat. Lines 27–29 read three arrays back in the same order they were written. Since readObject() returns Object, casting is used to cast the objects into int[], String[], and JButton[].

16.10 Random Access Files (Optional)

read-only
write-only
sequential

All of the streams you have used so far are known as *read-only* or *write-only* streams. The external files of these streams are *sequential* files that cannot be updated without creating a new file. It is often necessary to modify files or to insert new records into files. Java provides the RandomAccessFile class to allow a file to be read from and written to at random locations.

The RandomAccessFile class implements the DataInput and DataOutput interfaces, as shown in Figure 16.21. The DataInput interface shown in Figure 16.15 defines the methods (e.g., readInt, readDouble, readChar, readBoolean, readUTF) for reading primitive type values and strings, and the DataOutput interface shown in Figure 16.16 defines the methods (e.g., writeInt, writeDouble, writeChar, writeBoolean, writeUTF) for writing primitive type values and strings.

When creating a RandomAccessFile, you can specify one of two modes ("r" or "rw"). Mode "r" means that the stream is read-only, and mode "rw" indicates that the stream allows both read and write. For example, the following statement creates a new stream, raf, that allows the program to read from and write to the file **test.dat**:

```
RandomAccessFile raf = new RandomAccessFile("test.dat", "rw");
```

If **test.dat** already exists, raf is created to access it; if **test.dat** does not exist, a new file named **test.dat** is created, and raf is created to access the new file. The method raf.length() returns the number of bytes in **test.dat** at any given time. If you append new data into the file, raf.length() increases.

TIP

Open the file with the "r" mode if the file is not intended to be modified. This prevents unintentional modification of the file.

---

file pointer

A random access file consists of a sequence of bytes. There is a special marker called *file pointer* positioned at one of these bytes. A read or write operation takes place at the location of the file pointer. When a file is opened, the file pointer is set at the beginning of the file. When you read or write data to the file, the file pointer moves forward to the next data item. For example, if you read an int value using readInt(), the JVM reads four bytes from the file pointer and now the file pointer is four bytes ahead of the previous location, as shown in Figure 16.22.

For a RandomAccessFile raf, you can use raf.seek(position) method to move the file pointer to a specified position. raf.seek(0) moves it to the beginning of the file, and raf.seek(raf.length()) moves it to the end of the file. Listing 16.13 demonstrates RandomAccessFile.

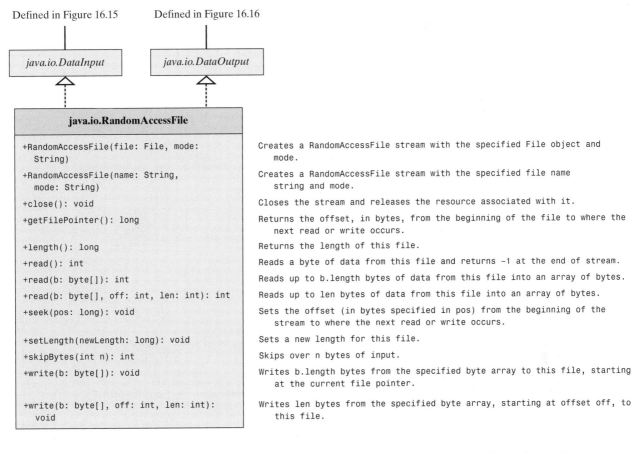

Defined in Figure 16.15

Defined in Figure 16.16

java.io.DataInput

java.io.DataOutput

java.io.RandomAccessFile

+RandomAccessFile(file: File, mode: String)	Creates a RandomAccessFile stream with the specified File object and mode.
+RandomAccessFile(name: String, mode: String)	Creates a RandomAccessFile stream with the specified file name string and mode.
+close(): void	Closes the stream and releases the resource associated with it.
+getFilePointer(): long	Returns the offset, in bytes, from the beginning of the file to where the next read or write occurs.
+length(): long	Returns the length of this file.
+read(): int	Reads a byte of data from this file and returns −1 at the end of stream.
+read(b: byte[]): int	Reads up to b.length bytes of data from this file into an array of bytes.
+read(b: byte[], off: int, len: int): int	Reads up to len bytes of data from this file into an array of bytes.
+seek(pos: long): void	Sets the offset (in bytes specified in pos) from the beginning of the stream to where the next read or write occurs.
+setLength(newLength: long): void	Sets a new length for this file.
+skipBytes(int n): int	Skips over n bytes of input.
+write(b: byte[]): void	Writes b.length bytes from the specified byte array to this file, starting at the current file pointer.
+write(b: byte[], off: int, len: int): void	Writes len bytes from the specified byte array, starting at offset off, to this file.

FIGURE 16.21 *RandomAccessFile implements the* DataInput *and* DataOutput *interfaces with additional methods to support random access.*

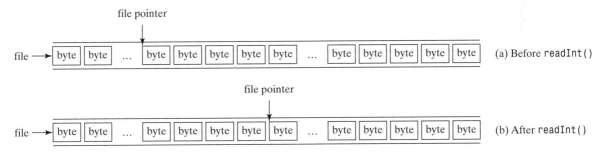

FIGURE 16.22 *After reading an* int *value, the file pointer is moved four bytes ahead.*

LISTING 16.13 TestRandomAccessFile.java (Random Access of File)

```
1 import java.io.*;
2
3 public class TestRandomAccessFile {
4   public static void main(String[] args) throws IOException {
5     // Create a random access file
6     RandomAccessFile inout = new RandomAccessFile("inout.dat", "rw");    RandomAccessFile
7
8     // Clear the file to destroy the old contents if exists
9     inout.setLength(0);                                                  empty file
```

```
10
11      // Write new integers to the file
12      for (int i = 0; i < 200; i++)
13        inout.writeInt(i);
14
15      // Display the current length of the file
16      System.out.println("Current file length is " + inout.length());
17
18      // Retrieve the first number
19      inout.seek(0); // Move the file pointer to the beginning
20      System.out.println("The first number is " + inout.readInt());
21
22      // Retrieve the second number
23      inout.seek(1 * 4); // Move the file pointer to the second number
24      System.out.println("The second number is " + inout.readInt());
25
26      // Retrieve the tenth number
27      inout.seek(9 * 4); // Move the file pointer to the tenth number
28      System.out.println("The tenth number is " + inout.readInt());
29
30      // Modify the eleventh number
31      inout.writeInt(555);
32
33      // Append a new number
34      inout.seek(inout.length()); // Move the file pointer to the end
35      inout.writeInt(999);
36
37      // Display the new length
38      System.out.println("The new length is " + inout.length());
39
40      // Retrieve the new eleventh number
41      inout.seek(10 * 4); // Move the file pointer to the eleventh number
42      System.out.println("The eleventh number is " + inout.readInt());
43
44      inout.close();
45  }
46 }
```

write

move pointer
read

close file

◆ A RandomAccessFile is created for the file named inout.dat with mode "rw" to allow both read and write operations in Line 6.

◆ inout.setLength(0) sets the length to 0 in Line 9. This, in effect, destroys the old contents of the file.

◆ The for loop writes 200 int values from 0 to 199 into the file in Lines 12–13. Since each int value takes four bytes, the total length of the file returned from inout.length() is now 800 (Line 16), as shown in Figure 16.23.

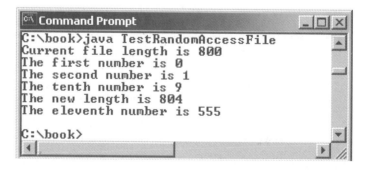

FIGURE 16.23 *TestRandomAccessFile manipulates a RandomAccessFile.*

✦ Invoking `inout.seek(0)` in Line 19 sets the file pointer to the beginning of the file. `inout.readInt()` reads the first value in Line 20 and moves the file pointer to the next number. The second number is read in Line 23.

✦ `inout.seek(9 * 4)` (Line 26) moves the file pointer to the tenth number. `inout.readInt()` reads the tenth number and moves the file pointer to the eleventh number in Line 27. `inout.write(555)` writes a new eleventh number at the current position (Line 31). The previous eleventh number is destroyed.

✦ `inout.seek(inout.length())` moves the file pointer to the end of the file (Line 34). `inout.writeInt(999)` writes a 999 to the file. Now the length of the file is increased by 4, so `inout.length()` returns 804 (Line 38).

✦ `inout.seek(10 * 4)` moves the file pointer to the eleventh number in Line 41. The new eleventh number, 555, is displayed in Line 42.

◈ 16.11   Case Study: Address Book (Optional)

Now let us use `RandomAccessFile` to create a useful project for storing and viewing an address book. The user interface of the program is shown in Figure 16.24. The *Add* button stores a new address at the end of the file. The *First*, *Next*, *Previous*, and *Last* buttons retrieve the first, next, previous, and last addresses from the file, respectively.

Random access files are often used to process files of records. For convenience, *fixed-length records* are used in random access files so that a record can be located easily, as shown in Figure 16.25. A record consists of a fixed number of fields. A field can be a string or a primitive data type. A string in a fixed-length record has a maximum size. If a string is smaller than the maximum size, the rest of the string is padded with blanks.

fixed-length record

Let **address.dat** be the file to store addresses. A `RandomAccessFile` for both read and write can be created using

```
RandomAccessFile raf = new RandomAccessFile("address.dat", "rw");
```

FIGURE 16.24 *AddressBook stores and retrieves addresses from a file.*

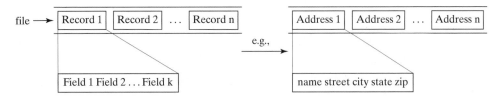

FIGURE 16.25 *Random access files are often used to process files of fixed-length records.*

Let each address consist of a name (32 characters), street (32 characters), city (20 characters), state (2 characters), and zip (5 characters). If the actual size of a field (e.g., name) is less than the fixed maximum size, fill it in with blank characters. If the actual size of a field is greater than the fixed maximum size, truncate the string. Thus the total size of an address is $32 + 32 + 20 + 2 + 5 = 91$ characters. Since each character occupies two bytes, one address takes $2 * 91 = 182$ bytes. After an address record is read, the file pointer is 182 bytes ahead of the previous file pointer.

For convenience, Listing 16.14 contains two methods for reading and writing a fixed-length string.

LISTING 16.14 FixedLengthStringIO.java (Fixed-Length String Binary I/O)

```
1 import java.io.*;
2
3 public class FixedLengthStringIO {
4   /** Read fixed number of characters from a DataInput stream */
5   public static String readFixedLengthString(int size,
6       DataInput in) throws IOException {
7     // Declare an array of characters
8     char[] chars = new char[size];
9
10    // Read fixed number of characters to the array
11    for (int i = 0; i < size; i++)
12      chars[i] = in.readChar();
13
14    return new String(chars);
15  }
16
17  /** Write fixed number of characters to a DataOutput stream */
18  public static void writeFixedLengthString(String s, int size,
19      DataOutput out) throws IOException {
20    char[] chars = new char[size];
21
22    // Fill in string with characters
23    s.getChars(0, s.length(), chars, 0);
24
25    // Fill in blank characters in the rest of the array
26    for (int i = Math.min(s.length(), size); i < chars.length; i++)
27      chars[i] = ' ';
28
29    // Create and write a new string padded with blank characters
30    out.writeChars(new String(chars));
31  }
32 }
```

read characters

fill string

fill blank

write string

The writeFixedLengthString(String s, int size, DataOutput out) method writes a string in a fixed size to a DataOutput stream. If the string is longer than the specified size, it is truncated; if it is shorter than the specified size, blanks are padded into it (Lines 26–27). In any case, a new fixed-length string is written to a specified output stream. Since RandomAccessFile implements DataOutput, this method can be used to write a string to a RandomAccessFile. For example, invoking writeFixedLengthString("John", 2, raf) actually writes "Jo" to the RandomAccessFile raf, since the size is 2. Invoking writeFixedLengthString("John", 6, raf) actually writes "John " to the RandomAccessFile raf, since the size is 6.

The readFixedLengthString(int size, InputOutput in) method reads a fixed number of characters from an InputStream and returns as a string. Since RandomAccessFile implements InputOutput, this method can be used to read a string from a writeFixedLengthString(String s, int size, DataOutput out).

The rest of the work can be summarized in the following steps:

1. Create the user interface.

2. Add a record to the file.

3. Read a record from the file.

4. Write the code to implement the button actions.

The program is shown in Listing 16.15.

LISTING 16.15 AddressBook.java (Write/View Address)

```java
1  import java.io.*;
2  import java.awt.*;
3  import java.awt.event.*;
4  import javax.swing.*;
5  import javax.swing.border.*;
6
7  public class AddressBook extends JFrame implements ActionListener {
8    // Specify the size of five string fields in the record
9    final static int NAME_SIZE = 32;
10   final static int STREET_SIZE = 32;
11   final static int CITY_SIZE = 20;
12   final static int STATE_SIZE = 2;
13   final static int ZIP_SIZE = 5;
14   final static int RECORD_SIZE =
15     (NAME_SIZE + STREET_SIZE + CITY_SIZE + STATE_SIZE + ZIP_SIZE);
16
17   // Access address.dat using RandomAccessFile
18   private RandomAccessFile raf;
19
20   // Text fields
21   private JTextField jtfName = new JTextField(NAME_SIZE);
22   private JTextField jtfStreet = new JTextField(STREET_SIZE);
23   private JTextField jtfCity = new JTextField(CITY_SIZE);
24   private JTextField jtfState = new JTextField(ZIP_SIZE);
25   private JTextField jtfZip = new JTextField(ZIP_SIZE);
26
27   // Buttons
28   private JButton jbtAdd = new JButton("Add");
29   private JButton jbtFirst = new JButton("First");
30   private JButton jbtNext = new JButton("Next");
31   private JButton jbtPrevious = new JButton("Previous");
32   private JButton jbtLast = new JButton("Last");
33
34   public AddressBook() {
35     // Open or create a random access file
36     try {
37       raf = new RandomAccessFile("address.dat", "rw");
38     }
39     catch(IOException ex) {
40       System.out.print("Error: " + ex);
41       System.exit(0);
42     }
43
44     // Panel p1 for holding labels Name, Street, and City
45     JPanel p1 = new JPanel();
46     p1.setLayout(new GridLayout(3, 1));
47     p1.add(new JLabel("Name"));
48     p1.add(new JLabel("Street"));
49     p1.add(new JLabel("City"));
50
51     // Panel jpState for holding state
52     JPanel jpState = new JPanel();
53     jpState.setLayout(new BorderLayout());
54     jpState.add(new JLabel("State"), BorderLayout.WEST);
55     jpState.add(jtfState, BorderLayout.CENTER);
```

constant

raf

GUI component

open file

create UI

```
56
57      // Panel jpZip for holding zip
58      JPanel jpZip = new JPanel();
59      jpZip.setLayout(new BorderLayout());
60      jpZip.add(new JLabel("Zip"), BorderLayout.WEST);
61      jpZip.add(jtfZip, BorderLayout.CENTER);
62
63      // Panel p2 for holding jpState and jpZip
64      JPanel p2 = new JPanel();
65      p2.setLayout(new BorderLayout());
66      p2.add(jpState, BorderLayout.WEST);
67      p2.add(jpZip, BorderLayout.CENTER);
68
69      // Panel p3 for holding jtfCity and p2
70      JPanel p3 = new JPanel();
71      p3.setLayout(new BorderLayout());
72      p3.add(jtfCity, BorderLayout.CENTER);
73      p3.add(p2, BorderLayout.EAST);
74
75      // Panel p4 for holding jtfName, jtfStreet, and p3
76      JPanel p4 = new JPanel();
77      p4.setLayout(new GridLayout(3, 1));
78      p4.add(jtfName);
79      p4.add(jtfStreet);
80      p4.add(p3);
81
82      // Place p1 and p4 into jpAddress
83      JPanel jpAddress = new JPanel(new BorderLayout());
84      jpAddress.add(p1, BorderLayout.WEST);
85      jpAddress.add(p4, BorderLayout.CENTER);
86
87      // Set the panel with line border
88      jpAddress.setBorder(new BevelBorder(BevelBorder.RAISED));
89
90      // Add buttons to a panel
91      JPanel jpButton = new JPanel();
92      jpButton.add(jbtAdd);
93      jpButton.add(jbtFirst);
94      jpButton.add(jbtNext);
95      jpButton.add(jbtPrevious);
96      jpButton.add(jbtLast);
97
98      // Add jpAddress and jpButton to the frame
99      getContentPane().add(jpAddress, BorderLayout.CENTER);
100     getContentPane().add(jpButton, BorderLayout.SOUTH);
101
102     jbtAdd.addActionListener(this);
103     jbtFirst.addActionListener(this);
104     jbtNext.addActionListener(this);
105     jbtPrevious.addActionListener(this);
106     jbtLast.addActionListener(this);
107
108     // Display the first record if it exists
109     try {
110       if (raf.length() > 0) readAddress(0);
111     }
112     catch (IOException ex) {
113       ex.printStackTrace();
114     }
115   }
116
117   /** Write a record at the end of the file */
118   public void writeAddress() throws IOException {
119     raf.seek(raf.length());
120     FixedLengthStringIO.writeFixedLengthString(
121       jtfName.getText(), NAME_SIZE, raf);
122     FixedLengthStringIO.writeFixedLengthString(
123       jtfStreet.getText(), STREET_SIZE, raf);
124     FixedLengthStringIO.writeFixedLengthString(
125       jtfCity.getText(), CITY_SIZE, raf);
```

register listener

first record

```
126      FixedLengthStringIO.writeFixedLengthString(
127        jtfState.getText(), STATE_SIZE, raf);
128      FixedLengthStringIO.writeFixedLengthString(
129        jtfZip.getText(), ZIP_SIZE, raf);
130    }
131
132    /** Read a record at the specified position */
133    public void readAddress(long position) throws IOException {
134      raf.seek(position);
135      String name = FixedLengthStringIO.readFixedLengthString(
136        NAME_SIZE, raf);
137      String street = FixedLengthStringIO.readFixedLengthString(
138        STREET_SIZE, raf);
139      String city = FixedLengthStringIO.readFixedLengthString(
140        CITY_SIZE, raf);
141      String state = FixedLengthStringIO.readFixedLengthString(
142        STATE_SIZE, raf);
143      String zip = FixedLengthStringIO.readFixedLengthString(
144        ZIP_SIZE, raf);
145
146      jtfName.setText(name);
147      jtfStreet.setText(street);
148      jtfCity.setText(city);
149      jtfState.setText(state);
150      jtfZip.setText(zip);
151    }
152
153    /** Handle button actions */
154    public void actionPerformed(ActionEvent e) {
155      try {
156        if (e.getSource() == jbtAdd) {                               add address
157          writeAddress();
158        }
159        else if (e.getSource() == jbtFirst) {                        first address
160          if (raf.length() > 0) readAddress(0);
161        }
162        else if (e.getSource() == jbtNext) {                         next address
163          long currentPosition = raf.getFilePointer();
164          if (currentPosition < raf.length())
165            readAddress(currentPosition);
166        }
167        else if (e.getSource() == jbtPrevious) {                     previous address
168          long currentPosition = raf.getFilePointer();
169          if (currentPosition -  2 * RECORD_SIZE > 0)
170            // Why 2 * 2 * RECORD_SIZE? See the follow-up remarks
171            readAddress(currentPosition - 2 * 2 * RECORD_SIZE);
172          else
173            readAddress(0);
174        }
175        else if (e.getSource() == jbtLast) {                         last address
176          long lastPosition = raf.length();
177          if (lastPosition > 0)
178            // Why 2 * RECORD_SIZE? See the follow-up remarks
179            readAddress(lastPosition - 2 * RECORD_SIZE);
180        }
181      }
182      catch(IOException ex) {
183        System.out.print("Error: " + ex);
184      }
185    }
186
187    public static void main(String[] args) {
188      AddressBook frame = new AddressBook();
189      frame.pack();
190      frame.setTitle("AddressBook");
191      frame.setDefaultCloseOperation(JFrame.EXIT_ON_CLOSE);
192      frame.setVisible(true);
193    }
194  }
```

✦ A random access file, **address.dat**, is created to store address information if the file does not yet exist (Line 37). If it already exists, the file is opened. A random file object, `raf`, is used for both write and read operations. The size of each field in the record is fixed and therefore defined as constants in Lines 9–15.

✦ The user interface is created in Lines 44–100. The listeners are registered in Lines 102–106. When the program starts, it displays the first record, if it exists, in Lines 109–114.

✦ The `writeAddress()` method sets the file pointer to the end of the file (Line 119) and writes a new record to the file (Lines 120–129).

✦ The `readAddress()` method sets the file pointer at the specified position (Line 134) and reads a record from the file (Lines 135–144). The record is displayed in Lines 146–150.

✦ To add a record, you need to collect the address information from the user interface and write the address into the file (Line 157).

✦ The code to process button events is implemented in Lines 156–180. For the *First* button, read the record from position 0 (Line 160). For the *Next* button, read the record from the current file pointer (Line 165). When a record is read, the file pointer is moved 2 * `RECORD_SIZE` number of bytes ahead of the previous file pointer. For the *Previous* button, you need to display the record prior to the one being displayed now. So, you have to move the file pointer two records before the current file pointer (Line 179). For the *Last* button, read the record from the position at `raf.length() - 2 * RECORD_SIZE`.

KEY TERMS

binary I/O 577	sequential access file 600
deserialization 598	serialization 598
file pointer 600	stream 577
random access file 600	text I/O 577

KEY CLASSES AND METHODS

✦ **java.io.File** is a wrapper class for the filename and its directory path. A `File` object contains the meta-information about a file, but it does not have the methods for reading/writing the file contents. You can use the `exist()` method to check whether a file exists.

✦ **java.io.Reader** is an abstract base class for reading characters.

✦ **java.io.Writer** is an abstract base class for writing characters.

✦ **java.io.FileReader** is a class for reading characters from a file.

✦ **java.io.FileWriter** is a class for writing characters to a file.

✦ **java.io.BufferedReader** is a class for reading characters from a buffer.

✦ **java.io.BufferedWriter** is a class for writing characters to a buffer.

✦ **java.io.PrintWriter** is a class for writing primitive values, strings, and strings as text.

✦ **java.io.PrintStream** is a class similar to `PrintWriter`, used for console output.

✦ `java.io.InputStream` is an abstract base class for a byte input stream.

✦ `java.io.OutputStream` is an abstract base class for a byte output stream.

✦ `java.io.FileInputStream` is a class for reading bytes from a file.

✦ `java.io.FileOutputStream` is a class for writing bytes to a file.

✦ `java.io.DataInputStream` is a class for reading primitive data values and strings.

✦ `java.io.DataOutputStream` is a class for writing primitive data values and strings.

✦ `java.io.BufferedInputStream` is a class for reading bytes from a buffer.

✦ `java.io.BufferedOutputStream` is class for writing bytes to a buffer.

✦ `java.io.ObjectInputStream` is a class for reading objects.

✦ `java.io.ObjectOutputStream` is a class for writing objects.

✦ `java.io.Seriablizable` is a marker interface that enables objects to be serializable.

✦ `java.io.RandomAccessFile` is a class for reading/writing from/to random access files.

CHAPTER SUMMARY

✦ The `File` class is used to obtain file properties and manipulate files. To read/write data from/to files, you have to use I/O classes.

✦ I/O can be classified into text I/O and binary I/O. Text I/O interprets data in sequences of characters. Binary I/O interprets data as raw binary values. How text is stored in a file is dependent on the encoding scheme for the file. Java automatically performs encoding and decoding for text I/O.

✦ The `Reader` and `Writer` classes are the roots of all text I/O classes. `FileReader`/`FileWriter` associates a file for text input/output. `BufferedReader`/`BufferedWriter` can be used to wrap on any text I/O stream to improve performance.

✦ The `PrintWriter` and `PrintStream` classes can be used to write primitive values, strings, and objects as text.

✦ The `InputStream` and `OutputStream` classes are the roots of all binary I/O classes. `FileInputStream`/`FileOutputStream` associates a file for binary input/output. `BufferedInputStream`/`BufferedOutputStream` can be used to wrap on any binary I/O stream to improve performance. `DataInputStream`/`DataOutputStream` can be used to read/write primitive values and strings.

✦ `ObjectInputStream`/`ObjectOutputStream` can be used to read/write objects in addition to primitive values and strings. To enable object serialization, the object's defining class must implement the `java.io.Serializable` marker interface.

✦ The `RandomAccessFile` class enables you to read and write data to a file. You can open a file with the `"r"` mode to indicate that it is read-only, or with the `"rw"` mode to indicate that it is updateable. Since the `RandomAccessFile` class implements `DataInput` and `DataOutput` interfaces, many methods in `RandomAccessFile` are the same as those in `DataInputStream` and `DataOutputStream`.

REVIEW QUESTIONS

Section 16.2 The *File* Class

16.1 What is wrong about creating a File object using the following statement?

```
new File("c:\book\test.dat");
```

16.2 How do you check whether a file already exists? How do you delete a file? How do you rename a file? Can you find the file size (the number of bytes) using the File class?

16.3 How do you obtain the file separator and path separator for the current system?

Section 16.3 How Is I/O Handled in Java?

16.4 Can you use the File class for I/O?

16.5 How do you read or write data in Java? What is a stream?

16.6 What is a text file, and what is a binary file? Can you view a text file or a binary file using a text editor?

Section 16.4 Text I/O

16.7 How is a Java character represented in the memory, and how is a character represented in a text file?

16.8 What value is returned from read() for text input? Is this the exact value stored in the file?

16.9 Is the exact Unicode value written into the file using write(int) for text output?

16.10 How do you create an input stream using FileReader? What happens if a file does not exist? How do you create an output stream using FileWriter? What happens if a file already exists? Can you append data to an existing file?

16.11 Why do you have to declare to throw IOException in the method or use a try-catch block to handle IOException for Java IO programs?

16.12 What is written to a file using write("91") on a FileWriter?

16.13 Why should you always close streams?

16.14 Is the line separator the same on all systems? How do you obtain a system-specific line separator?

16.15 Why should you use BufferedReader/BufferedWriter? How do you create a buffer stream for text I/O. Are the following the valid statements?

```
PrintWriter output1 = new PrintWriter(
  new BufferedWriter(new FileWriter("out1.txt")));

BufferedWriter output2 = new BufferedWriter(
  new PrintWriter(new FileWriter("out2.txt")));
```

Is the line separator the same on all systems? How do you obtain a system-specific line separator?

16.16 When should you use PrintWriter and PrintStream? How do you create a PrintWriter? What are the data types for System.in, System.out, and System.err? When you invoke System.out.println(), you don't have to place it in a try-catch block. Why?

16.17 How do you write a primitive value in BufferedWriter and in PrintWriter?

Section 16.6 Binary I/O

16.18 What are the differences between byte streams and character streams?

16.19 `InputStream` reads bytes. Why does the `read()` method return an int instead of a byte? Find the abstract methods in `InputSteam` and `OutputStream`?

16.20 Does `FileInputStream/FileOutputStream` introduce any new methods? How do you create a `FileInputStream/FileOutputStream`?

16.21 What will happen if you attempt to create an input stream on a nonexistent file? What will happen if you attempt to create an output stream on an existing file? Can you append data to an existing file?

16.22 Suppose input is a `DataInputStream`, `input.available()` returns 100. After invoking `read()`, what is `input.available()`? After invoking `readInt()`, what is `input.available()`? After invoking `readChar()`, what is `input.available()`? After invoking `readDouble()`, what is `input.available()`?

16.23 What is written to a file using `writeByte(91)` on a `FileOutputStream`?

16.24 How do you check the end of a file in a binary input stream (`FileInputStream`, `DataInputStream`)?

16.25 What is wrong in the following code?

```java
import java.io.*;

public class Test {
  public static void main(String[] args) {
    try {
      FileInputStream fis = new FileInputStream("test.dat");
    }
    catch(IOException ex) {
      ex.printStackTrace();
    }
    catch(FileNotFoundException ex) {
      ex.printStackTrace();
    }
  }
}
```

16.26 Suppose you run the program on Windows using the default ASCII encoding. After the program is finished, how many bytes are in the file t.txt? Show the contents of each byte.

```java
import java.io.*;

public class Test {
  public static void main(String[] args) throws IOException {
    FileWriter output = new FileWriter("t.txt");
    output.write("1234");
    output.write("5678");
    output.close();
  }
}
```

16.27 After the program is finished, how many bytes are in the file t.dat? Show the contents of each byte.

```java
import java.io.*;

public class Test {
  public static void main(String[] args) throws IOException {
    DataOutputStream output = new DataOutputStream(
      new FileOutputStream("t.dat"));
    output.writeInt(1234);
    output.writeInt(5678);
    output.close();
  }
}
```

16.28 For each of the following statements on a DataOutputStream out, how many bytes are sent to the output?

```
output.writeChar('A');
output.writeChars("BC");
output.writeUTF("DEF");
```

16.29 What are the advantages of using buffered streams? Are the following statements correct?

```
BufferedInputStream input1 =
  new BufferedInputStream(new FileInputStream("t.dat"));

DataInputStream input2 = new DataInputStream(
  new BufferedInputStream(new FileInputStream("t.dat")));

ObjectInputStream input3 = new ObjectInputStream(
  new BufferedInputStream(new FileInputStream("t.dat")));
```

Section 16.9 Object I/O

16.30 What types of objects can be stored using the ObjectOutputStream? What is the method for writing an object? What is the method for reading an object? What is the return type of the method that reads an object from ObjectInputStream?

16.31 Is it true that any instance of java.io.Serializable can be successfully serialized? Are the static variables in an object serialized? How do you mark an instance variable not to be serialized?

16.32 Can you write an array to an ObjectOutputStream?

16.33 Is it true that DataInputStream/DataOutputStream can always be replaced by ObjectInputStream/ObjectOutputStream?

16.34 What will happen when you attempt to run the following code?

```
import java.io.*;

public class Test {
  public static void main(String[] args) throws IOException {
    ObjectOutputStream output =
      new ObjectOutputStream(new FileOutputStream("object.dat"));

    output.writeObject(new A());
  }
}

class A implements Serializable {
  B b = new B();
}

class B {
}
```

Section 16.10 Random Access Files (Optional)

16.35 Can RandomAccessFile streams read and write a data file created by DataOutputStream? Can RandomAccessFile streams read and write objects?

16.36 Create a RandomAccessFile stream for the file **address.dat** to allow the updating of student information in the file. Create a DataOutputStream for the file **address.dat**. Explain the differences between these two statements.

16.37 What happens if the file **test.dat** does not exist when you attempt to compile and run the following code?

```
import java.io.*;

public class Test {
  public static void main(String[] args) {
```

```
    try {
      RandomAccessFile raf =
        new RandomAccessFile("test.dat", "r");
      int i = raf.readInt();
    }
    catch(IOException ex) {
      System.out.println("IO exception");
    }
  }
}
```

PROGRAMMING EXERCISES

Section 16.4 Text I/O

16.1* (*Counting characters, words, and lines in a file*) Write a program that will count the number of characters, including blanks, words, and lines, in a file. The filename should be passed as a command-line argument, as shown in Figure 16.26.

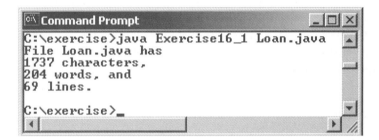

```
C:\exercise>java Exercise16_1 Loan.java
File Loan.java has
1737 characters,
204 words, and
69 lines.

C:\exercise>
```

FIGURE 16.26   *The program displays the number of characters, words, and lines in the given file.*

16.2   (*Processing scores in a text file*) Suppose that a text file **Exercise16_2.txt** contains an unspecified number of scores. Write a program that reads the scores from the file and displays their total and average. Scores are separated by blanks.

 HINT

Read the scores one line at a time until all the lines are read. For each line, use StringTokenizer or Scanner to extract the scores, and convert them into double values using the Double.parseDouble method.

16.3* (*Displaying country flag and flag description*) Example 13.6, "Using Combo Boxes," gives a program that lets users view a country's flag image and description by selecting the country from a combo box. The description is a string coded in the program. Rewrite the program to read the text description from a file. Suppose that the descriptions are stored in the file **description0.txt**, . . . , and **description8.txt** for the nine countries Canada, China, Denmark, France, Germany, India, Norway, the United Kingdom, and the United States, in this order.

16.4** (*Reformatting Java source code*) Write a program that converts the Java source code from the next-line brace style to the end-of-line brace style. For example, the following Java source uses the next-line brace style:

```
public class Test
{
  public static void main(String[] args)
  {
    System.out.println("Welcome to Java!");
  }
}
```

Your program converts it to the end-of-line brace style, as follows:

```
public class Test {
  public static void main(String[] args) {
    System.out.println("Welcome to Java!");
  }
}
```

Your program can be invoked from the command line with the Java source code file as the argument. It converts the Java source code to a new format. For example, the following command converts the Java source code file **Test.java** to the end-of-line brace style.

```
java Exercise16_4 Test.java
```

16.5*   (*Removing a given string from a text file*) Write a program that removes a specified string from a text file. Your program reads the file and generates a new file without the specified string, copies the new file to the original file, and passes the string and the file name from the command line, as follows:

```
java Exercise16_5 John Exercise16_5.txt
```

This command removes string John from **Exercise16_5.txt.**

16.6**   (*Creating a histogram for occurrences of letters*) In Example 13.10, "Creating Multiple Windows," you developed a program that displays a histogram to show the occurrences of each letter in a text area. Reuse the Histogram class created in Example 13.10 to write a program that will display a histogram on a panel. The histogram should show the occurrences of each letter in a text file, as shown in Figure 16.27. Assume that the letters are not case-sensitive.

◆ Place a panel that will display the histogram in the center of the frame.

◆ Place a label and a text field in a panel, and put the panel in the south side of the frame. The text file will be entered from this text field.

◆ Pressing the Enter key on the text field causes the program to count the occurrences of each letter and display the count in a histogram.

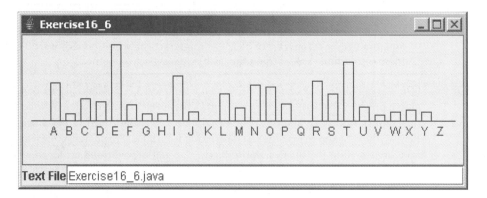

FIGURE **16.27** *The program displays a histogram that shows the occurrences of each letter in the file.*

16.7*   (*Scanning data from a file*) Write a program to create a file named **Exercise16_7.txt** if it does not exist. Write one hundred integers created randomly into the file using text I/O. Integers are separated by spaces in the file. Use StringTokenizer or Scanner to read the data back from the file and display the sorted data.

Section 16.6 Binary I/O

16.8*   (*Creating a binary data file*) Write a program to create a file named **Exercise16_8.dat** if it does not exist. If it exists, append new data to it. Write one hundred integers created randomly into the file using binary I/O.

16.9*   (*Summing all the integers in a binary data file*) Suppose a binary data file named **Exercise16_9.dat** has been created using `writeInt(int)` in `DataOutputStream`. The file contains an unspecified number of integers. Write a program to find the total of the integers.

16.10*   (*Converting a text file into UTF*) Write a program that reads lines of characters from a text and writes each line as a UTF string into a binary file. Display the sizes of both text file and binary file. Use the following command to run the program:

```
java Exercise16_10 Welcome.java Welcome.utf
```

Section 16.9 Object I/O

16.11*   (*Storing objects and arrays into a file*) Write a program that stores an array of five `int` values 1, 2, 3, 4 and 5, a `Date` object for current time, and the double value 5.5 into the file named **Exercise16_11.dat**.

16.12*   (*Storing* `Loan` *objects*) The `Loan` class, introduced in Section 6.15, "Case Study: The Loan Class," does not implement `Serializable`. Rewrite the `Loan` class to implement `Serializable`. Write a program that creates five `Loan` objects and stores them in a file named **Exercise16_12.dat.**

16.13*   (*Restoring objects from a file*) Suppose a file named **Exercise16_13.dat** has been created using the `ObjectOutputStream`. The file contains `Loan` objects. The `Loan` class, introduced in Section 6.15, "Case Study: The Loan Class," does not implement `Serializable`. Rewrite the `Loan` class to implement `Serializable`. Write a program that reads the `Loan` objects from the file and computes the total of the loan amount. Suppose you don't know how many `Loan` objects are in the file. Use `EOFException` to end the loop.

Section 16.10 Random Access Files (Optional)

16.14*   (*Updating count*) Suppose you want to track how many times a program has been executed. You may store an `int` to count the file. Increase the count by 1 each time this program is executed. Let the program be **Exercise16_14** and store the count in **Exercise16_14.dat.**

16.15**   (*Updating address*) Modify `AddressBook` in Listing 16.15 on page 605 to add an *Update* button, as shown in Figure 16.28, to enable the user to modify an address that is being displayed.

FIGURE **16.28**   *You can update the address record that is currently displayed.*

APPENDIXES

Appendix

Java Keywords

The following fifty keywords are reserved for use by the Java language:

abstract	double	int	super
assert	else	interface	switch
boolean	enum	long	synchronized
break	extends	native	this
byte	for	new	throw
case	final	package	throws
catch	finally	private	transient
char	float	protected	try
class	goto	public	void
const	if	return	volatile
continue	implements	short	while
default	import	static	
do	instanceof	strictfp*	

The keywords goto and const are C++ keywords reserved, but not currently used, in Java. This enables Java compilers to identify them and to produce better error messages if they appear in Java programs.

The literal values true, false, and null are not keywords, just like literal value 100. However, you cannot use them as identifiers, just as you cannot use 100 as an identifier.

assert is a keyword added in JDK 1.4 and enum is a keyword added in JDK 1.5.

---

*The strictfp keyword is a modifier for method or class to use strict floating-point calculations. Floating-point arithmetic can be executed in one of two modes: *strict* or *nonstrict*. The strict mode guarantees that the evaluation result is the same on all Java Virtual Machine implementations. The nonstrict mode allows intermediate results from calculations to be stored in an extended format different from the standard IEEE floating-point number format. The extended format is machine-dependent and enables code to be executed faster. However, when you execute the code using the nonstrict mode on different JVMs, you may not always get precisely the same results. By default, the nonstrict mode is used for floating-point calculations. To use the strict mode in a method or a class, add the strictfp keyword in the method or the class declaration. Strict floating-point may give you slightly better precision than nonstrict floating-point, but the distinction will only affect some applications. Strictness is not inherited; that is, the presence of strictfp on a class or interface declaration does not cause extended classes or interfaces to be strict.

THE ASCII CHARACTER SET

Tables B.1 and B.2 show ASCII characters and their respective decimal and hexadecimal codes. The decimal or hexadecimal code of a character is a combination of its row index and column index. For example, in Table B.1, the letter A is at row 6 and column 5, so its decimal equivalent is 65; in Table B.2, letter A is at row 4 and column 1, so its hexadecimal equivalent is 41.

TABLE B.1   ASCII Character Set in the Decimal Index

	0	1	2	3	4	5	6	7	8	9
0	nul	soh	stx	etx	eot	enq	ack	bel	bs	ht
1	nl	vt	ff	cr	so	si	dle	dcl	dc2	dc3
2	dc4	nak	syn	etb	can	em	sub	esc	fs	gs
3	rs	us	sp	!	"	#	$	%	&	'
4	(	)	*	+	,	−	.	/	0	1
5	2	3	4	5	6	7	8	9	:	;
6	<	=	>	?	@	A	B	C	D	E
7	F	G	H	I	J	K	L	M	N	O
8	P	Q	R	S	T	U	V	W	X	Y
9	Z	[	\	]	^	−	'	a	b	c
10	d	e	f	g	h	i	j	k	l	m
11	n	o	p	q	r	s	t	u	v	w
12	x	y	z	{	|	}	~	del		

TABLE B.2   ASCII Character Set in the Hexadecimal Index

	0	1	2	3	4	5	6	7	8	9	A	B	C	D	E	F
0	nul	soh	stx	etx	eot	enq	ack	bel	bs	ht	nl	vt	ff	cr	so	si
1	dle	dcl	dc2	dc3	dc4	nak	syn	etb	can	em	sub	esc	fs	gs	rs	us
2	sp	!	"	#	$	%	&	'	(	)	*	+	,	−	.	/
3	0	1	2	3	4	5	6	7	8	9	:	;	<	=	>	?
4	@	A	B	C	D	E	F	G	H	I	J	K	L	M	N	O
5	P	Q	R	S	T	U	V	W	X	Y	Z	[	\	]	^	−
6	'	a	b	c	d	e	f	g	h	i	j	k	l	m	n	o
7	p	q	r	s	t	u	v	w	x	y	z	{	|	}	~	del

Appendix
C

OPERATOR PRECEDENCE CHART

The operators are shown in decreasing order of precedence from top to bottom. Operators in the same group have the same precedence, and their associativity is shown in the table.

Operator	Name	Associativity
( )	Parentheses	Left to right
( )	Function call	Left to right
[ ]	Array subscript	Left to right
.	Object member access	Left to right
++	Postincrement	Right to left
--	Postdecrement	Right to left
++	Preincrement	Right to left
--	Predecrement	Right to left
+	Unary plus	Right to left
-	Unary minus	Right to left
!	Unary logical negation	Right to left
(type)	Unary casting	Right to left
new	Creating object	Right to left
*	Multiplication	Left to right
/	Division	Left to right
%	Remainder	Left to right
+	Addition	Left to right
-	Subtraction	Left to right
<<	Left shift	Left to right
>>	Right shift with sign extension	Left to right
>>>	Right shift with zero extension	Left to right
<	Less than	Left to right
<=	Less than or equal to	Left to right
>	Greater than	Left to right

>=	Greater than or equal to	Left to right
instanceof	Checking object type	Left to right
==	Equal comparison	Left to right
!=	Not equal	Left to right
&	(Unconditional AND)	Left to right
^	(Exclusive OR)	Left to right
¦	(Unconditional OR)	Left to right
&&	Conditional AND	Left to right
¦¦	Conditional OR	Left to right
?:	Ternary condition	Right to left
=	Assignment	Right to left
+=	Addition assignment	Right to left
−=	Subtraction assignment	Right to left
*=	Multiplication assignment	Right to left
/=	Division assignment	Right to left
%=	Remainder assignment	Right to left

Appendix

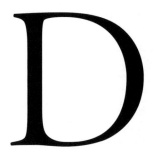

D

JAVA MODIFIERS

Modifiers are used on classes and class members (constructors, methods, data, and class-level blocks), but the final modifier can also be used on local variables in a method. A modifier that can be applied to a class is called a *class modifier*. A modifier that can be applied to a method is called a *method modifier*. A modifier that can be applied to a data field is called a *data modifier*. A modifier that can be applied to a class-level block is called a *block modifier*. The following table gives a summary of the Java modifiers.

Modifier	class	constructor	method	data	block	Explanation
(default)*	√	√	√	√	√	A class, constructor, method, or data field is visible in this package.
public	√	√	√	√		A class, constructor, method, or data field is visible to all the programs in any package.
private		√	√	√		A constructor, method or data field is only visible in this class.
protected		√	√	√		A constructor, method or data field is visible in this package and in subclasses of this class in any package.
static			√	√	√	Define a class method, or a class data field or a static initialization block.
final	√		√	√		A final class cannot be extended. A final method cannot be modified in a subclass. A final data field is a constant.
abstract	√		√			An abstract class must be extended. An abstract method must be implemented in a concrete subclass.
native			√			A native method indicates that the method is implemented using a language other than Java.
synchronized			√		√	Only one thread at a time can execute this method.
strictfp	√	√				Use strict floating-point calculations to guarantee that the evaluation result is the same on all JVMs.
transient				√		Mark a nonserializable instance data field.

*Default access has no modifier associated with it. For example: `class Test {}`.

UML GRAPHICAL NOTATIONS

This appendix summarizes the UML notations used in this book.

Classes and Objects

A class is described using a rectangle box with three sections.

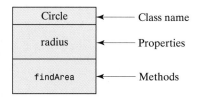

The top section gives the class name, the middle section describes the fields, and the bottom section describes the methods. The middle and bottom sections are optional, but the top section is required.

An object is described using a rectangle box with two sections.

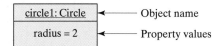

The top section is required. It gives the object's name and its defining class. The second section is optional; it indicates the object's field values.

The Modifiers `public`, `private`, `protected`, and `static`

The symbols +, −, and # are used to denote, respectively, `public`, `private`, and `protected` modifiers in the UML. The static fields and methods are underlined.

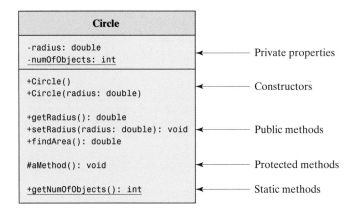

Class Relationships

The relationships of the classes are association, aggregation, and inheritance.

An *association* is illustrated using a solid line between the two classes with an optional label that describes their relationship.

Each class involved in an association may specify a multiplicity. A multiplicity is a number or an interval that specifies the number of objects of the class that are involved in the relationship. The character * means that the number of objects is unlimited, and an interval 1..u means that the number of objects should be between 1 and u, inclusive.

A filled diamond is attached to the composed class to denote the composition relationship, and a hollow diamond is attached to the aggregated class to denote the *aggregation* relationship, as shown below.

Inheritance models the is-a relationship between two classes, as shown below. An open triangle pointing to the superclass is used to denote the inheritance relationship between the two classes involved.

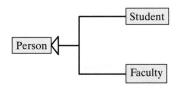

Abstract Classes and Interfaces

Abstract class names, interface names, and abstract methods are italicized. Dashed lines are used to link to the interface, as shown below:

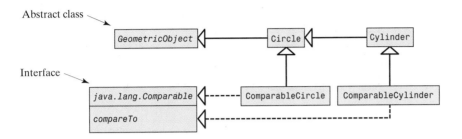

Sequence Diagrams

Sequence diagrams describe interactions among objects by depicting the time ordering of method invocations. The sequence diagram shown below consists of the following elements:

♦ Class role represents the role an object plays. The objects at the top of the diagram represent class roles.

♦ Lifeline represents the existence of an object over a period of time. A vertical dashed line extending from the object is used to denote a lifeline.

♦ Activation represents the time during which an object is performing an operation. Thin rectangles placed on lifelines are used to denote activations.

♦ Method invocation represents communications between objects. Horizontal arrows labeled with method calls are used to denote method invocations.

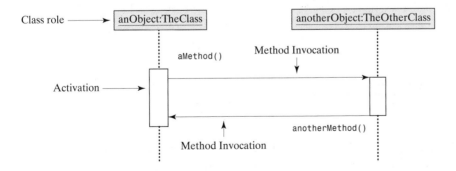

Statechart Diagrams

Statechart diagrams describe the flow of control of an object. The statechart diagram shown below contains the following elements:

◆ State represents a situation during the life of an object in which it satisfies some condition, performs some action, or waits for some event to occur. Every state has a name. Rectangles with rounded corners are used to represent states. The small filled circle is used to denote the initial state.

◆ Transition represents the relationship between two states, indicating that an object will perform some action to transfer from one state to the other. A solid arrow with appropriate method invocation is used to denote a transition.

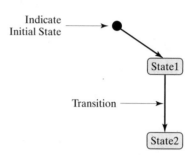

Appendix

Special Floating-Point Values

Dividing an integer by zero is invalid and throws `ArithmeticException`, but dividing a floating-point value by zero does not cause an exception. Floating-point arithmetic can overflow to infinity if the result of the operation is too large for a `double` or a `float`, or underflow to zero if the result is too small for a `double` or a `float`. Java provides the special floating-point values `POSITIVE_INFINITY`, `NEGATIVE_INFINITY`, and `NaN` (Not a Number) to denote these results. These values are defined as special constants in the `Float` class and the `Double` class.

If a positive floating-point number is divided by zero, the result is `POSITIVE_INFINITY`. If a negative floating-point number is divided by zero, the result is `NEGATIVE_INFINITY`. If a floating-point zero is divided by zero, the result is `NaN`, which means that the result is undefined mathematically. The string representation of these three values are Infinity, -Infinity, and NaN. For example,

```
System.out.print(1.0 / 0); // Print Infinity
System.out.print(-1.0 / 0); // Print -Infinity
System.out.print(0.0 / 0); // Print NaN
```

These special values can also be used as operands in computations. For example, a number divided by `POSITIVE_INFINITY` yields a positive zero. Table F.1 summarizes various combinations of the `/`, `*`, `%`, `+`, and `−` operators.

TABLE F.1   Special Floating-Point Values

x	y	x/y	$x*y$	$x\%y$	$x + y$	$x - y$
Finite	± 0.0	$\pm \infty$	± 0.0	NaN	Finite	Finite
Finite	$\pm \infty$	± 0.0	$\pm \infty$	x	$\pm \infty$	∞
± 0.0	± 0.0	NaN	$\pm \infty$	NaN	± 0.0	± 0.0
$\pm \infty$	Finite	$\pm \infty$	$\pm \infty$	NaN	$\pm \infty$	$\pm \infty$
$\pm \infty$	$\pm \infty$	NaN	$\pm \infty$	NaN	$\pm \infty$	∞
± 0.0	$\pm \infty$	± 0.0	NaN	± 0.0	$\pm \infty$	± 0.0
NaN	Any	NaN	NaN	NaN	NaN	NaN
Any	NaN	NaN	NaN	NaN	NaN	NaN

 Note
If one of the operands is NaN, the result is NaN.

Appendix

G

BIT OPERATIONS

To write programs at the machine-level, often you need to deal with binary numbers directly and perform operations at the bit-level. Java provides the bitwise operators and shift operators defined in Table G.1.

TABLE G.1

Operator	Name	Example (using bytes in the example)	Description
&	Bitwise AND	10101110&10010010 yields 10000010	The AND of two corresponding bits yields a 1 if both bits are 1.
¦	Bitwise inclusive OR	10101110¦10010010	The OR of two corresponding bits yields a 1 if either bit is 1.
^	Bitwise exclusive OR	10101110^10010010 yields 00111100	The XOR of two corresponding bits yields a 1 only if two bits are different.
~	One's complement	~10101110 yields 01010001	The operator toggles each bit from 0 to 1 and from 1 to 0
<<	Left shift	10101110 << 2 yields 10111000	Shift bits in the first operand left by the number of bits specified in the second operand, filling with 0s on the right.
>>	Right shift with sign extension	10101110 >> 2 yields 11101011 00101110 >> 2 yields 00001011	Shift bit in the first operand right by the number of bits specified in the second operand, filling with the highest (sign) bit on the left.
>>>	Right shift with zero extension	10101110 >>> 2 yields 00101011 00101110 >>> 2 yields 00001011	Shift bit in the first operand right by the number of bits specified in the second operand, filling with 0s on the left.

The bit operators apply only to integer types (`byte`, `short`, `int`, and `long`). A character involved in a bit operation is converted to an integer. All bitwise operators can form bitwise assignment operators, such as =, ¦=, <<=, >>=, and >>>=.

INDEX